Swiss Energy Governance

Peter Hettich • Aya Kachi
Editors

Swiss Energy Governance

Political, Economic and Legal Challenges and Opportunities in the Energy Transition

Springer

Editors
Peter Hettich
Institute of Public Finance, Fiscal Law and Law and Economics - IFF-HSG
University of St. Gallen
St. Gallen, Switzerland

Aya Kachi
University of Basel
Faculty of Business and Economics
Basel, Switzerland

ISBN 978-3-030-80786-3 ISBN 978-3-030-80787-0 (eBook)
https://doi.org/10.1007/978-3-030-80787-0

Published with the support of the Swiss National Science Foundation

This Springer imprint is published by the registered company Springer Nature Switzerland AG.
The registered company address is: Gewerbestrasse 11, 6330 Cham, Switzerland

Foreword

Concerns about climate change and the risks induced by nuclear power have led many countries to induce a transition toward an energy system based mostly on renewables. This transition is likely to take several decades, to require substantial investments, and to be at least partially enabled by changes in individual behavior.

Given the challenges involved in such a transition, several countries have decided to provide dedicated research funding for large-scale projects that result in insights and innovations for accelerating the energy transition or reducing its costs. In Switzerland, this has resulted in the creation of eight Swiss Competence Centers for Energy Research (SCCER), among which the Center for Energy, Society and Transition (SCCER CREST) is conducting research on non-technical aspects of the energy transition.

This collective volume presents results from several research groups that have worked on the *governance of energy transitions* in the context of the SCCER CREST. It illustrates the unique possibilities arising in large-scale projects that span more than the usual 3–4 years and that involve researchers with strongly differing backgrounds and perspectives. Furthermore, it exemplifies how to successfully navigate the pitfalls that arise when academic research is confronted with demands to provide simple and unified answers.

The contributions to this volume cover a wide range of topics in energy governance. Some contributions relate to the international context of energy policy—for example, analyzing the question of how non-EU countries like Switzerland can influence the development of EU energy policy. Other contributions investigate national regulatory strategies—for example, whether past ideas, such as unbundling, are still appropriate in a decentralized system or how legal settings can inhibit or foster the development of new technologies. Finally, there are contributions that connect policy and individual behavior, as illustrated by the study on the effects of policy risks on wind power development as well as by the study of media coverage of energy policy and its influence on voting behavior. Despite using different perspectives and approaches, the studies published here do not only cover a wide range of topics, but they do so in a way that provides an overall picture of challenges and potential solutions in governing an energy transition.

This illustrates important advantages of large-scale research projects: the ability to decide jointly which topics are to be covered, to conduct research on similar topics simultaneously, and to exchange results between individual teams early on. Due to this coordination and exchange, individual research projects provide added value to each other, and the overall achievement becomes more than the sum of the individual projects.

The above examples also point to another important advantage of large-scale projects: Such projects provide the funding required to analyze important questions not only from a single but from several disciplinary perspectives. Imagine a collective volume on energy governance written solely by political scientists, solely by legal scholars, or solely by economists. Even if all of these imagined books were based on top-quality research, all of them would be impecunious compared to the volume you are reading. Each of the above disciplines has its own way of perceiving the world, of analyzing problems, and of inferring solutions. These ways overlap only partially. Joining these perspectives provides a picture that is, albeit more expensive in terms of research funding, much more informative.

But this scale of funding is not only a chance but also a challenge. Often, large-scale research projects are asked to not only analyze a question from different perspectives and compare results but also to arrive at joint results, preferably based on joint approaches. Such demands are important for communicating overarching recommendations to persons outside academia.

But, if taken too far, such demands impoverish research. Progress in science stems from controversies, from the unwillingness of researchers to accept easily what they perceive to be false, from the drive to convince others who hold different views. If contrasting views have to be merged, results become vague and consensual with little prospect to provoke new ideas. If disciplinary methods are exchanged completely for "interdisciplinary" approaches, the precision on which scientific work hinges is diluted, and the ability to place results in an appropriate scientific context is lost. Finally, the false ideal might be served (once again) that there is a single "scientifically correct" answer to societies' needs and questions.

This collective volume exemplifies how to step around these pitfalls. The contributions are based on perceptions and methods stemming from different disciplines. They do not seek consensus at all costs but feel free to provide diverging, and, in some instances, even contrasting, perspectives and conclusions. Yet, it is clearly visible that the contributions originate from a joint project, that the authors have fruitfully engaged in discussions, and that they work toward common goals. The collective volume thus provides a picture of energy governance that is not a total perspective, where each element is configured to be a designated part of the whole, but rather a coordinated arrangement of individual perspectives. This provides the contrast and the level of detail that lead to a vibrant and informative picture.

In addition to these points, the collective volume provides a compelling argument that research on energy governance has a vital role in facilitating a timely and efficient transition to a new energy system.

It is a futile hope that technological innovations will automatically induce a broad deployment of "green" technologies or that large-scale transitions will not have to rely on changes in individual behavior. Consequently, a timely energy transition will require adjustments to policies, institutions, and framing conditions. But the transition will still take decades and will require the active engagement of a large and highly diverse set of actors. Therefore, such adjustments have to be developed taking into account the necessity of maintaining public support, of keeping essential actors engaged, of integrating new policies and institutions in the context of existing ones, and of ensuring coherence with international developments.

The contributions to this volume show how difficult it is to meet these challenges but also how much research in energy governance can contribute toward easing the energy transition. Even though research on energy governance has no shiny new technologies to show, its impact on the success of the current energy transition is likely to be substantial.

In summary, this collective volume is a remarkable achievement, thanks to the quality of the contributions and to the efforts of Prof. Hettich and Prof. Kachi, who not only initiated and edited this volume but also created and coordinated the work package in the SCCER CREST that provided the frame for the research published here.

Faculty of Business and Economics, Environmental Economics, University of Basel, Basel, Switzerland
Spring 2021
e-mail: frank.krysiak@unibas.ch

Frank C. Krysiak

Acknowledgments

This book is part of the activities of SCCER CREST (Swiss Competence Center for Energy Research), which is financially supported by Innosuisse under Grant No. KTI. 1155000154 and is published with the support of the Swiss National Science Foundation. Many researchers of this book have also been involved in and been funded by the National Research Program "Energy Turnaround" (NRP 70) of the Swiss National Science Foundation (SNSF). The editors and authors of this book wish also to express their gratitude to the many academic institutions as well as the public and private entities which have generously leveraged the funds provided by Innosuisse.

We also thank Dr. Nicole Pohl, Julie Freyer, MLaw, and Michael Vierbauch, B.A. HSG in Law, for their careful review and comments. The contents of and the mistakes in this book are the individual authors' sole responsibility. They do not necessarily represent the views of other contributors to this volume or of other members of SCCER CREST. We are grateful to receive any comments which our careful readers may have.

Acknowledgements

Contents

Introduction

Peter Hettich and Aya Kachi

Contents

1 Swiss Competence Center for Research in Energy, Society and Transition (SCCER CREST)

In 2014, the Swiss Confederation established the Swiss Competence Center for Research in Energy, Society and Transition to respond to important challenges posed by the Swiss energy transition, envisaged by the so-called "Energy Strategy 2050". It was only in 2017 that 55 researchers within SCCER CREST decided to form a specific work package dealing with energy governance. The work package aims at identifying and providing recommendations to overcome governance challenges, thereby making energy governance more effective, efficient, and transparent. The researchers seek to achieve impact by scientific analysis, by the provision of data or legal recommendations on governance arrangements as well as by the active

P. Hettich (✉)
Institute of Public Finance, Fiscal Law and Law and Economics, University of St. Gallen, St. Gallen, Switzerland
e-mail: peter.hettich@unisg.ch

A. Kachi
Faculty of Business and Economics, International Political Economy and Energy Policy, University of Basel, Basel, Switzerland
e-mail: aya.kachi@unibas.ch

P. Hettich, A. Kachi (eds.), *Swiss Energy Governance*,
https://doi.org/10.1007/978-3-030-80787-0_1

engagement with stakeholders, and by creating new networks within governance systems themselves. This book comprises some of their most important insights from their research during the seven years of SCCER CREST.

To be effective, research on governance needs to cut through the several disciplines that make up the social sciences. As a consequence, our research in energy governance is essentially interdisciplinary: In SCCER CREST, researchers mostly from political science, law, and management contributed to the work package. Nevertheless, research on governance necessarily draws upon frameworks of other disciplines such as sociology and psychology, for instance. Only a broad perception of governance allows us to evaluate, for example, the social acceptance of (energy) regimes or to analyze the changes in investor behavior to complement existing research findings from behavioral economics.

Involving such a great number of disciplines results in the use of a variety of different methods, from normative to qualitative and quantitative empirical methods. These methods include, but are not limited to, content analyses, comparative case studies, network analyses, and interviews, as well as predictive analyses that are based on theoretical modelling and simulations. Sometimes, different problem perceptions, approaches, and methods give rise to conflicting results – this is to be expected and inherent to the scientific process and not to be judged or resolved by the coordinators of a scientific research project.

The variety of researchers involved in CREST's work package on energy governance introduces a specific set of challenges to overcome barriers to collaboration. First of all, in order to pursue the jointly set goals of our research, a shared perception of the term "governance" is needed (Sect. 2.1). Second, a common understanding of the abilities and limits of the different research methods is required to see what research on "energy governance" might possibly achieve; we provide an overview on the research presented in this book in Sect. 2.2. Furthermore, and inherent to state-sponsored research projects, there is the understandable urge to provide accountability for the research funds spent: Bureaucrats easily succumb to the fallacy that, among any group of researchers, there should be a commonly accepted vision of the future and a commonly accepted way forward; since this is mostly not the case, we conclude this introduction with some thoughts on "narratives" (Sect. 3).

2 Research on Energy Governance

2.1 On "Governance"

Theories on "governance" have emerged in and have been transfused between many of the social sciences. The term is used in many different ways today by different researchers (as well as non-academics) and its meaning seems to be quite imprecise and open to many different interpretations. That may be the reason, as Adrian Rinscheid has put it, why various researchers representing different disciplines (social sciences, law, economics) can cooperate under this "umbrella term". For the purpose of this research project, we have incompletely theorized the term "governance" in order to start the contemplated research of the energy system and not to lose time trying to unify the several underlying governance theories.

In general, we see that the transformation of a whole industry requires overcoming legal, political, and behavioral obstacles—that is, overcoming situations in which the current state of governance impedes the transformation towards the policy goal and in which more adequate policies, regulations, and processes could facilitate the transformation. Against this backdrop, a common point of reference for our research might have been set by Elinor Ostrom, who would "ask where the rules that individuals use in action situations originate".[1] The policy process theories applied by Raphael Klein and Matthias Finger basically still use that approach to understand why actors behave as they do; of course, because actors are not totally rational and the policy process is complex, their approach has undergone some refinement.

Applying this perception of governance, we analyze obstacles to good governance by highlighting the role of key actors including the results they achieve. The key actors in energy governance are inherently heterogeneous in their policy preferences as well as in their practices of handling, steering, and defining policies and markets. These actors are also multi-leveled: Some are nested state actors (municipalities, cantons, and federal government), others are non-state and transnational (e.g., individuals, market participants, political parties and interest groups, industry associations, and NGOs). Incorporating this broad battery of actors into a comprehensive—legal, political, and economic—framework of analysis helps to investigate not only formal procedures, such as political and democratic processes, but also market behavior and societal practices. As evidenced in the contribution by Lena Schaffer and Alessio Levis, researchers of energy governance are not only interested in the policies and institutions that have to be implemented and designed for a successful energy transition; they are also investigating how the relevant actors discuss energy policy within the public sphere—that is, how these actors establish governance mechanisms from discourses.

Keeping this in mind, we understand why scholars of political science like Adrian Rinscheid refer to Rod Rhodes in order to shed light on the various understandings of governance, stipulating that governance is a new (at that time) and different (or "complementary") mode or process of governing that can be distinguished from markets and hierarchies as governing structures.[2] Governance, according to Rhodes, is described as "self-organizing, interorganizational networks" that are somewhat autonomous from the state and resist central guidance; the "challenge for government is to enable these networks and to seek out new forms of

[1] Ostrom (2005), p. 19.

[2] Rhodes (1996), p. 652.

co- operation".[3] This approach is more comprehensive than those we sometimes find in the economic literature.[4]

Thus, most of our research on energy governance analyzes how the behavior and practices of the actors in the energy industry influence policy implementation and how they feed back into the existing legal, political, and economic framework, reshaping the dynamic energy governance system. Consequently, we focus on the behavior as well as the positive and normative framework of political actors, bureaucracies, courts, international organizations, lobby groups, civil society, economic actors, and individuals; our analysis comprises the emergence of new policies, the enabling of such policies by use of legal instruments and procedures, and the implementation of such policies including their feedback loops. For legal scholars like Markus Schreiber, this requires to look beyond governmental or legislative behavior and to take into account the actions of private actors, including public-private hybrids, and the possibilities for cooperation between the state and the private sector.[5] For legal scholars, the governance perspective has the advantage of analyzing the actual state of affairs, without being narrowed down too early by preconceived, normative notions such as the rule of law or democracy[6]—this, of course, does not preclude the inclusion of normative elements such as "good governance". Nevertheless, and again referring to Rhodes, governance by self-organizing networks may be seen as a challenge to democratic accountability, but it might also be seen as a mode of governing that empowers citizens.[7]

2.2 *The Governance of the Energy Industry*

This book is structured in three parts. Part I deals with the interactions between the Swiss and European energy systems and policies, taking into account the Swiss system of multi-level governance. Against the backdrop of these and other framework conditions, in Part II, we take a closer look at state and non-state actors that drive (or are affected by) the energy transition; actors, which might use certain catalysts or which might face obstacles. The first two parts place greater emphasis on international and domestic institutions, laying out legal, political, and business contexts in which incentives and behaviors of various actors are considered. Based on the observed behavior of these actors, in Part III, we illuminate some of the emerging and more detailed questions to be answered with regard to two types of key actors: voters and other stakeholders such as industry players and interest groups. The overarching question that runs through Part III is what type of issues we need

[3] Rhodes (1996), p. 666.

[4] See, e.g., Williamson (2000), p. 597.

[5] Cf. Hoffmann-Riem (2011), p. 18.

[6] Müller (2008), p. 58 et seq.; Schuppert (2008), p. 13, 27.

[7] Rhodes (1996), p. 666 et seq.

solve in order to mitigate policy and acceptance risks that are expected in the process of an energy transition in Switzerland.

2.2.1 Interactions Between the Swiss and the European Energy System in the Context of the Swiss System of Multi-Level Governance (Part I)

Developments in international energy governance are important and often neglected conditions for the success of the Energy Strategy 2050. Such developments potentially comprise global climate policy, the changing institutional landscape of energy governance, changes in the political economy of renewable energies and European energy geopolitics, developments of global oil trade and markets, and new transnational challenges provoked by a global digital revolution (e.g., cyber security of smart grids). In this first part of the book, we analyze how the Energy Strategy 2050 interacts with such developments: Which developments on the global and European level will impact the success of Swiss energy governance? And how can Switzerland leverage its assets and strengths to support an energy transition on the European or even a global scale? Such questions, of course, are more easily answered by learning from experiences abroad, as seen in the comparative analysis by Sebastian Heselhaus, who describes the quest of the EU and Switzerland to shape the future energy mix: Should these entities combat climate change or prioritize security of supply? In the global context, energy governance also points to quite complex interactions between different actors at multiple levels, which is clearly visible in the field of climate change law: The chapter by Julia Hänni and Tienmu Ma seeks to provide an overview of how this interaction—involving judicial, legislative, and executive actors at the national, European, and international levels—has shaped how the area of climate change is regulated in Switzerland and beyond.

As the contribution by Benjamin Hofmann, David Kolcava and Philipp Thaler shows, Switzerland may be seen as a shaper in European electricity governance: Swiss influence is especially visible in matters related to grid management and cross-border electricity trade. Despite being a non-EU country, Switzerland has relatively high access to important European governance bodies. Switzerland also possesses structural power in serving as a European transit hub for electricity and as an important source of technical expertise. However, the authors highlight uncertainties resulting from the present lack of an electricity agreement between Switzerland and the EU, giving rise to a recommendation to strive for viable forms of energy cooperation with the EU and to strengthen the transit function and technical expertise of the country. Putting a policy transfer from Europe on display, Leonore Haelg, Tobias S. Schmidt and Sebastian Sewerin observe how policy instruments to boost the deployment of RE have diffused from frontrunner countries like Germany to jurisdictions like Switzerland: Switzerland implemented its first comprehensive support policy with the adoption of a cost-covering and technology-specific feed-in tariff in 2009, following Germany's example. Nevertheless, policy designs look very different in both countries, which makes it interesting to examine the reasons for these policy design differences.

2.2.2 Catalysts and Obstacles for State and Non-state Actors Driving the Energy Transition (Part II)

Given the Swiss federalist system, the enabling of policies in the context of a multi-level governance structure provides interesting insights as well. Martin Föhse emphasizes the fact that the energy sector has been subject to regulation since ancient times, with the cantons as primary drivers of lawmaking in Switzerland. Recently, however, more and more competencies have been transferred to the federal level. This transfer, together with the increasing complexity of the subject matter, has led to a legal framework that is difficult to understand and to apply, even for legal experts. It becomes clear that the Energy Strategy is the result of different energy strategies and networks of affected stakeholders and shaped not only by legalistic considerations of good lawmaking but very much also by dynamics of power, agency, and politics. Particularly, we see that Swiss multi-level governance affects the formulation and implementation of energy policy goals, for instance, because of the necessity to achieve sufficient socio-political acceptance for certain policy instruments. In this context, Raphael Klein and Matthias Finger investigate the impact that the electorate can have on the transition towards carbon neutrality, in particular looking at the Swiss electricity market. They use a hybrid agent-based model that allows them to study which policy instruments are more likely to be implemented depending on the Swiss electricity market progression and on policy actors' interests. They show that the electorate has a limited impact on the policy chosen and on the electricity market. Overall, an environmentally conscious electorate leads policy actors to select the carbon tax as a policy most often, which has the adverse effect to increase the electricity price and to exacerbate the import dependency in winter. At the same time, this is not sufficient to stem the construction of gas turbine power plants.

Confronted with visible state action driving energy governance, we easily lose sight of bottom-up approaches that enact decentralized, local energy strategies. While the energy sector is moving away from a traditional utility regulation to a market regime, we may identify private arrangements that coexist with public-sector regulation. Consequently, it is important to know how legal and political processes are influenced by and impact the practices and processes of local and private actors in the governance system. This way, we account for the fact that energy governance not only comprises state institutions but a broad variety of stakeholders that have their own agendas and interests—e.g., private service providers, existing market participants, and municipalities that all work towards the creation of self-sufficient energy regions or that adopt localized energy strategies. Thus, we acknowledge that these actors construct governance arrangements that do not involve governmental actors (e.g., area networks or virtual power plants using privately owned heat pumps).

One of the newly emerging hybrid actors in energy markets are utilities that not only carry out the public tasks assigned to them by the legislator but that are also active as entrepreneurial entities in the private sector. Andreas Abegg and Phil Baumann shed light on these activities, which range from electricity products for large customers, photovoltaic and e-mobility installations to services in the field of building services engineering, internet offerings, and the sale of household appliances and which can give rise to distortions of competition. As they point out, it is not only cross-subsidization but also financing advantages, exceptions to taxation, and considerable economies of scope that need to be considered when allowing such entities to operate on private markets. In this context of new business models, Mary Jean Bürer, Matthieu de Lapparent, Massimiliano Capezzali, and Mauro Carpita point out that we continue to measure progress on energy transitions in a superficial and extremely limited way, while the study of smart second-generation policies for the energy transition is neglected in the literature. Understanding how to redesign energy governance to allow for business model reconfiguration among incumbents and how to stimulate business model innovation from start-ups and new entrants is important for a viable energy transition in the long term. Existing laws will often not be suited to accommodate a new technology or business model, and the legislator may be slow in reacting to these new challenges. As evidenced in the contribution by Peter Hettich, many innovative business models with a potential of benefiting the consumer might be preempted by overcautious regulation, e.g., looking at the restrictions in the use of smart meter data or taking into account the effects of grid charges. However, as Markus Schreiber shows in his contribution, legal provisions may also serve to promote innovation: In his view, laws which stipulate favorable conditions for renewable energy sources might serve as an obvious example. In his contribution, Markus Schreiber investigates how the legislator, regulatory agencies, and private standard-setting bodies are responding to three different energy innovations: new renewable energy sources, new storage systems, and smart grids. He seeks not only to analyze commonalities and differences in the approach but also to identify best practices.

In summary, these contributions show that a thorough understanding of the agendas, interests, and arrangements of actors involved in the energy transition helps to make recommendations for a suitable legal, political, and business framework for the transformation of energy systems—a framework that fosters the goals of energy market regulation on all levels of the state and strengthens private autonomy at the same time. In particular, we have to ask which innovative forms of governance (e.g., network governance and forms of self-regulation) help to achieve a sustainable energy future, enabling adaptive and interactive systems which are able to learn and improve.

2.2.3 Understanding the Pressure Points of Policy and Acceptance Risks in the Context of Everchanging Framework Conditions (Part III)

In order to find more effective policies, it is important to know how interests and practices of key stakeholders can influence energy policymaking. Only if the role played by competing domestic interests is understood, can a sustainable transformation of energy systems succeed. In light of the asymmetric redistribution effects generated by a transformation of the energy system, we again need to look beyond state actors and make inquiries about the socio-political acceptance of certain policies by a variety of stakeholders such as voters, interest groups, and individual companies. Moreover, energy governance needs to respond to the puzzle that public acceptance for renewable energy technologies and policies is high, whereas the implementation of policy innovations is slow, particularly compared to other countries. In order to trace the socio-political barriers of a sustainable transformation of the energy system, we therefore need to examine strategic choices and other sources of influence asymmetries among different interests. With this in mind, the first two chapters of Part III look into challenges around voter perceptions, and the last two chapters focus on other stakeholders such as interest groups and individual companies.

Moving beyond the topic of diffuse public support, this part of the book first identifies two specific factors of energy policymaking in Switzerland that need to be addressed with regard to voter preferences. Here, media coverage of certain issues plays an important role: Adrian Rinscheid and Linards Udris investigate the patterns in media coverage in Swiss energy policymaking and the extent to which the media influence voters' decisions at the ballot. Based on the media coverage in the run-up to three recent energy-related referenda (2015 initiative "Energy tax instead of VAT"; 2016 nuclear phase-out initiative; 2017 referendum on the federal Energy Strategy 2050), they demonstrate that the three energy policy referenda are characterized by patterns similar to non-energy votes but also have distinct features. They find that the failure of the phase-out initiative can be partly explained by exposure to newspaper coverage: One in four left-wing voters who had initially been in favor of the popular initiative but were exposed to strongly negative coverage about it during the "hot" campaign phase changed their initial voting intention. Looking at the evolution of public discourses on energy policy in general, Lena Schaffer and Alessio Levis analyze another important factor reflecting policy discussion and contestation within the political arena from a more macroscopic viewpoint: They make a case for the disaggregation of energy policy and its public perception to add to our understanding of energy transition pathways, allowing for a more comprehensive understanding of the idiosyncrasies of Swiss energy policy regarding temporal as well as sectoral variation. In their contribution, they argue that an increased politicization of energy policy may affect future policy choice, and thus any account on energy transition policy needs to scrutinize potential feedback effects from policies that will manifest in policy discourses.

Another crucial factor for achieving the objectives of the Swiss Energy Strategy 2050 is to mobilize sufficient amounts of capital. While investments in energy infrastructure used to be exclusively the domain of electric utilities, recent experience shows a rise in investor diversity, suggesting an increasing importance of institutional investors, such as pension funds and insurance companies and community finance. However, despite the entrance of new investors and significantly reduced technology cost, "soft costs"—e.g., the policy risk premium and the cost of capital—still hamper the financing of projects in Switzerland. Lowering these costs—which are perceived differently depending on investor type—may be important for achieving Swiss energy policy targets.

Looking specifically at wind energy, we see that the administrative processes in Switzerland are particularly long and complex, with the planning phase taking up to a decade, more than twice as long as the European average. Against the backdrop of the slow development of wind energy projects in Switzerland, Anna Ebers Broughel and Rolf Wüstenhagen quantify the risk premium that lengthy permitting processes imply for wind energy investors in Switzerland; they suggest ways to reduce policy risk, i.e., ways to design "investment-grade" policies. They have empirically investigated the policy risk premium for financing renewable energy projects to get a realistic understanding of how capital flows from different investor groups (e.g., institutional investors vs electric utilities vs retail investors) will change under various policy scenarios. Their model shows that the highest profitability risks are related to the availability of feed-in tariffs, but other changes in the permitting process can also have a critical impact on the project's bottom line. The findings illustrate that energy project developers in Switzerland face a significant policy risk premium in the pre-construction stage.

Part III closes with the work by Duygan et al. by zooming out and providing a bird's eye view of perceptions on the energy strategies pursued by various interest groups, companies, and cantonal administrations in Switzerland. With regard to issue dimension, too, their work provides a rare opportunity for us to peruse through those actors' perceptions on a wide range of transition measures that have been debated in the context of the Energy Strategy 2050: electric vehicles, wind energy, deep geothermal energy, hydropower, and feed-in tariffs. By using novel data from an original survey conducted with more than 300 energy actors, they show that there is large variance in how realistic these actors think the Energy Strategy 2050 measures are in each of the aforementioned energy subdomains. Some actors believe strongly that the considered measures are absolutely realistic, while others believe the opposite. In some cases, such beliefs are correlated with the degree to which the actors are engaged with media-related activities, implying that what voters see in the media could reflect only the perception that is on one end of the stakeholder perception spectrum. As Rinscheid and Udris find out, voter opinions can depend substantially on what is covered by mainstream media. Therefore, these findings combined, we illuminate an emerging challenge that policymakers will face in the near future: How can they make sense of the divergence in energy stakeholder perceptions about the transition paths, and how can they communicate on it with voters without biases?

In short, Part III of this volume covers the concluding elements of the regulatory cycle, evaluating the impact of specific energy policies on various actors and their views. It also reminds us of the fact that, in addition to designing and implementing specific energy policies, policymakers in Switzerland will likely be required to better communicate the diverging views and preferences held by energy actors to their own voters. Elections and referenda will then determine the level of public acceptance for each of these measures, all of which gives rise to new issues on diverse political agendas that will let new legislation emerge.

3 A Narrative for the Energy Transformation?

Given the plethora of findings and recommendations compiled in this volume, the reader rightly will ask whether these can be stitched together into an integrated narrative, thereby providing guidance on how to transform an energy industry.

In general, public funding agencies nowadays are keen on having such narratives because they make it easier to explain to politicians and taxpayers how research projects have contributed to the achievement of political goals. For communication purposes, significant funds are reserved for image videos and shiny brochures, even in basic research, even in the social sciences. On the upside, a decreasing distance to politicians makes it easier for social scientists to obtain third party funding to pursue their research interests. On the downside, such funds rarely are granted without strings attached. When funding research in the social sciences, politicians are not only deprived of photo opportunities in laboratories or high-tech industrial plants; they will also have a hard time to accept that most research that is done in the social sciences will materialize just in text and will not be commercialized: There are no technologies to be explored and developed, no innovations to be developed for commercialization.

In contrast to technical research producing technical innovation, the research results in the social sciences are less tangible. In particular when pursuing controversial political projects, politicians might still hope that social scientist help them to achieve "social innovation"—that is, to find ways to increase the social acceptance of the government's plans for the energy industry. It is questionable, however, whether a government should ask researchers to engage in such "social engineering". Commonly accepted policy goals (e.g., a carbon-free energy supply) should not be mixed up with political goals (i.e., the Energy Strategy 2050). A statement by Henry Kissinger comes to mind:

> [I]n some respects the intellectual has never been more in demand; that he makes such a relatively small contribution is not because he is rejected but because his function is misunderstood. He is sought after enthusiastically but for the wrong reasons and in pursuit

of the wrong purposes. . . . [A]ll too often what the policymaker wants from the intellectual is not ideas but endorsement.[8]

Of course, politicians wish their policy proposals to appear science-based and, consequently, without alternative. Vice versa, researchers always have to fear that their research could be steered or channeled to support a political goal. Such fears are fomented when, as it is often done these days, the research results of very diverse research groups are boiled down into simple narratives that tell readers, briefly, how funded research contributed to one or another political goal. As John Kay and Mervyn King recently phrased this phenomenon:

> Our need for narratives is so strong that many people experience a need for an overarching narrative – some unifying explanatory theme or group of related themes with very general applicability. These grand narratives may help them believe that complexity can be managed, that there exists some story which describes 'the world as it really is'. Every new experience or piece of information can be interpreted in the light of that overarching narrative.[9]

Drawing from the intriguing allegory of the hedgehog and the fox, Kay and King circumscribe beautifully what is wrong with such an approach:

> The hedgehog knows one big thing, the fox many little things. The hedgehog subscribes to some overarching narrative; the fox is skeptical about the power of *any* overarching narrative. The hedgehog approaches most uncertainties with strong priors; the fox attempts to assemble evidence before forming a view of 'what is going on here'. We both have the experience of dealing with researchers for radio and television programmes: if you profess an opinion that is unambiguous and – for preference – extreme, a car will be on its way to take you to the studio; if you suggest that the issue is complicated, they will thank you for your advice and offer to ring you back. They rarely do. People understandably like clear opinions but the truth is that many issues inescapably involve saying 'on the one hand, but on the other'.[10]

In order to provide some closure to this extensive research project, the editors of this volume would very much like to provide the readers with the two or three "most important" recommendations for decision makers. However, this would devalue, even deface, the work of our researchers. In order to properly consolidate the results contained in this volume, the assumptions and value judgments that are the foundations of our work would need to be discussed extensively. It is very unlikely that a consensus could be reached on only a few of the many parameters that influence the success of the energy transformation. With good reasons, for example, the assumptions of the government regarding the electricity demand in 2050 may be regarded as frivolous by some or as well-founded by others. Consequently, with an aggregation of our results and a push for consensus, recommendations will become much more generic and, therefore, meaningless. Even if such consensus could be achieved, good advice for decision-makers would require not only a reference narrative but also an

[8] Kissinger (1959), p. 30, 33.

[9] Kay and King (2020), p. 219.

[10] Kay and King (2020), p. 222.

admission that this narrative could be false; we would therefore need to provide decision-makers with a set of alternative narratives that might be relevant, as well.[11] Since, in this volume, the overarching narrative is set by the government in the form of its Energy Strategy 2050, it seems indeed a formidable task for researchers to challenge the government's narrative in every conceivable way in order to detect misconceptions and potentials to make it more resilient to alternate futures. This would constitute a huge task in itself and a task that does not form part of the research design chosen here.

While the urge to disseminate the results of large (and expensive) research projects to the wider public is innocuous, the push for integrated narratives is not. The Oxford English Dictionary defines a narrative as "a story or representation used to give an explanatory or justificatory account of a society, period, etc." Based on this definition, Nobel Prize-winning economist Robert Shiller shows, in his recently published book, how such narratives may go viral and cause or support changes in the economy and in economic behavior.[12] For political scientists familiar with narrative studies, this is nothing new: Already in 2012, our research partner Giorel Curran emphasized that narratives and discourses are central to how we interpret and understand the world:

> The capacity to construct and disseminate compelling stories about particular issues is hence critical to an agent's capacity to advance their interests (sic!).[13]

In policy studies, the relevance of narratives has even led to the development of a distinct research program, bound together by the "Narrative Policy Framework", which has resulted in several hundred academic publications over the past decade.[14] These studies focus on the power of narratives in various ways, for instance in terms of their influence on public perceptions. As Elizabeth A. Shanahan and colleagues put it:

> Policy narratives are the lifeblood of politics. These strategically constructed 'stories' contain predictable elements and strategies whose aim is to influence public opinion toward support for a particular policy preference.[15]

Giorel Curran rightly points out that "[t]he capacity to shape the main knowledge claims of discourses so that the interests of some actors are promoted while others are contained thus connotes a considerable exercise of power."[16] Such power has not been granted to the editors of this volume. In order to form a narrative, we would need to select the supporting elements suitable for the composition of a storyline, bypassing a process that normally is, at least in part, left to the peer review process that validates contributions to the progress of science. Conflicting results, that

---

[11] Kay and King (2020), p. 285.

[12] Shiller (2019).

[13] Curran (2012), p. 236.

[14] E.g., Shanahan et al. (2011), p. 535 et seq.; Shanahan et al. (2018), p. 173 et seq.

[15] Shanahan et al. (2011), p. 374.

[16] Curran (2012), p. 236.

normally would point to possibilities for further research, would most probably find their place based on how they fit the overarching narrative. Furthermore, connecting the research results of this volume towards an integrated narrative would necessarily be a construct, since the individual researchers involved never have intended that their results should support a general storyline. In short: Joint visions and common narratives are not indispensable parts of the scientific method but rather political instruments.

The analysis of discourses and narratives in a certain field of interest *ex post* is completely different from drafting and constructing narratives for the use of agencies and policymakers *ex ante*. While the *ex post* analysis of narratives is an accepted field of scientific research, the *ex ante* construction of narratives forms part of a playground for public affairs departments and spin doctors. We are confident that the readers of this volume will understand our qualms, that they will accept our conclusion that there is no easy recipe to follow here, and that they will enjoy the diversity of insights furnished to them when reading this book.

References

Curran G (2012) Contested energy futures: shaping renewable energy narratives in Australia. Glob Environ Change 22(1):236–244

Hoffmann-Riem W (2011) Die Governance-Perspektive in der rechtswissenschaftlichen Innovationsforschung. Nomos, Baden-Baden

Kay J, King M (2020) Radical uncertainty: decision-making beyond the numbers. W.W. Norton & Company, New York

Kissinger HA (1959) The policymaker and the intellectual. Reporter 5(1959):30–35

Müller M-M (2008) Raum, Herrschaft und die Produktion von (Un-)Sicherheit in Mexiko. In: De La Rosa S, Höppner U, Kötter M (eds) Transdisziplinäre Governanceforschung. Nomos, Baden-Baden, pp 58–80

Ostrom E (2005) Understanding institutional diversity. Princeton University Press, Princeton

Rhodes RAW (1996) The new governance: governing without government. Polit Stud XLIV:652–667

Schuppert GF (2008) Governance — auf der Suche nach Konturen eines "anerkannt uneindeutigen Begriffs". In: Schuppert GF, Zürn M (eds) Governance in einer sich wandelnden Welt. VS Verlag für Sozialwissenschaften, Wiesbaden, pp 13–40

Shanahan EA, Jones MD, McBeth MK (2011a) Policy narratives and policy processes. Policy Stud J 39(3):535–561

Shanahan EA, McBeth MK, Hathaway PL (2011b) Narrative policy framework: the influence of media policy narratives on public opinion. Polit Policy 39(3):373–400

Shanahan EA, Jones MD, McBeth MK, Radaelli CM (2018) The narrative policy framework. In: Weible CM, Sabatier PA (eds) Theories of the policy process. Routledge, London, pp 173–213

Shiller R (2019) Narrative economics: how stories go viral and drive major economic events. Princeton University Press, Princeton

Williamson OE (2000) The new institutional economics: taking stock, looking ahead. J Econ Liter 38(3):595–613

Peter Hettich is Director with the Institute of Public Finance, Fiscal Law and Law & Economics (IFF-HSG) and Professor for public law at the University of St. Gallen, St. Gallen, Switzerland.

Aya Kachi is Associate Professor for International Political Economy and Energy Policy, University of Basel, Faculty of Business and Economics, Basel, Switzerland.

Part I
Interactions Between Swiss and European Energy Systems and Policy

Swiss Climate Change Law

International and European Context

Julia Hänni and Tienmu Ma

Contents

This chapter provides an overview of the state of Swiss, European, and international climate change law, up to and including January 2021 when the chapter was submitted to the publisher.

J. Hänni (✉)
Swiss Federal Supreme Court, Lausanne, Switzerland

University of St. Gallen Law School, St. Gallen, Switzerland
e-mail: juliafranziska.haenni@unisg.ch

T. Ma
University of Lucerne Faculty of Law, Lucerne, Switzerland
e-mail: tienmu.ma@unilu.ch

P. Hettich, A. Kachi (eds.), *Swiss Energy Governance*,
https://doi.org/10.1007/978-3-030-80787-0_2

Abstract This chapter explores the relationship between Swiss climate change law and the international and European climate change regimes. At the international level, the chapter reviews the three major international agreements regulating the field: the United Nations Framework Convention on Climate Change (UNFCCC), the Kyoto Protocol to the UNFCCC, and the Paris Agreement. And at the national and regional levels, the chapter briefly describes the CO_2 Act—often considered the heart of Swiss climate change policy—and questions whether it will prove effective in achieving its explicitly stated emissions reduction targets. The chapter then reviews the most significant recent innovation in the evolution of Swiss climate change policy: joining the Emissions Trading System (ETS) established by the European Union. Due to long-standing problems afflicting the ETS, the authors raise doubts about whether Switzerland's joining the scheme will lead to meaningful reductions in the country's greenhouse gas emissions. As an alternative to an ETS-centric approach, the authors refer to an approach centered on human rights. Drawing on the jurisprudence of the European Court of Human Rights (ECtHR), the major international climate change agreements, other sources of international law, and the recent *Urgenda* decision of the Supreme Court of the Netherlands, the authors argue that under the human rights approach, Switzerland would be obligated to take stronger measures to reduce emissions than it could hope to achieve through the ETS and the CO_2 Act alone.

1 Introduction

Perhaps more than in other areas, the field of climate change law involves a complex interaction among different actors at multiple levels of governance. This chapter seeks to provide an overview of how this interaction—involving actors at the national, European, and international levels—has shaped the way in which the field of climate change is regulated in Switzerland. The aim of the chapter, then, will be to explore the relationship between Swiss climate change law and the international and European climate change regimes; and a further aim will be to show how Switzerland's approach to regulating this area might be improved in light of recent developments in the field of human rights law.

The chapter is divided into four main parts. The first part (Sect. 2) presents an overview of the international climate change regime as embodied in the United Nations Framework Convention on Climate Change (UNFCCC), the Kyoto Protocol to the UNFCCC, and the Paris Agreement. Switzerland is a state party to all three agreements. The second part (Sect. 3) describes the current version of the CO_2 Act—often considered the heart of Swiss climate change policy—and questions whether it will prove effective in achieving its explicitly stated emissions reduction targets. Section 3 then discusses the most significant recent innovation in the evolution of Swiss climate change policy: joining the Emissions Trading System (ETS) established by the European Union. It will be argued in the third part (Sect. 4), however, that the long-standing problems afflicting the ETS raise doubts about whether joining the scheme will lead to meaningful reductions in Switzerland's greenhouse gas emissions. As an alternative to an ETS-centered approach, the fourth and final part of the chapter (Sect. 5) suggests the possibility of a reorientation: Drawing on the jurisprudence of the European Court of Human Rights (ECtHR), the major international climate change agreements, other sources of international law, and the recent *Urgenda* decision of the Supreme Court of the Netherlands, it argues that under the human rights approach, Switzerland would be obligated to take stronger measures to reduce emissions than it could hope to achieve by joining the ETS and implementing the CO_2 Act.

2 Switzerland and the International Climate Change Regime

Switzerland does not rank as one of the main emitters of greenhouse gases in the world today: According to official data reported in 2015, it is only responsible for around 0.1% of today's global greenhouse gas emissions, which amounts to approximately 6.4 tons per capita per year.[1] In spite of this, the effects of global warming are felt to a greater degree in Switzerland than in many other countries, both in terms of the raw increase in temperature and in terms of the life-threatening ramifications of that increase. Thus, according to Proclim (*Akademie der Naturwissenschaften Schweiz*)/IPCC Switzerland,[2] the average annual temperature in Switzerland has, in the last 150 years, risen about twice as much as the global mean, with a global mean temperature increase of about 0.85 °C, as compared to a mean increase of 1.8 °C in Switzerland.[3] These significant rises in temperature over such a short period of time—considerably more rapid than the relatively gradual temperature changes of pre-industrial times—are suspected of causing deadly natural events, such as mudslides and landslides in mountainous areas of Switzerland.[4]

[1] See "Switzerland's intended nationally determined contribution (INDC) and clarifying information," available at the UNFCCC website at: https://www.unfccc.int.

[2] IPCC Switzerland, run by ProClim on behalf of the Federal Office of the Environment, aims to provide specific information on the IPCC that is relevant to Swiss researchers and stakeholders, as well as to the general public in and from Switzerland.

[3] See Swiss Academies of Arts and Science (2016), p. 14, summarizing national studies in Switzerland prepared for the IPCC AR5 (https://www.ipcc.ch/report/ar5). The IPCC was established by the United Nations Environment Programme (UNEP) and the World Meteorological Organization (WMO) in 1988 with the aim of providing the world with a scientific view on the current state of knowledge on climate change and its potential environmental and socio-economic impacts (https://www.ipcc.ch/about). The most recent data from the Swiss Federal Office of Meteorology and Climatology, from 2019, indicates an even larger increase of 2.1 °C in the previous 150 years. See "Climate Change in Switzerland," available at https://www.meteoswiss.admin.ch.

[4] See, e.g., McClanahan (2019); see also "Klimaseniorinnen reichen Klage ein", *Neue Zürcher Zeitung* (25 October 2016), available at https://www.nzz.ch, which describes the first climate change–related lawsuit filed in Switzerland. The lawsuit was filed by a group of elderly women

Despite not being a major greenhouse gas emitter, Switzerland has reacted sensitively to the global problem of climate change. It has ratified the UNFCCC, the Kyoto Protocol, and the Paris Agreement. All of these agreements impose greater obligations and expectations on Switzerland and other developed countries than the corresponding obligations they impose on developing countries. The following three subsections review and compare the respective agreements.[5]

2.1 *The United Nations Framework Convention on Climate Change (UNFCCC)*

2.1.1 Overview and Main Purpose

The UNFCCC was opened for signature at the 1992 Rio Conference and has been in force since 1994, with 195 parties. The UNFCCC is a framework convention, in the sense that it sets the most important guidelines but does not impose any substantive targets.

According to Art. 2 of the Convention, preventing dangerous human interference with the climate system is the aim of the UNFCCC. The primary objective is "*to achieve (...) stabilization of greenhouse gas concentrations in the atmosphere at a level that would prevent dangerous anthropogenic interference with the climate system. Such a level should be achieved within a time frame sufficient to allow ecosystems to adapt naturally to climate change, to ensure that food production is not threatened and to enable economic development to proceed in a sustainable manner.*"

2.1.2 Main Principles

In their actions to achieve these aims, the Parties to the UNFCCC are to be guided by four main principles (Art. 3 UNFCCC).

First, the Convention states that the Parties should "*protect the climate system for the benefit of present and future generations of humankind, on the basis of equity*

---

claiming that the Swiss government violated their human rights by failing to take adequate measures to reduce greenhouse gas emissions. According to the plaintiffs, this failure has contributed to increasingly intense and frequent heat waves in Switzerland as a result of global warming, thereby putting the plaintiffs' life and health at risk. For a comprehensive overview of the litigation, see Bär et al. (2018), p. 194. The Swiss Federal Supreme Court, First Public Law Division, dismissed the lawsuit; see the Court's judgment no. 1C_37/2019, issued on 5 May 2020. On 26 November 2020, the plaintiffs filed an application before the ECtHR, challenging the Federal Supreme Court's ruling. A copy of the application can be found at KlimaSeniorinnen Schweiz's website: https://klimaseniorinnen.ch.

[5]For an overview of the UN climate treaties, see Hänni (2020), pp. 619–620, as well as Hänni (2019), pp. 3–6, for further details.

and in accordance with their common but differentiated responsibilities. Accordingly, the developed country Parties should take the lead in combating climate change and the adverse effects thereof" (Art. 3 para. 1 UNFCCC). This distinction between the obligations of developed countries and those of all countries in addressing the problem of climate change is an example of the principle of "*common but differentiated responsibilities.*"

Second, the UNFCCC incorporates a version of the *precautionary principle*, obligating state Parties to take "*precautionary measures to anticipate, prevent or minimize the causes of climate change and mitigate its adverse effects*" (Art. 3 para. 3 UNFCCC).[6] Significantly, Article 3 also makes clear that, where there is a threat of serious or irreversible damage, the absence of full scientific certainty should not be considered a reason to postpone the precautionary measures.

Third, according to the *integration principle*, "*The Parties have the right to, and should, promote sustainable development. Policies and measures to protect the climate system ... should be integrated with national development programmes, taking into account that economic development is essential for adopting measures to address climate change*" (Art. 3 para. 4). This principle attempts to strike a careful balance between, on the one hand, the right of countries—especially developing countries—to pursue their own economic development and, on the other hand, the expectation that these countries will take steps to ensure that this development proceeds in such a fashion that it does not impede the achievement of climate protection goals.

And fourth, the *principle of cooperation* states that "*[t]he Parties should cooperate ... to address the problems of climate change*" (Art. 3 para. 5). Climate change is a global problem, and this provision recognizes that it requires a global solution, involving cooperation among all parties, with each party doing its fair share. As we shall see below, this principle gains in significance when climate change is viewed from a human rights perspective.[7]

The first principle—the principle of "*common but differentiated responsibilities*"—is perhaps the most important of the four. The principle finds expression not only in the UNFCCC but also in the Kyoto Protocol and the Paris Agreement. And it also provides a key to understanding the substantive obligations these conventions impose on developed and developing countries, respectively.

---

[6]The term *mitigation* refers to all efforts to reduce or prevent emission of greenhouse gases. Mitigation can mean using new technologies and renewable energies, making older equipment more energy-efficient, or changing management practices or consumer behavior (see Art. 3 para. 3; Art. 4 para. 1 subpara. b; Art. 4 para. 1 subpara. f; Art. 4 para. 2 subpara. a UNFCCC). A secondary objective of the Convention is *adaptation* to the change. This refers to helping communities and ecosystems cope with changing climate conditions (Art. 4 para.1 subpara. b, Art. 4 para.1 subpara. e and Art. 4 para. 4 UNFCCC). Examples of adaptation include the more efficient use of water resources due to climate change—induced droughts and the building of physical defenses against floods caused by rising sea levels.

[7]See note 68 below and Sect. 5 generally.

The differing responsibilities imposed on developed and developing countries are a reflection of the fact that the former countries are the source of most past and current greenhouse gas emissions.[8] Therefore, industrialized countries are expected to contribute the most to cutting emissions on home ground, in this way taking the lead in modifying anthropogenic emissions of greenhouse gases consistent with the objective of the UNFCCC (Art. 4 para. 2 subpara. a UNFCCC). These countries are called Annex I countries, which are those belonging to the Organization for Economic Cooperation and Development (OECD), including Switzerland, as well as 12 countries considered to be "*economies in transition*."

In line with this, Art. 4 of the Convention sets up a system of differentiated commitments applying to developed countries and developing countries respectively. For example, the industrialized countries listed in Annex I are required to adopt national policies to mitigate climate change by limiting greenhouse gas emissions through the protection and enhancement of greenhouse gas sinks and reservoirs (Art. 4 para. 2 subpara. a UNFCCC).[9] The aim is to individually or jointly return to their 1990 level of anthropogenic emissions of carbon dioxide and other greenhouse gases not controlled by the Montreal Protocol (Art. 4 para. 2 subpara. b UNFCCC). However, it must be noted that the Convention does not contain any information on concrete measures, nor does it include a binding definition of the reduction target (level of 1990 until the year 2000). Concrete legal implications come only with the Protocols.

According to Art. 4 para. 2 subparas. a and b UNFCCC, industrialized countries shall individually or "*jointly*" return to their 1990 level of anthropogenic emissions of carbon dioxide and other greenhouse gases. The concentration of greenhouse gases in the atmosphere does not depend on where they are emitted or reduced. Industrialized states may therefore implement the required measures "*together with other states*," and measures can be taken where the marginal cost is the lowest. This clause has opened the Convention to criticism on the part of developing countries, as it allows the most powerful industrial states to find ways around their duties of reduction.

Annex II of the Convention deals with new financial resources. The UNFCCC directs new funds to climate change activities in developing countries as a duty of countries listed in Annex II, which is a shorter list, also including Switzerland. Thus, industrialized nations listed in Annex II agree to support climate change activities in developing countries by providing new financial support for action on climate change, above and beyond any financial assistance they already provide to these countries (Art. 4 para. 3 UNFCCC). Furthermore, a system of grants and loans has been set up through the Convention and is managed by the Global Environment

---

[8] See, e.g., Center for Global Development (2015); see also Rocha et al. (2015).

[9] According to Art. 1 paras. 7 and 8, respectively, a "reservoir" is defined as "a component or components of the climate system where a greenhouse gas or a precursor of a greenhouse gas is stored"; and a "sink" is defined as "any process, activity or mechanism which removes a greenhouse gas, an aerosol or a precursor of a greenhouse gas from the atmosphere."

Facility (Art. 21 para. 3 UNFCCC). Developing countries are to be supported with regard to costs of adapting to the adverse effects of climate change (Art. 4 para. 4 UNFCCC). And industrialized countries agree to share environmentally sound technologies and know-how with developing countries to enable the implementation of the Convention (Art. 4 para. 3, Art. 4 para. 5, Art. 4 para. 8 UNFCCC).

Despite the more stringent duties imposed on the developed countries, the UNFCCC also imposes some duties on developing countries, such as establishing inventories of anthropogenic emissions by sources and removals by sinks, and developing and implementing national/regional programs to mitigate climate change and to communicate information related to implementation (Art. 4 para. 1 subparas. a, b and j UNFCCC).[10]

Such duties, however, are subject to a relationship of conditionality vis-à-vis the developed countries' fulfillment of their duties. Art. 4 para. 7 UNFCCC states:

> The extent to which developing country Parties will effectively implement their commitments under the Convention will depend on the effective implementation by developed country Parties of their commitments under the Convention related to financial resources and transfer of technology and will take fully into account that economic and social development and poverty eradication are the first and overriding priorities of the developing country Parties.

2.1.3 Conference of the Parties

The Conference of the Parties (COP) is the supreme body of the Convention, as provided for by Art. 7 UNFCCC. The COP is charged with the following responsibilities:

- regular review of the implementation of the convention, that is, periodic examination of the Parties' obligations (Art. 7 para. 2 let a UNFCCC);
- providing and facilitating exchange of information on measures adopted by the Parties to address climate change (Art. 7 para. 2 subpara. b UNFCCC);
- making recommendations on matters necessary for implementation (Art. 7 para. 2 subpara. g UNFCCC).

Ordinary COPs are to be held every year (Art. 7 para. 4 UNFCCC). All states that are Parties to the Convention are represented at COP meetings, and the admission of observers (agencies of the UN, NGOs) is also possible. Meetings of the COP are

---

[10] For example, the Fourth National Communication of Mexico to the United Nations Framework Convention on Climate Change (Mexican Interministerial Commission on Climate Change [2011]) describes updates to its National Greenhouse Gas Inventory (pp. 55–103) as well as various efforts at mitigation and adaptation, such as a National Water Program that aims "*to reduce the risks associated with meteorological and hydrometeorological extremes and address their impacts*" (p. 116). Switzerland's greenhouse gas inventory is available at the website of the Federal Office for the Environment, https://www.bafu.admin.ch.

numbered in the order in which they are held. For example, "COP 13" represents the thirteenth Conference of the Parties.

The COP also has the power to adopt related legal instruments. Thus, "*the Conference of the Parties may, at any ordinary session, adopt protocols to the Convention*" (Art. 17 para. 1 UNFCCC). Protocols[11] can contain regulations concerning specific air pollutants or groups of air pollutants as well as provisions on concrete quantitative reduction targets. The most important related instruments are the Kyoto Protocol to the UNFCCC (Kyoto Protocol) and recently the Paris Agreement.

2.2 The Kyoto Protocol

2.2.1 Overview

The first meeting of the Conference of the Parties (COP 1) took place in Berlin in 1995. There, the Parties agreed to produce a Protocol containing quantitative measures and reduction targets. Two years later, COP 3 in Kyoto adopted a Protocol to the UNFCCC, containing legally binding reduction targets and imposing time limits on industrialized states concerning greenhouse gases (Art. 3 in conjunction with Annexes A and B Kyoto Protocol). The Protocol entered into force on 16 February 2005.

Recognizing again that developed countries are principally responsible for the current high levels of greenhouse gas emissions in the atmosphere as a result of more than 150 years of industrial activity, the Protocol places a heavier burden on developed nations under the aforementioned principle of "*common but differentiated responsibilities*." The Kyoto Protocol currently has 192 Parties, including Switzerland.[12] The negotiations were difficult, and some major countries have still not become parties to the Protocol, including the United States and Canada.

2.2.2 Emission Reduction Mechanisms

Art. 3 para. 1 of the Protocol states:

> The Parties included in Annex I shall, individually or jointly, ensure that their aggregate anthropogenic carbon dioxide equivalent emissions of the greenhouse gases listed in Annex A do not exceed their assigned amounts, calculated pursuant to their quantified emission limitation and reduction commitments inscribed in Annex B and in accordance with the

[11] This is not to be confused with the Montreal Protocol of 1987, whose aim was to protect the ozone layer from depletion (SR 0.814.021).

[12] See the Kyoto Protocol's status of ratification, available at: https://unfccc.int/process/the-kyoto-protocol/status-of-ratification.

provisions of this Article, with a view to reducing their overall emissions of such gases by at least 5 per cent below 1990 levels in the commitment period 2008 to 2012.

States listed in UNFCCC Annex I must therefore individually or jointly ensure that they do not exceed the emission limitations listed in Annex B of the Kyoto Protocol. The industrialized states listed in UNFCCC Annex I are required to achieve different quantitative reduction targets listed in the Kyoto Protocol's Annex B in order to achieve the aim of the Protocol.

According to Art. 2 para. 1 subpara. a of the Protocol, industrialized states must develop and implement national measures to reduce CO_2 emissions, adopting policies of energy efficiency, reforestation, and sustainable agriculture, and to phase out fiscal incentives, tax exemptions, and subsidies that run counter to the aims of the UNFCCC and the Kyoto Protocol.

But the Protocol also offers additional means to meet emission reduction targets. These include joint implementation and fulfillment, the Clean Development Mechanism, and international emissions trading.

Art. 3 para. 10 and Art. 3 para. 11 of the Protocol, in conjunction with Art. 6, foresee *joint implementation*, allowing states listed in UNFCCC Annex I to transfer emission reduction units to other states listed in Annex I. When financing emission reductions in another state, the respective emission reduction units are attributable to their own reduction targets.

The Protocol also provides for *joint fulfillment*. According to Art. 3 para. 1, in conjunction with Art. 4 of the Protocol, states can meet reduction targets in groups (the sum of individual reduction targets can be met by the whole group of states), e.g., the countries of the European Union.

The Kyoto Protocol's *Clean Development Mechanism* is delineated in Art. 12. It allows a country with an emission reduction or emission limitation commitment (Annex B country) to implement an emission reduction project in a developing country. Such projects can earn saleable certified emission reduction credits, which can then be counted towards meeting the Protocol's targets.

The Clean Development Mechanism represents the first global environmental investment and credit scheme of its kind. It might involve, for example, a rural electrification project using solar panels or the installation of more energy-efficient boilers. The mechanism stimulates sustainable development and emission reductions, while giving industrialized countries some flexibility in meeting their emission reduction or limitation targets.

2.2.3 Emissions Trading

As indicated above, another major innovation of the Kyoto Protocol is emissions trading, covered under Art. 17: "*The Parties included in Annex B [industrialized states] may participate in emissions trading for the purposes of fulfilling their commitments under Art. 3 [compliance with their reduction targets].*"

Emissions trading allows countries that have emission units to spare—i.e., permitted emissions left unused—to sell this excess capacity to countries that are over their targets. Art. 17 rests on two main premises: (1) emissions trading is open to states subject to the commitments in Annex B; and (2) trading must be supplemental to domestic actions. Since carbon dioxide is the principal greenhouse gas, emissions trading is often referred to as the "carbon market."

2.3 The Paris Agreement

2.3.1 Overview

In terms of effectiveness, the Kyoto Protocol had the advantage of a top-down prescriptive nature, as well as an implementation clause. However, in the end it proved not to be as effective as initially hoped. This is in large part due to the fact that, as noted above, it has failed to gain the support of some of the countries that contribute the most to worldwide greenhouse gas emissions.

In December 2015, the 21st Conference of the Parties to the UNFCCC adopted the "*Paris Agreement*," a new collective treaty to fight anthropogenic climate change. The Agreement is an instrument linked to the UNFCCC. After 25 years of UN climate diplomacy, the Paris Agreement was the first treaty to envisage climate action by all nations. Notably, the Agreement's preamble makes an explicit link between climate change and the fulfillment of human rights obligations.[13]

2.3.2 The 2 °C Limit

Article 2 of the Paris Agreement proposes some ambitious objectives. The long-term goal of the Agreement is to keep global temperature rise "well below 2°C" (Art. 2 Paris Agreement). This is a strengthened goal in comparison with earlier language. According to recent science (IPCC), the 2 °C limit would probably—though not certainly—prevent the most severe effects of climate change. Article 2 also contains the aim to "*pursu[e] efforts to limit the temperature increase to 1.5°C above pre-industrial levels*", as proposed by small island states and least developed countries. This will be a challenge, especially for countries that have yet to lift the majority of their citizens from poverty.

[13] See Preamble para. 11 Paris Agreement: "Acknowledging that climate change is a common concern of humankind, Parties should, when taking action to address climate change, respect, promote and consider their respective obligations on human rights, the right to health, the rights of indigenous peoples, local communities, migrants, children, persons with disabilities and people in vulnerable situations and the right to development, as well as gender equality, empowerment of women and intergenerational equity."

How, then, can the "well below 2°C" goal be reached? First, Parties aim to reach "*global peaking of greenhouse gas emissions as soon as possible*" (Art. 4 para. 1 Paris Agreement). However, no peaking dates and no percentage reductions are mentioned, recognizing that peaking will take longer for developing countries. Second, rapid reductions are foreseen thereafter: achieving a balance between anthropogenic emissions by reducing the emission of greenhouse gases during the second half of the century (Art. 4 para. 1, Art. 5 para. 1 Paris Agreement). Third, Parties shall formulate and implement long-term low greenhouse gas emission development strategies (Art. 4 para. 19 Paris Agreement). And fourth, stronger mitigation is provided for through so-called Nationally Determined Contributions (NDCs; Art. 3 Paris Agreement).

2.3.3 Nationally Determined Contributions

Let us take a closer look at this last mechanism, the Nationally Determined Contributions (NDCs). The Paris Agreement states that "*[e]ach Party shall prepare, communicate and maintain successive nationally determined contributions that it intends to achieve. Parties shall pursue domestic mitigation measures, with the aim of achieving the objectives of such contributions*" (Art. 4 para. 2 Paris Agreement). The Agreement contains no binding concrete contribution—only an expectation. It is, however, binding in the sense of an obligation of conduct in good faith (Parties are required to "prepare," "intend to achieve," etc.).[14] The NDC scheme therefore represents a "bottom-up approach," unlike its predecessor, the Kyoto Protocol.

According to the Agreement, developed countries should continue to take the lead by undertaking an "*absolute emission reduction target*"; developing countries are to continue enhancing mitigation (Art. 4 para. 2, Art. 4 para. 4 Paris Agreement).

Furthermore, each successive NDC is to represent a progression beyond the previous and to reflect the "*highest possible ambition*." This means that adjustment of the contributions is possible only in the direction of enhancing the level of ambition (see Art. 4 para. 3 Paris Agreement; "*ambition*" or "*ratchet mechanism*"). But again, the "*highest possible ambition*" is left to national determination. The efforts of all Parties are to represent a progression over time (Art. 3 Paris Agreement; collective requirement).

2.3.4 International Linkage and Adaptation

Article 6 of the Paris Agreement provides for a Sustainable Development Mechanism. International linkage under this provision gives the Parties a "green light" to develop carbon markets to promote the mitigation of greenhouse gas emissions while fostering sustainable development. Thus, similar to the Kyoto Protocol,

[14] See Hänni (2019), p. 4, for a detailed discussion.

emission reductions occurring outside of a Party's territory can be counted toward achieving the Party's Nationally Determined Contribution (Art. 6 para. 4 subpara. c Paris Agreement). This enables both the formation of coalitions and bottom-up heterogeneous linkage.[15] Different forms of emissions trading, explicitly provided for in the Kyoto Protocol, are therefore also possible under the Paris Agreement.

Article 7 of the Paris Agreement deals with mechanisms for adaptation, that is, instruments for dealing with the inevitable effects of climate change. The Paris Agreement establishes a global goal on adaptation, including through support for and international cooperation on adaptation efforts (Art. 7 paras. 1 and 6 Paris Agreement). Developing country Parties will receive enhanced support for adaptation actions (Art. 7 para. 7 Paris Agreement). All Parties are expected to engage in adaptation planning and to submit and periodically update an adaptation communication on their priorities, implementation and support needs, plans and actions (Art. 7 para. 10 Paris Agreement).

2.3.5 Loss and Damage and Global Stocktake

Article 8 of the Paris Agreement, concerning loss and damage, provides for yet another mechanism for climate action, in addition to mitigation and adaptation. Thus, the Paris Agreement builds on the Warsaw International Mechanism by providing for formal recognition and comprehensive risk management approaches to address loss and damage associated with the adverse effects of climate change. This new mechanism has not, however, been fully developed and will have to be concretized by future COPs in order to serve as an effective basis for compensation. Most recently, the mechanism was subject to intense negotiations at COP 25, where a key sticking point was the issue of how to finance the mechanism. There was consensus among the Parties that financing to avert, minimize, and address loss and damage must be "*scaled up*."[16] But the Parties could not come to an agreement to obligate developed countries in particular to fund this scaling up.[17]

[15] There are three relevant types of heterogeneity. First, there may be heterogeneity of policy instruments: It is possible not only to link two cap-and-trade systems, for example, but also a cap-and-trade system and a carbon tax system. Second, there may be heterogeneity in the formulation of the countries' respective NDCs themselves: Some NDCs, for example, might specify an aggregate emissions cap, while others might have only a cap on emissions per unit of economic activity. And third, there may be heterogeneity of jurisdiction: The systems to be linked can exist at regional, national, or sub-national jurisdictions. The agreement linking the EU and Switzerland's respective emissions trading systems (see Sect. 3 below) is an example of this kind of heterogeneity. The various types of heterogeneity are explained in Stavins (2016), pp. 54–55.

[16] See Decision 2/CMA.2, Warsaw International Mechanism for Loss and Damage associated with Climate Change Impacts and its 2019 review, §§ 30, 32, 33, and 35.

[17] For an account of the negotiations, see Pierre-Nathoniel, Siegele, et al., "Loss and Damage at COP25 – a hard fought step in the right direction," The Climate Analytics Blog (20 December 2019), available at: https://climateanalytics.org.

The Paris Agreement also provides that each Party is to report information on mitigation, adaptation, and support; the agreement requires that the information submitted by each Party undergo international review. A "*global stocktake*" is slated to take place in 2023 and every 5 years thereafter to assess collective progress toward fulfilling the purpose of the agreement (Art. 14 Paris Agreement). The outcomes of the stocktake will inform Parties in updating and enhancing their own national actions as well as international cooperation.

In 2018, a facilitative dialogue took place in order to encourage collective progress towards the long-term emission reduction goal of Art. 4 Paris Agreement. The dialogue was officially named the "*Talanoa Dialogue*," inspired by the Fijian tradition of dialogue in an inclusive and participatory manner. The dialogue culminated in the "*Talanoa Call for Action*" issued jointly by the Presidents of COP 23 and COP 24. The call was directed towards a wide range of actors and stakeholders, including state institutions, the private sector, and civil society, reiterating the goal of the Paris Agreement "*to hold temperature rise well below 2 degrees Celsius and to pursue efforts to limit it to 1.5 degrees.*"[18]

2.3.6 Assessment of the Paris Agreement as Compared to Its Predecessors

The Paris Agreement is distinctive in a number of ways as compared to its two predecessors, the UNFCCC and the Kyoto Protocol. The guiding principles stated in the UNFCCC are put into more or less concrete form in the Paris Agreement. But unlike the Kyoto Protocol, the Paris Agreement does not take a top-down, prescriptive approach—an approach that, as noted above, has thus far proved politically unsuccessful in gaining the support of some of the world's most important countries in terms of greenhouse gas emissions, though it remains to be seen whether this will change in the future.[19] The Paris Agreement instead takes a bottom-up facilitative approach[20] as a starting point, with national contributions constituting the bottom, and with rules of transparency, reporting, and so on constituting the top elements.[21] The Paris Agreement represents a facilitative rather than a prescriptive instrument. It tries to find a balance between, on the one hand, ensuring autonomy for states in the determination of their contributions and, on the other hand, strengthening oversight

---

[18] See the "Talanoa Call for Action," available at https://unfccc.int.

[19] It should be noted, however, that the Paris Agreement has also run into difficulties in this respect: It lost the support of the United States during the Trump Administration, which filed a formal withdrawal notice on 4 November 2019. The withdrawal took effect one year later, in accordance with Art. 28 para. 2 Paris Agreement. The United States' withdrawal ended up being a temporary one: On his first day in office, President Biden signed an executive order rejoining the Paris Agreement. See Milman, "Biden returns US to Paris climate accord hours after becoming president," The Guardian (21 January 2021), available at https://www.theguardian.com.

[20] This term is also used in Dehm (2018), p. 74.

[21] On the combination of bottom-up and top-down elements, see also Rajamani (2016), p. 502.

of these contributions through a robust transparency system, a global stocktake process (leading to the incremental adjustment of Nationally Determined Contributions in service of the long-term goals), and a compliance mechanism. However, the Agreement leaves mechanisms to be finalized by the Parties. And there are no clear and specific goals in relation to finance, technology and capacity-building.[22]

3 Swiss Climate Policy and the EU Emissions Trading System

3.1 The CO_2 Act and the Agreement on Linking the Emissions Trading Systems of the EU and Switzerland

The heart of Swiss climate policy is commonly considered to be the Federal Act on the Reduction of CO_2 Emissions, or simply the CO_2 Act. The current version of the Act, of 23 December 2011, entered into force on 1 January 2013 and has been subjected to occasional revisions in the interim,[23] whereas a new version of the Act, of 25 September 2020, has been approved by the Parliament but has yet to enter into force, pending the results of a popular referendum.[24]

The aim of the Act, stated in Article 1, is to reduce greenhouse gas emissions and in particular CO_2 emissions resulting from the use of fossil fuels in energy. Echoing Article 2 of the Paris Agreement, the Act aims to contribute to limiting the increase in global temperatures to well below 2 °C compared to pre-industrial levels and to contribute to efforts to limit that increase to below 1.5 °C.

More specifically, Article 3 of the Act also stipulates concrete emission reduction goals for Switzerland: a target of 50% in emission reduction compared to 1990 levels, by 2030, with a 35% reduction over the period of 2021–2030. It is worth noting that, in addition to these statutory aims, the Federal Council has set an even more ambitious post-2030 goal: net-zero emissions by 2050. This commitment has

[22] As noted by Arens et al. (2015), p. 4: "*The Paris Agreement only contains vague language concerning concrete financing contributions for mitigation and adaptation in developing countries. Legal bindingness of financing contributions in the Paris Agreement has been sacrificed due to pressure by the USA.*"

[23] *Bundesgesetz über die Reduktion der CO_2-Emissionen (CO_2-Gesetz; SR 641.71) vom 11. Dezember 2011.*

[24] *Bundesgesetz über die Verminderung von Treibhausgasemissionen (CO_2-Gesetz) vom 25. September 2020.* Unless otherwise stated, references to the Act will henceforth be to this, the latest version. Regarding the popular referendum, see "Climate and Covid laws set to come to public vote," SWI Swissinfo.ch (12 January 2021), available at https://www.swissinfo.ch. As the article notes, opponents of the law appear to have gathered more than enough signatures to force a referendum, but this has yet to be officially confirmed.

been confirmed in Switzerland's official communication to the UNFCCC under the Paris Agreement.[25]

That the CO_2 Act is considered the heart of Swiss climate policy is affirmed in its own text, which states that the aforementioned emission reduction target is to be achieved primarily through the Act's provisions (Art. 4 para. 1). One of the central instruments for the achievement of that target is the CO_2 levy, which imposes a tax on the production, extraction, and import of thermal fuels (Art. 34–41). The resultant increase in the price of fossil fuels creates an incentive to use them more economically, as well as to choose more low-carbon energy sources. And in a major revision of the previous version of the Act, the latest version adds a tax to be imposed on airline tickets and on aviation operations generally (Art. 42–52).

Furthermore, the Act aims to contribute to the reduction of emissions through the improvement of building standards (Art. 9–10) and the imposition of more stringent limits on vehicle emissions (Art. 11–20). Article 19 of the Act provides for fines on vehicle manufacturers that fail to abide by these limits.

In line with the flexible mechanisms of the Kyoto Protocol—specifically, the aforementioned Clean Development Mechanism and joint implementation—the Act allows for emission reductions achieved abroad to count toward the overall emission target (Art. 5), though it stipulates that 75% of the reductions must come by way of measures undertaken in Switzerland (Art. 3 para. 2). Notably, however, the Act does nothing to address emissions in the agricultural sector, which is responsible for 12.9% of Switzerland's overall emissions, according to recent data.[26]

The Act foresees an emissions trading system (Art. 21–33). Companies in specific categories that operate installations with high greenhouse gas emissions are required to participate in the scheme (Art. 21), as well as operators of aircraft taking off from or landing in Switzerland (Art. 22). The permits are allocated to the companies free of charge to the extent that the emissions are necessary for greenhouse gas–efficient production, whereas further permits are auctioned (Art. 26). Each year, companies must surrender emission permits or emission reduction certificates equal to the emissions caused (Art. 21 para. 2). The Federal Council determines in advance the quantity of emission permits available each year until 2030, taking into account comparable international regulations (Art. 25 para. 1). For emissions that exceed the permits, companies must pay 220 CHF per tonne CO_2 equivalent (CO_2eq), and the missing emission permits must be surrendered to the Confederation in the following year (Art. 29).

The Act also establishes a special Climate Fund based on the proceeds raised from the CO_2 levy, the airline and general aviation taxes, the auctions of emission permits, and the penalties paid by vehicle manufacturers failing to abide by vehicle emissions limits (Art. 53–61). The Act specifies how these proceeds are to be spent,

---

[25] See "Communication and update on Switzerland's NDC in accordance with UNFCCC decision 1/CP.21, § 24-25" (submitted in 2020, reaffirming the 50% reduction goal by 2030 and declaring a new goal of net-zero emissions by 2050), available at https://www.unfccc.int.

[26] See Federal Office of the Environment (2020), p. 282.

such as for initiatives aimed at further reduction of greenhouse gas emissions or at the prevention of damage to persons or property as a result of climate change (Art. 53 para. 2 and Art. 53 para. 3).

As noted above, the version of the CO_2 Act currently in force has been in place since 2013. Its effectiveness, however, has been called into serious question. The Act had set a national target of a 20% emissions reduction, compared to 1990 levels, by 2020 (Art. 3). But according to current projections, Switzerland has probably fallen short of that goal: The Federal Office of the Environment has reported that the reduction in emissions from the base year 1990 until 2018 was only 14%; it thus deems the 2020 goal unlikely to be achieved and declares the current evolutionary trend to be "*unsatisfactory*."[27] There is also reason to worry that Switzerland will miss the even more ambitious 50% reduction target set by the new CO_2 Act for the year 2030. At least one independent analysis predicts that, even on the assumption that the new version of the Act is approved by the popular referendum, enters into force, and is fully implemented, the country would only manage a 37.5% emissions reduction compared to 1990 levels.[28]

3.2 *Agreement on Linking the Emissions Trading Systems of the EU and Switzerland*

As noted above, the emissions trading system is one of the main mitigation measures foreseen by the CO_2 Act. Recently, Switzerland has taken a major step toward linking that system with the European Union's parallel scheme. Along these lines, the "*Agreement between the European Union and the Swiss Confederation on the linking of their greenhouse gas emissions trading systems*" was ratified, and it entered into force on 1 January 2020.[29] The effect of the agreement is that companies in the Swiss scheme are now permitted to trade on the EU ETS market.

[27] Federal Office for the Environment, "Climate: Indicators," available at: https://www.bafu.admin.ch.

[28] Climate Action Tracker, Country Summary: Switzerland (30 November 2020); see section entitled "Current Policy Projections," available at: https://climateactiontracker.org/countries/switzerland.

[29] *Abkommen zwischen der Schweizerischen Eidgenossenschaft und der Europäischen Union zur Verknüpfung ihrer jeweiligen Systeme für den Handel mit Treibhausgasemissionen*, SR 0.814.011.268.

3.3 EU ETS and the "European Green Deal"

Let us take a more detailed look at the EU Emissions Trading System. The ETS is a regional realization of emissions trading as foreseen in Article 17 of the Kyoto Protocol and Article 6 of the Paris Agreement.

The point of departure of the emissions trading system is to ask: What if pollution had a financial price? The "*cap and trade system*" created by economists has three main elements. First, authorities limit the amount of CO_2 emissions that industries are allowed to produce; this is the "*cap*." Permits to pollute are then distributed to companies; if a company emits more than its limit, it is required to pay a fine, thereby creating an incentive to find cleaner ways of operating. Finally, if a company emits less than it is permitted to, it can sell its permission to other companies; this is the "*trade*."

Every year the total number of permits is reduced; there is thus a "*declining cap*," entailing that it will become increasingly expensive to pollute.

In 2005, the EU introduced the world's biggest carbon trading system to date. The system represents the European Union's main effort at reducing overall emissions. The legal basis of the system is Directive 2003/87/EC of the European Parliament and of the Council of 13 October 2003 establishing a scheme for greenhouse gas emission allowance trading within the Community and amending Council Directive 96/61/EC.

The Directive adopts the market-based approach characteristic of cap-and-trade systems: Emitters operate under a declining emission cap and CO_2 is priced. The aim is to generate financial incentives to reduce greenhouse gas emissions. The ETS limits emissions from power stations, industrial plants, and airlines, encompassing more than 11,000 such entities, which together comprise nearly half of the EU's CO_2 emissions.

Heavy CO_2 emitting companies in the EU receive emission permits ("*cap*"), with each permit granting the holder the right to emit one ton of CO_2 or the equivalent amount of two more powerful greenhouse gases, nitrous oxide (N_2O) and perfluorocarbons (PFCs).

At the end of each year a company must surrender enough allowances to cover all of its emissions; otherwise, fines are imposed. If a company reduces its emissions, it can keep the spare permits to cover its future needs or sell them to another company that is short on permits ("*trade*"). Like Switzerland, the EU has set ambitious goals for emission reduction: The European Commission has proposed a minimum 55% reduction in emissions by 2030 as compared to 1990 levels and no net emissions by 2050.[30] The ETS remains the centerpiece of the EU's effort to achieve these goals; and indeed, the Commission foresees an expanded role for the ETS going forward.[31]

3.4 *Details of the Scheme*

The EU ETS covers the following gases and sectors:

(1) Carbon dioxide (CO_2) from power and heat generation; energy-intensive industry sectors including oil refineries, steel works and production of iron, aluminum, metals, cement, lime, glass, ceramics, pulp, paper, cardboard, acids; and commercial aviation;
(2) Nitrous oxide (N_2O) from production of nitric, adipic and glyoxylic acids and glyoxal (production of nylon, fertilizers, disinfectants, antibiotics etc.);
(3) Perfluorocarbons (PFCs) from aluminum production.

The EU ETS has proceeded thus far in three phases. The first phase, described as the "*learning-by-doing*" phase, began on 1 January 2005 and ended on 31 December 2007. Among the key features of Phase 1 were:[32]

(1) It covered only CO_2 emissions from power generators and energy-intensive industries.
(2) Almost all allowances were given to businesses for free.
(3) The penalty for non-compliance was 40€ per ton.

Phase 2 of the EU ETS overlapped with the first commitment period of the Kyoto Protocol, which had set concrete reduction targets for state Parties. The European Commission identifies the following key features of Phase 2 of the EU ETS:

(1) There was a lower cap on allowances (approximately 6.5% lower compared to Phase 1).
(2) Iceland, Liechtenstein, and Norway joined the scheme.
(3) Nitrous oxide emissions from nitric acid production were included by some countries in the scheme.
(4) Free allocation of allowances fell to 90%.
(5) Several countries held auctions of allowances.
(6) The non-compliance penalty was increased to 100€ per ton.
(7) Businesses were permitted to buy international credits amounting to approximately 1.4 billion tons of CO_2-equivalent.

---

[30] See European Commission (2020).

[31] European Commission (2020), pp. 13–16.

[32] These are the key features of Phase 1, as identified by the European Commission. See "Phases 1 and 2 (2005–2012)," (https://ec.europa.eu/clima/policies/ets/pre2013_en#tab-0-0).

(8) A Union-wide registry replaced national registries and the European Union Transaction Log replaced the Community Independent Transaction Log.
(9) The aviation sector was brought into the ETS on 1 January 2012.[33]

Phase 3 of the EU ETS ran from 2013 to 2020. The European Commission has pointed to four main changes from the previous two phases:

(1) A single, EU-level cap has been imposed in place of the previous national caps.
(2) Auctioning has replaced free allocation as the default method of allocating allowances, and a unified set of rules now governs allowances that are distributed for free.
(3) More sectors and gases have been included.
(4) 300 million allowances have been set aside in the New Entrants Reserve to fund the deployment of innovative, renewable energy technologies and carbon capture and storage.[34]

The current phase of the ETS, Phase 4, is expected to run from 2021 to 2030. In order to achieve even a 40% reduction in emissions compared to 1990 levels—which is significantly lower than the European Commission's proposed 55% reduction ambition noted above—the Commission calculates that the sectors included in the EU ETS would have to reduce their emissions by 43% compared to 2005 levels.[35]

With this target in mind, the Commission plans to implement a number of revisions to the scheme. Among the key revisions are:

(1) Increasing the pace of annual reductions in allowances to 2.2% as of 2021;
(2) Strengthening the Market Stability Reserve;[36]
(3) Continuing the free allocation of allowances to ensure the competitiveness of industrial sectors, while at the same time ensuring that free-allocation rules are in line with technological progress;
(4) Aiding industries and the power sectors with low-carbon funding measures.[37]

---

[33] These are the key features of Phase 2, as identified by the European Commission, in "Phases 1 and 2 (2005–2012)."

[34] These features are the key features identified by the European Commission in its description of the EU ETS (https://ec.europa.eu/clima/policies/ets_en).

[35] See "Revision for phase 4 (2021–2030)" (https://ec.europa.eu/clima/policies/ets/revision_en).

[36] The Market Stability Reserve is a mechanism that began operating near the end of Phase 3, in January 2019, with the aim of reducing the allowances surplus in the carbon market and improving the scheme's resilience to future shocks. See "Market Stability Reserve" at the European Commission's Climate Action website (https://ec.europa.eu/clima/policies/ets/reform_en). The mechanism is described in further detail in Sect. 4.3 below.

[37] These key features of Phase 4 are identified on the Commission's Climate Action website, "Revision for phase 4 (2021–2030)."

4 Criticisms of the Emissions Trading System

4.1 Far More Modest Reduction than Required

The ETS is the EU's flagship emissions reduction scheme, in operation for the past 15 years. As noted above, the fourth phase of the scheme, running from 2021–2030, has already begun. And yet, critics of the scheme have raised significant doubts about its success and viability.

The most important criticism is that the ETS has failed to reduce the EU's greenhouse gas emissions anywhere near the levels that were hoped for or that are required under international climate change conventions, such as the Kyoto Protocol's requirement that developed Annex I countries reduce their overall emissions of such gases by at least 5% below 1990 levels. In this respect, the results of Phase 1 of the scheme were disappointing. Rather than achieving a reduction in emissions, the aggregate emissions data for participating countries actually showed a slight increase, from 2034 billion tons of CO_2 in 2006 to 2050 billion tons in 2007.[38] Even on an optimistic recent scientific assessment covering the period 2008–2016, the EU's scheme has led to only a 3.8% greater reduction in emissions than if the scheme did not exist at all.[39] This is a far more modest reduction than is necessary to meet EU countries' obligations already under the Kyoto Protocol. It is also far more modest than both Switzerland's and the EU's ambitious plans for a 50% or 55% reduction in emissions by 2030 compared to 1990 levels and net-zero emissions by 2050.

4.2 Windfall Profits

Another significant criticism is that the ETS allows energy companies to generate windfall profits due to the allocation of allowances. This calls into question the fundamental fairness of the carbon-trading scheme, which is also compounded by the problem of increased energy costs for consumers. A study by Matthew Sinclair, Research Director of the UK's Taxpayer Alliance, explains the problem as follows:

> Allowances are given to the firms for free but they are scarce and have a value, as can be seen from the price in the carbon market. That means that, whether firms are buying the allowances in the market or using those they have been freely allocated, the need to hold them pushes up the cost of production relative to not producing and selling the allowance or not buying it in the first place. Increasing the opportunity costs of production increases the price those firms charge consumers.[40]

There is thus a double unfairness at work here: On the one hand, by receiving the allowances for free and having the opportunity to sell them to the market, the

[38] European Commission (2008), p. 2.

[39] Bayer and Aklin (2020), p. 117.

[40] Sinclair (2009), p. 11. On this point, see also Ellerman and Joskow (2008), pp. 24–26.

companies in question are able to secure windfall profits and are therefore unfairly advantaged; and on the other hand, consumers are unfairly required to pay increased prices due to the energy companies' having the opportunity to trade the freely allocated permits.

An important question raised by this issue is whether European judicial institutions—and the European Court of Justice (ECJ) in particular—can adapt to the challenges posed by the ETS or at least allow EU countries sufficient leeway to address such challenges themselves.

The ECJ has ruled on the effort of at least one EU country, Slovakia, to deal with the problem of windfall profits. Slovakia had decided, in 2011, to tax emission allowances (allocated free of charge) which had been sold or which had not been used at 80% of their value. The question presented in the case was whether Slovakia's actions were in conformity with the EU ETS (Directive 2003/87/EC).

The ECJ's judgment, issued on 12 April 2018 (C-302/17, PPC Power a.s.), answered this question in the negative. According to the Court, states are not permitted to undermine the objectives of the Directive 2003/87/EC. The ETS aims to encourage enterprises to reduce their greenhouse gas emissions, specifically by allowing them to trade the emission allowances they do not need. A tax of 80% on these allowances eliminates nearly all of their economic value, which would upset the delicate balance of incentives that the ETS is meant to create. The result of this judgment, however, is that national governments are prevented from addressing the problem of windfall profits that has been created by the ETS. This case provides an indication that the ECJ may not be so willing to allow the necessary flexibility in the operation of the ETS to address some of its most significant problems.

4.3 Instability and Volatility

Another common criticism is that the price of emission allowances has been subject to significant instability and volatility. As Ellerman et al. explain in a review article of the first two phases of the ETS, the first 10 years of the scheme saw extreme fluctuations in the price of emissions allowances, ranging from a few Euro cents to almost EUR 30.[41]

The problem with such price volatility is that it undermines the incentives that the ETS provides to companies to invest in emission reduction technologies. In general, the environmental effectiveness of an emissions trading scheme depends on the ability of the scheme and its regulations to provide consistent and stable incentives for companies to invest in such technologies. With highly volatile prices, however, "*no clear investment signal is provided and hence firms' decision-making and planning is rendered difficult*."[42] By undermining incentives to invest in clean

[41] Ellerman et al. (2016), pp. 96–97.

[42] Köppl et al. (2011), p. 3.

energy technologies, price fluctuations therefore end up undermining the very goal of the ETS, namely that of the reduction of emissions.

In order to address the problem of instability and volatility, in January 2019 a so-called "Market Stability Reserve" (MSR) began operating within the ETS. The idea underlying the MSR is a simple one: When the number of allowances in circulation exceeds a specified upper limit, the mechanism automatically withdraws allowances and stores them in the reserve. And when the number of circulating allowances falls below a specified lower limit, the withdrawn allowances are again released into the market. The MSR is designed to advance two main objectives: (1) to reduce the short-term excess in allowances, and (2) to stabilize the ETS in the long term, especially when demand for allowances falls during economic slowdowns.[43] The European Commission emphasizes that the reserve operates according to pre-defined rules, leaving no discretion to the Commission or to member states in the MSR's implementation.[44]

How effective the MSR will be in ensuring market stability in the ETS remains to be seen. One significant problem, noted by a number of commentators, is that the adjustments made by the MSR are subject to a delay vis-à-vis the behavior of market participants that the adjustments are meant to influence.[45] Imagine, for instance, that at the end of a given year, the MSR determines that there is a surplus of allowances in the market, which has led to an excessively low price per unit of carbon. In response, the MSR reduces the number of allowances on the market, thereby pushing up the price. By that time, however, it is possible that external economic factors will already have influenced the price in the same direction, thereby leading to an overcorrection. In any case, because the MSR began operating only in 2019, it is still too early to tell whether it will be effective at achieving its goal of stabilizing the ETS market.

4.4 Undue Political Pressure

Also undermining the effectiveness of the ETS has been the problem of undue political pressure, especially in the context of the free allocation scheme. One economic analysis found signs that the initial allocation of emission permits had been influenced by lobbying: "*Under the EU ETS, governments influenced by special interests made a tradeoff between the quantity of quotas issued and the decision to auction or to grant them for free.*"[46] The result was that the allocation of permits for 2005 exceeded real CO_2 emissions by approximately 100 million tons.[47]

---

[43] Andor et al. (2016), p. 90.

[44] "Market Stability Reserve" at the European Commission's Climate Action website (https://ec.europa.eu/clima/policies/ets/reform_en).

[45] See, e.g., Andor et al. (2016), p. 90; and Richstein et al. (2015), p. 3.

[46] Hanoteau (2014), p. 83.

[47] See Kettner et al. (2008), pp. 41–61.

In this way, the lobbying efforts of industries have damaged the effectiveness of the ETS itself. This goes some way toward explaining why the scheme has failed to achieve significant emission reductions.

One interesting question, however, is whether lobbying has continued to damage the effectiveness of the ETS even in Phase 3, where free allocation of permits has been almost completely replaced by an auction scheme. According to one analysis, the shift to an auction-based allocation of permits has not solved the problem but merely shifted the target of lobbying efforts. As part of the auction process in Phase 3 of the ETS, allocations are now made by reference to EU-wide "*benchmarks*" for emissions per unit of production.[48] But this seemingly objective process was, in the end, again biased by the power of lobbyists:

> Despite the quasi-scientific veneer of technical benchmarks, the decisions on how to define the categories and which criteria to adopt remain subject to the power politics of the industry lobby. Those with access to Brussels decision makers, or to national government departments willing to push their agenda, did best.[49]

The seemingly endless problems and recalibrations of each successive phase of the EU ETS raise a legitimate question: Could it be the case that the problem with the ETS lies not in the details of how it is designed but rather more fundamentally in the very idea of a carbon trading scheme? One potential explanation that merits further attention is the following: The ETS encourages not only companies but also the entire EU public to view greenhouse gas emissions as a problem that one can simply buy one's way out of, while minimizing the impact on the bottom line. Given that the scheme encourages such a profits-based mindset, it is no surprise that companies have felt emboldened to use their lobbying efforts to exploit every facet of the scheme to their maximal advantage. Perhaps, then, what the EU and Switzerland must do in order to effectively reduce greenhouse gas emissions is to focus not on further recalibrations of the ETS scheme but on a fundamental reorientation in how the challenges of climate change and emission reductions are conceived of. The next section will present one possible reorientation of this kind.

---

[48] "To set these new standards, the EU split the whole range of industrial goods into 53 categories, such as newsprint, coloured glass bottles, and roof tiles. An emissions limit was defined for each product that was intended to reflect the standards achieved by the most efficient 10 per cent of factories in the EU." Carbon Trade Watch (2011), p. 5; see also Jung (2010).

[49] Carbon Trade Watch (2011), pp. 5–6.

5 A Human Rights Approach to Climate Change

5.1 Link to the Human Rights Approach in the Paris Agreement

One approach to the problem of climate change that has recently been gaining attention is the human rights approach,[50] and as has already been noted, the Paris Agreement itself explicitly casts climate change as a human rights issue. It is of course impossible to do full justice to the human rights approach in this short space. So we shall instead focus briefly on how the human rights instrument most relevant to Switzerland and the EU—the European Convention on Human Rights (ECHR)—can be seen to generate strong obligations to reduce greenhouse gas emissions.

5.2 Art. 2 and 8 ECHR and ECtHR Case Law

The key provisions in the ECHR in connection with climate change are Art. 2 and 8. Art. 2 para. 1 guarantees the right to life, stating, in relevant part, that "[e] veryone's right to life shall be protected by law." And Art. 8 para. 1 states the following: "*Everyone has the right to respect for his private and family life, his home and his correspondence*." Although not expressly specified in the wording of Art. 8, the ECtHR's case law has made clear that the provision includes physical and psychological integrity within the scope of its protection.[51] Thus, while Art. 2 guarantees the right to life, Art. 8 guarantees a certain quality of life.[52]

Art. 2 has not infrequently been invoked by the ECtHR in environmental cases. Much of the Court's Article 2 jurisprudence in the environmental arena deals specifically with industrial hazards and dangerous activities. However, foreseeable environmental disasters can also fall within the scope of the provision. According to the jurisprudence of the ECtHR, a contracting state is obligated under Article 2 to take appropriate measures if there is a real and immediate risk to life and the state is aware of this risk, and this includes risks due to environmental hazards.[53]

Traditionally, Art. 2 and 8 have been understood as *negative rights*: They prohibit the state from engaging in certain forms of life-threatening conduct (Art. 2) or from

---

[50] For more details, see Hänni (2019), pp. 1–20.

[51] See Hänni (2020), p. 617; Vöneky and Beck (2017), p. 146.

[52] See ECtHR 7 April 2009, No. 6586/03, *Brânduşe v. Romania*, § 67. For similar provisions in the Swiss Constitution, see Art. 10 and 13.

[53] See, e.g., ECtHR 20 March 2008, Nos. 15339/02, 21166/02, 20058/02, 11673/02 and 15343/02, *Budayeva v. Russia*, para. 133; ECtHR 24 July 2014, Nos. 60908/11, 62110/11, 62129/11, 62312/11 and 62338/11, *Brincat v. Malta*, paras. 85 and 102; ECtHR 28 February 2012, Nos. 17423/05, 20534/05, 20678/05, 23263/05, 24283/05 and 35673/05, *Kolyadenko v. Russia*, para. 212; and ECtHR [GC] 30 November 2004, No. 48939/99, *Öneryildiz v. Turkey*, paras. 89–90.

unjustifiably interfering with an individual's private and family life (Art. 8). In this sense, the state has so-called "negative duties" toward individuals. Negative duties correspond to an individual's rights against state interference. However, the ECtHR has also interpreted Art. 2 and 8 as more than just negative rights. Indeed, it has ruled that a state's failure to protect individuals against adverse environmental effects—even those brought about by private third-parties—can constitute a violation of the right to life, as well as of the right to respect for private and family life. This results in so-called *positive duties* for member states under the Convention.[54]

For example, in the case of *López Ostra*,[55] a complainant (successfully) filed suit on the basis of Art. 8 because of the failure of Spanish authorities to act to prevent fumes that were being emitted from an industrial plant, causing health problems for a number of nearby residents. In a later case, the ECtHR held Italy responsible for failing to provide a functioning garbage collection system, even though there was no proof of a health hazard; the fact that a *private company* was responsible for the collection did not, in the eyes of the court, exempt Italy from its duty to protect its citizens under Art. 8;[56] for the situation tolerated by the state led to a deterioration in the applicants' quality of life, constituting a violation of their right to respect for private life.[57] The foregoing cases demonstrate that in the area of environmental protection the Court has recognized that the state has a *positive duty of protection*. In light of this positive duty of protection, states can in principle be held responsible for damages to the quality of life that result from their failure to reduce greenhouse gas emissions sufficiently—as long as this failure can be traced back to the breach of some legal duty.

5.3 Landmark Judgment in The State of the Netherlands v. The Urgenda Foundation

The ECtHR itself has not yet ruled on whether the failure to reduce greenhouse gas emissions constitutes a breach of a legal duty—specifically the positive duty of protection—leading to a violation of the Convention. But in December 2019, for the first time, the highest court of a state party to the ECHR—the Supreme Court of the Netherlands—made precisely such a finding in its landmark judgment in the case of *The State of the Netherlands (Ministry of Economic Affairs and Climate Policy) v. The Urgenda Foundation*.[58]

[54] See Hänni (2019), pp. 7–9. For overviews of the ECtHR's jurisprudence on positive obligations, see Sudre (1995), p. 363; Mowbray (2004), Klatt (2011), p. 691.

[55] ECtHR 9 December 1994, No. 16798/90, *López Ostra v. Spain*, § 51.

[56] ECtHR 10 January 2012, No. 30765/08, *Di Sarno and Others v. Italy*, §§ 104–108.

[57] See *Di Sarno*, § 108.

[58] See Hänni (2020), pp. 617–633, for a detailed analysis of the judgment.

One of the most important contributions of the *Urgenda* judgment is that it develops a powerful link between Art. 2 and 8 ECHR, on the one hand, and international climate change obligations, on the other. It does this via the "*common ground*" interpretive approach. Thus, quoting from the ECtHR's judgment in the case of *Demir and Baykara v. Turkey*,[59] the Supreme Court writes:

> The Court, in defining the meaning of terms and notions in the text of the Convention, can and must take into account elements of international law other than the Convention, interpretation of such elements by competent organs, and the practice of European States reflecting their common values. The consensus emerging from specialised international instruments and from the practice of contracting States may constitute a relevant consideration for the Court when it interprets the provisions of the Convention in specific cases.[60]

The common-ground interpretive principle therefore opens the door for the consideration of other elements of international law in the interpretation of Art. 2 and 8 ECHR. Two such elements are especially relevant in the climate-change context.

The first is the so-called "*no harm*" principle, which was developed in the Trail Smelter arbitration case from the first half of the twentieth century[61] and is now part of customary international law. According to that principle, states are under an obligation not to allow any activities within their jurisdiction that could cause harm to other states, including individuals in other states. Given that the damages resulting from activities causing global warming are not contained within the states in which such activities take place, the no harm principle can provide a powerful basis for interpreting Art. 2 and 8 to account for damages resulting from climate change.

Second, Article 47 of the International Law Commission's Draft articles on Responsibility of States for Internationally Wrongful Acts provides that when several states are responsible for an internationally wrongful act, each state may be held partially responsible for the resulting harms. In this way, partial fault gives rise to partial responsibility. This provides a way of holding individual countries accountable for their excessive greenhouse gas emissions, independent of whether

[59] ECtHR [GC] 12 November 2008, No. 34503/97, para. 85.

[60] Supreme Court of the Netherlands, Supreme Court Judgment, 20 December 2019, *The State of the Netherlands (Ministry of Economic Affairs and Climate Policy) and Stichting Urgenda*, 19/00135, § 5.4.2 (English version).

[61] *Trail Smelter Case*, the United States v. Canada, 1938 and 1941, Report of International Arbitral Awards, vol. III, p. 1905 at p. 1965: "No State has the right to use or permit the use of its territory in such a manner as to cause injury by fumes in or to the territory of another or the properties or person therein, when the case is of serious consequence and the injury is established by clear and convincing evidence."

each country's emissions—taken in isolation—are sufficient to bring about climate-related harms.[62]

This notion of partial responsibility sets the stage for the next step of the Supreme Court's argument, which is that "*Articles 2 and 8 ECHR relating to the risk of climate change should be interpreted in such a way that these provisions oblige the contracting states to do 'their part' to counter that danger.*"[63] In determining what it means for contracting states to do "*their part*" in combating climate change, the Supreme Court invokes a firm international consensus that UNFCCC Annex I countries would need to undertake significant reductions in order to avoid the most severe consequences of global warming. The linchpin of the Court's analysis is the IPCC scenario in AR4 in 2007. The Court writes: "*This scenario provides for Annex I countries to reduce greenhouse gas emissions by 25% to 40% in 2020 and by 80% to 95% in 2050, both compared to 1990 emissions.*"[64] The judgment goes on to marshal a dazzling array of other international sources in support of this significant level of reduction, including the Bali Action Plan, which emerged from the Bali Climate Change Conference in 2007 (COP 13); a resolution passed at the Cancún Climate Change Conference in 2010 (COP 16); another resolution passed at the Durban Climate Change Conference in 2011 (COP 17); and the Doha Climate Change Conference in 2012 (COP 18).[65] All of these conferences referred back to the IPCC scenario for AR4 as a benchmark for UNFCCC Annex I countries. In addition, the Court also cites the fact that "*[s]everal EU bodies — the Council, the Commission and the Parliament — expressed the scientifically supported necessity of reducing emissions by 30% in 2020 in comparison to 1990.*"[66]

In light of this international consensus, the Supreme Court held that the state of the Netherlands, as an Annex I country, has a human-rights based obligation to meet precisely these targets for significant reduction. As stated in the Court's summary of its judgment:

> All in all, there is a great degree of consensus on the urgent necessity for the Annex I countries to reduce greenhouse gas emissions by at least 25–40% in 2020. The consensus on this target must be taken into consideration when interpreting and applying Article 2 and 8 ECHR. The urgent necessity for a reduction of 25–40% in 2020 also applies to the Netherlands on an individual basis.[67]

---

[62] International Law Commission (2001), Art. 47 para. 1. This provision is explicitly invoked at *Urgenda*, § 5.7.6. See also Nollkaemper et al. (2020), p. 16, Principle 2, which explicitly recognizes shared responsibility for injuries due to "cumulative contributions," in which "the conduct of multiple international persons together results in an injury that none could have caused on their own" (p. 25, para. 5 of Commentary to Principle 2).

[63] *Urgenda*, § 5.8.

[64] *Urgenda*, § 7.2.1.

[65] These conferences are referred to at *Urgenda*, §§ 7.2.2 and 7.2.3.

[66] *Urgenda*, § 7.2.6.

[67] *Urgenda*, summary of §§ 6.1–7.3.6 of the Court's judgment.

It is often said that climate change is a global problem that necessitates a global cooperative solution, rather than a problem that any one country can solve on its own.[68] Nonetheless, the Court found that a 25–40% reduction by 2020 was the minimum reduction required for the Netherlands to *individually* do "its part" in that global effort to reduce greenhouse gas emissions.[69] Failure to attain this benchmark would, according to the Court, constitute a breach of the Netherlands' obligations under Art. 2 and 8 of the ECHR.[70]

5.4 Future Prospects of the Human Rights Approach

It is too early to tell what the implications of the landmark *Urgenda* judgment will be for other Annex I countries such as Switzerland. This will depend on at least two related factors: (1) whether the highest courts in other European countries will follow the lead of the Supreme Court of the Netherlands in imposing the same requirements on state institutions, and (2) whether the ECtHR will eventually step in to impose such requirements on all, or at least some, Council of Europe states, including Switzerland.[71]

[68] Recall the principle of cooperation, Art. 3 para. 5 UNFCCC, discussed in Sect. 2.1.2, herein.

[69] *Urgenda*, summary of §§ 5.6.1–5.8 of the Court's judgment.

[70] It is noteworthy that the Supreme Court found that the applicability of Articles 2 and 8 ECHR to the context of climate change was sufficiently clear, such that it explicitly refrains from requesting an advisory opinion from the ECtHR in accordance with Protocol No. 16 of the Convention, which states, in relevant part: "Highest courts and tribunals of a High Contracting Party, as specified in accordance with Article 10, may request the Court to give advisory opinions on questions of principle relating to the interpretation or application of the rights and freedoms defined in the Convention or the protocols thereto" (Art. 1 para. 1). See *Urgenda*, § 5.6.4.

[71] These two factors are related because the ECtHR often looks to the existence of a "European consensus" among member states in order to determine each state's "margin of appreciation" in state actions and policies that affect human rights fulfillment. On this principle, see *Goodwin v. The United Kingdom*, no. 28957/95 (2002), §§ 85–86; *Tekeli v. Turkey*, no. 29865/96 (2004), § 61; *Handyside v. The United Kingdom* [Plenary], no. 5493/72 (1976), § 48. At least two high-profile cases are now pending before the ECtHR, both involving Switzerland. First, in September 2020, six Portuguese youths filed an application to the Court against 33 states, including Switzerland, claiming violation of the ECHR due to the failure to take sufficient action for the prevention of climate change. A copy of the application in the case is available at https://youth4climatejustice.org. Because of the urgency of the case, the Court has granted it priority consideration under Rule 41 of the Rules of the Court. (Rule 41 states, in relevant part: "In determining the order in which cases are to be dealt with, the Court shall have regard to the importance and urgency of the issues raised on the basis of criteria fixed by it.") The governments of the 33 states have also been ordered to respond to the applicants' claims. See the Court's communication of 13 November 2020 (published 30 November 2020), in the case of *Duarte Agostinho and Others v. Portugal* and 32 Other States, no. 39371/20, available at http://hudoc.echr.coe.int. And in the second case, mentioned previously (see note 4 above), KlimaSeniorinnen has filed an application against Switzerland, though the Court has not yet issued a communication regarding that application.

Even before these questions are definitively settled, however, this chapter has aimed to provide a basis for further exploration of whether Switzerland's human rights obligations might require it to achieve a far greater reduction in greenhouse gas emissions than participation in the EU's Emissions Trading System and implementation of the CO_2 Act would be able to produce on their own.[72]

References

Andor MA, Frondel M, Sommer S (2016) Reforming the EU emissions trading system: an alternative to the market stability reserve. Intereconomics 51(2):87–93

Arens C, Hermwille L, Kreibich N, Mersmann F, Obergassel W, Ott HE, Wang-Helmreich H (2015) The Paris Agreement: kick-off for true global climate cooperation. Wuppertal Institute for Climate, Environment and Energy, Wuppertal

Bär CC, Brunner U, Casper K, Lustig SH (2018) KlimaSeniorinnen: lessons from the Swiss senior women's case for future climate litigation. J Human Rights Environ 9(2):194–221

Bayer P, Aklin M (2020) The European Union emissions trading system reduced CO2 emissions despite low prices. Proc Natl Acad Sci 117(16):8804–8812

Carbon Trade Watch (2011) EU Emissions Trading System: failing at the third attempt, April 2011. Available at https://corporateeurope.org

Center for Global Development (2015) Developed Countries are Responsible for 79 Percent of Historical Carbon Emissions, 18 August 2015. Available at https://www.cgdev.org

Dehm J (2018) Reflections on Paris: thoughts towards a critical approach to climate law. Revue québécoise de droit international 1(1), Hors-série septembre 2018 – Terre à terre: Environnement et approches critiques du droit, pp 61–91

Ellerman A, Joskow P (2008) The European Union's emissions trading system in perspective. Pew Center on Global Climate Change, Arlington

Ellerman AD, Marcantoniniy C, Zaklan A (2016) The European Union emissions trading system: ten years and counting. Rev Environ Econ Policy 10(1):89–107

European Commission (2008) Emissions trading: 2007 verified emissions from EU ETS businesses. European Commission Press Release, 23 May 2008

European Commission (2020) Communication from the Commission to the European Parliament, the Council, the European Social and Economic Committee and the Committee of the Regions – Stepping up Europe's 2030 climate ambition: Investing in a climate-neutral future for the benefit of our people, COM/2020/562 final, 17 September 2020

Federal Office for the Environment (2017) Emissions perspectives of greenhouse gases. Available at https://www.bafu.admin.ch

Federal Office of the Environment (2020) Switzerland's Greenhouse Gas Inventory 1990–2018: National Inventory Report and reporting tables (CRF). Submission of April 2020 under the United Nations Framework Convention on Climate Change and under the Kyoto Protocol. Available at: https://www.bafu.admin.ch

Hänni J (2019) Menschenrechtsverletzungen infolge Klimawandels – Voraussetzungen und Herausforderungen / Dargestellt am Beispiel der EMRK. Europäische Grundrechte-Zeitschrift 46(1–6):1–20

Hänni J (2020) Menschenrechtsschutz in der Klimakrise – Das Leiturteil Urgenda. Europäische Grundrechte-Zeitschrift 47(20–21):616–633

[72]For further details on the human rights approach, especially in the context of the European Convention on Human Rights, see Hänni (2019), pp. 1–20.

Hanoteau J (2014) Lobbying for carbon permits in Europe. Recherches économiques de Louvain 80 (1):61–87
International Law Commission (2001) Draft articles on Responsibility of States for Internationally Wrongful Acts, with commentaries, adopted by the International Law Commission at its fifty-third session. Yearbook of the International Law Commission, 2001, vol. II, Part 2
Jung A (2010) Dealing in hot air: the Pitfalls of Europe's new emissions trading system. Spiegel International, 30 December
Kettner C, Köppl K, Schleicher S, Therius G (2008) Stringency and distribution in the EU emissions trading scheme. The 2005 evidence. Clim Policy 8(1):41–61
Klatt M (2011) Positive obligations under the European Convention of Human Rights. Heidelberg J Int Law 71(4):691–718
Köppl K, Kettner C, Kletzan-Slamani D (2011) Price Volatility in Carbon Markets: Why it Matters and How it Can be Managed. Österreichisches Institut für Wirtschaftsforschung, Working Paper No. 409/2011, Wien
McClanahan P (2019) The Bondo Landslide and the Future of Climate Disasters, 19 August 2019. Available at https://www.outsideonline.com
Mexican Interministerial Commission on Climate Change (2011) Fourth National Communication of Mexico to the United Nations Framework Convention on Climate Change, Mexico City
Mowbray A (2004) The development of positive obligations under the European Convention on Human Rights by the European Court of Human Rights. Hart, Oxford
Nollkaemper A, d'Aspremont J, Ahlborn C, Boutin B, Nedeski N, Plakokefalos I (2020) Guiding principles on shared responsibility in international law. Eur J Int Law 31(1):15–72
Rajamani L (2016) Ambition and differentiation in the 2015 Paris Agreement: interpretive possibilities and underlying politics. Int Comp Law Q 65(2):493–514
Richstein JC, Chappin ÉJL, de Vries LJ (2015) The market (in-)stability reserve for EU carbon emission trading: why it might fail and how to improve it. Utilit Policy 35:1–18
Rocha M, Krapp M, Gütschow J, Jeffery L, Hare B, Schaeffer M (2015) Historical responsibility for climate change – from countries emissions to contribution to temperature increase. Climate Analytics, Berlin
Sinclair M (2009) The expensive failure of the European Union emissions trading scheme. Taxpayers Alliance, London. Available at https://www.taxpayersalliance.com
Sudre F (1995) Les "Positive Obligations" dans la Jurisprudence Européenne des Droits de l'Homme. Revue trimestrielle des Droits de l'homme 23:363–384
Stavins RN (2016) Market mechanisms in the Paris climate agreement: international linkage under Article 6.2. In: Stavins RN, Stowe RC (eds) The Paris Agreement and beyond: international climate change policy post-2020. Belfer Center for Science and International Affairs, Cambridge, pp 53–56
Swiss Academies of Arts and Science (2016) Brennpunkt Klima Schweiz. Grundlagen, Folgen und Perspektiven. Swiss Academies Reports, 11/5, Bern
Vöneky S, Beck F (2017) Umweltschutz und Menschenrechte. In: Proelss A (ed) Internationales Umweltrecht. De Gruyter, Berlin, pp 133–181

Julia Hänni is a Justice of the Swiss Federal Supreme Court (Lausanne, Switzerland) and Honorary Professor at the University of St. Gallen Law School (St. Gallen, Switzerland).

Tienmu Ma is an Academic Assistant at the University of Lucerne Faculty of Law (Lucerne, Switzerland).

The Quest for the Future Energy Mix in the EU and in Switzerland

Fighting Climate Change and/or Promoting Security of Supply?

Sebastian Heselhaus

Contents

Abstract Switzerland and the European Union (EU) face similar challenges when it comes to the decarbonisation and securing of energy supply. Both lack sufficient domestic energy resources, apart from nuclear energy. But nuclear energy has become controversial after the nuclear meltdown accident at Fukushima, Japan, in 2011. Without reconsidering nuclear energy as a future energy resource, the cooperation in the energy market between the EU and Switzerland becomes even more vital for securing energy supply. While in the past, Switzerland has fulfilled an important function in securing energy supply in neighbouring EU Member States, lately, the EU has provided for its own governance for emergency situations. However, Switzerland will maintain its function as an interface in the electricity sector. This is even more true, since the new focus on renewable energies fosters the demand for flexible cross-boundary solutions. An electricity agreement between Switzerland and the EU might provide a stable legal framework for these developments. The price to pay for Switzerland will be a further opening of the market, offering the private consumer a choice of energy providers. The good news for Swiss

S. Heselhaus (✉)
University of Lucerne, Faculty of Law, Lucerne, Switzerland
e-mail: sebastian.heselhaus@unilu.ch

P. Hettich, A. Kachi (eds.), *Swiss Energy Governance*,
https://doi.org/10.1007/978-3-030-80787-0_3

strategies for promoting renewable energies is that EU Member States are still allowed to take a flexible approach towards national promotion measures, especially in designing them to their territory. Therefore, the cooperation between Switzerland and the EU offers some advantages in terms of flexibility in the quest for security of supply while fighting climate change.

1 Similar Challenges

As highly industrialized European states, Switzerland and the Member States of the European Union contribute to climate change based on the greenhouse effect in a similar way. Both respond to this responsibility by similar self-binding commitments for reducing the emissions of greenhouse gases under the Paris Agreement, like before under the Kyoto Protocol, especially concerning CO_2 emissions.[1] At the same time, both have to fulfill their constitutional resp. primary law based obligations to secure an adequate supply of energy in the national[2] resp. supranational[3] framework.

Notwithstanding the diversity of the EU Member States, the EU and Switzerland face comparable challenges. Moreover, during the period covered by our research in SCCER CREST (since 2013), they have responded to these challenges in a similar manner, despite their autonomous, independent policy approaches. An important reason for this is that—although differences in detail may exist—neither the EU Member States nor Switzerland possesses significant domestic energy resources. Notwithstanding nuclear energy and the important, but limited, part of hydropower, Switzerland cannot rely solely on domestic energy resources. Similarly, nuclear energy still plays a decisive role in the EU. Besides, some Member States can rely on coal resources. But this energy resource is detrimental to the climate and too small to secure energy supply in the Union. Furthermore, it is a cost-intensive energy resource. In addition, natural gas available in some EU Member States has

[1] Switzerland ratified the Paris Agreement on 6 October 2017 and has accepted reduction targets of 50% by 2030 as compared to 1990. For 2050, there is a common reduction target of 70 to 85% as compared to 1990. Both targets include a partial use of emission reductions abroad. See Federal Office for the Environment (FOEN), The Paris Agreement, available at https://www.bafu.admin.ch. The EU ratified the Paris Agreement on 5 October 2016. In the Nationally Determined Contributions (NDC) of the EU in the framework of the Paris Agreement, the reduction target for greenhouse gas emissions amounts to 40% by 2030 as compared to 1990. See European Commission, Paris Agreement, available at https://ec.europa.eu.

[2] See the objective of a sufficient ("*ausreichenden*") energy supply according to Art. 89 para. 1 Federal Constitution (FC) as a task for the Swiss Federation as well as for the Swiss cantons.

[3] See the task to "ensure security of energy supply in the Union" according to Art. 194 para. 1 lit. b TFEU.

diminished considerably over the last years.[4] Last but not least, the petroleum in the North Sea is less profitable due to the low prices for petroleum on the world market.

Against this background, it is understandable that the EU and Switzerland are eager to conclude a bilateral electricity agreement. Despite the great mutual understanding in the negotiations, these have been stopped due to the demand by the EU to first conclude an Institutional Framework Agreement, which would grant the European Court of Justice (ECJ) a considerable role in legal disputes.[5]

Hereinafter, the focus will be on the development of interests of the negotiation partners with regard to promoting certain energy resources. Regularly, the objectives of the EU are identified as promoting security of supply—especially with reference to the blackout in Italy in September 2003—, stable and affordable prices and balancing effects with regard to the feed-in of electricity from renewable energies as well as fostering competition.[6] From a Swiss point of view, with reference to the Energy Strategy 2050[7] one has to mention the fostering of security of supply, better market access, especially for so-called balancing energy, as well as stabilizing the Swiss function of an "electricity hub for Europe".[8]

2 Development of Energy Resources

2.1 Nuclear Energy

The EU only has a limited legal basis for regulating the choice of energy resources. The provisions on energy regulation in Art. 194 TFEU leave a lacunae in this regard. But under the competences on the environment, Art. 192 para. 2 TFEU allows for regulating the choice of energy resources; however, unanimity is required. Therefore, any single Member State can block a legislative decision. It is true that promoting nuclear energy is a task of the EU, provided for by the Euratom Treaty. However, the treaty does not include an obligation for Member States to do so. The focus of the work under that treaty has shifted to safety in the field of nuclear energy.[9]

In the end, the possible acceptance of nuclear energy in the Member States has never been harmonized on the EU level, allowing for a divergent development. While some Member States, such as the so-called Visegrad-States and the United

---

[4] Heselhaus and Becker (2019), p. 249, 256 et seq.

[5] For details, see Hettich et al. (2015), pp. 3–4.

[6] Hettich et al. (2015), p. 6, with further references.

[7] Federal Council Dispatch on the Swiss Energy Strategy 2050 (*Energiestrategie 2050*), see Federal Council (2013), p. 7580 et seq.

[8] Weber and Kratz (2009), § 7 n. 25.

[9] Classen (2011), n. 16.

Kingdom, opt for modernizing and enlarging nuclear power plants,[10] others, such as France, have decided to reduce nuclear energy at least in some parts, even if supply remains on a comparatively high level. Other Member States have never been into nuclear energy, like Austria and Italy, or are exiting from nuclear energy in the aftermath of the nuclear meltdown in Fukushima in 2011, like Germany, where the last reactors will be taken off the net in 2022.[11]

So, the development of the EU policy in the area of nuclear energy is ambivalent. After Fukushima, the basis for running reactors has been to pass the so-called stress test, designed to check the security of all reactors in use. At the request of the European Council in 2011, the group of national surveillance authorities ENSREG (European Nuclear Safety Regulators Group) set up methods, the extent and the procedure of the stress test.[12] After the completion of the tests in 2012, all reactors could be kept in use. In the recent past, some reactors have been put off the net due to minor incidents. In a Belgian case, the ECJ decided that restarting the operation of a nuclear power station that had previously been shut down is basically allowed, even after a longer period of time. However, an environmental impact assessment has to be carried out.[13] In the European legal context, that leads to the participation of the public. Therefore, the risks of re-operation of nuclear power plants will be discussed in public.

According to a ruling by the Swiss Federal Nuclear Safety Inspectorate (*Eidgenössisches Nuklearsicherheitsinspektorat* [ENSI]), the operators of Swiss nuclear power plants were required to take part in the EU stress test, too. In their assessment of the Swiss country report on the EU stress test, the EU experts concluded that the Swiss nuclear power plants fulfil all the international requirements in all areas. Emphasis was put on the proactive measures of the Swiss Federal Nuclear Safety Inspectorate after Fukushima, on the seven safety layers of the Swiss nuclear power plants, as well as on the protection against a loss of the ultimate heat sink, i.e. cooling the reactor. Only with regard to extreme weather conditions and hydromanagement in case of severe accidents, the experts recommended further testing.[14] According to ENSI, there is an adequate framework for a systematic management of ageing in Swiss nuclear power plants. So, possible damages by ageing can be detected already in an early stage and countermeasures can be taken.[15]

---

[10] Heselhaus and Becker (2019), p. 249, 256 et seq.

[11] *13. Gesetz zur Änderung des Atomgesetzes*, regulating the exit from nuclear energy and accelerating the energy U-turn, German BGBl. 2011 I p. 1704 ff.

[12] ENSREG (2011).

[13] ECJ, C-411/17, ECLI:EU:C:2018/972 – Inter-Environnement Wallonie et Bond Beter Leefmilieu Vlaanderen.

[14] Swiss Federal Nuclear Safety Inspectorate (2012a); see in addition Swiss Federal Nuclear Safety Inspectorate (2012b). See also ENSREG (2012).

[15] ENSI has written the country report for Switzerland and, by the end of 2017, submitted it to the European Nuclear Safety Regulators Group ENSREG. Besides, ENSI has identified some areas for optimisation, see Swiss Federal Nuclear Safety Inspectorate (ENSI) (2018); Swiss Federal Nuclear Safety Inspectorate (ENSI) (2017).

In reaction to the meltdown incident in Fukushima, Germany put most of its nuclear power plants preliminarily off-line and then regulated the legally binding exit from nuclear technology.[16] In Switzerland, the Federal Council first took a basic decision in favour of a phase-out of nuclear energy on 25 May 2011. According to this, the existing nuclear power plants should go off-line at the end of their safety-related operational lifespan and shall not be replaced by new nuclear power plants. A necessity for an early exit from nuclear energy has not been identified.[17] With the slow phase-out, there is more time at hand for implementing the new energy policy and the conversion of the existing energy system.[18] In a second phase, the applicable laws have been changed: According to Art. 12a KEG[19] since 1 January 2018, the granting of general licenses for the construction of new, and according to Art. 106 para. 1bis KEG for the modification of existing, nuclear power plants has been prohibited. Although it is up to Parliament to change these rules for the future, the relevant law would be subject to a people's referendum. The decommissioning of a nuclear power plant is regulated in Art. 26 KEG und Art. 45 KEV. The proprietor has to decommission a plant if it has been definitely taken out of operation or the operating license has not been issued, has been withdrawn or has expired according to Art. 68 para. 1 lit. a or b KEG and the responsible authority (DETEC: Federal Department of the Environment, Transport, Energy and Communications) has ordered the installation to be decommissioned (Art. 26 para. 1 KEG). Pursuant to Art. 27 KEG the proprietor of the plant has to submit a project for the decommissioning of the plant to the authorities. The supervisory authority will set a deadline for this. Then the competent department (DETEC) will decide on the measures for the decommissioning (Art. 28 KEG). After the decommissioning activities have been completed, the department will decide whether the plant is no longer a source of radiological dangers and therefore will not be subject to the legislation on nuclear energy anymore (Art. 29 KEG). The first of the five Swiss nuclear power plants, the Mühleberg Nuclear Power Plant, has been shut down at the end of 2019.[20] Other dates for a shutdown of power plants have not yet been set resp. have been postponed.[21] Because of the step-by-step approach the situation of energy supply in Switzerland is, at the moment, less volatile than in Germany. However, in the mid term one has to deal with the loss of nuclear energy in Switzerland as an energy resource contributing to a stable basic supply.

---

[16] *13. Gesetz zur Änderung des Atomgesetzes*, German BGBl. 2001 I p. 1704 ff.

[17] Federal Council (2013), p. 7592.

[18] Federal Council (2013), p. 7608.

[19] Nuclear Energy Act (*Kernenergiegesetz KEG*) of 21 March 2003 (SR 732.1).

[20] See Federal Department for the Environment, Transport, Energy and Communications (2018).

[21] See Banholzer et al. (2019).

2.2 Fossil Energy Resources

In the European Green Deal, the European Commission calls for a fast exit from coal.[22] During the past seven years, the Commission has succeeded in building a strong consensus among Member States in favour of an exit from the coal industry.[23] Poland with its huge resources of coal is the only Member State still abstaining. However, under EU competences this single vote is enough to stop any direct regulation concerning the choice of energy resources in the Member States. The political reasoning by Poland is understandable when compared to the development in Germany. There, after long political discussions, a compromise on the exit from coal has finally been reached. However, the remaining operation period until 2038 is rather long and the financial payments are rather generous.[24] In the end, it becomes obvious that all states are hesitant to abstain from using their own energy resources. The strategy behind the Green Deal becomes clear when taking into account the financial mechanism.[25] The acceptance of Poland could be reached by offering payments in other areas. However, the enormous amount of financial resources necessary to cope with the COVID-19 pandemic makes it rather doubtful that the financial mechanism will be realised as envisioned.

In Switzerland, there are no coal-fired power plants and the small share of coal in the Swiss energy mix is due to electricity imports.[26] However, Swiss private enterprises are still investing in the coal industry abroad, primarily in Germany.[27] But a further decline is expected in Switzerland due to the high burden of CO_2 levies.[28]

In the EU, the pressure on coal has been increased indirectly by issuing stricter emission limits for coal power plants. Based on the Directive on Industrial Emissions (or IED), the Commission Implementing Decision 2017/1442[29] adopts the instrument of BAT (best available techniques) conclusions.[30] The BAT conclusions strengthen the limits set up by the IE Directive and call for stricter limits in case of new plants.

[22] European Commission (2019), no. 2.1.2., 7.

[23] Heselhaus and Becker (2019), p. 249, 256 et seq.

[24] In June 2020, the deliberations took place in the German Parliament (*Deutscher Bundestag*); also see Franzius (2018), p. 1585 et seq.

[25] For details, see Heselhaus (2020).

[26] Schweizerische Energie-Stiftung, *Kohlekraft in der Schweiz*, available at https://www.energiestiftung.ch. Coal accounted for 0.5% of gross energy consumption in 2017 and 2018, see Swiss Federal Office of Energy (2019c), p. 2.

[27] See the website of the Swiss Federal Office of Energy regarding fossil fuels and coal, available at https://www.bfe.admin.ch.

[28] The CO_2 levy on coal of CHF 60 per tonne of CO_2 equals CHF 150 per tonne of coal; see the website of the Swiss Federal Office of Energy regarding fossil fuels and coal, available at https://www.bfe.admin.ch.

[29] OJ. EU 2017, L 212, p. 1.

[30] For details, see Vollmer (2017), p. 822.

In addition, the technique of unconventional fracking is under debate in the EU and likewise in Switzerland.[31] The method applied for extracting gas or petroleum comprises a cocktail of water and hazardous substances pressed with high pressure into the earth in order to pump fossil energy resources to the surface. In the EU, there was a strong political debate whether fracking should be allowed at all or at least be strictly regulated. The European Parliament had at least asked for a duty for an environmental impact assessment.[32] In 2014, the European Commission opted in favour of a compromise and issued only a recommendation that left the decision on allowing fracking to the Member States.[33] Especially, it is only recommended to carry out a strategic environmental assessment or an environmental impact assessment (EIA).

Concerning the duty to carry out an EIA with regard to fracking operations, there is no explicit rule on such operations in the EIA Directive.[34] Therefore, the judiciary has been asked whether indirectly an EIA may be a precondition for drilling operations. In 2015, the ECJ decided that in case of a test drilling with a test extraction an EIA has to be carried out. While annex I no. 14 EIA Directive was not applicable in the case at hand for not reaching the threshold for daily extractions, the ECJ applied annex II no. 2 lit. d EIA Directive concerning deep drilling.[35] Furthermore, cumulative impacts of other operations in the vicinity, not necessarily of the same kind, have to be taken into account in the assessment.[36] Otherwise a danger would exist that relevant impacts on the environment would not be considered adequately.

Subsequently, several EU Member States have enacted fracking laws. In 2017, in Germany specific provisions have been added to the Federal Water Act (*Wasserhaushaltsgesetz*). They provide for broad prohibitions of fracking and limitations concerning the use of fracking techniques.[37] Especially unconventional fracking operations for commercial reasons are not allowed. However, the economic interests in fracking have diminished sharply because this complicated technique is not cost-efficient in comparison to the low prices for mineral oil.

In Switzerland, the competence for regulating fracking lies primarily with the cantons.[38] But not all of them have enacted specific legislation with regard to the utilization of the subsurface. Some cantons have opted for a prohibition or a moratorium on fracking in general or on fracking for extraction of unconventional

[31] See for the perils Gassner and Buchholz (2013), p. 143 et seq.

[32] European Parliament (2013).

[33] Recommendation 2014/70/EU, OJ. EU 2014, L 39, p. 72.

[34] Directive 2011/92/EU, OJ. L 26, p. 1.

[35] ECJ, C-531/13, ECLI:EU:C:2015:79—Marktgemeinde Straβwalchen.

[36] ECJ, C-531/13, n. 39, 43.

[37] *Gesetz zur Änderung wasser- und naturschutzrechtlicher Vorschriften zur Untersagung und zur Risikominimierung bei den Verfahren der Fracking-Technologie*, German BGBl. 2016 I 1972.

[38] Schweizerische Energie-Stiftung, *Fossile Energien, Fracking: Förderung unkonventioneller fossiler Rohstoffe*, available at https://www.energiestiftung.ch.

gas.[39] On the federal level, basic principles can be regulated.[40] So, the Swiss Federation could enact a general moratorium on fracking on the basis of Art. 74 and 76 FC.[41] Notwithstanding the legal possibility, fracking in Switzerland is not profitable from an economic point of view for the time being.

2.3 Renewable Energies

Concerning the promotion of renewable energies in the EU, two areas of action have to be differentiated: on the one hand, defining national targets (for the promotion of renewable energy in the Member States) and, on the other hand, controlling national measures under EU competition and economic law (for the latter, see Sect. 4). With regard to the development goals for renewable energies, the Renewable Energy Directive 2009/28/EC of 2009 (RE Directive 2020) has set up a goal for 2020 of a 20% share of renewable energies in the gross final energy consumption in the EU.[42] Since the potential in the Member States for promoting renewable energies varies considerably, the RE Directive 2020 provides for specific goals for each Member State.[43] In 2016, the European Commission stated in a report that Member States are likely to reach these goals by 2020.[44] As a promoting measure, the Commission recommended to streamline procedures for licensing. It took several years of intense political debate to modify the RE Directive 2020 in 2019. In the new RE Directive 2030 (Directive (EU) 2018/2001[45]), an overall goal of 32% of renewable energies in 2030 has been established.[46] Furthermore, the electricity from renewable energies shall be cost-efficient, market-based and facilitated by financial instruments.[47] In addition, administrative procedures should be streamlined, including so-called one-stop shops,[48] and the system of proof of origin has been optimized.[49]

In Switzerland, Art. 2 EnG does not provide percentages for the promotion of renewable energies, but points of reference ("*Richtwerte*"). According to them, an expansion of the average domestic production of electricity from hydropower to at least 37,400 GWh in 2035 is envisaged. Concerning other renewable energies, the

[39] Federal Council (2017), p. 3.

[40] Federal Council (2017), p. 6 et seq.

[41] Federal Council (2017), p. 3.

[42] Directive 2009/28/EC, OJ. EU 2009, L 140, p. 16.

[43] Annex I Directive 2009/28/EC.

[44] European Commission (2015).

[45] OJ. EU 2018, L 328, p. 82.

[46] Art. 3 para. 1 (new) Directive (EU) 2018/2001.

[47] Art. 4 para. 3 (new) Directive (EU) 2018/2001.

[48] Art. 15 (new) Directive (EU) 2018/2001.

[49] Art. 19 (new) Directive (EU) 2018/2001.

promotion target is set for 4400 GWh in 2020 and for 11,400 GWh in 2035. Targets referring to reductions of energy consumption are established in Art. 3 EnG.

In 2018, the share of renewable energies in Swiss energy consumption amounted to approximately 23%.[50] The share of renewable energies in final energy consumption for heat generation amounted to 22%. With respect to electricity consumption, 56% originated from renewable energies. With regard to national energy production, a share of 58.7% relied on renewable energies in 2018 with the major part being contributed by hydropower. The share of solar power, biomass, biogas, wind, and waste usage amounted to only 6.1% of energy production.[51] Not included in these figures are electricity imports. Differentiating according to energy resources, especially solar power has gained weight.

Still, hydropower is the major contributor to the Swiss electricity supply and according to the Energy Strategy 2050, it shall be further expanded. In 2035, according to the reference value in the Energy Act hydropower should at least produce on average 37,400 GWh.[52] There is no reference value set for 2020. In order to reach these targets, an average annual increase of 83 GWh will be necessary. It is true that the reference value will be in reach based on the practice so far, but that would mean to realize the whole potential of hydropower envisaged for 2050 in Switzerland already by 2035.[53]

In 2020, the Federal Council announced even more ambitious targets. On 3 April 2020, it decided to modify the energy law. The public consultation was open until 12 July 2020. Some of the main modifications will include the following measures: The already existing reference values ("*Richtwerte*") for expanding hydropower and other renewable energies for 2035 will be declared legally binding targets.[54] Likewise investment contributions in solar power, biomass, and hydropower, today limited until 2030, will be prolonged until the end of 2035. Further, another target for 2050 shall be included in the energy law.[55]

---

[50] See Swiss Federal Office of Energy (2019a), p. 5 et seq.

[51] Swiss Federal Office of Energy (2019b), p. 16.

[52] Art. 2 para. 2 EnG.

[53] Swiss Federal Office of Energy (2019b), p. 17.

[54] Federal Council (2020).

[55] The draft provision reads as follows (in German):

E-EnG Art. 2 Ziele für den Ausbau der Elektrizität aus erneuerbaren Energien

1. *Die Produktion von Elektrizität aus erneuerbaren Energien, ausgenommen aus Wasserkraft, hat im Jahr 2035 mindestens 11 400 GWh und im Jahr 2050 mindestens 24 200 GWh zu betragen.*
2. *Die Produktion von Elektrizität aus Wasserkraft hat im Jahr 2035 mindestens 37 400 GWh und im Jahr 2050 mindestens 38 600 GWh zu betragen. Bei Pumpspeicherkraftwerken ist nur die Produktion aufgrund von natürlichen Zuflüssen in diesen Werten enthalten.*
3. *Der Bundesrat kann gesamthaft oder für einzelne Technologien weitere Zwischenziele festlegen.*

The overall situation for a decarbonized energy production in the EU and in Switzerland is precarious. However, there are major differences with regard to specific renewable energies like wind power, which has been strongly developed in Germany but only plays a minor role in Switzerland. In many countries, nuclear power is still relevant for the basic and consistent supply of energy. This also holds true for Switzerland in the phase exiting out of this technology.

Attempts to make use of deep geothermal energy for producing electricity in Switzerland have so far all been unsuccessful. Therefore, for both parties to a possible bilateral electricity agreement there is a great interest in a stronger cooperation in the energy and electricity sector because that would allow to more easily balance the specific characteristics of individual energy resources in the overall energy mix. In this scenario, the already existing function of Switzerland as an electricity hub of Europe could be further strengthened. Instead, if the cooperation diminished by not concluding the agreement, there would be a strong likelihood that the debate on the use of nuclear power for a stable basic energy supply would resurface in Switzerland. Otherwise, Switzerland would have to accept a stronger dependency on its neighbouring countries.[56]

3 Security of Supply

The challenges faced by the specific energy resources raise the question of how to secure energy supply with a new energy mix. For the time being, in Switzerland the supply is estimated as sufficient.[57] In this regard, many see a specific interest of the EU in improving the technical side of security of supply by a strengthened cooperation with Switzerland.[58] This argument usually highlights the blackout in Italy of 2003 as well as the disruptions in parts of the Western European network system in 2006.

More recently, a new peril for security of supply has emerged in the Eastern part of the EU, in the gas sector. The political tensions between Russia and the Ukraine, which is granted special conditions as a gas transit country, form the background to this instable situation.[59] Reductions in the volume of transported gas were used as an instrument of political power in this dispute, leading to perils for the secure supply of energy for the neighbouring EU Member States. This has been a driving factor behind the German-Russian cooperation on establishing a second gas pipeline in the Baltic Sea—the much disputed Nord Stream 2 project.

---

[56] For the latter alternative, see Hettich et al. (2015), p. 44 et seq.

[57] Breitenmoser and Weyenath (2014), n. 659; see Hettich et al. (2015), p. 44 et seq.

[58] Hettich et al. (2015), p. 6.

[59] For details, see Heselhaus and Knaul (2015), p. 253, 260.

In 2019, the EU has responded to this challenge by enacting Regulation (EU) 2019/941 on risk-preparedness in the electricity sector.[60] This regulation has the objective to better protect the EU citizens from shortages of energy supply or electricity blackouts. To this end, Member States have to set up national plans to assess possible shortages,[61] which must comprise measures for providing for a regional crisis management. Therefore, regional crisis coordinators have to be designated for assisting regional network operators.[62] In addition, the governance framework of the regulation includes the Electricity Coordination Group (ECG).[63] In case of a crisis, the European Commission and the other Member States have to be informed immediately.[64] The costs for assistance in case of a crisis have to be borne by the Member State concerned.

From a Swiss point of view, this strengthening of the cooperation between EU Member States has a positive effect, as it secures a stable supply in the neighbouring states as well. However, by this measure of self-help the significance of Switzerland for the security of supply in EU Member States will diminish. Therefore, Switzerland will lose an ace in the negotiation poker with the EU concerning the electricity agreement, which it could have played earlier, if the negotiations had not been delayed.

4 Competition

Assuring adequate competition is an important objective of the EU single market. In the overall view, Switzerland is way behind in opening up the energy market, since the second step in liberalising the electricity market for the private consumer has not been accomplished so far.[65] In consequence, competitors from the EU are excluded from that part of the Swiss market. At the same time, Swiss enterprises can realize additional gains in these areas. Although there are some limitations to transfer the surplus to other parts of the electricity market,[66] it might be used as a reserve to be invested in renewable energies. From this point of view, it is of high interest to assess the leeway for EU Member States under EU law in promoting renewable energies. The same leeway could be demanded by Switzerland in a bilateral electricity agreement.

[60] OJ. EU L 158, p. 1. For details, see Heselhaus and Becker (2019), p. 249, 254.

[61] Art. 7 Regulation (EU) 2019/941.

[62] Art. 12 Regulation (EU) 2019/941.

[63] Art. 3 para. 2 Regulation (EU) 2019/941.

[64] Art. 14 Regulation (EU) 2019/941.

[65] Schleiniger et al. (2019), p. 20.

[66] BGE 142 II 451, E. 5.2.4. and E. 5.2.8.

4.1 *Promoting the Decommissioning or Construction of Nuclear Power Plants*

In Germany, considerable payments have been made to compensate utility companies for the decision to phase out nuclear energy. From the viewpoint of the EU, this situation has highlighted the problematic issue of decommissioning nuclear power plants, which has long been foreseen. Deconstruction not only has a technical side, but it has a competition law side as well. The existing funds for deconstruction in the Member States are often not sufficient for bearing all of the costs. Therefore, in Germany additional payments from the government have been provided, which privilege this industry sector in comparison to other energy sectors.[67] In this regard, the European Commission only issued a communication, in which a framework for measures by the Member States is set up, leaving them a broad margin for appreciation.[68]

In Switzerland the decommissioning of nuclear power plants is regulated by Art. 26–29 KEG.[69] In a specific chapter, the rules for securing the financial resources for the decommissioning are laid down. (Art. 77–82 KEG). The notion of decommissioning ("*Stilllegung*") is rather broad in Swiss law and comprises all measures after the operation of a plant from the stop of operations to the complete deconstruction of the facility.[70] The costs of decommissioning have to be borne by the proprietor.[71] A decomissioning fund ("*Stilllegungsfonds*") has been established, which secures the financing of the decommissioning, of the dismantling of obsolete nuclear installations and of the disposal of the resulting waste material ("*Stilllegungskosten*").[72] The costs of the decommissioning are governed by the ordinance on the decommissioning and disposal funds ("*Stilllegungs- und Entsorgungsfondsverordnung*", SEFV [Decommissioning and Waste Disposal Funds Ordinance]).[73] According to Art. 2 SEFV, the cost of the decommissioning comprises all costs which occur during the decommissioning of a power plant, especially the costs for the technical preparation of the facility, for the maintenance, for the decontamination and deconstruction of the site and the shredding of active and contaminated pieces thereof, for the transport and the disposal of the radioactive waste. These costs have to be differentiated from the disposal costs

[67] Heselhaus (2014), p. 201, 208 et seq.

[68] European Commission (2013).

[69] Nuclear Energy Act (*Kernenergiegesetz KEG*) of 21 March 2003, SR. 732.1.

[70] Hoppenbrock (2009), p. 157.

[71] Hoppenbrock (2009), p. 160.

[72] Art. 77 KEG.

[73] Ordinance of 7 December 2007 on the Decommissioning Fund and the Disposal Fund for Nuclear Installations (*Verordnung über den Stilllegungsfonds und den Entsorgungsfonds für Kernanlagen* [SEFV]), SR. 732.17.

("*Entsorgungskosten*"), which include all costs for the disposal of the radioactive operation waste and of the spent nuclear fuel after the final shutdown.[74]

The fund has legal personality and is supervised by federal authorities.[75] The main task of the fund is to guarantee the necessary financial resources.[76] According to Art. 77 para. 3 KEG, the proprietors of nuclear installations are obliged to pay contributions. The liability starts with the start of the operation and ends with the completion of the decommissioning.[77] The amount of the contributions is defined in Art. 4 and 8a SEFV. Furthermore, every 5 years, the proprietors have to undertake a study in order to review the predicted costs of decommissioning and disposal of waste.[78] Pursuant to Art. 8a SEFV, contributions have to be set at an amount which is sufficient to bear all of the said costs. According to information by BKW, the firm has already contributed around 40 million CHF to the costs by 2017 before the final decommissioning of the nuclear power plant in Mühleberg.[79] Therefore, financing should be secured.[80] In comparison to the EU, there are no relevant distortions of competition.

In the EU, there are some Member States eager to promote nuclear energy and to establish new facilities, like the United Kingdom and Hungary. In both countries, over the last years, considerable amounts of aid were granted by the state, which had to be checked by the European courts. The upgrading of the British nuclear power plant at Hinkley Point has been subject to some claims, which all were lost before the European courts. The European General Court (GC) accepted the state aid by the United Kingdom as permissible under EU state aid law, thus backing the former decision by the European Commission.[81] In second instance, the ECJ upheld the decision of the General Court.[82]

In Hungary, the construction of a new nuclear power plant has given rise to several legal issues under EU public procurement law. First, the European Commission allowed Hungary to rely on an exemption clause concerning the direct award of the contract to a Russian enterprise. Second, the Commission classified the financial contribution by Hungary as a permissible state aid.[83]

---

[74] Art. 3 SEFV.

[75] Art. 81 para. 1 KEG.

[76] Hoppenbrock (2009), p. 163.

[77] Art. 7 para. 1 and 2 SEFV.

[78] Art. 4 para. 1 SEFV.

[79] BKW (2018), p. 14.

[80] BKW (2018), p. 14.

[81] GC, T-382/15, ECLI:EU:T:2016:589.

[82] ECJ, C-640/16 P, ECLI:EU:C:2017:752.

[83] European Commission (2017).

4.2 Promoting Renewable Energies

When considering the EU rules for promoting renewable energies, one has to look not only at the regulations, which provide for certain mechanisms, but also at the jurisprudence, which controls national measures as well. The competence to promote renewable energies is laid down in Art. 194 para. 1 lit. c TFEU under the Lisbon Treaty of November 2009. Already at the beginning of 2009, and therefore still based on the (predecessor) competences for the environment, Directive 2009/28/EC[84] on the promotion of the use of energy from renewable sources was enacted. It lays down the legal framework for the promotion of renewable energy until 2020 (RE Directive [2020]). These provisions have been complemented by Directive (EU) 2018/2001[85] (RE Directive [2030]).

According to the RE Directives, Member States can enact their own measures for the promotion of renewable energies in order to reach their development targets.[86] Furthermore, Member States might cooperate with other Member States or third states through "cooperation mechanisms".[87] This includes the "statistical transfer", by which renewable energies in one country could be used for the achievement of development targets in another, if a compensatory payment has been disbursed.[88] However, in practice this mechanism is hardly used, although renewable energies would be promoted in a cost-efficient manner.

The RE Directive (2030) regulates the promotion of renewable energies in the EU from 2021 until 2030. In addition to adopted contents of RE Directive (2020), it aims at securing competition in promoting renewable energies and to avoid market distortions.[89] To this end, the promotion should be set up in an open, transparent, non-discriminatory and cost-effective manner, which fosters competition.[90] In the literature, doubts have been raised whether the directive will reach these objectives.

Like the European Commission, the European Courts have qualified the national promotion measures as state aids, which have to comply with the rules of EU competition laws. Furthermore, of all the national promotion measures only the German mechanism has not been qualified as an unjustified interference with the free movement of goods because in this mechanism, the financial means of the contribution always remained in the hands of private parties and never came under the control by the state.[91] In 2019, the ECJ has confirmed this view with regard to the German so-called "*EEG-Umlage*" in German energy laws.[92]

---

[84] OJ. EU 2009, L 140, p. 16.

[85] OJ. EU 2018, L 328, p. 82.

[86] Art. 3 para. 3 lit. a RE Directive (2020); Art. 4 para. 1 RE Directive (2030).

[87] Art. 3 para. 3 lit. b RE Directive (2020); Art. 8–13 RE Directive (2030).

[88] Art. 6 RE Directive (2020); Art. 8 RE Directive (2030).

[89] Art. 1 and 4 RE Directive (2030).

[90] Art. 4 para. 4, Art. 6 RE Directive (2030).

[91] ECJ, C-379/98, ECLI:EU:C:2001:160—PreussenElektra.

[92] ECJ, C-405/16 P, ECLI:EU:C:2019:268—Germany/Commission.

In a case of 2015 with reference to Switzerland, the ECJ decided that the RE Directive does not allow Member States to accept electricity from third countries as green electricity in the framework of the national promotion mechanisms.[93] Otherwise, the objectives of the directive, especially the decarbonisation of the energy supply, could be impaired.[94]

From the view of competition law, it has to be stressed that the ECJ interprets the RE Directive to allow for a territorial/regional limitation of the promoting measures.[95] These measures do interfere with the free movement of goods pursuant to Art. 34 TFEU, but they could be legitimate, i.e. proportionate.[96] On the one hand, the ECJ points out that each of the Member States has taken on specific targets for the production of electricity from renewable energies. Therefore, the Member States should be competent to decide on the implementing measures. On the other hand, the ECJ identified big differences in the potential for renewable energies of each Member State, which would call for a national nature of the promoting measures.[97] In 2017, the ECJ confirmed these principles, although reserving a strict test of proportionality of the mechanisms in place in a certain case.[98] An important element of this test is that the financial advantages of the measure must be directly attributed to the producers.[99] The basic argument of the ECJ cannot be underestimated because normally the ECJ rejects any attempt to justify a direct discrimination, i.e. a less favourable treatment based on the origin of a good, in the framework of the free movement of goods.

5 Conclusion

In conclusion, it has to be noted that the EU and Switzerland face similar challenges in the quest for the future energy mix. Without a reintroduction of nuclear energy, the European energy market becomes even more important for Switzerland and a secure energy supply. On the one hand, since the EU has set up new measures to stabilize energy supply in the Member States, the function of Switzerland as an energy reserve has been diminished. On the other hand, the function of Switzerland as a European electricity interface has been strengthened because the increase in renewable energies calls for a flexible cross-border balancing of supply. To this end, a bilateral energy and electricity treaty between Switzerland and the EU would establish a reliable legal framework. The price to pay for Switzerland would be the

[93] ECJ, C-66/13, ECLI:EU:C:2014:2399—Green Network SpA.

[94] ECJ, C-66/13, n. 59 et seq.

[95] ECJ, C-573/12, ECLI:EU:C:2014:2037—Ålands Vindkraft.

[96] ECJ, C-573/12, n. 82.

[97] ECJ, C-573/12, n. 93 and 94.

[98] ECJ, C-492/14, ECLI:EU:C:2016:732—Essent Belgium NV.

[99] ECJ, C-492/14, n 112.

second step in the liberalisation of the energy market with regard to private consumers. With regard to the Energy Strategy 2050 and the envisaged energy transition, the analysis has established that the EU gives its Member States considerable leeway for regional/national promotion mechanisms. Therefore, the quest for security of energy supply and the objective of fighting climate change can be flexibly combined in a closer cooperation with the EU.

References

Banholzer S, Iten T, Epprecht N (2019) Treiber für Stilllegungsentscheide in der Schweizer Atomindustrie - eine Analyse. Schweizerische Energie-Stiftung, Zurich

BKW (2018) Stilllegung Kernkraftwerk Mühleberg, Update 2018. Available at https://www.bkw.ch

Breitenmoser S, Weyenath R (2014) Europarecht - Unter Einbezug des Verhältnisses Schweiz – EU, 2nd edn. Dike Verlag, Zurich/St. Gallen

Classen CD (2011) Energiepolitik. In: Oppermann T, Classen CD, Nettesheim M (eds) Europarecht, 5th edn. Beck Verlag, München, § 23

ENSREG (2011) Declaration of ENSREG – EU Stress Tests Specifications, 31 May 2011. Available at http://www.ensreg.eu

ENSREG (2012) Switzerland – Peer review country report, Stress tests performed on European nuclear power plants, 26 April 2012

European Commission (2013) Communication from the Commission to the European Parliament and the Council on the use of financial resources earmarked for the decommissioning of nuclear installations, spent fuel and radioactive waste, COM(2013) 121, Brussels, 8 March 2013

European Commission (2015) Communication from the Commission to the European Parliament, the Council, the Economic and Social Committee and the Committee of the Regions, Renewable energy progress report, COM(2015) 293, Brussels, 15 June 2015

European Commission (2017) Hungary's support for Paks II compatible with EU aid rules, press release, 6 March 2017. Available at https://ec.europa.eu/commission/presscorner/home/en

European Commission (2019) Communication from the Commission to the European Parliament, the European Council, the Council, the Economic and Social Committee and the Committee of the Regions, The European green deal, COM(2019) 640, Brussels 11 December 2019

European Parliament (2013) Fracking: Umweltverträglichkeitsprüfung vor jedem neuen Projekt, press release, 9 October 2013. Available at https://www.europarl.europa.eu/news/de

Federal Council (2013) Botschaft vom 4. September 2013 zum ersten Massnahmenpaket der Energiestrategie 2050 (Revision des Energierechts) und zur Volksinitiative "Für den geordneten Ausstieg aus der Atomenergie" (Atomausstiegsinitiative). Federal Gazette BBl 2013 7561

Federal Council (2017) Fracking in der Schweiz, Bericht des Bundesrates in Erfüllung des Postulats Trede 13.3108 vom 19. März 2013. Available at https://www.bafu.admin.ch

Federal Council (2020) Bundesrat will einheimische erneuerbare Energien stärken und Strommarkt öffnen, press release, 3 April 2020. Available at https://www.admin.ch

Federal Department of the Environment, Transport, Energy and Communications (DETEC) (2018) Verfügung des Eidgenössischen Departements für Umwelt, Verkehr, Energie und Kommunikation UVEK vom 20. Juni 2018 betreffend Gesuch vom 18. Dezember 2015 auf Anordnung der Stilllegung für das Kernkraftwerk Mühleberg. Available at https://www.bfe.admin.ch

Franzius C (2018) Rechtsprobleme des Kohleausstiegs. Neue Zeitschrift für Verwaltungsrecht (NVwZ) 21:1585–1591

Gassner H, Buchholz G (2013) Rechtsfragen des Erdgas-Fracking - Grundwasserschutz und UVP. Zeitschrift für Umweltrecht (ZUR) 2013(3):143–150

Heselhaus S (2014) Aktuelle Entwicklungen im Europäischen Energierecht. In: Epiney A, Diezig S (eds) Schweizerisches Jahrbuch für Europarecht (SJER). Schulthess Verlag/Stämpfli Verlag, Zurich/Bern, pp 201–221

Heselhaus S (2020) Die Bedeutung des EU-Green Deal für die Energiebranche: verdeckte Revolution oder heisse Luft? In: Heselhaus S, Schreiber M (eds) 3. Tagung zum Recht und Management in der Energiewirtschaft (to be published)

Heselhaus S, Becker E (2019) Aktuelle Entwicklungen im Europäischen Energierecht. In: Epiney A, Hehemann L, Zlatescu PE (eds) Schweizerisches Jahrbuch für Europarecht (SJER) 2018/2019. Schulthess Verlag/Stämpfli Verlag, Zurich/ Bern, pp 249–274

Heselhaus S, Knaul A (2015) Aktuelle Entwicklungen im Europäischen Energierecht. In: Epiney A, Kern M, Hehemann L (eds) Schweizerisches Jahrbuch für Europarecht (SJER) 2014/2015. Schulthess Verlag/Stämpfli Verlag, Zurich/Bern, pp 253–280

Hettich P, Walther S, Schreiber Tschudin S (2015) Schweiz ohne Stromabkommen. Dike Verlag, Zurich/St. Gallen

Hoppenbrock V (2009) Finanzierung der nuklearen Entsorgung und der Stilllegung von Kernkraftwerken. Nomos, Baden-Baden

Schleiniger R, Betz R, Winzer C (2019) Der schweizerische Strommarkt zwischen Liberalisierung und Regulierung. Dike Verlag, Zurich/St. Gallen

Swiss Federal Nuclear Safety Inspectorate (ENSI) (2012a) EU-Stresstest: Hohes Sicherheitsniveau der Schweizer Kernkraftwerke bestätigt, press release, 26 April 2012. Available at http://www.admin.ch

Swiss Federal Nuclear Safety Inspectorate (ENSI) (2012b) EU Stress Test: high safety level of Swiss nuclear power plants is confirmed, 26 April 2012. Available at https://www.ensi.ch

Swiss Federal Nuclear Safety Inspectorate (ENSI) (2017) Ageing management in nuclear power plants, Topical Peer Review, Swiss National Assessment Report, Brugg

Swiss Federal Nuclear Safety Inspectorate (ENSI) (2018) Ageing management in nuclear power plants: Swiss National Assessment Report submitted to the European Commission, press release, 8 January 2018. Available at https://www.ensi.ch

Swiss Federal Office of Energy (SFOE) (2019a) Schweizerische Statistik der erneuerbaren Energien, Ausgabe 2018, preliminary. Available at https://www.bfe.admin.ch

Swiss Federal Office of Energy (SFOE) (2019b) Energiestrategie 2050, Monitoring-Bericht 2019, ausführliche Fassung. Available at https://www.bfe.admin.ch

Swiss Federal Office of Energy (SFOE) (2019c) Schweizerische Gesamtenergiestatistik 2018. Available at https://www.bfe.admin.ch

Vollmer M (2017) Die Kommission macht ernst: Der Durchführungsbeschluss 2017/1442. Natur und Recht (NuR) 39:822–826

Weber RH, Kratz B (2009) Stromversorgungsrecht, Ergänzungsband Elektrizitätswirtschaftsrecht. Stämpfli Verlag, Bern

Sebastian Heselhaus is Professor for International Law, European Law, Public Law and Comparative Law and Director of the Center for Law and Sustainability at the Faculty of Law at the University of Lucerne, Lucerne, Switzerland.

The Role of Switzerland in European Electricity Governance

Shaper, Follower, or Outsider?

Benjamin Hofmann, David Kolcava, and Philipp Thaler

Contents

Abstract This chapter explores the political influence of Switzerland as a non-EU country in European electricity governance. We argue that the influence of non-EU countries depends on their access to European governance institutions and their structural power resources. We further posit that the type of structural power resources circumscribes the specific areas of influence. The empirical analysis assesses these variables qualitatively based on interview and other primary data. First, it shows that Switzerland has relatively high access to important European governance bodies. Second, it reveals that Switzerland possesses structural power in serving as a European transit hub for electricity and an important source of technical expertise. Third, it confirms our theoretical expectation that Switzerland acts as a

The chapter draws on previous findings published as: Hettich et al. (2020); Hofmann et al. (2019).

B. Hofmann · D. Kolcava · P. Thaler (✉)
University of St. Gallen, Institute of Political Science, St. Gallen, Switzerland
e-mail: benjamin.hofmann@unisg.ch; philipp.thaler@unisg.ch

P. Hettich, A. Kachi (eds.), *Swiss Energy Governance*,
https://doi.org/10.1007/978-3-030-80787-0_4

shaper in European electricity governance. Swiss influence is especially seen in matters related to grid management and cross-border electricity trade. Limitations to Swiss influence are often rooted in the legal principles of the EU internal market. Our findings qualify claims about a marginalization of Switzerland in European electricity governance. At the same time, we highlight uncertainties resulting from the present lack of an electricity agreement between Switzerland and the EU. Our chapter recommends Swiss policy-makers to strive for viable forms of energy cooperation with the EU and to strengthen the transit function and technical expertise of the country.

1 Introduction

The Swiss energy transition takes place in a context of Europeanization.[1] For non-EU countries, Europeanization is often conceived of as a one-way street in which they are forced to adopt EU rules.[2] The EU's regulatory dominance over non-members rests on conditional infrastructure investments and its ability to grant or restrict access to its large internal energy market.[3] However, not all third countries are passive policy-takers in energy governance. We reiterate the argument made elsewhere that third countries can assume the roles of shapers, followers, outsiders, or challengers in European energy governance.[4] Switzerland is an interesting case in this respect because it is probably more embedded in the European energy system than any other non-member. This is especially true in the electricity sector whose importance is set to grow as mobility and heating are increasingly electrified. At the same time, the bilateral agreements between Switzerland and the EU still do not cover energy issues. Although the two parties have been negotiating a comprehensive electricity agreement since 2007, its conclusion remains blocked at the time of writing.

This chapter explores whether Switzerland currently acts as a shaper, follower, outsider, or challenger in European electricity governance. We build on the argument that the role of non-EU countries like Switzerland depends on their access to European governance institutions and their structural power resources.[5] We refine this argument by stressing that structural power characteristics of third countries define the specific areas in which they can wield political influence. Our empirical study shows that Switzerland has access to important European governance bodies. It further reveals that Switzerland possesses structural power in serving as a European transit hub and an important source of technical expertise. We probe the

[1] Hettich et al. (2020).

[2] Börzel (2011); Gawrich et al. (2010); Schimmelfennig and Sedelmeier (2005); Subotic (2011).

[3] Damro (2012), p. 695; Goldthau and Sitter (2015a); Lavenex (2004), p. 693.

[4] Hofmann et al. (2019).

[5] Ibid.

resulting expectation that Switzerland acts as a shaper in European electricity governance. In particular, it should be able to exert influence on European policies that address technical aspects of grid management and cross-border electricity flows. The empirical case study largely confirms these theoretical expectations while also identifying limits to Swiss influence in Europe. The findings qualify claims about a marginalization of Switzerland in European electricity governance.[6]

This chapter speaks to practitioners and scholars of Swiss and European energy governance alike. For practitioners of the Swiss energy transition, European electricity policy constitutes an important contextual factor because of Switzerland's high interconnectedness and seasonal import dependence.[7] For practitioners abroad, the Swiss case provides potential lessons for energy relations between the EU and other third countries, including post-Brexit EU-UK relations. For researchers, the chapter sheds light on the conditions under which Europeanization is not a one-way street and even non-members can shape EU policies.

The remainder of this chapter proceeds as follows: Section 2 outlines our theoretical argument about the role of third countries in EU energy governance. Section 3 briefly introduces the Swiss case and the empirical material we collected and analyzed. Section 4 describes the access of Swiss actors to key institutions of European electricity governance. Section 5 assesses the structural power resources of Switzerland in the electricity sector in relation to the EU. Section 6 presents evidence for a moderate shaper role of Switzerland in European electricity governance. Section 7 discusses how the conclusion or failure of an electricity agreement with the EU would change this role. Section 8 summarizes our findings and draws conclusions for policy-makers and researchers.

2 Third Countries in EU Energy Governance

This section presents our theoretical argument on the possible roles and sources of influence of third countries in EU energy governance. European integration in the energy domain has made increasing progress since the late 1980s.[8] EU institutions, bodies, and Member States have created a comprehensive set of legislation, legal acts, and court decisions relevant for the area of energy that is commonly known as the EU's *energy acquis*. Increasing supranationalization of the sector not only shaped the internal energy market but soon resulted in growing external influence beyond Union territory.[9] In this respect, academic contributions have highlighted the Europeanization of energy sectors of third countries, including Switzerland,[10]

[6] Van Baal and Finger (2019), p. 13.

[7] Ibid., 11; Hettich et al. (2015), p. 7.

[8] Buchan (2015); Thaler (2016).

[9] Cf. Thaler and Pakalkaite (2020).

[10] Van Baal and Finger (2019); Jegen (2009).

Norway,[11] and contracting parties of the Energy Community.[12] A common argument is that European market and regulatory power pushes many of these countries to approximate their domestic legislation to EU rules, taking over parts of or even the entire EU *energy acquis*.[13]

We put this EU-centric approach into perspective by arguing that third countries can play active roles in European energy governance. We understand governance very basically as the capacity "to develop some means of making and implementing collective choices".[14] Only few contributions have argued that third countries are not mere passive takers of EU rules but—under certain conditions — can actively influence EU energy policy.[15] This chapter builds on the conceptual framework developed by Hofmann et al.[16] According to this framework, the ability of third countries to upload their preferences to the EU level depends on two variables: access to venues and actors of EU energy policy-making and structural power resources.

Access—whether formal or informal—is a necessary precondition to generate influence. The formal access of a third country to venues and actors of EU energy policy-making is closely linked to its institutional arrangement with the EU. Countries of the European Economic Area (EEA) and of the Energy Community incorporate relevant parts of the *energy acquis* into their domestic legislation. This intimate institutionalized relationship provides them with regular access to bodies of EU energy governance. Switzerland, in contrast, has no institutionalized energy relationship with the EU, even though the entanglement of the two energy systems requires close cooperation. As this chapter will demonstrate, much of the access Switzerland currently enjoys may become subject to the conclusion of an electricity agreement with the EU that has been negotiated for several years. Finally, third countries without a dedicated energy agreement typically lack access to venues and actors of EU energy policy-making.

Structural power resources provide third countries with the political weight necessary to turn access into influence. Following the conceptualization of Hofmann et al., four different sources define the structural power of a country in the energy domain.[17] First, physical interdependencies with the EU can create political leverage for third countries. This structural power resource is closely related to the EU's import dependency and is typically possessed by suppliers of oil, gas, and electricity.[18] Second, third countries gain structural power when they serve as transit countries for energy supplies. The extent of political leverage depends on their

[11] Jevnaker (2016); Austvik (2019).

[12] Buschle (2014); Petrov (2012).

[13] Goldthau and Sitter (2015b, 2019).

[14] Peters and Pierre (2009), p. 91.

[15] Godzimirski (2019); Hofmann et al. (2019).

[16] Hofmann et al. (2019).

[17] Ibid., 154–155.

[18] Godzimirski (2019), pp. 106–107.

geographical location, grid interconnectedness, and the availability of alternative supply routes.[19] Third, structural power can be a consequence of the surge in renewable energies in the EU which requires flexible supply options. Non-EU countries can serve as much-needed flexibility providers based on their installed flexible generation and storage capacity, natural gas production,[20] and sufficient grid interconnectedness.[21] Finally, third countries can gain leverage through technological knowledge, regulatory expertise, and experience. Utilized in direct interactions by state and non-state actors with their EU counterparts, these qualities can shape discourses and create leadership.[22]

The combination of access and structural power determines the influence of a third country. We understand influence as the ability of a country to shape EU electricity policies along the lines of its own preferences. We assume that these preferences primarily reflect the strategic energy objectives of a country. In this chapter, we focus on the upload of third country preferences onto the EU *energy acquis*.[23] Third countries can assume four different roles in this respect.[24] Shapers have institutional access and make use of their high structural power to influence EU policy formulation. Followers also have access but lack the structural power resources to shape EU policies. Challengers lack formal access, but their high structural power resources, often a result of supply or transit functions, still provide them with influence on EU energy policy. Outsiders have neither access nor structural power and hence cannot exert any tangible influence.

We refine the initial argument by stressing that the type of structural power resources circumscribes the specific areas of influence. For instance, a strong transit function in an interconnected grid is a source of influence on matters related to common grid management. In addition, first-mover domestic experiences in electricity market liberalization or in the expansion of renewables are an asset for shaping EU policies on these issues. Finally, technical knowledge in the development of trading platforms can be a source of influence on the terms of cross-border electricity trading. The next section explains why and how we analyzed Switzerland as a case of third country influence in European electricity governance.

[19] Casier (2011), p. 496; Haghighi (2007).

[20] Natural gas can be viewed as a flexible supply option where it temporarily bridges gaps in electricity supply resulting from the phase-out of coal and nuclear power that cannot be filled by renewable electricity generation or other flexibility options (e.g., batteries, pump storage, or demand-side management).

[21] Lund et al. (2015), pp. 797–798.

[22] Bouwen (2004).

[23] Another form of influence not covered here is the customization of EU provisions when implementing them into domestic legislation, cf. Thomann (2015).

[24] Hofmann et al. (2019), pp. 155–156.

3 The Case: Switzerland in European Electricity Governance

Switzerland constitutes a salient case for investigating the role of non-EU countries in European electricity governance. On the one hand, Switzerland is an important third country for the EU because of its central position in the European electricity grid.[25] Its strategic importance may be a source of Swiss influence in European electricity governance. On the other hand, the institutional relationship between Switzerland and the EU seems to be deteriorating. The existing bilateral treaties do not cover electricity issues. Ad-hoc arrangements currently define Swiss participation in bodies of European electricity governance. The conclusion of a comprehensive electricity agreement is still pending after more than a decade of negotiations. Previous research has noted that, without an electricity agreement, Switzerland will increasingly be excluded from European cooperation.[26] It is thus not obvious that Switzerland as a non-EU country can play an active role in European electricity governance.

Our analysis follows a qualitative approach. First, we describe Swiss access to five important institutions in European electricity governance: the European Commission, the Council of Ministers, the Agency for the Cooperation of Energy Regulators (ACER), the European Network of Transmission System Operators for Electricity (ENTSO-E), and the Pentalateral Energy Forum (PLEF). We also consider other access points where relevant. Our description takes into account the formal institutional status of Swiss representatives (e.g., voting rights, membership, or observer status) as well as informal forms of access (e.g., loose contacts with decision-makers). We obtained data on formal and informal access from 16 interviews conducted with Swiss and European governance actors between June 2018 and March 2019 (see Annex). We complemented this data with relevant legal documents. We shared and reviewed our assessment with Swiss and European governance actors during a workshop in May 2019.[27]

Second, we assess the four structural power resources for Switzerland in the realm of electricity. For electricity supply, we analyze whether Switzerland has a positive electricity trade balance with the EU, taking into account seasonal patterns as well as emerging developments. For electricity transit, we consider whether Switzerland occupies a strategic location in EU supply corridors, whether its grid is highly interconnected with the EU grid, and whether alternative supply routes are scarce. For flexibility provision, we examine whether Switzerland has large installed capacities of hydropower or gas power plants, high storage capacities, and a high number and capacity of grid interconnectors. For expertise, we assess to what extent Swiss actors can contribute high levels of technical knowledge, governance experience,

[25] Hettich et al. (2015), p. 6.

[26] Van Baal and Finger (2019); Hettich et al. (2020); Jegen (2009).

[27] #REMforum 2019 Pre-Conference Workshop: "Swiss Energy Strategy 2050 and EU Clean Energy Package: Stronger Together?" 23 May 2019, St. Gallen.

and manpower to European governance processes. We collected data on these structural power resources from primary sources, including Swiss electricity statistics and interviews, as well as from relevant secondary sources.

Third, we provide and discuss anecdotal evidence for and against Swiss influence in European electricity governance. In accordance with our theoretical framework, we probe Swiss influence in areas where Switzerland has institutional access and possesses structural power resources. As the first two parts of the empirical analysis will suggest, these are primarily the areas of cross-border electricity flows and grid management. Again, our interviews were the main data source on Swiss influence activities, their success, and failure. We verified interview data on instances of Swiss (non-)influence by reviewing relevant pieces of European electricity legislation. Notably, we checked whether the legal provisions indeed seemed to (not) reflect Swiss interests.

The case study of Switzerland is relevant in its own right, but it can also provide lessons for energy relations between the EU and other non-members. The Swiss experience may be particularly interesting for the future role of the UK in European electricity governance after Brexit. Furthermore, it may be used for comparison to non-EU countries that cooperate with the EU under different institutional models, such as the EEA and Energy Community members. While acknowledging that our single case study cannot be generalized easily, we hope it provides input for further reflection and research.

4 Swiss Access to European Governance Institutions

This section describes Swiss access to European electricity governance. The governance of electricity in the EU is a complex process that involves various EU institutions, bodies, and actors. Moreover, forums not directly linked to the EU's institutional hierarchy shape the EU *energy acquis*. We focus on five key institutions and bodies to which Switzerland has varying degrees of access, as well as on some additional access points. As the executive, the European Commission defines the central lines of European energy policy. The Council of Ministers is one of the two co-legislators and the main forum for coordinating EU Member State positions. The Agency for the Cooperation of Energy Regulators (ACER) and the European Network of Transmission System Operators for Electricity (ENTSO-E) carry important functions in the elaboration of electricity regulation. In contrast to these four forums, the Pentalateral Energy Forum (PLEF) is not linked to the EU's institutional structure but has evolved into an important regional governance body.

4.1 European Commission

The European Commission is a central actor in EU energy governance. It develops proposals for energy legislation for adoption by the European Parliament and the Council. Concerning technical standards, it reviews network code proposals from ACER and ENTSO-E before sending them to the comitology process.[28] As Guardian of the Treaty, the Commission also oversees the implementation of EU energy law by the Member States and negotiates agreements with third countries such as Switzerland. Within the European Commission, the Directorate-General for Energy (DG ENER) is responsible for electricity-related matters. Furthermore, the Electricity Coordination Group (ECG) is an important Commission expert group that coordinates the implementation of electricity policies with cross-border impacts. The ECG comprises energy authorities and national regulators of EU Member States as well as representatives of ACER and ENTSO-E. A further venue for discussing issues related to the EU's internal market for electricity is the European Electricity Regulatory Forum (EERF or Florence Forum). Participants in the EERF include governmental and private actors from EU Member States and selected third countries.[29]

The Swiss Federal Office of Energy (SFOE) represents Swiss interests vis-à-vis the Commission and in the EERF but lacks access to the ECG. The SFOE cultivates a regular exchange with DG ENER, which is perceived as recognizing the importance of Switzerland for the EU's internal electricity market. For instance, Swiss decision-makers are optimistic that DG ENER would find ways to accommodate Swiss concerns in case of further integration.[30] However, this constructive relationship is instable for three reasons. First, the number of officials familiar with the Swiss dossier within DG ENER is small and shrinking, rendering future exchanges vulnerable to personnel fluctuations.[31] Second, the Commission is unwilling to compromise on the legal principles forming the basis for the EU internal market.[32] Third, the future institutional access of Switzerland will be decided upon on higher levels of the Commission, implying a close connection between Brexit and the Swiss issue.[33] This increasingly constrains the ability of the SFOE to find pragmatic solutions with the European Commission outside of formal arrangements.

[28] Interview 15.

[29] Interview 1.

[30] Interview 2.

[31] Interview 8, 13.

[32] Interview 8, 9.

[33] Interview 8, 9.

4.2 Council of Ministers

The Council of Ministers (Council) consists of the EU Member States and takes important decisions on major parts of EU energy policy and legislation. Discussions begin at the technical level of the Energy Working Party before continuing on the political level of the Committee of Permanent Representatives (COREPER). The final vote takes place in the Transport, Telecommunications and Energy Council configuration (TTE). Regulations are discussed and adopted in the comitology process in the Electricity Cross-Border Committee. Importantly, this procedure applies to the so-called Network Codes. Network Codes are sets of rules which are prepared by ENTSO-E, ACER, and the European Commission and contribute to harmonizing the European electricity market.[34] The Cross-Border Committee is presided by the Commission and comprises representatives of the EU Member States and the countries of the European Economic Area (EEA). The latter have an observer status without the right to vote, but presence tends to be more relevant than voting rights.[35]

Switzerland does not have formal access to any level of the Council hierarchy. It also lacks access to meetings of the Cross-Border Committee. As a consequence, Switzerland is excluded from many technical and political discussions that shape future amendments to the EU *energy acquis*. Swiss access is limited to occasional invitations to informal, technical meetings of energy attachés and informal meetings of energy ministers. The latter are independent of the Council hierarchy but are organized twice a year by the Council Presidency. Discussions in this setting have a rather general, political character.[36] Switzerland is represented by the federal councilor responsible for energy or a member of the SFOE. Overall, the scope for uploading Swiss preferences on the level of the Council of Ministers is slim.

4.3 Agency for the Cooperation of Energy Regulators (ACER)

The European Agency for the Cooperation of Energy Regulators (ACER) is an EU agency that formally brings together the energy regulators of the Member States.[37] The agency was established in 2011 in Ljubljana, Slovenia. It is integrated into the Union's institutional hierarchy and possesses regulatory powers. It coordinates the work of national regulatory authorities (NRAs) and contributes to the creation of network rules. Decision-making in ACER involves various forums at different levels

[34] Interview 8.

[35] Interview 8, 10.

[36] Interview 1.

[37] Regulation 2019/942 of the European Parliament and of the Council of 5 June 2019 establishing a European Union Agency for the Cooperation of Energy Regulators, OJ L 158, 14 June 2019, 22–53.

in the organizational hierarchy. Discussions usually begin in informal ad-hoc task forces and pass through one of the three working groups (electricity; gas; market integrity and transparency) before a final decision is taken in the Board of Regulators.[38]

The Swiss Federal Electricity Commission (ElCom) represents Switzerland in some forums of ACER as an observer. Following the conclusion of a Memorandum of Understanding (MoU) in 2015,[39] it participates in the electricity working group and its task forces. This allows ElCom to contribute to technical discussions and provides access to important information. For instance, Switzerland has been involved in the development of the Network Codes, which are an important element of European electricity regulation.[40] At the same time, the observer status sets limits in this respect. Unlike EU countries with full ACER membership, ElCom is excluded from the Board of Regulators. It also lacks access to the Board of Appeal, even when Switzerland is directly and adversely affected by ACER decisions.[41] Thus, Swiss access to ACER is best described as partial.

4.4 European Network of Transmission System Operators for Electricity (ENTSO-E)

The European Network of Transmission System operators for Electricity (ENTSO-E) encompasses 42 transmission system operators (TSOs), including the Swiss TSO Swissgrid.[42] The primary role of ENTSO-E lies in facilitating technical cooperation among European TSOs and in preparing secondary legislation for adoption in the EU comitology process. More specifically, the legal mandate of ENTSO-E comprises promoting the internal electricity market, facilitating cross-border trade and network development, and ensuring the secure and reliable operation of the European transmission system.[43] ENTSO-E consists of an Assembly, a Board, and five committees.[44] Its role in the development of Network Codes for cross-border network and market integration is preparatory. Yet, many of its decisions endure the

[38] Interview 5, 7.

[39] ElCom (2015), p. 5; Recital 25 Regulation 2009/713 of the European Parliament and of the Council of 13 July 2009 establishing an Agency for the Cooperation of Energy Regulators, OJ L 211, 14 August 2008, 1–14 (no longer in force).

[40] Interview 2, 3, 5, 8.

[41] Interview 5, 7, 12, 13.

[42] ENTSO-E Member Companies, available at https://www.entsoe.eu/about/inside-entsoe/members.

[43] Art. 28 Regulation 2019/943 of the European Parliament and of the Council of 5 June 2019 on the internal market for electricity, OJ L 158, 14 June 2019, 54–124.

[44] ENTSO-E, Articles of Association, chap. III, available at https://www.entsoe.eu/about/inside-entsoe/governance.

subsequent regulatory process.[45] The work of ENTSO-E affects Switzerland in many ways. For instance, decisions on cross-border capacity allocation have an impact on the amount of loop flows in the Swiss grid and on Swiss import capacity (see Sect. 6).[46] By planning the development of cross-border network infrastructure, ENTSO-E also influences Switzerland's role in the European electricity grid in the long run.[47]

Swissgrid is a founding member of ENTSO-E, takes part in all of its relevant bodies, and even holds a seat on the Board.[48] However, Swissgrid does not have voting rights in ENTSO-E.[49] This is due to Switzerland's third country status towards the EU. Nevertheless, Swissgrid is reported to be one of the most involved members in ENTSO-E[50] and consequentially, Switzerland's most important technical voice in Europe.[51] Compensating for its lack of voting rights, Swissgrid seeks to participate effectively with its extensive technical knowledge.[52] Representing Swiss interests in this way is further facilitated by the consensual decision-making practiced in ENTSO-E.[53] Hence, ENTSO-E represents a major access point for Switzerland on the European level.

4.5 Pentalateral Energy Forum (PLEF)

The Pentalateral Energy Forum (PLEF) is a voluntary format for regional cooperation on energy issues outside of the EU hierarchy. Established in 2005 by Belgium, France, Germany, Luxembourg, and the Netherlands, it promotes cooperation in electricity market integration and security of supply. Austria and Switzerland joined the forum in 2011. The functioning of the PLEF is laid down in two Memorandums of Understanding (MoU)[54] and two Political Declarations.[55] It consists of national

[45] Interview 15.

[46] Interview 13.

[47] Art. 48 Regulation 2019/943 of the European Parliament and of the Council of 5 June 2019 on the internal market for electricity, OJ L 158, 14 June 2019, 54–124.

[48] Interview 14.

[49] Interview 12.

[50] Interview 1, 3, 12.

[51] Interview 16.

[52] Interview 12.

[53] Interview 8, 12, 13.

[54] PLEF (2007), Memorandum of Understanding of the Pentalateral Energy Forum on Market Coupling and Security of Supply in Central Western Europe; PLEF (2017), Memorandum of Understanding of the Pentalateral Energy Forum on Emergency Planning and Crisis Management for the Power Sector. Both available at https://www.benelux.int/nl/kernthemas/holder/energie/pentalateral-energy-forum/.

[55] PLEF (2013), Political Declaration of the Pentalateral Energy Forum; PLEF (2015), Second Political Declaration of the Pentalateral Energy Forum of 8 June 2015. Both available at https://www.benelux.int.

ministries, NRAs, TSOs, power exchanges, and a Market Parties Platform from the participating countries, with close involvement of the European Commission. The significance and influence of the PLEF stems from this inclusive setup. This setup facilitates dialogue and agreement on energy issues of concern among neighboring countries, such as electricity cross-border flows. Indeed, many of the rules that eventually become part of the EU's *energy acquis* are first elaborated and tested within the regional context of the PLEF. For example, PLEF cooperation and discussions with the Commission have reportedly influenced parts of the Clean Energy Package. This includes areas such as market coupling, generation adequacy assessments, capacity mechanisms, risk preparedness, and flexible short-term markets.[56]

Unlike all other participants, Switzerland is only an observer in PLEF. This status is linked to its non-EU membership. Switzerland may not join certain discussions reserved for the EU members but otherwise enjoys the same rights as full members. The flexible institutional framework of the PLEF rewards active players. Switzerland serves as the co-chair of a standing expert group and is represented in various ad hoc groups.[57] Furthermore, the focus of the PLEF on deliberation and decision-making by consensus means that expertise and technical knowledge are valued. Participation in the PLEF gives Switzerland access to first-hand information and to preparatory negotiations of EU energy policy. Swiss representatives can also raise their concerns in direct exchanges with influential EU Member States and the European Commission. Such opportunities are usually unavailable to non-members in formal EU bodies.[58] Therefore, the PLEF is another major access point of Switzerland in European electricity governance.

4.6 Other Access Points

Swiss actors have additional access points to European electricity governance. One of them are formal relations with the European Parliament. Swiss relations with the European Parliament are cultivated by the Mission of Switzerland to the European Union in Brussels. The mission is part of the Federal Department of Foreign Affairs (FDFA). Moreover, delegations of the Swiss Federal Assembly and the European Parliament have regular exchanges, for instance, through working group sessions.[59] Besides this, most other Swiss access points on the European level are either informal or independent of EU institutions. They include informal collaboration of Switzerland with EU Member States, personal ties between energy attachés, contacts

[56] Interview 11.

[57] Interview 3, 11.

[58] Hofmann et al. (2019).

[59] Federal Department of Foreign Affairs (2019).

between ElCom and other regulators as well as contracts between Swissgrid and other TSOs.

Bilateral relations between Switzerland and EU Member States in the energy policy domain have been most fruitful with two sets of countries. On the one hand, neighbors like Austria or Italy share certain Swiss concerns because of their geographical proximity. On the other hand, small countries with limited resources, such as Luxembourg, have advocated interests based on Swiss technical expertise.[60] A further channel of informal access lies in personal relationships between diplomats. Reportedly, these contacts enable indirect access for Swiss attachés in the form of an efficient flow of information.[61] With respect to ElCom and other regulators, the Council of European Energy Regulators (CEER) is a forum for voluntary collaboration outside of the EU institutional framework. The most relevant issues for national regulators are usually discussed in ACER though.[62] Last, TSOs can deepen their cooperation through contracts under private law in the broader framework of ENTSO-E. Swissgrid seeks to harness such contracts for finding solutions to technical problems resulting from political disagreements between Switzerland and the EU.[63] However, the compatibility of such arrangements with European law is uncertain—an issue that is likely to be closely monitored by the European Commission.[64] The importance of these additional channels of Swiss access varies depending on the topic and context.

To sum up the preceding analysis, Switzerland has a relatively high level of access to European governance institutions despite not being an EU member. Major Swiss access points are ENTSO-E, the PLEF, and to some extent also the European Commission. Access is partial in case of ACER and minimal with respect to the Council of Ministers. Bilateral contacts with certain EU Member States, their regulatory authorities, and TSOs complete the picture.

5 Swiss Structural Power

Our theoretical argument posits that only structural power allows third countries to transform access to European governance bodies into influence. To what extent does Switzerland possess structural power in the realm of electricity? A first power resource to be assessed is electricity trade. In 2018, Switzerland exhibited an export surplus of 1.6 TWh, whereas it had been a net importer in 2017.[65] However, seasonal patterns are more important. Switzerland is highly dependent on electricity imports

[60] Interview 3, 4.

[61] Interview 3.

[62] Interview 5.

[63] Interview 13.

[64] Interview 8, 13.

[65] Swiss Federal Office of Energy (2019b), p. 4.

from the EU in winter. It usually roughly compensates this seasonal trade deficit with exports in spring and summer by activating its hydropower resources. The phase-out of all nuclear power plants in Switzerland foreseen in the Swiss Energy Strategy 2050[66] is likely to reinforce the import dependence in winter.[67] This is due to the higher contribution of non-seasonal nuclear energy to domestic power generation in winter.[68] Therefore, adequate Swiss import capacity is necessary for the implementation of the strategy. Also, given the vast scale of the European electricity market, Swiss generation capacities only play a minor role for meeting European demand. Switzerland thus yields little to no structural power stemming from electricity trade balances with the EU.

A second conceivable resource of Swiss structural power is electricity transit. Historically, the Swiss grid has been highly interconnected with neighboring countries' power grids. A reason for this is Switzerland's central geographic position in between Germany in the North, France in the West, and Italy in the South. As a consequence, the Swiss grid fulfills an important transit function. It carries 10% of all cross-border electricity flows in continental Europe and accounts for one fifth of the European interconnector capacity.[69] Italy is particularly dependent on Switzerland for its integration into efficiency-enhancing market coupling mechanisms.[70] Furthermore, up to 30% of the electricity traded between Germany and France flows through the Swiss grid,[71] putting considerable stress on Swiss infrastructure.[72] In recent years, the relative importance of Swiss transits has decreased somewhat because of the expansion of the Continental Synchronous Area.[73] However, the EU plans to further increase cross-border electricity trade among its Member States.[74] Electricity transits through Switzerland thus continue to play a critical role for the European internal market for electricity.

Constituting a third structural power resource, flexibility provision is crucial for integrating volatile electricity generation from renewable energy sources. Flexibility provision can be understood in two ways. Firstly, flexible generation or storage capacities can be mobilized on demand for stabilizing grid operation and for preventing supply shortages. With respect to gas, Switzerland depends heavily on imports[75] and a potential construction of gas power plant capacities is currently only

---

[66] Federal Council (2013), p. 7594.

[67] Schmid and Cheng (2019).

[68] Swiss Federal Office of Energy (2019b), p. 14.

[69] Marcus et al. (2017), p. 43; Pattupara and Kannan (2016), p. 153.

[70] Interview 6, Interview 16 (VSE).

[71] ElCom (2017), p. 2.

[72] Interview 13.

[73] Interview 13.

[74] Art. 15 Regulation 2019/943 of the European Parliament and of the Council of 5 June 2019 on the internal market for electricity, OJ L 158, 14 June 2019, 54–124.

[75] Swiss Federal Office of Energy (2019a), p. 2.

discussed for domestic use.[76] More importantly, installed hydropower capacity in Switzerland amounted to 16 GW[77] in 2018, which accounts for 55.4% of total domestic power generation.[78] Despite the vital domestic role of Swiss hydropower, the capacity of Swiss storage plants is small compared to the overall installed capacity in the European internal market.[79] Affordable alternatives for flexibility provision are available for the EU.[80] The use of Swiss storage capacity therefore does not seem indispensable for the EU at the moment. It may become more interesting though in conjunction with the phase-out of nuclear energy and coal in Germany and the EU-wide efforts to decarbonize electricity generation.

Furthermore, Switzerland's extensive grid infrastructure—including a total of 41 interconnectors at the borders—provides flexibility for EU countries. Flow-based market coupling within the EU increases cross-border capacities and actual cross-border electricity flows.[81] This expands the import capacities of EU countries and improves their ability to smoothen intermittent electricity flows. Although Switzerland is excluded from flow-based market coupling, a substantial amount of the additional electricity flows occurs in the Swiss grid. In that respect, the Swiss grid is an important building block of a flexible European electricity grid.[82]

A fourth structural power resource is expertise. Expertise can be used strategically to further national interests. Its use relies on access to the platforms where relevant policy discussions take place. Additionally, the expertise of Swiss actors must be judged in relation to the expertise of EU actors. In the domain of electricity trade, Switzerland has been a latecomer in market liberalization.[83] There is ample evidence, however, that Swiss actors have led the way in designing cross-border market platforms.[84] Concerning transit, Swissgrid possesses high expertise in grid management as demonstrated by its ability to maintain grid stability in spite of extensive loop flows. According to accounts received, the expertise of the Swiss TSO has been valued highly in ENTSO-E and the PLEF.[85] With respect to flexibility and renewables, the evidence is inconclusive. On the one hand, Switzerland co-chairs an expert group on flexibility in the PLEF.[86] Furthermore, Swiss regulations related to promoting renewables and energy efficiency are monitored by other countries and the

---

[76] Stalder (2019).

[77] Swiss Federal Office of Energy (2019c).

[78] Swiss Federal Office of Energy (2019b), p. 14.

[79] Hettich et al. (2015), p. 6.

[80] Swissgrid (2015), p. 95.

[81] Interview 13.

[82] See Heselhaus (2021).

[83] Van Baal and Finger (2019), p. 10. See also Föhse (2021) and Hettich (2021).

[84] Interview 5, 13.

[85] Interview 11, 12.

[86] Interview 11.

European Commission.[87] On the other hand, it is unclear how Swiss expertise in this domain compares to the knowledge of EU experts.

In sum, Switzerland possesses a moderately high level of structural power vis-à-vis the EU. Main sources of structural power are the transit function of its transmission grid and the technical expertise in grid management. Swiss grid elements also contribute to flexibility in the European electricity grid. By contrast, flexibility from Swiss hydropower as well as seasonal electricity exports seem too limited to make a difference.

6 Swiss Influence in European Electricity Governance

This section assesses the actual role of Switzerland in European electricity governance. The institutional access and structural power resources of Switzerland lead us to expect that it can act as a shaper in European electricity governance. Especially, Swiss actors should be able to influence issues related to grid management and cross-border electricity flows. These expectations are empirically evaluated below.

At first sight, empirical evidence suggests that Switzerland has no influence in European electricity governance. A prominent example in this respect is the exclusion of Switzerland from European market coupling. Market coupling is a cornerstone of the EU internal market for electricity. It increases efficiency by bringing together formerly separate transactions—the cross-border trading of electricity and the purchase of cross-border transmission rights.[88] The EU pursues market coupling for both day-ahead and intraday trading. In December 2014, the European Commission excluded Switzerland from day-ahead market coupling in Central Western Europe. This prevents a more efficient allocation of capacities at the Swiss border and thereby limits the country's import capacity.[89] In December 2016, the European Commission excluded Switzerland from cross-border intraday market coupling under the so-called XBID project. As an economic consequence, costs for intraday trading increased and the Swiss intraday market collapsed.[90] The main reason for the exclusion of Switzerland is that it does not transpose the EU *energy acquis*. The European Commission is unwilling to grant market access to any third country that does not commit to the rules of the EU internal electricity market.[91]

An even more serious issue for Switzerland is that its grid elements are not considered in the capacity calculation for cross-border electricity trade. The implementation of flow-based market coupling within parts of the EU has increased the electricity volumes traded between Germany and France. This has markedly

---

[87] Interview 1.

[88] Pellini (2012), p. 323.

[89] Interview 13.

[90] ElCom (2019a), pp. 15–16.

[91] Interview 8.

increased unscheduled electricity flows through the Swiss transmission grid.[92] The Swiss grid has only a limited physical capacity to deal with these so-called loop flows. Regardless of these limitations, ACER decided in November 2016 that Swiss grid elements would not be considered in the capacity calculation of the so-called European Core region.[93] This decision reflects the inferior observer status of ElCom in ACER and its lack of rights of appeal.[94] The Swiss grid is thus essentially treated as a "copper plate" that is able to absorb almost unlimited electricity flows. The resulting grid congestion and the limitations to import capacity threaten the security of supply in Switzerland.

At closer inspection, however, we also find empirical evidence for Swiss influence in European electricity governance. Three aspects deserve mention. First, the Electricity Balancing Guideline, which regulates access to European balancing power, addresses Swiss concerns about unscheduled flows and grid stability. The guideline states that "the European platforms for the exchange of standard products for balancing energy may be opened to TSOs operating in Switzerland [. . .] if the exclusion of Switzerland may lead to unscheduled physical power flows via Switzerland endangering the system security of the region".[95] This provision was the result of intense and coordinated lobbying by SFOE, Swissgrid, and ElCom in the various European governance bodies.[96] Its phrasing reflects the present physical situation in which disruptions of Swiss grid stability would be likely to spill over to the entire region, especially to Italy. Italian representatives have therefore been very supportive of Swiss positions on the European level.[97]

Second, a "technical approach" seems to be emerging for the management of unscheduled electricity flows through Switzerland.[98] For the winter 2018/19, Switzerland reached an interim solution with the NRAs of Central-West Europe. This solution allowed for temporary capacity restrictions in electricity trading between Central Europe and France if needed for ensuring Swiss grid stability.[99] For the future, the European Commission and ACER envisage that electricity flows through non-EU states like Switzerland may be considered in capacity calculation.[100] The consideration of third countries is conditional on the conclusion of operational agreements among the relevant TSOs. These agreements have to be in line with EU law and should address cost-sharing of any remedial actions. The development of this technical approach has been driven by the Swiss representation in the PLEF

[92] ElCom (2017); Swissgrid (2018), p. 10.

[93] ACER (2019), p. 24.

[94] Interview 5.

[95] Art. 1 para. 6 Commission Regulation 2017/2195 of 23 November 2017 establishing a guideline on electricity balancing, OJ L 312, 28 November 2017, 6-53.

[96] Interview 3.

[97] Interview 1, 13, 16.

[98] Interview 13.

[99] ElCom (2019b), p. 1.

[100] ACER (2019), p. 7.

and in ENTSO-E.[101] Its emergence again reflects the considerable interdependencies between the Swiss and EU electricity grids.

Third, Switzerland has also shaped other aspects of European energy governance. In the technical realm, Swissgrid has contributed to the development of electricity trading platforms and to outputs of ENTSO-E, such as the draft Network Codes.[102] Swissgrid has had a say in the development of these technical products and regulations because of its recognized expertise.[103] In the political realm, the SFOE provided inputs into the legislative process around the Clean Energy Package. It contributed to preparatory policy discussions within the PLEF and injected Swiss positions into EU negotiations via selected Member States.[104] It is admittedly difficult to identify the specific Swiss achievements in these complex and multifaceted technical and political processes. However, an EU official involved in high-level EU energy policy-making confirmed that "the de-facto power and representation of Switzerland without voting rights is many times higher than that of a small Eastern European Member State with voting rights".[105]

Overall, despite not being an EU member, Switzerland is a moderate shaper in European electricity governance. Swiss actors have mostly shaped technical policies related to grid stability. This influence has been rooted in three factors: the good access of Swiss actors to ENTSO-E and the PLEF; the physical interdependencies between the electricity systems of Switzerland and the EU; and the technical expertise of Swissgrid. Swiss influence has been more limited in the political realm. Reasons for this have been: the weak access of Swiss actors to ACER and EU legislative institutions; the reluctance of the EU to compromise on the legal principles of its internal market; and the lack of Swiss bargaining chips in terms of contributions to the EU electricity market beyond electricity transits and expertise. It follows that while Switzerland can shape certain technical policies, tensions arise when the legal or political foundations of the EU internal market are touched upon.

7 Outlook: A Swiss-EU Electricity Agreement?

This section provides an outlook on how the Swiss role in European electricity governance may evolve in the future. At present, the lack of a legal framework for Swiss-EU electricity cooperation threatens the moderate shaper role of Switzerland. The critical question here is whether the electricity agreement between Switzerland and the EU will be concluded or not. Negotiated since 2007, this agreement seeks to address regulatory gaps in Swiss-EU electricity relations and would grant

[101] Interview 11, 13.

[102] Interview 5, 13.

[103] Interview 12.

[104] Interview 4.

[105] Interview 8.

Switzerland full access to the EU electricity market. While the electricity agreement is virtually ready for adoption, the current Swiss political context renders its conclusion unlikely. The main obstacle is that the EU has made the adoption of an overarching institutional framework agreement a precondition for an electricity agreement. However, the Swiss government is hesitant to conclude the institutional framework agreement, which is highly controversial among the Swiss public and risks being rejected in a referendum. At the same time, the scope for alternative arrangements is limited. In the context of Brexit, the EU has adopted a principled approach to defend the integrity of its internal market and prevent "cherry-picking" by partners.[106] Consequently, the future role of Switzerland in relation to the EU's electricity market is defined by two possible scenarios, i.e., with and without an electricity agreement.

With an electricity agreement, Switzerland would be required to implement key parts of the EU *energy acquis*. At the same time, this kind of top-down Europeanization would be paralleled by new possibilities to shape European energy governance from the bottom. The reason is that an electricity agreement would consolidate and even expand access of Swiss actors to coordination forums of European energy policy. An electricity agreement is likely to necessitate more exchange and thus facilitate access of the SFOE to the Commission.[107] Switzerland may also gain access to the Electricity Coordination Group (ECG).[108] In the Council, a Swiss observer status at the technical level appears possible when changes to the *energy acquis* are discussed that may affect Swiss energy legislation.[109] An electricity agreement would also expand Switzerland's current form of cooperation with ACER, notably providing ElCom with access to discussions in all working groups and task forces,[110] as well as to the Board of Appeal and the dispute settlement mechanism.[111] In ENTSO-E, the electricity agreement would not only secure the strong position of Swissgrid[112] but possibly enhance it through voting rights.[113] Since the PLEF is independent from the EU's institutional framework, the role of Switzerland therein would remain unaffected by the electricity agreement. Overall, an electricity agreement would provide Switzerland with more formal access.

Conversely, without an electricity agreement, Switzerland is at risk of reduced access to important bodies of European energy governance. While this process has already started, its full extent remains uncertain. This is due to the fact that decisions on access of third countries are highly political and dependent on developments in the context of Brexit. Without an electricity agreement, access to the Commission

[106] Thaler (2020).

[107] Interview 9.

[108] Interview 1.

[109] Interview 3.

[110] Interview 3, 4, 7, 8.

[111] Interview 5, 7.

[112] Interview 1, 8, 12.

[113] Interview 1, 13.

Table 1 Present and future Swiss access to European electricity governance. Source: authors' own data; Hettich et al. (2020), pp. 88–89

Access point	Swiss actors	Present status	With agreement	Without agreement
ACER	ElCom	Partial observer	Full observer	Risk of exclusion
Council of Ministers	SFOE/ FDFA	Occasional participant on informal technical level	Observer at formal technical level	Risk of less access
Electricity cross-border committee	–	–	Observer	–
Informal meeting of EU energy ministers	Federal councilor or SFOE	Observer	Observer	Risk of less access
ENTSO-E	Swissgrid	Member with partial voting rights	Member with full voting rights	Risk of exclusion
TSO agreements	Swissgrid	Contracting party	Contracting party	Risk of tighter legal review
European Commission	SFOE/ FDFA	Bilateral contacts	More access	Less access
Electricity coordination group	–	–	Participation	–
Florence forum (EERF)	ElCom, SFOE	Observer	Observer	Risk of exclusion
PLEF	SFOE, ElCom, Swissgrid	Observer	Observer	Observer

and the Council will likely become more difficult. In addition, formal access points may be put at risk, including ACER and forums under the European Commission. Regarding the particularly important participation in ENTSO-E, an exclusion of Swissgrid or a downgrade of its status are looming.[114] Informal access points, such as the PLEF, may gain in importance for Switzerland but will be unable to fully compensate for the loss of formal access. Table 1 summarizes how the conclusion or non-conclusion of an electricity agreement changes Swiss access to European electricity governance (Annex).

Expected changes in Swiss access to European institutions have implications for its future role in EU electricity governance. The increasing access under an electricity agreement would strengthen Switzerland's role as a shaper. By contrast, the loss of formal access without an electricity agreement implies that Switzerland would cease to be a moderate shaper. The future role of Switzerland would then mainly depend on its structural power resources. If these power resources remained stable or

[114]Interview 8, 13.

grew, Switzerland could become a moderate challenger. For example, Switzerland might choose to reduce cross-border capacities to secure the stability of its grid. Such a decision would negatively affect electricity trade within the EU internal market. If the structural power resources of Switzerland diminished, an outsider role would appear most likely. Outsiders pursue their own policy directions while being unable to shape EU energy policy. In an interconnected European grid, Switzerland would continue to face loop flows and domestic grid congestion. This would endanger the stability of the Swiss grid. Furthermore, it would reduce the import capacities that Switzerland needs to meet electricity demand under increasing intermittent production from renewables. The future Swiss role in European electricity governance thus also has implications for the country's ability to achieve the objectives of its Energy Strategy 2050.[115]

8 Conclusion: Moderate Shaper with an Uncertain Future

This chapter asked what role Switzerland plays in European electricity governance. We argued that the role of third countries depends on their access to European governance bodies and their structural power resources. The empirical analysis has shown that Switzerland has formal or informal access to important governance bodies (especially ENTSO-E and the Pentalateral Energy Forum) and possesses relevant structural power resources. The analysis has confirmed the resulting expectation that, although not a member of the EU, Switzerland can shape certain aspects of European electricity policy. We also argued that structural power characteristics circumscribe the specific areas of third country influence. Switzerland serves as an electricity transit hub and possesses considerable technical expertise in grid management and cross-border electricity trade. Our empirical analysis has confirmed the expectation that Switzerland has been able to shape European electricity policy most successfully in these areas. Examples are provisions in the Electricity Balancing Guideline and the emerging "technical approach" to unscheduled flows in non-EU countries that consider Swiss interests. However, Swiss influence usually ends where its preferences conflict with legal principles of the EU internal market. The exclusion of Switzerland from EU electricity market coupling illustrates this. Moreover, the future of Switzerland as a moderate shaper in European electricity governance is highly uncertain. The reason is the blocked electricity agreement and the related risk of losing institutional access.

Our findings suggest three policy recommendations for Swiss practitioners. First, to maintain its constructive voice in European electricity governance, Switzerland needs to safeguard its continued access to governance institutions. The conclusion of an electricity agreement with the EU would formalize and enhance the institutional access of Switzerland. If the electricity agreement continues to be blocked, viable

[115] See also Heselhaus (2021).

alternatives need to be developed. The European Green Deal announced by the European Commission in December 2019 might create opportunities for new forms of "softer" cooperation.[116] Second, to secure its political influence in the long run, Switzerland should value and expand its interconnection with the EU electricity grid. The country's high level of integration in the European grid is not only a necessity for the implementation of the Energy Strategy 2050. It is also a source of structural power vis-à-vis the EU as long as alternative electricity supply routes to Italy remain scarce. Third, to consolidate its leading role in grid management and cross-border electricity flows, Switzerland should further strengthen its expertise in these fields. The EU values such expertise which is instrumental in developing its internal market and reaching its climate and energy targets. The Swiss TSO, Swissgrid, is particularly well placed to develop and provide this kind of technical expertise.

Our analysis also suggests lessons for practitioners abroad, especially in the UK. At present, the UK remains less interconnected with the EU than Switzerland and risks losing access to European governance bodies following Brexit.[117] According to our framework, this may turn the UK into a real outsider in European electricity governance. To avoid an outsider position, the UK would need to increase its structural power resources and safeguard its institutional access. Structural power can be increased by accelerating the implementation of planned interconnectors.[118] Institutional access can be safeguarded by concluding dedicated agreements with the EU. Given that both UK-EU and Swiss-EU relations are currently in flux, a model of future bilateral relations emerging in one case may come to guide solutions in the other.

Finally, this chapter has implications for future research. Its findings underline that the relationship between the EU and non-EU countries is multifaceted. Europeanization is not necessarily a one-way street through which third countries simply adopt centralized EU rules. Instead, it is a two-way street enabling even third countries to occasionally shape European policies. A limitation of our study is its exclusive focus on electricity. In reality, the political relations between the EU and non-members like Switzerland are multidimensional. Swiss structural power resources in one sector may be cancelled out by one-sided dependence on the EU in other sectors. An analysis of energy relations in the broader context of the institutional framework negotiations may help to overcome this barrier. Of course, as our analysis relied on a single case, we also caution against hasty generalization of our findings. Yet, previous short case studies of Norway and the members of the Energy Community suggest that our theoretical argument may be applicable more widely.[119] We therefore encourage more research into the sources, channels, and instances of third country influence in European energy governance and beyond.

[116] European Commission (2019), p. 20; Thaler (2020).

[117] Lockwood et al. (2017), pp. 139–142; Interview 8, 12.

[118] Ibid., 139.

[119] Hofmann et al. (2019).

Annex

List of interviewees

Interview number	Relevant present (or former) affiliation
1	SFOE
2	SFOE
3	(SFOE)
4	(SFOE)
5	NRA
6	NRA
7	ACER
8	European Commission
9	European External Action Service
10	Public sector
11	Public sector
12	ENTSO-E
13	TSO
14	TSO
15	(TSO)
16	Private sector association (2 interviewees)

References

Agency for the Cooperation of Energy Regulators (2019) Recommendation No 01/2019 of the European Union Agency for the cooperation of energy regulators on the implementation of the minimum margin available for cross-zonal trade pursuant to Article 16(8) of Regulation (EU) 2019/943: 08 August 2019

Austvik OG (2019) Norway: small state in the great European energy game. In: Godzimirski JM (ed) New political economy of energy in Europe: power to project, power to adapt. Springer International Publishing, Cham, pp 139–164

Börzel T (2011) When Europe hits . . . beyond its borders: Europeanization and the near abroad. Comput Eur Polit 9:394–413

Bouwen P (2004) Exchanging access goods for access: a comparative study of business lobbying in the European Union institutions. Eur J Polit Res 43:337–369

Buchan D (2015) Energy policy: sharp challenges and rising ambitions. In: Wallace H, Pollack MA, Young AR (eds) Policy-making in the European Union, 7th edn. Oxford University Press, Oxford, pp 344–366

Buschle D (2014) Exporting the Internal Market - Panacea or Nemesis for the European Neighbourhood Policy? Lessons from the Energy Community. EU Diplomacy Paper 2/2014

Casier T (2011) Russia's energy leverage over the EU: myth or reality? Perspect Eur Polit Soc 12:493–508

Damro C (2012) Market power Europe. J Eur Public Policy 19:682–699

Electricity Commission (2015) Reports on the activities of ElCom 2015. Available at https://www.elcom.admin.ch

Electricity Commission (2017) Technical report on unscheduled flows in the Swiss grid. Available at https://www.elcom.admin.ch
Electricity Commission (2019a) Market Transparency 2018 – ElCom Report. Available at https://www.elcom.admin.ch
Electricity Commission (2019b) Newsletter 03/2019. Available at https://www.elcom.admin.ch
European Commission (2019) Communication from the Commission to the European Parliament, the European Council, the European Economic and Social Committee and the Committee of the Regions, The European Green Deal, COM(2019) 640 final. Brussels, 11 December 2019. Available at https://ec.europa.eu
Federal Council (2013) Botschaft vom 4. September 2013 zum ersten Massnahmenpaket der Energiestrategie 2050 (Revision des Energierechts) und zur Volksinitiative "Für den geordneten Ausstieg aus der Atomenergie (Atomausstiegsinitiative)". Federal Gazette BBl 2013 7561
Federal Department of Foreign Affairs (2019) The European Parliament – a new political reality. Available at https://www.eda.admin.ch
Föhse M (2021) Decentralisation of energy generation, centralisation of energy Lawmaking. In: Hettich P, Kachi A (eds) Swiss energy governance. Springer, New York
Gawrich A, Melnykovska I, Schweickert R (2010) Neighbourhood Europeanization through ENP: the case of Ukraine. JCMS J Common Mark Stud 48:1209–1235
Godzimirski JM (2019) Channels of influence or how non-members can influence EU energy policy. In: Godzimirski JM (ed) New political economy of energy in Europe: power to project, power to adapt. Palgrave Macmillan, London, pp 105–137
Goldthau A, Sitter N (2015a) Soft power with a hard edge: EU policy tools and energy security. Rev Int Polit Econ 22:941–965
Goldthau A, Sitter N (2015b) A liberal actor in a realist world: the European Union regulatory state and the global political economy of energy. Oxford University Press, Oxford
Goldthau A, Sitter N (2019) Regulatory or market power Europe? EU leadership models for international energy governance. In: Godzimirski JM (ed) New political economy of energy in Europe: power to project, power to adapt. Palgrave Macmillan, London, pp 27–47
Haghighi SS (2007) Energy security: the external legal relations of the European Union with major oil and gas supplying countries. Hart, Oxford
Heselhaus S (2021) The quest for the future energy mix in the EU and in Switzerland. In: Hettich P, Kachi A (eds) Swiss energy governance. Springer, New York
Hettich P (2021) Governing decentral energy systems. In: Hettich P, Kachi A (eds) Swiss energy governance. Springer, New York
Hettich P, Walther S, Schreiber Tschudin S (2015) Schweiz ohne Stromabkommen. Dike, Zurich, St. Gallen
Hettich P, Thaler P, Camenisch L, Hofmann B, Petrovich B, Wüstenhagen R (2020) Europeanization of the Swiss energy system. Dike, Zurich, St. Gallen
Hofmann B, Jevnaker T, Thaler P (2019) Following, challenging, or shaping: can third countries influence EU energy policy? Polit Gov 7:152–164
Jegen M (2009) Swiss energy policy and the challenge of European governance. Swiss Polit Sci Rev 15:577–602
Jevnaker T (2016) Norway. In: Skjærseth JB, Eikeland PO, Gulbrandsen LH, Jevnaker T (eds) Linking EU climate and energy policies: decision-making, implementation and reform. Edward Elgar Publishing, Cheltenham
Lavenex S (2004) EU external governance in 'wider Europe'. J Eur Public Policy 11:680–700
Lockwood M, Froggatt A, Wright G, Dutton J (2017) The implications of Brexit for the electricity sector in Great Britain: trade-offs between market integration and policy influence. Energy Policy 110:137–143
Lund PD, Lindgren J, Mikkola J, Salpakari J (2015) Review of energy system flexibility measures to enable high levels of variable renewable electricity. Renew Sust Energ Rev 45:785–807

Marcus JS, Petropoulos A, Sapir S, Tagliapietra S, Terzi A, Veugelers R, Zachmann G (2017) Review of EU-Third Country Cooperation on Policies Falling within the ITRE Domain in Relation to Brexit: Study for the ITRE Committee, June 2017
Pattupara R, Kannan R (2016) Alternative low-carbon electricity pathways in Switzerland and it's neighbouring countries under a nuclear phase-out scenario. Appl Energy 172:152–168
Pellini E (2012) Measuring the impact of market coupling on the Italian electricity market. Energy Policy 48:322–333
Peters BG, Pierre J (2009) Governance approaches. In: Wiener A, Diez T (eds) European integration theory, 2nd edn. Oxford University Press, Oxford, pp 91–104
Petrov R (2012) Energy community as a promoter of the European Union's 'energy acquis' to its neighbourhood. Leg Issues Econ Integr 39:331–355
Schimmelfennig F, Sedelmeier U (eds) (2005) The Europeanization of central and Eastern Europe. Cornell University Press, Ithaca
Schmid S, Cheng K (2019) Energiewende? Ja, die Schweiz schafft das. In: republik.ch, Energie der Zukunft, Teil 5, 20 November 2019. Available at https://www.republik.ch
Stalder H (2019) Elcom-Präsident: "Gaskraftwerke müssen enttabuisiert werden". NZZ, 20 December 2019. Available at https://www.nzz.ch
Subotic J (2011) Europe is a state of mind: identity and Europeanization in the Balkans. Int Stud Q 55:309–330
Swiss Federal Office of Energy (2019a) Schweizerische Elektrizitätsstatistik 2018. Available at https://www.bfe.admin.ch
Swiss Federal Office of Energy (2019b) Künftige Rolle von Gas und Gasinfrastruktur in der Energieversorgung der Schweiz. Available at https://pubdb.bfe.admin.ch
Swiss Federal Office of Energy (2019c) Statistik der Wasserkraftanlagen der Schweiz. Available at https://www.bfe.admin.ch
Swissgrid (2015) Technischer Bericht zum Strategischen Netz 2025. Available at https://www.swissgrid.ch
Swissgrid (2018) Annual Report 2018. Available at https://www.swissgrid.ch
Thaler P (2016) The European Commission and the European council: coordinated agenda setting in European energy policy. J Eur Integr 38:571–585
Thaler P (2020) Energy cooperation between the EU and Switzerland: Partners by destiny in search of a new model. GovTran Policy Brief 01/2020. Available at https://www.govtran.eu
Thaler P, Pakalkaite V (2020) Governance through real-time compliance. The supranationalization of European external energy policy. J Eur Public Policy
Thomann E (2015) Customizing Europe: transposition as bottom-up implementation. J Eur Public Policy 22:1368–1387
Van Baal PA, Finger M (2019) The effect of European integration on Swiss energy policy and governance. Polit Gov 7:6–16

Benjamin Hofmann is Postdoctoral Researcher at Eawag, the Swiss Federal Institute of Aquatic Science and Technology, Dübendorf, Switzerland, and Lecturer in Political Science at University of St. Gallen, St. Gallen, Switzerland.

David Kolcava is Junior Project Manager and Researcher at the W.I.R.E. think tank in Zurich, Switzerland, and former Researcher at the Institute of Political Science at University of St. Gallen, St. Gallen, Switzerland.

Philipp Thaler is Senior Research Fellow at the Institute of Political Science at University of St. Gallen, St. Gallen, Switzerland.

The Design of the Swiss Feed-In Tariff

Policy Transfer and Accommodation

Leonore Haelg, Tobias S. Schmidt, and Sebastian Sewerin

Contents

Abstract In light of climate change mitigation and the transformation of the energy sector, many jurisdictions have adopted deployment policies for renewable energy (RE) technologies. Several RE deployment policy instruments have diffused from frontrunner countries to other jurisdictions. Switzerland implemented its first comprehensive RE support policy with the adoption of a cost-covering and technology-specific feed-in tariff in 2009, following Germany's example. Yet, policy designs look very different in the two countries and, importantly, also result in different policy outcomes. In this chapter, we examine the reasons for these policy design differences. We unpack the design of the Swiss feed-in tariff and analyze which of the policy's elements were directly adopted from Germany and which were accommodated to the Swiss context and why. In particular, we compare the specific instrument designs for two renewable power generation technologies, solar

---

L. Haelg (✉)
ETH Zurich, Energy Politics Groups, Department of Humanities, Social and Political Sciences, Zurich, Switzerland
e-mail: leonore.haelg@zhaw.ch

T. S. Schmidt · S. Sewerin
Zurich University of Applied Sciences (ZHAW), Research Group for Renewable Energy, Institute of Natural Resource Sciences, Wädenswil, Switzerland
e-mail: sebastian.sewerin@gess.ethz.ch

P. Hettich, A. Kachi (eds.), *Swiss Energy Governance*,
https://doi.org/10.1007/978-3-030-80787-0_5

photovoltaics (PV) and biomass, and study the role of technology-related actors in shaping these policy designs. We draw from the policy diffusion and policy transfer literatures and offer important extensions to the literature by showing that, instead of entire policies, it is possible that only certain design elements of a policy diffuse from one jurisdiction to another. Additionally, we find that the composition of the existing technology-related actor bases in the donor and recipient countries is important in determining whether the accommodation of the design elements to the domestic context occurs.

1 Introduction

Climate change mitigation requires the implementation of new policies to incentivize innovation in and the deployment of low-carbon energy technologies. Besides carbon pricing (addressing the negative pollution externality), R&D support policies and deployment policies for clean technologies should be part of this policy mix to address the various positive innovation externalities.[1] Frontrunner countries therefore started experimenting with technology deployment policies as early as the 1990s. These policy schemes have the goal of creating demand for novel technologies, such as renewable energy (RE) technologies, by increasing incentives for investments in these technologies.[2] For instance, the UK implemented the Non-Fossil Fuel Obligation in 1990, which offered RE technologies the possibility to compete for a premium price per unit of generated electricity.[3] Another example is RE standards, which were adopted by a number of US states in the 1990s and which require electricity suppliers to source a specific quantity of electricity from RE sources.[4]

Swiss policymakers did not remain dormant in this early phase of RE policy support. In 1991, they implemented an early version of an RE feed-in tariff.[5] A feed-in tariff supports RE deployment by offering guaranteed grid access as well as long-term and cost-covering remuneration of the generated electricity.[6] Yet, the 1991 feed-in tariff in Switzerland only offered grid access and a tariff on the basis of the avoided cost of conventional power plants rather than covering the cost incurred by RE electricity generation. In doing so, the instrument was designed to promote the deployment of small-scale hydropower and did so somewhat successfully. Other RE

[1] Jaffe et al. (2005); Van Benthem et al. (2008); Lehmann, Söderholm (2018).

[2] Schmidt et al. (2016).

[3] Mitchell (2000).

[4] Wiser et al. (2007); Carley et al. (2018).

[5] Haelg et al. (2020).

[6] Jacobs (2014).

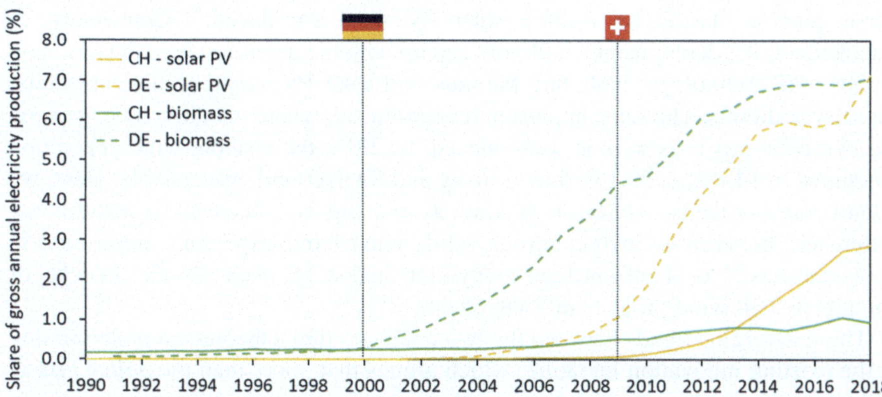

Fig. 1 Share of gross annual electricity production of the two RE technologies, solar PV (in yellow) and biomass (in green), in Germany (dashed line) and Switzerland (solid line). The dotted lines and flags represent the implementation year of the comprehensive feed-in tariff in the respective country. Data sources: BMWi (2019); Swiss Federal Office of Energy (2019)

technologies did not experience substantial capacity additions under this early feed-in tariff scheme.

Since the early 2000s, the number of jurisdictions that implemented RE deployment policies increased considerably. The most popular policy instrument at that time was the feed-in tariff.[7] The rise in policy support was followed by a surge in RE investments.[8] Germany, as one of the first countries to implement a comprehensive feed-in tariff (*Erneuerbare-Energien-Gesetz EEG*) in 2000, represents a frontrunner in RE capacity additions, specifically for solar photovoltaics (PV). Given the German policy's high effectiveness, more jurisdictions followed suit and also adopted feed-in tariffs. In Switzerland, where the development of non-hydro RE technologies was still very limited in the early 2000s, the process of completely revising the RE support policy was started in 2004 and finalized in 2009 with the implementation of a cost-covering, technology-specific feed-in tariff (*kostendeckende Einspeisevergütung KEV*) based on the German example.[9]

Even though many jurisdictions adopted the same RE support *instrument*, the policy *instrument designs* between these jurisdictions featured important differences. These design differences affected the respective policies' outcomes regarding RE deployment rates, which look very dissimilar in comparison. Particularly striking are the differences between Switzerland and Germany, which both implemented a feed-in tariff (see examples in Fig. 1). In Germany, biomass was already deployed before the EEG adoption but subsequently saw an increase in the deployment rate, while solar PV took off in terms of capacity additions after the EEG amendment in 2004,

[7]REN21 (2005).

[8]REN21 (2012).

[9]Haelg et al. (2020); see also Heselhaus (2021).

when generous tariffs for rooftop solar PV were introduced.[10] Conversely, in Switzerland, RE deployment could not keep up with the dynamics seen in Germany. No new RE technology, including biomass and solar PV, could secure substantial capacity additions. The same applies to onshore wind, where the difference between the two countries is even more pronounced. In 2018, the onshore wind generation amounted to 14.3% and 0.18% in Germany and Switzerland, respectively. Here, we do not consider the case of onshore wind, as it is largely influenced by institutional differences between the two countries: while wind farms experience opposition in both countries,[11] local citizens have many more and stronger possibilities to delay or completely halt wind projects in Switzerland.

These diverging trends between the two countries find a theoretical underpinning in the existing innovation literature, which argues that, more than the *policy instrument type* itself, the specific *instrument design* is often decisive for a policy's effectiveness.[12] Besides the instrument choice, the policy design includes specific policy settings and instrument calibrations, which represent the specific formulation and implementation of a policy.[13] For instance, while the feed-in tariff is a policy instrument, it includes specifications about which technologies are eligible to receive the tariff as well as the tariff's monetary value, which represent the policy's more specific design elements.[14]

In this chapter, we examine the reasons for the different policy designs in Germany and Switzerland. To do so, we unpack the design of the Swiss feed-in tariff and analyze which of the policy's elements were directly adopted from Germany and which were accommodated to the Swiss context and why. In particular, we compare the specific instrument designs for two renewable power generation technologies, solar PV and biomass, and study the role of technology-related actors in shaping these policy outputs. We draw from the policy diffusion and policy transfer literatures and offer important extensions to these literature streams by showing that, instead of entire policies, it is possible that only certain elements of a policy diffuse from one jurisdiction to another. We therefore invite policy diffusion and policy transfer scholars to take a design perspective in future research. The chapter also has direct implications for policymakers concerned with technology-related policy designs. In Switzerland, where additional low-carbon technology policies can be expected to be adopted soon in other sectors, such as mobility, heating, and carbon-intensive industries, policymakers will likely draw from experiences abroad. This chapter's findings may help identify on a more general level which type of design elements may be directly adopted and which are likely to be accommodated to the specific context.

---

[10] Hoppmann et al. (2014).

[11] Ebers and Wüstenhagen (2017); Sonnberger and Ruddat (2017).

[12] E.g., Kemp and Pontoglio (2011); Haelg et al. (2018); Polzin et al. (2019).

[13] Cashore and Howlett (2007).

[14] Haelg et al. (2018).

2 Review of the Policy Diffusion and Transfer Literatures

In this chapter, we draw from the policy diffusion and transfer literatures. The two are closely related in that they both analyze how policies spread across jurisdictions.[15] The policy diffusion literature focuses on the quantitative analysis of the drivers of policy spread across many jurisdictions, particularly studying structural factors, such as domestic institutions, political systems, and economic circumstances.[16] The policy transfer literature qualitatively analyzes the process by which experiences of and knowledge about a policy in one jurisdiction influence policymaking in another jurisdiction, mainly moderated by transnational or domestic agents.[17] The policy diffusion and transfer literatures overlap at the intersection of the structural factors and the involved agents, which are interdependent and exert influence on each other,[18] as well as the mechanisms responsible for a policy being adopted by many jurisdictions.[19]

With climate change and related environmental issues becoming more pressing, the literature on environmental and energy policies and their diffusion has seen substantial additions.[20] These studies' main focus lies on macro-level characteristics and processes, such as the type of diffusing instruments,[21] the drivers for the diffusion of specific instruments,[22] and the instrument characteristics fostering their diffusion.[23] However, these studies remain unclear about the specific designs of policy instruments.[24] In other words, how micro-level policy instrument design diffuses or is accommodated to the local context is underexplored.[25] This is particularly surprising in light of the above outlined differences in policy outcomes between jurisdictions and the literature pointing toward policy design as being decisive in influencing these outcomes. Only Biesenbender and Tosun[26] address this gap by analyzing the adoption and subsequent modifications of NOx emission standards in OECD countries. They find that different diffusion mechanisms are at play when a policy is newly adopted and when it is subsequently accommodated to the domestic context and that parliamentarians and their party affiliations have an effect on the willingness to adopt a new policy.

---

[15] Newmark (2002); Marsh and Sharman (2009).

[16] Gilardi and Füglister (2008); Berry and Berry (2014); Jordan and Huitema (2014).

[17] Dolowitz and Marsh (1996); Benson and Jordan (2011).

[18] Matisoff (2008); Marsh and Sharman (2009).

[19] Braun and Gilardi (2006).

[20] E.g., Tews et al. (2003); Holzinger et al. (2011).

[21] Stoutenborough (2008); Stadelmann and Castro (2014).

[22] E.g., Strebel (2011); Matisoff and Edwards (2014); Schaffer and Bernauer (2014).

[23] Busch et al. (2005).

[24] Jordan and Huitema (2014).

[25] Biesbroek et al. (2010); Biesenbender and Tosun (2014).

[26] Biesenbender and Tosun (2014).

We build on this finding but expand this understanding about the adoption and accommodation processes regarding the specific design elements of a policy instrument. Additionally, we include a perspective on the role of parliamentarians but also of other actors active in the policymaking process, such as interest groups. We follow Biesenbender and Tosun[27] and define policy accommodation as "a process of adapting a policy innovation to a domestic institutional and policy context".[28] While the role of interest groups in policymaking, including the implementation of environmental policies, comprises an entire branch of literature,[29] their influence on the specific instrument design[30] as well as the role of policy diffusion is underexplored.

Here, we intend to fill this research gap by analyzing how and why the design of a diffused policy instrument is accommodated upon and after its adoption with a specific focus on the effects of local technology-related actors, namely technology suppliers and technology users, on the process of designing the policy instrument. We analyze technology deployment policies because they are a type of environmental policy considered greatly effective in incentivizing investments in RE technologies[31] and because technology-related actors are highly important in this policy field as well as for other sectors that need to be decarbonized, such as transport, heating, and carbon-intensive industries.

3 The Case: Switzerland's Feed-in Tariff

We use inductive qualitative case study research[32] to unpack the design elements of the Swiss feed-in tariff and to analyze how policy transfer and accommodation played out.

3.1 Comparing the Swiss and German RE Policies

We conduct an in-depth analysis of the Swiss feed-in tariff (KEV), comparing the cases of two renewable power generation technologies, solar PV and biomass.[33]

[27] Biesenbender and Tosun (2014).

[28] Biesenbender and Tosun (2014), p. 424.

[29] E.g., Cheon and Urpelainen (2013); Markard et al. (2016); Jacobsson and Lauber (2006); Dumas et al. (2016).

[30] To our knowledge, Stokes (2013) and Haelg et al. (2020) are the only studies analyzing how politics can influence policy instrument design.

[31] Couture and Gagnon (2010).

[32] Eisenhardt (1989).

[33] In our analysis, we only look at biomass power generation from resources such as wood, agricultural waste, etc. Hence, we exclude the feed-in tariffs provided for power from waste incineration and landfill and sewage gas. For Switzerland, the analyzed resource here is "other

Specifically, we study how the feed-in tariff instrument has diffused from Germany to Switzerland and how and why its design has undergone accommodations due to the influence of technology-related actors. We limit the analysis to the revision of the Energy Act (*Energiegesetz EnG*) adopted by the Swiss parliament in 2007 and implemented in 2009 and the corresponding Energy Ordinance (*Energieverordnung EnV*), which were superseded by a new act and a new ordinance in 2018, following the parliamentary debate and the referendum on the Energy Strategy 2050 on May 21, 2017.

These cases are particularly suited for several reasons: First, the feed-in tariff is an instrument type that can easily be tailored to differentiate between technologies or applications by offering them different tariffs.[34] By analyzing the feed-in tariff design for different technologies, we can perform a comparative case study with different actors involved in the policymaking process *ceteris paribus*.

Second, Germany was the first country to introduce a technology-specific feed-in tariff in 2000. In the following, the instrument has diffused to many countries.[35] Switzerland implemented its feed-in tariff only recently in 2009 and has largely drawn from frontrunner countries, such as Germany. Moreover, both countries already implemented a technology-neutral feed-in tariff in the 1990s,[36] mainly to trigger the construction of small hydropower plants, and therefore had equal opportunity to learn from this early version of the later policy instrument. Yet, besides these similarities, the specific design of the technology-specific feed-in tariff has proven to be different in Germany and Switzerland in terms of application specificity and subtechnology specificity.

Third, the rationale for the technology selection is based on the different initial industry and technology user environments in Germany and Switzerland, allowing for the analysis of different actor bases. While in the field of biomass, the two countries have shown similarities in terms of technology suppliers, fuel suppliers, and the technological demand to employ agricultural residues even before the policy's implementation, this was different for solar PV. In the 1990s, several firms were already active in solar PV cell production in Germany,[37] leading to a 30% share of the solar PV cell production in Europe by 2000.[38] Additionally, German firms have also been highly active in solar PV module production. Switzerland, conversely, has never been host to a substantial solar PV cell production industry, and before the implementation of the feed-in tariff, only a few firms were

biomass" (*übrige Biomasse*) (EnV 2011). For Germany, resources included in the biomass feed-in tariff are listed in the Biomass Ordinance (*Biomasseverordnung*).

[34] Schmidt et al. (2016); Haelg et al. (2018).

[35] Jacobs (2012); REN21 (2016).

[36] See Hettich (2021).

[37] Jacobsson and Lauber (2006).

[38] Schmela and Kreutzmann (2001).

active in the market.[39] Yet, these existing firms were predominantly manufacturers of building-integrated PV (BIPV) modules.

Fourth, the policymaking process in Switzerland includes a public consultation process (*Vernehmlassungsverfahren*) during which interested associations and interest groups as well as individuals and firms may comment on the draft of every new law or ordinance. The ministry in charge of the proposed policy then compiles a report summarizing the participants' concerns about and approval of the consultation process. These documents are publicly available and add to the good availability of data on the policymaking process in Switzerland.

3.2 Method and Sampling

We proceeded in two steps. First, we conducted comprehensive desk research, scanning academic literature and policy documents, such as draft and final versions of the German Renewable Energy Sources Act (EEG), the Swiss Energy Act (EnG), and the corresponding Energy Ordinance (EnV), transcripts of parliamentary debates and of meetings by the parliamentary energy commissions, statements on the public consultation process, and public and technical reports cited during the parliamentary debates.

Second, we conducted interviews with bureaucrats, parliamentarians, and representatives of industry associations to gain insights into processes not publicly available. We interviewed a sample of 17 persons who were involved in the Swiss policymaking process. Two additional actors preferred to give a written statement by e-mail rather than being interviewed. We used theoretical sampling to identify relevant interview partners,[40] who were then contacted via e-mail. The interviews were conducted in person or by phone, lasted between 30 and 120 min, and were transcribed.

4 Evolution of the Feed-In Tariff Design in Germany and Switzerland

This section summarizes the results of this study. We start with a section (4.1) on the implementation of the feed-in tariff as a policy instrument to support RE technologies in Switzerland and on the transfer of the instrument design from Germany. This is followed by Sect. 4.2 presenting more detailed results on the two technologies biomass and solar PV, respectively. All sections are subdivided into two parts presenting how and why the feed-in tariff design came about.

---

[39] IEA (2009).

[40] Eisenhardt (1989).

4.1 Feed-In Tariff Implementation

In 1999, the Swiss parliament implemented the EnG following the addition of the Energy Article to the Swiss constitution after a popular vote. The Energy Article requires the federal government to "establish principles on the use of local and RE sources and on the economic and efficient use of energy".[41] The EnG replaced the earlier Resolution on Energy Use, incorporating the principle of supporting RE with guaranteed grid access and a tariff reflecting the cost of electricity from new conventional power production plants. Requests by a minority of members of the Social Democratic Party (SP) and the Green Party (GP) to offer a cost-covering remuneration for solar PV and wind power were dismissed at that time.

In a referendum in 2002, the majority of Swiss voters rejected a framework law for the liberalization of the Swiss electricity market against which the labor unions, supported by French-speaking SP representatives, had taken the optional referendum. After the vote, however, the European Union continued to push for electricity market liberalization in Switzerland. A new draft was therefore elaborated by the Swiss Federal Office of Energy (SFOE) and published by the Federal Council in 2004 and subsequently dealt with by the two chambers of parliament. In this context, SP parliamentarians, backed by RE industry associations and the GP, seized the window of opportunity opened by the first rejection of the market liberalization law to push for an EnG revision including comprehensive support for RE. This had become feasible because the left-wing parties threatened to relaunch a referendum against market liberalization, aided by complementary developments, such as blackouts in California and an increasing oil price, which caused many center and right-wing parliamentarians to consider RE as a means of ensuring the security of supply. Importantly, experiences in other countries where RE already received policy support—specifically Germany—were also invoked to argue in favor of RE in Switzerland. Supportive center and right-wing parliamentarians, particularly those with relations to technology users or suppliers, were specifically concerned by the Swiss industry losing market shares. Hansjörg Walter (National Councilor, Swiss People's Party [SVP], head of the Farmers' Union) stated during the debate in 2005,

> We have already lost a lot compared to Germany and Austria, where the support for alternative energies, particularly for biomass, is strong.[42]

Yves Christen (National Councilor, Radical Democratic Party (FDP), President of Swissolar) stated during the same debate,

> In Germany, roughly 150,000 jobs have been created since the introduction of the cost-based feed-in tariff. This is the last moment for us to enter this market by creating a domestic market and by promoting access to renewable energies.[43]

---

[41] Federal Constitution of 18 April 1999 of the Swiss Confederation, Art. 89 para. 2.

[42] Walter, Plenary Session, OB NC 2005, 1091.

[43] Christen, Plenary Session, OB NC 2005, 1078.

In the first draft of the new EnG, the SFOE and the Federal Council included a set of different instruments to support RE, including voluntary quotas and competitive auctions. However, the parliament finally opted, in principle, for the adoption of a feed-in tariff in 2007 after many rounds of debates.[44] The SP and GP parliamentary groups, who unanimously voted in favor of the feed-in tariff, did not have a majority in the parliament. Yet, they were supported by a great number of parliamentarians from other parties who were, besides others, representatives of farmers and businesses and saw opportunities for their constituents in comprehensive RE support. The KEV was thus adopted. The experience in Germany was invoked by many proponents to support their choice. Specifically, they referred to Germany as an example where the feed-in tariff proved to be effective in increasing RE deployment. Two RE associations (Renewable Energy Agency (AEE) and Holzenergie Schweiz) stated during the public consultation process,

> The cost-based feed-in tariff is evidentially (see the example of Germany and others) the only truly effective instrument for the promotion of renewable energies.[45]

Adrian Stiefel (Head of Climate and Energy Policy at WWF) stated in an interview,

> [We] had a look at Germany and some other countries to see what [instrument] they used, how effective were the different instruments, where was [RE deployment] increased, where did we see the desired development, and finally where could we see scalability. We soon realized that the feed-in tariff was the right instrument for our situation.

Roger Nordmann (National Councilor, SP) stated in an interview,

> Germany was a very important role model because it showed that this scheme could achieve [broad RE deployment].

Martin Bäumle (National Councilor, Green Liberal Party [GLP]) stated during the parliamentary debate,

> The feed-in model is an internationally well-proven model, and the majority of our neighboring countries and competitors in this technology sector have this model. RE capacity additions, for instance, in Germany, prove that it is successful.[46]

Once the parliament had decided on the policy instrument, it discussed the specificities of the feed-in tariff to be written into the EnG. One such discussion emerged around the RE technologies to be included in the feed-tariff, specifically around the question of whether solar PV should be removed from the scheme. On this issue, the bill shuttled between the two chambers of parliament many times and triggered heated debates. Finally, a compromise was achieved, linking the amount of support for solar PV to its cost. This meant that solar PV would only receive little support while its cost was still very high, but that this support could grow when the cost fell below predefined thresholds. Specifically, the share of support for individual

[44] Haelg et al. (2020).

[45] AEE (2004); HES (2004).

[46] Bäumle, Plenary Session, OB NC 2005, 1089.

technologies was limited to 50% for small hydropower and 30% for other technologies, while solar PV could receive between 5% and 30%.[47] Interestingly, proponents of both opinions looked at Germany for arguments. On the one hand, actors in favor of entirely excluding solar PV argued that the solar PV boom in Germany was inefficient, as the technology's cost was still quite high, and were thus afraid to incur high costs. On the other hand, actors in favor of including solar PV argued that the development in Germany had created many jobs in the solar PV industry and that the cost for solar PV was declining at a high rate. David Stickelberger (Managing Director of Swissolar) stated in an interview,

> The opposite coalition certainly used [Germany as an example]. We used it, too. We pointed out that in Germany, the market started to grow and the cost decreased. It started at 1 euro per kWh or even more and then decreased considerably.

Yves Christen (National Councilor, FDP, President of Swissolar) stated in an interview,

> [To convince others to include solar PV], I talked a lot about the small and medium enterprises. The idea was to show that in Germany they had created thousands of jobs.

Another discussion emerged around the surcharge imposed on electricity consumers to finance the feed-in tariff. Unlike in Germany where the consumer surcharge was uncapped, that is, limited only by the number of installations applying for the feed-in tariff, the Swiss parliamentarians decided very early on in the policymaking process to cap the surcharge and thus set a limit to the number of installations that could be supported. The main debate then emerged around the level at which the surcharge should be capped. SP and GP parliamentarians supported a high ceiling, while important representatives of the SVP, FDP, and CVP, especially in the National Council, argued for a lower cap. Finally, the Council of States compromised on a medium ceiling of 0.6 Rp./kWh, and the National Council followed suit. Here, the proponents of a low cap used Germany as an example where unlimited RE support had led to a high EEG charge and thus to high electricity prices for consumers. Rolf Hegetschweiler (National Councilor, FDP) stated during the debate,

> We are ready to invest a lot of money in the RE deployment. The consumer will have to pay for this. We should not be surprised if we experience the same as Germany, for instance: the experience that [the electricity market] is liberalized, but that electricity prices finally rise because we pass the surcharge on to the consumer.[48]

Related to the consumer surcharge ceiling, the parliament decided to substantially exempt electricity-intensive businesses from the consumer surcharge. With the issue being largely uncontested, the main discussion emerged around the question of whether these businesses should be entirely or only substantially exempted and thus around fairness. While other countries, including Germany, had implemented

[47] EnG Art. 7a (2009).

[48] Hegetschweiler, Plenary Session, OB NC 2006, 1784.

a similar design element in their feed-in tariff schemes, they were not used as an argument in favor of or against the exemption in parliament. Yet, SFOE representatives stated in a commission meeting that they had used the German exemption for electricity-intensive businesses as a blueprint to formulate their proposal, which was adopted by the parliament with few amendments.

Finally, the EnG amendment including a technology-specific feed-in tariff for RE generation, as adopted by the federal parliament, was implemented in 2009. Further design specificities of the instrument, such as the individual tariffs, were left to the SFOE and the Federal Council, who defined them separately in the EnV.

4.2 Feed-In Tariff Designs Specific to Individual Technologies

One of the key design elements of a feed-in tariff is how it supports specific technologies and their applications in different markets.[49] Here, we analyze the two specific technologies biomass and solar PV to understand which design elements were transferred and which were accommodated.

While the new EnV was implemented along with the amended EnG in 2009, preparatory work on it started much earlier, in 2006, in fact before the EnG was approved by parliament. The subscription process for installations to receive the feed-in tariff opened in April 2008, even though the feed-in tariff was not introduced until January 2009. The surcharge cap was reached within 6 months, that is, before the feed-in tariff had become active.[50] The consumer surcharge has therefore been increased several times since the EnG's implementation in 2009 to reduce the number of projects on the waiting list.

As parliament was pushing for a prompt implementation of the feed-in tariff, the deadlines for the SFOE to draft the specific designs for the individual technologies were short. For this reason and because Germany had already gained experience with its feed-in tariff design, the policymakers at the SFOE analyzed with interest what was working and what was not in the neighboring country, including design elements related to specific technologies and applications. Michael Kaufmann (Head of Renewable Energies, SFOE) stated in an interview,

> We analyzed a lot and had many experts from Germany who showed us how things worked and also did not work. We tried to avoid many misdirected incentives that were present in Germany.

[49] Schmidt et al. (2016); Haelg et al. (2018).

[50] SFOE (2008).

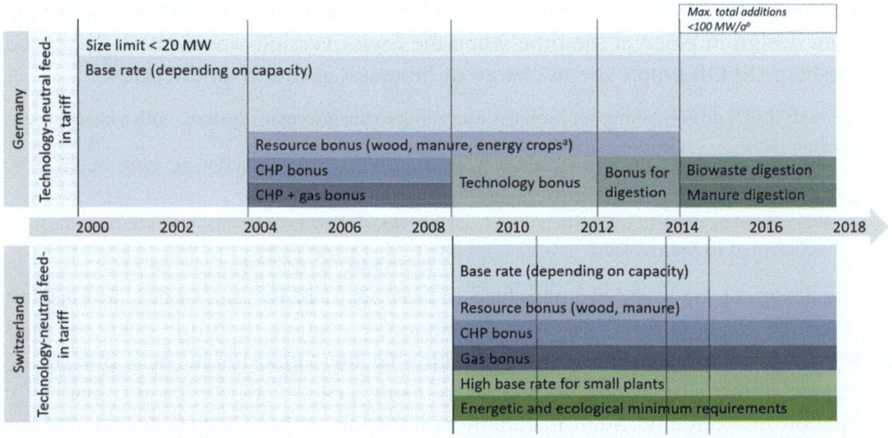

Fig. 2 Design elements of the biomass feed-in tariff in Germany (top) and Switzerland (bottom). The elements that only appear in one country's design are colored in green. The vertical black lines disclose the major amendments of the policies in Germany and Switzerland. [a]Energy crops (*nachwachsende Rohstoffe [NaWaRo]*) are crops specifically grown for power generation; [b]the total gross additions are limited to 100 MW, and the tariffs provided to biomass installations were adapted to achieve this goal

4.2.1 Specific Design of the Biomass Feed-In Tariff

Supporting biomass was never contested either in Switzerland or in Germany due to the farmers' strong lobby and the relatively centralized and dispatchable nature of biomass power production. As Rudolf Rechsteiner (National Councilor, SP) stated in an interview,

> This may sound exotic today, but at that moment, biomass, biogas, and geothermal power formed the majority in parliament [leading to the adoption of the feed-in tariff].

Work on the design of the Swiss biomass feed-in tariff started in 2006, with the finalized tariffs implemented in the context of the EnV amendment in 2009. The Swiss tariff structure was similar to the structure in place in Germany at the time (see Fig. 2, below). It consisted of a base rate depending on the installation's electric capacity complemented by bonuses for more costly feedstocks, combined heat and power technology, and the electrification of biogas. In Switzerland, the base rate differentiated between capacities lower than 50 kW and capacities between 50 kW and 100 kW. It was considerably higher than in Germany, where the base rate was the same for all installations below 150 kW. The tariff structure persisted throughout subsequent amendments of the EnV even though some actors made advances to add a high bonus for entirely manure-based installations. Additionally, the biomass installations supported by the feed-in tariff had to fulfill minimum energetic and ecological requirements, such as the use of the process heat for feedstock drying and the exclusion of primary renewable feedstock from the support.

The design of the Swiss biomass feed-in tariff displays striking similarities to the German design in place at the time when the Swiss version was drafted. As Bruno Guggisberg (SFOE employee in charge of biomass) stated in an interview,

> We said, 'Let's do something for biomass according to the [German] system, with a base rate and bonuses.'
>
> "The deadline was so short [...], we did not need to reinvent the wheel. So we looked across the border [...] mainly to Germany."
>
> We looked at the EEG specifications [...] and decided to take [them] and see how they can be adapted to Switzerland.

The design of the Swiss biomass feed-in tariff featured two minor deviations from the German design. First, biomass installations needed to fulfill energetic and ecological minimum requirements to be eligible for support. This was due to the increasing number of installations directly using primary RE crops for electricity production in Germany. Such installations led to decreasing social acceptance for biomass installations in Germany and to the implementation of these minimum requirements in Switzerland. As Bruno Guggisberg (SFOE employee in charge of biomass) stated in an interview,

> Those installations using energy crops, we did not want to support those. [...] We wanted to introduce ecological minimum requirements to prevent these [installations] which do not fulfill those requirements.

As Stefan Mutzner (Managing Director of Ökostrom Schweiz) stated in an interview,

> [Energy crop plants] do not make sense in Switzerland. In Germany, they served to avoid a surplus of certain grains and to use fallow land to grow energy crops for biogas plants. We don't have that in Switzerland.[51]

Second, small installations receive considerably higher base rates. As Bruno Guggisberg (SFOE employee in charge of biomass) stated in an interview,

> The Germans had different classifications. They also had larger installations. We felt that those did not fit for Switzerland.
>
> According to the RE statistics, the existing installations were mostly 30 kW, 50 kW, 80 kW.

This is confirmed by an industry representative who, however, stated that small plants expand their capacity nowadays and newly-built plants are all above 200 kW.

4.2.2 Specific Design of the Solar PV Feed-In Tariff

As outlined in Sect. 4.1, the support for solar PV was highly contested in the parliamentary debate that led to the introduction of the feed-in tariff in Switzerland. In 2009, the specific design of the solar PV feed-in tariff initially differentiated between rooftop, open-space, and building-integrated solar PV and varied with the

[51] Swiss agriculture supplies only 64% of the country's gross food consumption, Walser (2013).

installed capacity. The tariffs were continuously adapted to the solar PV price reductions. With the amendment of 2014, a one-off investment grant for small-scale rooftop installations was introduced. Since then, installations below 10 kW no longer obtain a feed-in tariff but a one-off investment grant consisting of a base rate and a capacity-dependent rate. Owners of installations between 10 kW and 30 kW have the choice between the feed-in tariff and the investment grant. Finally, the most recent amendment in 2015 granted the same tariff for rooftop and open-space installations.

Similar to the German solar PV feed-in tariff design, the Swiss design differentiated between rooftop and open-space installations. This is intriguing since the support for open-space installations was in fact disfavored. As David Stickelberger (Managing Director of Swissolar) stated in an interview,

> Even more than today, we saw open-space installations as compromising the reputation [of solar PV].
>
> We did not have special interest in the open-space installations. I remember that the Federal Office [of Energy] introduced it, and we thought, do it if you want to.

In later amendments, both countries adapted the design to provide equal tariffs to (large-scale) rooftop and open-space installations. In Switzerland, the distinction between large- and small-scale was abolished in that very small-scale installations no longer received a feed-in tariff. The rationale behind consolidating the two categories was the investment cost for the different installation types, which had largely converged in previous years and therefore did not require further tariff differentiation.[52]

Besides the similarities, the Swiss solar PV feed-in tariff design exhibits several differences from the German case (Fig. 3). First, the small-scale investment grant was introduced as a reaction to the high number of small-scale rooftop solar PV installations on the waiting list to receive the feed-in tariff. The waiting list was a direct result of the investment cap for solar PV.

Second, unlike the German feed-in tariff, the Swiss solar PV feed-in tariff has always extensively supported BIPV installations. In fact, Switzerland was the home of a small BIPV industry that emerged in the 1990s as a result of the strong research and development support policies in this sector. This Jenny (State Councilor, SVP) stated in a debate in 2007,

> [The BIPV] market grows very quickly: the revenues increase every year by 45%. [. . .] But sadly the [Swiss] products are only exported; sadly they only go abroad – we need a domestic market.[53]

Urs Wolfer (SFOE employee in charge of solar PV) stated in an interview,

> If you never start to push [building-integrated PV], nothing is ever going to be developed. Therefore, we set this incentive.

[52] SFOE (2014).

[53] Jenny, Plenary Session, OB CoS 2007, 52.

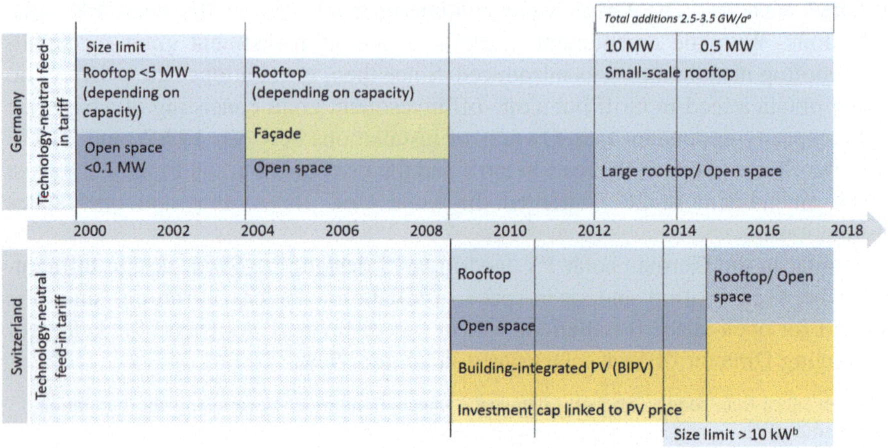

Fig. 3 Design elements of the solar PV feed-in tariff in Germany (top) and Switzerland (bottom). The elements that only appear in one country's design are colored in yellow. The vertical black lines disclose the major amendments of the policies in Germany and Switzerland. [a]The total gross additions are limited to 2.5–3.5 GW (2012–2014) and 2.5 GW (since 2014), respectively, and the tariffs provided to solar PV installations adapted to achieve this goal; [b]since 2014, solar PV installations below 10 kW no longer obtain a feed-in tariff but a one-off investment grant consisting of a base rate and a capacity-dependent rate. Owners of installations between 10 kW and 30 kW have the choice between the feed-in tariff and the investment grant

David Stickelberger (Managing Director of Swissolar) stated in an interview,

> Our stance was always consistent in that we wanted the BIPV tariff. [BIPV] was the USP [unique selling point] of the Swiss PV industry and even an export good in the initial period of the feed-in tariff.
>
> The other argument was the social acceptance. Our position was to fulfill higher aesthetic standards, much higher than [those] abroad.

This design feature was introduced for two reasons. First, the Swiss PV industry lobbied to include their main product, BIPV modules, in the policy scheme. Therefore, this design element originated from domestic factors that influenced path-dependent policymaking and therefore from emerging actors. Second, this design feature was also introduced due to concerns about losing shares in the transnational BIPV market.

Finally, even though revisions of the EnV and thus the tariffs for the individual technologies and installations were decided upon only by the Federal Council, they still underwent a public consultation process. Stakeholders opposing high tariffs for solar PV even used Germany as an example to solicit for lower tariffs. Urs Näf (Head of Energy Policy, Economiesuisse) stated in an interview,

> [Germany] was the most important case for us to obtain reference prices. We always analyzed whether the Swiss prices were far from their [Germany's] prices. I remember having noticed that solar PV received double the amount in Switzerland than in Germany at one point. [. . .] We tried to pressure for lower tariffs, but it did not work. [. . .] Therefore, solar PV was hopelessly overpaid for very long.

5 Discussion and Conclusion

A considerable body of research has analyzed how policies are transferred from one country to another. However, very few studies have examined how and why the design of a transferred policy is accommodated upon adoption in the recipient country. In this chapter, we have focused on the Swiss feed-in tariff policy instrument and explored which of this instrument's design elements were transferred and which were accommodated upon adoption and how. We studied the evolution of the Swiss feed-in tariff in general as well as its specific design for biomass and solar PV technologies. We find that Swiss policymakers have drawn much from the experience with the feed-in tariff in Germany. On the instrument level, policymakers were influenced by this experience and the resulting boom in RE installations and its industry. For biomass, where similar technology users and suppliers exist in both countries, the design of the feed-in tariff was adapted to the Swiss context only to a limited extent. For solar PV, however, the design has been largely accommodated to the Swiss context, on the one hand, due to learning from the German experience and, on the other hand, due to the different industry base present in the two countries. We hence find that technology-related actors take an important role in the policy transfer process. This chapter thus complements the existing literature on policy diffusion and transfer, with a focus on instrument design and its accommodation upon adoption.

These findings have policy implications on a broader technology governance level, especially given the increasing role of technology in both creating and solving problems in various policy fields,[54] specifically climate and energy policy. The diffusion of policy instruments is more likely to happen *without* a specific design accommodation between jurisdictions if they share the same technology-related actor base. This finding allows us to speculate about other sectors in Switzerland that need decarbonization. For instance, policy transfer without major accommodation is likely in the field of low-carbon heating technologies between the cantons in Switzerland or between Switzerland and Austria. These jurisdictions not only share a similar current technology stock and suppliers, they are also host to important manufacturers of low-carbon heating technologies, such as heat pumps and wood-fired heating devices. In contrast, the accommodation of design elements can be expected between jurisdictions with different technology-related actor bases. For instance, policy transfer with major accommodations between Switzerland and its larger neighboring countries is likely regarding electric mobility, which will probably become relevant in the very near future. While France, Germany, and Italy are all home to important automotive industries with their own interests regarding electric mobility, such actors are lacking in Switzerland. These implications are important for policymakers, as they may help them foresee technology-related differences in the positions of their actor bases regarding policy design elements.

[54] Jaffe et al. (2002).

This may help policymakers identify actors with similar interests as well as pinpoint issues where resources may be bundled to obtain the desired policy output.

The contributions of our study are fourfold. First, we unpack and analyze the policy design elements of a deployment policy and their diffusion from one country to another and, hence, expand the focus of the policy diffusion and transfer literatures to these micro-level elements. Second, we show the influence of technology-related actors in policy adoption and accommodation. These actors initially only emerge upon (early) technology deployment and therefore coevolve with policy.[55] Third, we contribute to the literature on RE policies with an in-depth analysis of the Swiss feed-in tariff, specifically for biomass and solar PV technologies. Fourth, and more broadly, we contribute to discussions about designing policies that are effective in the long run, for example, by creating positive policy feedback from targeted or nurtured actors.[56]

To test our results, future research should expand our approach to other cases, that is, more RE technologies, other countries, or even other policy fields. Quantitative studies could analyze to what extent our results are generalizable. This is however tricky since comparatively measuring the dependent variable, policy design output, is challenging[57] and has only recently been tackled.[58]

References

AEE (2004) Vernehmlassungsantwort - Vernehmlassung AEE zum Stromversorgungsgesetz. Agentur für erneuerbare Energien und Energieeffizienz

Benson D, Jordan A (2011) What have we learned from policy transfer research? Dolowitz and Marsh Revisited. Polit Stud Rev 9:366–378

Berry FS, Berry WD (2014) Innovation and diffusion models in policy research. In: Sabatier PA, Weible CM (eds) Theories of the policy process, 3rd edn. Westview Press, Boulder/CO, pp 307–359

Biesbroek GR, Swart RJ, Carter TR, Cowan C, Henrichs T, Mela H, Morecroft MD, Rey D (2010) Europe adapts to climate change: comparing national adaptation strategies. Glob Environ Change 20:440–450

Biesenbender S, Tosun J (2014) Domestic politics and the diffusion of international policy innovations: how does accommodation happen? Glob Environ Change 29:424–433

BMWi (2019) Zahlen und Fakten - Energiedaten. Bundesministerium für Wirtschaft und Energie, Berlin

Braun D, Gilardi F (2006) Taking "Galton's Problem" seriously: towards a theory of policy diffusion. J Theor Polit 18:298–322

Busch P-O, Jörgens H, Tews K (2005) Regulatory instruments: the making of a new international environmental regime. AAPSS Ann 598:146–167

[55] Schmidt and Sewerin (2017).

[56] Voss et al. (2009); Jordan and Matt (2014); Capano and Woo (2017).

[57] Schaffrin et al. (2015).

[58] Schmidt and Sewerin (2019).

Capano G, Woo JJ (2017) Resilience and robustness in policy design: a critical appraisal. Policy Sci 50:355–382
Carley S, Davies LL, Spence DB, Zirogiannis N (2018) Empirical evaluation of the stringency and design of renewable portfolio standards. Nat Energy 3:754–763
Cashore B, Howlett M (2007) Punctuating which equilibrium? Understanding thermostatic policy dynamics in pacific northwest forestry. Am J Pol Sci 51:532–551
Cheon A, Urpelainen J (2013) How do competing interest groups influence environmental policy? The case of renewable electricity in industrialized democracies, 1989–2007. Polit Stud 61:874–897
Couture T, Gagnon Y (2010) An analysis of feed-in tariff remuneration models: implications for renewable energy investment. Energy policy 38:955–965
Dolowitz DP, Marsh D (1996) Who learns what from whom: a review of the policy transfer literature. Polit Stud 44:343–357
Dumas M, Rising J, Urpelainen J (2016) Political competition and renewable energy transitions over long time horizons: a dynamic approach. Ecol Econ 124:175–184
Ebers A, Wüstenhagen R (2017) Local acceptance of wind energy in Switzerland, Estonia and Ukraine. A cross-country analysis based on choice experiments. Universität St. Gallen, St. Gallen
Eisenhardt KM (1989) Building theories from case study research. Acad Manag Rev 14:532–550
Gilardi F, Füglister K (2008) Empirical modeling of policy diffusion in federal states: the dyadic approach. Swiss Polit Sci Rev 14:413–450
Haelg L, Waelchli M, Schmidt TS (2018) Supporting energy technology deployment while avoiding technological lock-in. Environ Res Lett 13:104011
Haelg L, Sewerin S, Schmidt TS (2020) The role of actors in the policy design process: introducing design coalitions to explain policy output. Policy Sci 53:309–347
HES (2004) Vernehmlassungsantwort - Bundesgesetz über die Stromversorgung und Revision des Elektrizitätsgesetzes. Holzenergie Schweiz, Zurich
Heselhaus S (2021) The quest for the future energy mix in the EU and in Switzerland. In: Hettich P, Kachi A (eds) Swiss energy governance. Springer, New York, pp 43–60
Hettich P (2021) Governing decentral energy systems. In: Hettich P, Kachi A (eds) Swiss energy governance. Springer, New York, pp 155–170
Holzinger K, Knill C, Sommerer T (2011) Is there convergence of national environmental policies? An analysis of policy outputs in 24 OECD countries. Environ Polit 20:20–41
Hoppmann J, Huenteler J, Girod B (2014) Compulsive policy-making - the evolution of the German feed-in tariff system for solar photovoltaic power. Res Policy 43:1422–1441
IEA (2009) National Survey Report of PV power applications in Switzerland 2008. International Energy Agency, Paris
Jacobs D (2012) Renewable energy policy convergence in the EU - the evolution of feed-in tariffs in Germany, Spain and France. Ashgate Publishing Limited, Farnham
Jacobs D (2014) Policy invention as a process of evolutionary tinkering and codification: the emergence of feed-in tariffs for renewable electricity. Environ Polit 25:755–773
Jacobsson S, Lauber V (2006) The politics and policy of energy system transformation—explaining the German diffusion of renewable energy technology. Energy Policy 34:256–276
Jaffe AB, Newell RG, Stavins RN (2002) Environmental policy and technological change. Environ Resour Econ 22:41–70
Jaffe AB, Newell RG, Stavins RN (2005) A tale of two market failures: technology and environmental policy. Ecol Econ 54:164–174
Jordan A, Huitema D (2014) Innovations in climate policy: the politics of invention, diffusion, and evaluation. Env Polit 23:715–734
Jordan A, Matt E (2014) Designing policies that intentionally stick: policy feedback in a changing climate. Policy Sci 47:227–247
Kemp R, Pontoglio S (2011) The innovation effects of environmental policy instruments — a typical case of the blind men and the elephant? Ecol Econ 72:28–36

Lehmann P, Söderholm P (2018) Can technology-specific deployment policies be cost-effective? The case of renewable energy support schemes. Environ Resour Econ 71:475–505
Markard J, Suter M, Ingold K (2016) Socio-technical transitions and policy change – advocacy coalitions in Swiss energy policy. Environ Innov Soc Trans 18:215–237
Marsh D, Sharman JC (2009) Policy diffusion and policy transfer. Policy Stud 30:269–288
Matisoff DC (2008) The adoption of state climate change policies and renewable portfolio standards: regional diffusion or internal determinants? Rev Policy Res 25:527–546
Matisoff DC, Edwards J (2014) Kindred spirits or intergovernmental competition? The innovation and diffusion of energy policies in the American states (1990 – 2008). Environ Polit 23:795–817
Mitchell C (2000) The England and Wales Non-Fossil fuel obligation: history and lessons. Annu Rev Energy Environ 25:285–312
Newmark AJ (2002) An integrated approach to policy transfer and diffusion. Rev Policy Res 19:151–178
Polzin F, Egli F, Steffen B, Schmidt TS (2019) How do policies mobilize private finance for renewable energy? — a systematic review with an investor perspective. Appl Energy 236:1249–1268
REN21 (2005) Renewables 2005 Global Status Report. REN21 Secretariat, Paris
REN21 (2012) Renewables 2012 Global status report. REN21 Secretariat, Paris
REN21 (2016) Renewables 2016 Global status report. REN21 Secretariat, Paris
Schaffer LM, Bernauer T (2014) Explaining government choices for promoting renewable energy. Energy Policy 68:15–27
Schaffrin A, Sewerin S, Seubert S (2015) Toward a comparative measure of climate policy output. Policy Stud J 43:257–282
Schmela M, Kreutzmann A (2001) Marktwachstum gewinnt an Fahrt. Phot. Das Solarstrom-Magazin 4:12–15
Schmidt TS, Sewerin S (2017) Technology as a driver of climate and energy politics. Nat Energy 2:17084
Schmidt TS, Sewerin S (2019) Measuring the temporal dynamics of policy mixes – an empirical analysis of renewable energy policy mixes' balance and design features in nine countries. Res Policy 48:103557
Schmidt TS, Battke B, Grosspietsch D, Hoffmann VH (2016) Do deployment policies pick technologies by (not) picking applications? — a simulation of investment decisions in technologies with multiple applications. Res Policy 45:1965–1983
Sonnberger M, Ruddat M (2017) Local and socio-political acceptance of wind farms in Germany. Technol Soc 51:56–65
Stadelmann M, Castro P (2014) Climate policy innovation in the South – domestic and international determinants of renewable energy policies in developing and emerging countries. Glob Environ Change 29:413–423
Stokes LC (2013) The politics of renewable energy policies: the case of feed-in tariffs in Ontario, Canada. Energy Policy 56:490–500
Stoutenborough JW (2008) Encouraging pollution-free energy: the diffusion of state net metering policies. Soc Sci Q 89:1230–1251
Strebel F (2011) Inter-governmental institutions as promoters of energy policy diffusion in a federal setting. Energy Policy 39:467–476
Swiss Federal Office of Energy (2008) Das neue Fördersystem für grünen Strom stösst an seine Grenzen. Press release, 28 November 2008
Swiss Federal Office of Energy (2014) Revision der Energieverordnung per 1. Januar 2015. Press release, 05 November 2014
Swiss Federal Office of Energy (2019) Schweizerische Gesamtenergiestatistik 2018. Swiss Federal Office of Energy, Bern
Tews K, Busch P-O, Jörgens H (2003) The diffusion of new environmental policy instruments. Eur J Polit Res 42:569–600

Van Benthem A, Gillingham K, Sweeney J (2008) Learning-by-doing and the optimal solar policy in California. Energy J 29:131–151
Voss JP, Smith A, Grin J (2009) Designing long-term policy: rethinking transition management. Policy Sci 42:275–302
Walser B (2013) Hat die Schweiz genügend Boden, um alle satt zu machen? Tages-Anzeiger, 21 November 2013
Wiser R, Namovicz C, Gielecki M (2007) The experience with renewable portfolio standards in the United States. Electr J 20:8–20

Leonore Haelg is Scientific Collaborator at Zurich University of Applied Sciences (ZHAW), Research Group for Renewable Energy, Institute of Natural Resource Sciences, Campus Grüental, Wädenswil, Switzerland. She conducted her PhD thesis with the Energy and Technology Policy Group at the Department of Humanities, Social and Political Sciences at ETH Zurich, Zurich, Switzerland

Tobias S. Schmidt is Associate Professor at the Department of Humanities, Social and Political Sciences at ETH Zurich, Zurich, Switzerland and head of the Energy and Technology Policy Group.

Sebastian Sewerin is a senior researcher and a lecturer with the Energy and Technology Policy Group at the Department of Humanities, Social and Political Sciences at ETH Zurich, Zurich, Switzerland.

Part II
Actors Driving the Energy Transition

Decentralisation of Energy Generation, Centralisation of Energy Lawmaking

Reflections About the Origins and Evolution of Swiss Energy Law

Martin Föhse

Contents

Abstract The energy sector has been subject to regulation since ancient times. The mechanisms of regulatory activity in this sector run like a red thread through history. New regulations are often born out of necessity (for example because of limited energy resources or today because of climate objectives). Switzerland's energy law was originally a cantonal matter. Over the course of time, more and more competences have been transferred to the federal level. This, together with the increasing complexity of the subject matter of regulation, has led to a conflicting legal

M. Föhse (✉)
University of St. Gallen, IFF-HSG, St. Gallen, Switzerland
e-mail: martin.foehse@unisg.ch

P. Hettich, A. Kachi (eds.), *Swiss Energy Governance*,
https://doi.org/10.1007/978-3-030-80787-0_6

framework that renders it nearly impossible, even for experts, to answer everyday questions of competence with the necessary clarity and without much effort.

1 Introduction

The development of regulation in the Swiss energy sector has been and continues to be a constant process, strongly driven by technical progress. In his fundamental work "Energy Law" from 2005, Jagmetti identifies four successive priorities of regulation for Switzerland, starting with industrialisation in the late nineteenth century: (1) security aspects, (2) supply, (3) conservation of nature and landscape and finally (4) the market.[1] However, these domains have not evolved as separate fields. Rather, they have complemented each other. This has been accompanied by an increase in complexity and growing conflicts of interest and by a steady increase in the density of regulation.[2]

Jagmetti's observations also reveal another aspect: to support his remarks, he refers primarily to laws enacted on the federal level. As will be shown below, in the context of Switzerland's federal structure and organisation, this means that regulatory activity has increasingly been transferred from the cantons to the federal level. We are therefore dealing with a form of centralisation. At the same time, paradoxically, energy supply in Switzerland is—politically desired—developing (again) in exactly the opposite direction, namely towards electricity that is largely produced on a decentralised basis and as far as possible in a climate-friendly manner. This primarily concerns photovoltaic systems.

With a view to the desired decarbonisation of energy supply, electricity is the key energy source today, already accounting for 25% of Switzerland's total final energy consumption.[3] This article therefore primarily focuses on the development of the regulation of the electricity industry since the founding of the state, but not without establishing cross-references to other areas of energy legislation and the time before that, insofar as they appear to be useful for understanding the overall context. In the following, the legislator's approach to the challenges of regulating the electricity industry in a federal context will be critically examined and finally illustrated with examples. It will be demonstrated that the increasing complexity of the energy sector has had an important impact on the evolution and quality of energy regulation in Switzerland.

To present the development of Swiss energy law in a comprehensive manner would go far beyond the scope of this contribution. In over 150 years of development, there have been countless important events, technical, economic and political

[1] Jagmetti (2005), p. 11.

[2] Jagmetti (2005), p. 16.

[3] Swiss Federal Office of Energy (2019b), p. 4.

developments, from industrialisation and two world wars to the digital age. This is also not a historical investigation, especially since I limit myself mainly to the analysis of typical legal sources, namely the legislative materials, mainly produced by the Federal Council, which automatically narrows the perspective. However, since the focus is on the creation of federal competences and on the way in which these competences were used by the legislator, this approach seems to be appropriate here. From this perspective, the following are just a few of the highlights that I believe have a certain significance for the electricity industry. The selected highlights also form a kind of temporal bracket around the entire Swiss energy law, i.e. the basic regulation on the use of hydropower[4] around 1900 on the one hand and the electricity market regulation at the beginning of the twenty-first century on the other.

2 Energy Law: Origins and Essence

2.1 Subject Matter of Energy Law

The term "energy law"—like the term "regulation of the energy sector"—cannot be defined conclusively. However, for the purpose of this paper, it is necessary to provide a consistent framework for the terms used.

From a material point of view, it would be quite justifiable to describe all law as energy law that has a connection to the topic of energy production and use. The large scope of this field is, however, demonstrated by the four main areas of regulation or "tendencies",[5] as Jagmetti calls them (security, supply, conservation of nature and landscape as well as the market). From a political point of view, this ranges from climate and environmental policy (coping with climate change and the conservation of natural resources) to economic policy (security of supply and competitiveness) and social and structural policy (affordable energy supply and fair distribution of revenues).

As already mentioned, this article deals with the regulation of the electricity industry and there primarily with what I would like to call "nominal energy law" or "energy law in the narrow sense". I am referring to the law that "wants to be" energy law, i.e. the law that directly regulates, for example, the use of hydropower. Occasionally, however, cross-references are made to "functional energy law" or "energy law in the broader sense". This refers to norms that primarily have a different focus, such as environmental law, including water protection, regional planning law or antitrust and competition law, but which also have a material connection to energy.

---

[4] Hydropower accounts for a good 55% of today's domestic electricity production (Swiss Federal Office of Energy 2019a, p. 2).

[5] Jagmetti (2005), p. 11.

2.2 Energy Regulation as a Historical Constant

The topic of energy supply and use has already occupied our extinct ancestor Homo Erectus since he learned to control fire about one million years ago.[6] Regulation in the broad sense of the term also began early on. For example, the use of wood was already subject to antique regulations. In the third century, the Roman Emperor Alexander Severus assigned forest management to the same institution that was responsible for the administration of the public baths. Haas suspects that this was a new regulation of the supply of firewood, which had previously been carried out via intermediaries.[7] It is possible that the excessive use of resources from the operation of these same thermal baths had resulted in bottlenecks in the supply of wood, which even then had a connection to ancient social and environmental policies.[8]

The use of water power to drive mills and saws can also be traced back to ancient times.[9] One example from the baroque era is Zurich, whose Grand Council made the use of wood the subject of regulation by means of so-called "mandates". This was intended to guarantee both the supply of wood and the protection of wood as a natural resource.[10] In the *Hoch-Obrigkeitliche[n] Mandat, Betreffend die Versorg- und Beschirmung der Holz- und Waldungen* from 1717, for example, the following lines can be found (loosely translated from the original text formulated in old German language):

> To our great regret, we have had to learn that in many places of our territory the inhabitants are robbing themselves of this treasure by excessive and unsustainable consumption and extinction of the woods. It is time to understand that if this danger is not recognised, there is reason to worry about such a general damage to the land, which our descendants would have to pay a great deal for [. . .].[11]

Here, too, the close links with other areas of interest and policy, in particular the aspect of intergenerational sustainability of natural resource use, are evident. Finally, water rights that are still valid today and that recently occupied the Federal Supreme Court of Switzerland also go back to the time of the so-called Ancien Régime.[12] These arbitrarily selected examples show that since ancient times there seems to

---

[6] Berna et al. (2012), p. 1215 et seq.

[7] Haas (2006), p. 130, with a reference to a calculation of the consumption of firewood on page 244.

[8] Haas (2006), p. 244 et seq. and 252; he remains skeptical with regard to the link to environmental considerations.

[9] Grewe (2009), p. 429 et seq.

[10] Schindler (2019), p. 279.

[11] Mandat (1717), p. 204 et seq.: "*Weilen wir aber zu unserm nicht geringen Bedauern in Erfahrung bringen müssen, wie dass an vielen Orten unserer Bottmässigkeit unsere Angehörige durch übermässiges und landesverderbliches Geuden und Austoten der Hölzern sich dieses Kleinods also berauben, dass wann hierwider nicht erforderliches Einsehen gethan wurde, nicht unzeitig zu besorgen wäre, es möchte hieraus ein solcher allgemeiner Landsschaden erwachsen, dessen unsere Nachkommen sich nicht wenig zu entgelten haben wurden.*"

[12] BGE 145 II 145; Föhse (2019), p. 444 et seq.

have been a need to establish rules for the use of energy sources for various motives. This article will not go back too far in time. Rather, it begins with the founding of the Swiss Confederation in 1848. In the following sections, the rough constitutional lines will be delineated and compared with the regulatory priorities mentioned by Jagmetti.

3 Milestones in the Regulation of the Electricity Industry

3.1 Levels of Government and Basic Jurisdiction

Switzerland ("the Swiss Confederation" [*Schweizerische Eidgenossenschaft*]) has a federal structure consisting of 26 cantons (Art. 1 BV).[13] In accordance with the Swiss system of federalism, the cantons are sovereign "except to the extent that their sovereignty is limited by the Federal Constitution" (Art. 3 BV)—this norm is already found with almost identical wording in the first constitution of 12 September 1848 (there also in Art. 3).[14] With regard to the competences under constitutional law, this means that the Confederation and the cantons must share "sovereignty". Moreover, it implies that the Confederation must (only) fulfil duties in those areas where limits to cantonal sovereignty are provided by the Federal Constitution (Art. 42 BV). The Confederation should only take on those tasks "that the Cantons are unable to perform or which require uniform regulation by the Confederation" (Art. 43a para. 1 BV). In view of the history of modern Switzerland, which in 1848—apart from the short period of the Helvetic Republic from 1798–1803—emerged from a federation of sovereign states (the cantons) of strongly contrasting socio-cultural areas, this can be regarded as an obvious decision.[15]

In the following sections, the tendency towards centralisation in energy law regulation will be documented. For this purpose, it will be necessary to trace the development of the relevant federal competences in the constitution. In the absence of federal competence, the member states, i.e. the cantons, are entitled to legislate. The following overview of the development of constitutional competences will be based on the three federal constitutions since the founding of the Swiss Confederation, i.e. those of 1848, 1876 and 1999, and it will take the regulation of hydropower as its starting point. Moreover, the focus will be on the main areas of regulation mentioned by Jagmetti. Cantonal law will only be included on a selective basis where it seems appropriate.

[13] Federal Constitution of the Swiss Confederation *("Bundesverfassung der Schweizerischen Eidgenossenschaft" vom 18. April 1999 [BV, SR 101]).*

[14] However, the term "sovereignty" was subject to intensive debates in the so-called *Tagsatzung*, the assembly that was responsible for drafting the first Swiss constitution (Kölz 1992, p. 578; Schweizer 2014, p. 83; Jaag 2015, p. 149).

[15] Tschannen (2016), p. 95.

3.2 *Hydropower*

3.2.1 From Wood to Coal

Even at the time when the state was founded around 1850, wood was still the main energy source in Switzerland, accounting for 88% of the total. This was followed by peat (9%) and coal (3%). Hydropower accounted for only 1%.[16] As far as the first constitution of 1848 is concerned, one can be brief about energy law. There are no competence norms that would concern nominal energy law, nor are there any that would concern functional energy law. The constitution of the young nation (understandably) had other focal points, above all the question of the structure of the federal parliament as a unicameral national representation, as a "*Tagsatzung*" or in a bicameral system based on the model of the United States of America, the question of the structure of electoral law and the three powers, or the fundamental relationship between the Confederation and the cantons.[17] Conversely, this means that "energy" as a potential subject matter of regulation was entirely in the hands of the cantons.

Barely 26 years after the founding of the state, the totally revised constitution of 29 May 1874 was the second constitution to come into force in Switzerland. The constitution of 1874 is a key enactment for energy law. At the beginning, however, it was also free of energy law ballast (not considering Art. 24 BV 1874, which provides for the supervision of the hydraulic engineering and forest police, which for the time being was still limited to the high mountain areas, and the legislative competence regarding fisheries according to Art. 25 BV 1874).

For various reasons,[18] however, wood-based energy supply came to an end as early as the 1860s. Wood and peat were increasingly replaced by coal. Swiss coal consumption rose exponentially from this point on and flourished from the early years of the twentieth century until the mid-1960s, when it disappeared just as quickly and was replaced mainly by oil.[19] The main consumers of coal were—before electrification—initially the railways, gas works (for the production of so-called "town gas" by coal gasification, especially for public lighting) and industry (steam engines). From the beginning of the twentieth century, heating systems in residential buildings were also added.[20]

[16] Kupper and Pallua (2016), p. 16; today the shares in total energy consumption are as follows: petroleum fuels (13.9%), motor fuels (35.4%), electricity (25.0%), gas (13.5%), remainder (12.2%) (Swiss Federal Office of Energy 2019b, p. 4).

[17] Kölz (1992), p. 554 et seq.

[18] Kupper and Pallua (2016), p. 16 et seq.

[19] Kupper and Pallua (2016), p. 22 et seq.; Swiss Federal Office of Energy (2019b), p. 3.

[20] Kupper and Pallua (2016), p. 32 et seq.

3.2.2 The Beginnings of Electrification: The Struggle for Water

Electrification began in the early 1880s.[21] At that time, electricity was also generated from hydropower in Switzerland for the first time. In contrast to coal, which had to be imported, hydropower provided a domestic source for renewable energy. This opened up completely new opportunities but also raised fundamental questions about water sovereignty, the granting of rights of use and the distribution of the revenues.[22] The Federal Council's comments from 1905 are illustrative of this:

> As a mountainous country, Switzerland possesses a number of relatively easily exploitable hydropower sources, which constitute a considerable part of the national wealth and whose value has risen significantly since electricity has begun its global conquest and the technology of converting hydropower into electrical energy has experienced a tremendous upswing. Thanks to this progress, we in Switzerland are able to replace coal, which we have to purchase from abroad, by hydropower as a source of power to a very significant extent. [. . .] This means that the national authorities must also concern themselves more than before with the issue of Swiss hydropower. Our primary responsibility is to ensure that, when Switzerland switches over to the electrical operation of its railways [. . .], the hydropower that is necessary for this purpose will be available.[23]

In accordance with the basic constitutional order, the cantons were initially competent for regulation. The enactment of a corresponding framework regulation by the Confederation was politically complex and therefore difficult.[24] It began with a petition (*Gesuch*) from the "Central Executive Committee of the Swiss Frei-Land Company" (*Centralvorstand der schweizerischen Gesellschaft Frei-Land*) in April 1891, whose main concern was to monopolise hydropower at the federal level and to state, among other things, that the use of hydropower and the transmission of electricity generated from hydropower should be a federal matter.[25] The Federal Council took this concern as an opportunity to have the subject examined in greater depth in a report that appeared 3 years later (1894) and which, as it turned out afterwards, provided guidance for the future organisation of water use in

---

[21] Kupper and Pallua (2016), p. 37 and 53; Föhse (2015), p. 126.

[22] See also Jagmetti (2005), p. 410 et seq.

[23] Federal Council (1905), p. 223: "*Die Schweiz besitzt als Bergland eine Summe von verhältnismässig leicht verwertbaren Wasserkräften, welche einen erheblichen Teil des Nationalvermögens ausmachen und deren Wert bedeutend gestiegen ist, seitdem die Elektrizität ihren Siegeszug durch die Welt angetreten und die Technik der Umwandlung der Wasserkraft in elektrische Energie einen ungeheuren Aufschwung genommen hat. Durch diesen Fortschritt erreichen wir in der Schweiz, dass in einem sehr bedeutenden Masse die Steinkohle, welche wir aus dem Ausland beziehen müssen, als Krafterzeugerin durch die Wasserkraft ersetzt werden kann. [...] Daraus ergibt sich die Notwendigkeit, dass sich auch die Landesbehörden mehr als bisher mit der Angelegenheit der schweizerischen Wasserkräfte beschäftigen. Wir haben in erster Linie dafür zu sorgen, dass, wenn die Schweiz zum elektrischen Betrieb ihrer Bahnen [...] übergehen wird, die nötige Wasserkraft zu diesem Behufe zur Verfügung steht.*"

[24] Federal Council (1905), p. 224.

[25] Federal Council (1894), p. 820.

Switzerland,[26] even though it took almost 25 years to draft the new regulation[27] before it came into force with the Water Rights Act (WRA)[28] on 1 January 1918.[29] This includes the creation of the necessary constitutional basis in the form of the new Art. 24bis BV 1874 (which was promoted by a popular initiative)[30] and a mandatory constitutional referendum on 25 October 1908.[31]

In the run-up to the vote, the Federal Council rejected a popular initiative, which called for extensive centralisation at the federal level, and basically confirmed its position, already formulated in the 1894 report, that water sovereignty and regulatory powers should essentially remain with the cantons.[32] The parliament responded to the initiative with a counter-proposal prepared by a commission of experts, which was further adapted during the parliamentary debate. The initiative committee subsequently withdrew its proposal.[33] With Art. 24bis BV 1874, adopted on 25 October 1908, it was now laid down at constitutional level that the Confederation should (at least) have basic legislative competence in the field of hydropower.[34] Furthermore, the Confederation was supposed to act as the licensing authority in intercantonal relations in the event of a dispute as well as in international relations. In contrast, the fees and charges arising from water use were the responsibility of the cantons (see Art. 24bis BV 1874).[35] This is still the case today (Art. 76 para. 4 BV).

3.3 *The Safety of Electrical Installations as a Milestone?*

As is not uncommon, the work of the legislator was overtaken by events during the discussions surrounding water sovereignty. The dangers of using electricity were soon recognised. As early as 1902, the Federal Council therefore felt compelled[36] (in my opinion without the necessary constitutional basis)[37] to regulate the safety of

[26] Federal Council (1894), p. 820.

[27] Federal Council (1912), p. 669.

[28] Water Rights Act *(Bundesgesetz vom 22. Dezember 1916 über die Nutzbarmachung der Wasserkräfte, Wasserrechtsgesetz [WRG, SR 721.80])*.

[29] See AS 1933 189.

[30] Federal Council (1907), p. 624.

[31] Federal Council (1912), p. 45.

[32] Federal Council (1894), p. 821.

[33] Federal Council (1908b), p. 475.

[34] Federal Council (1912), p. 672.

[35] Federal Council (1908a), p. 7 et seq.; Jagmetti (2005), p. 410 et seq.

[36] Federal Council (1899), p. 787.

[37] Federal Council (1899), p. 790. From a legal point of view, the reasons given in the Federal Council dispatch for the legitimacy of the legislation do not seem very convincing (the dispatch states that the Federal Assembly had already decided this beforehand and that, in the meantime, legislation in civil and criminal matters had also become a federal competence). It goes without saying that the Federal Assembly cannot give itself competences that it does not have under the

electrical installations by means of a federal law (the EleG[38])—an issue that may have become more urgent after a fire had broken out in the Zurich telephone exchange on 2 April 1898 due to a lack of safety precautions.[39] As Jagmetti points out,[40] the fact that the issue of security was initially reflected in (centralised) federal law was probably due in large part to the complexity of hydropower from a political point of view and to coincidence, rather than to a deliberate strategy, although the problem had been known for some time. The necessary constitutional basis was not established until 1908, when the constitutional provision on hydropower was introduced in Art. 24bis para. 9 BV 1874 (now Art. 91 para. 1 BV).

3.4 *The Issue of Energy Supply as a Milestone?*

Electricity began its triumphal advance after the First World War, after it had still been considered a luxury good at the turn of the twentieth century. Initially, it was used primarily for public lighting or the operation of trams in the cities.[41] The lack of fuel made the dependence on foreign countries obvious, so that industrial enterprises also began to replace coal with electricity. Efforts to bring electricity into the home also began in the 1920s. But it took until the 1950s and 1960s before electrification was fully implemented.[42] In 1945, for example, only 1% of households had a vacuum cleaner or refrigerator; by 1970, these figures had risen to 86 and 82% respectively (electric cookers and, in particular, electric irons had been quite common since the pre-war period).[43]

When the constitutional basis for the use of hydropower was created in 1908 and the Federal WRA came into force in 1918, the focus was probably less on supplying the general population with electricity (in the sense of a basic supply), but rather on the use and expansion of hydropower itself and the hoped-for reduction of dependence on hard coal imports from abroad.[44] On the one hand, this picture emerges from the Federal Council dispatch on the constitutional amendment, in which the issue of supply is at best indirectly reflected (in particular in the form of the obligation to obtain a permit for the transfer of electricity abroad and the probably

---

Constitution. To what extent the competence to legislate on civil and criminal law is relevant here is difficult to see, unless one assumes an enormously broad concept, especially of civil law, under which one could subsume almost any regulatory activity. It rather seems as if the matter has been taken on by necessity—regardless of the division of competences defined in the constitution.

[38] Electricity Act *(Bundesgesetz vom 24. Juni 1902 betreffend die elektrischen Schwach- und Starkstromanlagen, Elektrizitätsgesetz [EleG, SR 734.0])*.

[39] Federal Council (1899), p. 787.

[40] Jagmetti (2005), p. 11.

[41] Kupper and Pallua (2016), p. 42.

[42] Swiss Federal Office of Energy (2019b), p. 3.

[43] Kupper, Pallua (2016), p. 44 et seq. and 53.

[44] Jagmetti (2005), p. 411.

desired reduction of foreign dependency).[45] On the other hand, there is the dispatch on the WRA, where the Federal Council makes a pointed statement on what it considers to be the central aspect of the "exploitation" of hydraulic power—namely the "interest of the general public in this national resource". Just as important—as already in the debate on the constitutional provision—was the social and economic component, the question of participation in the new resource as "national wealth" and the prevention of price increases for fiscal purposes or through speculation.[46]

Finally, this is also in line with the state of technical development and the degree of electrification at the time, which had not yet reached households. From the federal government's point of view, the focus was on railways as potential customers, as well as cities for public lighting and trams and, increasingly, industry.[47] At the time, Switzerland was still a "coal country" and thus became increasingly dependent on foreign countries at the turn of the twentieth century.[48] Consistent energy supply policy only began later, after the Second World War.[49]

However, it is interesting to note that Art. 55 let. d WRA stipulates that hydropower concessions can also contain provisions "on the tariffs for the supply of the generated power, on the power to be supplied free of charge or at preferential prices, on the reduction of electricity prices in case of increased profit, [and] on the supply of power to a region". The standard obviously aims at avoiding that fiscal objectives of the state or speculative activities hinder the development of power plant capacity. With approximately the same wording, it is still part of the WRA today (only the term "power" was replaced by "electrical energy" as of 1 May 1997). Today, however, it is obviously in conflict with the new electricity market regulation, which has been in force since 2008. In the course of the drafting of the StromVG,[50] the rule seems to have been overlooked. As a result, Parliament has made more or less unsuccessful attempts to improve it. The rule should, however, have been deleted.[51]

The topic of supply therefore came into focus later. From an energy history perspective, the 1950s seem to have been a decisive turning point in this respect. In step with strong economic growth, energy consumption also increased exponentially,[52] so that historians see these years as an epochal change or a threshold period from industrial to consumer society.[53] The Federal Council's 1957 dispatch in

---

[45] Federal Council (1907), p. 624 et seq.

[46] Federal Council (1912), p. 674.

[47] Federal Council (1912), p. 676.

[48] Kupper and Pallua (2016), p. 24 (about coal extraction in Switzerland).

[49] Kupper and Pallua (2016), p. 64.

[50] Electricity Supply Act *(Bundesgesetz vom 23. März 2007 über die Stromversorgung, Stromversorgungsgesetz [StromVG, SR 734.7]).*

[51] Kratz (2016), p. 434. Kratz sees the problem, but does not comment on it.

[52] Swiss Federal Office of Energy (2019b), p. 3.

[53] Kupper and Pallua (2016), p. 55.

favour of the creation of a constitutional provision on nuclear energy is a good illustration of the new emphasis on "security of supply".

> Keeping pace with the development of nuclear research and technology has become crucial for our country. Without its own oil and coal deposits, Switzerland has shifted to the intensive exploitation of the country's most important energy sources, namely hydropower. However, our own energy sources are currently only able to satisfy about 33 percent of our total raw energy requirements (hydropower 24, firewood 9), and we are dependent on imported energy sources for the rest.[54]

After the creation of the constitutional basis on 24 November 1957[55] and with the definition of exclusive federal competence, things moved quickly. On 23 December 1959 the Federal Assembly passed the Atomic Energy Act (*Atomgesetz*).[56] In 1964, for example, the energy supply company BKW announced that it was planning to build a nuclear power plant in Mühleberg near Bern. Construction began just 3 years later, in 1967. Test operations began in 1971, and the nuclear power plant was connected to the grid in 1972 (the Beznau I nuclear power plant went into operation in 1969).[57] The Mühleberg power plant was taken off the grid at the end of 2019. From a political point of view, nuclear energy remains controversial, and the applicable law aims primarily at the protection of public policy interests, such as public safety (the safe operation of power plants) and security (the protection of the population) and public health. From a legal point of view, centralisation is less problematic in this field, both from a federalist perspective and in view of the legal challenges. On the contrary, it was the right choice.

Also in the 1950s (1958), the electricity networks of Germany, France and Switzerland were connected at the substation in Laufenburg. This laid the foundations for Switzerland's international electricity trading and significantly increased the volume of (already existing) cross-border electricity exchange, while at the same time strengthening grid stability—and thus the security of supply.[58] Electricity now made its way into households, and coal was replaced by oil, which in the early

[54] Federal Council (1957), p. 1148: "*Für unser Land ist es nachgerade zu einer Schicksalsfrage geworden, mit der Entwicklung der Atomforschung und der Atomtechnik Schritt zu halten. Ohne eigene Erdöl- und Kohlenvorkommen hat sich die Schweiz auf die intensive Auswertung der wichtigsten landeseigenen Energiequellen, nämlich die Wasserkräfte, verlegt. Unsere eigenen Energiequellen vermögen aber zur Zeit nur etwa 33 Prozent des gesamten Rohenergiebedarfs zu befriedigen (Wasserkraft 24, Brennholz 9), und für den Rest sind wir auf importierte Energieträger angewiesen.*"

[55] See AS 1957 1027. Available at https://www.amtsdruckschriften.bar.admin.ch.

[56] Atomic Energy Act *(Bundesgesetz vom 23. Dezember 1959 über die friedliche Verwendung der Atomenergie, Atomgesetz [AtG, AS 1960 541])*. Available at https://www.amtsdruckschriften.bar.admin.ch.

[57] Föhse and Drittenbass (2017), p. 169.

[58] Föhse (2014), p. 8; Kupper, Pallua (2016), p. 50 et seq.

1970s, shortly before the oil crisis, accounted for around 80% of Switzerland's total energy consumption.[59]

3.5 Spatial Planning, Nature and Heritage Conservation

As far as nominal energy law is concerned, after the creation of the EleG and WRA, the Confederation—apart from the legislation on nuclear energy—for a long time abstained from the temptation to intervene in the electricity industry in a regulatory manner. For the sake of completeness, only the constitutional provision for pipelines for the transport of liquid or gaseous fuels (*Rohrleitungsanlagen zur Beförderung flüssiger oder gasförmiger Brenn- oder Treibstoffe*) of 5 March 1961 and the Pipelines Act (*Rohrleitungsgesetz*) that was based on this provision should be mentioned as exceptions.[60] Apart from this, the Confederation left the field to the cantons, particularly with regard to electricity supply. The cantons usually considered the supply of electricity to be a public task and largely took charge of it themselves.[61] Today, the electricity industry is still cantonal and municipal, i.e. state-dominated.[62] The entire electricity supply in Switzerland was therefore initially established and managed under cantonal and municipal aegis and responsibility—in terms of legislation, supply and enforcement.

However, the strong economic growth from the 1950s onwards also had equally strong external effects on the land requirements of settlements and urban areas, on waste generation, pollution of the environment and the emission of greenhouse gases. This brought spatial planning, nature conservation and environmental protection more and more into the focus and led to a series of constitutional and legislative changes with varying degrees of centralisation, which are primarily attributable to functional energy law and also affect the electricity industry.[63] However, these issues did not only gain relevance as late as the 1960s but already in the early 1950s with the creation of the constitutional provision for water protection in 1953,[64] whereupon the Federal Assembly passed the Water Protection Act on 16 March 1955 (*Gewässerschutzgesetz*).[65] This was followed by a constitutional amendment on the protection of nature and heritage (27 May 1962), the basis for the Nature and

---

[59] Kupper and Pallua (2016), p. 55 and 59; Jagmetti (2005), p. 13; Swiss Federal Office of Energy (2019b), p. 3.

[60] Federal Council (1960), p. 1581; Pipelines Act *(Bundesgesetz vom 4. Oktober 1963 über Rohrleitungsanlagen zur Beförderung flüssiger oder gasförmiger Brenn- oder Treibstoffe, Rohrleitungsgesetz [RLG, SR 746.1]).*

[61] Jagmetti (2005), p. 12.

[62] Swiss Federal Office of Energy (2019a), p. 41 et seq.

[63] Jagmetti (2005), p. 14 and 32, provides a survey.

[64] Federal Council (1953), p. 240.

[65] Federal Council (1955), p. 552.

Cultural Heritage Protection Act (*Natur- und Heimatschutzgesetz*[66]) of 1 July 1966, and a constitutional amendment on spatial planning (14 September 1969),[67] the basis for the 1979 Spatial Planning Act (*Raumplanungsgesetz, RPG*[68]). Moreover, the constitutional basis for the 1983 Environmental Protection Act (*Umweltschutzgesetz*) was adopted by the people and the cantons already on 7 February 1971.[69]

It was not until 23 September 1990 that the Energy Article (after a first attempt in 1983 had failed)[70] was adopted—again a constitutional provision that is part of nominal energy law (Art. 24octies BV 1874), the predecessor of today's Art. 89 BV.[71] This was followed by the Decree on Energy Use (*Energienutzungsbeschluss*)[72] and in 1998/1999 finally by the first Federal Energy Act (*Energiegesetz*),[73] which has already been replaced by the current Energy Act (EnG)[74] that was passed by the Federal Assembly on 30 September 2016.

3.6 The Market

Around the turn of the millennium, market liberalisation increasingly became the focus of electricity sector regulation. An initial attempt was made to open up the electricity market by, among other things, granting everyone the right to use the network of a third party—as had already been done in the gas sector.[75] However, the Electricity Market Act (*Elektrizitätsmarktgesetz, EMG*)[76] did not survive the referendum, so that this project was postponed.[77] It was only in a second attempt—and under the new title Electricity Supply Act (*Stromversorgungsgesetz, StromVG*)—

[66] Nature and Cultural Heritage Protection Act *(Bundesgesetz vom 1. Juli 1966 über den Natur- und Heimatschutz [NHG, SR 451])*.

[67] Federal Council (1969), p. 568.

[68] Spatial Planning Act *(Bundesgesetz vom 22. Juni 1979 über die Raumplanung, Raumplanungsgesetz [RPG, SR 700])*.

[69] Federal Council (1970), p. 1609.

[70] Federal Council (1984), p. 902.

[71] Federal Council (1989), p. 902.

[72] *Bundesbeschluss vom 14. Dezember 1990 für eine sparsame und rationelle Energienutzung*. See AS 1991 1018. Available at https://www.amtsdruckschriften.bar.admin.ch.

[73] Energy Act *(Energiegesetz vom 23. Juni 1998 [EnG, SR 730.0])*. See AS 1999 197. Available at https://www.amtsdruckschriften.bar.admin.ch.

[74] Energy Act *(Energiegesetz vom 30. September 2016 [EnG, SR 730.0])*.

[75] As provided by the Pipelines Act *(Bundesgesetz vom 4. Oktober 1963 über Rohrleitungsanlagen zur Beförderung flüssiger oder gasförmiger Brenn- oder Treibstoffe, Rohrleitungsgesetz [RLG, SR 746.1])*.

[76] Electricity Market Act, *Elektrizitätsmarktgesetz*, referendum proposal (Federal Council 2000, p. 6189).

[77] Jagmetti (2005), p. 14 et seq.

that the rules on market opening made it into the official compilation of federal legislation. However, the electricity market had already been partially opened up, as the Federal Supreme Court decided by interpretation of the Cartel Act (*Kartellgesetz*)[78]—that means by interpretation of functional energy law. One might almost say that Switzerland has stumbled into the partial opening of the electricity market. From a regulatory point of view, however, this StromVG is of great significance. What was cantonal for decades has now been taken over by the Confederation—in this long series of newly created federal competences, this is probably the most significant encroachment on cantonal competences. At that point, however, the regulatory environment had become much more complex than it had been when the WRA or EleG was adopted. The StromVG was not only intended to open up the electricity market. It also had to take into account the objectives of the constitution for a "sufficient, diverse, safe, economic and environmentally sustainable energy supply" and an "economic and efficient use of energy" (Art. 89 para. 1 BV), as well as the standards on nature and heritage protection and those on spatial planning. As if this were not enough, the provisions of the European Union were now also to be taken into account. The interconnection of energy systems means that EU regulation is also having an increasing influence on Swiss energy law.[79] The problems this has caused will be examined in the following overview.

3.7 Conclusion

The development of regulatory activity on the basis of the constitutions shows that, during the first 150 years of its existence, the Confederation has acquired more and more regulatory powers in nominal and functional energy law. The use of these powers has resulted in more or less far-reaching federal interventions. However, particularly in the area of hydropower, which is crucial to the electricity industry, the federal government has been reluctant to encroach on cantonal competences. Similarly, electricity supply remained firmly in cantonal and municipal hands until the StromVG was created. Since the new constitution of 18 April 1999 came into force on 1 January 2000, no new federal powers have been added, but the federal legislature has nevertheless intervened massively in the historically evolved structure of cantonal regulation of electricity supply.[80]

Overall, viewed from a distance, the development seems to have been less driven by political and strategic action, but rather by the needs of the times. This is illustrated beautifully by the example of the safety of electrical installations, which would probably not have got onto the political agenda so quickly without certain

[78] BGE 129 II 497, Cartel Act *(Bundesgesetz über Kartelle und andere Wettbewerbsbeschränkungen vom 6. Oktober 1995, Kartellgesetz [KG, SR 251])*.

[79] Hettich et al. (2020), p. 7 et seq. and 49 et seq.

[80] Föhse (2015), p. 131 et seq.

accidents, by impending supply shortages in the 1950s or environmental pollution later on, both of which were also countered by regulatory means. Interestingly, the same pattern can already be seen in the examples of ancient Rome and of Zurich during the Ancien Régime mentioned at the beginning. The same is true if we look at the recent total revision of the Energy Act and the ensuing decision to phase out nuclear power, which originated in a submarine earthquake followed by a tsunami in Japan that resulted in a nuclear disaster.[81]

4 Centralised Regulation of Electricity Supply

4.1 Three Perspectives on Centralisation

As explained above, the StromVG is the most severe form of intervention in cantonal competences by the federal legislator to date. As a consequence, important regulatory competences have been transferred to the federal level. The following section illustrates how the legislature of the Swiss Confederation has dealt with the complexity of the subject of energy in historically grown federal structures. This will be done by analysing three topics that can be regarded as challenges: (1) the past, (2) legal doctrine and (3) federal structures.

4.2 The Challenge of the Past

Historical developments show that electricity supply was traditionally based on a monopolistic structure with vertically integrated companies, while at the same time it was understood as a public task already early on.[82] Even today, the Swiss electricity industry is almost exclusively state-owned. Even though more and more players are now dressed up in the guise of stock companies, the state remains the dominant shareholder in most cases.[83]

From a legal point of view, this raises some fundamental questions, most notably that of state responsibility in this context. Art. 6 para. 2 EnG (heading: Concept and responsibility), states that it is for the energy industry to ensure the production, transformation, supply and distribution of energy. However, this very "energy industry" is under state control or the actors are either themselves "states" or shares of energy suppliers are state property. If one puts this in the context of the principle of legality (which is related to the rule of law), according to which "all activities of the state are based on and limited by law" (Art. 5 para. 1 BV), i.e. all state action

[81] Föhse (2014), p. 6.

[82] Föhse (2014); Föhse (2015), p. 4 and 126; Jagmetti (2005), p. 19.

[83] Swiss Federal Office of Energy (2019a), p. 41.

requires a legal basis, this means that electricity supply is a task that is ascribed to the state (here the cantons and, if applicable, the municipalities) and that is a state responsibility.

This role of the state has now been strengthened by the StromVG, Article 6 of which stipulates an obligation for grid operators to provide a basic supply, i.e. to supply the desired quantity of electricity of the required quality at all times. This also seems to imply that the state has a responsibility to ensure the supply of electricity (in German "*Gewährleistungsverantwortung*"), if not to say that the state is directly responsible to fulfil this task, i.e. to supply electricity (in German "*Erfüllungsverantwortung*").[84] The new federal energy law does not provide a clear answer with regard to the role of the state in electricity supply; so far the issue has not even been discussed. This is despite the fact that the question would be both fundamental for the future of energy supply and also entails certain legal consequences, which will be briefly discussed below.

4.3 The Challenge of the Legal Doctrine

Legal doctrine distinguishes between public and civil law. Whereas in civil law relationships one basically assumes structures in which contracting parties meet on an equal footing and can in principle freely regulate their legal relationships in the form of contracts, the situation is different in public law. Public law is characterised by unilateral and binding action by public authorities, primarily in the form of rulings[85] (*Verfügungen*). While civil law disputes are decided by a civil court, in administrative law, state authorities decide in the first instance, after which the legal dispute goes to specialised administrative courts.

It is precisely the typical power gap in public law (the relationship between the state and its citizens) that calls for special mechanisms for legal protection. Thus, Art. 35 para. 2 BV states that "[w]hoever acts on behalf of the state is bound by fundamental rights and is under a duty to contribute to their implementation". With regards to electricity supply, the situation is such that the supplier is usually state-controlled or directly state-owned and has a monopoly on supply.[86] Accordingly, the old Energy Act of the Canton of Bern, for example, expressly assigned the legal relationships in the supply of electricity to public law (Art. 32 para. 2 of the old EnG BE) and, if necessary, made the municipalities responsible for supply (Art. 8 para. 2 of the old EnG BE). According to Bernese practice, the electricity suppliers also had the right to decide certain aspects by ruling.

[84] Föhse (2015), p. 142.

[85] Art. 5 para. 1 of the Federal Act on Administrative Procedure *(Bundesgesetz vom 20. Dezember 1968 über das Verwaltungsverfahren, Verwaltungsverfahrensgesetz [VwVG, SR 172.021]).*

[86] Föhse (2015), p. 140 et seq.; Jagmetti (2005), p. 20, also considers legal relations under civil law to be a valid option.

Swiss electricity supply law now suffers from the fact that the legislator has failed to make a statement concerning the role of the state in the context of the new regulation, not to mention the missing clarification of the classification as civil law or public law. In the meantime, the Federal Court also had to deal with the matter—and correctly assigned the basic supply of electricity to public law under the StromVG.[87] However, a number of elementary issues remain unsatisfactorily resolved, including that of jurisdiction over disputes arising from the electricity supply relationship.[88] When centralising regulatory responsibilities, the Confederation has thus simply ignored legal doctrine in important areas, which leads to problems in legal practice.[89]

4.4 The Challenge of Federal State Structures

The principle of sovereignty of the cantons in Switzerland, insofar as it "is not limited by the Federal Constitution" (Art. 3 BV), creates a further challenge because it results in a complex system of overlapping responsibilities of the Confederation, the cantons and even the municipalities. The wide variety of federal competences that have accumulated over the years in the constitution has led over time, via the implementing legislation, to an increasingly dense federal legal network of nominal and functional energy law, which in part consciously or unconsciously overlaps with cantonal law. The cantons, in turn, also have the option of delegating certain regulatory powers to the third level, the municipalities (Art. 50 para. 1 BV).

The current rules regarding the allocation of grid costs are a good example for uncertainty arising from the complex distribution of competences. In itself, one could assume that the StromVG, which aims to increase competition in electricity markets, conclusively regulates this essential question. However, a closer look reveals that there are massive uncertainties concerning the allocation of grid costs in the context of the connection of properties to the electricity grid, both with regard to the competence to issue rules and with regard to the rules themselves or their implementation. This is due, among other things, to the fact that this topic in the StromVG overlaps with spatial planning law, where we have primarily cantonal or even municipal responsibilities (Art. 75 para. 1 BV), and, on top of that, with another federal competence in the area of promoting home ownership (Art. 108 para. 1 BV) and the relevant law (WEG[90]).[91]

---

[87] BGE 144 III 111 E. 5.2; Föhse (2018), p. 1235 et seq.

[88] Föhse (2018), p. 1242.

[89] Föhse (2018), p. 1245.

[90] Federal Act of 4 October 1974 on the Promotion of Housing Construction and Home Ownership *(Wohnbau- und Eigentumsförderungsgesetz vom 4. Oktober 1974 [WEG, SR 834]).*

[91] Föhse (2018), p. 1230.

The problem here is that these norm conflicts were not resolved by federal legislation in the course of centralisation. What remains is a chaos of norms and responsibilities which renders it nearly impossible, even for experts, to answer everyday questions of competence with the necessary clarity and without much effort.[92]

5 Conclusion

It is precisely the historically grown responsibilities, the constant increase in federal competences and the simultaneous increase in regulatory complexity that make electricity market regulation an extremely demanding task. Unfortunately, the Confederation has not been entirely successful in managing this challenge. Federal law is now similar to "a worn-out old carpet that covers some parts of cantonal law, but that can't prevent other parts from shining through or from (intentionally or unintentionally) coming to light".[93]

Regulation of the electricity market would have required a prudent approach and, first and foremost, a review of the initial situation, along the lines of the questions of responsibilities, competences, legal spheres and tasks. Looking back in history, an interesting pattern can be detected: in many cases, the interventions of federal law to date have been born out of necessity or a situation of distress, so to speak. As a rule, legislation of the Confederation has been relatively cautious, and the cantons have retained considerable powers (except in the case of environmental protection or regulations that primarily aim at the protection of public policy interests, such as the EleG or the Atomic Energy Act). The StromVG is different—a necessity was and is not apparent here. Rather, it appears as if a situation of distress has been created without a necessity.

References

Berna F, Goldberg P, Kolska Horwitz L, Brink J, Holt S, Bamford M, Chazan M (2012) Microstratigraphic evidence of in situ fire in the Acheulean strata of Wonderwerk Cave, Northern Cape province, South Africa. PNAS:1215–1220. https://doi.org/10.1073/pnas.1117620109

Federal Council (1894) Bericht und Antrag vom 4. Juni 1894 betreffend die Monopolisierung der Wasserkräfte. Federal Gazette BBl 1894 II 820

Federal Council (1899) Botschaft vom 5. Juni 1899 über den Erlass eines Bundesgesetzes betreffend die elektrischen Schwach- und Starkstromanlagen. Federal Gazette BBl 1899 III 786

Federal Council (1905) Botschaft vom 4. Dezember 1905 betreffend die Verwertung inländischer Wasserkräfte ins Ausland. Federal Gazette BBl 1905 VI 223

[92] Föhse (2018), p. 1239.

[93] Föhse (2018), p. 1236.

Federal Council (1907) Botschaft vom 30. März 1907 betreffend die Bundesgesetzgebung über die Wasserkräfte. Federal Gazette BBl 1907 II 624
Federal Council (1908a) Botschaft vom 24. November 1908 über die eidgenössische Volksabstimmung vom 25. Oktober 1908 betreffend Aufnahme eines Artikels 24bis (Wasserkräfte) in die Bundesverfassung. Federal Gazette BBl 1908 VI 7
Federal Council (1908b) Verhandlungen des Bundesrates vom 10. Juli 1908. Federal Gazette BBl 1908 IV 465
Federal Council (1912) Botschaft vom 19. April 1912 zum Entwurfe eines Bundesgesetzes über die Nutzbarmachung der Wasserkräfte. Federal Gazette BBl 1912 II 669
Federal Council (1953) Bundesbeschluss vom 30. September 1953 über die Ergänzung der Bundesverfassung durch einen Artikel 24quater betreffend den Schutz der Gewässer gegen Verunreinigung. Federal Gazette BBl 1953 III 240
Federal Council (1955) Bundesgesetz vom 16. März 1955 über den Schutz der Gewässer gegen Verunreinigung. Federal Gazette BBl 1955 I 552
Federal Council (1957) Botschaft vom 26. April 1957 über die Ergänzung der Bundesverfassung durch einen Artikel betreffend Atomenergie und Strahlenschutz. Federal Gazette BBl 1912 II 669
Federal Council (1960) Bundesbeschluss vom 14. Dezember 1960 über die Ergänzung der Bundesverfassung durch einen Artikel 26bis betreffend Rohrleitungsanlagen zur Beförderung flüssiger oder gasförmiger Brenn- oder Treibstoffe. Federal Gazette BBl 1960 II 1581
Federal Council (1969) Bundesbeschluss vom 21. März 1969 über die Ergänzung der Bundesverfassung durch die Artikel 22ter und 22quater (Verfassungsrechtliche Ordnung des Bodenrechts). Federal Gazette BBl 1969 I 568
Federal Council (1970) Bundesbeschluss vom 18. Dezember 1970 über die Ergänzung der Bundesverfassung durch einen Artikel 24septies betreffend den Schutz des Menschen und seiner natürlichen Umwelt gegen schädliche oder lästige Einwirkungen. Federal Gazette BBl 1970 II 1609
Federal Council (1984) Bundesratsbeschluss vom 2. November 1984 über das Ergebnis der Volksabstimmung vom 23. September 1984 (Atom-Initiative; Energie-Initiative). Federal Gazette BBl 1984 III 900
Federal Council (1989) Bundesbeschluss vom 6. Oktober 1989 über die Ergänzung der Bundesverfassung. Federal Gazette BBl 1989 III 902
Federal Council (2000) Elektrizitätsmarktgesetz vom 15. Dezember 2000. Federal Gazette BBl 2000 6189
Föhse K (2014) Die rechtliche Ausgestaltung der nationalen Netzgesellschaft im Stromversorgungsgesetz (StromVG). Dissertation, University of Bern
Föhse K (2015) Die Leiden der jungen Strommarktordnung – aktuelle Probleme des StromVG unter besonderer Berücksichtigung der Rechtsprechung zu Netzgebietszuteilung und Grundversorgung. recht 2015/3: 125–143
Föhse K, Drittenbass J (2017) Parteistellung und Rechtsschutz natürlicher Personen im Umfeld von Kernkraftwerken. SR 3(2017):167–177
Föhse M (2018) Grundversorgung mit Strom – ein Überblick zu Rechtsverhältnissen und Zuständigkeiten. AJP 10(2018):1235–1250
Föhse M (2019) Kommentierung von BGE 145 II 140. ZBl 8(219):436–447
Grewe K (2009) Die Reliefdarstellung einer antiken Steinsägemaschine aus Hierapolis in Phrygien und ihre Bedeutung für die Technikgeschichte. In: Bachmann M (ed) Bautechnik im antiken und vorantiken Kleinasien. Ege Yayinlari, Istanbul
Haas J (2006) Die Umweltkrise des 3. Jahrhunderts n. Chr. im Nordwesten des Imperium Romanum: Interdisziplinäre Studien zu einem Aspekt der allgemeinen Reichskrise im Bereich der beiden Germaniae sowie der Belgica und der Raetia. Dissertation, University of Stuttgart
Hettich P, Thaler P, Camenisch L, Hofmann B, Petrovich B, Wüstenhagen R (2020) Europeanization of the Swiss Energy System. Dike, Zurich

Jaag T (2015) Kompetenzverteilung zwischen Bund und Kantonen. In: Biaggini G, Gächter T, Kiener R (eds) Staatsrecht, 2nd edn. Dike, Zurich, pp 149–159

Jagmetti R (2005) Energierecht. In: Koller H, Müller G, Rhinow R, Zimmerli U (eds) Schweizerisches Bundesverwaltungsrecht, Band VII. Helbing & Lichtenhahn, Basel

Kölz A (1992) Neuere Schweizerische Verfassungsgeschichte: Ihre Grundlinien vom Ende der Alten Eidgenossenschaft bis 1848. Stämpfli, Bern

Kratz B (2016) Kommentar zu Art. 55 WRG. In: Kratz B, Merker M, Tami R, Rechsteiner S, Föhse K (eds) Kommentar zum Energierecht, Band I: WRG /Ele G/StromVG/RLG. Editions Weblaw, Bern

Kupper P, Pallua I (2016) Energieregime in der Schweiz seit 1800, Schlussbericht im Auftrag des Bundesamts für. Energie, Innsbruck

Sammlung der Bürgerlichen und Policey-Geseze und Ordnungen, Lobl. Stadt und Landschaft Zürich (1757-1793), Bd. 3 (1757), No. XXIII. Hoch-Obrigeitliches Mandat, betreffend, die Versorg- und Beschirmung der Holz- und Waldungen (1717). Orell und Comp, Zurich: 204 ["Mandat (1717)"]

Schindler B (2019) Kontinuität und Wandel im Verwaltungsrecht: Miszelle zum Energierecht der Barockzeit. In: Hottelier M, Hertig Randall M, Flückiger A (eds) Études en l'honneur du Professeur Thierry Tanquerel. Schulthess, Geneva/Zurich/Basel, pp 277–286

Schweizer RJ (2014) Kommentar zu Art. 3 BV. In: Ehrenzeller B, Schindler B, Schweizer RJ, Vallender K (eds) Die Schweizerische Bundesverfassung, St. Galler Kommentar. Dike, Zurich

Swiss Federal Office of Energy (2019a) Schweizerische Elektrizitätsstatistik 2018. Available at https: //www.bfe.admin.ch

Swiss Federal Office of Energy (2019b) Schweizerische Gesamtenergiestatistik 2018. Available at https://www.bfe.admin.ch

Tschannen P (2016) Staatsrecht der Schweizerischen Eidgenossenschaft. Stämpfli, Bern

Martin Föhse was Assistant Professor at the University of St. Gallen and Researcher at the IFF HSG, St. Gallen, Switzerland, from 2016-2021. Now he practises as a lawyer and partner at the law firm Kellerhals Carrard.

The Long-Term Impact of the Electorate on the Swiss Electricity Market Transition

Raphael Klein and Matthias Finger

Contents

Abstract The Swiss government, through its Energy Strategy 2050, is engaged on a path to transition Switzerland to become a carbon-neutral country by the year 2050. In this chapter, we look at the impact that the electorate can have on this transition and on the Swiss electricity market. This is done using hybrid agent-based modelling. We model the Swiss electricity market and we add to this a model of the policy-making process. This allows us to study which policy instruments are more likely to be implemented depending on the Swiss electricity market progression and on the policy actors' interests. The results have shown that the electorate has a limited impact on the policy chosen and on the electricity market. Overall, an environmentally conscious electorate leads policy actors to select the carbon tax as a policy more often. This, however, has the adverse effect to increase the electricity price and increase import dependency in winter. In high demand growth scenarios, the carbon

R. Klein (✉) · M. Finger
EPFL, CDM-MIR, Lausanne, Switzerland
e-mail: r.klein-1@tudelft.nl; matthias.finger@epfl.ch

P. Hettich, A. Kachi (eds.), *Swiss Energy Governance*,
https://doi.org/10.1007/978-3-030-80787-0_7

tax policy is not sufficient to stem the construction of gas turbine power plants. We also show that because the electricity model does not consider an extended demand response option or technology advancement, the knowledge gained from this model is limited. This drives the behaviour of the model into scenarios which are unlikely to happen, such as a large increase of the gas turbine power plants. Overall, we conclude that, in their current form, even with an environmentally conscious electorate, the electricity market conditions do not allow Switzerland to reach its emissions targets.

1 Introduction

On 21 May 2017, the Swiss population voted for the revised Federal Energy Act, also dubbed Energy Strategy 2050 (ES2050).[1] With the ES2050, the government pledged to shut down all nuclear power plants, to increase the amount of investment in renewable energy such as solar, wind and geothermal, and to increase electricity efficiency throughout the economy. Beyond this, in August 2019, the government also set the goal for Switzerland to be carbon-neutral by 2050.[2] In Switzerland, most of the electricity production is already low-carbon. In 2018, a majority of 55% of the electricity was produced by hydropower plants. The rest was produced by nuclear power plants (36%) and a mix of solar, wind, biomass and thermal power plants (9%).[3] However, the rest of the energy sector is powered mostly by fossil fuels.

The Swiss electricity mix is bound to change in the coming years. Nuclear power plants are to be shut down relatively soon. Promoted by the government, efficiency measures and investments in renewable energy sources are meant to bridge the gap in electricity production. Additionally, more imports of electricity from neighbouring countries could also be used if that were to be needed. The current goals of the government are to see the renewable energy supply reach 40% by 2050, on top of existing hydropower production.[4] These targets were designed to achieve goals set by the Federal Council that wants to see Switzerland carbon-neutral by 2050.[5] Reaching these targets would require a drastic increase in the amount of solar and wind production, along with the wide-scale adoption of geothermal power wherever it is possible.

Additionally, when it comes to electricity production, Switzerland has strong seasonal variations in electricity supply. The demand in winter is higher than the supply; therefore, imports are often needed from neighbouring countries.

[1] Swiss Federal Office of Energy (2018a).

[2] RTS (2019).

[3] Swiss Federal Office of Energy (2018b).

[4] Swiss Federal Office of Energy (2019).

[5] Wuthrich (2019).

Meanwhile, there is a surplus of electricity in the summer leading to the export of the Swiss electricity production. A lot of this is driven by the behaviour of hydroelectric plants. In the future, with the current renewable energy production goals, this seasonal imbalance could be further reinforced with a higher deficit in winter, rendering Switzerland more dependent on its neighbours for its security of supply for parts of the year.

Future electricity demand scenarios also need to take into account the electrification of the energy system with a potential growth in demand in the electricity system due to a shift in energy sources in the heating and mobility sectors. At the moment, the electricity production sector accounts for only one third of total Swiss energy consumption, with another third of the energy used for heating and the last third used for mobility. A large shift of energy sources in both these sectors is needed to achieve the carbon neutrality goals set by the government. But this could lead to significant electricity demand growth even if there is an increase in efficiency measures.

So far, the population has been keen on a sustainable transition, but politicians have been slower to follow. Recent parliamentary elections in 2019 have shown that the composition of the Swiss parliament has been affected by this upswell in voters' environmental concerns. However, it remains unclear how this will affect policymaking within the country in the future. More importantly, it is unclear what impact a change in the belief of the policymakers will have on the Swiss electricity sector considering the current policies that are available. This chapter aims at understanding exactly this: *What impact can the Swiss electorate have on the Swiss electricity system and its transition?*

A hybrid model is used to answer this question. This model is a combination of a Swiss electricity market model and a model of the policy-making process. Each of these models is based on previous work with the Swiss electricity market model being a converted existing system dynamics model[6] and the policy-making process model taking inspiration from a forthcoming paper by Klein.[7] This hybrid modelling approach enables the endogenisation of the policy-making process in a socio-technical system simulation for the first time.

In this chapter, the research that has been performed when it comes to the modelling and simulation of electricity markets and of the policy-making process is presented in Sect. 2. A description is then provided of the hybrid model in Sect. 3. In Sect. 4, an outline of the experiments that were performed with the model is given and the results of the simulations are presented. Section 5 discusses the implications of the results and the conclusions that can be drawn from them. Finally, in Sect. 6, the paper is concluded and an outline of the work that remains to be done in the future is given.

---

[6] Van Baal (2016, 2019a)

[7] Klein et al. (forthcoming).

2 The Research Up to Now

The hybrid approach that is pursued in this chapter is novel; however, the study of electricity markets using simulation and the study of the policy-making process are each not new developments in the literature. A high number of electricity market models are present throughout the literature. They were built with the aim to answer specific research questions and are often tailored to their geographic specificities. As for the policy-making process, policy theories have been developed and detailed over the past decades to study this process. A forthcoming paper by Klein has also presented an approach where the theories of the policy process can be used to establish a common language for simulation modellers that can in turn be used to craft models of the policy-making process.[8] These are all detailed in this section.

2.1 *Modelling Electricity Markets*

Studies of electricity markets using simulation are common throughout the literature. As early as the late 90's, Ford[9] looked at the construction cycles in the western US electricity market using system dynamics.[10] This study concluded that the construction cycles can lead to major changes in market prices. It also highlighted how such problems could be dealt with using a constant capacity alongside the market clearing price.

Since then, studies have varied in focus, geographical region, scope, and methods. This includes looking at fuel mix diversification incentives using a mean-variance portfolio optimisation approach.[11] It also includes looking at nuclear energy policy in Belgium after the Fukushima nuclear accident using system dynamics.[12] Other models focused on capacity mechanisms.[13] In the case of Bhagwat et al.,[14] EM-Lab, an agent-based model, was used to investigate a number of different research questions including those related to capacity mechanisms.[15] Finally some models were part of much larger projects looking at transitions in general. In the case of Trutnevyte et al.,[16] the hybrid model studied was built from a

[8] Klein et al. (forthcoming).

[9] Ford (1999).

[10] Sterman (2001).

[11] Roques et al. (2008).

[12] Kunsch and Friesewinkel (2014).

[13] Bhagwat et al. (2014); Bhagwat (2016); Bhagwat et al. (2016); Chao and Lawrence (2009); De Vries and Heijnen (2008).

[14] Bhagwat et al. (2014).

[15] De Vries et al. (2013).

[16] Trutnevyte et al. (2014).

number of other models. The model was used to study storylines within the transition of the UK power system.

In a lot of cases, these models are built for the purpose of exploring current or future policies and they assess their impact individually. In the case of Kunsch and Friesewinkel,[17] for example, policies were embedded directly into the system dynamics model and tested for a set of alternative policies. These policies were tested against one another and the results were compared to see what outcomes were obtained for each of the policies. A similar approach was used in Fagiani et al.,[18] where the dynamic interactions between two different policies were tested. In this case, the policies were adaptive, therefore taking information from the system to adjust themselves.

The Swiss electricity market has also been studied using a number of different simulation methods. Densing et al.[19] have looked at a number of these studies and compared the resulting scenarios. In their paper, results from a number of different studies from various organisations that have used a variety of modelling approaches were compared. The goal was for stakeholders to better understand the impact of their modelling assumptions. One of the results of this paper was to show that, overall, the different studies that have been used over the years result in a wide array of scenarios that are deeply influenced by their underlying assumptions.

In separate studies, Ochoa and Van Ackere, Van Ackere and Ochoa, and Osorio and Van Ackere[20] have also studied the Swiss electricity market using system dynamics models. Ochoa and Van Ackere[21] focused on the need for policies to limit the dependence on imports and to foster capacity expansion. This was illustrated for a number of different scenarios, some of which have now come to pass. Van Ackere and Ochoa[22] modelled the Swiss hydroelectric power plants using system dynamics to better study how different production policies impact production and price patterns. This is important as Switzerland is heavily influenced by its hydroelectric power plant park. Finally, Osorio and Van Ackere[23] looked at the impact of the nuclear phase-out and the addition of renewable energy sources into the market on the electricity mix. The outcomes showed that the removal of nuclear energy is mostly replaced by solar production and imports, along with a rise of the electricity price.

Separate studies have also been ongoing at the Paul Scherrer Institute (PSI).[24] The model used in this case is the Swiss TIMES[25] model. This model is a large linear

[17]Kunsch and Friesewinkel (2014).

[18]Fagiani et al. (2014).

[19]Densing et al. (2016).

[20]Ochoa and Van Ackere (2009); Van Ackere and Ochoa (2010); Osorio and Van Ackere (2016).

[21]Ochoa and Van Ackere (2009).

[22]Van Ackere and Ochoa (2010).

[23]Osorio and Van Ackere (2016).

[24]Kannan and Turton (2011, 2012, 2013); Paul Scherrer Institute (2012).

[25]The Integrated MARKAL EFOM System.

programming optimisation model made of a number of modules. It was used to study the electricity system, but was not limited to it, also looking at the different sector couplings. Within this model for example, Kannan and Turton studied different technological pathways and their impacts on the overall market.[26]

Overall, simulation and modelling has been an approach that has been used extensively to study electricity markets, including the Swiss market in particular. And for the most part, the use of policies is exogenous within these models, that is, the policy selection process is not integrated within the electricity market models. In the present chapter, we propose to extend this body of literature by looking at a model that considers the electricity market but also the policy-making process that is followed to select the policies to be implemented.

2.2 Policy Process Theories

There are a large number of theories of the policy process within the literature.[27] These theories help provide insights into all aspects of the policy process, whether it concerns the actors and their behaviours, the steps that are followed within the process, or the differences that can be found upon implementation of policies. One of the strengths of these theories is that each theory looks at a different part of the process. For example, the theory of the policy cycle focuses on the steps that the policy process follows.[28]

In a forthcoming paper, Klein has presented a common language based on a number of theories that can be used to model and simulate the policy-making process.[29] The paper argues why such a model can be useful and the present chapter is one such example. Because of the disparities in the focus of the different theories, it is impossible to use one theory to simulate the entire policy process. It is not possible to combine all of the theories for simulation either, as the theories can sometimes be incoherent, overlapping or lack specifics on how certain parts of the policy process work. The common language is meant to remedy these issues by providing a specific language to model these theories. This language is suggested by the authors, but it is in no way the only approach possible. It is based on the theory of the policy cycle,[30] the multiple streams framework,[31] and the advocacy coalition framework.[32] It is organised along four main elements which are: time, the policy arena, the agents and the interactions. These are detailed below.

---

[26] Kannan and Turton (2013).

[27] Sabatier (2007).

[28] Jann and Wegrich (2007).

[29] Klein et al. (forthcoming).

[30] Jann and Wegrich (2007).

[31] Zahariadis (2007).

[32] Sabatier (1987).

Time is the first key element considered. It is required to define a sequence for the policy process. This is needed for the simulation. A computer requires a sequence of steps to perform a simulation. It cannot operate events that happen at the same time. One process that can be considered is one that follows the theory of the policy cycle for example. This would include steps like the agenda setting, the policy formulation, the policy implementation and the policy evaluation.

The policy arena is the second key element. The policy arena defines boundaries for the model that is studied. The selection of a policy arena leads to the selection of the broader topic of the simulation. The policy arena also defines geographical boundaries. From this, the modeller can select the appropriate agents but also the policies and issues that should be discussed by the agents within the model.

The agents and their specific roles come next. Different roles can be considered within the policy-making process. For example, the policymaker's role is always included as it selects the policy instruments. But other roles like the media, the electorate or policy entrepreneurs can sometimes be omitted depending on the research questions that the model is used for. Different policy arenas might also call for specific and more detailed roles for the agents. Beyond their roles, agents also have a belief system. This belief system is a representation of the environment for the agents. It is what the agents use to choose the policy instruments to be implemented.

Finally, the fourth and last key element is related to interactions. First, there are interactions between the agents and the environment. The environment informs the agents on their beliefs. The flip side is that the policymakers can affect the environment by implementing policies. Beyond this, agents can also influence one another on their beliefs in the hope to advance their respective interests. According to the theories, they can also assemble into coalitions to further advance their interests. A wide array of strategies and behaviours can be included within the modelling of the policy process.

3 The Hybrid Electricity Model

To study the impact of policymaking on the Swiss electricity market, a hybrid modelling approach is used. This approach uses an already verified and validated electricity model along with a model of the policy process that has been demonstrated and tested through a theoretical approach. In this section, we detail how the hybrid model that uses both models was constructed. We first detail each of the models separately, before outlining how they were connected to one another.

3.1 The Electricity Model

Numerous electricity models have already been built, tested and used over the years. This is also the case for the study of the Swiss electricity market: van Baal has built one of these models using a system dynamics modelling approach.[33] The model was upgraded to a hybrid agent-based/system dynamics model to better consider the investment portion of the electricity market and to study the potential for a strategic reserve in Switzerland.[34]

For the purpose of this chapter, we re-use the same modelling formalisation and assumptions. The model that was built is one that was entirely based on the one presented in van Baal[35] but that was implemented into an agent-based modelling paradigm. Similarly, the inputs that are used to initialise and historically validate the model are the same. The main reason for this new implementation of the same model was to simplify the connection of this model to the policy-making process model which is also an agent-based model. Additionally, this also leads to a more modular model allowing for easier reusability and the potential for extensions. Finally, the new implementation was made in Python, which is an open source programming language, thus making the model more accessible.[36]

The model is composed of two main modules: the spot market module, where supply is matched to demand, and the investor module, where investors can manage their existing assets and invest in new production assets.

3.1.1 The Spot Market Module

The spot market is responsible for matching supply and demand. Demand is comprised of two parts: inelastic demand, which is an input of the model and which represents the Swiss domestic electricity consumption, and elastic demand, which relates to the variable demand that can arise from imports, exports, and from hydroelectric power pumping plants.

The supply is provided by the power plants that are present in the system, the model being initialised with the Swiss electric generation park from 2016 that includes hydroelectric, hydroelectric-pumping, solar, wind, Combined Cycle Gas Turbines (CCGT), waste incineration, run-of-river, and nuclear power plants. Each power plant is instantiated as a separate agent. To participate in the spot market, each asset has a certain bidding price. This calculation is different for all technology types. For wind, solar and run-of-river power plants, the price is equal to the variable costs. For waste incineration, nuclear and CCGT power plants, the fuel costs are added to the variable costs. Depending on the policies, emissions can also add to the costs of the CCGT power plants.

The bidding costs for the hydroelectric and hydroelectric pumping power plants are different as the costs have to take into account the reservoirs, and therefore the

[33] Van Baal (2016).

[34] Van Baal (2019a).

[35] Van Baal (2019b).

[36] The model can be found on Github: https://github.com/kleinrap/SwissElectricityMarket.

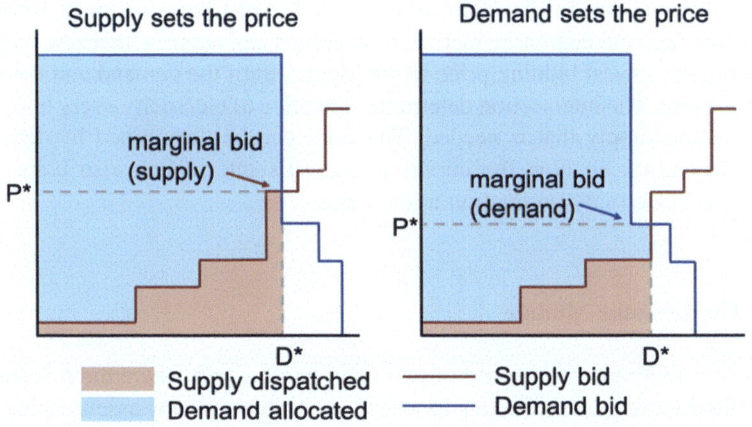

Fig. 1 Merit-order dispatch of the spot market, reproduced with authorisation from Van Baal (2019a)

costs of water. These are referred to as opportunity costs, and the equation that is used to calculate them is based on the work in Van Baal.[37] It is given by:

$$P_{bid} = (1 - f) \cdot \left(P_{ref} - MC\right) + MC \tag{1}$$

where f represents the amount of energy left in the reservoir, P_{ref} is the reference price that the investor uses to bid and MC are the marginal costs of the installation (which include the variable costs for a hydroelectric power plant).

This equation was designed in such a way that assets will have some water left in their reservoirs at all times for periods of very high electricity prices. When the reservoir is full, the investor is likely to bid for a lower price and vice versa.

The imports and exports are also an important part of the spot market. First, Switzerland has long-term contracts with France. This consists of options that Switzerland can exercise depending on the spot market price and which are introduced into the model through historical inputs. Beyond this, Switzerland has a certain number of connections with its neighbours that allow it to import or export electricity. Within the model, each country is considered as an agent of its own, and countries can bid on the spot market. That bid is dependent on the net transfer capacity between the two countries and the price is set by the price of electricity in the neighbouring country, which is itself based on a historical yearly profile. Note that these interconnections are also used by the long-term contract for the case of France, an element that can further limit the capacity available for other suppliers.

The spot market, where supply is matched to demand, is operated using a merit-order dispatch algorithm. A graphical illustration of this algorithm is shown in Fig. 1. This algorithm makes sure that there is as much supply as there is demand. The

[37] Van Baal (2016).

maximum price allowed is the Value of Lost Load (VoLL) and it is set at 3000 CHF/MWh. If the demand cannot be met, then blackouts can occur. Otherwise, supply is added from the lowest bidding price to the highest until the demand and the supply curves intersect. The intersection determines the price of electricity every hour, and it determines the supply that is needed. The price can be determined by demand or supply, depending on how the curves cross. This intersection also helps assign revenues and electricity production to the assets.

3.1.2 The Investor Module

The investor module is composed of two main parts: a part where the investors can manage their current assets and a part where investments in new assets can be made. These investments are limited to the solar, wind and CCGT technologies. The assumption is that these are the only viable technological options for Switzerland. The country is planning to retire its nuclear power generation, and, in the current political climate, coal power plants are out of the question.

Investment analyses are performed by the agents on a regular basis. These are done on discrete power plants for each of the three technologies. The investment decision is based on a profitability index, with the assumption that the investors have access to the general market prices along with their respective asset-level data. The profitability index is given as follows:

$$PI = \frac{NPV}{IC} = \frac{\sum_{n=0}^{N} C_n (1+r)^n}{IC} \tag{2}$$

where C_n is the cash flow at time step n, r is the discount rate and IC are the investment costs.

After the initial decision to invest, the planned assets go through a number of steps that include planning time, re-assessment of the profitability index, and construction of the asset. These steps can delay the introduction of a new power plant significantly.

Investors can also manage their assets. This happens mostly towards the end of life of the assets. Investors periodically re-assess the profitability of their assets, so they can decide whether they should mothball the asset or keep it online. In cases where the asset is close to its end of life, the investors can also decide on whether to retire and decommission the asset or extend its life, an action that is limited in number.

3.2 The Policy Emergence Model

The policy process model is specified according to the four key elements that were outlined earlier: time, policy arena, agents and interactions. The main choice that is left to the modeller is to decide how much complexity needs to be integrated into each of these elements to answer the research question. In the present case, only a limited amount of complexity is required. This leads to a relatively simple policy-making process model. It is detailed in this section.

For the time element, we consider a two-step policy-making process consisting of an agenda-setting and a policy formulation step. The agenda-setting step is the first step and consists of the agents selecting an issue to place on the agenda to narrow down further discussions. This agenda is then used to limit the policy instruments that can be evaluated for implementation. During the policy formulation step, the policymakers select a policy instrument and implement it with the aim of affecting the outcomes of the electricity model.

The policy arena is the Swiss electricity market model. This policy arena helps define the issues that can be considered within the belief system of the agents. It further limits the agents that can be considered to policymakers that are related to the electricity market. It also helps define the policy instruments that can be considered within this model. The policy core issues that are selected are the environment and the economy, following insights gained from Markard et al.[38] The secondary issues are extracted directly from the electricity model, along with the policy instruments, which are derived from exogenous parameters. These are detailed in the next section.

For the agents, only two roles are introduced: the policymakers and the electorate. The policymakers are agents that decide what should go on the agenda and what policies should be implemented. They base their decisions on their preferred states and their beliefs for each issue in the belief tree. They focus on the issues that they consider to be the most urgent to deal with, which means issues that have the largest gap between preferred state and belief. The electorate on the other hand can only perform one action: they influence the preferred states of the policy makers. This is a progressive influence that can vary in strength based on the parameters defined by the modeller.

When it comes to the interactions, only three are considered. As outlined in the previous paragraph, the first interaction is the electorate influencing the policymakers. The second and third interactions are then inherent in the construction of the hybrid model: the environment—in the electricity market model—influences the beliefs of the policymakers, and the policymakers influence the electricity market through policy instruments.

---

[38] Markard et al. (2016).

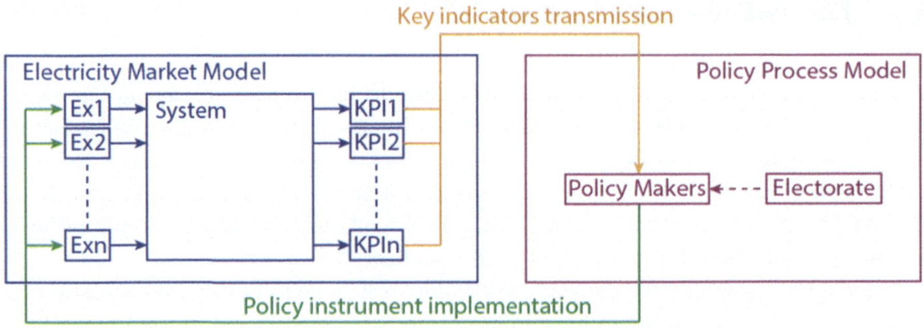

Fig. 2 Conceptual representation of the hybrid model and the interaction between the two models

3.3 The Hybrid Model

To study the impact of the policy process on the electricity market, we need to connect both models. How this is done conceptually is illustrated in Fig. 2. The models are connected through one link in each direction. After the electricity model has been simulated for a pre-defined amount of time, a number of key indicators are extracted from the electricity model and used to inform the beliefs of the policymakers. These are indicators that will help policymakers make a decision on what, if any, policy instrument should be implemented such that their preferred states are reached for all their issues. The policy instrument implementation is the second connection linking the policy-making model to the electricity model. Each policy instrument corresponds to a change of a set of exogenous parameters within the electricity model. These changes in turn affect the outcome of the electricity model. Overall, this forms a loop that includes the two models, thus creating a hybrid model.

In the present case, the indicators that are taken from the electricity model to inform the policymakers' beliefs are the following:

- KPI1—The total renewable energy production [MWh]
- KPI2—The year averaged electricity price [CHF/MWh]
- KPI3—The total renewable energy investments as a percentage of the overall investments [%]
- KPI4—The total domestic emissions [ton]
- KPI5—The total imported emissions [ton]

The policymakers can act through policy instruments that can change the following exogenous parameters:

- Ex1—Solar subsidy [CHF/MWh]
- Ex2—Wind turbine subsidy [CHF/MWh]
- Ex3—Investor's hurdle rate [%]
- Ex4—Carbon tax on domestic emissions [CHF/ton]
- Ex5—Carbon tax on imported emissions [CHF/ton]

4 Experiments, Simulations and Results

The simulation of the model is used to answer the research question. The scenarios are designed with this in mind. In this section, we also present the results obtained, including main metrics from the electricity market model and the policy selected by the policymakers in the policy emergence model. The results are then analysed to better understand what the impact of the electorate is on the policy makers and whether that influence leads to policy change.

4.1 Scenarios

For the construction of the scenarios, we look at varying only two parameters, one in each model: the influence rate of the electorate and the electricity demand growth.

Depending on how strong the electorate influence is, the beliefs of the policymakers will vary at a slower or quicker pace. Varying the strength of the influence can help illustrate a sense of urgency in the general public as we are currently witnessing in the context of climate change for example. We select scenarios where the electorate has zero influence and therefore the policymakers do not change their beliefs, a scenario where the policymakers' beliefs change towards the beliefs of the electorate by 5% of the difference in both agents' beliefs every round, and a scenario where this change is 50%. This helps represent a range of scenarios with a very weak and a very strong electorate.

The second parameter, the electricity demand growth, is part of the Swiss electricity market model. The demand growth for the electricity sector is so far predicted to be stable or negative in the coming years.[39] This can be attributed to an increase in efficiency in the heating sector and in general appliances. However, in the future and to meet the carbon neutrality pledge of the confederation, there is an expectation of the electrification of society. This includes the mobility sector using electricity as its main energy source and the building sector. We therefore assume that the growth will remain non-negative. To take into account these scenarios, we look at three scenarios of electricity demand growth: 0%, 1.5% and 3%.

4.2 Model Initialization

Both models are initialised following a different approach related to their use. The Swiss electricity market model is initialised with data used previously by van Baal et al. in their work.[40] This consists of mostly historical data including data on the

[39] Swiss Federal Office of Energy (2013).

[40] Van Baal (2019a).

import and export capacity and prices, the demand, and the technology costs. This data was compiled for several years, from 2015 to 2017. The model simulation itself is run from the year 2016 onwards. Furthermore, it is also important to note that this model was historically validated using this same data.

For the policy-making process model, only the preferred states of the policymakers and the electorate have to be initialised. The number of agents considered does not make a difference regarding the complexity. For the preferred states of the electorate, it was decided to select preferred states that reflect the targets of the Swiss government in 2050, which means carbon neutrality, investments limited only to renewable energy sources and affordable electricity prices. For the policymakers, their initial preferred states were set to the current levels in the model. This assumes that the agents are content with the current levels of the indicators.

4.3 Model Simulation

The models are simulated in series in a loop. The electricity model runs on an hourly time step while the policy-making process model is simulated every three years. This means that every 3 years, the electricity model simulation is halted and the policy emergence model is simulated. Once this is done, the policy selected is implemented and the electricity model resumes. This is done for a period of thirty years starting in the year 2016—due to the availability of historical data to initialise the model. Furthermore, for each combination of scenarios, the hybrid model is repeated fifty times to obtain results from which conclusions can be drawn.

4.4 Results

We present the results based on three main figures. In Fig. 3, the monthly averaged electricity price for all of the scenario combinations considered is plotted. Each of the three demand growth scenarios is plotted for each of the electorate influence parameter values. Figure 4 presents the electricity supplied by solar, wind and CCGT power plants. The results are split per growth demand scenario. The demand is also plotted as a reference. Finally, the third figure presents the sum of policies implemented across 50 simulations for the three different electorate influence rates for a demand growth of 3%. This is presented in Fig. 5.

Figure 3 shows that prices are bound to go up over time, regardless of the scenario, though this increase is less pronounced for smaller demand growth scenarios. This shows that the price rise is linked to demand growth and not so much to electorate influence. The highest growth in prices is related to the 3% demand growth scenario as could be expected. In this scenario, Switzerland's demand would roughly double from 10 to 20 GW, an additional demand that would have to be fulfilled by a combination of new investments and additional imports from

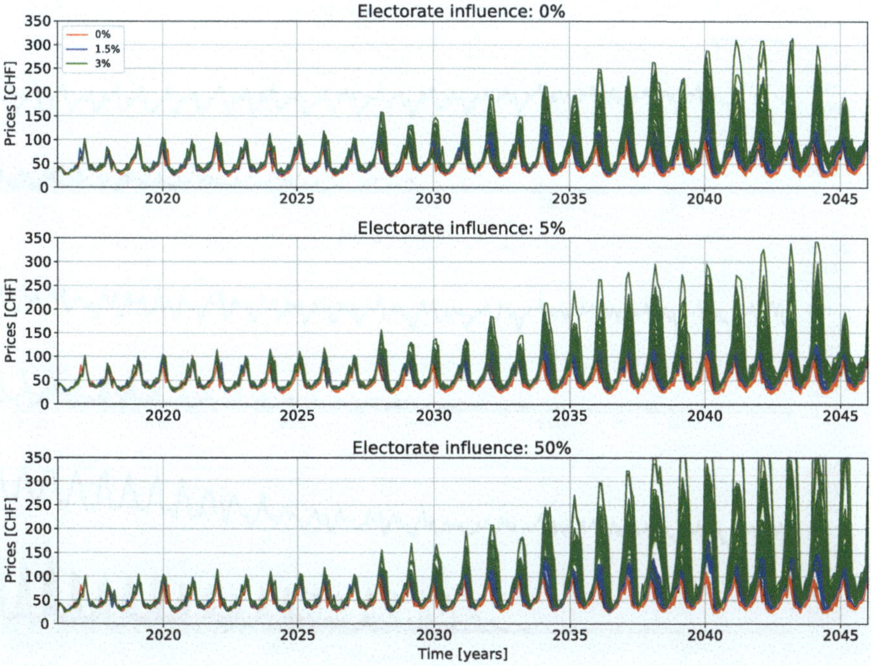

Fig. 3 Monthly averaged electricity prices, split according to the three electorate influence rates and for the three demand growth scenarios

neighbouring countries as shown in Fig. 4. This would imply electrification of a significant share, if not of the entire energy sector. We can conclude from this that prices of electricity across the country will depend heavily on the speed of the electrification in Switzerland and, in some respect, on the speed of efficiency increases as well.

Figure 4 outlines the supply from solar, wind and CCGT, and therefore, by proxy, the investments in those technologies over time. One can see that the difference in the energy mix is mostly driven by demand growth and not so much by electorate influence. In fact, the electorate influence has so little impact on the results that it is difficult to even differentiate the different electorate influence scenarios in the plots. For the scenario with 0% growth, most of the investments are limited to wind and solar. Note that, within the electricity model, solar and wind each have a cap of installed capacity based on numbers from the Swiss Federal Office of Energy (SFOE), for wind at 2282 MW and for solar at 19,702 MW. It was also assumed that there is no growth in import and export capacity as this would have a large impact on the security of supply and the introduction of CCGT power plants.[41] There is some investment in CCGT for this scenario, but overall gas plants are not considered financially viable and are therefore avoided. The electricity prices are

[41] Van Baal (2019b).

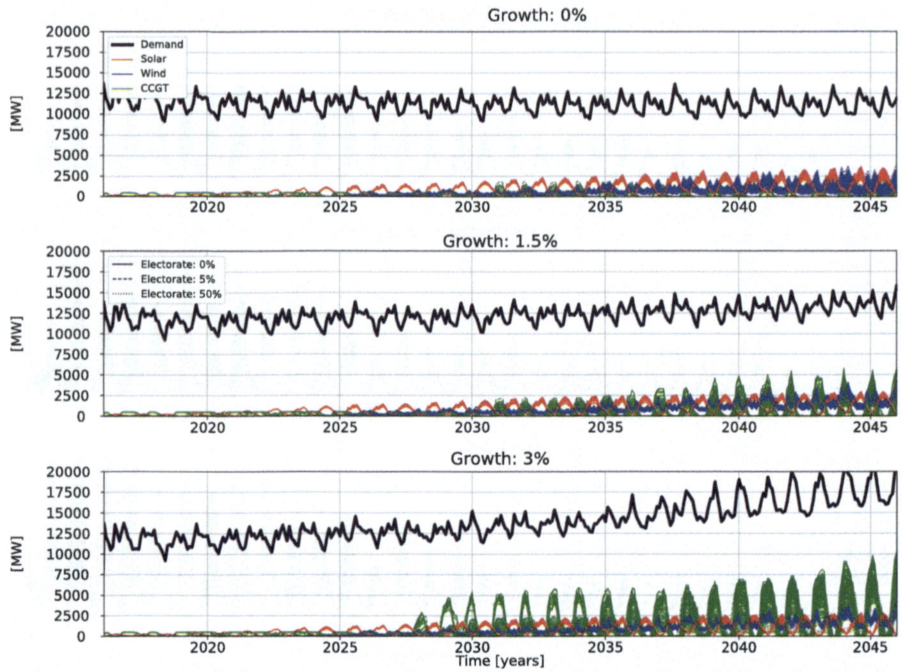

Fig. 4 Overall demand with the electricity supplied by solar, wind and CCGT sources for all scenarios

too low. Things change in the case of the 1.5% and the 3% demand growth scenarios. For the 1.5% scenario, there is a clear investment in CCGT capacity around the time when solar and wind are maxed out. This is justified by an increasing demand and rising prices. For the 3% scenario, the rise in prices is so quick that investments in CCGT occur early on, even before solar and wind have been maxed out. CCGT is viable early on and is seen as the only possible technology able to bridge the demand gap considering that only a limited increase in imports and exports is possible and considering the other boundaries of the model.

Finally, Fig. 5 is the only figure that describes the outcome of the policy-making process model. The figure was made by summing, for each time step, the policy instrument implemented by the policymakers. This allows us to see what policy instruments are favoured by the policymakers and at which time steps. Only the 3% demand growth scenario results are presented here because these results provide the most insights. The results for the other scenarios are similar in nature. One can observe that actors overall prefer the use of the carbon tax policy, may it be domestic or foreign. This is the case for all growth scenarios with one difference between them: the timing at which the taxes are imposed. In the case where the electorate has an important influence on the policymakers, the taxes are implemented very early on. In fact, it is the only scenario where the tax is imposed in the second step in 2021. This happens for forty of the fifty simulations. For the other scenarios, where the

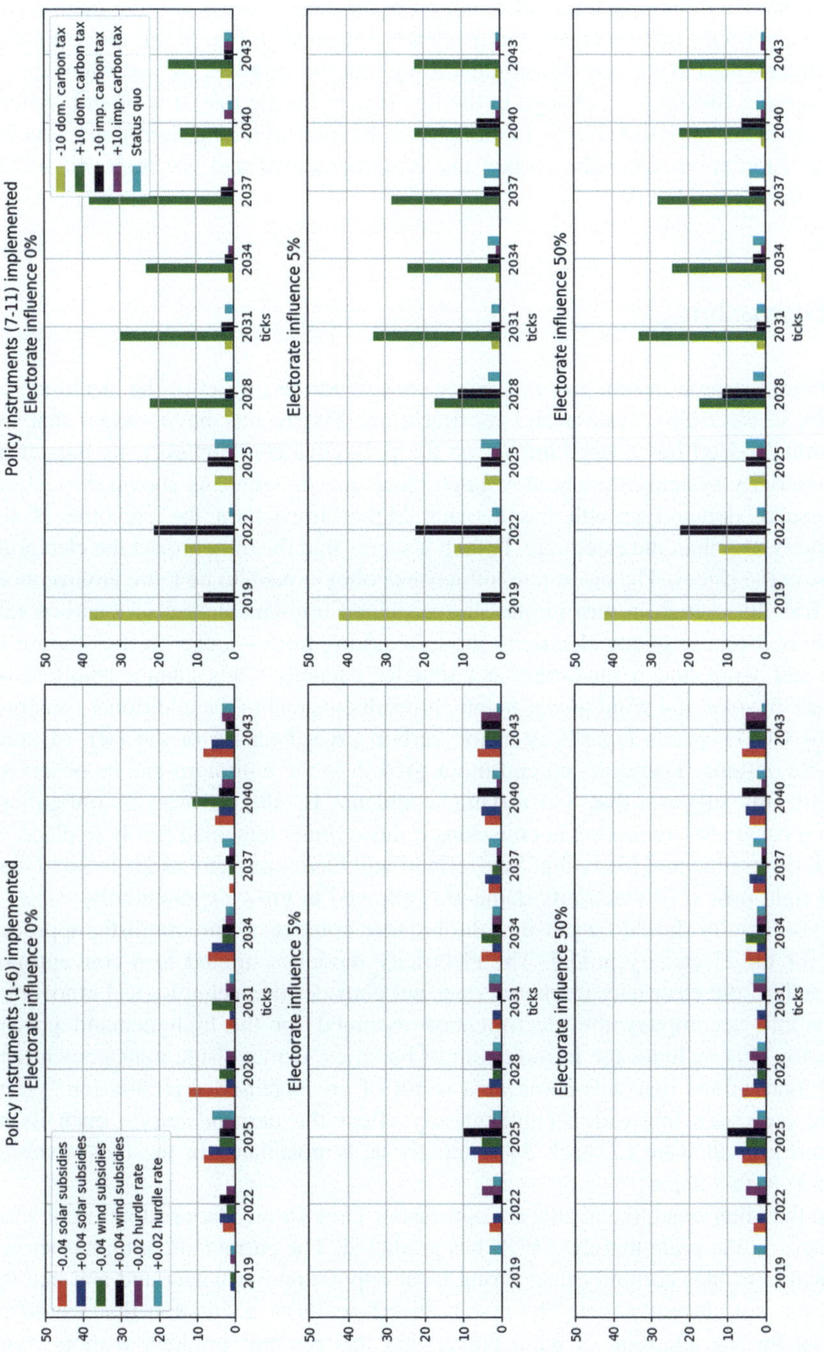

Fig. 5 Cumulative policy instrument selection for a 3% electricity demand growth scenario for all fifty repetitions for each simulation

electorate has less or no influence on the policymakers, it takes more time for the tax to be considered. Note that the introduction of the carbon tax is also the main driver for the electricity price increase that is clearly reflected in Fig. 3. All other policies are implemented at a much slower rate throughout the simulations, and when agents implement a subsidy or a change in the investment hurdle rate, it is often balanced out later by an opposite change in that policy, having little long-term impact on the overall simulation. Only the carbon tax is implemented and not removed for all simulations considered.

5 Discussion

The main research question of this paper concerned the impact of the electorate on the Swiss electricity system and its transition. The results have shown that the electorate indeed has a large impact on the policymakers. However, its impact on the electricity system as a whole is much more questionable. As shown throughout the results, demand growth has a much higher impact on the outcome of the electricity mix than the electorate. In fact, it seems that the only impact the electorate has is on the prices. The electorate influences policymakers to be more environmentally friendly, which in turn implies the sustained implementation of a carbon tax. However, because of the electricity model's assumptions—a cap on the amount of solar and wind and a maximum net transfer capacity—this cannot result in an increase in solar and wind power plants. It results instead in the additional construction of CCGT plants regardless of the carbon price because of the lack of other possible options. Therefore, an enormous growth in the emissions can be observed. Overall, this suggests that Switzerland would not be able to meet its obligations when it comes to a reduction in emissions if those limits remained firmly in place. In fact, it is possible and likely that Switzerland will have more emissions in 2050 than it has right now if its electricity demand is allowed to grow exponentially.

These results should be put into the broader context of the simplistic approach used for the electricity model. The electricity model is limited to a conventional approach of the electricity market. It does not consider the technological innovation that would accompany the electrification assumed for the high demand growth scenario. This includes the introduction of batteries, demand side management and other innovations that will come as a result of an increased digitalisation. When considered, such innovation could greatly affect the demand curve, even if the demand growth were to reach 3% annually as is postulated in the most extreme scenario in this paper.

On the other hand, the results are optimistic. They show a large adoption of wind turbines, on the scale that the SFOE has predicted. The current situation has shown that wind turbines currently face strong local opposition in Switzerland and that the goals are not currently met. The results therefore show a situation that would be optimal for the adoption of wind power; but this remains unlikely without more social acceptance, accompanied by significant regulatory and legal change.

Besides the optimistic increase of wind turbines, the model suggests that a large number of CCGT power plants will be constructed in Switzerland. These results are purely based on economics and do not reflect the politics, or acceptance, of such technology. In fact, it is likely that proposals for the construction of a CCGT power plant would face the same amount of rejection as a wind turbine, if not more. Highlighting this issue, and especially in a 1.5% or 3% demand growth scenario, it is important to note that the production stemming from CCGT power plants would need to be filled by other electricity sources. From the results of this model, it is unclear what that could be.

The results also depict Switzerland as a country that is even more dependent, seasonally, on its neighbours. The decrease in nuclear power production, accompanied by more solar power and the potential of demand growth means that Switzerland will be even less able to supply its entire electricity in the winter period and will further depend on its neighbours for its security of supply. This is an issue that is politically sensitive considering the current negotiations between Switzerland and the European Union.[42] Nonetheless, it is an issue that will become more important as time passes as the results suggest.

Elements related to the policy-making process model have also affected the results. Within the policy-making process model, the policymakers are only able to select one policy instrument at a time. This is an assumption that is made based on insights gained from punctuated equilibrium theory.[43] A different implementation could have seen policymakers negotiating to introduce a policy package that would include a number of different policy instruments. This might affect the results as it could include the introduction of subsidies for solar power plants and an increase of carbon taxes by policymakers. However, considering the net difference between the amount of times the carbon tax policy instruments are selected and the other instruments, it is unlikely that considering such a policy package would make a large difference.

Beyond the potential for policy packages, the policy-making process model used within this paper is inherently simple. In fact, most of the model could have been replaced by one agent whose preferred states change over time and who tests policy instruments, selecting the best and implementing it. One of the reasons for the use of this model was to present a novel approach for the study of socio-technical system simulations. The other reason was the research question. The policy-making model used is sufficient to answer the question.

For other research questions and more policy-focused research questions, the policy-making model can be made to incorporate more complexity. For example, Markard et al. (2016) have shown that coalitions play an important role in the shaping of the electricity market policies. To investigate the impact of coalitions on the electricity system, the policy-making process model would need to incorporate aspects such as coalitions, policy entrepreneurs, agent on agent interactions, and

[42] Van Baal and Finger (2019).

[43] Baumgartner et al. (2014).

potential additional elements such as imperfect knowledge transfer. The approach presented here allows for that when needed. However, this complexity increase would bring limitations of its own but would allow for answering many more research questions.

Overall, the study presented here was the first time that such an approach was utilised. This has allowed us to gain a better understanding of the feedback effects between the policy-making process and the electricity system, despite the simplicity of both models. It has also shown that there is room for improvement, mostly through an increase in complexity in either model. Increasing complexity in the electricity model would allow for more insightful results and could help guide the design of new regulations. A more complex policy-making process would allow for more insights on the dynamics between the different coalitions that are present in the Swiss electricity market and for a better understanding of how this might impact policy selection.

6 Conclusion

In this paper, we have presented a novel approach to study the Swiss electricity market by also considering the policy-making process. We have presented a hybrid model that combines two agent-based models: one of the electricity market and another of the policy-making process. By connecting these two models we were able to study the impact that the electorate has on the Swiss electricity market through the policy-making process.

Overall, the results show that the electorate has an impact on the electricity market though not necessarily along its goals—or preferred states as they are named in the model. The results also show that despite using a simple policy-making process model, it is the simplicity of the electricity market model that constrains the possible results. The results highlight the fact that the electorate only has a finite amount of influence and that, without the presence of new innovative technologies and the accompanying regulations, the current course is unlikely to allow Switzerland to fulfil its emissions obligations. Moreover, the model demonstrates that the confederation is likely to be seasonally highly dependent on its neighbours.

Within the scope of this model, the policymakers opted in the majority of time for a carbon tax to achieve their goals, may it be on domestic energy supply or on imports. This had the perverse effect to push the prices up. We have shown that the main reason why the actors chose the carbon tax policy instrument was the fact that there were no other good alternatives provided to them—the electricity model does not allow for more effective policy instruments.

In future work, complexity will be added to the electricity market model to allow for the possibility of demand side management and prosumers and to take into account the potential for more batteries within the electrical system. Future work will also expand the research questions that can be answered using this hybrid approach by exploring the impact of coalitions on the Swiss electricity market.

References

Baumgartner FR, Jones BD, Mortensen PB (2014) Punctuated equilibrium theory: explaining stability and change in public policymaking. In: Sabatier PA, Weible CM (eds) Theories of the policy process, 3rd edn. Westview Press, Boulder, pp 59–103

Bhagwat P (2016) Security of supply during the energy transition: the role of capacity mechanisms. Dissertation, Delft University of Technology

Bhagwat PC, Iychettira K, De Vries LJ (2014) Cross-border effects of capacity mechanisms. In: 11th International Conference on the European Energy Market (EEM14), 1–5

Bhagwat PC, Richstein JC, Chappin EJ, De Vries LJ (2016) The effectiveness of a strategic reserve in the presence of a high portfolio share of renewable energy sources. Utilit Policy 39:13–28

Chao H, Lawrence DJ (2009) How capacity markets address resource adequacy. In: 2009 IEEE Power & Energy Society General Meeting, 1–4

De Vries LJ, Heijnen P (2008) The impact of electricity market design upon investment under uncertainty: the effectiveness of capacity mechanisms. Utilit Policy 16(3):215–227

De Vries LJ, Chappin EJ, Richstein JC (2013) EMLab-Generation - an experimentation environment for electricity policy analysis (Version 1.0). Technical report, Delft University of Technology

Densing M, Panos E, Hirschberg S (2016) Meta-analysis of energy scenario studies: example of electricity scenarios for Switzerland. Energy 109:998–1015

Fagiani R, Richstein JC, Hakvoort R, De Vries LJ (2014) The dynamic impact of carbon reduction and renewable support policies on the electricity sector. Utilit Policy 28:28–41

Ford A (1999) Cycles in competitive electricity markets: a simulation study of the western United States. Energy Policy 27(11):637–658

Jann W, Wegrich K (2007) Theories of the policy cycle. In: Fischer F, Miller GJ, Sidney MS (eds) Handbook of public policy analysis: theory, politics, and methods. Routledge, New York, pp 43–62

Kannan R, Turton H (2011) Documentation on the development of the Swiss TIMES Electricity Model (STEM-E). Technical report, PSI

Kannan R, Turton H (2012) Swiss Electricity Supply Options. Energy Economics Group, Laboratory for Energy Systems Analysis. Technical report, PSI

Kannan R, Turton H (2013) A long-term electricity dispatch model with the TIMES framework. Environ Model Assess 18(3):325–343

Klein R, Ashkenazy A, Nikolic I, Bots PWG (forthcoming) Developing a common language of the policy process for modellers. Policy Studies Journal (under review)

Kunsch PL, Friesewinkel J (2014) Nuclear energy policy in Belgium after Fukushima. Energy Policy 66:462–474

Markard J, Suter M, Ingold K (2016) Socio-technical transitions and policy change: Advocacy coalitions in Swiss energy policy. Environ Innov Soc Trans 18:215–237

Ochoa P, Van Ackere A (2009) Policy changes and the dynamics of capacity expansion in the Swiss electricity market. Energy Policy 37(5):1983–1998

Osorio S, Van Ackere A (2016) From nuclear phase-out to renewable energies in the Swiss electricity market. Energy Policy 93:8–22

Paul Scherrer Institute (2012) The new swiss energy policy: Where will the electricity come from? Energie-Spiegel, No. 21 (November)

Roques FA, Newbery DM, Nuttall WJ (2008) Fuel mix diversification incentives in liberalized electricity markets: a mean–variance Portfolio theory approach. Energy Econ 30(4):1831–1849

RTS (2019) La Suisse doit viser la neutralité carbone dès 2050, 28 August 2019. Available at https://www.rts.ch

Sabatier PA (1987) Knowledge, policy-oriented learning, and policy change: an advocacy coalition framework. Knowledge 8(4):649–692

Sabatier PA (2007) Theories of the policy process, 2nd edn. Westview Press, Boulder

Sterman JD (2001) System dynamics modeling: tools for learning in a complex world. California Manage Rev 43(4):8–25

Swiss Federal Office of Energy (2013) Energieperspektiven 2050. Technical report, available at https://www.bfe.admin.ch

Swiss Federal Office of Energy (2018a) Energiestrategie 2050 nach dem Inkrafttreten des neuen Energiegesetzes. Presentation, available at https://www.bfe.admin.ch

Swiss Federal Office of Energy (2018b) Gesamte Erzeugung und Abgabe elektrischer Energie 2018. Technical report, available at https://www.bfe.admin.ch

Swiss Federal Office of Energy (2019) The energy strategy 2050. Presentation

Trutnevyte E, Barton J, O'Grady Á, Ogunkunle D, Pudjianto D, Robertson E (2014) Linking a storyline with multiple models: a cross-scale study of the UK power system transition. Technol Forecast Soc Change 89:26–42

Van Ackere A, Ochoa P (2010) Managing a hydro-energy reservoir: a policy approach. Energy Policy 38(11):7299–7311

Van Baal PA (2016) Business implications of the energy transition in Switzerland. MSc Thesis, EPFL

Van Baal PA (2019a) Effectiveness of a strategic energy reserve during the energy transition: the case of Switzerland. Competition and Regulation in Network Industries. https://doi.org/10.1177/1783591719879365

Van Baal PA (2019b) Policy analysis during socio-technical energy transitions: three essays on the Swiss electricity sector. Dissertation, EPFL

Van Baal PA, Finger M (2019) The effect of European integration on Swiss energy policy and governance. Polit Gov 7(1):6–16

Wuthrich B (2019) La suisse décrète la neutralité carbone en 2050. Le Temps (online), 28 August 2019. Available at https://www.letemps.ch/suisse/suisse-decrete-neutralite-carbone-2050

Zahariadis N (2007) The multiple streams framework: structure, limitations, prospects. In: Sabatier PA (ed) Theories of the Policy process, 2nd edn. Westview Press, Boulder, pp 65–69

Raphael Klein is Post-doctoral researcher at the Faculty of technology, Policy and Management at Delft University of Technology, Delft, The Netherlands.

Matthias Finger is Professor at the College of Management of Technology at École Polytechnique Fédérale de Lausanne, Lausanne Switzerland.

Governing Decentral Energy Systems

Triangulating Between Uniform European and National Standards and Locally Optimized Energy Regimes

Peter Hettich

Contents

Abstract Against the backdrop of an energy system moving from vertically integrated monopolies towards a decentral system with a multitude of actors in ever-changing roles, we observe a gradual strengthening of central governance mechanisms on the nation-state and on the European level. Such a top-down approach to the governance of the energy system might have been necessary to open up energy markets to competitive processes and innovation. With social goals shifting and security of supply and environmental concerns gaining importance, the governance of the energy system has to be reshaped anew, enabling, e.g., the optimization of regional energy systems by local actors. In particular, strict unbundling rules may hinder or preclude system-serving behavior, to the detriment of all market participants and consumers. Lawmakers and regulators should provide some leeway to cooperative approaches, such as the empowerment of local actors to devise their own energy regimes.

P. Hettich (✉)
Institute of Public Finance, Fiscal Law and Law and Economics, University of St. Gallen, St. Gallen, Switzerland
e-mail: peter.hettich@unisg.ch

P. Hettich, A. Kachi (eds.), *Swiss Energy Governance*,
https://doi.org/10.1007/978-3-030-80787-0_8

1 Introduction

The design of a country's electricity supply system can be centralized or decentralized. In Switzerland, discussions on this subject began at the turn of the nineteenth century, with the advent of electrification.[1] For the understanding of the present paper, it is important that the different designs of the supply systems in individual countries are not the result of a search and discovery process initiated by market competition, but the result of a deliberative political decision of intervention or non-intervention. In Switzerland, a decision of non-intervention by the federal authorities gave rise to a mostly centralized electricity supply system governed by the cantons; this system is slowly becoming more decentralized, mostly driven by federal and European regulation. Thus, the central governance mechanisms inherent in federal and European regulations have provided important boosters to transform the energy system. However, central governance may also frustrate local initiatives and take away opportunities to modify and optimize the performance of local energy systems. Thus, decision-making at a higher level may help to steer communities towards a common goal, but it might come with losses of efficacy and efficiency.

Consequently, this chapter explores frictions, sometimes quite hidden, at the interfaces of the European, federal, cantonal, and communal level, which affect the behavior of participants in the energy market. While the current shift towards a decentralized and more renewable electricity supply would not have been possible without a kickstart on the European and federal level, this author argues that rigid legislation on the central level hinders—somewhat counterintuitively—further progress towards an environmentally sustainable electricity supply.

At first, we will look at the development of a more interventionist approach at the central levels of government before we discuss the obstacles which the current set of rules and regulations pose for a more sustainable electricity system. We conclude with proposals that could lift these obstacles, providing more leeway for local actors while safeguarding the public interests that might be seen threatened by a less interventionist approach.

2 Decentralization of the Swiss Energy System

2.1 Vertically Integrated State-Owned Monopolies

Theoretically, competitive markets realize the economic welfare optimum. In reality, however, particularly looking at grid-bound energy supply, various plausible reasons for market failure and other "market imperfections" exist. These market imperfections may justify economic policy interventions.

---

[1] Walther (2014), p. 31.

Network effects in energy markets give rise to natural monopolies, which tend to form vertically integrated energy suppliers. These suppliers extend the reach of their grid monopolies into upstream and downstream markets (i.e., into the markets for energy production and energy distribution).

Further, the long-term nature of investment decisions gives rise to concerns as to whether the private markets create sufficient incentives for investments. In particular, prices in electricity markets are linked to short-term marginal costs of production due to the lack of storage. Consequently, the fixed costs of production are considered as "sunk" and as not relevant to the decision on the use of a power plant. The recovery of the full costs of a power plant in the electricity market is only achieved by temporary price peaks; these peak prices are the most important refinancing source for power plant investments. If such phases with higher prices do not occur or if such phases are counteracted by regulation, incentives for new investments are strongly reduced. This so-called "missing money problem" may trigger interventions by the state to encourage new investments. Indeed, the public sector (in Switzerland the cantons and municipalities) provides for a large share of the capital of the electricity and the gas industry. Even compared with institutional investors, the public sector has a high capacity to bear the long-term risks associated with investments in the energy sector.[2] Still, there are concerns regarding the survival of the Swiss hydropower plants: Because of its historically large profits, this backbone of the Swiss electricity supply does not profit so much from subsidies but is rather subject to taxation (fees for water rights, "*Wasserzins*"); efforts to change this or to adapt the current system of taxation have not made much progress, so far.

The Swiss Confederation enacted legislation on the electricity sector already in 1902 (Electricity Act, *Elektrizitätsgesetz*); legislation on the oil and gas sector was enacted in 1963 (Pipelines Act, *Rohrleitungsgesetz*). However, these legislative acts are mainly concerned with the planning and safety of electricity lines and pipelines. Consequently, most issues that are relevant to the organization of the energy markets have been left to cantonal legislation. For the reasons stated above, the cantons and municipalities were invested heavily in the energy markets; they had little interest in regulating the energy sector, since this would only serve to limit the entrepreneurial leeway that their state-owned monopoly enterprises had so far enjoyed. The market structure resulting from this non-intervention policy was shaped by nearly 800 municipal and cantonal energy suppliers, which enjoyed local and regional monopoly powers. These state-owned enterprises were deeply enmeshed in politics, which resulted in moderated pricing. Since there was no competition for consumers, horizontal cooperation was abundant, resulting, for example, in many joint electricity power plants in the Swiss alps (mostly pump storage power plants).

[2] Hettich et al. (2017), p. 26 et seq.

2.2 Gradual Strengthening of Decentral Producers

The Resolution on Energy Use of 1990 (*Energienutzungsbeschluss*) forced grid operators to purchase the electricity offered by small producers. The provision significantly strengthened the position of renewable electricity producers, since suppliers had to purchase "energy not produced on a regular basis" as well. Small hydroelectric power plants as well as producers using new renewable energies (solar energy, biomass including biogas, geothermal energy, wind, etc.), waste energy, and combined heat and power generation were able to benefit from the provision. The Federal Council held that these producers would help to secure and to diversify energy supply, in particular in times of crisis. The remuneration that had to be paid was not intended to subsidize renewable energy producers; nevertheless, these producers were compensated (initially) with 0.16 CHF/kWh.[3] This first timid step towards decentralization was enshrined in permanent law with the Energy Act of 1998 (*Energiegesetz*); since then, independent producers have a legal right to feed their electricity into the grids. Starting 2005, grid operators were allowed to ask for a surcharge on the transmission costs of their grids in order to finance the remuneration of the independent producers (Additional Cost Financing, *Mehrkostenfinanzierung*). By implementing this change, a proto-system to decentralize electricity supply was put in place.

While the European Union enabled electricity consumers to freely choose their electricity supplier, the first attempt of the Swiss Confederation to liberalize its markets failed. In order to overcome the resistance of the socialist party and the trade unions, the Swiss legislator significantly enhanced the feed-in rights of independent suppliers. In contrast to the situation in 1990, the enhanced feed-in rights were meant to increase the share of renewable energy in the electricity system; the reliability of the energy infrastructure and the ability of energy providers to meet current and future demand were less a concern. The improved prospect for renewable energy providers was enough to secure the political acceptance necessary to liberalize the electricity markets for large consumers. Since then, a plethora of subsidies have been paid out not only to small but also to large renewable energy producers. Nevertheless, in 2020, the share of decentral producers in electricity generation was still timid: 3.97% photovoltaics, 0.22% wind, and 0.87% biomass.[4] The share of new renewables in primary energy consumption is negligible.[5] In fact, the decarbonisation of the energy supply has not even really started yet. Despite the energy system mostly producing in central power plants at this point in time, we acknowledge that the buildup of photovoltaic capacity has been impressive during the last years; electricity generation by photovoltaics constitutes the main driver for the decentralization of the energy system.

[3] Federal Council (1988), p. 515 et seq.

[4] Swiss Federal Office of Energy (2021), p. 6.

[5] Swiss Federal Office of Energy (2021), p. 5.

This being said, decentralization is not a goal per se, but rather seen as an instrument to maintain a carbon-free (mostly renewable) electricity supply in Switzerland, even after the phaseout of the nuclear energy plants. A mix of mostly legal factors, which are explained below in more detail, contributes to the rapid expansion of photovoltaics: a provision of direct subsidies, even for large electricity suppliers; a secure legal status for independent prosumers (feed-in rights); as well as consumption-based grid charges that benefit prosumers (consumption-based grid charges generate a cross-subsidy that is paid by normal households; the depressing effects on profits of the utilities are also known as the "utility death spiral").[6] Of course, other factors—declining costs of generation, increasing social acceptance, utilities located in progressive cities investing in new renewables, etc.—have contributed to this development as well.

3 Centralization of Swiss Energy Governance

The shift towards decentralization, although still timid, is enabled by regulation, mostly enacted on the federal level. In addition, European regulation is strongly influencing the shape of federal regulation, despite the fact that Switzerland is not a member of the European Union.

3.1 Energy Governance on the Federal Level

Federal regulation sets the most important parameters for decentralization: The law defines decentral producers by setting a cap on capacity and power generation. Decentral producers below this cap have an unrestricted right to feed their energy into the grid for free, regardless of actual electricity demand and regardless of production by other producers (priority of dispatch).[7] The basic compensation that the grid operator is required to pay to decentral producers is fixed by law as well;[8] although the basic compensation is not intended to subsidize decentral producers, some "progressive" utilities set a higher basic rate in order to incentivize decentral production. For decentral producers participating in the Swiss support scheme, a subsidy is paid out to cover the actual costs of production and to alleviate market risks; today, the subsidy takes the form of a one-off contribution or of a sliding market premium (replacing the earlier fixed feed-in premium model).[9]

[6] Hettich and Walther (2015), p. 24 et seq.

[7] Art. 15 para. 1 and 2 Energy Act (*Energiegesetz*).

[8] Art. 15 para. 3 Energy Act (*Energiegesetz*).

[9] Art. 19 and 25 Energy Act (*Energiegesetz*).

Since the subsidies are declining and, if the government keeps its promise, due to be phased out, other factors have become important for decentral producers. In particular, the number of prosumers (mostly decentral solar electricity generators making use of their right for self-consumption) has risen due to the structure of grid tariffs for low-voltage households. Federal law holds that grid charges for households shall predominantly be consumption-based.[10] Consequently, prosumers participate only to a partial extent in the effective costs they cause to the distribution network, since these effective costs are mainly caused by installed capacity. Hence, prosumers benefit from an (indirect) subsidy that can be regarded as a cross-subsidization by other users of the distribution network (i.e., people who do not own real estate).[11]

Last but not least, many decentral producers are households that profit from legal provisions protecting "vulnerable consumers". The tariff for electricity supply as well as the grid charges are cost-based and, in principle, fixed for the duration of a whole year.[12] The law basically bans discriminating tariffs between normal households and prosumers. Households and small businesses have a legal right to purchase all the electricity they need, thereby rendering demand-side management of households virtually impossible.[13]

3.2 Energy Governance on the European Level

At the time of writing, Switzerland is neither a member of the European Union (EU) nor is it bound to adhere to EU law due to bilateral cooperation agreements. Nevertheless, EU law deeply affects the shape of Swiss energy regulation due to effects of indirect "Europeanization".[14] Since 2007, Switzerland and the EU have been negotiating an electricity agreement that would allow Switzerland to participate in the mechanisms of European energy governance and to trade electricity on an equal footing with its European competitors. With only a few points of the electricity agreement remaining controversial, the main obstacle to conclude the agreement are open institutional questions. Negotiations on an institutional agreement have been ongoing since 2012; their successful conclusion, farther away than ever, is a precondition for any new agreement on market access.[15]

During the negotiations, the EU's internal energy market has evolved considerably, having reached a high degree of formalization of its institutions and

[10] Art. 14 para. 3 Electricity Supply Act (*Stromversorgungsgesetz*) and Art. 18 para. 3 Electricity Supply Ordinance (*Stromversorgungsverordnung*).

[11] Hettich and Walther (2015), p. 24 et seq.

[12] Art. 6 para. 3 and 4 Electricity Supply Act (*Stromversorgungsgesetz*).

[13] Art. 6 para. 1 Electricity Supply Act (*Stromversorgungsgesetz*).

[14] See for mechanisms of "Europeanization" Knill and Lehmkuhl (2002), p. 255 et seq.

[15] Hettich et al. (2020), p. 92.

regulations. In November 2016, the European Commission brought forward a package of legislative proposals ("Clean Energy for all Europeans"), which was adopted by the European Parliament and Council and entered into force in 2018 and 2019. In contrast, Switzerland has not yet fully implemented the 3rd package on the internal energy market, which was adopted by the EU already in 2009. Although the draft electricity agreement has never been published, it may reasonably be expected that Switzerland would have to adapt its energy governance to the one of the EU.

An electricity agreement would contain rules on state aid, as required by the draft institutional agreement.[16] However, the recast renewable energy directive still allows for subsidy schemes for electricity generation from renewable sources, as long as these subsidy schemes are as non-distortive as possible for the functioning of the electricity markets. In particular, the directive exempts small (decentral) installations from market-based allocations of subsidies in order to support their rollout.[17] Despite the fact that most support schemes fall within the scope of the European state aid rules,[18] the Guidelines of the European Commission on State aid for environmental protection and energy for the years 2014–2020[19] provide for ample scope when designing subsidy schemes (the adoption of new Guidelines is foreseen for the end of 2021). Further and somewhat unexpected, the European Court of Justice, in a landmark decision issued on 28 March 2019, has ruled that the German promotion scheme does not constitute "state aid" according to European law.[20] Since Switzerland has modeled its own subsidy scheme on Germany's promotion scheme, it might retain considerable autonomy when supporting renewable energy generators.[21]

With regard to the indirect support of decentral producers through the exemption from grid charges, the Commission recognizes the wide variety of tariff structures across the EU; so far, the EU has refrained from harmonizing distribution tariff structures and methodologies.[22] A proposal to empower the European Commission to adopt delegated acts concerning the establishment of network codes in the area of harmonized transmission and distribution tariff structures and connection charges has been dropped in the course of the negotiations on the Electricity Regulation. However, after trilogue negotiations, the Commission and the Council agreed that the Agency for the Cooperation of Energy Regulators (ACER) "shall provide a best practice report on transmission and distribution tariff methodologies while taking account of national specificities"; the Agency's recommendation shall be taken duly into consideration by regulatory authorities when approving or fixing transmission

[16] Art. 8A–8C Draft Institutional Agreement between Switzerland and the EU.

[17] Recital 17 et seq. Directive 2018/2001 of the European Parliament and of the Council of 11 December 2018 on the promotion of the use of energy from renewable sources, OJ L 328, 21 December 2018, 82–209.

[18] Art. 107 of the Treaty on the Functioning of the European Union.

[19] OJ C 200, 28.6.2014, 1–55.

[20] Bundesrepublik Deutschland v Europäische Kommission, ECJ C-405/16 of 28 March 2019.

[21] Hettich et al. (2020), p. 8.

[22] European Commission (2016), p. 164 and 171.

or distribution tariffs.[23] Although this indicates some move towards more central governance, the impact of the new electricity regulation on grid charges in the EU member states as well as in Switzerland seems rather small.[24]

4 Obstacles and Frictions

The specific regulations mentioned above do not touch on cross-border trade with electricity. Looking at small electricity generators, the new European regulations in this area are hardly required to guarantee the functioning of the EU's internal electricity market. Thus, while indeed providing a strong boost to the rollout and deployment of decentral renewable energy infrastructures, we also need to analyze the drawbacks that come with increased central—i.e., European—governance of the electricity markets. In order to identify legal obstacles and frictions towards the transformation of a carbon-free energy system (the Swiss electricity system is mostly carbon-free already), our institute has participated in a field test of the Swiss Federal Office of Energy, the results of which will be discussed in detail in this chapter.[25]

4.1 *Field Test "aliunid"*

The enterprise "aliunid" is a joint venture of several energy providers, grid operators and energy producers; as a white-label-product, it provides smart home and smart business solutions to households and SMEs. For utilities, aliunid analyzes energy flows in households, boroughs, municipalities as well as larger regions. Based on real-time data, aliunid helps to optimize local and regional energy supply and consumption, thereby saving grid costs and electricity for balancing.

Aliunid tries to exploit a weakness of a predominantly renewable energy system. Looking at electricity supply, renewable energy systems rely on many small, decentral electricity producers, which mainly make use of solar and wind energy. This renders the energy system highly dependent on the weather. Since production can no longer easily be adjusted to demand, flexibilities on the demand side and storage options become more important.

Households, in particular prosumers with photovoltaic arrays and storage devices (at-home batteries, electric vehicles, heat pumps, electric water boilers), dispose of many small but—if aggregated—significant flexibilities. At best, these flexibilities

[23] Art. 18 para. 9 et seq. Regulation 2019/943 of the European Parliament and of the Council of 5 June 2019 on the internal market for electricity, OJ L 158, 14 June 2019, 54–124.

[24] Hettich et al. (2020), p. 27.

[25] See Moeller, press release of 7 May 2019, available at https://energeiaplus.com/2019/05/07/aliunid-startet-feldtest-mit-iot-plattform.

are used to optimize the household's electricity or overall energy consumption. By using its flexibility options, a household may save on electricity and grid costs. However, such an optimization does not necessarily reduce system costs. The electricity cost of the supplier depends on system-wide demand, with prices rising sharply during peak times; peak times on the system level do not necessarily correlate with peak demand on the household level. Furthermore, grid costs of households depend on the maximum capacity that is provided; an optimization of electricity demand on the household level focusing on saving individual grid costs does not necessarily reduce the peak capacity—maybe required just once a year—of a specific household. That households are left indifferent to situations of peak demand constitutes a negative externality. Thus, incentives for households to include system costs into their optimization efforts are needed.

One purpose of aliunid is to bundle a large number of flexibility options. This enables internal offsetting of flexibilities (e.g., by using the battery storage of a household to reduce peak demand in a certain region); bundling also reduces transaction costs, enabling aliunid to market its flexibilities on a wholesale basis and to generate revenues. Taking into account the needs of households, municipalities and regions at the same time, aliunid may indeed help to save on grid costs, at least in the long run. With many smart devices connected to the home's smart meter, aliunid generates an additional revenue flow by providing smart home solutions. Needless to say, this business model is heavily dependent on real time data; in an ideal world, this data would update every 1–5 s.

4.2 *Possible (Legal) Obstacles to Implement the Business Model*

There are several obstacles to overcome in order to turn aliunid into a sweeping success; unfortunately, many of these obstacles are "self-inflicted", unnecessary regulatory burdens.

4.2.1 Low Market Value of Flexibility

First of all, the efficient marketing of flexibility options may help the transformation of the energy system, but the financial rewards are limited at this point in time, for several reasons. Flexibility options compete with the costs of generating additional electricity, which are, despite recent price hikes, still quite low throughout Europe; generation from wind and solar plants has risen sharply while fossil power plants, in particular coal power plants, are still operating. Consequently, looking at Switzerland, the purchase price for flexibility options is capped by the costs of importing additional electricity from neighboring countries. In a peculiar way, the abstention of Switzerland from the EU's common market in energy helps to make flexibility options more profitable, since transaction costs for cross-border trade of electricity remain high.[26]

4.2.2 Postage Stamp Principle for Grid Charges

Another reason for the low value of flexibility lies with the structure of the grid charges: The law requires grid operators to apply the "postage stamp principle" on their tariffs, meaning that network usage tariffs are to be calculated independently of the distance between entry and exit point of the electricity.[27] The "postage stamp principle" is sensible for a centralized energy system because it protects captured consumers from monopolistic suppliers that purchase electricity from afar; against this backdrop, the "postage stamp principle" embodies considerations of equity and fairness. The cantons may even choose to establish a fund to compensate for unequal grid charges, though no canton has taken such measures so far.[28] In a decentral energy system, however, uniform grid charges provide no incentives to optimize the energy system on a local or regional level. Given the fact that local electricity producers indeed may help to obviate expansions of the electricity grid, the "postage stamp principle" does not reward investments in local electricity generation, thereby rendering local consumers of electricity indifferent to the costs of "their" electricity network.

In 2019, the independent regulatory agency for the electricity markets (ElCom—Electricity Commission) issued a notice on "innovative and dynamic grid usage and energy supply tariffs".[29] It held that consumers may be offered a choice of grid tariffs; however, these tariffs need to fulfill the legal requirements, somewhat limiting the range of possible choices. It also held that dynamic tariffs are "not per se illegal", but need to adhere to the (inherently static) principles set by the law. "Smart Grid Ready" tariffs need to observe a range of requirements, which gives rise to legal risks when they are used. There are no incentives to optimize the local energy system, since—according to ElCom—it is illegal to reward such optimization by reimbursing consumers with parts of the avoided grid costs.[30] At least, network-serving and system-serving behavior of consumers using smart control systems may be rewarded by providing financial incentives.[31] Finally, the Electricity Commission held that dynamic electricity pricing might be illegal in light of universal service

[26] For a detailed description of cross-border trade with the European Union and the mechanism of "market coupling", see Hettich et al. (2015), p. 21 et seq. See for cost estimates Van Baal et al. (2019), p. 38.

[27] Art. 14 para. 3 lit. b Electricity Supply Act (*Stromversorgungsgesetz*).

[28] See for the structure of grid charges Federal Council (2005), p. 1652 et seq.

[29] ElCom (2019), p. 3 et seq.

[30] ElCom (2019), p. 5.

[31] Art. 8c para. 2 Electricity Supply Ordinance (*Stromversorgungsverordnung*).

obligations.[32] A flat rate for electricity supply, however, is in line with the legal requirements; of course, such a flat rate provides no incentives to adapt electricity consumption at all.[33]

4.2.3 Restrictive Use of Smart Meter Data

Smart energy and smart home services require data. Accumulating and processing the data enables the effective and efficient functioning of the smart grid. In order to provide its energy services, aliunid needs data about actual electricity consumption, actual electricity production, as well as a home's potential for additional electricity consumption and additional production; due to privacy concerns, this data only is available to aliunid in a condensed and aggregated form. In order to provide additional smart home and smart business services, aliunid further needs smart meter data from all smart devices and home appliances, as well as from additional sensors and security systems; for the same privacy concerns, most of this data will only be stored and analyzed locally.

Nevertheless, the gathering of data touches on sensitive issues: On the one hand, data is collected from end consumers, whose personal rights must be protected; on the other hand, information on the operation of the power supply system is exchanged, which can be critical for system stability. Data protection, in the sense of protecting personal data against misuse, and data security, in the sense of protecting data against loss, falsification, damage or deletion by organizational and technical measures and by software, must therefore be guaranteed.[34] Furthermore, the law states that economically sensitive information obtained from the operation of the electricity grids shall be treated confidentially by the electricity supply companies, subject only to statutory disclosure obligations; hence, this data must not be used for other areas of economic activity (so-called "informational unbundling").[35]

As a basic principle, the use of intelligent control systems requires the consent of the affected final consumers, producers and storage facilities.[36] Network operators may process the data gathered from intelligent control systems without consent for the management of the grid: First, they may legally use personality profiles and personal data in pseudonymized form, including load profiles of fifteen minutes and more, for the measurement of electricity flows, for the control and regulation of the grid, for the use of tariff systems, and for the operation, balancing and planning of

[32] See for this interpretation of Art. 6 para. 3 Electricity Supply Act (*Stromversorgungsgesetz*); ElCom (2019), p. 8.

[33] ElCom (2019), p. 7 et seq.

[34] A consortium with participation of the University of St. Gallen has conducted two studies on data protection and data security of the smart grid, the results of which are summarized in Hettich and Rechsteiner (2014), n. 1.

[35] Art. 10 para. 2 Electricity Supply Act (*Stromversorgungsgesetz*); see also Hettich and Rechsteiner (2014), n. 5.

[36] Art. 17b para. 3 Electricity Supply Act (*Stromversorgungsgesetz*).

the network. Second, they may also use personality profiles and personal data in non-pseudonymized form, including load profile values of fifteen minutes or more, for billing purposes (billing for energy supply, grid usage and remuneration for the use of the control systems).[37] According to a recent draft amendment for the Electricity Supply Act, all processing of smart meter data, which is not necessary for fulfilling the task of electricity supply, may only be carried out with the express consent of the persons concerned.[38]

Against the backdrop of these restrictions, the express consent seems required for all personal data with a higher granularity than fifteen minutes (if available at all), as well as for all data that is not required for billing purposes or for grid management.[39] Such a regime is even more rigid than the general data protection laws, which also allow for data processing if a legitimate interest of the concerned business is involved.[40] Thus, it is reasonable to say that network operators and other players in the smart grid may not be able to easily tap the huge potential of data from intelligent systems, e.g., for smart home and security services or for personalized advertising.[41] Such enhanced services, however, may be necessary to generate a reasonable return on the investments of the utilities in the smart grid. Looking generally at the current regime of data protection, a move towards a more risk-based approach and a holistic system of information governance might be required to enhance many of the information-based services provided today.

4.3 Workarounds and Legal Recommendations

Aliunid is one of many smart energy providers that have developed business models to support the transformation towards a carbon-free energy system.[42] Because of current policies, this transformation is accompanied by a decentralization of the energy system. This move towards a decentral energy system is not reflected in the current regulatory framework. There is no specific incentive to optimize local grid usage: Because of the "postage stamp principle", transporting electricity over long distances costs the same as using local production. There is no specific incentive to adapt consumption to current demand because the reward for flexibility is so low.

---

[37] Art. 8d para. 1 Electricity Supply Ordinance (*Stromversorgungsverordnung*).

[38] Draft Amendment of 18 June 2021 for Art. 17b^{quater} and 17c Electricity Supply Act; see also, more clearly, the earlier Draft Amendment of 17 October 2018 for Art. 17b^{ter} Electricity Supply Act (*Stromversorgungsgesetz*).

[39] Federal Council (2018), p. 70; Federal Council (2021), p. 102.

[40] See Rechsteiner and Steiner (2018), n. 56 et seq., arguing for a more expansive application of the law.

[41] Rechsteiner and Steiner (2018), n. 42.

[42] Looking at Switzerland, the electricity system is mostly carbon-free at this point in time, thanks to large generation capacities that make use of nuclear and hydro energy. The challenge will be to maintain this environmentally friendly status despite the planned nuclear phaseout.

There are rather weak incentives for small prosumers to adapt electricity generation to current demand because their subsidies are mostly fixed and their marginal costs of production are very low. There are no specific provisions on storage (e.g., batteries, Power2X), making it difficult to distinguish self-serving and system-serving storage devices; without such distinction, rewarding the flexibility provided by storage is hardly feasible. Last but not least, the commercial use of smart meter data is very much dependent on consent, which needs to be freely given on an informed basis.

On the upside, the current regulatory framework does not preclude innovative business models in the energy sector. Financial incentives to reward system-serving behavior via dynamic grid charges and electricity tariffs are possible, although quite limited because of the legal requirements that have to be adhered to. Available flexibilities of consumers and prosumers may be harnessed by using contractual arrangements.

The legal requirements for informational unbundling are more challenging to meet: Economically sensitive information obtained from the operation of the electricity grids may not be used for other areas of commercial activity. Aliunid, however, does not qualify as a grid operator; it obtains the required data via an open interface of the smart meter (offered on a non-discriminatory basis by the network operator to all interested parties). Consequently, obtaining consent is the most important obstacle for the use of smart meter data. If the required consent may be obtained, smart meter data may be used to provide smart home and security services as well as enhanced commercial offers (e.g., personalized advertisements).

5 Concluding Remarks

Current electricity market regulation makes use of a plethora of instruments that deal—each on its own—with different aspects of the energy and electricity market design. There is a law on electricity market regulation, on the promotion of renewable energy, on the use of hydropower, on the mitigation of greenhouse gas emissions; soon, there will also be a law on the gas market. The transformation path envisioned by the federal government, however, makes it necessary that these instruments operate as one system, enabling easy conversions from one form of energy into another. Although there are no legal impediments to conduct these conversions, there are no legal norms to facilitate conversions, either.

Current electricity market design focuses on breaking up vertically integrated monopoly structures by strict unbundling rules. As a matter of principle, these rules may take different forms: the incumbents either may be broken up along the value chain, or they may be forced to provide access to their networks. Successfully implemented in telecommunication markets, unbundling regulation helps competitors to enter the markets which are upstream and downstream to a network (i.e., the electricity grid). Unbundling, however, raises transaction costs (cost of regulation and enforcement, cost of lost synergies, etc.). In contrast to telecommunication markets, the electricity grid and electricity generation are not only complements but also substitutes: A lack of electricity in a certain area may be countered by ramping up generation or by adding grid capacity. Consequently, unbundling electricity markets requires procedures to coordinate the buildup of grid and generation capacity; these procedures need to replace the internal coordination within the integrated energy supplier. Since such outside coordination is costly, there is a vast literature that indicates that unbundling may not be so efficient, after all.[43] Thus, efficient coordination of the participants in the electricity market may be difficult to achieve in a centralized energy system. In a decentralized energy system with many participants in ever-changing roles, efficient coordination may be impossible to obtain, in particular when using traditional command-and-control regulation. New instruments and procedures for adjudication and dispute settlement are needed but not within reach.

Many regulatory principles that govern energy and electricity markets have been developed for other infrastructure sectors—sectors that are also prone to network effects. The "postage stamp principle" that governs grid charges, e.g., has an obvious predecessor in postal markets; unbundling network access services from other services has been implemented in the telecommunication markets. These principles had their use when the monopolies in these network industries had to be broken up and when room had to be made for some competition. Today, other social goals have taken preeminence, such as security of supply and the mitigation effort regarding greenhouse gases. As the case study "aliunid" shows clearly, some of the old instruments hinder the transformation of the energy industry.

In the past, the energy industry was often not able to position itself at the forefront of innovation. This has changed, as the industry enters unchartered waters. To find effective and efficient solutions for the energy transformation, difficult first-order problems have to be solved: Centralized command-and-control regulation, on the national or on the European level, may not be suited to seek, find, and implement the most efficient solutions. To optimize a local "energy environment", locally adapted regimes might be needed.[44] Research pioneered by Elinor Ostrom shows that local actors that are responsible for a localized resource may also solve second-order problems: They are able to develop and implement local rules and regimes that effectively and efficiently manage their resources, e.g., their local energy system.[45] Today, such voluntary regimes, e.g., concluded by contracts or devised in communal regulation, are easily frustrated by the current top-down approach to the regulation of the energy system.[46] Of course, fair access to these localized systems and appropriate protection of captive consumers will remain important and will remain a task for

[43] Hettich (2020), n. 38; Föhse (2014), n. 504.

[44] Ostrom (2005), p. 255 et seq.; see also Ostrom, Stein Rokkan Lecture, "Protecting Institutional Diversity", St. Gallen, 16 April 2011.

[45] See, e.g., Ostrom (1998), p. 2; Schlager (2002), p. 804.

[46] Ostrom (1990), p. 21 et seq.; see also Ostrom, Stein Rokkan Lecture, "Protecting Institutional Diversity", St. Gallen, 16 April 2011.

central governance regimes. However, such goals also may be enforced by performance benchmarks and by processes to replace failing local regimes.[47]

Not every problem of the energy sector requires a European solution. But what is sure: The regulatory innovation needed to manage a rapidly transforming energy system may not be found by sticking to traditional bureaucratic processes and procedures.[48] We need approaches that are systemic, that provide leeway for learning as well as trial and error processes, and that are quickly able to identify and scale successful experiments as well as to shut down the ineffective ones.

References

Electricity Commission (2019) Fragen und Antworten zu neuartigen und dynamischen Netznutzungs- und Energieliefertarifen: Februar 2019 (Update September 2019). Available at https://www.elcom.admin.ch

European Commission (2016) Commission Staff Working Document accompanying the proposal for the Directive on common rules for the internal market in electricity, the Regulation on the electricity market, the Regulation establishing a European Union Agency for the Cooperation of Energy Regulators, the Regulation on risk preparedness in the electricity sector, SWD(2016) 410 final, Brussels 30 November 2016

Federal Council (1988) Botschaft vom 21. Dezember 1988 betreffend den Bundesbeschluss über eine sparsame und rationelle Energieverwendung (Energienutzungsbeschluss, ENB). Federal Gazette BBl 1989 I 497

Federal Council (2005) Botschaft vom 3. Dezember 2004 zur Änderung des Elektrizitätsgesetzes und zum Stromversorgungsgesetz. Federal Gazette BBl 2005 1611

Federal Council (2018) Revision des Stromversorgungsgesetzes (volle Strommarktöffnung, Speicherreserve und Modernisierung der Netzregulierung). Erläuternder Bericht zur Vernehmlassungsvorlage (Oktober 2018). Available at https://www.admin.ch

Federal Council (2021) Botschaft zum Bundesgesetz über eine sichere Stromversorgung mit erneuerbaren Energien. Federal Gazette BBl 2021 1666

Föhse KS (2014) Die rechtliche Ausgestaltung der nationalen Netzgesellschaft im Stromversorgungsgesetz (StromVG). Dike, St. Gallen

Hettich P (2014) Kooperative Risikovorsorge: Regulierte Selbstregulierung im Recht der operationellen und technischen Risiken. Schulthess, Zurich

Hettich P (2020) Infrastrukturverfassung. In: Diggelmann O, Hertig Randall M, Schindler B (eds) Verfassungsrecht der Schweiz. Schulthess, Zurich 2020, Vol. III, VIII.9

Hettich P, Rechsteiner S (2014) Datensicherheit und Datenschutz im Smart Grid. Jusletter 27 October 2014. Available at https://jusletter.weblaw.ch

Hettich P, Walther S (2015) "Hype" um Batterien lässt das Verteilnetz vergessen: Skizzen zu einer sachgerechteren Anlastung der Netzkosten. Bulletin SEV/VSE 106(12):24–26

Hettich P, Walther S, Schreiber Tschudin S (2015) Schweiz ohne Stromabkommen. Dike, St. Gallen

Hettich P, Walther S, Wohlgemuth D, Camenisch L, Drittenbass J (2017) Strommarkt 2023: Quotenmodelle im Zieldreieck von Umweltverträglichkeit, Wirtschaftlichkeit und Versorgungssicherheit. Dike, St. Gallen

[47] Karkkainen (2002), p. 193 et seq.; Karkkainen (2006), p. 893; Sabel and Simon (2004), p. 1020, 1062.

[48] See for cooperative approaches to regulation Hettich (2014), p. 269 et seq.

Hettich P, Thaler P, Camenisch L, Hofmann B, Petrovich B, Wüstenhagen R (2020) Europeanization of the Swiss Energy System. Dike, St. Gallen

Karkkainen BC (2002) Collaborative ecosystem governance: scale, complexity, and dynamism. Virginia Environ Law J 21:189–243

Karkkainen BC (2006) Information-forcing environmental regulation. Florida State Univ Law Rev 33:861–902

Knill C, Lehmkuhl D (2002) The national impact of European Union regulatory policy: three Europeanization mechanisms. Eur J Polit Res 41(2):255–280

Ostrom E (1990) Governing the commons: the evolution of institutions for collective action. Cambridge University Press, New York

Ostrom E (1998) A behavioral approach to the rational choice theory of collective action. Am Polit Sci Rev 92:1–22

Ostrom E (2005) Understanding institutional diversity. Princeton University Press, Princeton

Rechsteiner S, Steiner T (2018) Datenschutz bei intelligenten Mess- und Steuersystemen. Jusletter 11 June 2018. Available at https://jusletter.weblaw.ch

Sabel CF, Simon WH (2004) Destabilization rights: how public law litigation succeeds. Harv Law Rev 117:1015–1101

Schlager E (2002) Rationality, cooperation, and common pool resources. Am Behav Sci 45:801–819

Swiss Federal Office of Energy (2021) Schweizerische Statistik der erneuerbaren Energien: Ausgabe 2020. Available at https://www.bfe.admin.ch

Van Baal P, Finger M, Fischer M, Maggetti M, Morger L, Pflieger G, Refle J-E (2019) The Swiss energy transition and the relationship with Europe: Complementary study NRP70 Energy Turnaround (unpublished report)

Walther S (2014) Kooperative Steuerungsinstrumente im schweizerischen Stromversorgungsrecht. Dike, St. Gallen

Peter Hettich is Director with the Institute of Public Finance, Fiscal Law and Law and Economics (IFF-HSG) and Professor for public law at the University of St. Gallen, St. Gallen, Switzerland.

Governance of Energy Innovations

Markus Schreiber

Contents

Abstract Innovation plays an important role in the transition towards a more sustainable energy system. The law is often thought of as an inhibiting factor for innovation. However, legal provisions may also serve to promote innovation. Laws which stipulate favourable conditions for renewable energy sources are an obvious example. Finally, existing laws will often not be suited to accommodate a new technology or business model, and the legislator may be slow in reacting to these new challenges. This increases the importance of government agencies as well as non-state governance.

M. Schreiber (✉)
University of Lucerne, Center for Law and Sustainability, Lucerne, Switzerland
e-mail: markus.schreiber@unilu.ch

P. Hettich, A. Kachi (eds.), *Swiss Energy Governance*,
https://doi.org/10.1007/978-3-030-80787-0_9

Therefore, a closer look at the governance of innovations in the energy sector seems warranted. This chapter will investigate how the legislator, regulatory agencies and private standard-setting bodies are responding to three different energy innovations: new renewable energy sources, new storage systems and smart grids. This chapter will serve not only to analyse commonalities and differences in the approach, but also to identify best practices.

1 Introduction

1.1 Overview

A successful energy transition as envisaged by the Swiss Federal Government's Energy Strategy 2050[1] will not only require major changes in behaviour, but also the market introduction of innovative technologies. The law is often thought to inhibit innovation.[2] In a survey for the German-speaking countries Germany, Austria and Switzerland among energy utility companies, 74% named "regulation" as the biggest obstacle to innovation, closely followed by "political framework" with 71%, making these two by far the most often named factors.[3]

However, the law may also function as a catalyst of innovation. An example are legal provisions that promote renewable energy sources, e.g. by implementing quotas, subsidies or other privileges. Either way, no innovation will succeed if the legal framework discourages its use.[4] The governance[5] of energy innovation not only involves legislative measures, but also those taken by regulatory bodies. These include both governmental regulatory agencies as well as private regulatory bodies, such as industry associations.

This chapter will provide an overview of how the different governing actors in Switzerland have dealt with and are dealing with energy-related innovation. Past treatment of innovation will be explained by a short look at the first electrification as well as the innovation of nuclear energy. Current developments which will be assessed are new renewable energy sources, new storage systems and smart grids. But first, it seems appropriate to provide a concise overview of the different functions the law may serve in relation to (primarily technological) innovation.

[1] Swiss Federal Office of Energy (2018).

[2] For a discussion of the term "innovation" in a legal context, see Schreiber (2019), p. 12 et seq.

[3] BDEW, Ernst & Young GmbH (2015), p. 38. Also cf. Schreiber (2019), p. 1.

[4] For a general discussion of the topic, see Schreiber (2019).

[5] For a discussion on the governance of innovation from a legal perspective, see Hoffmann-Riem (2011a). For a general description of the term, see Schuppert (2008). Concerning the difficulties which legal scholars encounter in dealing with the governance concept, cf. Trute et al. (2008), p. 173, 178 (who are otherwise optimistic); also see the opportunities described by Kötter (2008).

1.2 Law and Innovation

The interrelation between law and technological innovation has been investigated at least as early as the 1970s.[6] However, especially in Germany starting in the mid-to-late 1990s, a broader research interest in law and innovation has taken hold.[7] This "jurisprudential innovation research"[8] distinguishes between different functions that the law serves in relation to innovation.

First, the law has to *enable* innovation.[9] This means that the legal framework does not prohibit the innovation and allows all of the actions which are necessary to implement the innovation.[10] In energy law, the introduction of the Atomic Energy Act (*Atomgesetz*, current title: *Kernenergiegesetz*, SR 732.1) first enabled the innovation of nuclear energy production in Switzerland. Before, the trade restrictions in nuclear fuels made this impossible.[11]

In addition, the law may *stimulate* innovation.[12] This means that the law not only enables the innovation but also incentivizes it.[13] Energy-related examples are legal privileges for renewable energy sources such as quotas, feed-in tariffs etc.[14]

I have argued that when the law prescribes the innovation (or at least a certain level of innovation) in a binding way, it is no longer adequate to refer to this as a mere stimulating function. Instead, I have suggested that one may refer to this as an *enforcement* function.[15] An example of this is *technology forcing*, where the law stipulates requirements which cannot be fulfilled by the existing technologies.[16] This happened when new energy efficiency requirements for lamps effectively outlawed traditional light bulbs in the EU and subsequently in Switzerland.[17]

The law also serves to protect society from *undesired incidental effects* associated with an innovation.[18] This limiting function[19] has traditionally been served by safety regulations and is one of law's traditional functions.[20]

---

[6] Schreiber (2019), p. 3 et seq. See for example OTA (1979), p. 45; Stewart (1981).

[7] Hoffmann-Riem and Schmidt-Assmann (1994); Hoffmann-Riem and Schneider (1998); Eifert and Hoffmann-Riem (2002); Hoffmann-Riem (2011a); Gattermann (2012); Hoffmann-Riem (2016).

[8] "*Rechtswissenschaftliche Innovationsforschung*" in German.

[9] The enabling function or "*Ermöglichungsfunktion*" in German.

[10] Cf. Schreiber (2002), p. 235; Schreiber (2019), p. 90 et seq.

[11] Schreiber (2019), p. 91.

[12] The stimulating function or "*Stimulierungsfunktion*" in German.

[13] Schreiber (2002), p. 242; Hoffmann-Riem and Schneider (1998a, b), p. 396; Schreiber (2019), p. 92 et seq. Also cf. Ashford and Hall (2011), p. 272, who call for "legal interventions".

[14] Cf. Schreiber (2019), p. 92.

[15] Schreiber (2019), p. 93 et seq. ("*Durchsetzungsfunktion*" in German).

[16] Gerard, Lave (2005).

[17] Hettich (2015); Nusser (2010); Schreiber (2019), p. 93.

[18] Schreiber (2002), p. 249.

[19] "*Nebenfolgenbegrenzungsfunktion*" in German.

[20] Murswiek (1990), p. 208 et seq.; Schreiber (2019), p. 95 et seq.

The undesired effects of an innovation may be so far-reaching that the legislator decides to ban the innovation altogether. I have argued that this constitutes a new category, the *blocking function*.[21] An example from the energy industry is the ban of nuclear energy in Austria, which never introduced the technology.[22]

Finally, the law's main function is to resolve conflicts. The *conflict resolution function* also becomes relevant with regards to innovation.[23] For example, the new Swiss Energy Act (*Energiegesetz*, SR 730.0) stipulates a national interest in the use of renewable energies in Article 12, which may help to address conflicts with other public interests (such as the environment or landscape conservation).[24]

2 History of Swiss Energy Innovation Governance

A short review of Switzerland's past regulatory responses to innovation will show how the government's approach has changed since the late nineteenth century.

2.1 First Electrification

The first electrification in Switzerland started in the late 1870s and progressed quickly in the 1890s, driven by hydropower plants.[25] However, the legislator remained passive for a long time, only enacting legislation to resolve conflicts between the new power lines and existing telegraph lines (in the latter's favour).[26] This passivity was a conscious choice, as "the final word" on the new technology had not yet been spoken and regulation would therefore have to wait.[27]

Thus, the regulation of the new (and dangerous) technology fell upon private organisations. The Swiss Electrotechnical Association (*Schweizerischer Elektrotechnischer Verein*, SEV) created safety rules for high-voltage installations in 1896.[28] The same association later founded a technical auditing body (Technical Inspectorate, *Technisches Inspektorat*) that even offered inspections of private

---

[21] "*Blockierungsfunktion*" in German, Schreiber (2019), p. 97 et seq.

[22] At the time when the "*Atomsperrgesetz*" (Federal Act on the ban of using nuclear fission for Austria's energy supply) was introduced in 1978, the Austrian people had already voted against the commissioning of an already-built nuclear power plant in Zwentendorf.

[23] Hoffmann-Riem and Schneider (1998a, b), p. 397; Schreiber (2019), p. 98 et seq.

[24] For a discussion of Article 12 Energy Act, see Gerber (2019).

[25] For an overview of Switzerland's early electrification, see Gugerli (1994a, 1996); Wyssling (1946); see also Föhse (2021).

[26] Wyssling (1946), p. 120, 276; Schreiber (2019), p. 98 et seq.

[27] Sten. Bull 1894 S 321, 327; see also Gugerli (1994b), p. 14; Schreiber (2019), p. 436.

[28] Wyssling (1946), p. 279; Schreiber (2019), p. 436 et seq.

household installations for a fee.[29] Thus, in the absence of government regulation, the private economy supplied its own regulatory system. This also shows that private governance is by no means a new phenomenon.[30] The Swiss Electricity Act (*Elektrizitätsgesetz*, SR 734.0) only entered into force in 1903, two decades after the corresponding British Act was introduced.[31]

The formerly private Technical Inspectorate has now become the Federal Inspectorate for Heavy Current Installations (*Eidgenössisches Starkstrominspektorat*, ESTI). This body is still operated by Electrosuisse, but it has been endowed with a public mandate and can issue administrative decisions (*Verfügungen*, cf. Article 16 para. 2 lit. a Electricity Act).

2.2 Nuclear Energy

In stark contrast to the first electrification, the introduction of nuclear energy was not passively observed by the legislator. As mentioned in Sect. 1.2 above, there could not have been an introduction of this innovation without the legislator's initiative, since trade restrictions on nuclear fuels hindered the private market participants.

As nuclear energy was heralded as the solution to the world's energy problems, the Swiss legislator was poised to move quickly. The legislator intervened at the earliest possible stage by promoting research in nuclear energy.[32] The constitution was amended to allow for rules at the federal level, since the topic of nuclear energy was deemed to be of national significance.[33] Also, regulatory oversight had to take place at the federal level, since in the early stages of the technology, not enough experts would have been available to staff a large number of cantonal authorities.[34] On the basis of this new federal legislative power, the Atomic Energy Act entered into force in 1960.

The initial intent of the new law was to promote nuclear energy, corresponding with the enabling and stimulating function of innovation-related law (see Sect. 1.2

[29] Wyssling (1946), p. 280; Schreiber (2019), p. 437.

[30] Contrary to the apparent opinion of Benz (2004a), p. 13 et seq., who seems to emphasize actual changes in the governance responsibilities between government and private actors as one of the reasons for the popularity of the term "governance".

[31] Electric Lighting Act 1882, 45&46 Vict c 56. See Gugerli (1994b), p. 13 et seq.; Schreiber (2019), p. 437.

[32] The legislative materials for the necessary changes to the Swiss constitution concluded that without significant public involvement, even research into the new technology would be doomed to failure. See Federal Council (1957), p. 1159 et seq.; Schreiber (2019), p. 438.

[33] Art. 24quinquies of the former (1874–2000) constitution was adopted to grant legislative powers regarding nuclear energy to the federation. See Federal Council (1957), p. 1139; Schreiber (2019), p. 438 et seq. The same content is now found in Art. 90 Federal Constitution (*Bundesverfassung der Schweizerischen Eidgenossenschaft*).

[34] Federal Council (1957), p. 1139.

above). Thus, rules on the procurement of nuclear fuels provided a legal framework in which, for the first time, nuclear energy could be exploited in Switzerland (*enabling* function).[35] Also, massive public investments into nuclear energy research and development were made possible under the new legal provisions (*stimulating* function).

However, the new laws were not only intended to promote this innovation. Instead, the potential risks of nuclear energy were already well-known. Hence, the new legislative framework was also created to reduce these risks as much as possible.[36] This corresponds with the *limiting* function of the law. For example, the construction of nuclear energy installations was made subject to a detailed approval procedure.[37] The Atomic Energy Act also introduced liability provisions.[38] Still, even here the promotion of the new technology was part of the focus, since the liability was limited.[39]

In addition, the Atomic Energy Act established the supervision of all nuclear energy installations at the federal level. Therefore, there was no need for industry associations to establish their own regulatory bodies.

Finally, it is interesting to note that some hesitance by the federal legislator to regulate a completely new technology can be noticed as well. For example, the legislator saw the problems of having to use exact legal definitions at a time when much of the relevant terminology was still in flux.[40] This problem was diminished by defining several technical terms at the ordinance level, which made it easier to quickly make amendments as they became necessary.[41] This is a legislative technique that is still used frequently today when regulating innovative technologies[42] and that was also part of the regulation during the first electrification.[43] At the same time, it also raises questions as to which parts of the regulation are so important that under constitutional law, they must be implemented in a formal (parliamentary) law.[44] In general, however, the Swiss legislator was much more willing to regulate nuclear energy in its infancy, compared to the "wait-and-see" approach favoured during the first electrification.

The Atomic Energy Act has been replaced by the Nuclear Energy Act, which entered into force in 2005. The regulatory oversight is currently exercised by the Federal Nuclear Safety Inspectorate (*Eidgenössisches*

[35] Schreiber (2019), p. 439.

[36] Federal Council (1957), p. 1139, 1141 et seq.; Federal Council (1958), p. 1522 et seq.

[37] In Articles 4–7, see Federal Council (1958), p. 1538 et seq.

[38] In Article 11, see Federal Council (1958), p. 1544 et seq.

[39] Federal Council (1958), p. 1544 et seq.

[40] Federal Council (1958), p. 1535 et seq.

[41] Federal Council (1958), p. 1535 et seq.

[42] Schreiber (2019), p. 79, 392.

[43] Schreiber (2019), p. 393.

[44] Regarding the general question of which rules may be implemented in an ordinance, see Müller (2020), p. 48 et seq.

Nuklearsicherheitsinspektorat, ENSI). This demonstrates the importance of regulatory agencies not only for competition-oriented market regulation, but also for safety regulation (cf. the *ESTI* discussed in Sect. 2.1 above).

2.3 Interim Conclusions

The comparison between the regulatory approaches to the first electrification and the introduction of nuclear energy has shown remarkable differences. During the first electrification, the legislator remained largely passive. The regulation of high-voltage installations was therefore first implemented by the private sector through industry associations. These associations later played an important part in the preparation of the first electricity-specific laws.[45]

In contrast, the peaceful use of nuclear energy was accompanied by the legislator from the very beginning. This included provisions to support research and development. The regulation and supervision took place at the federal level from the start, due to the significance of the innovation and the potential risks involved. The public sector was thus deeply involved in the new industry, and there was little room for private self-regulatory[46] governance.

What is the reason for the difference in these two approaches? The first electrification did not collide with many legal provisions since the overall "regulatory density"[47] was not nearly as high in the late nineteenth century as it is today. Thus, the private market participants were able to employ the new technology without facing prohibitory restrictions.

On the contrary, nuclear energy faced a prohibitory legal framework that prevented the private industry from ever implementing the new technology without government intervention. Since even the trade of nuclear fuels was prohibited, a completely new legal framework was necessary in order to enable the innovation.

It may be presumed that, given the ever-increasing regulatory density especially in the energy sector, current innovations will rather fall into a similar category as nuclear energy. This would mean that the legislator would interfere at an early stage, maybe even before the innovation has entered the market. The following discussion of current innovation governance in the energy sector will, among other things, shed light on this question.

---

[45] Wyssling (1946), p. 281 et seq.; Schreiber (2019), p. 437.

[46] For discussion of self-regulation, see Hettich (2014), p. 269 et seq.

[47] For a discussion of this term, see Citi, Justesen (2014), p. 713 et seq., 716 et seq.

3 Governance of Current Energy Innovations

3.1 New Renewable Energy Sources

The term "new renewable energy sources" is used in Switzerland to designate all renewable energies other than the long-established hydropower.[48] Increasing the production from new renewable energy sources has been one of the main focuses of the Swiss Energy Strategy 2050.[49] Several options exist to promote renewable energy production, including quotas[50] and auctions.[51] The Swiss legislator opted for a feed-in tariff system, the "feed-in remuneration at cost" (*Kostendeckende Einspeisevergütung*, KEV).[52] In recent years and with the introduction of the completely revised Energy Act in 2018, the system has taken on a more market-oriented approach. Under the new feed-in tariff system (*Einspeisevergütungssystem*, EVS), renewable energy producers, as a basic principle, have to directly market the electricity they produce (Article 21 Energy Act).[53]

Thus, the federal legislator has played a crucial role in the promotion of (new) renewable energy sources. This is complemented by cantonal and municipal subsidies for renewable energy installations, especially for solar heating in households.[54]

However, the multi-level governance[55] of renewable energy not only extends to provisions that promote this innovation. Often, authorities at the cantonal or municipal level will be tasked with the implementation of other provisions that *interfere* with renewable energy projects. With regards to solar installations, for example, the federal legislator has introduced Article 18a of the Spatial Planning Act (*Raumplanungsgesetz*, SR 700). In its current version, the provision stipulates that certain well-integrated rooftop solar systems do not need a building permit. This—constitutionally controversial[56]—provision was partly a response to the strict application of cantonal and municipal rules for listed historic buildings and townscape protection (*Denkmal- und Ortsbildschutz*). The tensions between the federal legislator's intent to promote solar energy and the cantons' and municipalities' wish to

---

[48] Cf. Article 2 para. 1 Energy Act (*Energiegesetz*), which does not use the term "new renewable energy" but still only applies to all renewable energy sources "except for hydropower".

[49] Federal Council (2013), p. 7594.

[50] Which have notably been used in the UK for a long time under the "renewables obligation" scheme.

[51] Such as those now used in Germany under the Renewable Energy Sources Act (*Erneuerbare-Energien-Gesetz*—EEG 2017).

[52] For a critical assessment of the KEV system, see Hettich and Walther (2011).

[53] For a detailed discussion of the Swiss feed-in tariff system, see Haelg et al. (2021).

[54] A list of the available support schemes can be found on the website https://www.energie-experten.ch/de/energiefranken.html.

[55] For a general discussion of this concept, see Benz (2004b). In the context of the energy transition, see Thaler et al. (2019).

[56] Cf. Hettich and Peng (2015). For a more general discussion, see Müller and Vogel (2012).

protect their townscapes are a good example of problems inherent in multi-level governance.[57]

3.2 New Storage Systems

With the rising share of variable renewable energy sources, at some point in the future, storage capacity may be needed.[58] Until recently, the only large-scale storage technologies were pump hydropower storage systems. With the increasing need for storage capacity and the lack of suitable locations for new pump hydropower plants, new energy storage technologies (e.g. batteries, compressed air storage or even Power-to-Gas)[59] will become more relevant.

Compared to some other countries and the EU,[60] the Swiss legislator has so far remained relatively passive in the governance of new storage systems.[61] One important obstacle for new storage technologies is the existing legal framework for pump hydropower storage. Pump hydropower is exempted from the final consumer status under Article 4 para. 1 lit. b Electricity Supply Act (*Stromversorgungsgesetz*, SR 734.7). This, most importantly, means that pump hydropower plants do not have to pay grid fees under Article 14 Electricity Supply Act. If—as I have argued[62]—this exemption did not apply to new storage technologies, that would be a major impediment to the diffusion of new storage systems.

The Federal Council had originally planned to clarify that all storage systems with the exception of pump hydropower plants are final consumers.[63] This provision was later removed from the draft ordinance due to negative responses in the consultation.[64] Since the executive level of governance therefore refrained from clarifying the legal status of storage systems, this burden now falls back on the legislator.

Meanwhile, the private Swiss Association of Electric Power Producers and Distributors (*Verband Schweizerischer Elektrizitätsunternehmen*, VSE) has published a "Handbook Storage", which stipulates that storage systems that take electricity from the public grid and later feed electricity back into the grid at the same

[57] Also cf. Thaler et al. (2019), p. 3.

[58] See Schreiber (2019), p. 167 et seq. Only a long-term need for storage is seen by Hewicker et al. (2013). For a detailed discussion of storage-related governance, see Walther (2019).

[59] For a detailed description of new storage technologies, see Sterner and Stadler (2017).

[60] Cf. Schreiber (2019), p. 276 et seq., 409, 427 et seq.

[61] Also cf. Kratz (2018); Walther (2019).

[62] Schreiber (2019), p. 234 et seq. But cf. Kratz (2018), p. 73, 94 et seq.; Walther (2019), p. 30.

[63] In a revised Article 2 para. 3 Electricity Supply Ordinance (*Stromversorgungsverordnung*), see Federal Department of the Environment, Transport, Energy and Communications (2018), p. 6.

[64] Schreiber (2019), p. 276. For the statements from the consultation, see "*Strategie Stromnetze: Änderungen auf Verordnungsstufe*", available at https://www.admin.ch.

location should be exempt from paying grid fees.[65] This is particularly noteworthy as under the Swiss principle of subsidiarity, private industry associations play an important role in energy governance (Article 3 Electricity Supply Act). It may therefore be argued that, where the legislator does not provide clear stipulations, the industry association's interpretation of the law should prevail.[66] The regulatory agency ElCom has recently confirmed the VSE's interpretation,[67] while the Federal Council still pursues plans to explicitly state in the law that only pump hydropower plants are exempt from grid fees.[68]

Regardless of how binding the industry association's rules are, they are another good example of private (self-regulatory) governance in the absence of specific legislation.

In addition, regulatory authorities may become important for storage systems as well. If grid operators were allowed to install their own storage systems (which is currently unclear under unbundling rules),[69] the question would arise whether the costs could be recovered under the Swiss "cost-plus" regulation (Art. 15 Electricity Supply Act). The regulatory agency ElCom has in the past refused to accept costs for certain innovative measures as they were not seen as "currently" necessary.[70] The same problem may arise with investments in storage capacity that may only be truly needed in the future. This shows that a conservative approach by regulatory agencies may inhibit innovation in regulated industries.

3.3 Smart Grids

In a new, more sustainable energy industry with decentralised, variable renewable energy sources, storage systems and "prosumers" that produce as well as consume electricity, digital technology may help to connect all these different market actors. In such a "smart grid", information on energy demand and production, the current grid situation and other important data could be used, inter alia, to match electricity production and consumption despite the variability of renewables.[71]

However, the vast amount of data necessary for such a smart grid has led to data protection concerns.[72] The governance of smart grids must therefore take into

[65] Verband Schweizerischer Elektrizitätsunternehmen (2017), p. 8.

[66] See Walther (2019), p. 30. But cf. Schreiber (2019), p. 266 et seq.

[67] Electricity Commission (2020), p. 17 et seq.

[68] Swiss Federal Office of Energy (2020), p. 5.

[69] Kratz (2018), p. 96 et seq.; Walther (2019), p. 11 et seq.; Schreiber (2019), p. 361 et seq.

[70] See Electricity Commission (2011) for smart grid technology. Also cf. Walther (2014), p. 171 et seq.; Schreiber (2019), p. 381 et seq.

[71] For the potential uses of smart grid technologies in Switzerland, see BET Dynamo Suisse (2014).

[72] See McKenna et al. (2012).

account both the stimulating as well as the limiting functions of innovation-related law.

The Swiss federal legislator has chosen exactly this two-pronged approach. On the one hand, the law stimulates and, to a significant extent, even enforces the implementation of smart grid technology. The latter aspect especially applies to smart meters. Here, the law enforces a smart meter rollout, according to which grid operators have to replace 80% of the meters in their grid area with smart meters by January 1, 2028 (Article 17a para. 2 Electricity Supply Act, Articles 8a, 31e and 31l Electricity Supply Ordinance).

On the other hand, the law also fulfils a limiting role with regards to the potential dangers that a smart grid poses for data protection. Real-time electricity consumption data could be used to learn about a household's income, the number and age of people in the household and the times at which a house is left empty.[73] For this reason, Article 17c Electricity Supply Act declares that the federal Data Protection Act is applicable to all smart metering data.[74]

In addition, Article 8b Electricity Supply Ordinance demands that all smart metering systems have been successfully tested for their data security by the Federal Institute of Metrology. Article 8d Electricity Supply Ordinance stipulates in which manner the data may be used. Inter alia, the time resolution may only be fifteen minutes or more (para. 1) and personal data may generally only be used in pseudonymised or aggregated form (para. 2). However, such data usage does not require the respective person's consent. This makes large-scale use of smart metering data practically feasible and thus serves a stimulating function.

3.4 Interim Conclusions

The survey of current energy innovations has shown two different approaches: With new renewable energy sources and smart grids, the legislator has played an early role in promoting these technologies. This is reminiscent of the historic approach to nuclear energy. For smart meters, the federal law has even implemented a mandatory roll-out. This shows that the law has partially evolved from a mere stimulating tool for innovation to an enforcer of innovation.

However, in the case of new energy storage systems, the Swiss legislator has taken a much more cautious approach. So far and unlike in some neighbouring

[73] Newing et al. (2015); Anderson et al. (2017).

[74] This is relevant since the number of privately organised but publicly (often at the cantonal level) dominated energy utility companies leads to the question whether cantonal or federal data protection laws are applicable. The federal law only applies to data handled by private persons or federal authorities, Article 2 para. 1 Data Protection Act (*Bundesgesetz über den Datenschutz*). Therefore, it does not apply to data handled by cantonal authorities. The latter are governed by the cantonal data protection laws.

countries,[75] no storage-specific supportive legislation has been implemented. As has been shown, the first (and ultimately aborted) attempt to regulate storage systems was intended to cement the existing special status of the incumbent technology, pump hydropower storage. In the absence of legal provisions, a private industry association has introduced rules on storage systems in a technical document. This legislative passivity, coupled with an increased governance role of private institutions, is similar to the first introduction of electricity in Switzerland.

4 Best Practices of Innovation Governance

The different historic and current governance approaches to innovation lead to the question whether best practices can be identified. While more research seems warranted, the following section will highlight some key factors.

4.1 Analysis of the Existing Framework

When deciding on whether a proactive or a passive legislative approach should be chosen, the existing legal framework must be taken into account. A passive approach will only work if the existing framework allows the innovation to be implemented. If the existing rules prohibit the innovative solution or render it economically unattractive, a passive approach will likely prevent the innovation's widespread adoption. Hence, the first electrification of Switzerland was possible despite the legislator's passivity, since no existing laws prevented the innovation from being implemented.

Contrary to this, a similar approach would not have been possible with nuclear energy, since existing international rules prevented fuels from being obtained by private market actors. Therefore, the existing legal framework must be analysed as to its impact on the innovation. If the innovation seems desirable but the existing framework would severely hinder its implementation, a passive approach is not a feasible option.[76]

In this context, it should also be noted that minor changes to the existing framework which remove the legal obstacles might be preferable to specific support schemes or other legal privileges for the innovation.[77]

---

[75] See § 111 para. 3 of the Austrian *Elektrizitätswirtschafts- und -organisationsgesetz* 2010; § 118 para. 6 of the German *Energiewirtschaftsgesetz*.

[76] Cf. Schreiber (2019), p. 441 et seq.

[77] Schreiber (2019), p. 389 et seq.

4.2 Technology-Neutral Rules

When a decision is made to enact legislation to support (or, in the case of negative effects, limit) the innovation, the exact design of the new rules is critical. For example, if legal privileges are introduced for a narrowly defined innovation, other (potentially better) technologies may not benefit from these. This would grant an unfair advantage to the innovation supported by the legislator. The rules should therefore be technology-neutral to ensure fair competition that leads to the best market outcome.[78]

That is why, for example, legal definitions should be broad enough to include not just the specific innovation but also other innovative options. This is also important since new technologies may be invented faster than the legislator can react. This is commonly referred to as "legal lag".[79] The rules should thus also take into account potential new inventions that are not yet available when the rules are drafted. One could call these "technology-open" rules.[80]

4.3 Flexibility

The "legal lag" problem just described above is often coupled with another phenomenon: the lack of knowledge on the legislator's part. The legislator cannot know in advance whether an innovation will be successful or whether new, even better technologies or processes will be introduced in the future.[81] For this reason, the legislator will often prefer flexible rules at the ordinance level that can be quickly adapted to changing circumstances.[82] Despite the advantages that ordinances offer in terms of flexibility, the principle of legality demands, inter alia, that the basic stipulations are contained in a formal (parliamentary) enactment (*Gesetz im formellen Sinne*).[83] The ordinance's comparative lack of democratic legitimation may also become a political burden when compared with parliamentary enactments.

[78] Cf. Kratz (2018), p. 46, 228 et seq.; Hettich et al. (2017), p. 177 et seq.; Schreiber (2019), p. 391.

[79] This term has been used, inter alia, in the context of product liability rules concerning innovative products; Zech (2016), p. 15 et seq.; Vieweg (2011), p. 337.

[80] Sailer and Reuter (2014), p. 13; Schreiber (2019), p. 390.

[81] Stewart (1981), p. 1275; Hoffmann-Riem (2011b), p. 316; Schreiber (2019), p. 75 et seq.

[82] Schreiber (2019), p. 392 et seq.

[83] For a discussion of the principle of legality in the context of energy law, see Jagmetti (2005), p. 108 et seq.; Petrik-Haltiner (2017), p. 14 et seq. In the context of innovation, see Schreiber (2019), p. 101 et seq.

4.4 Multi-Level Governance

Another important decision is whether the innovation should be regulated at the federal, cantonal or municipal level. Often, this decision will be shaped by the constitutional definition of competencies and responsibilities. However, some ground-breaking innovations may even justify changes to the constitutional framework, as was the case with nuclear energy in Switzerland. Where competing federal and cantonal competencies exist, the federal legislator must decide whether to act on its powers and therefore preclude conflicting cantonal rules.

One advantage of federal laws may be that the innovation will face the same legal framework in the entire country. This might help with standardisation and could increase investors' confidence. However, cantonal or municipal laws may have the benefit that several legal frameworks could compete with one another. "First-mover" cantons or municipalities would be able to implement new rules, which could then be observed by the others. This might enable a competition to see which rules best aid the innovation's implementation.

Cities are often especially interested in innovations and offer the advantage of many potential users who might adopt the innovation, as well as an advanced infrastructure. They thus seem like a well-suited "playground" for new innovations. It may therefore be desirable to allow cities to adopt specific rules to help with a new innovative project. This is only possible where federal and cantonal laws provide enough room for municipal enactments.

Despite the potential advantages of multi-level governance with regards to innovation, the Swiss energy sector has seen a steady development towards more centralised rules at the federal level in recent decades.[84] This calls into question to which degree these potential advantages may actually be exploited.

4.5 Public or Private Governing Bodies

In the absence of legislation, private bodies may offer a good alternative to implement rules on the innovation. Private governing bodies such as industry associations often have more information on the innovation than the legislator and they understand better how it might be implemented. They can therefore draft rules which fit the innovation very well.

However, the involvement of private governing bodies may also have disadvantages. For example, established industry associations may seek to hinder innovations that they regard as threatening to their business models.[85] For a simple thought experiment to illustrate this, just imagine the taxi drivers' union drafting rules on

[84] See Föhse (2021).

[85] Cf. Schreiber (2019), p. 86.

Uber.[86] The problem of incentives is exacerbated where private associations do not represent all market actors.[87]

In addition, private rule-making may raise questions as to the rules' validity. The existing legislation may be unclear on the subject of the innovation. When private associations implement rules, it becomes difficult to judge whether the law does indeed make stipulations on the innovation or whether there was sufficient room for the private body to create its own rules. This is the case for storage technology, where it seems questionable whether the VSE's rules are compatible with the existing laws.[88]

It is also worth noting that there is no strict dichotomy between private and public governing bodies. An example of this, which has been discussed here, is the safety regulatory agency for the electricity market, the *ESTI*, which was originally founded as part of a private technical association but which has now been granted powers similar to those of a government institution.

5 Conclusions

The governance perspective draws attention to the interplay of state and non-state actors at multiple vertical and horizontal levels. The discussion has shown that these factors also affect the relationship between law and innovation in the energy sector.

While some energy innovations were driven by legislation early on, others met a mostly passive legislator. In these cases, private governing bodies such as industry associations have played an important role in shaping the innovation's regulatory environment. The interplay between private and public actors becomes especially apparent when formerly private institutions are endowed with regulatory powers by the state, as was the case with the *ESTI*.

Innovation may be governed effectively at multiple vertical levels, which could lead to a competition between different cantons and municipalities as to the most innovation-friendly legal framework. However, a disadvantage is the potential patchwork of laws that might deter investments. Also, different priorities between the federal, cantonal and municipal level may cause problems, as was the case with photovoltaic installations. In recent years, the energy sector has witnessed a development towards more laws at the federal level, with less and less room for cantonal laws.

The "regulatory density" in the energy industry has increased significantly in the last few decades. For this reason, a legislative "wait-and-see" approach as favoured

[86] Regarding the regulatory environment for Uber in Switzerland, see Abegg and Bernauer (2018); Meier (2018); Riemer-Kafka and Studer (2017); Sieber-Gasser (2017).

[87] Cf. Schreiber (2019), p. 273 et seq.

[88] See Walther (2019), p. 30, on the one hand and Schreiber (2019), p. 267 et seq., 275, on the other hand.

during the early electrification may no longer be feasible. Where innovative technologies and business models meet legal provisions that were never intended to govern them, changes to the legal framework may be inevitable in order for the innovation to succeed.

Despite this apparent need for regulatory intervention, it is crucial to design technology-neutral rules that do not favour any specific innovation over another and that are open to future developments. Otherwise, laws and regulations may drive an inferior solution's success while blocking more innovative approaches.

References

Abegg A, Bernauer C (2018) Welchen neuen Regulierungsbedarf schaffen Airbnb, Uber & Co.? Aktuelle Juristische Praxis 27:82–88

Anderson B, Lin S, Newing A, Bahaj A, James P (2017) Electricity consumption and household characteristics. Comput Environ Urban Syst 63:58–67

Ashford NA, Hall RP (2011) The importance of regulation-induced innovation for sustainable development. Sustainability 3:270–292

Benz A (2004a) Governance. In: Benz A (ed) Governance – Regieren in komplexen Regelsystemen. VS Verlag, Wiesbaden, pp 11–28

Benz A (2004b) Multilevel Governance. In: Benz A (ed) Governance – Regieren in komplexen Regelsystemen. VS Verlag, Wiesbaden, pp 125–146

BET Dynamo Suisse (2014) Kosten und Nutzenaspekte von ausgewählten Technologien für ein Schweizer Smart Grid im Auftrag des Bundesamtes für Energie. Aachen, Zofingen

Bundesverband der Energie- und Wasserwirtschaft e.V. (BDEW), Ernst & Young GmbH (2015) Gewohnte Wege verlassen – Innovation in der Energiewirtschaft, Stadtwerkestudie Juni 2015. Dusseldorf

Citi M, Justesen MK (2014) Measuring and explaining regulatory reform in the EU. Eur J Polit Res 53:709–726

Eifert M, Hoffmann-Riem W (eds) (2002) Innovation und rechtliche Regulierung. Nomos, Baden-Baden

Electricity Commission (2011) Anfrage betreffend Kostentragung für Glasfasern für Smart Metering / Smart Grid, 952-11-025. Bern, available at https://www.elcom.admin.ch

Electricity Commission (2020) Fragen und Antworten zur Energiestrategie 2050, Bern

Federal Council (1957) Botschaft vom 26. April 1957 über die Ergänzung der Bundesverfassung durch einen Artikel betreffend Atomenergie und Strahlenschutz. Federal Gazette BBl 1957 I 1137

Federal Council (1958) Botschaft vom 8. Dezember 1958 betreffend den Entwurf zu einem Bundesgesetz über die friedliche Verwendung der Atomenergie und den Strahlenschutz. Federal Gazette BBl 1958 II 1521

Federal Council (2013) Botschaft vom 4. September 2013 zum ersten Massnahmenpaket der Energiestrategie 2050 (Revision des Energierechts) und zur Volksinitiative "Für den geordneten Ausstieg aus der Atomenergie (Atomausstiegsinitiative)". Federal Gazette BBl 2013 7561

Federal Department of the Environment, Transport, Energy and Communications (DETEC) (2018) Bundesgesetz über den Um- und Ausbau der Stromnetze (Strategie Stromnetze), Teilrevision der Stromversorgungsverordnung. Erläuternder Bericht, Bern

Föhse M (2021) Decentralisation of energy generation, centralisation of energy lawmaking. In: Hettich P, Kachi A (eds) Swiss energy governance. Springer, New York

Gattermann J (2012) Produktverantwortung nach dem Elektrogesetz und der Altfahrzeugverordnung. Kassel

Gerard D, Lave LB (2005) Implementing technology-forcing policies. Technol Forecast Soc Change 72:761–778
Gerber A (2019) Art. 12 Energiegesetz. In: Heselhaus S, Hänni J, Schreiber M (eds) Rechtsfragen der Energiewirtschaft. Dike, Zurich, St. Gallen, pp 77–106
Gugerli D (ed) (1994a) Allmächtige Zauberin unserer Zeit. Chronos, Zurich
Gugerli D (1994b) Der Ausbau der äussern Organisation. In: Gugerli D (ed) Allmächtige Zauberin unserer Zeit. Chronos, Zurich, pp 9–23
Gugerli D (1996) Redeströme. Chronos, Zurich
Haelg L, Schmidt TS, Sewerin S (2021) The design of the swiss feed-in tariff. In: Hettich P, Kachi A (eds) Swiss energy governance. Springer, New York
Hettich P (2014) Kooperative Risikovorsorge. Schulthess, Zurich
Hettich P (2015) Die Glühbirne – Lucifer neuer Zeiten. Schweizerisches Zentralblatt für Staats- und Verwaltungsrecht 116:567–588
Hettich P, Peng GL (2015) Erleichterte Bewilligung von Solaranlagen in der Rechtspraxis. Aktuelle Juristische Praxis 24:1427–1438
Hettich P, Walther S (2011) Rechtsfragen um die kostendeckende Einspeisevergütung (KEV) für Elektrizität aus erneuerbaren Energien. Schweizerisches Zentralblatt für Staats- und Verwaltungsrecht 112:143–171
Hettich P, Walther S, Wohlgemuth D, Camenisch L, Drittenbass J (2017) Strommarkt 2023: Quotenmodelle im Zieldreieck von Umweltverträglichkeit, Wirtschaftlichkeit und Versorgungssicherheit. Dike, Zurich, St. Gallen
Hewicker C, Raadschelders J, Werner O, Ebert M, Engelhardt C, Mennel T, Verhaegh N (2013) Energiespeicher in der Schweiz. SFOE, Bern
Hoffmann-Riem W (2011a) Die Governance-Perspektive in der rechtswissenschaftlichen Innovationsforschung. Nomos, Baden-Baden
Hoffmann-Riem W (2011b) Rückblick auf das Projekt "Recht und Innovation". In: Eifert M, Hoffmann-Riem W (eds) Innovation, Recht und öffentliche Kommunikation. Duncker & Humblot, Berlin, pp 295–321
Hoffmann-Riem W (2016) Innovation und Recht – Recht und Innovation. Mohr Siebeck, Tübingen
Hoffmann-Riem W, Schmidt-Assmann E (eds) (1994) Innovation und Flexibilität des Verwaltungshandelns. Nomos, Baden-Baden
Hoffmann-Riem W, Schneider J-P (1998a) Zur Eigenständigkeit rechtswissenschaftlicher Innovationsforschung. In: Hoffmann-Riem W, Schneider J-P (eds) Rechtswissenschaftliche Innovationsforschung. Nomos, Baden-Baden, pp 389–412
Hoffmann-Riem W, Schneider J-P (eds) (1998b) Rechtswissenschaftliche Innovationsforschung. Nomos, Baden-Baden
Jagmetti R (2005) Energierecht. Helbing & Lichtenhahn, Basel
Kötter M (2008) Rechtsordnung und Regelungsstrukturen. In: De La Rosa S, Höppner U, Kötter M (eds) Transdisziplinäre Governanceforschung. Nomos, Baden-Baden, pp 212–229
Kratz B (2018) Speicher als Schlüsselkomponente der Energiewende. Dike, Zurich, St. Gallen
McKenna E, Richardson I, Thomson M (2012) Smart meter data. Energy Policy 41:807–814
Meier A (2018) Risques de précarisation des travailleurs induits par les plateformes. Aktuelle Juristische Praxis 27:302–315
Müller G (2020) Wie steuert der Gesetzgeber die Verordnung? Schweizerische Juristen-Zeitung 116:47–53
Müller G, Vogel S (2012) Kompetenzverteilung zwischen Bund und Kantonen auf den Gebieten der Energie-, Umwelt- und Raumordnungspolitik. Erlinsbach, Fällanden
Murswiek D (1990) 2. Bericht. In: Ipsen J, Murswiek D, Schlink B (eds) Die Bewältigung der wissenschaftlichen und technischen Entwicklungen durch das Verwaltungsrecht. De Gruyter, Berlin, pp 207–234
Newing A, Anderson B, Bahaj A, James P (2015) The role of digital trace data in supporting the collection of population statistics. Populat Space Place 22:849–863
Nusser J (2010) Zwei Jahre EBPG. Zeitschrift für Umweltrecht 2010:130–136

Office of Technology Assessment (OTA) (1979) OTA Priorities 1979. Washington D.C
Petrik-Haltiner TS (2017) Spannungsfelder rund um die Stromkosten und -tarife. Schulthess, Zurich
Riemer-Kafka G, Studer V (2017) Digitalisierung und Sozialversicherung. Schweizerische Zeitschrift für Sozialversicherung und berufliche Vorsorge 11:354–384
Sailer F, Reuter S (2014) Rechtliche Rahmenbedingungen für Stromspeicher. VDI, Würzburg
Schreiber L (2002) Innovationsgeeignetheit von Technikrecht am Beispiel der Signaturregulierung. In: Eifert M, Hoffmann-Riem W (eds) Innovation und rechtliche Regulierung. Nomos, Baden-Baden, pp 216–263
Schreiber M (2019) Rechtliche Innovationssteuerung am Beispiel der Power-to-Gas-Stromspeichertechnologie. Schulthess, Zurich
Schuppert GF (2008) Governance. In: Schuppert GF, Zürn M (eds) Governance in einer sich wandelnden Welt. VS Verlag, Wiesbaden, pp 13–40
Sieber-Gasser C (2017) Wirtschaften im rechtlichen Graubereich. Zeitschrift für Europarecht 19:4–15
Sterner M, Stadler I (eds) (2017) Energiespeicher. Springer, Berlin
Stewart RB (1981) Regulation, innovation, and administrative law. California Law Rev 69:1256–1377
Swiss Federal Office of Energy (2018). Energy Strategy 2050. Available at https://www.bfe.admin.ch
Swiss Federal Office of Energy (2020) Faktenblatt Bundesgesetz für eine sichere Stromversorgung mit erneuerbaren Energien. Bern
Thaler P, Hofmann B, Abegg A, Bornemann B, Braunreiter L, Burger P, Dörig L, Ejderyan O, Heselhaus S, Opitz C, Petrovich B, Rinscheid A (2019) Schweizer Energiepolitik zwischen Bund, Kantonen und Gemeinden. SCCER CREST White Paper 7. Basel, St. Gallen
Trute H, Kühlers D, Pilniok A (2008) Governance als verwaltungsrechtswissenschaftliches Analysekonzept. In: Schuppert GF, Zürn M (eds) Governance in einer sich wandelnden Welt. VS Verlag, Wiesbaden, pp 173–189
Verband Schweizerischer Elektrizitätsunternehmen (VSE) (2017) Handbuch Speicher. Aarau
Vieweg K (2011) Produkthaftungsrecht. In: Schulte M, Schröder R (eds) Handbuch des Technikrechts. Springer, Berlin, pp 337–383
Walther S (2014) Kooperative Steuerungsinstrumente im schweizerischen Stromversorgungsrecht. Dike, Zurich, St. Gallen
Walther S (2019) Regulierung von Energiespeichern in der Schweiz. Dike, Zurich, St. Gallen
Wyssling W (1946) Die Entwicklung der schweizerischen Elektrizitätswerke und ihrer Bestandteile in den ersten 50 Jahren. SEV, Zurich
Zech H (2016) Haftungsregeln als Instrument zur Steuerung von "emerging risks". In: Fuhrer S (ed) Jahrbuch SGHVR 2016. Schulthess, Zurich, pp 1–23

Markus Schreiber is Senior Academic Assistant at the Center for Law and Sustainability, University of Lucerne, Lucerne, Switzerland.

Governance Drivers and Barriers for Business Model Transformation in the Energy Sector

Mary Jean Bürer, Matthieu de Lapparent, Massimiliano Capezzali, and Mauro Carpita

Contents

Abstract Smart second-generation policies for energy transition governance have been less studied and reviewed in the literature. They are also difficult to compare or measure in terms of their effectiveness with regard to the energy transition, not only because each country's objectives and underlying drivers for an energy transition are different. Technological innovation and new technology deployment are only the tip of the iceberg. Understanding how to redesign energy governance to allow for business model reconfiguration among incumbents and how to stimulate business

M. J. Bürer (✉) · M. de Lapparent · M. Capezzali · M. Carpita
Haute école d'ingénierie et de gestion du canton de Vaud, HES-SO, Yverdon-les-Bains, Switzerland
e-mail: maryjean.burer@heig-vd.ch; matthieu.delapparent@heig-vd.ch; massimiliano.capezzali@heig-vd.ch; mauro.carpita@heig-vd.ch

P. Hettich, A. Kachi (eds.), *Swiss Energy Governance*,
https://doi.org/10.1007/978-3-030-80787-0_10

model innovation by start-ups and new entrants is key for an effective and sustainable energy transition in the long term. However, beyond this, countries must address the underlying driving forces such as consumption patterns and the financial system. Therefore, business model transformation is not the only solution, but it is an important one and it requires well-designed policies. It also requires the involvement of all stakeholders at all levels of the economic fabric of each region and country. At the same time, we continue to measure progress on energy transitions in a superficial and extremely limited way. Policies must now be smarter, not just more ambitious in terms of appearances, and the measurement of energy transition progress must evolve as well. We discuss the full story of an energy transition to the extent possible in a single chapter. For example, we will review business models in different sub-sectors, policies that either block or promote such changes in each sub-sector chosen, and the elements that are necessary for energy transitions to become successful and sustainable without long-term government intervention and financial support. Finally, we also provide insights from an expert workshop held in 2019 and we outline our upcoming work on an Energy Transition Preparedness Index.

1 Introduction

There is no commonly accepted conceptual framework or unambiguous definition of energy transition and different timeframes and transition paths can be observed in different countries. It encompasses the political and increasingly social willingness to gradually phase out fossil energy resources in favor of low-emission sources, while putting in place measures for energy efficiency across all application sectors. However, besides these overarching objectives, there is no consensus on crucial aspects such as the time schedule of such a transition and its phasing, the role of state authorities, and the level of regulation. There is also no consensus on the very technologies that will indeed lead to the desired change. Addressing consumption patterns is also part of the solution but has not been a popular solution as countries continually seek economic growth and increasing purchasing power for their constituents. The place of natural gas and nuclear energy within the energy transition is vehemently disputed, within a broader discussion that also involves the need to decrease greenhouse gas (GHG) emissions, while satisfying expectations for continuous increases of purchasing power—a difficult nut to crack in any country.

A large number of studies have delved into the analysis of the conditions that could sustain the energy transition, covering a broad spectrum of possibilities from emerging technologies—e.g., in the field of energy storage or even new energy vectors such as hydrogen or methanol—to social behavior.[1] As is the case with any major change, the energy transition will not happen if it does not involve all the

[1]Rieple et al. (2019).

stakeholders at all levels of the economic fabric of each region and country. While certain measures can be sustained for a given period of time by state subsidies and policies—as has been the case in almost all industrialized countries with respect to renewable energy sources such as PV—, eventually the transition and its choices will gravitate towards clear market opportunities, those prospering without financial support mechanisms. Perhaps new, robust business models,[2] combined with innovative regulations, tariff structures and market design, and reductions in consumption can lead to a true transition and sustain it over time.

Creative uses of technological innovations, innovative business models, and proactive corporate sustainability strategies can sustain the energy transition. These tools apply to the supply side but also to the demand side, addressing consumption as much as possible. Research conducted in the past has shown that the success of the energy transition relies more on other factors (social or business-related) and not just on technological innovation.[3] The successful implementation of the energy turnaround thus requires business model innovation as one of the key drivers.[4] In the energy sector, business model innovation has increasingly become a priority for the long-term profitability of utilities.[5]

Various recent scientific works have looked at the role of business model innovation in supporting fundamental value propositions and value creation changes to promote the energy transition. Loock used choice experiments with investment managers for renewable energy to identify which business models could succeed in the market.[6] This work has provided some evidence that business models that focus on customers and that propose high-quality services are more attractive than business models oriented to low prices and state-of-the-art technologies. Richter explored existing business model approaches adopted by utilities with regard to renewable energy and found that utilities have developed viable business models for large-scale renewable energy generation but should invest further to take advantage of forthcoming business opportunities related to smaller distributed generation projects.[7]

Still business model innovation alone will have limited power to change things without corresponding policies that increase the potential for change among incumbents and the impetus for change from start-ups and new entrants. There is a chicken-and-egg problem where policies are needed to support decision-making on business model reconfiguration (among incumbents mostly); meanwhile, new business

[2]The most widely used definition is the one given by Osterwalder and Pigneur (2010), p. 14: "A business model describes the rationale of how an organization creates, delivers, and captures value".

[3]Boo et al. (2016).

[4]Boo et al. (2017).

[5]Castaneda et al. (2017) demonstrate the potential impact of renewable energy sources (RES) on electricity systems. The authors look in particular at how solar rooftop generation can be a threat to utilities.

[6]Loock (2012).

[7]Richter (2012, 2013).

models are needed first to stimulate such policy developments. Often these new business models come from start-ups and new entrants, but they themselves struggle with the lack of clear policy frameworks because they often rely heavily on strategic partnerships with incumbent energy players to succeed.

The more important step to support the change process seems to be to create the right policy frameworks that support business model change.

In interviews that were conducted with utilities and other key energy sector corporate players throughout the last 5 years, executives agreed across the board that new business models are needed for the energy transition but that these new models will not gain momentum unless new policies and measures that support and partly guarantee their success are also implemented. This is especially true when we speak about business model reconfiguration (when a company changes its existing business model to a new one). The energy sector is very dependent on regulatory frameworks. Some authors have looked at the entire spectrum of regulatory frameworks for supporting renewable energy.[8] Others have analyzed specific technologies that could enable the energy transition, like storage technologies.[9] Finally, the fact that new business models will have to be backed by supporting regulatory frameworks has been confirmed by other research, such as by Facchinetti et al.[10]

In our continuing work on the energy transition, we aim at measuring the preparedness level of countries and key economic actors with respect to the energy transition. We assume that a successful energy transition will require both business model reconfiguration and business model innovation. Both incumbents (existing players like utilities) and new stakeholders such as innovative start-ups exploring new technologies and approaches are among the actors that will shape the transition. In this chapter, we review new business models coming from start-ups and new entrants as well as areas where business model reconfiguration is happening among incumbents.

Some work already exists to categorize business models by sub-sector.[11] However, little work has tried to categorize business models by types of players. We will start this process by looking at business models that are most relevant to large incumbents on the one hand and business models that are more relevant to start-ups and new entrants on the other hand.

We then provide examples of policies or legislation that are either blocking business model developments or supporting such changes. The chapter is not able to provide a fully comprehensive view of all sub-sectors. Therefore, only a few

[8]Rubino et al. (2016).

[9]Broeckx et al. (2019).

[10]Facchinetti et al. identified favorable business conditions (that spurred investment in comprehensive business models) such as supportive policy scenarios, a growing economy, new development projects involving multiple energy carriers in areas characterized by a high building density, and target customers with a high willingness to pay (Facchinetti et al. 2016, p. 11).

[11]E. g. Burger and Luke (2016) review business models for Distributed Energy Resources (DER) and define business model archetypes for the three largest DER categories: demand response (DR) and energy management systems (EMS), electrical and thermal storage, and solar PV.

sub-sectors are explored, with some focus on the power sector and innovative solutions in this sector allowing for decentralized energy systems, increased flexibility, and optimization of such systems, e.g., via different options for storage or "smart" energy management.

This chapter also reviews the existing literature to understand what drives business model transformation in the energy sector. We are assuming that an energy transition of a country or region (at least for the average OECD or European country) typically requires both: (1) business model reconfiguration among incumbents and (2) business model innovation among start-ups and new entrants. Both kinds of business model change require sustainability strategies combined with business model innovation that can vary from reactive to proactive strategies. Schaltegger et al. review such reactive to proactive sustainability strategies and identify sustainability strategies that must be combined with business model innovation.[12] In order to better analyze business model changes in the context of the energy transition and understand what the antecedents for each kind of change are, we decided early in our research that it was important to obtain indicators for change related to two separate phenomena—business model reconfiguration and business model innovation.[13] We suppose that for an energy transition to happen rapidly and with economic success, we need policies and support mechanisms that stimulate and allow both kinds of business model change to occur and that enable synergies between the two.[14]

A good business environment for entrepreneurship and innovation of course supports business model innovation among start-ups and new entrants, but it also requires specific push factors relevant to the energy sector and the dynamics of each sub-sector where the business models apply. One of the key conditions is the right set of policies for a given country (regulations and new legislation), as well as on the regional level, and this is the focus of our work funded by the SCCER CREST, a consortium for socio-economic research on the energy transition in Switzerland.

Why is it important to look at this subject? We know a lot about technological innovation, but we know less about business model innovation. We are experimenting with it today—in real-time fashion. Many companies are even afraid of it, or at least very reluctant to engage in innovative market frameworks, especially

[12] Schaltegger et al. present three options for companies to combine strategic sustainability choices with business model innovation (Schaltegger et al. 2012, p. 110): "*Defensive strategies* with slight degrees of business model adjustment or adoption protect the current business model...; *[a] ccommodative strategies* go along with a change and some improvement of the business model, thus exerting some influence on business case drivers by experimenting within the current model...; [and] *proactive strategies* leading to (actual) business model redesign address many business case drivers strongly and continuously, with the effect of regular creations of business cases for sustainability."

[13] For definitions see Massa and Tucci (2014).

[14] For example, government support of start-ups with new business models can have a variety of effects: (i) incumbents can be encouraged to innovate and develop similar solutions, (ii) incentives can be created for incumbents to acquire innovative companies and internalize the innovation in their already existing business models, or (iii) innovation can inspire business model reconfiguration among incumbents.

in countries with uncertain and evolving regulatory conditions. They are afraid of how it may impact their business, which until today has been very stable and lucrative because of regulations that supported the "historical" business model based on maximizing the number of kWh of power or cubic meters of natural gas sold to final customers, while decreasing both CAPEX (capital expenditure) and OPEX (operating expenses) as far as possible.

1.1 Barriers for New Energy Transition Business Models

The energy system must confront several barriers (market and social, financial, regulatory, and innovation barriers) that slow down implementation towards a more sustainable energy structure. These barriers are explained in a report by Boo et al.[15] They explain that market and social barriers include the lack of knowledge, consumer engagement, and trust. The current system structure does not provide enough data to encourage consumers to change their behaviors. Innovative technologies such as smart meters and distributed generation can, however, enable customers to manage their own energy consumption. Another barrier is insufficient reference cases on new business models and approaches. Companies have a hard time to react when there are several new trends appearing at the same time and when uncertainty about the prospects of technologies or business models is high. Boo et al. also note that new business models face a difficulty in fitting the existing systems. There is a need for supporting infrastructures and technological changes. Internal management structures of large incumbent energy firms could add to the challenge. The implementation of new business models requires the collaboration of a number of different departments within a company that are likely to have different perspectives on change and to pursue their own objectives. There can be divisions between product and service developers or divisions between those who make investment decisions and those who supervise operations.

Financial barriers also hamper the transition. New financial models are therefore needed to meet investor needs and open up new pools of low-cost funds for energy projects. Other barriers mentioned in the literature are high upfront costs, especially for most energy efficiency measures that require more investment than conventional technologies. Decision-makers, including consumers such as private homeowners, might not be able or willing to make large upfront investments. In addition, it is difficult to access the necessary capital. A low return on investment is another barrier for new business models, especially for renewable technologies. Customers do not invest in renewable energy projects when the payback time is too long. Then, cumbersome regulation (and lack of clear legislation) is a clear barrier. The report by Boo et al. also describes restrictive rules that prevent companies from taking new approaches. In addition, permits for renewable energy installations are difficult to

---

[15] Boo et al. (2017).

obtain. In particular wind energy project developers in Switzerland face a significant policy risk premium in the pre-construction stage that obstructs investments.[16] Finally, there are innovation barriers, and with so many barriers to the innovation process, companies sometimes lose focus on market needs and the evolving needs of clients. Managements may have a historical bias and try to stick to the traditional business model for too long.[17]

1.2 Review of the Literature on the Energy Transition Progress

A recent report by the IEA on Energy Transition Indicators provides an overview of global energy investments and a comprehensive analysis that can be used for future work to develop an index showing the relative preparedness of countries for an energy transition. One point clearly made in this framework by the IEA is that one must look at data for the five underlying sectoral drivers (power generation, energy integration, industry, buildings, and transport) as well as both energy supply and energy demand indicators in order to assess the readiness of a country for an energy transition.[18] Focusing mainly on one part of the energy system, for example only the oil and gas sector, would be insufficient and could be misleading.

Furthermore, before trying to learn from existing assessments of energy transition progress, it is important to note that we must distinguish between developed markets that have substantial infrastructure lock-in to overcome and emerging markets, especially Sub-Saharan Africa, where technology leapfrogging is a distinct possibility.[19] Here we focus on the case of developed markets, those having infrastructure lock-in to overcome and entrenched business models supported by stable regulatory frameworks that have long existed. Indeed, energy transitions for countries where leapfrogging is possible require another focus and other policy frameworks. More research is needed in that area as well. In fact, an energy transition preparedness index is needed for such countries as well, but it is necessary to consider them separately. Mixing their energy transition analysis with that for developed countries could prove to be too challenging and lead to unsatisfactory results for all country types.

With regards to the energy transitions that most countries in developed markets are experiencing today, most work in the literature seems to focus on the transformation of markets in the short term. For example, Schleicher-Tappeser looks at how renewable energy will change the electricity markets in the next 5 years.[20] The

[16]Ebers Broughel and Wüstenhagen (2021).

[17]Boo et al. (2017).

[18]IEA (2019a).

[19]This difference is also emphasized by Smil (2010).

[20]Schleicher-Tappeser (2012).

author notes that increasing autonomy and flexibility of consumers challenge the top-down control logic of traditional power supply and push for a more decentralized and multi-layered system. The author explains that how rapidly and smoothly this transformation occurs depends largely on the adaptation speed of the regulatory framework and on the ability of market players to develop appropriate business models. Other pieces of work, such as Cross et al., have looked at progress in renewable energy and how this relates to targets in Europe.[21] Finally, some pieces of work have focused on specific market niches or specific applications and the opportunities they offer for increasing flexibility. Such developments could either create momentum towards a different type of energy system or simply allow our existing systems to operate more efficiently. The flexibility that "aggregators" offer to the existing system is an example for this.[22]

On the macro-level, energy transition assessments (and indicators) are now available from various international institutions like the IEA,[23] IRENA,[24] and the World Economic Forum.[25,26] Furthermore, other related indexes are valuable sources of energy- and policy-related indicators, such as the UN SDSN's SDG Index[27] and the 2019 SDG Index and Dashboards Report for European Cities.[28] However, individual institutes around the world also develop their own pieces of work evaluating countries' progress on the energy transition. It is important to provide a deeper analysis of countries' progress and movements towards an energy transition, sometimes with a smaller set of countries, and not just global assessments that tend to overlook important details and over-use aggregated data. An example of a deeper analysis undertaken with fewer countries is the work of the German *Forschungsstelle für Energiewirtschaft (FfE)* for a project called eXtremOS.[29] Researchers, of course, must accept a trade-off each time they start a project of

---

[21] Cross et al. (2015).

[22] An aggregator (also called a "virtual power plant") can create a sizable capacity similar to that of a conventional generator and it can operate many distributed renewable energy sources together. Aggregators can sell electricity or ancillary services in the wholesale market or in the system operator's ancillary services procurement. An aggregator contributes to the system's flexibility because it enables smoother integration of distributed energy resources into the power system (IRENA 2019a, p. 49).

[23] IEA (2019a).

[24] IRENA (2019a, b).

[25] The 2019 Energy Transition Index (ETI) "provides scores for 115 countries spanning the many dimensions of energy transition performance and enablers". The Index aggregates 40 energy transition indicators over these dimensions; this includes integrating information from data sources that describe country levels of energy pollution, prices, supply chains, infrastructure, political institutions, financial systems, human capital and more. "Country-specific scores are derived by normalizing the individual indicators and applying a weighting framework" (WEF 2019a, p. 9).

[26] Singh et al. (2019).

[27] Sachs et al. (2019).

[28] Lafortune et al. (2019).

[29] The main objective of this project was to investigate the value of flexibility related to European electricity market coupling (FFE 2020).

this type, between comprehensive treatment of countries, markets, and technology options as opposed to the deeper understanding brought by a focus on fewer elements.

There are various energy transition assessments that have a special focus, such as policy or climate pledge assessments. When it comes to policy reviews, the Regulatory Indicators for Sustainable Energy (RISE) benchmarks national policies and regulatory frameworks on energy access, energy efficiency, and renewable energy. Other pieces of work come from the IEA, PBL, and the Climate Action Tracker.[30]

What we found, however, is that few studies assess the capacity of countries for business model innovation (especially not as related to the energy sector). This is of course difficult to do with existing available indicators and data, but we must develop new approaches to take into account qualitative aspects that are so important for energy transitions, such as the ability to support business model change. One realization as we attempted to develop our own index to measure countries' progress on the energy transition and their preparedness for an energy transition is that just because an aspect cannot be easily tracked by available data and measured, this does not mean it should not be part of an assessment. Otherwise, if this were the case, countries (and companies) might tend to focus only on areas where measurement is possible, even if investing in other avenues would finally be more transformative. This dilemma is already hurting the reputation of Environmental, Social and Governance (ESG) reporting and other corporate sustainability reporting schemes.[31] The potentially negative influence of simplification (for communication purposes) on good decision-making does not only risk leading policy dialogues towards "quick fixes" that do not address the core problems of the system, but it also allows for an imbalanced importance of the media for consensus building and increases their power to influence the direction of political decisions, whether they are aware of it or not. The importance of the media and the need to manage governments' communications about their climate strategies ahead of time was demonstrated in Duygan et al.[32] Adding the needed complexity to existing index projects around the world,

[30]The IEA Policy and Measures databases offer access to information on energy-related policies and measures taken or planned to reduce greenhouse gas emissions, improve energy efficiency, and support renewable energy development and deployment. The PBL Netherlands Environmental Assessment Agency provides the Climate Pledge Nationally Determined Contribution (NDC) tool, which projects country-level emissions to 2030, under the scenario of full implementation of Paris Agreement NDCs and under the trajectory of current national climate and energy policies. Finally, the Climate Action Tracker tracks the emission commitments and actions of countries and provides an assessment of individual national pledges, targets and NDCs as well as currently implemented policies to reduce their greenhouse gas emissions (WEF 2018).

[31]Over the last years, many papers (e.g., Pojasek and Toolbox 2010; Hedstrom 2019) have looked at the counter-productive impacts of reporting schemes used today to measure corporate sustainability. Also, ESG reporting is shown to be taken-up by companies more due to a herding phenomenon, which means that companies that report are not driven to report for value creation purposes (Przychodzen et al. 2016). One could learn from this experience and avoid developing energy transition reporting tools that do not create real value for stakeholders.

[32]Duygan et al. (2021).

speaking about business model innovation as a key input for leadership, and not simply accepting an assessment just because it achieved consensus in a given industry setting is part of creating the appropriate dialogue needed for good policy-making around the energy transition.

1.2.1 Oil and Gas

According to the IEA's World Energy Investment Report of 2018, the oil and gas sector is changing for a number of reasons. The report states, for example, that there has been a broad shift in favor of projects with shorter construction times that limit capital at risk. In addition, the oil and gas sector is changing because people and investors are requesting it to change. The Oil and Gas Climate Initiative (OGCI), which brings together 13 of the world's top oil and gas companies, has pledged to reach its methane intensity target of 20% by 2025, and energy companies are increasingly shifting towards producing gas.[33] Power-to-X technology innovations also open up new opportunities for the oil and gas sector to integrate with the power sector and allow for business model change.

In the future, one could also imagine self-consumption communities or industrial parks working as microgrids and potentially producing excess energy that can be stored and traded. Hydrogen can store such excess electricity, for example. This would allow for revenue generation, even in the context of social housing projects if they operated on a renewable-based microgrid, using technologies to control and optimize demand and supply curves locally.[34]

The California Energy Commission (CEC) speaks about the experiences of several microgrid projects around the world. One of them is the ENGIE "Center of Excellence" microgrid in Singapore, where the most innovative aspect is probably the integration or use of hydrogen as an energy storage medium.[35] The report explains that the system is targeting off-grid customers.[36] Therefore, there are no opportunities for traditional revenue streams that are tied to the grid. However, the project proved the ability to use excess renewable energy to create hydrogen fuel for transportation. Of course, for any future microgrid project, stored hydrogen could be a potential revenue stream for other applications in the local, or regional, economy. Selling hydrogen for local ground or marine transportation could be one revenue stream. In terms of other areas of transition, energy efficiency has changed the game

[33] Bousso (2018).

[34] Cases and business models for microgrid projects, sometimes integrating the production of hydrogen or other products, have been studied by several research projects. One was conducted for the State of California in 2018 (CEC 2018), and more cases have emerged more recently around the world such as in Sweden (Ali 2019).

[35] Excess renewable energy generated from wind and solar is converted into hydrogen via electrolysis. Some of this hydrogen is diverted to motor vehicles, with the residual hydrogen combusted in a fuel cell.

[36] CEC (2018).

too. Prices for some efficient goods have continued to fall, and many energy efficient investments are already cost-effective with relatively short payback periods.

More innovative business model changes are also happening in this sector, and a transition from oil to gas is apparent in many countries around the world, having an important impact on carbon emissions; however, critics say the industry is not doing enough.[37] Some examples of more innovative business models being explored at least by certain companies are: (in the mobility business) capturing value by switching to a services model as opposed to today's traditional model of selling fuel for transportation, for example, by charging customers per kilometer, irrespective of the type of energy supplied.[38]

Some companies are exploring the possibility of "independent retailers". Such companies will not necessarily be involved in production activities, but they might engage in new activities including commercializing fuels, LPG and/or electricity.[39] Different business models will emerge. The authors of a recent report on the future of oil companies predict that many of the International Oil Companies (IOCs) will move in the direction of "energy holding" companies, while some large National Oil Companies (NOCs) may try to prolong their existence through scale advantages in the model of an "XXL oil company".[40] The report also notes that IOCs with limited access to fossil resources and high exposure to environmental topics and customer preferences will lead the "surpassing petroleum" trend.[41]

---

[37] Bousso (2018).

[38] Monzon et al. (2019), p. 68.

[39] They can also increasingly commercialize these fuels together with non-energy products and services. In fact, the value of an international brand for fuel retailing may be limited today (Monzon et al. 2019, p. 66). This is due to competitive barriers to capturing margins from new products and services at petrol stations that are largely owned by third parties. These factors represent major challenges for players that aspire to maintain their growth rates and levels of return on the capital employed. To remain competitive, a strong innovation capability is therefore needed in the sector to develop differentiated and viable customer-centric solutions.

[40] Monzon et al. (2019), p. 66.

[41] Monzon et al. (2019), p. 59.

The Coronavirus and the Impacts of the Oil Shock of 2020 As we are writing this chapter in March 2020, the coronavirus is rampaging country by country, and many analysts are trying to understand what could be the implications of the virus on the global economy. One of the sectors that is already affected is the energy sector. At first the renewable energy sector was affected (China holds elevated weight in the industry's supply chain), but the oil and gas markets were affected via the impact on demand for transport fuels, too. This worsened due to uncoordinated supply management among the largest oil producing countries. Some fear that meeting energy transition goals will become even more challenging all around the world, and especially in continents like Africa, if oil prices remain low. On the other hand, it is difficult to predict what will happen. Lower oil prices also could lead countries to undertake fossil fuel subsidy reforms more easily.[42] Nevertheless, after the coronavirus became a global pandemic in March 2020, some started to predict that the oil shock of 2020 would lead to further challenges with regard to meeting countries' energy transition goals.[43]

New business models for cleaner energy systems will help, but if oil is very cheap, even the best efforts to support business model innovation for clean energy sources will have a limited impact. The only way out of this problem is strict policies to support such business models for the energy transition, but this can hardly be expected in many developing countries, especially after a coronavirus pandemic and the various economic fallouts related to it. On the other hand, in certain countries some smaller markets may still boom. For example, today the off-grid solar market is booming around the world. 600 million people in Sub-Saharan Africa are currently without power.[44] Lease models or what are called "pay-as-you-go" models for stand-alone systems and other new business models combined with such technologies will most likely still have a market in Africa. Energy efficiency and business models for energy savings may have less uptake, but they will be valid in all cases, no matter which fuels dominate markets in the future. However, issues like transportation will become increasingly difficult to address all around the world if fuel prices are too low. The key to transportation is indeed to reduce the need for transportation or lower consumption, but we have seen how

(continued)

[42] Merrill et al. explain that it became easier to reform fossil fuel subsidies in the past when oil prices were low (IISD 2017, p. 2).

[43] Montgomery (2020).

[44] Sioshansi (2018).

countries have responded to low oil prices in terms of consumption patterns and choice of vehicle (e.g., the rise in SUV sales in the United States after the oil price collapse of 1986).[45] As we are writing this, we also hope that COVID-19 will not lead to a global economic downturn, resulting in job losses and potentially political and social unrest. We know that during economic downturns people can develop attitudes that help to fuel unrest, terrorism, or even war.[46] The energy transition will be more than a second priority under such scenarios.

1.2.2 Power Generation and Flexibility Markets

While there are many aspects that we cannot cover in one chapter, it is clear that in almost any energy transition the power sector integrates a high amount of renewable energy. In a report by IRENA, the importance of power system flexibility is highlighted.[47] The Association for Renewable Energy & Clean Technology (REA) evaluates a select number of countries regarding their flexibility services and other related transition factors.[48] These are specifically transition factors regarding flexibility that can predict readiness for an energy transition at least for power generation in a given country. The transition factors considered by REA are market access, socio-political support, and technology potential. Regarding market access one aspect that REA attempts to measure is whether regulation enables fair access for all providers. With regard to socio-political support, REA looks at whether flexibility needs are recognized but also if there is a supportive political and public consensus and if public policy and regulation are aligned. Finally, regarding technology potential, REA takes into account if the country enables grid accessibility, EV infrastructure deployment, digitalization, and innovation.

According to REA, power systems must be able to operate in circumstances where renewable energy output may vary significantly from hour to hour. As generators are replaced by renewable energy generation with more volatile outputs,

---

[45] Gately (1986).

[46] Liu (2018).

[47] The report (IRENA 2018, p. 23) notes: "A power system can be considered flexible if it can cost-effectively, reliably and across all time scales: (1) Meet the peak loads and peak net loads, avoiding loss of load. (2) Maintain the balance of supply and demand at all times, and ensure the availability of sufficient capability to ramp up and down, the availability of sufficient fast-starting capacity and the capability to operate during low net loads. (3) Have sufficient storage capacity . . . to balance periods of high VRE generation and periods of high demand but low VRE generation. (4) Incorporate capabilities to adjust demand to respond to periods of supply shortages or over generation."

[48] REA (2019). REA is the Association for Renewable Energy and Clean Technology in the UK. It is a not-for-profit trade association established in 2001 and a coalition built to be the voice for renewable energy and clean technology in the UK, with 550 member organizations representing every type of renewable energy.

new providers of flexibility services are emerging, including distributed generation, energy storage, and demand response.[49] However, providers face barriers such as limitations to access flexible power markets.

1.2.3 Coal

To measure any energy transition progress, it is key to look at how coal-fired power generation is phasing out or continuing. The IEA tracks coal-fired power and reports on trends.[50] It found that coal generation in Asia—particularly China and India—increased significantly, but it fell elsewhere, including in the United States and Europe. Coal remains the largest source of electricity generation worldwide, with a share of 38%.

The report notes that coal-fired power generation in the United States continued to drop in 2018 (by 60 TWh) despite strong electricity demand growth, as 15 GW of coal capacity were retired. As for Europe, coal generation also decreased (by 20 TWh), mainly because of strong renewables-based expansion. Some countries have announced coal phase-outs: Germany, the largest coal consumer in Europe, plans to be coal-free by 2038. However, many believe this is too late. Despite the complexity of the situation, involving job losses in parts of the country, the German public approves of the way the government has decided to deal with the coal and nuclear phase-out.[51]

In this book chapter, we consider business model change opportunities and policies to support these changes for different sub-sectors. For coal, the best option is perhaps not to innovate the business model that makes coal investments work but to rather slowly phase out of coal; but every country will have its strategy on what to do and how to do this. In the future, geopolitical changes may even make coal investments more attractive for some countries. As for those that are phasing out of coal, there are different strategies for dealing with such phase-outs.

Historically, the traditional utility business model of selling electricity from large-scale thermal power plants and expanding grids to meet rising demand has supported strong balance sheets. In many markets, utilities serve as reliable purchasers of power, and this facilitates investments by independent power producers. However, today, as we face other priorities including climate change, air pollution, and the energy transition, such investment decisions are becoming more complex. The business model is simply less attractive than in the past. However, regulatory frameworks can sometimes maintain business models which would otherwise

[49] REA (2019), p. 4.

[50] IEA (2019b).

[51] A look at the public approval of the energy transition law in Germany provides interesting insights. Referring to a study by the Potsdam Institute for Advanced Sustainability Studies (IASS), Wehrmann and Wettengel (2019) point out that "a surprising finding was that support for coal phase-out now enjoyed similar support as a nuclear phase-out, with approval by 63 percent of the population."

phase out on their own for economic reasons. How the business models of utilities interact with policies and market designs (including those that are now finally changing) will have huge implications on a country's energy and climate change goals, especially when it comes to large-scale investment decisions like whether to invest in and build new coal-fired power plants or not.

Decades ago, Europe started with the unbundling of vertically integrated companies and the establishment of wholesale markets and retail competition. In recent years, the success of energy efficiency contributed to weaker electricity demand, policies supporting renewables prompted competition from independent power companies, and other challenges emerged. In short, these changes have weakened price signals for investment in traditional energy projects (from energy-only markets) and reduced the profitability of existing generation assets that are dependent on wholesale market revenues.[52]

Today, innovations in the energy sector, such as virtual power plants allowing bilateral power exchange and increased roles for consumers and third parties to provide energy, capacity and flexibility services, facilitate new business models and allow for the reconfiguration of existing business models in the sector. New ways of trading energy are also emerging. For example, peer-to-peer (P2P) trading encourages more renewable energy distributed generation installations and increased local use of energy resources. However, the regulatory treatment—for example, regarding grid usage charges—must still evolve strongly before large-scale implementation of P2P trading would be likely to provide any benefits to consumers.[53] If P2P trading of energy were allowed and self-consumption communities were further developed, increasingly one could imagine a scenario where central thermal power plants will be humanity's energy solution of the past. Such thermal generation will have completely new economics in the case of increased carbon pricing and once the power market and its mechanisms evolve over time. New technologies, such as battery storage even for on-grid storage, electric vehicles offering opportunities for distributed storage, and other electrification trends have the potential to change investment needs and approaches, thus opening up new opportunities but also creating a completely different system to work with. These factors raise a number of uncertainties for thermal power plants. However, today experiments with alternative systems are still not sufficient, and only a few countries[54] are experimenting with the latest technologies such as P2P trading for the time being.

[52] IEA (2017).

[53] IRENA (2019a), p. 49.

[54] For example, countries where P2P projects are in place include: Bangladesh (SOLShare), Germany (Lumenaza, sonnenCommunity), the Netherlands (Vandebron, Powerpeers), the UK (Piclo – Open Utility), and the United States (TransActive Grid) (IRENA 2019a, p. 49).

1.3 The Impact of Digitalization

Digitalization is transforming every sector of the economy. Energy is no different. However, the way energy will be transformed by digitalization is likely to be more thought-through. The energy system requires reliable systems that have been well tested due to its high importance to all the sectors of any economy. In Bürer, de Lapparent, Pallotta et al., we elaborated on the risks that applying blockchain to the energy sector could impose on the electricity system and the caution needed as the reliability of service is so important for this sector. Meanwhile, there are many benefits to the energy transition if we increasingly take advantage of digitalization, for example with regard to energy efficiency. A range of challenging issues must be addressed if the world is to harness digitalization for greater energy efficiency.

1.3.1 Business Model Change Due to Digitalization in the Power Sector

Digitalization can convert data into value for the power sector. The application of digital monitoring and control technologies in the power generation and transmission domains has been an important trend for several decades. Switzerland aims to modernize its economy and society by embracing digitalization and plans to take a leading role in this domain. The Swiss digitalization action plan resonates with the Energy Strategy 2050, which supports (i) the optimization of the power system as opposed to only investing in traditional grid enforcement and (ii) the electrification and decentralization of the energy system through digitalization.

Wider usage of smart meters and sensors, the application of the Internet of Things and the use of large amounts of data with artificial intelligence have created opportunities to provide new services to the system. Digital technologies support the transformation of the power sector in several ways, including better monitoring of assets and their performance, operations that are more refined and control closer to real time, the implementation of new market designs, and the emergence of new business models.[55]

Several recent reports have put the grid in the center of the power system and discussed the issue of digitalization. Digital technologies can provide solutions for the energy transition because they can be used to (1) allow for better flexibility in energy systems, but also (2) to reduce energy intensity. For example, two reports from IRENA and the World Economic Forum (WEF) have recently underlined these aspects. IRENA indicates digitalization as a major driver for innovation and as a solution to energy sector challenges.[56] Meanwhile, a WEF report[57] calls for attention to the interconnectivity of the power system, in terms of both grid elements and

[55] IRENA (2019a), p. 31.

[56] IRENA (2019a).

[57] WEF (2019b).

associated stakeholders. It also brings to light what impact a breach in the grid, physical or cyber, can have on an entire economy and society.

Digital technologies like those used for communications, smart meters, and IT systems are considered as enabling technologies for flexibility markets and therefore for the integration of renewables into the energy system. In a report by REA, experts were asked about various aspects supporting energy transition preparedness in nine European flexible power markets. The report comes to the following conclusion:

> In high scoring countries, digital technologies i.e. communications, dispatch, smart meters, data standards, and IT systems across markets, are a key enabler for flexibility markets. In lower scoring markets not all this digital infrastructure is in place.[58]

The IEA believes digitalization will also impact energy intensity. IEA's "Energy Efficiency 2019" provides an overview of where every country stands and how well countries have done with regard to energy intensity.[59] Beyond that, their emphasis on digitalization as an enabler is of special interest to us. There is a benefit from digitalization; however, it must be said that there can also be a cost to digitalization in that digital technologies also consume energy. The report looks at various reasons for the recent deceleration in energy efficiency progress, including the increasing use of digital technologies around the world. However, the authors mostly focus on ways in which digitalization is transforming energy efficiency and increasing its value. The report explains that, through multiplying the interconnections between systems, digitalization enables benefits from such interconnections (among buildings, appliances, equipment and transport systems) to be tracked and efficiency gains to be measured and valued more quickly and accurately than before.

Finally, the IEA has identified a set of critical policy considerations within its new Readiness for Digital Energy Efficiency policy framework. This policy framework is designed to ensure that the benefits of digital energy efficiency are realized through policies that address a range of issues. These range from balancing data accessibility with data privacy to helping remove regulatory barriers to innovation. The framework also mentions policies to "encourage technology and business model innovation".[60]

Advancements in the decentralization of energy systems and electrification have made digitalization more relevant over the last years. The many new assets (such as many small generators on the supply side and many new loads from the electrification of heat and transport on the demand side) have an impact on the power system and make management and control very important for the energy transition and its success. Digitalization can therefore enable the management of large amounts of data and optimize systems with many small generation units.[61]

---

[58] REA (2019), p. 5.

[59] IEA (2019c).

[60] IEA (2019c).

[61] IRENA (2019c), p. 16.

According to the report by IRENA, digitalization allows for enhanced communication, control and eventually automated smart contracts based on blockchain technology[62] that will allow distributed energy resources to be bundled by "aggregators".[63] The authors say that digitalization will also enable enhanced controllability—if assets could be controlled remotely and used for demand response—, behind-the-meter generation, home energy management, and electric vehicles (EVs). Finally, the authors believe that digitalization can increase flexibility and enhance the ability to accommodate the intermittency of renewables. The report also explains that digital technologies unlock the flexibility from different sources. For example, the cost of grid integration can be cut by better managing various devices such as EVs, battery management systems, demand response, and other devices that intelligently control solar generation for daytime loads and storage for night-time uses.[64]

The Internet of Things (IoT) also allows for data hub developments to support electricity retail markets and other innovations.[65] The IoT enables real-time communication through the Internet, across the grid, and facilitates information gathering and exchange. It also facilitates exchange of information among devices in electricity demand centers (such as homes or commercial and industry facilities). According to IRENA, the IoT, together with optimization algorithms, could increase system flexibility by enabling remotely managed and/or rapid automatic changes in distributed resources and demand.[66] IoT can also allow for improved renewable energy forecasting and trading and decreasing uncertainty.[67]

In this area of digitalization and with regards to new business models, it is possible that the combination of new technologies (like blockchain) and new policies such as those that allow the trading of energy savings can lead to new business model opportunities.

Otherwise, in terms of trading energy, digital solutions, such as those based on blockchain, can also be applied. Currently, the most uncertain application for energy is peer-to-peer energy trading. However, business models that enable distributed energy resources to provide services to the grid are much stronger so far.[68] As for

---

[62] Blockchain is a distributed ledger technology that can be used to securely record all transactions taking place on a given network. Blockchain potentially allows: (1) increased direct trading and sharing of verifiable information, removing the need for the middleman and enabling newer / lower-cost operating models on a smaller scale; (2) flexibility in the system, enabling decentralized flexible energy sources to provide services to the electricity grid; (3) new markets and transactions with products with a certified and trustable energy footprint; and (4) potential cyber security benefits, IRENA (2019a), p. 46.

[63] IRENA (2019c), p. 16.

[64] IRENA (2019a), p. 45.

[65] NordREG (2018).

[66] IRENA (2019a), p. 45.

[67] IRENA (2019a), p. 45.

[68] Bürer et al. (2019) look at different use cases for blockchain in the energy sector and provide insights on the key risks and opportunities for blockchain in light of the energy transition.

peer-to-peer energy trading, blockchain technology allows transactions to be facilitated differently. Today they are facilitated by third parties, suppliers and system operators, whose main tasks are centrally compiling information on loads and generation or contracting supply and distribution services. Blockchain technology enables new ways of organizing decentralized persons without the immediate need for one centrally connecting entity, as explained in Diestelmeier.[69] However, this implies profound legal and policy consequences. Meanwhile, more research is needed and a better understanding is required regarding the potential of blockchain to enable a very different management system for electrical energy.[70] Diestelmeier identifies those main policy implications for EU electricity law and thereby adds to the discussion on how blockchain technology could facilitate "prosumers" to develop as independent market participants in the electricity sector from an energy law perspective.[71]

Finally, digitalization leading to more streaming, data centers, data networks, and other uses such as bitcoin also brings questions about increasing energy consumption from digitalization, and it must be managed properly in order for a country to be a leader in the energy transition.[72]

Digitalization offers some hope to companies that struggle (or will struggle) with the economic threats that come from potentially too rapid scenarios for the energy transition. This is explained in a WEF White Paper that provides examples of sectors and specific firms that suffered major losses after disruptions (e.g., GE that lost two-thirds of its capitalization in 2018 after it had to take a major write-down of its turbines division).[73] Digitalization has provided hope to such firms in some cases: "[R]ecent history has also shown that many incumbents, especially in the electricity sector, have been able to change business models and investment strategies to take advantage of new opportunities centered more around energy services to customer, renewables and the digitalization of energy."[74]

1.3.2 Business Model Change Due to Digitalization in the Mobility Sector

In Europe, data is available on electric vehicle charging points,[75] electrified rail lines,[76] private expenditure in R&D in transport,[77] the share of renewable energy in

69 Diestelmeier (2019), p. 189.

70 Bürer et al. (2019).

71 Diestelmeier (2019), p. 194.

72 Nouyrigat (2019).

73 WEF (2019c).

74 WEF (2019c), p. 24.

75 The Netherlands being the leader in this area, followed closely by Denmark.

76 Luxembourg, Belgium, the Netherlands, Sweden and Austria being leaders.

77 Germany being a clear leader here.

transport fuel consumption and the market share of electric passenger cars[78] and more. You can easily evaluate countries based on many indicators for which data is currently collected.[79] However, the mobility sector is quickly changing, pushed by new technologies, including digital technologies, new business models and a young generation that does not necessarily see the value in owning a car. Meanwhile, it is more difficult to measure and track business model innovation by country for this sector. One could track the uptake of digital technologies for the transportation sector, but it is more difficult to track new business models.

Navigant has put out a white paper that explains the concept of "value stacking" where business models are combined for innovative mobility concepts.[80] In this report, different business model options are reviewed from "infrastructure developer", "charging service provider" and "load orchestrator" to "mobility provider". The report comes to the conclusion that in the near term, data sharing between policymakers, utilities, and fleet operators could help anticipate needs for charging infrastructure as mobility service fleets electrify.[81] In terms of new business models facilitated by digital technologies or smart-grid control systems, several options and related business models are being conceived to support vehicle-to-grid (V2G) concepts, where EVs are integrated intelligently into microgrids and sometimes even used for distributed storage.[82]

Finally, a recent report by the European Joint Research Center (JRC) looks at the role of Distribution System Operators (DSOs) in Europe in the development of smart grid solutions.[83] This study looks at the charging stations implemented by DSOs. As the report says, remarkably, the vast majority of the DSOs in the dataset are not owners of the charging points.

> 10% of the DSOs with charging points in their territory have mentioned that they own a percentage of them. More than half of these DSOs operate less than the 9% of the charging points. It is expected that the number of charging points will increase in the close future with the expected increase of EVs. So far, the trend has been increasing.[84]

[78] Sweden being a clear leader in these two areas.

[79] European Commission (2019).

[80] Navigant (2019).

[81] This report and a report by the IEA (IEA 2019d) also speak about the intensive and distinct use patterns of shared and/or automated fleets. These use patterns imply higher (and different) needs for charging compared to private EVs. The availability and coverage of public and fast chargers could be a critical factor in how quickly these fleets become electric and how business models evolve around shared and/or automated mobility.

[82] It may also be worth mentioning that HEIG-VD is currently involved in a collaborative project with Planair, an energy consulting company. HEIG-VD has been charged to study and help industry stakeholders develop new business models in the context of V2G for a microgrid consisting of an innovation park where solar PV installations on the buildings provide power and EVs could provide distributed storage capacity to manage the microgrid.

[83] Prettico et al. (2019).

[84] Prettico et al. (2019), p. 56.

The fact that the charging points are mostly owned by other entities shows that business model change is potentially driven by forces outside the DSOs' own innovation ecosystem. Policies to support new business models using digital technologies from start-ups and new entrants in the mobility sector could be an important policy strategy to pursue at this time, at least in the short term. In addition, policies and funding programs allowing for experimentation (sandboxes) for the application of digital technologies in the mobility sector, preferably programs matching incumbents with start-ups, could allow for further exploitation of potential gains from digital technologies in the mobility sector.

2 Exploring the Regulatory Framework for Business Model Change

Policy framework conditions to achieve business model reconfiguration—i.e., changes in the business models of Distribution System Operators (DSOs), Distribution Network Operators (DNOs), and Transmission System Operators (TSOs)—are going to be different from the policy framework conditions that support business model innovation by start-ups, spin-offs, and new entrants. The same is the case for incumbents of the transportation sector (automakers, oil and gas distributors, retailers of vehicles, and traditional firms in public transport) versus start-ups with new business models in this field (e.g., start-ups offering car sharing with or without electric vehicles and charging infrastructure, regional bus companies offering new mobility services).

Furthermore, it is a combination of policies that is needed and a well coordinated set of policies so that there are no extensive unintended impacts on other innovations. One of the ways to block business model reconfiguration or innovation beyond local or individual developments is via uncoordinated policy frameworks for individual sub-sectors, as is currently the case for biomethane because each country has different biogas regulations and agreements are missing.[85] Meanwhile, each country must develop policies that match local needs and that correspond to the level of awareness of consumers.

The energy transition simply requires the participation of all stakeholders and this is why new approaches are needed to address this challenge, such as design thinking, co-creation, and systems thinking. This also means moving well beyond just carbon pricing, although carbon pricing has created important incentives to move away from fossil fuel energy sources and reduce consumption. In June 2019, 57 carbon pricing initiatives were implemented or scheduled for implementation.[86] Such developments are helpful as indirect market-pull measures; however, more direct

[85] Mediavilla et al. (2013).

[86] This consists of 28 emission trading systems (ETS) in regional, national and subnational jurisdictions and 29 carbon taxes, primarily applied on a national level. In total, these carbon

market-push and market-pull measures are needed now, especially those supporting business model innovation that has the potential to transform the industry while creating opportunities for growth.

We divide our discussion into examples of policies blocking business model developments and policies promoting business model developments for both actors (incumbents and start-ups or new entrants). Due to the limited space of this book chapter, we focus more on power generation and in particular on renewable energy. Therefore, an in-depth assessment including all sub-sectors cannot be provided. An overview of some business model innovation successes (and failures) in the transportation sector can be found in a paper by Wells.[87] In this paper, we explore progress with regard to business model changes in the area of electric vehicle charging.

Finally, we will discuss the results from our workshop and conclude with findings relevant to our ongoing work—the development of an Energy Transition Preparedness Index (the first version of which will be launched in 2021).

2.1 The Context for Business Model Change for DSOs in Europe

According to the IEA, electricity sector investments have a strong relationship with government policies. Furthermore, according to the IEA, around three-quarters of utility earnings now stem from segments that offer more stable and predictable cash flows, such as networks and generation (e.g., renewables, co-generation, and some thermal power plants) that benefit from contracted or regulated pricing.[88] European utilities are strategically re-orienting their businesses to adapt to the situation. Utility planning now emphasizes themes around business model transformation, enhanced operational efficiency, and improved financial management.

The European electricity industry association has also called for a new strategic vision for the sector. However, this ongoing change has not yet resulted in an earnings boost, according to the IEA. They explain that one reason is that business models for grids and renewables are capital-intensive, requiring continuous investment over time to expand revenues.[89] Some EU member countries also have trouble meeting their renewable energy targets because support levels offered for renewable energy sources are too low and may be below long-term marginal costs. Also, there

pricing initiatives cover 11 gigatons of carbon dioxide equivalent (GtCO2 e) or about 20% of global GHG emissions (CPLC 2020).

[87] Wells (2015).

[88] IEA (2017).

[89] IEA (2017).

is sometimes insufficient electricity grid capacity to integrate renewable energy sources.[90]

Meanwhile, as for investment capabilities, European utilities are increasing their expenditures. In November 2017, six utilities collectively called on the European Union to support a strengthened renewable energy target of 35% by 2030, compared with an originally proposed target of 27%.[91] At the same time, the electricity sector has also witnessed rapid growth in new, less capital-intensive business models that leverage digital technologies to provide system and consumer services.[92] However, current regulations do not necessarily provide the incentives for such investments and the value proposition for utilities, developers, and system operators is still not clear.

A report by the European Joint Research Center (JRC) also provides an overview of the situation of DSOs in Europe.[93] The context for business model transformation in the energy sector is very complex and different in each country. Some DSOs have the capacity for lower transaction costs under certain new business model scenarios, while others will have clearly higher transaction costs for certain technological innovations and business model opportunities until the framework conditions change. Others can benefit from scale and from their scope (and importance) in the country, allowing for creativity to develop into new business opportunities. Some countries allow sandboxes for experimentation. Other DSOs can more easily utilize synergies with network investments. There is no one-size-fits-all solution to developing regulations (and legislation) for business model innovation, but experiences in one country can be used in another to allow for increasingly intelligent policy-making over time. Some policies will open up opportunities for new entrants to play a role in offering services to individual communities, and perhaps other countries will develop policies allowing for start-ups to bring in new technologies and business models where incumbents continue to maintain their connection to the customer.

---

[90] Ali et al. (2017).

[91] Reuters (2017).

[92] One model is the Virtual Power Plant (VPP) model that aggregates and trades small-scale energy resources on wholesale markets and provides coordinated balancing and ancillary services to grid operators. Asset-light business models of this kind can limit the network size to meet peak demand and have the potential to defer expensive future capital upgrades; see IEA (2017).

[93] See Prettico et al. (2019).

2.2 Policies Blocking Business Model Developments

2.2.1 For the Electric Power Sector

The electric power sector includes many sub-sectors where important innovation is happening with regard to the energy transition and where policies can support, or block, innovations including business model innovation.

The Case of Microgrids and Local Energy Ownership Models

Many types of barriers exist for microgrids, from infrastructure to technical barriers, to public acceptance and environmental issues, to economic, market and financial barriers. But it is the regulatory and administrative barriers that remain the over-arching issue for microgrids. Administrative issues can arise from the length, complexity and non-transparency of permitting procedures or from the lack of clear responsibilities and skills within the local and national authorities. In many countries, microgrids as energy distribution systems are still within a grey area in terms of regulation and legal status.

> [T]here are no specific policies and regulations formulated for distributed generation (DG) and microgrid (MG) systems in the European Union. Each EU member state transposes the mentioned directives following the particularities of their national energy policies and regulatory frameworks for the promotion and development of renewable energies and microgrid systems.[94]

In Europe, managing a local distribution grid is a regulated activity. There are specific rules about who is allowed to deal with these configurations and in which cases. Completely islanded or grid-connected microgrids both represent a new development for energy regulators because they will entail updating the rules of the game. At the same time, regulators will need to completely reform the electricity tariff system that was established years ago for very centralized systems.

In a report by Gancheva et al. for the EC, lessons for local energy ownership models and an analysis of key barriers are also provided. The report explains that the first barrier relates to the legal standing of community energy, i.e., the constraints imposed by national legal frameworks that limit the conditions under which an energy community can be formed and operate. For example, securing access to the national electricity grid is vital for community energy projects. Examples showed that the costs, delays, and uncertainty associated with connection to the grid represent major barriers for groups developing community energy projects. Rules about the operation and connection of renewable energy sources and their systems in general affect the development of RE communities. As was shown in Germany, granting powers to local authorities by the national law helped the success of community energy in the federal states (*Bundesländer*). Therefore, the report

[94] Ali et al. (2017), p. 6.

concludes that clear definitions and rules are needed while keeping some flexibility in order to allow the various models of local energy ownership to flourish.[95]

The Case of Storage

Regulatory support for storage can be expected to vary around the world, but many feel it is a game changer for renewables and should be supported by specific policy frameworks. In a report by STORY, a Horizon 2020 funded project,[96] the authors explain that our energy system will have to tap into much-needed sources of flexibility if the EU's ambitious target of 32% renewables by 2030 is to be met. Energy storage will be a part of the mix to ensure the effective integration of intermittent renewable energy sources while maintaining grid stability. Energy storage can play a role in several areas: in the wholesale, the balancing, or the ancillary services market. However, for all areas, it is essential that barriers to entry be removed. The report explains that although market design changes may help to overcome certain obstacles, they are not enough to make the business case for energy storage viable. Similarly, appropriate tariffs are needed, but they are not sufficient by themselves. The report also explains that the EU has subsidized renewables, but it is not inclined to do the same for storage, where the EU seems to be banking on R&D support programs. The hope is that innovation alone will help to further reduce the costs of storage technologies. Meanwhile, the United States did not wait for the costs of storage to drop. It has set targets for energy storage, granting subsidies to support those targets, similarly to its policy on renewables. Several states have already imposed energy storage deployment targets and in other states, target processes are underway. An order by the US Federal Energy Regulation Commission FERC (issued in February 2018)[97] requires the creation of participation models for energy storage across the country in order to remove barriers to the participation of electric storage resources in the capacity, energy and ancillary services markets operated by regional transmission organizations and independent system operators. In specific states, different needs for storage have different regulatory implications. For example, in California, PG&E's landmark energy storage solicitation where batteries were to replace fossil fuel generation on the power grid attracted attention in past years.[98] It was the first time a utility and its regulators have sought to directly replace multiple

[95] Gancheva et al. (2018), p. 25.

[96] Broeckx et al. (2019), p. 18.

[97] Federal Energy Regulatory Commission (2018): Electric Storage Participation in Markets Operated by Regional Transmission Organizations and Independent System Operators, Order No. 841, 162 FERC ¶ 61,127, available at https://www.ferc.gov.

[98] Switching to batteries can lead to decreased reliance on gas. In the case of California, state regulators were already planning for three fossil fuel power plants to retire. They ordered PG&E to seek alternatives to the generators.

major power plants via battery storage. The request was approved by US federal regulators (FERC).[99]

In Switzerland there is also a legal framework supporting storage, but it is likely to evolve to facilitate the energy transition. Schreiber (2021) goes into more details about the current legal framework related to storage in Switzerland that exempts pump hydropower plants from paying grid fees but does not provide a clear framework for new storage technologies yet. He also explains the interesting role of private industry associations in the absence of a specific legislation on the other storage technologies. It is interesting to note that companies are driving the developments in this area probably because they see the potential for new business models related to other storage options in Switzerland.[100] A good overview of the political frameworks in place today, the legislation that is being introduced, and other developments is provided by Global Legal Insights.[101] Beyond federal legislation and regulation, since 1990, all cantons have drawn up their own energy legislation and regulations. In the Canton of Vaud, for example, one of the strategic axis areas in terms of infrastructure to support the energy vision of the Canton is to develop infrastructure for the storage of energy and to favor the convergence of grids.[102] New IT tools that are being developed and new management strategies and technologies will increasingly also allow the convergence of grids, including gas and power grids. Oversizing both networks is not the best solution when alternative approaches are apparent.[103] As tools continue to be developed to help cantons, cities, and individual companies better manage their grids and the existing infrastructure, innovations in business models will emerge together with new technological options (storage-related or other), and subsequently policy frameworks will be called to evolve in order to become better suited to energy transition strategies on the local, regional, and national levels.

Regarding the question whether Switzerland will follow or diverge from the EU on storage, the relationship between Swiss and EU legislation has to be analyzed. The recast Electricity Market Design Directive, part of the EU's Clean Energy for All legislative package, includes measures to adapt the EU electricity policy

---

[99] Bade (2018).

[100] The Swiss Federal Constitution (*Bundesverfassung*), the Energy Act (*Energiegesetz*), the CO_2 Act (*CO_2-Gesetz*), the Nuclear Energy Act (*Kernenergiegesetz*) and the Electricity Supply Act (*Stromversorgungsgesetz*) are all integral parts of the instruments defining a sustainable and modern Swiss energy policy. In addition, energy policies at the cantonal level as well as the federal level are also based on the presentation of energy perspectives as well as on strategies, implementation programs, and the evaluation of measures at the municipal, cantonal and federal levels. Therefore, policies in Switzerland will evolve to facilitate the transition in each canton.

[101] GLI (2020).

[102] DIREN (2019).

[103] We developed a software tool under a project supported by the H2020 (the Horizon 2020 European funding program) called IntegrCiTy for the optimized development and management of gas and power grids, see: http://iese.heig-vd.ch/projets/integrcity. For this project, we worked with industry stakeholders to develop business model options for the software in a design thinking workshop held with local gas and power industry stakeholders in 2018.

framework for the clean energy transition, including measures to enhance flexibility and enable consumer participation in energy markets.[104] Furthermore, energy storage is also recognized as a distinct asset class in the directive, separate from generation. The measures are expected to facilitate energy storage investments. However, individual Member States still need to implement this directive into national law, and Switzerland will pursue this direction as well. The consulting company Norton Rose Fulbright has produced a report about the situation for storage, including an analysis of the regulatory environment. They mention that "the provisions of the directive entitling transmission system operators (TSOs) and distribution system operators (DSOs) to own and operate storage assets under certain circumstances may result in narrower or broader markets for storage services offered by independent storage operators in different Member States." Member States can now make strategic decisions to enable consumers to shift their demand, to allow self-consumption (like in Switzerland) and storage, and to enable dynamic time-of-use tariffs as part of their implementation of this directive. The authors explain that the same is true for the role of aggregators and local energy communities addressed by the directive. Finally, the authors expect the rollout of smart meters to become increasingly important to enable the intended flexibility.[105]

Norton Rose Fulbright explore other examples of legal barriers for storage in their report.[106] For example, the report explains the current situation in France, where, except for pumped storage, energy storage remains limited, but a forecast recently published by CRE, the French energy regulator, reports a potential for energy storage of between 1 and 4 GW by 2030. The report covers several legal and commercial challenges for energy storage projects in France. Moreover, the French feed-in tariffs regime for electricity production favored the direct injection of electricity into the grid rather than its storage. Therefore, the report comes to the conclusion that multiple factors have hindered the emergence of an energy storage market in France.

2.2.2 For the Heating and Cooling Sector

In this section, we explore under which circumstances policies are blocking (or otherwise promoting) new business models and technologies in the heating and cooling sector, but also how sometimes other policies can cause unintended effects and reduce the incentives for such developments. According to a recent report on cities, two key elements are necessary for the sustainable energy transition to

[104] The directive aims to reduce the barriers to energy storage. It mandates fair rules in relation to network access and charging. It also mandates non-discriminatory and competitive procurement of balancing services. A wide definition of "energy storage" was chosen in the directive. That definition encompasses both reconversion to electricity and conversion into another energy carrier, like hydrogen gas; see NRF (2019).

[105] NRF (2019).

[106] NRF (2019).

succeed: first a more rapid deployment of renewables in the sector and second widespread electrification in all economic sectors. The report explains that cities have a unique role to play in this mission. First, the heating and cooling sectors are local markets. Second, cities have an influence at a local level, and they can encourage their residents and other citizens to support the energy transition. For heating and cooling systems, the development of urban renewable heating and cooling markets is key to decarbonizing these sectors, the report explains.[107]

The Energy Performance of Buildings Directive (EPBD) of the EU[108] outlines specific measures for the building sector, updating and amending many provisions from the 2010 EPBD. In Switzerland, many provisions exist to improve energy efficiency in buildings, but at present, approximately 50% of Switzerland's primary energy consumption is attributable to buildings: 30% for heating, air-conditioning and hot water, 14% for electricity and around 6% for construction and maintenance.[109] New business models, e.g., combining business models for renewable energy with investment models for energy efficiency improvements, could incite investors to invest more in insulation, refurbishments, etc. New business models for buildings are also tracked in a report by Boo et al.[110] and another review of business models for renewable energy in the built environment was conducted by Würtenberger and Bleyl.[111] Indeed business innovation in the building sector is occurring all along the industry value chain, starting with the re-design of project delivery models and energy performance solutions and including deep renovation. Service-oriented business models are leading the way towards a greener building industry, in which there is considerable cross-sectoral collaboration.[112]

Affordable and reliable options to decarbonize the provision of heating and cooling in urban areas now include solar thermal, bio-heat and geothermal technologies. Renewables combined with energy efficiency improvements in cities have enabled the development of "net zero" buildings and districts. Solar thermal systems on building façades and rooftops as well as modern biomass stoves and boilers are also stand-alone solutions now available in many cities.[113] A report prepared by the IEA about the German energy transition states that the government is still in the process of formulating a decarburization plan for the heating sector—which accounts for over 50% of final energy consumption.[114]

Nevertheless, in terms of energy efficiency, legal measures are starting to drive improvements in both Switzerland and Germany. In Germany, the Climate Action

[107] REN21 (2019b), p. 13.

[108] Directive 2010/31/EU of the European Parliament and of the Council of 19 May 2010 on the energy performance of buildings, Official Journal L153, 13–35.

[109] Swiss Federal Office of Energy (2019).

[110] Boo et al. (2017).

[111] Würtenberger and Bleyl (2012).

[112] Boo et al. (2017).

[113] REN21 (2019a), p. 22.

[114] IEA (2020).

Programme 2030 contains important measures for the heating sector.[115] However, policies and innovative measures that push for business model changes in the heating sector should be further explored in future research work. For example, there may be opportunities where new business models combined with innovative policy-making create incentives for energy efficiency improvements in existing buildings at the same time that investors invest in eco-villages or self-consumption communities, and this could be backed by specific policies and measures, locally or on the regional level.

2.3 *Policies Promoting Business Model Developments*

When we interviewed executives at the start of the SCCER CREST project, all executives across the board from technology providing firms to energy distribution companies to ICT firms in the energy business said that in order to have a successful energy transition, we need new business models, but in order to see these new business models emerge in the energy sector, we need new regulatory frameworks.[116] Indeed, according to the IEA, across all power sector investments, more than 95% of investment is now based on regulation or contracts for remuneration.[117] Investment in energy efficiency is particularly linked to government policy, often through energy performance standards. Likewise, it is clear and well-known that business models in the energy sector can only be successful if supported by regulatory frameworks and good legislation. Some examples of how policies support business model innovations are provided in this section.

2.3.1 For the Transportation Sector

Beyond the measures that are applied today (e.g., taxes for fuel, incentives for clean vehicles, and funding for public transportation), governments can also play a role in more directly creating business model change in the transportation sector in specific

[115] This includes measures such as tax relief for energy-efficient refurbishment of buildings. It also includes a premium for exchanging oil heaters for new, efficient heating systems. Finally, it includes the expansion of heat grids and district heating with a view to integrating renewable energy sources into heating networks (especially in densely populated areas). This strategy is also pursued in Switzerland in some regions. As for Germany, as the intended carbon tax will also apply to heating emissions, it is expected to bolster existing energy efficiency efforts in the sector (IEA 2020).

[116] Structured interviews were held with executives (or middle-managers) at ten major corporate entities in the energy sector, with interviews held from 2014 to 2016 and in different locations (Zurich, London, Lausanne, and on the phone with several other firms). For confidentiality, we have decided to withhold the names of the firms. They comprise firms in the energy technology business and the ICT business as well as utilities companies active in both distribution and production. We also interviewed two major auto manufacturers.

[117] IEA (2018a).

areas. Governments can transform their transportation concepts and promote electrification. Such electrification is a new type of power demand for utilities and helps to drive innovation and decarbonization.

Governments, particularly municipalities, can provide their communities with access to greater transportation and fueling options through the T2G (Transportation-to-Grid) platform. However, today this is not a full reality yet in many cities. Most cities are still experimenting with such concepts and platforms. These efforts could support municipality goals such as addressing climate change. More simply, municipalities could provide more and more charging points for the public in cities, as is being done on a pilot basis today in Basel.[118] Novel types of public-private partnerships with innovative financing schemes can be explored by cities, together with their local stakeholders. Another area for work to be done is defining new city planning rules to allow for both improved livability in a city and reduced emissions. Design thinking and co-creation workshops with urban dwellers could help develop solutions adapted to various specific sets of users. Comparing a city's status and accomplishments to general guidance and best practices for urban planners could be a starting point for deciding on where a city needs the most help and ideation inputs from inhabitants. Some guidelines are reviewed by Kodukula.[119]

In the transportation sector, standards for new vehicles sold or taxes to change the purchasing behavior of people with regard to vehicles help. However, they do not create special opportunities for business model developments or business model innovation. Policies in the transportation sector must start to become more strategic.

First, they must aim to decarbonize energy carriers and fuels, vehicles, and infrastructure. Second, incentives for such investments in infrastructure together with innovative local policies are needed. Furthermore, integrating public transport investments with private (passenger) transport business models needs to be further explored. If demonstrations prove these integrated concepts to be of interest to private investors, perhaps driven by prosumer-led business models intended for city inhabitants, then policies and specific programs could be developed to specifically promote such integration. For example, one idea is to use the DC network of public transport for the integration of Photovoltaics (PV) and as a charging point for electric vehicles (EV). The aim of this integration is to stabilize the DC network of public transport and to offer new services and modes of supply. Such a configuration and its potential is studied in the framework of a project conducted at our school (HES-SO) called Projet InterHubEN.[120] Third, policy frameworks can support strategic value chains and create conditions for new business models in terms of

---

[118] Some of these charging points are available in covered parking structures. Today just 10 parking places in the blue zone areas in the city are available with one hour more of parking than normally is the case in this blue parking zone and free unlimited parking during the night and the weekend. Each parking spot reserved for electric vehicles is equipped with a sensor so that users can use an application to know where public charging stations are available in the city.

[119] For cities that are revising their land-use plans or transport plans several recommendations such as linking land use and transport planning are made and summarized in Kodukula (2018).

[120] https://heig-vd.ch/rad/groupes-transversaux/hub-mobilit%C3%A9/ra-d/projet-interhuben.

supply chains. Policies can help reduce investment risks for the development of battery industry value chains, for example. Strengthened funding for battery manufacturing can be coupled with requirements regarding the sustainability of battery cell manufacturing and therefore improve the transparency of the raw material supply chains.[121] Such innovations are on the level of sustainable innovative supply chain management, but they could also integrate new commercial business models. Finally, policies could also be developed to support utilities and energy providers that wish to redefine themselves. Utilities as electric distribution providers have the opportunity to enter the transportation business by delivering electricity to plug-in electric vehicles (PEVs) and extending their networks to support PEV charging infrastructure. Transportation electrification is an opportunity for utilities to proactively redefine the nature of customer engagement in a new scenario where customers will increasingly have access to distributed renewables and energy storage and opportunities to engage with third-party energy service providers, thus threatening the utility business model.

2.3.2 For the Electric Power Sector

The basic context for DSOs in Europe and the changes they are experiencing regarding their business models were already discussed in the introduction to this section. We have also reviewed good governance frameworks for renewable energy,[122] although good governance of the electric power sector is much wider than just good governance regarding renewables. In IRENA's report on power system flexibility, the fact that flexibility in the system must respond according to the time scales that are relevant to renewable resources is explained. Many policies that support renewable energy, such as policies allowing for technologies adding flexibility in the market, were already reviewed in earlier sections of this chapter. Via the IRENA Knowledge Framework for power sector transition, IRENA has developed over twenty indicators allocated in the following macro-sectors (which indicate readiness for the energy transition): flexibility, transmission, demand response and storage, interconnectors, operation, and markets. More work is needed in each area to understand how new business models can apply in each case and which policies can be developed to support them.[123]

---

[121] IEA (2019e).

[122] Some elements of a good renewable energy governance for the electric power sector are highlighted in a report by IEA (2018b). According to the report, good governance of the energy transition should include: (1) renewable energy policies on end-use sectors, not just power generation, (2) support for heating and cooling applications of renewables by dedicated targets, technology mandates, financial incentives, generation-based incentives and carbon and energy taxes, (3) evolved policies in the power sector to address new challenges, (4) measures supporting the integration of variable renewable energy, and (5) consideration of holistic policies considering factors beyond the energy sector itself.

[123] IEA (2018b).

There is also a need to consider reforming the basic model that allows for investments in the grid. This is also important to keep renewable energy sources, which may be produced at distance, connected to the grid. Some countries are better prepared for increasing renewables integration in their grids and others less. One of the ways to better adapt a regulatory framework in the energy sector for renewables is to adapt the cost allocation schemes of a country, sometimes allowing for very shallow cost allocation schemes for cost allocation structures associated with connecting renewable generation to the existing transmission network. Madrigal and Stoft review various structures already implemented in some European countries.[124]

3 Insights from our Expert Workshop

On 20 January 2020, we conducted a workshop with experts from different parts of the energy sector—in equal numbers with regard to the type of stakeholder—from start-ups to small and medium-sized enterprises (SMEs) to DSOs to academics and consultants in the energy sector. In order to facilitate the workshop and allow for an open discussion of the results, 15 participants were invited to the workshop and finally 12 participants and two organizers were present. The ideation workshop took place over three hours and was comprised of a quick introduction to our work followed quickly by four break-out working sessions. In these sessions, the participants worked on different tasks. First, they worked on what they individually thought were the conditions for an energy transition in general and shared this with their group. Second, they identified (using post-its) the conditions in the short term versus the long term as well as conditions necessary for Switzerland versus other countries—organizing the thoughts from the first brainstorming session and categorizing them on the chart we drew on the white board. In these first two break-out groups, both groups followed the same task and their results were combined later on. Then groups were asked to mix again and work together to discuss the conditions for incumbents to create business model reconfiguration in a more detailed manner (in one group). The other group was asked to consider the conditions for start-ups, SMEs, and new entrants to bring new business models or business model innovation to the sector. Participants were also asked to provide measurable indicators that could be used in our research work for the building of our Energy Transition Preparedness Index.

The participants always worked in two groups with participants mixing each time a new task was started to form a new group dynamic and in order to mix expertise and create a maximum level of creative potential for each of the topics addressed. Finally, they were asked to divide again into new groups in order to provide their inputs on new sources of data that we can use for developing measurements or

[124]Madrigal and Stoft (2012).

indicators. Another group discussed methodologies that could be used to advance the research framework that had already been prepared by the research group.

The results of this workshop clearly showed that participants from across the value chain or ecosystem and across industries believed that policies were a key condition for driving business model change. Many policy options were suggested in the first and second brainstorming sessions. Both groups generated a diversity of policy suggestions to drive an energy transition. However, the most important findings for our research work concerned the conditions for business model reconfiguration versus business model innovation for start-ups and new entrants. These inputs will serve to inform the development of the Energy Transition Preparedness Index that we are building at HEIG-VD.

3.1 Energy Transition Pre-Requisites Based on Time and Country/Region Context

Time elements (such as the short term versus the long term) and space elements (such as geographical space considered) affect the assumptions one makes when considering what is needed for any given energy transition. From the workshop session on the time versus space perspective, Table 1 presents the combined results based on the time elements and space elements. We asked participants to note what were elements creating preparedness for an energy transition in each context and to try to indicate aspects that could be measured (as well as propose real indicators that could be used in our index).

3.2 Changes Needed to Support Business Model Reconfiguration

The key elements that participants viewed as important in terms of impacting business model reconfiguration were:

- lobbies (size, power, motivation)
- R&D investments
- country energy mix (production)
- organizational structure and impacts of companies (aspects such as culture, turnover, organizational structure, energy footprint, environmental impacts of plants and production)

What we learned from this was that especially a measure for lobbies in a country had not been taken into account in our preparation of the Energy Transition Preparedness Index. We will have to find a value or proxy for measuring the

Table 1 Elements important for an energy transition[a]

Selected elements important for Switzerland	
Elements important in the short term: • pilot projects with new tech & business models • spending on renewable research • consciousness of people • financial incentives • cheaper rail travel • technology to limit reinforcement of the electricity grid (maximize assets) • legal framework	Elements important in the long term: • preventing PV cannibalization (maintaining long-term profitability) • geopolitical independence • recycling infrastructure for PV • personal energy management conducted by residential consumers in the same way as financial management (user-friendly) • the financial sustainability of the energy transition model
Elements important for all countries	
Elements important in the short term: • policies to push renewables • regulation on the use of gas • push full EVs (not plug-in hybrids) • EU regulation for charging infrastructure at home • road tax for EVs not before 2026 • CO_2 standards for new vehicles sold • battery-powered trains • country-level investments in Distributed Energy Resources (DER) roll-out • digitalization vision at country level • change management inside of firms • consumer evolution towards prosumers • political consensus to move away from "dirty" production	Elements important in the long term: • get out of fossil fuel energies (coal, fuel) • lower CO_2 everywhere with incentives • competitive pressure on energy distributors (create urgency to act) Things that can be measured: • renewable installed capacity (power and heat generation) • tech innovation around energy production, exchange, local consumption • availability of new technologies for production and distribution • legal and regulatory framework (e.g., updated norms, incentives for housing refurbishment . . .) • charging infrastructure and other key infrastructure investments • education to raise awareness and social responsibility

[a]Based on the initial brainstorming by workshop participants on January 20, 2020 at HEIG-VD in Yverdon-les-Bains, Switzerland

power of lobbies eventually, but in the meantime, we could use the SDG Index to obtain measures for good governance.

3.3 Changes Needed to Support Business Model Innovation

The key changes that participants viewed as important for creating the conditions for business model innovation (for start-ups, SMEs and new entrants) were:

- grants and funds available for start-ups
- good universities = universities that produce a lot of entrepreneurs
- number of organizations that bridge start-ups and industry
- number of start-ups met by incumbent companies
- number/value of angel investors in energy

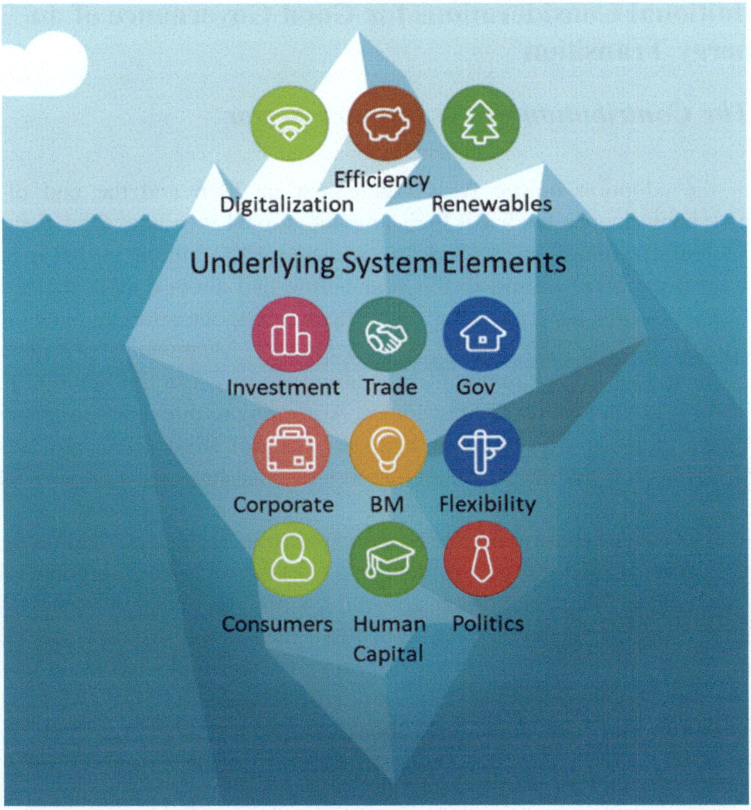

Fig. 1 Elements of an energy transition and its interacting systems

- funded mentors
- number of policies promoting innovation and helping to add urgency

Participants strongly believed that SMEs and start-ups must receive support to bridge the gap towards incumbents and that rather simple solutions such as increased numbers of mentors to link start-ups to incumbents could help in this respect. With regards to quantification and measurement of preparedness, the quality of mentorship (and other) programs will, however, be difficult to estimate.

In any case, the full results of this session combined with the knowledge we have gained from our ongoing database development will help us develop three sub-indexes of the Energy Transition Preparedness Index:

- Sub-Index 1: Comparing countries by their general infrastructure and investments
- Sub-Index 2: Comparing countries by antecedents for business model reconfiguration (for incumbents)
- Sub-Index 3: Comparing countries by antecedents for business model innovation (for start-ups, SMEs, and new entrants)

4 Additional Considerations for Good Governance of an Energy Transition

4.1 The Contribution of the Finance Sector

Between the adoption of the Paris Agreement in 2016 and the end of 2018, cumulative bank finance for fossil fuels amounted to $1.9 trillion. Global subsidies for fossil fuel consumption reached an estimated $300 billion in 2017, an 11% increase from the $270 billion in the year before and about double the estimated support for renewable power generation.[125] In addition, one estimate places the true cost of fossil fuels at upwards of $5.2 trillion.[126] Meanwhile, rich developed countries, including European countries, continue to invest in dirty energy projects around the world via export credit agencies. According to a review on financing for dirty energy projects, export credit agencies (ECAs) from G20 countries were responsible for $5.6 billion in annual support for coal projects between 2013 and 2015 or 57% of all public finance for coal.[127]

With regard to carbon pricing, the report explains in some detail that recognizing the cost of carbon emissions, governments are working on pricing carbon so that the market internalizes this cost and investment decisions are made accordingly. Meanwhile, public finance for the production of fossil fuels effectively acts as a negative price on carbon emissions. This is why reforming ECAs should happen in parallel to putting in place carbon pricing schemes around the world.

According to the WEF, the "rapid approach" to the energy transition does not deny that fossil fuels will continue to play a major role in energy markets for decades to come.[128] Growth in the core markets of major energy players may turn to decline and the effects may be priced by financial markets even before supply peaks. Moreover, the report explains that once a tipping point is reached, financial markets will tend to speed up the pace of change by constraining capital to declining industries and reallocating it to those that are growing. Moreover, regulations will most likely eventually change to reduce the lawsuits of companies and even state-owned companies against countries for their abrupt legal decisions regarding the energy transition.[129] But, of course, these effects do not happen alone. They happen

---

[125] IISD (2017).

[126] REN21 (2019a).

[127] According to Doukas et al. (2017), p. 4, a few country actors are responsible for the majority of this financing, with Japan and China in particular standing out along with South Korea and the United States. The report states that "Japan is the largest provider of public finance for fossil fuels – for both oil and gas, and coal – with $16.5 billion annually in support between 2013 and 2015 compared to $2.7 billion annually in support for clean energy."

[128] WEF (2019c).

[129] In a blog by IISD, the Energy Charter Treaty and its implications on countries wishing to change laws affecting investments in the nuclear or coal sector are explained (IISD 2019).

because of a concerted effort to get to the root of the problem—the way fossil fuels are financed and the level of investments in this sector.

Today countries can instead invest in green bonds and other green financial instruments with public money, while they reduce their investments in dirty energy projects. Green finance centers are emerging everywhere in the world from New York to London originally and to countries like South Africa, Morocco, Kazakhstan, and others today. Africa is expected to attract significant green investment as it starts to build up solar and wind power, taking advantage of the opportunity to leapfrog outdated fossil fuel energy systems. International banks are also moving ahead with green finance such as France's Credit Agricole that has surpassed Spain's Banco Santander recently for being the top underwriter of green bonds this year. France and China are contending as the biggest backers of green bonds in 2019 and 2020. As countries are increasingly decarbonizing their investments and at the same time shifting to green finance and allowing local finance centers to emerge to finance infrastructure projects at the local level, things will start to change.[130]

4.2 Consumption Patterns

The role of European countries' production and consumption patterns in contributing to the current state of planetary boundary[131] processes is a starting point to measure and assess how countries, or a given country, are doing with regard to their current state of production and consumption and how they are doing with regard to addressing this issue seriously. Input-output analyses combined with life-cycle analyses are another method to understand the contribution of production and consumption patterns of a country to various environmental issues. The level of consumption in Switzerland is already high compared to other countries in the world. The Swiss government is fully aware of this problem. The Swiss Federal Office for the Environment (FOEN) notes that the global impacts of Swiss consumption are primarily at the expense of the climate and biodiversity.[132] In terms of climate change, Switzerland's per-capita greenhouse gas footprint is currently around 14 tonnes of CO_2-equivalents per capita, well above the globally sustainable level, which scientific estimates place at 0.6 tonnes per capita for 2015.[133] If one also counts the impact of the financial sector, one of the country's biggest economic engines, one can calculate an even bigger footprint for Switzerland, compared to other countries. The point, however, is not to criticize Switzerland but rather to underline that any country's energy transition goals cannot be achieved (no matter

---

[130]Bloomberg (2019).

[131]Rockström et al. (2009).

[132]Swiss Federal Office for the Environment (2019).

[133]FOEN website (accessed in February 2020): https://www.bafu.admin.ch/bafu/fr/home/themes/economie-consommation/dossiers/impact-environnemental-du-commerce-international.html.

what technologies and business models are applied) without significant changes in consumption patterns.[134]

Population growth, economic growth, and the fact that Swiss consumption has risen disproportionately to population growth are among the key drivers and trends responsible for the situation. The Swiss Federal Office for the Environment explains that between 2000 and 2016, household consumption spending increased by 31%, almost twice as much as the population. At the same time, consumption patterns have worsened due to open market policies.[135]

Work reviewing transport consumption patterns for cities and urban areas is also available for various countries, and from this work it is clear that emissions from transport continue to be a major problem for most countries, in particular growth in emissions from passenger vehicles. To solve this problem, countries can consider recommendations for city planners to reduce emissions while making cities more livable for citizens. This is one way to deal with this type of consumption pattern, although one that is very challenging. For example, a set of recommendations is available in Kodukula (2018).[136]

More efficient, cost-deflated energy unlocks new consumption patterns. In the past, when a new energy source entered the global energy mix, there was an acceleration of energy demand.[137] In the future, it would be interesting to understand how new business models could help reduce energy demand along with revolutions on the supply side. Which business models offer benefits on both sides of the equation and what are the key policy-making solutions that would push such business models to become commonplace?

Also, while a country can reduce its consumption based on business-as-usual consumption patterns, policymakers must be aware that new scenarios can also lead to some increases in consumption due to new consumption patterns. In fact, some new business models may even lead to higher consumption, while others lead to unexpected changes in consumption behavior. More research would be needed to understand what the potential effects could be of various new business models. For example, blockchain-based business models in the energy sector could be overall beneficial in one way, but they could increase emissions on the other hand (perhaps emissions generated elsewhere) because of the architecture choices for blockchain (e.g., proof of work being the most energy-intensive choice).[138]

---

[134]Cassoret (2018).

[135]The environmental impact of opening up the market was reviewed by the Swiss Federal Office for the Environment (see Frischknecht et al. 2018). It mentions that in the context of international trade, the environmental impact of consumption is felt throughout the production and marketing chains, as shown by the example of Switzerland, which generates the largest part of its impact (more than 70%) abroad. The Swiss Federal Office for the Environment explains that for trade to be genuinely sustainable from an ecological point of view, producing countries should have environmental laws comparable to those of Switzerland—and respect them.

[136]Kodukula (2018).

[137]Fattouh et al. (2019).

[138]Bürer et al. (2019).

Table 2 Components of the energy transition preparedness index and interacting systems

Groups of elements	Components for the development of indicators
Tip of the Iceberg (elements often tracked already)	• energy efficiency progress (for various sub-sectors) • renewable energy progress (for various sub-sectors and using various indicators) • digitalization preparedness and management of digitalization trends
Energy-Economy System	• capital and investment • trade: exports (net exports of CO_2, but also embodied CO_2 in exports) and also indicators for imports[a] • institutions and governance with a focus on innovative activities and programs for both industry and start-ups together
Energy-Tech/Business System	• corporate commitment • innovative business environment supported for both business model innovation and business model reconfiguration • energy system structure including production (e.g., storage and flexibility of system for renewable energy)
Energy-Society System	• consumer participation • human capital • regulation and political commitment (including whether they address systemic issues)

[a]Today, markets are eerily interdependent. The international trade of oil and gas is an area where one country's self-interested strategy can have dramatic impacts on the entire world economy and the environment in general

4.3 Building an Energy Transition Preparedness Index

Based on our own work on the Energy Transition Preparedness Index,[139] we have defined the following key areas that we want to cover in our index. They are grouped by interacting systems (Table 2).

Using this basic framework, an Energy Transition Preparedness Index can be prepared with a variety of data sources and indicators from existing indexes around the world to compare countries on their energy transition progress to date. For each of the areas above, data and indicators can be aggregated with regard to different aspects such as clean energy, energy efficiency, mobility, climate and energy data, fossil fuels/nuclear power, and general economic or industrial policy indicators. A "country scorecard" is envisioned, which can provide an explanation of a country's ranking and suggestions on how it can improve. As for companies, a "company

[139]This work commenced in 2014 and it is ongoing. It includes (1) semi-structured interviews with executives and middle managers in the energy sector; (2) our own case study analysis of sub-sectors like on-grid storage, smart grid technologies, and microgrids; (3) an analysis of what we have discovered from existing energy transition assessment work and our literature review; (4) data collection and initial development of the index; and (5) an analysis of workshop results (one workshop on blockchain use cases in the energy sector held in June 2019 and another workshop on the index held in January 2020).

scorecard" can also be used to compare how prepared a company is compared to others in the given industry segment. Such scorecards could help both countries and companies monitor their progress on the energy transition and provide an incentive to improve over time. They can also be used to evaluate weaknesses in any given system and to understand how changes in one system might also influence other elements in the same interacting system or in another interacting system, or another country altogether. The emphasis of our scorecards will, however, be on business model transformation elements, meaning that part of the data collected and used for the work will have to be qualitative, not only quantitative or based on existing data and indicators from well-known sources.

For each country, each interacting system should be evaluated using all available data to the greatest extent possible. Once the results are available, weaknesses in any interacting system can be identified. How these weaknesses may influence other interacting systems can also be discussed. The objective of the index will be to create an open discussion about countries' key energy transition choices, based on scientific evidence.

Based on our analysis until now, we can say at least that top ranked countries in such an assessment should ideally have the following characteristics:

1. The country has effective governance of the energy transition—for example, the governance is transparent, participatory and resilient from (or less affected by) lobbying pressures. The country feels free to change its decisions on energy without fearing legal challenges. It has already made important capital and R&D investments towards supporting clean energy and transport and demonstrates a low carbon energy system compared to others. The country also shows constant improvement and verifiable action plans to move towards zero emissions in all areas and in cooperation with various stakeholders.
2. The country (and participating companies) actively invests in creating an innovative business environment in all sub-sector areas with a focus on innovation for a purpose, as opposed to innovation only for economic growth. Purpose-led missions are a means towards meeting economic objectives as well as environmental or social objectives of a country. The country has shown to be innovative in its governance framework conditions, and policies are made to evolve rapidly with technological and new business model opportunities. For example, the country allows sandboxes or specific temporary measures (aimed at supporting the emergence of innovative business models) in its regulatory framework.[140]
3. The country is not only investing in support mechanisms and programs for new business models and innovative technologies in the area of clean or low-carbon energy production, but also in the areas of energy productivity of industrial processes and buildings performance.

[140] An example is the co-ownership law scheme in Switzerland (RCP in French and ZEV in German) that provides a legal basis for self-consumption communities and allows for different tariff structures inside the community (from the normal regulated tariff structures).

4. The country already has a flexible energy system and is working to make it more flexible to allow for the increasing inclusion of renewables while fostering energy efficiency in all application domains in parallel with efforts to encourage the implementation of network convergence and sector coupling solutions.
5. The country is also active in addressing systemic roots of the problem, including consumption patterns of the population and the impact of financial institutions' investment decisions (especially for countries where the financial sector is important, like Switzerland). This means that the country has demonstrated its intentions through deeds and actions and it has displayed good governance in these two areas.
6. The country displays a high level of corporate engagement either via its private sector associations and/or via individual corporate leadership actions. Corporate commitment is demonstrated via indicators and data gathered by neutral parties.
7. The country also displays a high level of local leadership from cantons, cities, communes, and even schools with their individual activities and programs to include and involve citizens in the energy transition.
8. The country displays evidence of investing in human capital to address the energy transition, with a focus on supporting start-ups and entrepreneurs not only with technological innovations but also with business model innovations for the energy sector. The number of events that connect start-ups to incumbents is one indicator. Investments in programs that connect start-ups with incumbents in the energy sector and allow for mentoring start-ups that are introducing new business models and technologies, including digital innovations, are also important.
9. The country has a sufficient level of digital competitiveness, and it has plans and programs for the use of digital technologies towards strategic energy transition goals. At the same time, it is addressing increasing energy use from data centers, data networks, etc.
10. The country's spending on public transportation is sufficient and public satisfaction with public transport is high. Important investments such as electrified railway lines or other low-carbon means of transportation have been realized. Planning also integrates the interaction between transport and land use. The country also continues to support innovative concepts and business models for mobility.

The underlying systems represented in this figure are:

1. Energy-economy system: investment, trade and institutions/existing governance
2. Energy-technology/business system: corporate, business model innovation and reconfiguration, and flexibility of the energy system
3. Energy-society system: consumer participation, human capital, and regulatory and political commitment (including regulating and using the financial system appropriately)

These three systems and the underlying indicators and data sources for each will be compiled in the three sub-indexes explained earlier, allowing primarily for the above elements to be combined appropriately depending on which stakeholder the elements apply to (incumbents or start-ups, SMEs, and new entrants).

Metrics for each of the areas above now need to be developed based on available qualitative and quantitative data and integrated in a meaningful way. One way is using systems thinking which can then be used later for stakeholder value network analysis and other useful tools for the development of strategies. It is also important to understand which systems different players have control over in order to change them. In the World Economic Forum's work on the energy transition, three co-evolving and interacting systems were defined: (1) energy-economy, (2) energy-technology, and (3) energy-society.[141]

One could imagine an index developed for each system so that we can compare countries by interacting systems as well as elements relevant to each type of business model change. The results can then be compiled into one index for a general comparison. What is important to remember, however, is that the elements we will be measuring are not independent; they are interdependent, and this adds another challenge when building such an index.

However, if successful with such an approach, we can at least begin the process of uncovering all the elements hidden under the "tip of the iceberg" of energy transition assessments. Eventually specific companies' strategic responses to the energy transition can be analyzed using this tool as well.

5 Conclusions on Governing the Energy Transition via Business Model Change

In our research work conducted over the past years, we have aimed to understand business model transformation in the energy sector via a mix of methods. All governments must start working closely together with their business community members in innovative and transparent ways towards developing necessary regulatory frameworks and other means to promote and take the maximum advantage from new business models and new technologies. Each country (and community) will have its own pathway to finding the most appropriate solutions and investing in them. For an effective energy transition, new business models should be supported in the area of renewable energy integration but also in the areas of energy productivity of industrial processes and buildings performance. New or reconfigured business models must also address the problem of consumption patterns.

[141] WEF (2019a), p. 23, covers the three co-evolving and interacting systems above. For example, in the energy-society system the focus is on the collection of energy policies related to efficiency, security and energy equity/justice. The key players identified for this system are policymakers, consumers, and workers. The challenges identified for this system comprise competing priorities within different political parties and governments and changes in priorities over different time frames.

Indeed, this chapter shows that alternative business models are moving away from energy as a commodity (the push model) to energy as a service, where an end-customer can partner with (or replace) the provider. However, not all countries' energy sectors will evolve rapidly towards such business model transformation. Countries will proceed at different paces and should proceed at different paces, due to varying priorities. Apart from those higher-level insights, from our analysis of data and our workshop findings we have found that for an energy transition to happen many elements need to be put in place. In all areas, business model innovation and reconfiguration can play a huge role in creating the transition towards cleaner sources of energy. From our analysis, technological innovation, such as from digitalization, is also shown to provide future value to energy transitions, providing new opportunities for energy efficiency, new ways to trade and manage energy, and new strategies for a better management of the grid.

However, we also discussed that new technologies and business model transformation are not enough. Consumption patterns need to change as well and perhaps business models can help in that respect, but not on their own. New educational programs could be envisaged, youth could be more empowered to find innovative solutions through specific design thinking challenges and similar initiatives. These events could be co-sponsored by universities, companies, and other groups such as investors. However, whatever funding is available should require concrete results as well. The focus of such events should not only be on technological solutions, but mentors and coaches are needed to orient students, entrepreneurs, and professional participants towards thinking about how to use technologies in existing systems or how to combine multiple sources of energy. Design thinking sprints should not stop at the ideation stage, but they should allow for sufficient product demonstration and testing, or business model development and testing. Eventually the best ideas can then move on to deployment and testing in the market.

We have also learned that good energy transition governance is not only about pushing forward renewable energy investments and deployment of renewable energy to its maximum or about applying taxes, but it requires smart integrated policies and policies that address the systemic problems, such as the financial system, and consumption patterns. The latter are a kind of third generation of energy transition policies. New strategies for policy-making, participatory methods for policy development, and *innovation with a purpose* are required. Strategies must be increasingly developed by multiple stakeholders of society, and progress (or setbacks) and commitments by both the public and the private sectors should be monitored in a transparent and unbiased manner. That calls for new approaches based on open governance, co-creation, design thinking, and agile innovation on the part of governments, among incumbents, between institutions, and not only among start-ups.

Meanwhile, there is no perfect scenario and there is no perfect pathway to the energy transition of a country, just as there is no perfect country comparison. However, it is clear that more research and a better understanding are needed with regard to what governance frameworks inspire business model reconfiguration among incumbents on the one hand and business model innovation from start-ups and new entrants on the other hand and how these two phenomena influence each other. Dealing with the energy transition is extremely complex for a number of reasons. However, this complexity should not bar us from trying. A saying says: "Do not fear failure but rather fear not trying" (Roy T. Bennett).

6 Ideas for Future Research

Some ideas for future research that would appear to be valuable given our analysis of what is available today and what is missing are:

- Understand the systemic impacts of recent events on the energy transition and how far the power of new business model innovation can go in driving us towards an energy transition in each country context.
- Evaluate alternative ways to compile and compress all the relevant energy transition indicators into one measurement tool and allow the tool to generate different results based on the users' own opinions about each possible input to avoid bias.
- Look at what people are doing in each country: How are social movements affecting the energy transitions of different countries and how can the energy transition be managed in a democratic way, helping to increase the sense of cohesion of societies in a time of potential global unrest?
- Look into what people want from their energy transition (how this is different in countries), perhaps clustering countries by people's expectations for their energy transition.
- Produce more case studies to understand business model changes per sub-sector and the way policies are barring or promoting such developments in each case.
- Do more research on which business models offer benefits on both sides of the equation (the demand side as well as the supply side) and on the key policy-making solutions that would push such business models to become commonplace.
- How can public sector entities develop new business models themselves, and how can unprecedented changes be imagined by local leaders to significantly change business models on the local level?
- Carry out more interviews with executives to understand what makes their companies able to change their existing business models and what they think about regulations and legislation which could support business model developments for the energy transition, despite external shock factors such as a global oil price shock.
- Analyze the impact of energy transition pathways on people and how people in turn may impact the pathways, e.g., consider how young people are changing their consumption habits or modes of transport and how this will impact different sub-sectors and scenarios.

- Hold more design thinking workshops between different players—government, businesses, and even consumers—to work together on these issues and find solutions community by community.

Acknowledgements The authors are particularly grateful to the companies that kindly accepted to participate in this study via our design thinking workshop held in January 2020 and in the interviews, which we conducted with executives of companies in the energy sector inside and outside of Switzerland since the start of SCCER CREST in 2014.

References

Ali Y (2019) Sweden's Summer Sunshine Stored in Hydrogen for the Winter. Microgrid Knowledge, 17 December 2019. Available at https://microgridknowledge.com

Ali A, Li W, Hussain R, He X, Williams BW, Memon AH (2017) Overview of current microgrid policies, incentives and barriers in the European Union, United States and China. Sustainability 9(7):1146. https://doi.org/10.3390/su9071146

Bade G (2018) Storage will replace 3 California gas plants as PG&E nabs approval for world's largest batteries. Utility Dive, 9 November 2018. Available at https://www.utilitydive.com

Bloomberg (2019) The Rise of the Green Financial Hubs. Bloomberg Green, Newsletter by Bloomberg, 4 March 2020. Available at https://www.bloomberg.com

Boo E, Dallamaggiore E, Dunphy N, Morrissey J (2016) How innovative business models can boost the energy efficient buildings market. Int J Housing Sci Appl 40(2):73–83

Boo E, Molinero S, Sanvicente E, de Melo P, Landini A, Otal J, Melchiorre T, Melia A (2017) Report on novel business models and main barriers in the EU energy system, report for the ENTRUST project, January 2017

Bousso R (2018) Big Oil spent 1 percent on green energy in 2018. Reuters, 12 November 2018. Available at https://www.reuters.com

Broeckx S, Ramos A, Fernandez L, Meeus L (2019) Energy Storage – Our take on business models and regulation. STORY, A vision of our future energy system, Horizon 2020 project. Story Highlight, May 2019

Bürer M, de Lapparent M, Pallotta V, Capezzali M, Carpita M (2019) Use cases for blockchain in the energy industry opportunities of emerging business models and related risks. Comput Ind Eng 137. https://doi.org/10.1016/j.cie.2019.106002

Burger SP, Luke M (2016) Business models for distributed energy resources: a review and empirical analysis. An MIT Energy Initiative Working Paper, April 2016. Massachusetts Institute of Technology, USA

Cassoret B (2018) Transition énergétique – Ces vérités qui dérangent! De Boeck Supérieur, Paris

Castaneda M, Franco CJ, Dyner I (2017) Evaluating the effect of technology transformation on the electricity utility industry. Renew Sust Energ Rev 80:341–351. https://doi.org/10.1016/j.rser.2017.05.179

CEC (2018) Microgrid Analysis and Case Study Report, California, North America and Global Case Studies, August 2018. Navigant Consulting, Chicago

Cross S, Hast A, Kuhi-Thalfeldt R, Syri S, Streimikiene D, Denina A (2015) Progress in renewable electricity in Northern Europe towards EU 2020 targets. Renew Sust Energ Rev 52 (C):1768–1780

CPLC (2020) Who is using carbon pricing? Carbon Pricing Leadership Coalition. Available at https://www.carbonpricingleadership.org/who

Diestelmeier L (2019) Changing power: shifting the role of electricity consumers with blockchain technology – policy implications for EU electricity law. Energy Policy 128:189–196. https://doi.org/10.1016/j.enpol.2018.12.065

DIREN (2019) Conception cantonale de l'énergie, Adoptée par le Conseil d'Etat le 19 juin 2019, Canton of Vaud, DTE, DGE, DIREN

Doukas A, DeAngelis K, Ghio N (2017) Talk is Cheap: How G20 Governments are Financing Climate Disaster, July 2017. Oil Change International, Friends of the Earth U.S., the Sierra Club, and WWF European Policy Office. Available at http://priceofoil.org

Duygan M, Kachi A, Oeri F, Oliveira TD, Rinscheid A (2021) A survey of stakeholders' views and practices. In: Hettich P, Kachi A (eds) Swiss energy governance. Springer, New York, pp 369–396

Ebers Broughel A, Wüstenhagen R (2021) The influence of policy risk on swiss wind power investment. In: Hettich P, Kachi A (eds) Swiss energy governance. Springer, New York, pp 345–368

European Commission (2019) EU Transport Scoreboard. EU mobility indicators for years 2015–2017. European Commission. Available at https://ec.europa.eu

Facchinetti E, Eid C, Bollinger A, Sulzer S (2016) Business model innovation for local energy management: a perspective from Swiss utilities. Front Energy Res 4. https://doi.org/10.3389/fenrg.2016.00031

Fattouh B, Poudineh R, West R (2019) The rise of renewables and energy transition: what adaptation strategy exists for oil companies and oil-exporting countries? Energy Transit 3:45–58. https://doi.org/10.1007/s41825-019-00013-x

FFE (2020) Value of flexibility in the context of European electricity market coupling with extreme technological, regulatory and social developments. The Research Center for Energy Economics, Munich. Available at https://www.ffe.de

Frischknecht R, Nathani C, Alig M, Stolz P, Tschümperlin L, Hellmüller P (2018) Umwelt-Fussabdrücke der Schweiz – Zeitlicher Verlauf 1996–2015. Federal Office for the Environment, Bern

Gancheva M, O'Brien S, Crook N, Monteiro C (2018) Models of local energy ownership and the role of local energy communities in energy transition in Europe. Report for the Commission for the Environment, Climate Change and Energy, European Committee of the Regions, Brussels

GLI (2020) Energy Laws and Regulations - Switzerland. In: GLI - Global Legal Insights International legal business solutions. Available at https://www.globallegalinsights.com

Gately D (1986) Lessons from the 1986 oil price collapse. Brook Pap Econ Activity 17:237–284

Hedstrom GS (2019) Beware the 80/20 Governance Trap: Focus on the "G" in ESG. Available at https://esgnavigator.com

IEA (2017) Changing utility business models and electricity investment. IEA, Paris

IEA (2018a) World energy investment 2018. IEA, Paris. Available at https://www.iea.org

IEA (2018b) Renewable Energy Policies in a Time of Transition. IRENA, OECD/IEA and REN21

IEA (2019a) Energy Transitions Indicators. Tracking energy transitions. IEA, Paris, 2 December 2019. Available at https://www.iea.org

IEA (2019b) Tracking Power. IEA, Paris. Available at https://www.iea.org

IEA (2019c) Energy Efficiency 2019. IEA, Paris. Available at https://www.iea.org

IEA (2019d) Shared, automated... and electric? Commentary 28 March 2019. IEA, Paris. Available at https://www.iea.org

IEA (2019e) Global EV Outlook 2019. IEA, Paris. Available at https://www.iea.org

IEA (2020) Germany 2020 - Energy Policy Review. Country report – February 2020. IEA, Paris. Available at https://www.iea.org

IISD (2017) Fossil Fuel Subsidy Reform and Taxation- Stories for Success for the Talanoa Dialogue. IISD Global Subsidies Initiative submission to the UNFCCC Talanoa Dialogue, March 2017. Available at https://unfccc.org

IISD (2019) Modernizing the Energy Charter Treaty: A make-or-break moment for sustainable, climate-friendly energy policy, by Martin Dietrich Brauch, 13 November 2019. Available at https://www.iisd.org

IRENA (2018) Power system flexibility for the energy transition, Part 1: overview for policy makers. International Renewable Energy Agency, Abu Dhabi

IRENA (2019a) Innovation landscape for a renewable-powered future: solutions to integrate variable renewables. International Renewable Energy Agency, Abu Dhabi. Available at https://www.irena.org

IRENA (2019b) Renewable Energy Statistics 2019 and Renewable Capacity Statistics 2019. International Renewable Energy Agency, Abu Dhabi. Available at https://www.irena.org

IRENA (2019c) Solutions to integrate high shares of variable renewable energy (Report to the G20 Energy Transitions Working Group (ETWG)). International Renewable Energy Agency, Abu Dhabi. Available at https://www.irena.org

Kodukula S (2018) Integrated land use planning and Urban transport in low carbon cities. UNCRD Environmentally sustainable transport (EST) forum. Ulaanbaatar, Mongolia

Lafortune G, Zoeteman K, Fuller G, Mulder R, Dagevos J, Schmidt-Traub G (2019) The 2019 SDG Index and Dashboards Report for European Cities (prototype version). Sustainable Development Solutions Network (SDSN) and the Brabant Center for Sustainable Development (Telos)

Liu Q (2018) The next economic crisis could cause a global conflict. Here's why. World Economic Forum, 13 November 2018. Available at https://www.weforum.org

Loock M (2012) Going beyond best technology and lowest price: on renewable energy investors' preference for service-driven business models. Energy Policy 40:21–27

Madrigal M, Stoft S (2012) Transmission expansion for renewable energy scale-up: emerging lessons and recommendations, A World Bank Study. World Bank, Washington, D.C. Available at https://openknowledge.worldbank.org

Massa L, Tucci CL (2014) Business model innovation. In: Dodgson M, Gann DM, Phillips N (eds) The Oxford handbook of innovation management. Oxford University Press, Oxford, pp 420–441. https://doi.org/10.1093/oxfordhb/9780199694945.013.002

Mediavilla M, de Castro C, Capellán I, Javier Miguel L, Arto I, Frechoso F (2013) The transition towards renewable energies: physical limits and temporal conditions. Energy Policy 52:297–311. https://doi.org/10.1016/j.enpol.2012.09.033

Montgomery S (2020) The oil shock of 2020 appears to be here – and the pain could be wide and deep. In: theconversation.com, 13 March 2020. Available at https://theconversation.com

Monzon D, Guzman R, Kalkman J, Rogers S, Kinbaum A (2019) Shaping the oil company of the future. Arthur D Little Prism 1(2019):56–71. Available at https://www.adlittle.com

Navigant (2019) Transportation-to-Grid – New Business models to capture value in the energy cloud, published in 2019. Available at https://www.guidehouse.com

NordREG (2018) Implementation of data hubs in the Nordic countries. Status Report, June 2018

Nouyrigat V (2019) Streaming, bitcoin, IA: le délire énergétique! Science & Vie. Available at https://www.science-et-vie.com

NRF (2019) Regulatory progress for energy storage in Europe. Norton Rose Fulbright. Available at https://www.nortonrosefulbright.com

Osterwalder A, Pigneur Y (2010) Business model generation: a handbook for visionaries, game changers, and challengers. John Wiley & Sons, Hoboken

Pojasek RB, Toolbox Q (2010) Quality toolbox using leading indicators to drive sustainability performance. Environ Q Manage 18(4):87–93. https://doi.org/10.1002/tqem.20228

Prettico G, Flammini M G, Andreadou N, Vitiello S, Fulli G, Masera M (2019) Distribution System Operators observatory 2018 - Overview of the electricity distribution system in Europe, EUR 29615 EN, Publications Office of the European Union, Luxembourg. https://doi.org/10.2760/104777, JRC113926

Przychodzen J, Gómez-Bezares F, Przychodzen W, Larreina M (2016) ESG issues among fund managers—factors and motives. Sustainability 8:1078. https://doi.org/10.3390/su8101078

REA (2019) Energy Transition Readiness Index, A new report from the REA, commissioned by Eaton and Drax. Available at https://www.r-e-a.net

REN21 (2019a) Renewables 2019 Global Status Report. Renewable Energy Policy Network, REN21 Secretariat, Paris. Available at https://www.ren21.net/

REN21 (2019b) Just Launched: Our Renewables in Cities 2019 Global Status Report. Renewable Energy Policy Network, REN21 Secretariat, Paris. Available at https://www.ren21.net

Reuters (2017) European utilities urge EU to raise green energy targets, 6 November 2017. Available at https://uk.reuters.com

Richter M (2012) Utilities' business models for renewable energy: a review. Renew Sust Energ Rev 16(5):2483–2493. https://doi.org/10.1016/j.rser.2012.01.072

Richter M (2013) Business model innovation for sustainable energy: German utilities and renewable energy. Energy Policy 62:1226–1237

Rieple A, Sorg M, Meier G (2019) Ziel 2030: Anteil erneuerbarer Gase 30% im gasversorgten, Wärmemarkt für Gebäude, (1) Aktuelle Herausforderungen. Energie Zukunft Schweiz, Dezember 2019. Available at www.ezs.ch

Rockström J, Steffen W, Noone K, Persson Å, Chapin F, Lambin E et al (2009) Planetary boundaries: exploring the safe operating space for humanity. Ecol Soc 14(2):32. https://doi.org/10.5751/ES-03180-140232

Rubino A, Costa Campi MT, Lenzi V, Ozturk I (eds) (2016) Regulation and investments in energy markets. Elsevier, Academic Press. https://doi.org/10.1016/C2015-0-00384-7

Sachs J, Schmidt-Traub G, Kroll C, Lafortune G, Fuller G (2019) Sustainable development report 2019. Bertelsmann Stiftung and Sustainable Development Solutions Network (SDSN), New York

Schaltegger S, Lüdeke-Freund F, Hansen E (2012) Business cases for sustainability: the role of business model innovation for corporate sustainability. Int J Innov Sustain Dev 6:95–119. https://doi.org/10.1504/IJISD.2012.046944

Schleicher-Tappeser R (2012) How renewables will change electricity markets in the next five years. Energy Policy 48:64–75. https://doi.org/10.1016/j.enpol.2012.04.042

Schreiber M (2021) Governance of energy innovations. In: Hettich P, Kachi A (eds) Swiss energy governance. Springer, New York, pp 175–194

Singh HV, Bocca R, Gomez P, Dahlke S, Bazilian M (2019) The energy transitions index: an analytic framework for understanding the evolving global energy system. Energy Strategy Rev 26:100382. https://doi.org/10.1016/j.esr.2019.100382

Sioshansi F (2018) Three new energy companies finding value in three new business models, energypost.eu, 31 May 2018. Available at https://energypost.eu

Smil V (2010) Energy transitions: history, requirements, prospects. Praeger Publishers Inc, Santa Barbara, Calif

Swiss Federal Office for the Environment (2019) Economy and Consumption: In Brief. Available at https://www.bafu.admin.ch

Swiss Federal Office of Energy (2019) Energy in buildings. Available at https://www.bfe.admin.ch

WEF (2018) Fostering effective energy transition – a fact-based framework to support decision-making. World Economic Forum, Geneva

WEF (2019a) Fostering Effective Energy Transition 2019. Available at https://reports.weforum.org

WEF (2019b) Cyber resilience in the electricity ecosystem: principles and guidance for boards. World Economic Forum, Geneva. Available at https://www.weforum.org

WEF (2019c) The speed of the energy transition – gradual or rapid change, white paper, September 2019. World Economic Forum, Geneva. Available at https://www.weforum.org

Wehrmann B, Wettengel J (2019) Polls reveal citizens' support for Energiewende. Clean Energy Wire, 21 October 2019. Available at https://www.cleanenergywire.org

Wells P (2015) New business models and the automotive industry. In: Nieuwenhuis P, Wells P (eds) The global automotive industry. John Wiley & Sons, Boston, pp 209–217. https://doi.org/10.1002/9781118802366.ch18

Würtenberger L, Bleyl J (2012) Business models for renewable energy in the built environment. Energy Research Centre of the Netherlands. Available at http://iea-retd.org

Mary Jean Bürer is a senior researcher at the Haute école d'ingénierie et de gestion du canton de Vaud, HES SO at Yverdon-les-Bains, Switzerland.

Matthieu de Lapparent is a professor at the Haute école d'ingénierie et de gestion du canton de Vaud, HES SO at Yverdon-les-Bains, Switzerland.

Massimiliano Capezzali is a professor at the Haute école d'ingénierie et de gestion du canton de Vaud, HES SO at Yverdon-les-Bains, Switzerland.

Mauro Carpita is a professor at the Haute école d'ingénierie et de gestion du canton de Vaud, HES SO at Yverdon-les-Bains, Switzerland.

Electricity Utility Companies Entering Private Sector Markets

How to Avoid Distortions of Competition

Andreas Abegg and Phil Baumann

Contents

The chapter is based on previous findings published as Abegg and Baumann (2020).

A. Abegg (✉)
Zurich University of Applied Sciences, Centre for Public Commercial Law, Winterthur, Switzerland
e-mail: andreas.abegg@zhaw.ch

P. Baumann
University of Lucerne, Faculty of Law, Lucerne, Switzerland
e-mail: phil.baumann@unilu.ch

P. Hettich, A. Kachi (eds.), *Swiss Energy Governance*,
https://doi.org/10.1007/978-3-030-80787-0_11

Abstract On the one hand, energy utility companies (EUCs) fulfill public tasks assigned to them by the state. On the other hand, they are also often active as entrepreneurs in the free market. For example, they supply electricity products to major customers, install photovoltaic and e-mobility systems and provide services in the areas of building technology, metering and telecommunications. In such private sector activities, energy utility companies potentially enjoy unjustified advantages due to the fact that they are publicly controlled and perform public tasks: they receive particularly good financing conditions, are taxed on a privileged basis and benefit from economies of scope and information advantages when public and private sector tasks are carried out in parallel. Such privileges may distort competition or prevent companies from entering a market. This chapter examines the legal requirements for dealing with this issue and proposes specific measures with which legislators and authorities can avoid harmful effects of private sector activities by EUCs.

1 Introduction

In Switzerland, almost 90% of the electricity utility companies (EUCs) are public sector utilities and therefore belong to the state.[1] In the course of the partial opening of the electricity market that has already taken place and the intended complete opening thereof, these public utilities are faced with the challenge of compensating for revenue losses from traditional "monopoly" areas.[2] At the same time, energy supply companies are expected to make their contribution to increasing energy efficiency and expanding renewable energies within the framework of the federal Energy Strategy 2050.[3]

This is the backdrop against which EUCs are expanding their business activities by moving from their public service sectors into private markets and thus becoming hybrid operators. In Switzerland, state activity in the private sector is permitted in principle, in accordance with legal doctrine and case law.[4] However, EUCs' increased activities in the private sector are regularly the subject of controversial public debate.[5] The attention has been in particular on accusations of EUCs reaping unjustified competitive advantages and thus benefiting from an "unequal playing field" in competition with private providers.

---

[1] Swiss Federal Office of Energy (2018a), p. 1.

[2] See Graf and Waldmeier (2016), p. 12.

[3] See, e.g., Vettori et al. (2018), p. 4.

[4] BGE 138 I 378, E. 6.3.2 and 6.3.3. In particular, the Swiss Electricity Supply Act (*Stromversorgungsgesetz*) does not explicitly prohibit EUCs from carrying out certain private sector activities (Kratz 2018, p. 97).

[5] See for example Enz (2018), p. 1 et seq. and 11; Müller (2017), p. 19; Vonplon (2019), p. 13; see further Schneider (2016), p. 647 et seq.; see also the campaign "*Fair ist anders!*" of the Berne SME trade association, which is aimed in particular at BKW's private sector activities. Available at www.fair-ist-anders.ch.

The issue of competition distortions arising from private sector activities is not limited to the corresponding entrepreneurial activities of EUCs; it is a problem that occurs generally when state activities press into the private sector.[6] So far, however, a sector-specific analysis of the private sector activities of EUCs has not been conducted. In particular, it is unclear which private sector activities are being carried out by EUCs. In addition, the public discussion focuses on allegedly competition-distorting behavior of a particular EUC, while there is a lack of comprehensive analysis of the whole field.

This chapter aims to fill these gaps. The first step is to explain what the private sector activities of EUCs are all about and what motivates them (Sect. 2). In a second step, the chapter describes the distortions of competition that can potentially arise from EUCs' private sector activities. The individual distortions are illustrated with concrete examples from the field of activity of the EUCs (Sect. 3). In a third step, it is examined to what extent legal requirements exist for EUCs to avoid distortions of competition (Sect. 4). Finally, a fourth and last step illustrates the possible measures which can be taken by EUCs and their owners' associations over and above the legal requirements to avoid distortions of competition and ward off accusations thereof (Sect. 5).

2 Private Sector Activities of EUCs

2.1 Distinction from Public Tasks of EUCs

Public tasks are undertakings defined by the legislator to be fulfilled on its behalf.[7] The opposite case is when EUCs become active in the private sector by carrying out entrepreneurial activities outside the fulfillment of public tasks.[8]

There are about 630 EUCs in Switzerland. Their fields of activity differ greatly. For example, several EUCs are organized as multi-utility companies and operate not solely electricity networks but also water, gas, district heating or telecommunications networks.[9] Some EUCs produce their own electricity, while others obtain all their electricity requirements from upstream suppliers.[10] While the business

[6]See Baumann (2019), p. 85 et seq. and 137 et seq. for a comprehensive overview.

[7]Rütsche (2013), p. 157 et seq.; Rütsche (2016), p. 79; similar also the definition in Federal Council (2017a), p. 1895, according to which public tasks are all those tasks which the state has to fulfill on the basis of a legal statute.

[8]This reflects our understanding. In contrast to this, the prevailing doctrine contrasts private sector state activity with entrepreneurial state activity in the monopoly sector (see Krähenmann 1987, p. 122; Reich 2009, n. 909; Rhinow et al. 2011, § 18, n. 38; Vogel 2000, p. 22 and 75).

[9]For a summary history of EUCs, see Reich (2009), p. 205 et seq.

[10]Swiss Federal Office of Energy (2018b), p. 15 et seq.

activities of EUCs differ in detail, the common feature of EUCs is that they generally operate their own distribution network and supply electricity to end consumers.[11]

Distribution network operation includes the obligation to connect end consumers in the respective network area to the electricity network and to ensure its maintenance and renewal.[12] Distribution network operators thus perform a public task that has been assigned to them by the respective canton on the basis of federal law.[13]

Under current legislation, electricity supply, i.e. the delivery of electricity, can be divided into the universal service and the free market. In the universal service pursuant to Art. 6 of the Swiss Electricity Supply Act (*Stromversorgungsgesetz*), customers whose annual consumption is below the threshold of 100 MWh per year (so-called "fixed end consumers") and who are therefore not free to choose their provider are supplied with electricity at "reasonable tariffs" by the state-designated local distribution network operator. In the free market, on the other hand, end consumers who exceed the above-mentioned consumption threshold are free to choose their electricity provider (Art. 6 para. 2 and para. 6 Swiss Electricity Supply Act). End consumers who would in principle be entitled to a free choice of provider but do not claim market access remain in the universal service with the fixed end consumers.[14] Since Art. 6 para. 1 of the Electricity Supply Act stipulates that the local distribution network operator has a supply obligation vis-à-vis the fixed end consumers and the consumers who renounce market access, the universal service of electricity is correctly qualified as a public task by legal doctrine and case law.[15]

In addition to operating the distribution network and providing the basic electricity supply, some utility companies also fulfill other public tasks. Examples include waste disposal, water and gas supply, maintenance of public lighting and operation of fiber optic networks.[16]

For example, the *Werke Fehraltorf* utilities are responsible not only for electricity supply and distribution network operation but also for water supply, waste disposal and road maintenance in the municipality of Fehraltorf.[17] In

(continued)

[11] Electricity Commission (2018), p. 28; Swiss Federal Office of Energy (2018b), p. 12.

[12] Jäger and Scheidegger (2016), Art. 5 para. 1–4, Electricity Supply Act, n. 8.

[13] Föhse (2018), p. 1242; see also Stöckli (2016), p. 184 and 192.

[14] See Föhse (2018), p. 1236; Scholl (2015), n. 13.24.

[15] BGE 144 III 111, E. 5.2; VGer BE 100.2017.247 of 12 January 2018, E. 3.3; Diebold and Ludin (2018), n. 85; Föhse (2015), p. 142; see further Rütsche (2013), p. 160.

[16] Whether the construction and operation of fiber optic networks are public tasks to be performed by an EUC or an activity that should be carried out by the EUC, is to be examined according to applicable legal provisions.

[17] See http://www.fehraltorf.ch/werke/dokumente/?navid=119623119623.

turn, the City of Zurich's electricity utility *ewz* was given the task of building and operating a fiber optic network by the city council under a performance mandate.[18]

2.2 Examples of Private Sector Services Provided by EUCs

In addition to operating the distribution network and fulfilling other public tasks, utility companies are economically active in areas that do not constitute public tasks.[19] The extent to which such private sector services are offered varies considerably from one EUC to another.[20]

Numerous utility companies offer homeowners comprehensive services in the planning, installation and maintenance of photovoltaic systems.

For example, *Stadtwerk Winterthur* offers an "all-round carefree package" which includes planning, financing, installation of the solar system and obtaining the necessary permits.[21]

Many EUCs also offer e-mobility solutions, such as the installation of home charging stations for electric vehicles. This service is also offered along with the assembly of photovoltaic systems.[22]

The revised Energy Act created the regulatory framework for "prosumer" consumption of solar power, whereby prosumer consortia were made possible.[23] However, the accounting for the electricity consumption and production by the respective

[18] See Resolution by the Municipal Council Zurich of 20 December 2006 (Nr. 2006/200). See for another example the EUC Eniwa, which has been mandated by the city of Aarau with the supply of water, electricity, gas and heating/cooling (City Council Aarau 2000, p. 1 et seq.).

[19] See Sect. 2.1.

[20] See also the examples mentioned in Vaterlaus et al. (2017), p. 35.

[21] See https://stadtwerk.winterthur.ch/privatkundschaft/angebote/fotovoltaik. Similar services are being offered by *Industrielle Werke Basel (IWB)* (available at https://www.iwb.ch/Fuer-Zuhause/E-Mobilitaet/Laden-mit-Solarstrom.html), *Romande Energie* (available at https://www.romande-energie.ch/particuliers/habitat-et-services-energetiques/panneaux-solaires-photovoltaiques) or BKW (available at https://www.bkw.ch/unsere-kompetenzen/building-solutions/solarenergie).

[22] See for example the offers by IWB (available at https://www.iwb.ch) and *Romande Energie* (available at https://www.romande-energie.ch).

[23] See Art. 16 and 17 Energy Act (*Energiegesetz*).

users is associated with difficulties. Numerous utility companies compete with private providers to offer billing solutions for self-consumption of solar power.[24]

A wide range of offers in the field of building services engineering represents a broad private sector field of activity for EUCs. Building services engineering consists of all the technical installations in a building and thus includes in particular the sanitary, heating, air conditioning, ventilation, high and low voltage systems. In this context, utility companies offer electrical and plumbing services as well as heating installations, lighting solutions and alarm systems.[25]

Several utilities offer so-called energy contracting solutions. In this case, the EUC assumes responsibility for the planning, construction, operation and maintenance of the heating system or heating network. The customer undertakes to purchase a certain amount of energy annually at a calculable price. He does not become the owner of the heating system and does not have to worry about its maintenance.[26]

A particularly illustrative case of private sector activity is when utilities sell household and electrical appliances.

For example, *Groupe E* advertises a “wide range” of household appliances, including refrigerators, dishwashers, irons, coffee machines, grills, steam cleaners and vacuum cleaners.[27]

The construction and operation of a fiber optic network may be a public task. On the other hand, utilities become private sector operators when they offer their own data network products.

---

[24] See for a detailed analysis Probst et al. (2019), p. 7 et seq.

[25] Illustrative in this regard is the owner strategy for *Stadtwerk Winterthur* (Stadtwerk Winterthur 2013), p. 5, which obliges *Stadtwerk Winterthur* to provide services in the areas of heating, plumbing and electricity installations and to offer a 24-hour service hotline for these services; see further the respective services offered by CKW (available at https://www.ckw.ch) and by EKZ (available at https://www.ekz.ch).

[26] See the respective services offered by EKZ (available at https://www.ekz.ch/contracting), SAK (available at https://www.sak.ch/private/prosumer/energiecontracting) or *Stadtwerk Winterthur* (available at https://stadtwerk.winterthur.ch/geschaeftskundschaft/angebote/energie-contracting).

[27] See https://shop.groupe-e.ch/de/.

For example, various EUCs offer their own internet services, which can be obtained with additional options for TV and telecommunications.[28] *Elektrizitätswerk Altdorf* in turn offers its own cloud solution for data storage.[29]

It is hardly surprising that EUCs also offer electricity products for the already liberalized electricity market.[30] Larger EUCs, such as Canton of Zurich's EKZ, also offer smaller utilities support services for electricity procurement.[31]

2.3 Why Do EUCs Become Active in the Private Sector?

One of the main reasons for the private sector activities of EUCs is the partial market liberalization that has already taken place and the intention to fully open the electricity market. The partial liberalization of the market has put the EUCs in a difficult position between private sector activity and the fulfillment of public tasks. As distribution network operators, energy utility companies must continue to operate the network and provide the basic energy supply as part of their public tasks.[32] At the same time, however, they face private competition with regard to large customers who make use of free market access. Liberalization has also put pressure on the margins for electricity prices charged by EUCs.[33] As electricity as a product is difficult to differentiate, price adjustments are necessary to keep and win customers in the liberalized environment.[34] Against this background, the establishment of new business areas in private sector markets is considered strategically necessary in order to compensate for the loss of income from traditional fields of activity and to secure the company's existence in the long term.[35]

---

[28] See the respective services offered by IWB (available at https://www.iwb.ch/Fuer-Zuhause/Telekom/IWB-Internet.html), Eniwa (available at https://www.eniwa.ch/de/internet.html) or *Groupe E* (available at https://www.groupe-e.ch/de/intelligente-loesungen/multimedia/privatkunden).

[29] See https://www.ewa.ch/privatkunden/daten-produkte/urcloud.

[30] See for an example the services offered by EKZ (available at https://www.ekz.ch) and CKW (available at https://www.ckw.ch).

[31] See https://www.ekz.ch/de/unternehmen/target/evu.html.

[32] See Sect. 2.1.

[33] See Graf and Waldmeier (2016), p. 13; Sonderegger (2014), p. 27.

[34] See Swiss Federal Office of Energy (2018b), p. 42. 67% of the customers with free market access (which, however, account for 80% of the electricity consumed by free customers) have left the universal service (Swiss Federal Office of Energy 2018b, p. 62).

[35] Baumann (2019), n. 91; Vaterlaus et al. (2017), p. 35; see further Vogel (2000), p. 7, and Bürer et al. (2021), p. 219.

In addition, the Energy Strategy 2050 has shifted the focus of the energy business.[36] Alongside the classic universal service, new services such as energy consulting or contracting offers for photovoltaic systems and heat pumps are coming to the fore. Owner communities are expected to give their utilities a leading role in improving energy efficiency and implementing renewable energies.[37] The efforts of energy supply companies in this respect are considered[38] essential for the implementation of the Energy Strategy 2050 and are therefore receiving special attention.

For example, in a benchmarking project of the Swiss Federal Office of Energy (SFOE), contracting services for PV systems and heat pumps by utilities are considered to make a positive contribution to energy efficiency and the promotion of renewables.[39] In this respect, there is also political pressure for EUCs to move into business areas such as electromobility, for example, whose profitability prospects are negative or difficult to predict.[40]

In addition, imminent liberalization and advancing technology are opening up new business fields that overlap the areas of public service and the free market. The focus is on offers under the overarching theme "smart energy", which coordinate energy production, energy consumption and energy infrastructure according to demand.[41]

Furthermore, within the framework of the liberalization of the electricity market, the utilities and their management have been granted greater autonomy by their public owners.[42] Against the backdrop of declining earnings in the traditional business area, it makes sense for the managers of utility companies to take advantage of this additional entrepreneurial scope in private sector markets. There are also incentives for managers of public enterprises to expand the scope of activities of the public enterprise, as the size of the enterprise is sometimes seen to reflect on the capabilities of the management.[43]

Finally, the granting of additional entrepreneurial leeway is likely to take place against the background that the public owners hope that this will secure long-term

---

[36] Vaterlaus et al. (2017), p. 35.

[37] See for example Municipal Council Bern (2017), p. 1, according to which ewb must position itself as an implementer of renewable energies; see further Enz (2018), p. 1 et seq. and 11, according to whom the canton's ownership strategy requires SAK to take action in the field of efficient energy use.

[38] EY (2017), p. 2.

[39] See Vettori et al. (2018), p. 4 and 60.

[40] See with regard to the profitability of charging stations State Council Basel-Stadt (2019), p. 11 and 25, where it is noted that private operators are not currently setting up charging infrastructures, as the high investment costs cannot be recouped.

[41] See with regard to "smart energy systems" Lund et al. (2017), p. 560.

[42] See Sonderegger (2012), p. 16; see also Vaterlaus et al. (2017), p. 29.

[43] Sappington and Sidak (2003), p. 500.

revenues for the public sector. The profits of EUCs can be of considerable importance for the budget of the community concerned.[44] If the revenues of EUCs fall, unpopular budget cuts or tax increases might become inevitable.[45] Certain communities thus explicitly expect their EUCs to become active in private sector markets.[46]

3 Distortions of Competition

From an economic point of view, it is problematic if public companies—utility companies in particular—are unjustifiably privileged in the private sector compared to private providers. Unjustified competitive advantages can significantly impair the allocative efficiency in the market economy and thus reduce the welfare of society as a whole.[47] In particular, there is a risk that, as a result of unjustifiably privileged EUCs, efficient private operators will be forced out of the market or privately owned companies will be deterred from entering it.[48]

Unjustified competitive advantages are those that are not attributable to the EUCs' own contributions but that rather result from the fact that EUCs are controlled by the public authorities and/or perform public tasks. In this context, the term "state-related competitive advantages" is also aptly used.[49] The following provides an overview of the state-related competitive advantages that can be expected from private sector activities of EUCs.

3.1 *Financial Advantages*

EUCs may have lower financing costs for their private sector activities compared to private providers. There are potential advantages in both borrowing and raising equity.

EUCs benefit from lower borrowing costs if they are granted low-interest loans at non-market conditions by the community or state-controlled institutions.

[44] Illustrative in this regard are the comments made by a politician of the city council in Bern with regard to the ownership strategy of ewb. The politician states that ewb delivers great profits of over CHF 30 million to the city treasury every year and that without this contribution the City of Bern would not be able to fulfill its public tasks (Council Secretariat City of Bern 2006, p. 681).

[45] For instance, the City of Bern had to compensate for budget shortfalls resulting from lower distributions by ewb (Municipal Council Bern 2016).

[46] The State Council of the Canton of Basel-Stadt explicitly expects IWB to become entrepreneurially active outside its public tasks (State Council Basel-Stadt 2018, p. 4).

[47] See Baumann (2019), n. 252 et seq.; Friederiszick (2008), p. 652 et seq.

[48] See Friederiszick (2008), p. 653; Geddes (2004), p. 29; Sappington and Sidak (2004), p. 14.

[49] See Diebold (2014), p. 221; Federal Council (2017b), p. 9.

For example, the City of Bern raises capital on the financial market to the benefit of its utility *Energie Wasser Bern* (ewb). Due to the city's positive rating, ewb benefits from favorable interest rate conditions. In principle, ewb must compensate the risk imposed on the City of Bern by the raising of capital and the more favorable interest conditions in the form of an interest margin to the City of Bern. However, due to the tense market environment, the City of Bern recently decided not to charge the interest margin, which resulted in a competitive advantage for ewb.[50]

In addition, EUCs are granted more favorable conditions for borrowing if lenders assign them a higher credit rating due to their proximity to the state. For example, a higher creditworthiness may result from the fact that income or assets from the EUC's public tasks serve as collateral.[51] In addition, existing explicit or implicit state guarantees have a positive effect on the creditworthiness of EUCs.[52]

Not only in terms of borrowing costs but also in terms of equity capital costs, EUCs can have state-related competitive advantages. Private competitors have to pay interest on the equity provided to them by their owners to cover the investment risk. Private providers must generate a profit to pay such interest on equity. Consequently, they include a corresponding profit mark-up in their prices. If the public owners, on the other hand, do not demand an adequate return on equity, the EUC can offer its goods and services without the necessary profit component and thus at potentially lower prices than its private competitors.[53]

Sometimes the regulations by the public owners explicitly allow the waiver of a profit component.[54] It is similarly problematic if the public owners do not specify profit, dividend or return on equity targets for the utility company.[55] In this case, there is a risk that EUCs will not include a (sufficient) profit margin in their private sector offers.

[50] See Municipal Council Bern (2016).

[51] For instance, electricity distribution networks or utilities could be pledged. However, certain EUCs are not allowed to pledge their distribution networks (see Art. 3 para. 1 ewz regulation [*Verordnung über ewz*]).

[52] Geddes (2004), p. 30 et seq.; Nielsen (1981), p. 58; see also Waldmeier (2018), n. 538. Explicit state guarantees in favor of EUCs exist if the liability of the community for the EUC is stipulated by law. According to a study by Vaterlaus et al. (2017), p. 37, 30% of urban EUCs have an explicit state guarantee. In the case of implicit state guarantees, in contrast to explicit state guarantees, there is no legal liability of the community, but it can be concluded from the specific circumstances that the state will accept responsibility for the debts of the EUC.

[53] See Baumann (2019), n. 198 et seq.; Herrmann (2014), p. 413; see with regard to the relevance of the profit margin in public sector transportation Abegg, Seferovic (2018), n. 9 et seq.

[54] For instance, ewb must set cost-covering prices for its private sector services (Art. 13 ewb regulation [*ewb-Reglement*]).

[55] See Baumann (2019), n. 200.

Finally, there may be financing advantages from hybrid activity if EUCs can use the income from public service activities to make investments in their private sector activities. This is particularly problematic if the margins in the private sector do not allow the private providers to make corresponding investments and if the borrowing and equity capital required for this would also be too expensive at a risk-adjusted interest rate.[56]

It is argued, for example, that without the income from the monopoly business of Bern's power supplier, *Bernische Kraftwerke* (BKW) would not have had the necessary financial resources and stability to acquire various companies in the building technology sector.[57]

3.2 *Tax and Regulatory Advantages*

Private sector activities of EUCs may be unjustifiably favored by lower or no taxation.[58] A low tax burden on EUCs' private sector activities may result mainly from their legal form. The Confederation, the cantons and the communes, as well as the public institutions of these communities, are exempt from both direct federal taxes and, usually, from cantonal and communal taxes.[59] This means that dependent EUCs in particular, but also EUCs with the legal form of a legally independent institution, are not taxable, even if they carry out private business activities.[60] This unacceptable competitive advantage can be reduced by a provision in the organizational decree according to which the utility is liable to pay tax on its private economic activities.[61]

In addition to tax advantages, regulatory advantages for EUCs' private sector activities mainly offer benefits in the form of simplified licensing procedures, legal exemptions, specific bankruptcy decrees or special rights.[62]

---

[56] Baumann (2019), n. 201 et seq.

[57] Schneider (2016), p. 647 et seq.

[58] See Capobianco, Christiansen (2011), p. 5; see further Flatt and Zindel (2017), p. 1 et seq.

[59] Art. 56 let. a-c Federal Act on Direct Federal Taxation (*Bundesgesetz über die direkte Bundessteuer*).

[60] See Mayoraz (2018), n. 556. 17% of EUCs that have their own legal personality are constituted in the form of a public institution (Swiss Federal Office of Energy 2018b, p. 17 et seq.). On the other hand, tax exemptions for EUCs with a legal form under private law are only possible under strict conditions (see BGer 2C_206/2018 of 23 July 2019, E. 4.4).

[61] See Baumann (2019), n. 210.

[62] OECD (2016), p. 30.

3.3 Cross-Subsidies

In the case of EUCs with hybrid activities, there is a risk that the private sector activities of the EUC will be cross-subsidized. This involves shifting costs or revenues within the EUC to the benefit of the private sector activities and to the detriment of the public sector.[63]

EUCs operating hybrid systems can cross-subsidize the private sector mainly by misallocating costs.[64] The public sector has to bear costs that were actually incurred in the private sector. Such a cost shift occurs directly when the EUC's public service remit covers the deficit of its private sector activities at the end of the accounting period. On the other hand, it is more difficult to trace cross-subsidies that are implemented by means of common costs misallocation. Common costs are those that cannot be directly allocated to a product.[65] An example of this is the cost of an EUC's head office building, which serves both areas of activity. A clear allocation of common costs to the respective market segments is not possible in many cases and is difficult for the regulatory authority to verify.[66] This may provide a certain incentive for EUCs to charge too low a share of common costs to the private sector, thus cross-subsidizing it.[67]

3.4 Economies of Scope

EUCs operating hybrid systems are able to realize considerable economies of scope. These are savings in the average total costs that arise when different goods are provided together by one company. Where economies of scope exist, it is cheaper to produce two or more products together in a single company rather than separately in different companies.[68]

In perfect markets, economies of scope do not pose a problem because competitors could also enter the respective markets and thus benefit from the resulting cost savings. In contrast, economies of scope resulting from the hybrid activity of an EUC are problematic. As a rule, private competitors cannot enter the public domain due to legal restrictions, as the fulfillment of public tasks is regularly reserved for certain public EUCs. Private competitors are thus not in a position to realize the same

[63] Baumann (2019), n. 215 et seq. and 219.

[64] See European Commission (2010), p. 28.

[65] See with regard to common costs Fritsch (2018), p. 216.

[66] Brennan (1990), p. 40; Fritsch (2018), p. 216; Weber (1986), p. 420 et seq.

[67] See Geddes (2004), p. 30.

[68] See Fritsch (2018), p. 171 et seq.; Ghazarian (2018), p. 22; Peeperkorn and Verouden (2014), n. 1.49.

economies of scope and are consequently exposed to higher costs than their hybrid competitors.[69]

In principle, utilities can realize economies of scope across their entire value chain. If the private and public sectors need the same inputs, cost savings can be achieved through joint purchasing. Examples include volume discounts on the purchase of computers or vehicles or discounts in connection with joint office space rentals.[70]

Furthermore, an EUC can realize economies of scope if infrastructures, means of production or services can be used jointly by its private and public sectors.[71] Examples of this are the shared use of websites, vehicles, tools, software programs, HR departments or warehouses.

Economies of scope also result from the bundled offer of products from the private and public sectors. A bundled offer of several products by one utility company may well meet a customer need to obtain all services from one single source (so-called "one-stop shopping").[72] Cost advantages arise for the utility, for example through the joint use of sales staff or joint invoicing. The cost savings can then be (partially) returned to the customers for acquisition purposes.

For example, Lucerne's utility *Energie Wasser Luzern* (ewl) announced a new type of combined product at the end of 2017, which encompasses internet products and electricity that can be purchased for a monthly flat rate. A combination discount is granted, whereby customers pay CHF 150 less per year on a cumulative basis.[73]

This last example highlights the issue of economies of scope in hybrid activities of EUCs, since private competitors cannot make a corresponding combined offer (with the basic supply of electricity plus internet) to fixed end consumers.

Finally, economies of scope for EUCs can also derive from the joint use of intangible assets. An EUC can use its brand, which was initially created and strengthened in the public sector, for products and services in the private market (so-called "umbrella branding").[74] Umbrella branding has the advantage for EUCs that they do not have to build a new brand for their products offered in the private sector. This makes it easier for EUCs to enter private sector markets. Similarly, EUCs can use umbrella branding to transfer their high image recognition and trust values from the public sector to their private sector offerings.[75] It has been found that

[69] See Ghazarian (2018), p. 52 et seq.; Sappington and Sidak (2004), p. 13.

[70] See Baumann (2019), n. 232.

[71] See Barney and Hesterly (2015), p. 217.

[72] See Baumann (2019), n. 235 and 238.

[73] Ewl (2017).

[74] See for a detailed discussion of umbrella branding Baumann (2019), n. 234.

[75] See Scheda (2014), p. 34.

although "independent customers" often show a willingness to switch from the universal service to the market offer, they often remain with their incumbent EUC as it enjoys a high degree of credibility.[76]

3.5 Information Advantages

A further competitive advantage resulting from proximity to the state can come in the form of information advantages for EUCs. Due to their closeness to the state, their obligation to fulfill public tasks and personnel interrelations, EUCs have access to business-relevant information that is not available to private providers.[77] In particular, EUCs can potentially access customer data from the public sector, which allows them to tailor their own private sector offerings to specific customer needs.

For example, employees of the utility *Elektrizitätswerk Schaffhausen* used customer addresses from the monopoly sector for a marketing campaign for solar systems.[78]

Significant information advantages can result for EUCs from their function as (distribution) network operators. As distribution network operators, EUCs are given exclusive insights into the functioning and future development of the electricity system. They may therefore have an information advantage over private competitors, for example in the areas of storage requirements and flexibility.[79] In addition, network operators may obtain data from the customers' network connection, which can be used for new business models.[80] These include customized products, the sale of data to third parties (e.g. insurance companies) and new services.[81]

As a result of information advantages, an EUC can also give preference to its own private sector activities over private competitors.

For example, *Energie Wasser Bern* (ewb), in its function as a distribution network operator, must periodically request the owners of electrical

(continued)

[76] Swiss Federal Office of Energy (2018b), p. 62 et seq.

[77] See for a detailed discussion Baumann (2019), n. 247 et seq.

[78] The employees were subsequently fined by the Swiss Federal Office of Energy for this misconduct (see Vonplon 2019, p. 13).

[79] Kratz (2018), p. 158 et seq.

[80] Kratz (2018), p. 159.

[81] Beyeler (2017), p. 59.

installations to have their installations inspected. In principle, the owners may entrust inspections to any company authorized to do so. Unless the owners had previously decided on a particular inspection company, ewb passed on almost all inspection assignments to its own subsidiary. ewb also expressly referred on its website to the inspection offers of its own subsidiary but not to offers from other private suppliers.[82]

4 Legal Requirements for EUCs to Avoid Distortions of Competition

4.1 Constitutional Requirements

According to prevailing legal doctrine and case law, the private sector activities of state-owned companies and thus also especially those of EUCs must be conducted in a manner that is neutral to competition, respectively in a manner that does not distort competition.[83] The requirement of competitive neutrality results from the interaction of Art. 27 and 94 of the Swiss Federal Constitution (*Bundesverfassung*).[84] The private sector activities of the EUCs may be considered in compliance with the requirement of competitive neutrality if they have to face the same competitive conditions as private competitors do. Distortions of competition in the form of legal and de facto privileges for the private sector activities of EUCs must therefore be avoided. In particular, legal advantages such as the exemption from tax and insurance obligations, the granting of explicit state guarantees or exemptions from the relevant economic supervision and competition law are problematic.[85] Furthermore, de facto privileges such as the preferential provision of infrastructure, implicit state guarantees and cross-subsidization also conflict with the requirement of competitive neutrality.[86]

Although the requirement of competition neutrality is thus generally easy to understand, its concrete implementation and enforcement is much more difficult:

---

[82] See Competition Commission (2014), p. 79 et seq, n. 156 et seq., ewb.

[83] See for an overview of the requirements for private sector activities by the state Hangartner (2007), p. 241 et seq.; Hänni and Stöckli (2013), n. 1717 et seq.; Krähenmann (1987), p. 209 et seq.; Reich (2013), p. 1410; Rhinow et al. (2011), § 18 n.53 et seq.; Tschannen et al. (2014), § 10 n. 24 et seq.; Vogel (2000), p. 109 et seq., 116 and 125; BGE 138 I 378, E. 7-9.

[84] Schönbächler (1998), n. 86; Vogel (2000), p. 123; BGE 143 II 425, E. 4.2.

[85] See Hangartner (2007), p. 245 et seq.; Hänni, Stöckli (2013), n. 1720; Vogel (2000), p. 208 et seq.

[86] Rhinow et al. (2011), § 18 n. 106; Hangartner (2007), 245 et seq.; Uhlmann (1997), p. 213 et seq.; BGE 138 I 378, E. 9.1.

Firstly, it is apparent from case law that certain distortions of competition are not considered at all, or only to a certain extent, to be a violation of competitive neutrality. In fact, the case law on this matter does not always appear to be entirely consistent.[87] In the *Glarnersach* decision, the Federal Supreme Court classified factual competitive advantages, such as access to customer data in the monopoly sector or the possibility of offering combination products, as modest at best—which is why a significant distortion of competition was not considered to exist.[88] In contrast, in a more recent decision the Federal Supreme Court rightly assumed that the synergy effects resulting from the parallel fulfillment of a public task and the provision of private sector services constitute a distortion of competition to the detriment of competitors operating purely in the private sector.[89]

Secondly, it is difficult to conclusively derive from the condition of competitive neutrality what concrete measures are to be taken to avoid the respective distortions of competition. The handling of cross-subsidization provides an example of this. According to the Federal Supreme Court in the *Glarnersach* decision, the financial separation of the (public) monopoly sector from private sector services was sufficient for the enforcement of the ban on cross-subsidies.[90] In this context, the Supreme Court considered cross-subsidies via common cost allocation to be "hardly plausible" if the allocation keys are based on realistic cost estimates.[91] On the other hand, purely financial or accounting separation is considered insufficient in legal doctrine, which indeed postulates that, due to the uncertainties in cost allocation, a strict organizational separation of the two areas would also be required in order to effectively prevent cross-subsidies.[92]

Overall, the requirement of competitive neutrality so far results in only a few specific requirements for how EUCs organize their private sector activities. Clearly inadmissible are cross-subsidies, which means that the public service remit must be financially separated from the EUC's private sector activities. Tax, financing, economies of scope and information advantages are problematic in light of the requirement of competitive neutrality. However, concrete and consistent requirements for dealing with them cannot yet be derived from the existing case law.

[87] See Baumann (2019), n. 342 et seq.

[88] BGE 138 I 378, E. 9.4; see for critical discussions of this decision Hangartner (2012), p. 1821; Kraemer and Stöckli (2013), p. 29; Reich (2013), p. 1411 et seq.; see further Weber and Volz (2013), n. 2.650. It is, however, important to note that in the *Glarnersach* decision, the Federal Court only subjected the statute in question to a very broad review (so-called abstract norm review, in German *"abstrakte Normenkontrolle"*).

[89] See BGer 2C_1007/2015 of 10 May 2016, E. 5.2.

[90] BGE 138 I 378, E. 9.2.

[91] BGE 138 I 378, E. 9.3.3.

[92] Abegg and Frei (2018), p. 152; Kraemer and Stöckli (2013), p. 38 et seq.; Stoffel and Murith (2019), p. 34.

4.2 Antitrust Law

Electricity utilities, irrespective of their legal form, are subject to antitrust law if they carry out private sector activities outside their monopoly areas.[93] In the case of EUCs, it can be assumed in general that they have a dominant position on the market because of their public tasks and any monopoly rights associated with them. In this context, dominant companies behave unlawfully if, by abusing their dominant position in the market, they hinder other companies from starting or continuing to compete or disadvantage trading partners.[94] According to the practice of the competition authorities, this dominant position can also be abused in upstream or downstream or neighboring private markets.[95] If EUCs have a dominant position in the market, it must be examined to what extent the distortions of competition (described in Sect. 3 above) are to be qualified as abuse of a dominant position within the meaning of Art. 7 of the Swiss Cartel Act (*Kartellgesetz*).[96]

In the case of cross-subsidization, the discrimination of trading partners (Art. 7 para. 2 let. b Swiss Cartel Act) as well as the unlawful practice of price undercutting (Art. 7 para. 2 let. d Swiss Cartel Act) may be of relevance.[97]

In the case of discrimination of trading partners (Art. 7 para. 2 let. b Swiss Cartel Act), the EUC's own private sector division is given preference over its private competitors. The private sector division purchases services from the EUC at cross-subsidized conditions, while private providers have to pay the full price. However, this abuse presupposes that the cross-subsidized services in question are actually offered to or demanded by private competitors. This will often not be the case, particularly with respect to typical internal group or company services in the areas of IT, personnel administration, marketing or accounting.[98]

By contrast, in the case of price undercutting (Art. 7 para. 2 let. d Swiss Cartel Act), cross-subsidization is used to undercut prices or other trading conditions in order to weaken or drive current competitors out of the market or to prevent potential competitors from entering the market.[99] Abusive price undercutting is to be assumed if the revenues generated are not sufficient to cover the company's own costs in the

[93] Art. 2 para. 1 Swiss Cartel Act. See Competition Commission (2014), p. 79 et seq., n. 22 et seq., ewb; see also BGE 138 I 378, E. 9.3.3 and 9.4; see further Ducrey (2009), p. 76.

[94] Art. 7 para. 1 Swiss Cartel Act.

[95] Competition Commission (2014), p. 79 et seq., n. 66 et seq., ewb; Stäuble and Schraner (2018a), Art. 7 n. 239.

[96] See Competition Commission (2014), p. 79 et seq., n. 81, ewb.

[97] Competition Commission (2014), p. 79 et seq., n. 88 and 91. ewb; Borer (2011), Art. 7, n. 18. According to Amstutz, Carron (2010), Art. 7 n. 242, cross-subsidization may also constitute a form of unfair conditions of trade within the meaning of Art. 7 para. 2 let. c Swiss Cartel Act.

[98] See Competition Commission (2014), p. 79 et seq., n. 88 et seq., ewb; Stäuble and Schraner (2018b), Art. 7 n. 324.

[99] Competition Commission (2014), p. 79 et seq., n. 91, ewb; Zäch (2005), n. 684.

long term.[100] After successfully forcing the competitors from the market, the utility can then raise prices above the competitive level and compensate for losses (so-called "recoupment").[101] In addition to recoupment, abusive undercutting also requires that an undercutting strategy is implemented and that there are no justifications for the undercutting. Cross-subsidization on its own, however, does not constitute a requirement for price undercutting in the sense of Art. 7 para. 2 let. d Swiss Cartel Act. But it does make undercutting financially more bearable for the EUC employing the strategy, especially if funds from the public sector are used for cross-subsidization.[102]

According to the existing practice of the Secretariat of the Swiss Competition Commission (*Sekretariat der Wettbewerbskommission WEKO*), there are indications of abusive cross-subsidization, as can occur in the case of unequal treatment of trading partners or price undercutting, if (i) the private sector activities of EUC receive services from that EUC at non-market conditions, (ii) the EUC obtains services from the private sector at too high a price or without justification by not complying with public procurement law, or (iii) structural deficits of the private sector activities are covered with funds from the public task remit of the EUC.[103]

An abuse of market power within the meaning of Art. 7 Swiss Cartel Act can also exist when information advantages are being exploited by the EUC. In the case of hybrid activities, the transfer of information from the public sector activities to the private sector activities is problematic because the EUC has the relevant information due to its obligation to fulfill a public task and not due to its own economic capabilities. If the transfer of information within the EUC is based on an obstructionist strategy aimed at forcing competitors from a market or keeping them out of the private market, an abuse of a dominant position is likely to be assumed.[104] According to the Secretariat of the Competition Commission, an impermissible data exchange can also consist of an EUC recommending its own private sector services to its customers in the public sector.[105]

EUCs may unlawfully impede competitors in the meaning of Art. 7 para. 2 let. f Swiss Cartel Act if they couple private sector offers with services from the public sector. Such "coupling" can also be achieved by means of positive incentives, in particular discounts. In the case of hybrid EUCs, the abusive nature of coupling arises from the special legal status of the public service area.[106] Against this

---

[100] In determining whether prices are cost-covering, it must be examined whether the company is able to cover average variable costs during the period of price undercutting (Amstutz and Carron 2010, Art. 7 n. 377).

[101] Amstutz, Carron (2010), Art. 7 n. 322; Borer (2011), Art 7 n. 24; Stäuble and Schraner (2018b), Art. 7 n. 436.

[102] See Amstutz and Carron (2010), Art. 7 n. 365 and 372; Zäch (2005), n. 684.

[103] Competition Commission (2014), p. 79 et seq., n. 85 et seq. and 127 et seq., ewb.

[104] See Competition Commission (2014), p. 79 et seq., n. 145 et seq., ewb.

[105] See Competition Commission (2014), p. 79 et seq., n. 156 et seq., ewb.

[106] See Borer (2011), Art. 7 n. 27; Vogel (2000), p. 197 et seq.; Zäch (2005), n. 702; see further Competition Commission (2011b), p. 483 et seq., n. 159, Gebäudeversicherung Bern (GVB).

background, a combined product for the purchase of electricity and internet services would be problematic, especially if a combined discount is granted.[107] However, combined products from private sector activities and public tasks are hardly unobjectionable from an antitrust point of view, even without the granting of discounts, as private suppliers are unable to make an equivalent offer.[108]

In contrast, in an older decision from the year 2011 the Secretariat of the Competition Commission had considered it unproblematic under antitrust law for a hybrid company to apply umbrella branding. In accordance with the Secretariat's practice, the use of a common umbrella brand as well as the uniform design and reciprocal linking of the group's own websites in particular are to be classified as permissible conduct.[109] However, joint advertising campaigns for products of private sector activities and public services should be avoided.[110]

It follows from the above that the problematic practices punishable under antitrust law cover a subset of possible distortions of competition by EUCs. Distortions of competition such as cross-subsidization, information advantages and, to a lesser extent, economies of scope may form part of abusive practices, provided that the other elements of the relevant exclusionary conduct are given.[111] Moreover, it is necessary that the distortions of competition do not result in an obstructive effect that is merely minor in nature.[112] However, competitive advantages of EUCs that are due to state regulations, such as tax advantages and financing advantages, hardly fall within the scope of Art. 7 Swiss Cartel Act.[113]

---

[107] See Sect. 3.4 above with regard to a corresponding combination product intended to be launched by ewl.

[108] Against this background, *Gebäudeversicherung Bern* has undertaken not to offer any combination products (see Competition Commission 2011b, p. 483 et seq., n. 166 et seq., Gebäudeversicherung Bern [GVB]).

[109] Competition Commission (2011a), p. 87 et seq., n. 35, Switch/Switchplus; Competition Commission (2014), p. 79 et seq., n. 167 et seq., ewb; Competition Commission (2011b), p. 483 et seq., n. 165, Gebäudeversicherung Bern (GVB). Stoffel and Graber (2013), p. 853, on the other hand, consider the joint use of a website or a customer magazine to be actions in the grey area of competition law.

[110] For example, *Gebäudeversicherung Bern* has undertaken not to conduct any joint advertising campaigns for the compulsory buildings insurance and the private insurance offered (Competition Commission 2011b, p. 483 et seq., n. 167, Gebäudeversicherung Bern ([GVB]).

[111] Otherwise, the distortions of competition may still be subsumed under the general clause of Art. 7 para. 1 Swiss Cartel Act. According to Stoffel and Murith (2019), p. 45, cross-subsidizations are per se prohibited under antitrust law.

[112] Competition Commission (2011a), p. 87 et seq., n. 51, Switch/Switchplus.

[113] See Vogel (2000), p. 208 et seq.

4.3 Electricity Supply Law

The Swiss Electricity Supply Act (*Stromversorgungsgesetz*) addresses the risk of EUCs transferring their market power resulting from distribution network operation to competitive areas of activity with the following unbundling requirements.[114] According to Art. 10 para. 1 Swiss Electricity Supply Act, EUCs must ensure the independence of distribution network operation. To this end, the distribution network operations are to be unbundled from the other areas of activity, at least in accounting terms (Art. 10 para. 3 Swiss Electricity Supply Act).[115] In addition, Art. 10 para. 2 Swiss Electricity Supply Act provides for informational unbundling, according to which economically sensitive information obtained from network operation may not be used by EUCs for other areas of activity. Finally, cross-subsidization between network operation and the other areas of activity is explicitly prohibited.[116] The Federal Electricity Commission (ElCom) monitors compliance with these provisions.[117] Failure to comply with the requirements for accounting unbundling and the prohibition of use of sensitive information could result in fines of up to CHF 100,000.[118]

Art. 10 para. 1 Swiss Electricity Supply Act expressly prohibits cross-subsidization between distribution network operation and other areas of activity. The provision aims to ensure that revenues from the network sector are not used to cross-subsidize competitive activities.[119] However, the prohibition of cross-subsidization is largely unspecified. Due to the heterogeneity of the utilities, it was decided not to make specific regulatory requirements for the allocation of common costs.[120] However, according to Art. 7 para. 5 Electricity Supply Ordinance (*Stromversorgungsverordnung*), the cost allocation keys used must be appropriate, comprehensible and recorded in writing, and they must comply with the principle of consistency.[121]

Informational unbundling shall prevent that EUCs have a competitive advantage over their competitors arising from the knowledge of distribution network operation.[122] Economically sensitive information according to Art. 10 para. 2 Swiss Electricity Supply Act is information from the operation of electricity networks which is suitable for providing the EUC with a competitive advantage in the private

[114] Federal Council (2004), p. 1648.

[115] See also Art. 6 para. 3 and Art. 12 para. 2 Electricity Supply Act.

[116] Art. 10 para. 1 Electricity Supply Act.

[117] Art. 22 para. 1 Electricity Supply Act.

[118] Art. 29 para. 1 and 2 Electricity Supply Act. Accordingly, the Swiss Federal Office of Energy fined employees of *Elektrizitätswerke Schaffhausen* for misusing addresses from the monopoly sector for a marketing campaign for private sector activities (see Vonplon 2019, p. 13).

[119] See Federal Council (2004), p. 1648.

[120] See D'Arcy and Burri (2009), p. 133.

[121] See also VSE (2018), p. 10.

[122] Federal Council (2004), p. 1649; see also VSE (2018), p. 17.

sector.[123] An unjustified competitive advantage may arise if the information from the operation of the network leads, for example, to a reduction in costs, an advantage in time, an increase in revenue or an improvement in the product in the private sector activities of the utility.[124] The prohibition of use of economically sensitive information includes in particular the master data (name, address, etc.) and consumption data of network users as well as related meta and structural data.[125] Informational unbundling has gained in importance as a result of progressive digitalization and the introduction of intelligent metering systems.[126] In this context, the issue has also increasingly moved into the focus of ElCom's attention.[127]

The accounting unbundling of the distribution network operations from the other areas of activity serves to make the cost structure of network operations transparent to the regulator and thus preclude inadmissible cross-subsidization.[128] However, the legislator has left EUCs considerable leeway with regard to the systemic implementation of accounting unbundling.[129]

The provisions of the Swiss Electricity Supply Act described above are hardly sufficient to comprehensively avoid cross-subsidization and information advantages. Because the legislator has deliberately refrained from organizational unbundling of the distribution network business,[130] it remains permissible, for example, for the same persons to hold management positions in both the distribution network and competitive areas.[131] Economically relevant information flows between the areas of activity can therefore hardly be avoided. In the case of accounting unbundling, there are considerable differences in the EUC's overhead cost allocations. This makes it more difficult to monitor the ban on cross-subsidization. Finally, economies of scope are only addressed indirectly, namely via information unbundling and the ban on cross-subsidization. Ultimately, the Swiss Electricity Supply Act does not contain any provisions on the financing of and tax advantages for energy supply companies.

[123] Orelli and Thomann (2016), Art. 10 n. 9.

[124] Orelli and Thomann (2016), Art. 10 n. 9; VSE (2019), p. 17.

[125] VSE (2019), p. 18; see also for a detailed list of economically sensitive data Bundesnetzagentur (2007), p. 15.

[126] Lang (2019), p. 3.

[127] Electricity Commission (2018), p. 28; Lang (2019), p. 3.

[128] D'Arcy and Burri (2009), p. 130; Orelli and Thomann (2016), Art. 10 n. 18; VSE (2018), p. 9.

[129] Orelli and Thomann (2016), Art. 10 n. 20; see further D'Arcy, Burri (2009), p. 130 et seq.; Stillfried (2010), p. 182.

[130] Federal Council (2004), p. 1649.

[131] Orelli, Thomann (2016), p. 16.

5 Measures to Avoid Distortions of Competition

There are only few concrete guidelines for EUCs on how to deal with potential distortions of competition in their private sector activities (Sect. 4 above). This regulatory deficit weighs heavily, as on the one hand it is hardly to be expected that the private sector activities of EUCs will lose importance in the future.[132] On the other hand, many of the measures proposed here may become relevant regardless, particularly with a view to a possible electricity agreement with the EU. It is to be expected that Switzerland will have to adopt the requirements of EU state aid law and the electricity acquis to the greatest extent possible in order to participate in the EU's internal electricity market.[133] Distortions of competition, in particular tax and financing advantages, are incompatible with the EU ban on state aid in principle.[134]

The following lays out *de lege ferenda* measures to avoid the distortions of competition described above.[135] For EUCs that want to pro-actively ensure the competitive neutrality of their private sector activities, this catalogue of measures also offers a corresponding recommendation for action already today. This is not an exhaustive list. Depending on the area of activity of the utility, there are further distortions of competition which may result in an additional need for action.

5.1 Organizational Requirements

Avoiding distortions of competition effectively requires a structural separation between the public tasks and the private sector activities of the EUC. Structural separation can be carried out in different gradations. It may take the form of accounting, functional, organizational or even ownership unbundling.[136] At the time when the Swiss Electricity Supply Act was enacted, distribution networks were not organizationally separated due to the restrictions of smaller EUCs.[137] However, the distortions of competition described above are favored by the lack of organizational separation. If the private sector activities of an EUC are considerable, legal provisions to ensure the organizational outsourcing of these activities to a

[132] See Sect. 2.3.

[133] Federal Council (2013) p. 7582; see also Mayoraz (2018), n. 547; Hofmann et al. (2021), p. 85.

[134] Mayoraz (2018), n. 551 and 553 et seq.; Ziegler, Moser (2019), n. 58 and 77.

[135] In doing so, reference is made in particular to some of the relevant EU requirements.

[136] See OECD (2015), p. 46 et seq.; Petrik-Haltiner (2017), p. 44.

[137] Federal Council (2004), p. 1649; Orelli, Thomann (2016), Art. 10 n. 8. In contrast, Art. 26 para. 1 of Directive 2009/72 of the European Parliament and the Council of 13 July 2009 concerning common rules for the internal market in electricity and repealing Directive 2003/54/EC, OJ L 211, 14 August 2009, 55-93, requires distribution network operation to be carried out by a separate company. However, Art. 26 para. 4 of the Directive 2009/72/EC allows exemptions for vertically integrated EUCs with fewer than 100,000 customers.

separate company are necessary. In order to avoid tax advantages, the legal form of a private-law company limited by shares should be chosen in principle.[138]

However, in the case of EUCs with limited private sector activities, organizational separation may not be appropriate. In this case, the EUC should be required by law to separate the two sectors by function. To this end, the public sector and private sector activities must be managed as separate business units.[139] In order to meet the requirements of the Federal Supreme Court and Electricity Supply Act regarding the financial separation of public and private sector activities, at least the accounts of the two sectors must be kept separately.[140]

In any case, the separation of public tasks and private sector activities requires that the public tasks to be performed by the EUC are clearly defined. In particular, expansions that are not worthwhile from an entrepreneurial point of view but politically desired by the EUC's public owners must be defined by the latter as a public task.[141] The costs involved in undertaking such public tasks must be disclosed to the legislator so that it can make an informed decision on the cost-benefit ratio of the project.[142]

5.2 *Financial Advantages*

If private-sector activities of EUCs are financed by means of debt (loans, credits, etc.), the law must provide that the EUC has to pay interest at market rates in order to avoid financing advantages. On the one hand, an EUC may only grant loans to its private sector business divisions or subsidiaries at normal market conditions in order not to expose itself to the accusation of abusive cross-subsidization under antitrust law.[143] On the other hand, the public owners themselves can also ensure that there are no financing advantages by granting loans to an EUC for private sector activities only on market terms.

In order to determine the market rate, the interest rate that would apply to comparable private companies must be ascertained. To this end, EUCs should obtain appropriate benchmark ratings for all loans. The rating would determine the interest rate at which the public utility would have to take out the loan if it were operating as

[138] See Sect. 3.2; Mayoraz (2018), n. 556.

[139] See Finger et al. (2009), p. 22.

[140] See Sect. 4.3. According to Art. 4 para. 1 Directive 2006/111 of the European Commission of 16 November 2006 on the transparency of financial relations between Member States and public undertakings as well as on financial transparency within certain undertakings, OJ L 318, 17 November 2006, 17-25, the costs and revenues are to be allocated by means of uniformly applied, objectively justified and clearly defined cost accounting principles.

[141] See OECD (2012), p. 53.

[142] See OECD (2015), p. 47.

[143] Competition Commission (2014), p. 79 et seq., n. 115, ewb.

a private company. To ensure the independence of the ratings, they should not be issued by institutions that maintain a significant business relationship with the EUC.

It may prove disproportionately costly for EUCs to obtain such ratings, especially if the debt financing is negligible for the EUC's business. For this reason, it might be appropriate for the regulator to calculate the interest advantage resulting from state control for different categories of utilities. This would then be added to the interest rate actually granted in order to determine the market rate.

Interest rate adjustments are more difficult when utilities take out loans from third parties. As shown above, state guarantees in favor of EUCs lead to financing advantages. For this reason, explicit state guarantees for private sector activities of EUCs must be abolished as a first step. However, it can be presumed that even without an explicit state guarantee, third parties assume that there is a low risk of default of a state-owned utility. In order to avoid financing advantages, EUCs should be obliged to calculate the resulting interest advantage using the methods described above and then pay it to the state.

In addition, public authorities should only provide collateral for EUC loans at market conditions. Market conditions may normally be assumed if (i) the EUC is not in any financial difficulties, (ii) the collateral is linked to a specific transaction, (iii) the community also bears part of the risk and (iv) the utility pays a market price for the provision of the collateral.[144]

With regard to advantages in terms of return on equity, it is imperative for the community to expressly state in both the organizational decree and the owner strategy that private sector activities may only be taken up by the EUC if market returns are achieved.[145] A market return corresponds to the average expected return on an investment that the market requires on the basis of generally accepted criteria, taking into account in particular the risk involved in the investment, the financial situation of the firm and the specific characteristics of the economic activity concerned.[146]

For example, the calculation of the internal rate of return (IRR) is a widely accepted standard method for determining the annual return on capital.[147] The same results are usually obtained when the investment decision is evaluated on the

[144] See n. 114 Commission Notice on the notion of State aid as referred to in Article 107(1) of the Treaty on the Functioning of the European Union C/2016/2946, OJ C 262, 19 July 2016, 1–50.

[145] According to Schedler et al. (2016), p. 118, the return on equity must be regulated in the owner strategy.

[146] See n. 102 Commission Notice on the notion of State aid as referred to in Article 107(1) of the Treaty on the Functioning of the European Union C/2016/2946, OJ C 262, 19 July 2016, 1–50.

[147] See n. 102 Commission Notice on the notion of State aid as referred to in Article 107(1) of the Treaty on the Functioning of the European Union C/2016/2946, OJ C 262, 19 July 2016, 1–50. The IRR takes into account the future cash flows that an investor expects to receive during the investment period. It defines the discount rate at which the capital value of several cash flows is zero.

basis of its net present value (NPV).[148] The target return can also be derived from the weighted average cost of capital (WACC). According to this method, an EUC must at least generate returns that exceed its capital costs.[149] Ideally, EUCs generally examine their private sector projects using various methods to confirm the estimates.[150]

Especially for smaller EUCs, the calculation of a target return at market conditions is likely to be a challenge. It might be appropriate then to provide guidelines to EUCs with ranges of normal market returns for relevant private sector activities.

5.3 *Tax and Regulatory Advantages*

Private activities of EUCs must be subject to the same taxation as the corresponding activities of private operators. Tax advantages of EUCs mostly result from the fact that the tax preference is linked to a legal form which is not open to private competitors.[151] The maxim must be that the tax liability of EUCs has to be based on their activity and not on their organizational form.[152] To this end, the organizational decrees of public law institutions must stipulate as standard that utilities are taxable as private companies with regard to their private sector activities.[153]

However, even with a corresponding decree, preferential tax treatment at the level of federal taxes remains in place. Against this background, it is imperative that the private sector activities of EUCs be conducted only in the legal form of companies limited by shares under private law.[154] If such adaption of the legal form cannot be carried out, EUCs should be required by law to calculate the normal taxation for their private sector activities. The calculated tax advantage must then be compensated for by means of a compensatory payment to the public authorities.

If there are other regulatory advantages in favor of the private sector activities of EUCs, the relevant provisions must be repealed or adapted by the respective community. If regulatory preferences cannot be avoided, the advantage must be compensated to the community and taken into account in the pricing of the private sector offer.

---

[148] See n. 102 Commission Notice on the notion of State aid as referred to in Article 107(1) of the Treaty on the Functioning of the European Union C/2016/2946, OJ C 262, 19 July 2016, 1–50. In the case of NPVs, the difference between the positive and negative cash flows accruing during the investment period is discounted at an appropriate rate of return.

[149] See Art. 13 para. 3 let. b Electricity Supply Ordinance.

[150] See n. 105 Commission Notice on the notion of State aid as referred to in Article 107(1) of the Treaty on the Functioning of the European Union C/2016/2946, OJ C 262, 19 July 2016, 1–50.

[151] See Sect. 3.2.

[152] This is stated explicitly in the Guidelines of the Federal Council on Corporate Governance (Guideline 28) (Federal Council 2006, p. 8283).

[153] See Federal Council (2006), p. 8282.

[154] See Sect. 3.2.

5.4 *Cross-Subsidies*

As described above, the current prohibition of cross-subsidization is difficult to specify and verify with regard to the more than 600 EUCs in Switzerland. The following measures can also be taken to ensure that no cross-subsidization takes place.

The law should stipulate that services between the private and public sector business divisions of an EUC must be provided at arm's length and must be set out in contractual agreements.[155] In this way, EUCs can also ensure that they are not suspected of abusive practices under antitrust law in connection with cross-subsidization.[156]

Cross-subsidization resulting from a misallocation of overheads is particularly difficult to trace. For this reason, it is important that overhead costs are correctly broken down. In doing so, appropriate, comprehensible and written cost codes that comply with the principle of consistency must be used. As a result of the differences between the EUCs, it is hardly possible to provide uniform cost codes. However, it would be useful to use concrete, meaningful examples to show which requirements the overhead cost codes of the utility companies have to meet.

Within the framework of the "sunshine regulation" now provided for by law in accordance with Art. 22a of the Draft Electricity Supply Act, ElCom can also collect information on the relevant overhead costs (allocations) from the electricity utility companies and compare the data received.[157] The results of this comparison can then be published. EUCs whose overhead costs (allocations) differ significantly from the average are motivated to make adjustments to the cost allocation or to justify their chosen method convincingly.

Finally, EUCs should regularly check whether their private business activities are free of cross-subsidies. In practice, there are various methods to do so.[158] In the present case, it would make sense to follow a further development of the Faulhaber rule, as provided for in Art. 48(1) of the Swiss Postal Regulation.[159] Accordingly, there is an illegal cross-subsidization if the revenue from a particular good offered by the utility in the private sector is not sufficient to cover the incremental costs of this

---

[155] See European Commission, Interpretative Note on Directive 2009/72 of the European Parliament and the Council of 13 July 2009 concerning common rules for the internal market in electricity and repealing Directive 2003/54/EC, OJ L 211, 14 August 2009, 55-93, and Directive 2009/73 of the European Parliament and the Council of 13 July 2009 concerning common rules for the internal market in natural gas and repealing Directive 2003/55/EC, OJ L 211, 14 August 2009, 94–136; European Commission (2010), p. 25.

[156] See Sect. 4.2.

[157] See Swiss Federal Office of Energy (2018c), p. 33 et seq.

[158] See Baumann (2020), n. 12 et seq.; Spiekermann (2010), p. 28 et seq.

[159] See with regard to the further development of the Faulhaber rule Baumann (2020), n. 16; Platt (2005), p. 39.

good and there is a service or business division in the public sector whose revenue exceeds its stand-alone costs.[160]

5.5 *Economies of Scope*

In the case of economies of scope, the requirements regarding cross-subsidization and informational unbundling must always be observed.[161] This means that the private sector activities of the EUC can only provide shared services such as IT services and HR support if information unbundling is guaranteed and there is no risk of cross-subsidization.[162]

EUCs are to be prohibited by law from offering combined products or combination discounts from the public sector and private business activities. This is already required in view of the fact that they would otherwise expose themselves to risks under antitrust law.[163] "All-round carefree packages" that are offered by EUCs and include both public and private sector services must therefore be unbundled.

It can be assumed that the average customer is unaware of the fact that EUCs have public functions alongside private sector activities.[164] In order to avoid unjustified advantages in this respect, it must be clearly recognizable for the customer in each case whether a service is offered by an EUC's public sector or private sector activities. It is important to rule out any likelihood of confusion between the two areas.[165]

To this end, an EUC may be required by law to use a different brand in its private business activities than the one it uses for its public service activities.[166] The brands must thus be designed and also deployed in such a way that customers can recognize the services of the EUC and have no doubt about which of the two areas of activity the services belong to.[167] Measures to achieve this include, for example, different color choices, distinguishable fonts and the use of individual image components and unique names.[168]

---

[160] See Baumann (2020), n. 14 et seq., for a detailed description of incremental and stand-alone costs; see for the calculation of the stand-alone costs PostCom (2013), p. 3.

[161] See Sect. 4.3.

[162] See Bundesnetzagentur (2006), p. 19; European Commission (2010), p. 25.

[163] See Sect. 4.2.

[164] In a similar way Bundesnetzagentur (2012), p. 9.

[165] See Art. 26 para. 3 Directive 2009/72 of the European Parliament and the Council of 13 July 2009 concerning common rules for the internal market in electricity and repealing Directive 2003/54/EC, OJ L 211, 14 August 2009, 55–93; European Commission (2010), p. 27.

[166] Art. 26 para. 3 Directive 2009/72/EC.

[167] See Bundesnetzagentur (2012), p. 10. However, it should probably remain possible that customers conclude on the basis of the respective brands that the two divisions belong to the same company or group of companies.

[168] Bundesnetzagentur (2012), p. 10.

Likewise, the business correspondence and advertising material of EUCs are to be designed so as to avoid confusion. In the case of letters, faxes, emails, price lists, etc., it should be clearly visible for the customer whether these are messages related to the public tasks fulfilled by the EUC or from private customer care. In order to avoid any risk of confusion between the two areas, EUCs must generally refrain from publishing joint customer magazines, newsletters and the like.[169]

Finally, it has to be ensured that customers can easily see whether the information presented on the internet is part of the private sector activity or the public sector remit of the EUC. For this reason, a joint internet presence must be avoided and separate web addresses are to be maintained for the two areas. In order to avoid any risk of confusion, different email addresses or contact forms should be used for contact requests.[170] Corresponding principles must also apply to telephone communication. For the public sector and private sector activities, the EUC should have to set up separate service telephone numbers and make them known to customers.[171]

5.6 *Information Advantages*

For EUCs, the requirements for information unbundling according to the Swiss Electricity Supply Act are to be observed first and foremost. However, these requirements are rather general and only cover the use of information benefits from the network sector and the universal energy supply.[172] Against this background, it is necessary to provide for additional measures. Where possible, these can be integrated into existing internal company guidelines, processes and systems for data compliance and data governance.[173]

EUCs are to be obliged to identify and document the information relevant to competition in a first step. A corresponding analysis must be carried out for all the public service areas operated by the EUCs. It must also be determined where and by means of which processes this information is to be stored physically and electronically.[174] To the extent permitted by the applicable legal provisions, competition-relevant information from the public task areas must be disclosed to all private

---

[169] See Bundesnetzagentur (2012), p. 5.

[170] See Bundesnetzagentur (2012), p. 6.

[171] See Bundesnetzagentur (2012), p. 7. For example, EKZ has different service numbers for inquiries regarding power outages and the like and for inquiries with regard to electrical installations offered by EKZ Eltop.

[172] See Lang (2019), p. 3.

[173] See VSE (2019), p. 20 et seq.

[174] Bundesnetzagentur (2007), p. 8.

competitors on a non-discriminatory basis.[175] Ideally, such publications should use an easy to find, central link on the EUC's website.

In a second step, "Chinese Walls" are to be set up between the public and private sectors. The aim of these is to ensure that the private sector does not gain information benefits from the public tasks of the utility. From an organizational point of view, a functional and spatial separation of the areas of activity is possible. At the same time, access restrictions must be provided for, if necessary, and access rights to data relevant to competition must be regulated.[176]

To this end, employees must be clearly assigned to the individual areas of activity. Management positions should be filled differently for the public sector and private sector activities.[177] Competition-relevant information from the public task areas must only be accessible to employees who actually belong to the relevant public task area of the EUC.[178] The access rights to computer systems in which competition-relevant information of the public task area is managed must be restricted accordingly for employees of the private enterprise sector.[179] Consequently, employees in the private sector must not be able to access customer information (name, address, bank details, etc.) from the public sector in the integrated computer system.[180]

If services are provided for customers within the scope of the public remit, the EUC should not refer exclusively to its own private sector offer in this context.[181] For example, it is not permitted to draw the attention of a customer for whom the utility company provides a network connection to the utility company's own range of services regarding the installation of solar systems. Employees with customer contact should be trained in how to classify customers into their respective areas of responsibility and activity and how to deal with customer enquiries regarding the private sector offer.[182]

---

[175] Bundesnetzagentur (2007), p. 10; Finger et al. (2009), p. 22. For example, *Gebäudeversicherung Bern* has undertaken to offer data records from the monopoly sector which it makes available to its subsidiaries operating in the private sector to private providers on equal terms (Competition Commission 2011b, p. 483 et seq., n. 167, Gebäudeversicherung Bern [GVB]).

[176] Bundesnetzagentur (2007), p. 22; see further Ziegler and Moser (2019), n. 30.

[177] For example, *Gebäudeversicherung Bern* has committed itself to this (Competition Commission 2011b, p. 483 et seq., n. 167, Gebäudeversicherung Bern [GVB]).

[178] Bundesnetzagentur (2007), p. 8.

[179] Bundesnetzagentur (2007), p. 9.

[180] Bundesnetzagentur (2006), p. 24.

[181] Bundesnetzagentur (2007), p. 11.

[182] Bundesnetzagentur (2007), p. 11.

6 Summary and Outlook

Electricity utility companies today often operate in hybrid mode. On the one hand, they carry out the public tasks assigned to them by the legislator. On the other hand, apart from the fulfillment of public tasks, they are active as entrepreneurs and thus in the private sector. Private sector activities may range from electricity products for large customers, photovoltaic and e-mobility installations to services in the field of building services engineering, internet offerings and the sale of household appliances.

A utility's private sector activities can be associated with several potential distortions of competition. It is not only cross-subsidization, which is often at the forefront of discussions, that should be considered. Rather, EUCs potentially benefit from financing advantages and, due to their legal form, from significant exceptions to taxation. Furthermore, considerable economies of scope can be achieved by hybrid EUCs, as the public and private sectors can draw on joint company resources. As a result of the proximity to the state and their function as distribution system operators, EUCs have a competitive information advantage over private suppliers (Sect. 3 above).

Guidelines for dealing with the individual distortions of competition derived from constitutional, antitrust and electricity supply law are only partially binding. In particular, there is a lack of instruments for dealing with issues related to taxation, financing and economies of scope. In contrast, the requirements relating to cross-subsidization and the exploitation of information benefits for private sector activities are more comprehensive (Sect. 4 above).

The present contribution has set out (above in Sect. 5) *de lege ferenda* measures to avoid distortions of competition. Irrespective of the extent to which these reform proposals are implemented, it is imperative that EUCs and their public owners seriously address the problem of distortions of competition and the measures described. Otherwise, there is a risk that their private sector activities will increasingly be rejected and that their scope for economic development will be restricted by political considerations.

References

Abegg A, Baumann P (2020) Privatwirtschaftliche Tätigkeiten von Energieversorgungsunternehmen – wie Wettbewerbsverzerrungen vermieden werden. Schriften zum Energierecht, Band 15. Dike Verlag, Zurich/St. Gallen

Abegg A, Frei M (2018) Eintritt des Staates in den Wettbewerb. Recht – Zeitschrift für juristische Weiterbildung und Praxis 3(2018):142–154

Abegg A, Seferovic G (2018) Abgeltung ungedeckter Kosten im regionalen Personenverkehr unter besonderer Berücksichtigung von Konzernstrukturen. Sui Generis 2018:360–373

Amstutz M, Carron B (2010) Kommentar zu Art. 7 KG. In: Amstutz M, Reinert M, Honsell H (eds) Basler Kommentar Kartellgesetz. Helbing Lichtenhahn, Basel

Barney JB, Hesterly WS (2015) Strategic management and competitive advantage: concepts and cases. Pearson, Essex
Baumann P (2019) Wettbewerbsverzerrungen durch privatwirtschaftliche Staatstätigkeit. Dissertation, University of Lucerne
Baumann P (2020) Quersubventionierungen bei privatwirtschaftlicher Staatstätigkeit, Jusletter 9 March 2020. Available at https://jusletter.weblaw.ch
Beyeler F (2017) Verwirrung im (smarten) Daten-Dschungel. Bulletin SEV/VSE 12(2017):56–60
Borer J (2011) Kommentar zum Wettbewerbsrecht I, Schweizerisches Kartellgesetz. Orell Füssli, Zurich
Brennan TJ (1990) Cross-subsidization and cost misallocation by regulated monopolists. J Regul Econ 2(1):37–51
Bundesnetzagentur (2006) Gemeinsame Auslegungsgrundsätze zu den §§ 6-10 EnWG, 01 March 2006. Available at: https://www.bundesnetzagentur.de/
Bundesnetzagentur (2007) Gemeinsame Richtlinie der Regulierungsbehörden des Bundes und der Länder zur Umsetzung der informatorischen Entflechtung nach § 9 EnWG, 13 June 2007. Available at https://www.bundesnetzagentur.de
Bundesnetzagentur (2012) Gemeinsame Auslegungsgrundsätze III der Regulierungsbehörden des Bundes und der Länder zu den Anforderungen an die Markenpolitik und das Kommunikationsverhalten bei Verteilnetzbetreibern (§ 7a Abs. 6 EnWG), 16 July 2012. Available at https://www.bundesnetzagentur.de
Bürer M, de Lapparent M, Capezzali M, Carpita M (2021) Governance drivers and barriers for business model transformation. In: Hettich P, Kachi A (eds) Swiss energy governance. Springer, New York, p 219
Capobianco A, Christiansen H (2011) Competitive neutrality and state-owned enterprises: challenges and policy options. OECD Corporate Governance Working Papers No. 1. OECD Publishing, Paris
City Council Aarau (2000) Eignerstrategie des Stadtrats Aarau für die Eniwa Holding AG. Available at https://www.eniwa.ch
Competition Commission (2011a) Recht und Politik des Wettbewerbs 2011/1. Available at www.bundespublikationen.admin.ch
Competition Commission (2011b) Recht und Politik des Wettbewerbs 2011/4. Available at www.bundespublikationen.admin.ch
Competition Commission (2014) Recht und Politik des Wettbewerbs 2014/1. Available at www.bundespublikationen.admin.ch
Council Secretariat City of Bern (2006) Minutes of the City Council meeting of 11 May 2006. Available at https://ris.bern.ch
D'Arcy A, Burri S (2009) Das Rechnungswesen von Elektrizitätsversorgungsunternehmen (EVU) aus regulatorischer Sicht. In: Meyer C, Pfaff D (eds) Finanz- und Rechnungswesen - Jahrbuch 2009. WEKA, Zurich
Diebold N, Ludin M (2018) Öffentliche Beschaffungen von Strom im teilliberalisierten Stromversorgungsmarkt. Dike, Zurich/St. Gallen
Diebold NF (2014) Die öffentliche Ausschreibung als Marktzugangsinstrument. ZSR 133:219–252
Ducrey P (2009) Fallstricke für öffentliche Unternehmen im Wettbewerb. In: Hettich P (ed) Öffentliche Unternehmen zwischen Politik und Markt, Referate der Tagung vom 17. Februar 2009 in Zurich. Schriftenreihe des IRP-HSG, St. Gallen
Electricity Commission (2018) Reports on the activities of ElCom 2018. Available at https://www.elcom.admin.ch
Enz K (2018): Energiemarkt: Ostschweizer Netzbetreiber konkurrenziert private KMU. Ostschweiz am Sonntag, 7 January 2018. Available at https://www.tagblatt.ch
European Commission (2010) Interpretative Note on Directive 2009/72/EC concerning common rules for the internal market in electricity and directive 2009/73/EC concerning common rules for the internal market in natural gas, 22 January 2010. Available at https://www.ec.europa.eu

ewl (2017) ewl kombiniert Strom und Internetprodukt, press release, 24 November 2017. Available at: https://www.ewl-luzern.ch

EY (2017) Elektrizitätswerke-Studie Schweiz 2017, Verteilnetzbetreiber der Zukunft. Ernst & Young, Zurich

Federal Council (2004) Botschaft vom 3. Dezember 2004 zur Änderung des Elektrizitätsgesetzes und zum Stromversorgungsgesetz. Federal Gazette BBl 2004 1611

Federal Council (2006) Bericht vom 13. September 2006 zur Auslagerung und Steuerung von Bundesaufgaben. Federal Gazette BBl 2006 8233

Federal Council (2013) Botschaft vom 4. September 2013 zum ersten Massnahmenpaket der Energiestrategie 2050 und zur Volksinitiative "Für den geordneten Ausstieg aus der Atomenergie". Federal Gazette BBl 2013 7561

Federal Council (2017a) Botschaft vom 15. Februar 2017 zur Totalrevision des Bundesgesetzes über das öffentliche Beschaffungswesen. Federal Gazette BBl 2017 1851

Federal Council (2017b) Staat und Wettbewerb. Auswirkungen staatlich beherrschter Unternehmen auf die Wettbewerbsmärkte, Bericht des Bundesrates in Erfüllung der Postulate 12.4172 FDP-Liberale Fraktion vom 13.12.2012 und 15.3880 Schilliger vom 22.09.2015

Finger M, Jaag C, Lang M, Lutzenberger M, Trinker U (2009) Angemessenheit und Folgen einer funktionalen oder strukturellen Trennung von Swisscom, Studie im Auftrag von Swisscom – Schlussbericht. Swiss Economics, Zurich

Flatt M, Zindel T (2017) Steuerpflicht von Schweizer Energieversorgern, Kantonal geprägte, unterschiedliche Steuerpraxen im Kontext dynamischer Entwicklungen im Schweizer Energiemarkt. EVU Partners, Aarau

Föhse K (2015) Die Leiden der jungen Strommarktordnung – aktuelle Probleme des StromVG unter besonderer Berücksichtigung der Rechtsprechung zu Netzgebietszuteilung und Grundversorgung. Recht – Zeitschrift für juristische Weiterbildung und Praxis 3 (2015):125–143

Föhse M (2018) Grundversorgung mit Strom – ein Überblick zu Rechtsverhältnissen und Zuständigkeiten. AJP 10(2018):1235–1250

Friederiszick HW, Röller LH, Verouden V (2008) European state aid control: an economic framework. In: Paolo B (ed) Handbook of antitrust economics. MIT Press, Cambridge

Fritsch M (2018) Marktversagen und Wirtschaftspolitik, Mikroökonomische Grundlagen staatlichen Handelns. Vahlen, Munich

Geddes RR (2004) Case studies of anticompetitive SOE behavior. In: Geddes R (ed) Competing with the government: anticompetitive behavior and public enterprises. Hoover Press, Stanford

Ghazarian L (2018) Quersubventionen und Verbundvorteile im EU-Beihilferecht unter besonderer Berücksichtigung der beihilferechtlichen Zugangsregulierung und Infrastrukturförderung. Dissertation, University of Bonn

Graf P, Waldmeier N (2016) Wenn Geschäftsmodelle Rost ansetzen. kommunalmagazin.ch, 2:12–15

Hangartner Y (2007) Der Staat als Unternehmer. In: Rechtswissenschaftliche Abteilung der Universität St. Gallen (ed) Rechtliche Rahmenbedingungen des Wirtschaftsstandortes Schweiz, Festschrift 25 Jahre juristische Abschlüsse an der Universität St. Gallen (HSG). Dike, Zurich/St. Gallen

Hangartner Y (2012) Entscheidbesprechung zu BGer 2C_485/2010 vom 3. Juli 2012. AJP 12 (2012):1817–1823

Hänni P, Stöckli A (2013) Schweizerisches Wirtschaftsverwaltungsrecht. Stämpfli, Bern

Herrmann K (2014) Öffentliche Unternehmen, Eine ökonomische Analyse kommunaler Wirtschaftstätigkeit, List Forum für Wirtschafts- und Finanzpolitik 40:403–421

Hofmann B, Kolcava D, Thaler D (2021) The role of Switzerland in European Electricity Governance. In: Hettich P, Kachi A (eds) Swiss energy governance. Springer, New York, p 85

Jäger C, Scheidegger C (2016) Kommentar zu Art. 5 Abs. 1-4 StromVG. In: Kratz B, Merker M, Tami R, Rechsteiner S, Föhse K (eds) Kommentar zum Energierecht, Band I: WRG/EleG/StromVG/RLG. Editions Weblaw, Bern

Kraemer R, Stöckli A (2013) Grenzenlose Staatswirtschaft? Recht – Zeitschrift für juristische Weiterbildung und Praxis 1(2013):28–45
Krähenmann B (1987) Privatwirtschaftliche Tätigkeit des Gemeinwesens. Dissertation, University of Basel
Kratz B (2018) Speicher als Schlüsselkomponente der Energiewende. Dike, Zurich/St. Gallen
Lang L (2019) Informatorische Entflechtung als (weiterer) Treiber der Konsolidierung kleinerer EVU. EVU Partners, Aarau
Lund H, Østergaard P, Connolly D, Mathiesen BV (2017) Smart energy and smart energy systems. Energy 137:556–565
Mayoraz JF (2018) Staatliche Beihilfen in den Rechtsbeziehungen der Schweiz und der Europäischen Union, unter besonderer Berücksichtigung von ausgewählten Aspekten aus der schweizerischen Elektrizitätswirtschaft. Dissertation, University of Zurich
Müller A (2017) Die Berner breiten sich auch in Zürich aus, 1 December 2017. In: nzz.ch. Available at https://www.nzz.ch
Municipal Council Bern (2016) Neues Ausschüttungsmodell für ewb. Available at https://www.bern.ch
Municipal Council Bern (2017) Eignerstrategie Energie Wasser Bern (ewb). Available at https://www.bern.ch
Nielsen RP (1981) Competitive advantages of state owned and controlled businesses. Manage Int Rev 21(3):56–66
OECD (2012) Competitive neutrality, Maintaining a level playing field between public and private business. OECD Publishing, Paris
OECD (2015) OECD guidelines on corporate governance of state-owned enterprises. OECD Publishing, Paris
OECD (2016) State-owned enterprises as global competitors, A challenge or an opportunity? OECD Publishing, Paris
Orelli M, Thomann M (2016) Kommentar zu Art. 10 StromVG. In: Kratz B, Merker M, Tami R, Rechsteiner S, Föhse K (eds) Kommentar zum Energierecht, Band I: WRG/EleG/StromVG/RLG. Editions Weblaw, Bern
Peeperkorn L, Verouden V (2014) The economics of competition. In: Faull J, Nikpay A (eds) The EU law of competition. Oxford University Press, Oxford
Petrik-Haltiner TS (2017) Spannungsfelder rund um die Stromkosten und -tarife, Eine systematische Analyse der Rechtslage im Nachgang an die erste Etappe der schweizerischen Strommarktliberalisierung. Dissertation, University of Zurich
Platt D (2005) Quersubventionierung im Wettbewerbsrecht der Europäischen Union, Dissertation, University of Munich
PostCom (2013) Weisung 1/2013 der PostCom zuhanden der Schweizerischen Post betreffend den Nachweis der Einhaltung des Quersubventionierungsverbots im Einzelfall, 15 March 2013. Available at: https://www.postcom.admin.ch
Probst S, Känel L, Konersmann L (2019) Update 2019: Abrechnungslösungen für den Eigenverbrauch von Solarstrom, Eine Übersicht für Projektentwickler und Bauherren. Energie Zukunft Schweiz, Zürich
Reich J (2009) Grundsatz der Wirtschaftsfreiheit, Evolution und Dogmatik von Art. 94 Abs. 1 und 4 der Bundesverfassung der Schweizerischen Eidgenossenschaft vom 18. April 1999, Dissertation, University of Basel
Reich J (2013) Gebäudeversicherung und "negativ nachgeführte" Bundesverfassung. AJP 9 (2013):1399–1412
Rhinow R, Schmid G, Biaggini G, Uhlmann F (2011) Öffentliches Wirtschaftsrecht. Helbing Lichtenhahn, Basel
Rütsche B (2013) Was sind öffentliche Aufgaben? Recht – Zeitschrift für juristische Weiterbildung und Praxis 4(2013):153–162
Rütsche B (2016) Staatliche Leistungsaufträge und Rechtschutz. ZBJV 2(2016):71–113
Sappington DEM, Sidak GJ (2003) Competition law for state-owned enterprises. Antitrust Law J 71 (2):479–523

Sappington DEM, Sidak GJ (2004) Anticompetitive behavior by state-owned enterprises: incentives and capabilities. In: Geddes R (ed) Competing with the government: anticompetitive behavior and public enterprises. Hoover Press, Stanford
Scheda L (2014) Kantonale Gebäudeversicherer - neue “Wettbewerber” auf dem Privatversicherungsmarkt. In: Fuhrer S (ed) Jahrbuch SGHVR 2014/Annales SDRCA 2014. Schulthess, Zurich
Schedler K, Müller R, Sonderegger RW (2016) Führung, Steuerung und Aufsicht von öffentlichen Unternehmen, Public Corporate Governance für die Praxis. Haupt, Bern
Schneider H (2016) Staat und Wirtschaft im Wettbewerb. sic! Zeitschrift für Immaterialgüter. Informations- und Wettbewerbsrecht 12:641–649
Scholl P (2015) Elektrizität. In: Biaggini G, Häner I, Saxer U, Schott M (eds) Fachhandbuch Verwaltungsrecht. Schulthess, Zurich/Basel/Geneva
Schönbächler P (1998) Wettbewerbsneutralität staatlicher Massnahmen, Dissertation, University of Zurich
Sonderegger RW (2012) Eignerstrategie als Führungsinstrument bei öffentlichen Energieversorgern, Gründe und Wege für die Einführung. Bulletin SEV/VSE 2012(7):14–16
Sonderegger RW (2014) Führung, Steuerung und Aufsicht von öffentlichen Unternehmen in Schweizer Städten, Erkenntnisse der Studie zum Stand der Umsetzung von Public Corporate Governance in Städten und grösseren Gemeinden der Schweiz. IMP-HSG, St. Gallen
Spiekermann MK (2010) Vermeidung von Quersubventionen durch sektorspezifische Regulierung am Beispiel der deutschen Elektrizitätswirtschaft. Dissertation, University of Bonn
Stadtwerk Winterthur (2013) Eignerstrategie für Stadtwerk Winterthur. Available at https://www.stadtwerk.winterthur.ch
State Council Basel-Stadt (2018) Eignerstrategie für die IWB Industrielle Werke Basel 2019-2022. Available at https://www.bs.ch
State Council Basel-Stadt (2019) Ratschlag Gesamtkonzept Elektromobilität. Available at https://www.bs.ch
Stäuble L, Schraner F (2018a) Kommentar zu Art. 4 Abs. 2 KG. In: Zäch R, Arnet R, Baldi M, Kiener R, Schaller O, Schraner F, Spühler A (eds) DIKE Kommentar zum Bundesgesetz über Kartelle und andere Wettbewerbsbeschränkungen. Dike, Zurich/St. Gallen
Stäuble L, Schraner F (2018b) Kommentar zu Art. 7 KG. In: Zäch R, Arnet R, Baldi M, Kiener R, Schaller O, Schraner F, Spühler A (eds) DIKE Kommentar zum Bundesgesetz über Kartelle und andere Wettbewerbsbeschränkungen. Dike, Zurich/St. Gallen
Stillfried M (2010) Die energierechtliche Jahresrechnung gemäss Stromversorgungsgesetz, Offene Fragen und Lösungsvorschläge. Der Schweizer Treuhänder 84(4):180–187
Stöckli A (2016) Messwesen im Bereich der elektrischen Energie – geschlossener oder offener Markt? In: Die Schweizerische Vereinigung für Verwaltungsorganisationsrecht SVVOR (ed) Verwaltungsorganisationsrecht -Staatshaftungsrecht - öffentliches Dienstrecht, Jahrbuch 2015. Stämpfli, Bern
Stoffel WA, Graber N (2013) L’assurance incendie et le droit de la concurrence. In: Rumo-Jungo A, Pichonnaz P, Hürlimann-Kaup B, Fountoulakis C (eds) Une empreinte sur le Code civil. Stämpfli, Bern
Stoffel WA, Murith S (2019) Entreprises publiques et droit de la concurrence. In: Hochreutner I, Stoffel WA, Amstutz M (eds) 10ème Journée de droit de la concurrence/10. Tagung zum Wettbewerbsrecht. Growth Publisher Law, Bern
Swiss Federal Office of Energy (2018a) Faktenblatt 2 – Der Schweizer Strommarkt. Available at https://www.newsd.admin.ch
Swiss Federal Office of Energy (2018b) Markt- und Wettbewerbsanalyse Grundlagenpapier für den erläuternden Bericht zur Vernehmlassungsvorlage Revision StromVG vom Oktober 2018. Available at https://www.bfe.admin.ch
Swiss Federal Office of Energy (2018c) Revision des Stromversorgungsgesetzes (volle Strommarktöffnung, Speicherreserve und Modernisierung der Netzregulierung), Erläuternder Bericht zur Vernehmlassungsvorlage, October 2018. Available at https://www.admin.ch
Tschannen P, Zimmerli U, Müller M (2014) Allgemeines Verwaltungsrecht. Stämpfli, Bern

Uhlmann F (1997) Gewinnorientiertes Staatshandeln, Möglichkeiten und Zulässigkeit gewinnorientierter staatlicher Eigenbetätigung aus wirtschaftsverfassungsrechtlicher Sicht. Dissertation, University of Basel
Vaterlaus S, Zenhäusern P, Kaufmann C, Worm H (2017) Staat und Wettbewerb, Institutionelle und wettbewerbliche Aspekte bei kantonalen und kommunalen Unternehmen, Studie im Auftrag des Staatssekretariats für Wirtschaft SECO. Polynomics, Olten
Vettori A, Wunderlich A, Iten R, Bulgheroni R, Streit D, Camacho-Bütikofer M, Brandes C (2018) Benchmarking von Energieversorgungsunternehmen in den Bereichen Energieeffizienz und erneuerbare Energien, Resultate der Erhebungsrunde 2017/18. Energieschweiz, Bern
Vogel S (2000) Der Staat als Marktteilnehmer, Voraussetzungen der Zulässigkeit wirtschaftlicher Tätigkeit des Gemeinwesens in Konkurrenz zu Privaten. Dissertation, University of Zurich
Vonplon D (2019) Stromkonzern zapft Kundendatei ab. Neue Zürcher Zeitung, 28 June 2019. Available at https://www.nzz.ch
VSE (2018) Kostenrechnungsschema für Verteilnetzbetreiber der Schweiz, Branchensystematik für die Kostenermittlung im Zusammenhang mit der Netznutzung. VSE/AES, Aarau
VSE (2019) Data Policy in der Energiebranche, Rahmenwerk für den gesamtheitlichen Umgang mit Daten in der Energiebranche. VSE/AES, Aarau
Waldmeier D (2018) Insolvenz verselbständigter Verwaltungseinheiten von Bund und Kantonen, Unter besonderer Berücksichtigung staatlicher Einstandspflichten. Dissertation, University of St. Gallen
Weber RH (1986) Wirtschaftsregulierung in wettbewerbspolitischen Ausnahmebereichen, Studien zur staatlichen Wirtschaftsregulierung und zum Einsatz der Regulierungsinstrumente in den Transport-, Kommunikations- und Energiemärkten in der Schweiz und in den Vereinigten Staaten von Amerika, Habilitation University of Zurich. Nomos, Baden-Baden
Weber RH, Volz S (2013) Fachhandbuch Wettbewerbsrecht, Expertenwissen für die Praxis. Schulthess, Zurich
Zäch R (2005) Schweizerisches Kartellrecht. Stämpfli, Bern
Ziegler AR, Moser P (2019) Sind die kantonalen Gebäudeversicherungsmonopole "eurokompatibel"? Jusletter 12 August 2019. Available at https://jusletter.weblaw.ch

Andreas Abegg is Head of the Centre for Public Commercial Law at Zurich University of Applied Sciences, Winterthur, Switzerland.

Phil Baumann is Senior Academic Assistant at the University of Lucerne Faculty of Law, Lucerne, Switzerland.

Part III
Understanding the Pressure Points of Policy and Acceptance Risks

Referendum Campaigns in Swiss Energy Policy

A Comparative Analysis of Media Coverage and a Case Study of Media Influence on Voting Behavior

Adrian Rinscheid and Linards Udris

Contents

Abstract What are the patterns in media coverage in Swiss energy policy-making, and to what extent do the media influence voters' decisions at the ballot? In a first step, this chapter provides a comparative investigation of media coverage in the run-up to three recent energy-related referenda (2015 initiative "Energy tax instead of VAT"; 2016 nuclear phase-out initiative; 2017 referendum on the federal Energy Strategy 2050), with 31 other referenda between 2014 and 2018 as a benchmark. Based on a content analysis of articles published in 21 Swiss newspapers, our analysis demonstrates that the three energy-policy referenda are characterized by patterns similar to non-energy votes but also have distinct features. In a second step, we specifically focus on the 2016 nuclear phase-out initiative, which was characterized by balanced newspaper reporting, and explain voting behavior by linking data on media coverage and individual-level data from a panel survey (n = 1014). The

A. Rinscheid (✉)
Institute for Economy and the Environment, University of St. Gallen, St. Gallen, Switzerland
e-mail: adrian.rinscheid@unisg.ch

L. Udris
Department of Communication and Media Research and Research Center for the Public Sphere and Society, University of Zurich, Zurich, Switzerland
e-mail: l.udris@ikmz.uzh.ch

P. Hettich, A. Kachi (eds.), *Swiss Energy Governance*,
https://doi.org/10.1007/978-3-030-80787-0_12

analysis relies on "linkage analysis", a method that takes media contents as quasi-experimental stimuli to explain individual-level outcomes. We find that the failure of the phase-out initiative can be partly explained by exposure to newspaper coverage: one in four left-wing voters who had initially been in favor of the popular initiative but were exposed to strongly negative coverage about it during the "hot" campaign phase changed their initial voting intention. The analysis also suggests that the media coverage may have helped center/right-wing voters to learn about their preferred party's position so as to align their vote choice with their political predisposition.

1 Introduction

Direct democracy is an important component of Switzerland's political DNA. On average, Swiss citizens were called to vote on eight federal ballot propositions per year since the beginning of the century. In international comparison, there is no country in which direct democratic votes are held as frequently as in Switzerland. While energy topics had been absent from the voting agenda for more than a decade, a number of direct democratic votes with important implications for the country's energy system have been held at the federal level since 2015. In this chapter, we discuss two interrelated questions with respect to these direct democratic votes: First, what are the patterns of media coverage of energy topics in the run-up to direct democratic votes? And second, to what extent does media reporting influence citizens' vote decision?

Media coverage about referendum campaigns[1] has received increasing scholarly attention not only in Switzerland but also internationally. So far, most analyses fall into two camps, focusing either on the media as a "mirror" of society or as a "molder" of society. On the one hand, scholars analyze media coverage as a dependent variable, asking which factors actually shape the news. On the other hand, scholars use media coverage as an independent variable to examine possible effects on decision-making. In this vein, linkage studies often examine whether frames and arguments salient in media coverage can be linked to citizens' decision-making. Scholars also use the overall intensity and tonality of media coverage in order to explain voting behavior. Encompassing analyses, however, which examine the dual role of the media both as a dependent and independent variable are rare, with the study led by Hanspeter Kriesi being the most notable

[1] Throughout the text, we use the term "referenda" to refer to three distinct instruments of Swiss direct democracy: "popular initiatives" (popular votes launched by citizens to enact a constitutional amendment), "optional referenda" (popular votes to challenge a bill adopted by parliament) and "mandatory referenda" (popular votes on bills which by law have to be put on the ballot in any case).

exception.[2] In this chapter, we try to address this shortcoming by showing how media coverage about three energy-related proposals can be explained and by illuminating how media coverage about one energy policy-related proposal, the nuclear phase-out initiative, affected voting behavior.

The chapter is structured as follows. In Sect. 2, we first provide some context by reviewing research on media coverage in referendum campaigns. Next, we empirically investigate how three recent energy-related direct democratic votes were covered by the media, also in comparison with other direct democratic votes. Sect. 3 starts by deriving several theoretical expectations regarding the influence of media coverage on voting behavior, before using the case of the nuclear phase-out initiative (2016) to investigate these expectations empirically. The chapter concludes by discussing implications for Swiss energy governance and further research.

2 Media Coverage in Referendum Campaigns

2.1 Research on Media Coverage About Swiss Referenda

An important strand of research on the role of media in direct democracy focuses on media coverage as a dependent variable, evaluating the quality of media coverage[3] and asking which factors shape news reporting. When it comes to explaining actual media coverage, most data comes from the Swiss case. This is not surprising because the Swiss case offers excellent conditions for comparative analyses. This stream of research argues that media coverage largely reflects power structures in society and actual campaign activities, which is why media do not cover all votes, actors or arguments with the same intensity and tonality. Hence, media often quote political actors who hold important positions and have official roles in the campaigns (e.g., referendum committees), and they often report on actors' campaign activities such as press conferences.[4] In a comparative analysis, Linards Udris and colleagues found that the amount of media attention to a referendum in the "hot" phase of the campaign cannot be explained with the "real" degree of contestation (e.g., inner-party conflicts), the status of the challengers or the temporal proximity of the vote in parliament or at the polls (both opinion polls and final results).[5] Instead, media attention is higher if at least one of the following conditions is present: a) media attention was already high in an earlier phase, b) the referendum is about "identity politics" or the cultural dimension of political conflicts (e.g., the initiative against "mass immigration") rather than socio-economic issues, c) the challengers use

[2] Kriesi (2012).

[3] For instance, Dekavalla (2016); Ettinger and Imhof (2014); Marcinkowski and Donk (2012); Marquis et al. (2011); Renwick and Lamb (2013).

[4] Hänggli (2012).

[5] Udris et al. (2016, 2018).

populist rhetoric, or d) political advertising expenditures are high, which evidently favors political actors from the right, since they normally have a relatively large campaign budget.[6] Matthias Gerth and colleagues also argue that issue characteristics matter: familiar and uncomplex issues (e.g., asylum policy) trigger more attention than unfamiliar, complex issues (e.g., tax reform).[7]

At the same time, media do not merely follow political agendas but also shape news coverage according to their own logics. This is illustrated by the considerable differences in media attention among media types, for instance between tabloid and quality media, with the former investing fewer resources and producing fewer articles than the latter. These differences can be explained with different structural features of these media types and thus different organizational routines and logics.[8] Furthermore, ownership structures shape news coverage; media with close ties to political parties or milieus tend to take a political stance in their reporting, including on referenda.[9] Finally, with the ongoing commercialization of the media, media tend to frame politics, including referendum campaigns, as a "horse race" between political actors, stressing contestation and tactics instead of issue substance.[10] These findings point to certain deficits in the quality of media coverage. In sum, however, the empirical literature paints a rather positive picture of Swiss media coverage. Initiatives and referenda are considered "routine and ritualized business" for Swiss media and most votes are covered in a more or less substantial and objective way.[11]

Within the growing literature on referendum coverage in Swiss media, energy-related referenda, however, have not played a role recently. Scholars are either concerned with general patterns across policy issues[12] or have empirically investigated other policy fields such as social policy[13] or migration, traffic, and foreign policy.[14] The few available recent studies on Swiss energy policy do not focus on referendum debates in news media but on Twitter[15] or focus on media coverage not about a specific referendum campaign but on the aftermath of the Fukushima accident in general.[16]

This dearth of research is unfortunate because in recent years, the number of energy-related votes at the national level has increased. Since 2015, Swiss citizens have voted on three different energy-related proposals (see Table 1): the popular

[6] Hermann (2012).
[7] Gerth et al. (2012).
[8] Rademacher et al. (2012).
[9] Jandura and Udris (2019); Udris et al. (2020).
[10] Hänggli (2012).
[11] Kriesi (2012), p. 232.
[12] For instance, Udris et al. (2018).
[13] Marquis et al. (2011).
[14] Marcinkowski and Donk (2012).
[15] Arlt et al. (2019) on the nuclear phase-out initiative.
[16] Kepplinger and Lemke (2016); Kristiansen (2017).

Table 1 Energy-related direct democratic votes at the federal level since 2015

Title	Type (Sponsor)	Voting Day	Yes-votes (in percent)
Energy tax instead of VAT (*Energie-statt Mehrwertsteuer*)	Popular initiative (Green Liberal Party)	March 8, 2015	8.0
Nuclear phase-out (*Atomausstiegsinitiative*)	Popular initiative (Green Party)	November 27, 2016	45.8
Energy Strategy 2050 (*Energiestrategie 2050*)	Optional referendum	May 21, 2017	58.2

initiative "Energy tax instead of VAT" by the Green Liberal Party (GLP) in March 2015 (henceforth "GLP initiative"), the popular initiative on a nuclear phase-out ("Atomausstiegsinitiative") by the Green Party (GP) in November 2016 and the referendum on the national Energy Strategy 2050 in May 2017 (henceforth "ES2050").[17] After a break of more than a decade—energy-related referenda peaked between 2000 and 2003—these recent votes have brought energy policy back on the voting agenda. While two popular initiatives attempted to challenge the status quo by advocating for more renewable energies, the referendum against the federal Energy Strategy 2050 tried to keep the status quo by blocking an encompassing move away from nuclear energy and fossil fuels toward renewable energies. Is the growing importance of energy policy and the according conflict also reflected in media coverage? Knowing that public votes are, by and large, "routine business" for Swiss media, we expect the media, of course, to devote their attention also to these energy-related proposals. But how much and in which way is an open question which we investigate in Sect. 2.2.

2.2 Media Coverage of Recent Energy-Related Referenda

In order to determine and contextualize media attention to public votes and tonality towards these votes, we rely on data from the "*Abstimmungsmonitor*", a project at *fög—Forschungszentrum Öffentlichkeit und Gesellschaft* (University of Zurich), which has examined news coverage about national public votes in Switzerland since 2013. Data from the "*Abstimmungsmonitor*" (*monitor on public votes,* henceforth "monitor") has been used for case studies[18] and comparative analyses.[19] Short reports on each voting day are publicly available on the website of the research center.[20]

[17] The popular initiative on a "Green Economy" in the broader field of environmental policy also included some energy-related aspects. It was rejected in 2016.

[18] For instance, Udris et al. (2020).

[19] For instance, Udris (2016).

[20] See https://www.foeg.uzh.ch/de/forschung/Projekte/Abstimmungsmonitor.html.

In order to rely on the same media sample and time frame for each public vote, the monitor data is based on a standardized data collection approach. The entire sample now consists of news coverage about 34 different public votes between 2014 and 2018 published in 21 different news outlets during 11 weeks in the run-up to the vote (starting 12 weeks before voting day until 1 week before voting day). The sample yields 9951 news articles in total, 1046 of which relate to the three energy-related referenda. The newspaper sample covers a broad spectrum in terms of regional diversity, including 15 outlets from German-speaking Switzerland and 6 from French-speaking Switzerland, and in terms of media types, ranging from low-quality tabloid and commuter papers to more mid-market regional papers (e.g., Südostschweiz) to high-quality papers (e.g., Neue Zürcher Zeitung), and including daily papers, Sunday papers and one weekly magazine.[21]

Apart from the number of articles (a proxy for media attention), the monitor data includes information on tonality, which is measured at the article level. Each article is assigned a type of tonality, with "positive" indicating an article primarily conveying a message of support for the proposal, for instance an editorial or a report describing the press conference of the proponents; "negative" conveying rejection; and "ambivalent" including rather balanced (or ambivalent) messages. Next, an aggregated tonality score is constructed at the newspaper level by subtracting the number of negative articles from the number of positive ones, dividing the result by the overall number of articles (including articles with ambivalent tonality) and multiplying by 100. Hence, the aggregated tonality score is bounded between −100 and 100. In addition, for each article, the data includes up to three actors (individual or collective actors) with a statement on the proposal, including the stance an actor takes (positive, negative, ambivalent). In the data analysis, for each collective actor (e.g., SVP) or actor type (e.g., experts), a score that displays the overall acceptance towards the proposal is shown. This actor-level score is calculated in the same way as the article-level tonality score discussed above.

We now present the results from our comparative analysis of media coverage. First, we focus on media attention and tonality; second, we shed light on differences among media outlets; and third, we highlight actor constellations in the three energy-related referenda.

Table 2 shows the amount of media attention and the tonality towards the three recent energy-related proposals in comparison with 31 other votes. We display initiatives (*Volksinitiativen*) and referenda in the narrow sense (*Referenden* against federal proposals) separately, since they have different institutional characteristics (initiatives are initiated bottom-up, federal proposals top-down) and different tonality directions—support for challengers takes a positive tonality in the case of initiatives but a negative tonality in the case of federal proposals. The three referenda

[21] The 21 examined news outlets are listed alphabetically: 20 minuten; 20 minutes; 24-Heures; Aargauer Zeitung; Basler Zeitung; Berner Zeitung; Blick; Blick am Abend; Die Südostschweiz; Le Matin; Le Matin Dimanche; Le Temps; (Neue) Luzerner Zeitung; Neue Zürcher Zeitung; NZZ am Sonntag; Schweiz am Wochenende/am Sonntag; SonntagsBlick; SonntagsZeitung; Tages-Anzeiger; Tribune de Genève; Weltwoche.

Table 2 Media attention and tonality towards initiatives and referenda

	Media attention	Tonality
Initiative "Energy tax instead of VAT" (2015)	132	−41
Nuclear phase-out initiative (2016)	398	−1
18 other initiatives (average)	*296*	*−27*
Energy Strategy 2050 (2017)	516	8
13 other federal proposals (average)	*275*	*18*

Note: "Media attention" indicates the number of articles published on the respective public vote. "Tonality" indicates tonality (averaged over all newspapers) towards the respective vote

share common features, but they differ in terms of attention and tonality. The data shows relatively low media attention to the GLP initiative in 2015, while both the nuclear phase-out initiative in 2016 and the energy referendum ES2050 in 2017 triggered much more media coverage than other votes.

We argue that the following factors help explain these differences in media attention.[22] Political advertising expenditures, which usually correlate with overall media attention, were below average in the run-up to the GLP initiative and above average in the other two cases, with the number of political ads as a possible proxy.[23] Furthermore, only the two referenda with high media attention included debates on nuclear energy, while the GLP initiative focused more on renewable energy and on financial policy in general. This difference in issue characteristics is important, since nuclear energy has been found to be extensively and intensively covered by the media, especially after the accident at Japan's Fukushima Daiichi nuclear power plant.[24] In this sense, in gauging the newsworthiness of an issue in the "hot" phase, journalists use previous media attention as a yardstick.[25] We can also argue that the GLP initiative constituted a more technical and unfamiliar issue; hence it was less attractive and more difficult for the media to cover. The nuclear phase-out initiative and ES2050, on the other hand, with their focus on nuclear energy (in the case of the phase-out initiative including a date to end electricity generation based on nuclear energy) represented a more familiar and concrete issue.

As regards tonality, media coverage is, on average, negative towards initiatives and positive towards federal proposals (see Table 2). Given that federal proposals have, on average, good chances to withstand a referendum, while the majority of popular initiatives is rejected, this supports the finding that media typically reflect the majority view of political actors and the final voting result. However, the three energy proposals fit this pattern to different extents. Media coverage about the GLP initiative was indeed typical of media coverage about initiatives, even though criticism in this case was even more pronounced. (In this light, the very low approval rate at the polls is not surprising.) In comparison, the nuclear phase-out initiative

[22] See Udris et al. (2018).

[23] Heidelberger (2017).

[24] Kristiansen (2017).

[25] Udris et al. (2018).

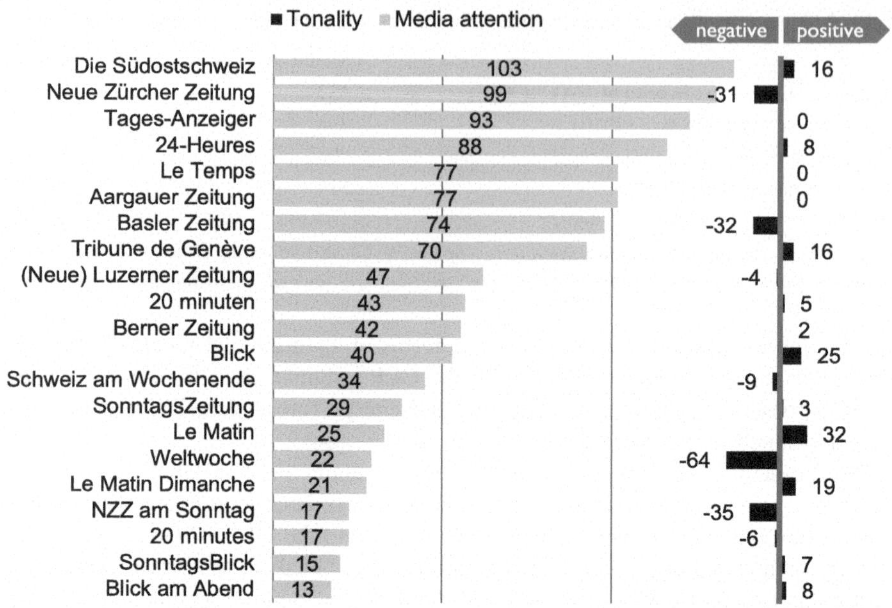

Fig. 1 Media attention and tonality in different newspapers—three energy-related proposals

found more support and less criticism in media coverage than expected. Unlike other initiatives, tonality towards the nuclear phase-out was ambivalent, i.e., the numbers of articles supportive and critical of the initiative were about equal. The Green Party as a challenger of the status quo thus managed to stimulate a salient and multifaceted debate, with their proposal finding more support in the media than average initiatives. Finally, on average, the media portrayed the ES2050 only in a slightly positive light compared to other federal proposals. Hence, the federal energy strategy was a hotly debated and controversial issue in the media, a finding that is mirrored by the diversity of views about the implementation of the ES2050 among stakeholders of the Swiss energy system, as documented by a stakeholder survey conducted within the work package "Energy Governance" of SCCER-CREST.[26]

At the same time, media coverage differed considerably among newspapers (see Fig. 1). This is not surprising, since each newspaper is embedded in a different context, reflecting both the specific political climate in cantons and regions and, above all, specific ownership and production structures. For the data analysis, we combined the three energy-related proposals, as positive tonality in all cases ultimately means support for more "green" policies and renewable energies. Through this comparison, large differences among newspapers become clear. *Weltwoche* (−64), *Neue Zürcher Zeitung (NZZ;* −31) and its sister paper *NZZ am Sonntag* (−35) and *Basler Zeitung* (−32) had the most negative tonality scores, while *Le*

[26] See Duygan et al. (2021).

Table 3 Share of media attention given to different collective actors and actor types in media coverage of the three energy-related proposals

	Initiative "Energy tax instead of VAT" (2015)	Nuclear phase-out initiative (2016)	Energy Strategy 2050 (2017)	Total
Media	13%	13%	24%	329
Economy	2%	15%	12%	220
SVP	6%	6%	13%	165
FDP	6%	5%	10%	138
Green party	6%	14%	2%	128
Civil society	4%	9%	6%	127
Federal Council	13%	6%	6%	120
Experts	3%	5%	6%	94
SP	9%	6%	3%	81
CVP	2%	5%	4%	76
Green Liberal party	19%	2%	2%	69
Other actors	16%	15%	11%	234
Statements all actors	*193*	*717*	*871*	*1781*

Matin (+32) and its sister paper *Le Matin Dimanche* (+19) and *Blick* (+25) displayed the most positive tonality scores. The positive tonality apparent in newspapers from Suisse romande (e.g., *Le Matin*, *Le Matin Dimanche, Tribune de Genève*) seems to reflect a political climate more favorable to renewable energies, as is also attested in the final voting results. As concerns negative tonality, ownership structures might indeed be another explanatory factor. *Weltwoche* and *Basler Zeitung* (at that time) were owned by political actors from the SVP, and *NZZ* is owned by shareholders who are obliged to be either members of the FDP or have a "liberal" ("*freisinnig-demokratisch*" in German, in the sense of *conservative liberalism*) worldview. Both SVP and FDP were more or less critical of renewable energy policies and of phasing out nuclear energy. In media coverage, journalists then seemed to align with the official or long-standing political stance of their newspapers, which is in line with earlier findings.[27]

Apart from media-specific factors, the overall support or rejection reflected in the tonality is a specific result of actor constellations and political conflict. This is illustrated by the media attention that was given to different actors (Table 3) and actors' acceptance of proposals (based on their statements; Table 4). With respect to the latter, +100 means that all statements of an actor are positive (indicating support), −100 means that all statements of an actor are negative (indicating rejection), and 0 means that either the actor uses ambivalent messages or there are various competing factions within a collective actor (e.g., within a political party). Table 3 (media

[27] See Jandura and Udris (2019); Udris et al. (2020); Kepplinger and Lemke (2016).

Table 4 Acceptance of energy-related proposals by different collective actors and actor types

	Initiative "Energy tax instead of VAT" (2015)	Nuclear phase-out initiative (2016)	Energy Strategy 2050 (2017)	Total
Media	−62	−2	−10	329
Economy	−100	−79	16	220
SVP	−100	−63	−85	165
FDP	−100	−78	−20	138
Green party	75	99	100	128
Civil society	13	51	−9	127
Federal Council	−88	−98	88	120
Experts	−40	15	2	94
SP	−100	93	100	81
CVP	−50	−74	63	76
Green Liberal party	92	87	88	69
Other actors	N/A	N/A	N/A	234
Statements all actors (n)	*193*	*717*	*871*	*1781*

attention) and Table 4 (acceptance) show that each referendum followed a specific pattern. The overall negative tonality towards the GLP initiative was also reflected in the actor constellation. Apart from the GLP, this initiative received some support only from the Green Party (6%; +75), while almost all other actor groups were quoted with primarily negative messages.

In contrast, the nuclear phase-out initiative and ES2050 proposal were much more contested, albeit with different conflict constellations. The nuclear phase-out received support not only from the Green Party but also from the GLP, the Social Democrats and parts of civil society and experts. Notably, when media used comments and their own evaluations, there was a balance between support and rejection—unlike in the case of the GLP initiative. In terms of media attention, the Green Party was highly visible (14%; +99), as were its opponents representing incumbent business interests such as those from the nuclear sector ("economy", 15%; −79) and the center-right parties including SVP, FDP and CVP (collective media attention: 16%). In sum, this media portrayal followed a rather "classic" energy- and environment-related conflict in the economic left-right dimension, with some support by the media themselves.[28]

Media coverage about ES2050 shows that the majority of actors used favorable messages, but two large parties, which were also the parties with the highest media attention, were either highly critical (SVP: 13%; −85) or internally divided (FDP:

[28] This is also supported by an analysis of the Statistical Office of the Canton of Zurich, available at https://statistik.zh.ch. Based on aggregate data on municipalities and voting results in these municipalities, Moser (2018), p. 3, finds that the vote can be explained much more on the economic dimension than on the cultural dimension.

10%; −20). Support from economic actors, which gained much media coverage, remained limited (12%; only +16), again pointing at competing positions and conflict among economic organizations. In addition, parts of civil society were somewhat skeptical towards ES2050 (−9), as were the media themselves (−10), especially right-wing leaning media from German-speaking Switzerland (cf. above). In sum, media portrayal of ES2050 did not follow a "classic" economic left-right conflict but rather showed internal conflict among the center-right and the economy.

Finally, when it comes to actual dynamics in media coverage about referenda in general, the overall campaign period is usually relatively short. The "hot" phase typically begins around 6 to 4 weeks before voting day and intensifies until a climax is reached around three to 1 week(s) before voting day. Dynamics in media reporting are usually linked to dynamics in campaign activities and to the timing of voters' decision-making. For instance, many citizens send out their ballots by mail during the "hot" campaign phase.[29] During this peak period, media publish more than three to four times as many articles per week compared to two or more months before the vote. At the same time, media coverage typically does not intensify any longer, the closer the voting day gets.

Broadly speaking, votes on energy policy are no exception to this rule. However, some interesting deviations can be observed (see Fig. 2). First, both ES2050 and the nuclear phase-out initiative showed an unusually marked increase in media attention even in the second week before voting day, while media coverage on the GLP initiative began to stagnate earlier on. Second, media attention to ES2050 started rather early, also because parliamentary debates on related issues (in particular hydropower) that were taking place at the same time were discursively linked to the ongoing referendum campaign. In this sense, the "hot" phase of the ES2050 lasted longer than on average, while the nuclear phase-out initiative showed the most intense, i.e., most "condensed" media coverage.

To conclude, media coverage about all three proposals reflected the actor constellations and foreshadowed the final voting result. Hence, the two initiatives were portrayed less favorably than the federal proposal. However, the GLP initiative found much less media attention and was rejected even more strongly than is typically the case for popular initiatives (both at the ballot and as measured through the tonality index), while the nuclear phase-out initiative, in contrast to other initiatives, was characterized by a balanced amount of supportive and critical newspaper articles. As the high level of media attention indicates, both the nuclear phase-out initiative and the ES2050 were heavily contested, and the latter triggered more criticism than the average federal proposal. The strong contestation was at the time also underlined by survey results indicating a close race between proponents and opponents a few weeks before the vote. But the nature of contestation differed

[29] See Milic et al. (2014), p. 290 et seq. One reason is that this is exactly the period when citizens receive their voting material, which consists of the official ballots and accompanying official brochures on the content of the votes. There is evidence suggesting that many citizens cast their vote by postal ballot right after they receive the voting material.

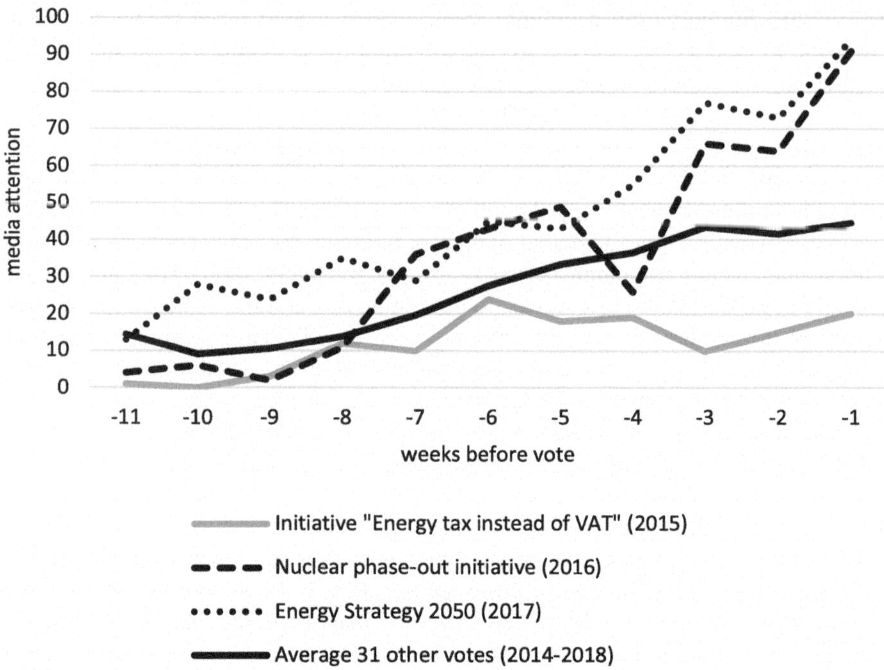

Fig. 2 Dynamics of media attention

between the cases. The ES2050 media coverage pointed at internal conflicts within the FDP and among economic actors, i.e., disagreements within political and economic elites. Media coverage about the nuclear phase-out initiative, on the other hand, reflected well-known conflict constellations with two antagonistic camps, i.e., between left-wing actors in favor of an expedited nuclear phase-out and economic and right-wing actors (plus the Federal Council) campaigning unitedly against such a measure.

3 The Role of Media Coverage in Explaining the Result of the Nuclear Phase-Out Vote

While Sect. 2 has provided insights into media coverage of energy-related referenda as a dependent variable, we now focus on media coverage as an independent variable. Based on a linkage approach, we test to what extent the tonality of media coverage affects citizens' decision-making and voting behavior. We do this by studying the case of the 2016 nuclear phase-out initiative. We selected this case because it allows, we believe, even better testing of several effects known from the literature on electoral choice. As shown above, media attention to the nuclear phase-out initiative was relatively high; thus, citizens were potentially confronted with a lot of information. This was also true for the ES2050, but not for the GLP initiative. Information on the nuclear phase-out initiative conveyed an almost "perfectly" ambivalent tonality in terms of support and rejection, while the ES2050 was characterized by a slightly positive aggregated tonality and the GLP initiative by a clearly negative one. Therefore, at the individual level, we assume to detect a lot of variation with respect to exposure to different kinds of tonality regarding the phase-out proposal. Moreover, unlike the media debate on the ES2050, the debate surrounding the nuclear phase-out initiative conveyed clear actor and conflict constellations well-known from partisan politics. In sum, citizens potentially received much information—"new" information regarding the (surprisingly) ambivalent tonality but also "old" information regarding the well-known actor constellation. We examine this configuration in light of the literature on campaign effects.

3.1 *Campaign Effects*

As noted by McCombs and Shaw almost half a century ago, "the pledges, promises, and rhetoric encapsulated in news stories, columns, and editorials constitute much of the information upon which a voting decision has to be made."[30] Despite the changes in the relevance of communication channels and media systems that have occurred since then, the news media still play a major role as a transmission belt in today's democracies in general and in helping citizens to form vote choices in particular.[31] For Switzerland's direct democratic system, it has been shown that voters rely strongly on the media (especially newspapers) as a source of information to form their voting preferences.[32]

What kinds of effects can be expected to be brought about by media coverage in the run-up to a direct democratic vote? Research on campaign effects often draws on the classical work of Lazarsfeld and colleagues.[33] Accordingly, an electoral campaign may have three distinct effects. First, it can lead to a *reinforcement* of voters' initial intentions; that is, voters have already formed certain intentions at the outset of a campaign and these become reinforced over the course of the latter. Second, voters may have no voting intentions at the beginning of a campaign, but the latter activates their latent political predispositions and thereby helps them to take a vote choice—a mechanism called *activation* or *crystallization*. As a third possibility, a campaign may induce voters to rethink their original voting intention, leading to a *conversion* in the sense that they take a choice that is different from their original voting intention. As Kriesi and Sciarini[34] pointed out, a campaign may bring about a fourth

[30] McCombs and Shaw (1972), p. 176.

[31] E.g., Kübler and Kriesi (2017); Wettstein and Wirth (2017).

[32] Bonfadelli and Friemel (2012); Tresch (2008).

[33] Lazarsfeld et al. (1944).

[34] Kriesi and Sciarini (2004).

effect: voters who have a specific voting intention at the outset of a campaign may finally refrain from casting a vote. This fourth campaign effect may be called *demobilization*.

When it comes to media effects, our baseline expectation is that exposure to positive coverage—i.e., news coverage favorable about the ballot proposition—increases the probability of voting in favor of it vis-à-vis casting a "no"-vote (hypothesis 1).

Positive coverage should reinforce the voting intentions of voters who already had favorable intentions before, especially by reinforcing known arguments in favor of the proposal and potentially providing new ones. For voters with initially negative voting intentions, one may expect positive coverage to lead to a persuasion effect. However, this view ignores voters' political predispositions including their partisan orientation, which can be expected to condition the effects of exposure to media coverage. Referendum campaigns not only help voters to gain issue-specific knowledge but also to learn about the positions political parties take on a ballot proposition.[35] Many voters use information about a party's stance on a political issue as shortcuts in forming their own preferences,[36] and the relevance of this partisan heuristic has also been demonstrated in the context of Swiss direct democratic votes.[37] In sum, in the context of the nuclear phase-out initiative, which was characterized by the long-standing ideological divide between (nuclear-skeptic) left-wing and (nuclear-friendly) right-wing parties,[38] we therefore expect exposure to positive media coverage about the phase-out proposal to reinforce positive voting intentions among left-party voters (hypothesis 2). For right-party voters with positive voting intentions, on the other hand, exposure to positive coverage may resonate with their prior intentions, but as the campaign advances, these voters are likely to become aware of the inconsistency between their political predisposition and their voting intention. This ambivalence can be expected to dampen any reinforcement effect.

As a mirror image to the second hypothesis, we expect exposure to negative coverage about the proposal to reinforce negative voting intentions among right-party voters (hypothesis 3). Again, we do not expect such an effect for left-party voters with initially negative voting intentions, due to the ambivalence that arises between growing awareness of one's preferred party's position and the original voting intention.

Based on our hypotheses, the subsequent analyses focus specifically on reinforcement effects. While we will also explore conversion and demobilization effects, our data are not suited to investigate activation effects, as will be further explained below.

[35] Selb et al. (2009).

[36] Arceneaux (2008); Nicholson (2012).

[37] Kriesi (2005).

[38] Dermont and Kammermann (2020).

3.2 Empirical Analysis of Media Effects in the Nuclear Phase-Out Vote

To examine media effects on voting behavior, we combine data from a panel survey with a content analysis of newspaper articles from the *monitor* database described above. We thus rely on "linkage analysis", an approach pioneered by Arthur H. Miller and colleagues in the 1970s that uses media content as a quasi-experimental stimulus to explain individual-level variables.[39] The idea behind the method is to link media content data with survey data after having matched survey respondents with the media they actually consume. Linkage analysis is suited to identify effects of media content on individual-level variables in real-world settings, but it might be prone to underestimating the true size of effects.[40] The approach is the state-of-the-art method in media effects research and has been applied extensively in studies of the impact of news consumption on political behavior.[41] In Sect. 3.2.1 we describe our survey data, which captures the outcome of interest (voting behavior) as well as several focal explanatory and control variables. Sect. 3.2.2 presents the media content data, and Sect. 3.2.3 presents the results of our regression analyses. We discuss the results in Sect. 3.3.

3.2.1 The Survey: Sampling Strategy and Relevant Variables

To gather data on individuals' voting behavior in the 2016 nuclear phase-out vote and other variables of interest, we fielded a panel survey with Swiss voters. The study participants were drawn from an online consumer panel operated by the Swiss market research agency Intervista. Participants were part of an entirely actively recruited pool, which included nearly 70,000 registered individuals in 2016.[42] We employed stratified random sampling with proportionate allocation to approximate a sample that demographically represents the Swiss voting population. The population was stratified by gender, age, education, partisan orientation and region, covering the German- and French-speaking parts of Switzerland.[43] Respondents were surveyed based on computer-assisted web interviews. The pre-vote questionnaire (t_0, $n = 1216$) was administered right at the outset of the "hot" campaign phase (October 10–19, 2016). The post-vote survey (t_1, $n = 1014$) started 1 h after the polling

[39] Miller et al. (1979).

[40] Scharkow and Bachl (2017).

[41] See De Vreese et al. (2017), who provide an excellent and hands-on overview on the method, and Fazekas and Larsen (2016).

[42] While opt-in panels consist of a self-selected sample of volunteers, Intervista's actively recruited panel comes close to a probability sample of the Swiss voting population. See https://www.intervista.ch/en/panel.

[43] The Italian-speaking region of Switzerland, in which only 6.1% of Swiss voters reside, was not covered by the survey.

stations had closed (November 27) and ended 4 days later (December 1). The drop-out rate between the waves was 16.6%.[44]

Dependent Variable

Our dependent variable captures voting behavior in the popular vote on the nuclear phase-out initiative in 2016. At t_1, we asked whether respondents had participated in the vote and, if they had, whether they had voted in favor or not. The dependent variable finally consists of three categories: voting in favor, voting against, and abstention.

Explanatory and Control Variables

In order to investigate the possible effects of newspaper coverage on voting behavior, the pre-vote survey included an item for measuring respondents' newspaper consumption. Respondents were given a list of 30 Swiss newspapers and asked to indicate which ones they consulted regularly to find out about political and economic issues. Respondents could choose as many papers as they wanted. These individual-level data were later on linked to data covering the tonality of newspaper reporting about the phase-out initiative (see Sect. 3.2.2).

In the post-vote survey, respondents were asked about the sources of information they had used to inform themselves about the phase-out initiative (see Fig. 4). Here, they could select among a number of sources, which also included the official governmental information booklet (*Bundesbüchlein*). To investigate the role government messaging might have played in shaping voting behavior, we use a dummy variable measuring whether voters had read the booklet or not.

Voters also receive advice from their social environment, e.g., through discussions with friends and family members.[45] To measure the intensity of respondents' exposure to these sources of information, the post-vote survey included an item asking respondents to indicate the frequency with which they had discussed the popular initiative with other people around them. For eight categories,[46] respondents indicated whether they had discussed the initiative "never" (coded as 0), "rarely" (1), "sometimes" (2) or "often" (3). These data were aggregated to an additive index of exposure to social voting cues.

To assess partisan orientation, respondents were asked to indicate (at t_0) which political party best represented their political views. Based on this information, we generated a variable capturing whether respondents leaned towards one of the parties

[44] More information on the survey data can be found in Rinscheid and Wüstenhagen (2018).

[45] Bonfadelli and Friemel (2012).

[46] The categories are: spouse/partner; own children; own parents; other relatives; friends; neighbors; workmates; acquaintances from clubs, associations or congregations.

supporting the initiative, a party without a clear stance, or one of the parties rejecting it. Information on stable sociodemographic variables including respondents' gender, age, education, and place of residence were also collected at t_0. Based on the latter, we generated two dummy variables. The first, "Danger Zone", captures whether the place of residence is within a radius of 20 kilometers from one of the country's nuclear reactors. This radius corresponds to the legally defined "danger zone", in which a serious nuclear incident can pose a threat to the population, for which protective measures are required.[47] The second, "Language Region", captures whether respondents live in the French- or German-speaking part of Switzerland. Finally, our analyses control for initial (t_0) voting intentions and the strength of these. At t_0, respondents were asked to indicate, on a 5-point scale, whether they intended to certainly (coded as 1) or rather (2) vote in favor of the initiative, had not formed a voting intention yet (3), or intended to rather (4) or certainly (5) vote against the initiative. We generated a dummy variable "Initial voting intention" to differentiate between voters intending to vote in favor and voters intending to vote against. We generated a second dummy variable "Strength of initial voting intention", distinguishing between voters with "weak" intentions in favor or against the initiative at t_0 (corresponding to "2" and "4" on the 5-point scale) and voters with "strong intentions" ("1" and "5").

3.2.2 Newspaper Data: Sample, Coding and Index Construction

In order to investigate the effects of newspaper coverage on voting behavior, the individual-level behavioral data on media consumption described in Sect. 3.2.1 were merged with data on newspaper coverage about the initiative. In general, for the latter, we relied on the newspaper-level tonality scores described in Sect. 2.2. However, our sample of newspapers used here deviates slightly from the monitor sample described in Sect. 2.2. First, the Sunday newspapers *SonntagsBlick* and *Le Matin Dimanche* were not included because they were not covered by the survey. Second, *L'Hebdo* was included in the linkage analysis, but was not used for the comparative analysis in Sect. 2.2 (including data between 2014 and 2018), since *L'Hebdo* ceased to exist in 2017. This leaves us with a sample of 10 subscription newspapers, 5 tabloid and free newspapers, and 5 Sunday newspapers. 6 of these newspapers appear in French and 14 in German.

Moreover, given that the implementation of the first survey wave was not finalized before October 20, 2016, our linkage analysis only used tonality data based on the 268 articles that were published between October 20 and November 20, 2016 (see Table 5). That way, we made sure to relate the mechanisms of reinforcement, conversion and demobilization to the newspaper coverage that

[47] Art. 3 para. 1 let. b Emergency Protection Ordinance (*Verordnung über den Notfallschutz in der Umgebung von Kernanlagen, Notfallschutzverordnung, NSFV, SR 732.33*).

Table 5 Classification of newspaper articles used for the study of media effects

Tonality towards phase-out initiative	No. of articles
Positive	58
Neutral/ambivalent	158
Negative	52

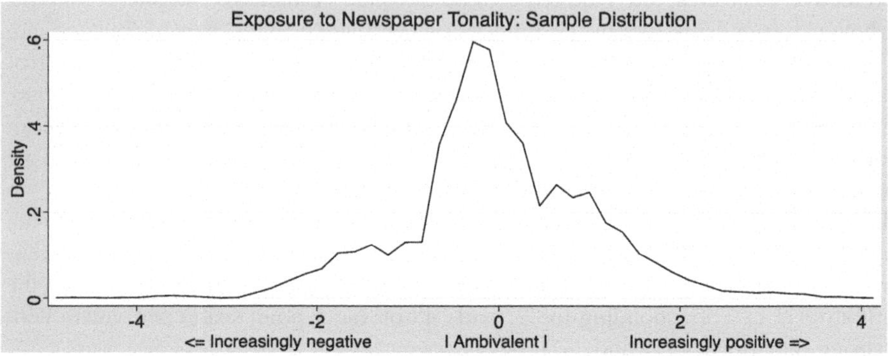

Fig. 3 Distribution of the tonality index (z-transformed) among study participants

happened precisely between the two survey waves. Our analysis thereby covers almost the entire "hot" phase of the referendum campaign (see Fig. 2).

Table 5 shows the numbers of articles with a positive, neutral/ambivalent or negative tonality with regard to the nuclear phase-out initiative used for the linkage analysis. The proportion of articles classified as positive (58, or 21.6%) was slightly higher than the proportion of articles classified as negative (52, or 19.4%) during the period of observation. The majority of articles (158, or 59%) was coded as neutral or ambivalent. Similar to the procedure described in Sect. 2.2, we computed tonality scores at the level of individual newspapers. These ranged from −33.3 (*20 minutes*) to +83.3 (*L'Hebdo*). To account for variations in the frequency with which different newspapers reported about the nuclear phase-out initiative, we multiplied the tonality scores by the number of articles about the nuclear phase-out initiative per publication day. The resulting normalized tonality score ranges from −18.5 (*Luzerner Zeitung*) to 18.5 (*L'Hebdo*). Next, for each respondent, we added the newspaper-level tonality scores for those newspapers that (s)he had indicated to use regularly to find out about political and economic issues. The distribution of the resulting (z-transformed) individual-level index of exposure to newspaper coverage about the nuclear phase-out initiative is shown in Fig. 3.

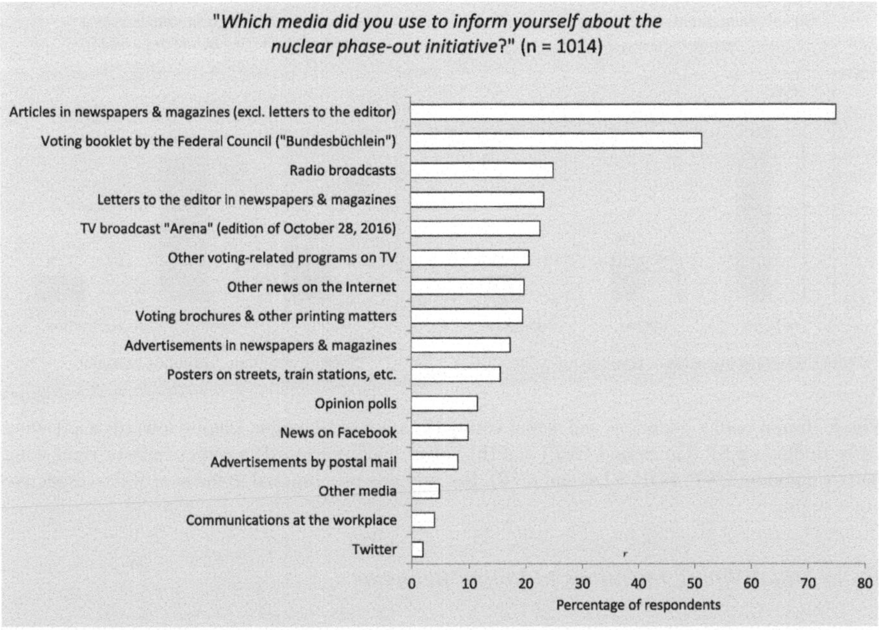

Fig. 4 Respondents' use of media in the context of the nuclear phase-out initiative

3.2.3 Data Analysis and Results

Frequencies: Relevance of Information Sources

In Switzerland, newspapers are perceived as (highly) important mass media channels. In a study on three referendum campaigns, newspapers were found to be among the three most important information sources, together with television and the governmental information booklet;[48] this pattern is confirmed by the regularly conducted VOTO (formerly VOX) analyses.[49] In our sample, 75% of respondents indicated that they used newspapers to inform themselves about the nuclear phase-out initiative, followed by the voting booklet published by the Federal Council (51%) and way ahead of further media like radio, television and internet sources (see Fig. 4). This underscores the importance of newspapers as a source of information in the run-up to the referendum.[50]

[48] Bonfadelli and Friemel (2012), p. 174.

[49] See Milic et al. (2014), p. 299.

[50] See also the contribution by Schaffer and Levis (2021) in this volume, which underscores the particularly prominent role of newspapers in shaping public opinion compared with other news media.

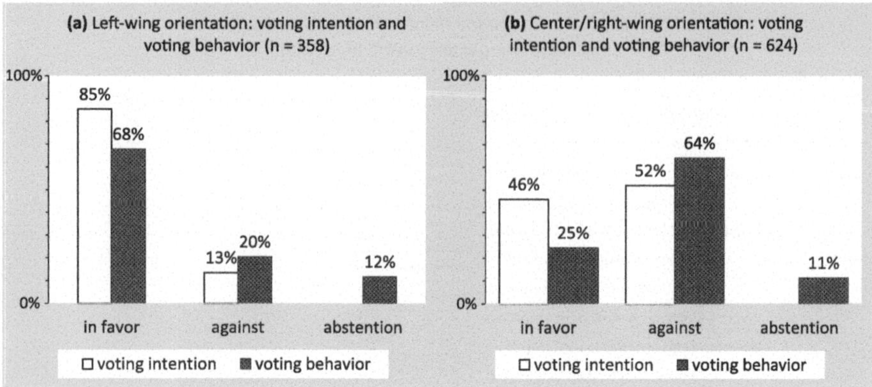

Fig. 5 Initial voting intentions and actual voting behavior of (a) voters leaning towards a left-wing party (including SP, Green and GLP) and (b) voters leaning towards a center-right or right-wing party (including CVP, FDP, BDP and SVP). Bar width is proportional to the size of the respective voter segment

From Initial Voting Intentions to Voting Behavior

Figure 5 indicates the extent to which initial voting intentions (t_0) were in line with actual voting behavior (t_1), differentiating between voters leaning towards the left-wing parties supportive of the popular initiative (a) and voters leaning towards the center-right parties that rejected the phase-out proposal (b). As Fig. 5 illustrates, there was considerable movement in voters' preferences on both sides of the political spectrum. While 85% of left-wing voters in our sample had expressed an intention to vote in favor of the popular initiative right before the "hot" campaign phase, only 68% finally voted in favor, with the remainder either voting against (20%) or not casting a vote at all (12%).

A different pattern can be observed for voters of the parties that rejected the initiative. While there was almost a balance between supporters (46%) and opponents (52%) of the initiative at t_0, only one in four right-wing voters finally voted "yes". Half of the voters who defected from their initial support did not participate and the other half voted against. On aggregate, the majority of voters participating in both survey waves (60.5%) had expressed an intention to vote in favor of the initiative at t_0, but only 45.7% of participating voters finally supported it at the ballot (compared with 45.8% in the electorate).[51] These patterns beg the question

[51] Our survey overestimates voter turnout (88.6% vs. 45.3% in reality). Such turnout gaps are a phenomenon typical of post-election studies, and the magnitude of the gap in our data is similar or slightly higher than turnout gaps documented in panel studies in the context of other Swiss referenda (Hänggli et al. 2012). The reasons are threefold: besides overrepresentation of politically interested citizens in political surveys and vote misreporting (Selb and Munzert 2013), politically active citizens are more likely to participate in a multi-wave survey (Sciarini and Kriesi 2003). One implication is that the numbers representing "voting behavior" in Fig. 5 are not representative of the entire electorate.

how the observed opinion swings on both sides may be explained and, in particular, what role media coverage of the phase-out initiative might have played in bringing about not only the erosion of the relatively strong cohesion of the political left between t_0 and t_1 but also the consolidation of the "no-camp" within the political right.

Regression Analysis

To analyze voting behavior, we start with a multinomial logistic regression analysis. This classification method is a generalization of logistic regression that can be applied if the dependent variable is categorically distributed. The dependent variable of our multinomial logit model consists of three categories corresponding to voting in favor of the phase-out initiative, voting against, and abstention. Table 6 contains the regression coefficients for the three contrasts: voting in favor versus against,

Table 6 Multinomial Logistic Regression coefficients: Voting behavior in the popular initiative on the nuclear phase-out (2016)

	Vote in favor versus against		Vote in favor versus abstention		Vote against versus abstention	
Independent variables						
Tonality about initiative	0.077	(0.094)	0.331**	(0.122)	0.255*	(0.120)
Government booklet	−0.430*	(0.197)	1.230***	(0.270)	1.660***	(0.271)
Partisan orientation	−0.620***	(0.106)	−0.221	(0.137)	0.399**	(0.145)
Social cues	0.124	(0.108)	0.866***	(0.152)	0.742***	(0.152)
Age	−0.114	(0.061)	0.200*	(0.081)	0.314***	(0.080)
Gender	0.233	(0.193)	−0.282	(0.254)	−0.515*	(0.251)
Education	−0.007	(0.207)	0.263	(0.273)	0.270	(0.277)
Danger zone	−0.304	(0.269)	−0.277	(0.334)	0.026	(0.329)
Language region	0.099	(0.232)	0.013	(0.299)	−0.085	(0.306)
Initial voting intention	3.365***	(0.258)	1.913***	(0.338)	−1.452***	(0.270)
Strength of initial voting intention	1.420***	(0.200)	1.058***	(0.254)	−0.362	(0.257)
Intercept	−2.867***	(0.578)	−1.613*	(0.731)	1.254	(0.688)
n	983					
Pseudo R^2	0.355					

Note: * $p < 0.05$, ** $p < 0.01$, *** $p < 0.001$; standard errors in parentheses

The following are dummy variables: Government booklet: consulted = 1 (51.5%)—not consulted = 0 | Gender: female = 1 (50.2%)—male = 0 | Education: attended high school = 1 (36.9%)—did not attend high school = 0 | Danger Zone: lives within danger zone = 1 (16.4%)—does not live within danger zone = 0 | Language Region: French-speaking = 1 (22.9%)—German-speaking = 0 | Initial voting intention: In favor = 1 (61.6%)—Against = 0 | Strength of initial voting intention: Strong = 1 (51.1%)—Weak = 0. Partisan orientation is 3-tiered (supporting a party in favor of initiative, without clear stance, against the initiative). Age has 6 categories (>29, 30–39, 40–49, 50–59, 60–69, 70+). Tonality about initiative (negative to positive) and Social cues (little to much exposure) are continuous voting in favor versus abstention, and voting against versus abstention. The coefficients of the third column are simply the result of subtracting the coefficients of the first column from those of the second.

The coefficients provide first clues with respect to the impact of the independent variables on voting behavior. Regarding the focal explanatory variable—exposure to newspaper coverage regarding the popular initiative—the results do not unambiguously support our first hypothesis. Contrary to what we had expected, exposure to increasingly positive tonality did not increase the probability to cast a "yes"-vote, at least in the contrast with voting "against" (first column). However, as can be seen from the coefficients in the second and third column, higher exposure to positive tonality led to a *higher probability of casting a vote at all.* While this finding seems counterintuitive in the case of rejecting the proposal, we conclude that positive coverage about the phase-out initiative generally had a mobilizing effect. Table 6 conveys some more interesting results. With respect to the government booklet, taking note of this publication had a mobilization effect, given that it significantly increased the probability to cast either a yes- or no-vote. Reading the booklet also significantly increased the probability of voting against, compared to voting in favor, which is hardly surprising given that the booklet advocated strongly against the popular initiative. With respect to partisan orientation, our model confirms that right-wing voters were significantly more likely to vote against the initiative. Moreover, both higher exposure to social voting cues and higher age operated in favor of participating in the vote but do not help explaining voting behavior as such. Finally, both the intention to vote in favor at t_0 and the strength of the initial intention were significantly (and strongly) related to approval of the initiative at t_1, while only the intention to reject the initiative (but not the strength of it) helps explain the mobilization of "no"-voters.

However, the results contained in Table 6 do not illuminate the ways in which the tonality of media reporting may have driven the three mechanisms introduced above. Therefore, in the next step, we computed predicted probabilities for different values of exposure to media coverage. We differentiated between voter segments corresponding to the mechanisms of reinforcement, demobilization and conversion in the following way:

- Voters who were in favor of the initiative throughout (i.e., at t_0 and t_1): *Reinforcement* of support (n = 379)
- Voters who intended to vote in favor of the initiative at t_0 but did not vote: *Demobilization* of support (n = 77)
- Voters who changed their preference from support (t_0) to rejection (t_1): *Conversion* of support (n = 148)
- Voters who rejected the initiative at t_0 and t_1: *Reinforcement* of rejection (n = 324)
- Voters who rejected the initiative at t_0 but either did not vote (*demobilization*) or changed their preference to support at t_1 (*conversion*; n = 56).

We pooled demobilization and conversion for initial opponents because these two subgroups would become too small for meaningful quantitative analyses if included separately in our models. The remaining 30 voters who participated in both survey waves either had no preference at t_0 or refused to indicate/did not remember their voting behavior at t_1. As only three (nine) voters who had no initial voting intention finally supported (rejected) the phase-out proposal t_1, we did not investigate potential activation effects.

Figure 6 shows predicted reinforcement, conversion, and demobilization effects for different values of the tonality index. For the computation of predicted probabilities, we converted the tonality index into five categories based on the quintiles of the distribution shown in Fig. 3: respondents exposed to strongly (1) or moderately (2) negative tonality about the phase-out initiative, respondents exposed to

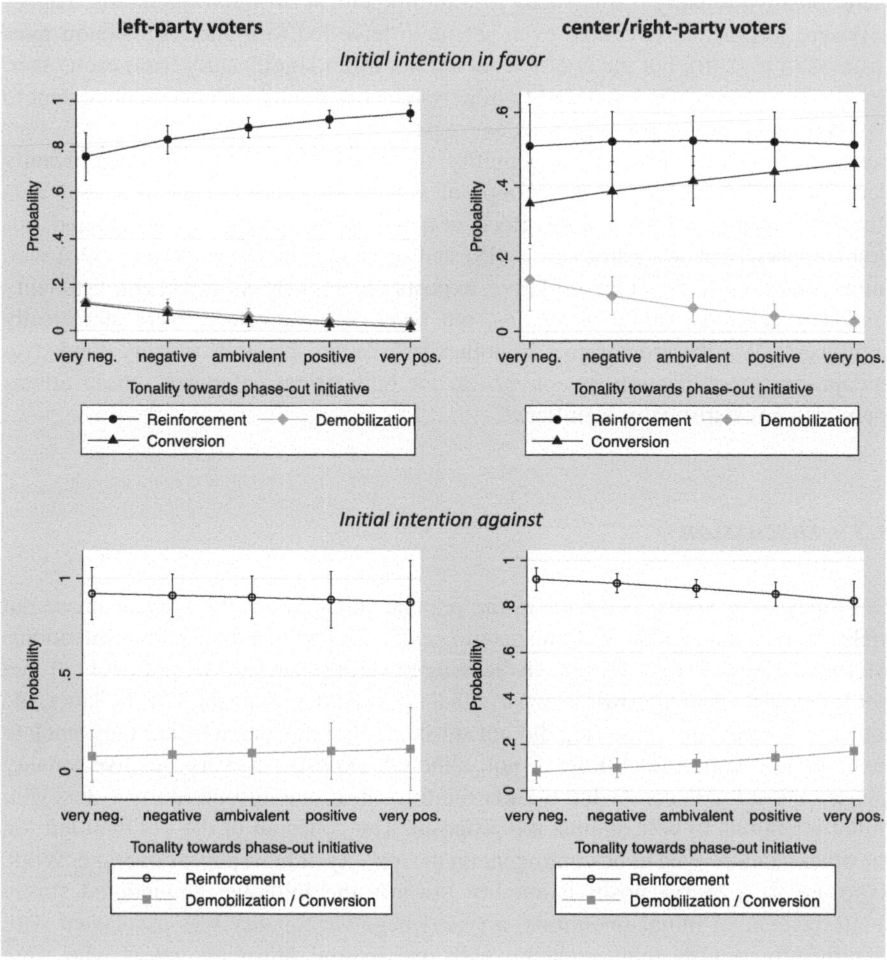

Fig. 6 Predicted reinforcement, demobilization, and conversion effects in the nuclear phase-out vote, 2016: the influence of newspaper coverage

ambivalent tonality (3), and respondents exposed to moderately (4) or strongly (5) positive tonality. In line with our expectation (hypothesis 2), the probability of casting a "yes"-vote increased for left-party voters who intended to vote in favor at t_0 ($n = 306$), as we move from very negative (0.76) to very positive (0.95) tonality. Conversely, both the probability of demobilization (0.12 to 0.03) and conversion (0.12 to 0.02) significantly decreased, the more positive the newspaper coverage about the initiative became. Hence, positive media reporting played a significant role in fostering left-party voters' initial voting intentions, and very negative reporting resulted in abstention or rejection of the initiative for a quarter of supporters of the political left who had initially intended to vote in favor. Looking at center/right-party voters with an initial intention to cast a "yes"-vote ($n = 285$), the pattern is different. Here, positive tonality did not lead to a reinforcement of initial intentions. Higher exposure to positive coverage even seems to have led to higher conversion rates (from 0.35 to 0.46), but the coefficients did not differ significantly from each other. Similar to voters of the left, tonality of newspaper reporting influenced the extent to which demobilization played a role: as we pass from a very negative (0.14) to a very positive (0.02) tonality, the probability to abstain from the vote significantly decreased. With respect to the groups of voters who opposed the proposal at t_0 (the lower panels in Fig. 6), little effects of newspaper coverage can be detected. For both supporters of left parties ($n = 48$) and of center/right parties ($n = 326$) with initial intentions to reject the initiative, exposure to an increasingly *negative* tonality tended to reinforce initial intentions, but none of these effects were statistically significant. We therefore reject hypothesis 3. While positive tonality tended to encourage demobilization or conversion for both groups of voters, these effects were also not statistically significant.

3.3 Discussion

Our analysis of voting behavior in the popular initiative on the nuclear phase-out yields three main results. With respect to *reinforcement* of initial voting intentions, we found a media effect for citizens leaning towards a party of the political left, but not for citizens leaning towards a party that opposed the proposal. For the latter, the tonality of newspaper reporting did not substantially influence whether they stuck to their original voting intentions or not, although exposure to very positive tonality was associated with somewhat weaker reinforcement among right-party voters with initial intentions to vote against the proposal. The cohesion of the political left, on the other hand, proved to be contingent on the tonality of newspaper coverage. While exposure to a (very) positive tonality towards the initiative engendered strong reinforcement of initial intentions, a (very) negative tonality was associated with significantly weaker reinforcement, with one in four left-wing voters who were exposed to strongly negative coverage during the "hot" campaign phase changing their initial voting intention. These voters either abstained from the vote or voted against. As we have shown elsewhere, an emphasis on the benefits of nuclear power (especially its better climate performance vis-à-vis imported coal power, which opponents of the initiative portrayed as the main alternative) may have caused many voters to rethink their initial preference.[52] Notwithstanding the deep partisan divide over nuclear power, which has recently been corroborated in a conjoint experiment by Dermont,[53] this finding suggests that the fundamental rejection of nuclear power is a less important part of the political DNA of the left than one may have assumed.

Second, in terms of *demobilization*, our multinomial logit model showed that exposure to positive tonality had a mobilizing effect. To put this finding into perspective, it needs to be highlighted that other variables including information sources such as the government booklet and social voting cues operated in favor of voter participation as well. What we deem worth to be emphasized, however, is that the more negative the tonality of media coverage about the initiative became, the less likely voters with an initial intention to cast a "yes"-vote were to participate in the vote. Given the rather low number of non-voters in our sample, future research should more closely investigate the role of media coverage in influencing turnout in the context of popular votes on energy topics and beyond.

Third, with respect to *conversion*, we found a significant effect of our exposure index for left-party voters but not for center- and right-wing voters. Nevertheless, as we showed in Fig. 5, many of the latter had initially supported the initiative but "defected" in the course of the campaign, voting in line with their preferred parties. Interestingly, they did this even when being exposed to newspaper coverage that was quite supportive of the initiative. Hence, while the tonality of newspaper coverage as such did not lead to conversion, it would be premature to conclude that the consolidation of the political right was independent of media coverage. As our regression analysis shows, partisan orientation was significantly related to voting behavior. This suggests that, for those voters, newspaper coverage in general may have helped them to learn about parties' positions on the proposal, leading to an alignment of their voting intentions and general political predispositions.[54]

To put the interpretation of results into context, two methodological issues should be noted. First, as is typically the case in applications of linkage analysis, the detected effects are very likely to represent lower-bound estimates of the true effects.[55] Given the high intensity of the campaign, the nuclear phase-out case can be seen as a most-likely case for identifying media effects in a referendum campaign,[56] which should have worked in favor of detecting any media effects at all. The fact that the effects are likely to be biased downwards is due to measurement limitations both in terms of media content analysis and media use. As a remedy, future studies on the role of media in citizens' decision-making should consider

[52] Rinscheid and Wüstenhagen (2018).

[53] Dermont (2019).

[54] On this argument, see Selb et al. (2009).

[55] Scharkow and Bachl (2017).

[56] Sciarini and Tresch (2011).

using more fine-grained (beyond tonality scores at the article level) and encompassing (in terms of included media) measurements of media content. With respect to media use, recent work has proposed a range of sophisticated data collection techniques that may be more reliable than the self-reported media use queries used in this study.[57] Second, one may wonder whether voters' decision to consume specific news media is an endogenous companion of socio-demographic characteristics and, most importantly, partisan orientation. To check for this possibility, we conducted a series of robustness analyses, including regressing the tonality index on the set of variables used in our main regression models as well as examining the average political leaning of readers of various newspapers. The main result of these analyses is that only geography, i.e., voters' place of residence, is significantly related with consumption of specific newspapers. With respect to the partisan orientation of newspapers' readership, we see differences for some newspapers, but these are overall quite small.

4 Conclusion

This chapter took a two-step approach. First, it investigated patterns of media coverage surrounding referendum campaigns in Swiss energy policy-making. Second, it asked to what extent the media have an effect on voters' decisions at the ballot. As regards media coverage, we saw that media attention and tonality towards three recent energy policy votes followed some typical patterns in referendum coverage but also showed proposal-specific features. Compared to typical patterns, the media paid considerably more attention to the nuclear phase-out initiative and the Energy Strategy 2050, while much less attention was given to the initiative by the Green Liberals. In line with the finding that the media tend to reflect the political constellation surrounding a given proposal, tonality towards the Energy Strategy, a federal proposal, was indeed more positive than tonality towards the initiatives brought forward by challengers of the status quo. Interestingly, however, tonality towards the nuclear phase-out initiative was less negative than is typically the case for popular initiatives, leading to balanced coverage of the proposal. Apart from tonality, our findings highlighted different actor constellations. Through a combination of indicators (attention, tonality, actors), we came to the conclusion that media coverage of the nuclear phase-out initiative constituted a salient and politically well-known debate, boiling down to a left-right conflict typical of previous debates in the energy domain.

Following recent suggestions to study how voters' acceptance of energy policies is formed by media coverage during political campaigns[58] and to combine media content analysis with survey research to examine the nexus between news media

[57] For an overview, see De Vreese and Neijens (2016).

[58] Carattini et al. (2017).

reporting and individual preference formation on nuclear power,[59] the second part of the chapter linked data on newspaper coverage of the phase-out initiative with a panel study. Using media content as a quasi-experimental stimulus allowed us to investigate the extent to which exposure to newspaper reporting had a bearing on changes in voting intentions among different groups of voters. Indeed, our analysis identified specific media effects regarding reinforcement and conversion of voting intentions and with respect to mobilization. While these effects were moderated by partisan orientation, they did not always play out as expected. Above all, for the important group of right-leaning voters who had initially supported the initiative but casted a "no"-vote, their vote choices were not contingent on their exposure to tonality as conveyed by newspapers. We concluded that media coverage affected voting behavior not only through its tonality (as for left-wing voters) but presumably through its volume (amount of media attention) and the cues on party positions, which future studies should more closely attend to. Again, we believe that these effects were issue- and proposal-dependent, given that popular initiatives usually receive a lot of support in their early stages but lose support as the campaigns go on. In this light, it would be interesting to examine media effects in the run-up to the vote on the Energy Strategy 2050, a much more "confusing" proposal from the perspective of citizens, as the center-right was itself divided. In general, combining manual content analysis of news articles provided by the *monitor* data with a panel survey in the context of a typical popular vote in Switzerland is a methodological innovation that should be taken up and refined in future research to even better understand the mechanisms through which media coverage helps voters to shape their vote choices on energy topics and beyond. Such an approach may also provide valuable insights into the dynamics of opinion formation in the context of local infrastructure siting decisions, most importantly perhaps in the context of wind turbine installations, where social acceptance risks and their roots need to be better understood and carefully managed in order to fulfill the goals of the ES2050.[60]

References

Arceneaux K (2008) Can partisan cues diminish democratic accountability? Polit Behav 30:139–160. https://doi.org/10.1007/s11109-007-9044-7

Arlt D, Rauchfleisch A, Schäfer MS (2019) Between fragmentation and dialogue. Twitter communities and political debate about the Swiss "Nuclear Withdrawal Initiative". Environ Commun 13:440–456. https://doi.org/10.1080/17524032.2018.1430600

Bonfadelli H, Friemel TN (2012) Learning and knowledge in political campaigns. In: Kriesi H (ed) Political communication in direct democratic campaigns. Palgrave Macmillan, Houndmills, Basingstoke, pp 168–187

[59] Kristiansen et al. (2016), p. 45; Rinscheid (2020).

[60] See Ebers Broughel and Wüstenhagen (2021).

Carattini S, Baranzini A, Thalmann P, Varone F, Vöhringer F (2017) Green taxes in a post-Paris world: are millions of nays inevitable? Environ Resour Econ 68:97–128. https://doi.org/10.1007/s10640-017-0133-8

De Vreese CH, Neijens P (2016) Measuring media exposure in a changing communications environment. Commun Methods Meas 10:69–80. https://doi.org/10.1080/19312458.2016.1150441

De Vreese CH, Boukes M, Schuck A, Vliegenthart R, Bos L, Lelkes Y (2017) Linking survey and media content data: opportunities, considerations, and pitfalls. Commun Methods Meas 11:221–244. https://doi.org/10.1080/19312458.2017.1380175

Dekavalla M (2016) Framing referendum campaigns: the 2014 Scottish independence referendum in the press. Media Cult Soc 38(6):793–810. https://doi.org/10.1177/0163443715620929

Dermont C (2019) Environmental decision-making: the influence of policy information. Env Polit 28:544–567. https://doi.org/10.1080/09644016.2018.1480258

Dermont C, Kammermann L (2020) Political candidates and the energy issue: nuclear power position and electoral success. Rev Policy Res:1–17. https://doi.org/10.1111/ropr.12374

Duygan M, Kachi A, Oeri F, Oliveira TD, Rinscheid A (2021) Energy policymaking in Switzerland. In: Hettich P, Kachi A (eds) Swiss energy governance. Springer, New York

Ebers Broughel A, Wüstenhagen R (2021) The influence of policy risk on Swiss wind power investment. In: Hettich P, Kachi A (eds) Swiss energy governance. Springer, New York

Ettinger P, Imhof P (2014) Qualität der Medienberichterstattung zur Minarett-Initiative. In: Scholten H, Kamps K (eds) Abstimmungskampagnen. Springer VS, Wiesbaden, pp 357–369

Fazekas Z, Larsen EG (2016) Media content and political behavior in observational research: a critical assessment. Br J Polit Sci 46:195–204. https://doi.org/10.1017/S000712341500006X

fög – Forschungsinstitut Öffentlichkeit und Gesellschaft / UZH (2019) Jahrbuch Qualität der Medien 2019: Schweiz – Suisse – Svizzera, Jubiläumsausgabe. Schwabe, Basel

Gerth MA, Dahinden U, Siegert G (2012) Coverage of the campaigns in the media. In: Kriesi H (ed) Political communication in direct democratic campaigns. Palgrave Macmillan, Houndmills, Basingstoke, pp 108–124

Hänggli R (2012) Key factors in frame building: how strategic political actors shape news media coverage. Am Behav Sci 56:300–317. https://doi.org/10.1177/0002764211426327

Hänggli R, Schemer C, Rademacher P (2012) Design of the study: an integrated approach. In: Kriesi H (ed) Political communication in direct democratic campaigns. Palgrave Macmillan, Houndmills, Basingstoke, pp. 39–53

Heidelberger A (2017) APS-Inserateanalyse der eidgenössischen Abstimmung vom 21. Mai 2017. Année Politique Suisse, Institut für Politikwissenschaft, University of Bern. Available at https://anneepolitique.swiss

Hermann M (2012) Das politische Profil des Geldes: Wahl- und Abstimmungswerbung in der Schweiz. Forschungsstelle sotomo am Geographischen Institut UZH, Zurich

Jandura O, Udris L (2019) Parteigänger oder neutrale Berichterstatter? Die Berichterstattung in Schweizer Printmedien vor den eidgenössischen Abstimmungstagen. MIP – Mitteilungen des Instituts für Deutsches und Internationales Parteienrecht und Parteienforschung 25:111–120

Kepplinger HM, Lemke R (2016) Instrumentalizing Fukushima: comparing media coverage of Fukushima in Germany, France, the United Kingdom, and Switzerland. Polit Commun 33:351–373. https://doi.org/10.1080/10584609.2015.1022240

Kriesi H (2005) Direct democratic choice: the Swiss experience. Lexington Books, Lanham

Kriesi H (2012) Conclusion. In: Kriesi H (ed) Political communication in direct democratic campaigns. Palgrave Macmillan, Houndmills, Basingstoke, pp 225–240

Kriesi H, Sciarini P (2004) The impact of issue preferences on voting choices in the Swiss Federal Elections, 1999. Br J Polit Sci 34:725–759. https://doi.org/10.1017/S0007123404000269

Kristiansen S (2017) Media and risk: a phase model elucidating media attention to nuclear energy risk. NEU - Nachhaltigkeits-, Energie- und Umweltkommunikation, vol 5. Universitätsverlag Illmenau, Illmenau

Kristiansen S, Bonfadelli H, Kovic M (2016) Risk perception of nuclear energy after Fukushima: stability and change in public opinion in Switzerland. Int J Public Opin Res 28:1–27. https://doi.org/10.1093/ijpor/edw021

Kübler D, Kriesi H (2017) Debate how globalisation and mediatisation challenge our democracies. Swiss Polit Sci Rev 23:231–245. https://doi.org/10.1111/spsr.12265

Lazarsfeld PF, Berelson B, Gaudet H (1944) The People's choice. How the voter makes up his mind in a presidential campaign. Columbia University Press, New York

Marcinkowski F, Donk A (2012) The deliberative quality of referendum coverage in direct democracy. Javn - Public J Eur Inst Commun Cult 19:93–109. https://doi.org/10.1080/13183222.2012.11009098

Marquis L, Schaub HP, Gerber M (2011) The fairness of media coverage in question: an analysis of referendum campaigns on welfare state issues in Switzerland. Swiss Polit Sci Rev 17:128–163. https://doi.org/10.1111/j.1662-6370.2011.02015.x

McCombs ME, Shaw DL (1972) The agenda-setting function of mass media. Public Opin Q 36:176–187

Milic T, Rousselot B, Vatter A (2014) Handbuch der Abstimmungsforschung. Verlag Neue Zürcher Zeitung, Zurich

Miller AH, Goldenberg EN, Erbring L (1979) Type-set politics: impact of newspapers on public confidence. Am Polit Sci Rev 73:67–84. https://doi.org/10.2307/1954731

Moser P (2018) Die Abstimmungen vom 10.6.2018 - eine Kurzanalyse. Zurich. Available at https://statistik.zh.ch

Nicholson SP (2012) Polarizing cues. Am J Pol Sci 56:52–66. https://doi.org/10.1111/j.1540-5907.2011.00541.x

Rademacher P, Gerth MA, Siegert G (2012) Coverage of the campaigns in the media. In: Kriesi H (ed) Political communication in direct democratic campaigns. Palgrave Macmillan, Houndmills, Basingstoke, pp 93–107

Renwick A, Lamb M (2013) The quality of referendum debate: the UK's electoral system referendum in the print media. Elect Stud 32:294–304. https://doi.org/10.1016/j.electstud.2012.10.013

Rinscheid A (2020) Business power in noisy politics: an exploration based on discourse network analysis and survey data. Polit Gov 8(2). https://doi.org/10.17645/pag.v8i2.2580

Rinscheid A, Wüstenhagen R (2018) Divesting, fast and slow: affective and cognitive drivers of fading voter support for a nuclear phase-out. Ecol Econ 152:51–61. https://doi.org/10.1016/j.ecolecon.2018.05.015

Schaffer L, Levis A (2021) Public discourses on (sectoral) energy policy in Switzerland. In: Hettich P, Kachi A (eds) Swiss energy governance. Springer, New York

Scharkow M, Bachl M (2017) How measurement error in content analysis and self-reported media use leads to minimal media effect findings in linkage analyses: a simulation study. Polit Commun 34:323–343. https://doi.org/10.1080/10584609.2016.1235640

Sciarini P, Kriesi H (2003) Opinion stability and change during an electoral campaign. Int J Public Opin Res 15:431–453

Sciarini P, Tresch A (2011) Campaign effects in direct-democratic votes in Switzerland. Journal of Elections. Public Opin Parties 21(3):333–357. https://doi.org/10.1080/17457289.2011.588334

Selb P, Munzert S (2013) Voter overrepresentation, vote misreporting and turnout bias in postelection surveys. Elect Stud 32:186–196. https://doi.org/10.1016/j.electstud.2012.11.004

Selb P, Kriesi H, Hänggli R, Marr M (2009) Partisan choices in a direct-democratic campaign. Eur Polit Sci Rev 1:155–172. https://doi.org/10.1017/S175577390900006X

Tresch A (2008) Öffentlichkeit und Sprachenvielfalt. Medienvermittelte Kommunikation zur Europapolitik in der Deutsch- und Westschweiz. Nomos, Baden-Baden

Udris L, Eisenegger M, Schneider J (2016) News coverage about direct-democratic campaigns in a period of structural crisis. J Inf Policy 6:68–104. https://doi.org/10.5325/jinfopoli.6.2016.0068
Udris L, Eisenegger M, Schneider J (2018) Medienresonanz von Abstimmungsvorlagen im Vergleich. In: Kübler D (ed) Medien und direkte Demokratie. Schulthess, Zurich, pp 65–88
Udris L, Eisenegger M, Vogler D, Häuptli A, Schwaiger L (2020, in print) Reporting when the current media system is at stake. Explaining news coverage about the initiative on the abolishment of public service broadcasting in Switzerland. In: Tandoc EC, Jenkins J, Thomas RJ, Westlund O (eds) Critical incidents in journalism: pivotal moments reshaping journalism around the world. Routledge, New York
Wettstein M, Wirth W (2017) Media effects: how media influence voters. Swiss Polit Sci Rev 23:262–269. https://doi.org/10.1111/spsr.12263

Adrian Rinscheid is International Postdoctoral Fellow and Lecturer at the Institute for Economy and the Environment at the University of St. Gallen, St. Gallen, Switzerland.

Linards Udris is Senior Research and Teaching Associate at the Department of Communication and Media Research and Research Center for the Public Sphere & Society at the University of Zurich (Zurich, Switzerland).

Public Discourses on (Sectoral) Energy Policy in Switzerland

Insights from Structural Topic Models

Lena Maria Schaffer and Alessio Levis

Contents

Abstract Energy transitions are based upon policy choices of sovereign nation states. Hence, politics plays a role in determining which policies governments implement and which sectors are targeted. Our chapter looks at the evolution of public discourse on energy policy as one important factor reflecting policy discussion and contestation within the political arena. Our descriptive and explorative analysis of the early public discourse in Swiss energy policy between 1997 and 2011 contributes to three main issues. First, it makes a case for the disaggregation of energy policy and its public perception to add to our understanding of energy transition pathways. We argue that looking at sectoral discourses as well as sectoral policy outputs allows for a more comprehensive understanding of the idiosyncrasies of Swiss energy policy regarding temporal as well as sectoral variation. Second, an increased politicization of energy policy may affect future policy choice, and thus any account on energy transition policy needs to scrutinize potential feedback effects from policies that manifest via policy discourse. Third, and on a more

L. M. Schaffer (✉)
University of Lucerne, Lucerne, Switzerland
e-mail: lena.schaffer@unilu.ch

A. Levis
ETH Zürich, Zürich, Switzerland

P. Hettich, A. Kachi (eds.), *Swiss Energy Governance*,
https://doi.org/10.1007/978-3-030-80787-0_13

methodological stance, we argue that our approach to use news media as a representation of the public discourse via structural topic models can help to explore and explain the evolving national policy priorities regarding energy transition.

1 Introduction

The most central task for effective climate policy is the fundamental restructuring of the way in which we produce and consume energy—a process generally referred to as energy transition. The policies associated with energy transition are needed for nations to fulfill their emission goals under the Paris Agreement, given that energy consumption for electricity generation, transport and heating and cooling of buildings is contributing massively to CO_2 emissions in most countries. To honor their international commitments, nations have implemented a plethora of different policies to convert their economies from using mainly fossil fuels to economies based on renewable energy consumption and an efficient use of energy within the past 30 years.

The resultant national energy governance, i.e. which policies governments implement and which sectors are targeted by these policies, is idiosyncratic. While most nations follow a rough pattern starting from green industrial policy to later add pricing policies and finally ratchet up the policy mix,[1] the concrete choices about which sectors are addressed to what extent vary widely between countries. In our contribution, we heed the calls of different scholars for the joint analysis of different sectors and their associated policies.[2] More precisely, we first make a case for the increased disaggregation of energy policy and its public perception and discourse to add to our understanding of energy transition pathways. To this end, we argue that our descriptive and explorative analysis of the public discourse in Swiss energy policy between 1997 and 2011 allows for a more comprehensive description and understanding of the idiosyncrasies of Swiss energy policy regarding temporal and sectoral variation.

Second, the path-dependent character of national energy policy, which has been stressed in previous scholarly work,[3] means that former decisions in energy policy have strong implications for future choices. In this chapter, we argue that comparative research should go beyond explaining policy adoption. Energy transitions are long-term policy projects that have distributive effects. If policies are increasingly contested and politicized, this may affect future policy choices. Politicization might be visible in increased discourse after policy-making. We suggest that researchers use public discourse to monitor contested policies.

[1] According to Meckling et al. (2017).

[2] Stokes and Breetz (2018).

[3] Aklin and Urpelainen (2013); Unruh (2002).

Third, our approach to use news media as a representation of the public discourse via structural topic models can help to explore and explain patterns within energy policy discussions and the evolving national policy priorities regarding the energy transition.

We descriptively map the development of the Swiss energy policy discourse over the years 1997–2011 by looking at different sectors and comparing discussions on different instruments. Our guiding questions are: How does media discourse develop over time and which factors are associated with (low) high levels of discourse? Drawing on an extensive news media content analysis of the two leading Swiss quality newspapers, we first show how climate change relevant energy policy was reflected within the media. We link our insights from these media discourses with actual policy outcomes as well as incidences of popular referendums on energy policy to gain some leverage over the question whether policy-making of the Swiss government has been more responsive to issues or sectors that loomed large on the public's agenda or whether we cannot establish any connection. Second, we depict how specific discourses and debates around energy policy developed over time. To explain this variation in the Swiss discourse on energy policy, we submit that through the discourse a potential political space opens for the formulation of and debate on alternative solutions.

2 How News Media Can Approximate Public Discourses

We measure our theoretical construct "public discourse" by texts in newspapers. Along with other research streams like politicization research[4] that heavily draw on news content to capture their phenomenon of interest, we do not equate concept and measurement. However, we want to explain directly why the news media appears to be the premium choice for our research interest, especially by highlighting the advantages of the text-as-data/content analysis approach on the basis of newspapers.

Newspaper reporting provides researchers with an accessible medium through which one can assess national tendencies in issue framing or general topics of discourses.[5] And although other media outlets such as TV or social media have gained tremendous ground over the past 30 years, newspapers still maintain their inter-media agenda-setting power.[6] This means that issues picked up by leading quality newspapers actually influence reporting in other outlets such as social media,[7] TV or radio. This ability of news media to influence the national conversation on certain policy issues is forcefully shown in the study by King et al.,[8] who find

[4]De Wilde et al. (2016).

[5]Broadbent et al. (2016), p. 6.

[6]Vliegenthart and Walgrave (2008); Golan (2006).

[7]King et al. (2017).

[8]King et al. (2017), p. 776.

that "exposure to the news media causes Americans to take public stands on specific issues, join national policy conversations, and express themselves publicly—all key components of democratic politics—more often than they would otherwise." This suggests that quality newspapers can serve as a valid proxy for the general media landscape.

Moreover, news media reporting impacts on individuals as well as policy-makers. On the one hand, publicly available information is crucial to the formation of individual political preferences.[9] Additionally, media content is often found to be closely linked to public opinion on given issues.[10] On the other hand, policy-makers tend to rely on opinions represented in the media when trying to gauge public opinion,[11] considering published opinion as an approximation of public opinion.[12] Thus, the news media is an important source of information for any inquiry on discourses in national energy politics.

For our contribution to this edited volume, we use data on Swiss newspaper reporting on climate change and energy transition policy as a starting point.[13] In recent years, text-as-data approaches have gained in popularity within political science research.[14] Especially topic models have come into use more often to analyze large amounts of data without having to refer to (expensive) human coders. The specific unsupervised automated content analysis method used in this contribution is called structural topic modeling (STM). It allows scholars to include covariates that affect the topical prevalence and furthermore analyze the effect of covariates on topic proportions on the document level.

In our contribution, we apply these automated content analysis tools to understand how the public discourse on energy policy has evolved over time and whether we can gain general insights into potential future discourses. In the following section, we present general assumptions on the development of energy policy discourses over time and across newspapers. We then introduce our data and STM as a novel method to study energy policy discourses via newspaper data. A discussion of our results and of possible avenues for future research concludes our chapter.

[9] Gilens (2001).

[10] Bauer (2005); Oehl et al. (2017); Sampei and Aoyagi-Usui (2009); Schaffer et al. (2021).

[11] Herbst (1998).

[12] Schaffer et al. (2021).

[13] Oehl (2015); Oehl et al. (2017); Schaffer et al. (2021).

[14] E.g. Tvinnereim and Fløttum (2015); Tvinnereim et al. (2017).

3 The Evolution of Public Discourse on Energy Transition Policies

While the transitions in the energy sector we have been observing globally over the past 20 years are certainly accelerated by technological progress, they are based upon policy choices of sovereign nation states. Certainly, outcomes of international climate negotiations, such as the Paris Agreement, act as an external accelerator of energy transitions. In the end, however, national governments are firmly in the driving seat with respect to the pathways towards decarbonizing their economies. As a result, politics is supposed to play a major role in energy transition pathways. We thus heed the call from transition scholars to more closely look into the politics of energy transition.[15]

3.1 *Explaining Energy Transition Policy*

Energy policy adoption and change are the outcomes that have primarily been analyzed in different literatures, including political science and political economy, but also within the public policy literature. With respect to the political science literature, scholars have argued that governments' energy policy choices depend on a plethora of factors such as domestic political institutions,[16] the national energy mix,[17] governing parties,[18] as well as coalitional politics.[19] In general, one would assume that public policy in democracies will depend on the public's stance towards the societal goal of energy transition. That is, according to normative theories of democracy, governments should be responsive to the public's demand on issues. Studies in the transition and political science literatures that focus on how public discourses as a dimension of demand shape policy change or how media discourses can be linked to feedback effects of policy, however, have so far been rare.[20]

Within the policy literature, the Advocacy Coalition Framework[21] or the multiple streams model have been prominent choices to describe when crucial events happened or "windows of opportunity" opened for policy change. Most notably, the Fukushima incident is portrayed as such a focusing event for accelerated energy transition pathways in many different countries.[22] Such focusing events may lead to

[15] E.g. Markard et al. (2016).

[16] Aklin and Urpelainen (2013).

[17] Schaffer and Bernauer (2014).

[18] Cao (2012); Schaffer and Bernauer (2014).

[19] Meckling and Jenner (2016).

[20] Notable exceptions include: Kern (2011); Isoaho and Markard (2020).

[21] Ingold (2011); Ingold and Fischer (2014); Markard et al. (2016).

[22] Hermwille (2016); Kammerer et al. (2020); Markard et al. (2016); Rinscheid (2015); Wittneben (2012).

policy change through public pressure and upcoming elections,[23] further exposing the importance of public opinion and media discourses for policy choice.

Our contribution seeks to add to both literatures by considering the relationship between public discourses and public policy as well as between public discourses and other political events.

We argue that there are two shortcomings within the literature that we address in a preliminary attempt here. First, energy policy and decarbonization pathways should not be addressed in an aggregated fashion. It becomes increasingly unsatisfactory to link broad measures of e.g. public demand for climate change or energy transition policies to an aggregated measure of policy output without differentiating whether the measure targets the transport or buildings sector or whether the policy instrument used is a carbon tax or an information campaign on energy efficiency.[24] Energy policy is not one monolithic block and we submit that disaggregating national energy policy choices into sectors, policy instruments or other meaningful units can add to our understanding of idiosyncratic pathways and delivers a more accurate representation of the whole picture. Second, research has overly focused on policy adoption.[25] In our view, research should move on from the study of what determines countries' energy policies to the question of what happens after policy adoption.[26] To this end, we stress the importance of contestation in politics and that researchers need to account for an increased politicization as it may impact on future policy choices.[27] In considering both discourses toward policy adoption and policy contestation as well as politicization in our descriptive analysis, we expect interesting first insights into the level of contestation of different policies. Eventually future contributions might seek to theorize a priori about different impacts of policies on their contestation and politicization within the policy discourse.

In the following paragraphs, we formulate assumptions about the evolution and development of public discourse on energy policy in general before we turn to our data and test our assumptions on the early media discourses in Switzerland.

3.2 Differences in Energy Policy Discourse

A public debate over issues that interest the general public is a key element of democracy. Especially regarding topics that newly emerge on the national agenda,

[23] Jahn and Korolczuk (2012); Kammerer et al. (2020); Wittneben (2012).

[24] Schaffer et al. (2021).

[25] Hughes and Urpelainen (2015); Jenner et al. (2012); Jenner et al. (2013); Schaffer et al. (2021); Ward and Cao (2012).

[26] Béland (2010); Schaffer and Bernauer (2014); Sewerin et al. (2020).

[27] Meckling et al. (2017); Béland et al. (2020); Isoaho and Markard (2020); Lüth and Schaffer (2021).

media discourse can shape public discourse which is observed by policy-makers.[28] Accordingly, scrutinizing the development of the public discourse on energy policy in its early stages can add interesting insights to the debate on policy adoption and change. As energy policy is becoming more central to achieve societal goals such as a reduction of CO_2 emissions, lower risk from nuclear energy, or energy independence, these policies become ever more salient in the public discourse. With the increased salience of climate change as a topic on the international as well as the national agenda, the importance of energy issues within the national public discourse should increase. Accordingly, we would expect that the overall prevalence of energy policy topics within newspapers should increase over time (*assumption 1*).

As we have emphasized above, seeing the discourse over energy policy as one monolithic block might not do justice to the differences that exist with regards to topics, sectors or instruments of energy policy. That is, beyond the overall changes in the prevalence of energy policy in public debate, we aim to disaggregate our data to consider variation in discourse between different energy sectors.

This leads to the following questions: Which sectors in energy policy are emphasized in the debate? What are the broader narratives that guide the discourse? We submit that differences in the public discourse may arise from two main reasons: (1) differences arise from policy-making and (2) differences arise from the independent role of news media.

On the level of policy-making (1), the strength of public discourse may change in the course of the legislative process. On the one hand, before policy-making takes place, general news media reporting varies with legislative activity as the news media report about parliamentary debates or governmental policy choices. On the other hand, legislative activity induces feedback effects after policy-making that will enter media discourse and politicize issues surrounding energy policy.

More concretely, the political decision in favor of the transition to a low-carbon economy and the policies associated with it give governments considerable leeway concerning their selection of instruments and sectors to target. This difference in policy-making focus of the government may result in varying reporting on different energy policy issues within news media. Thus, we expect that news media reporting mirrors policy-making activity (*assumption 2a*).

In line with the policy-cycle model,[29] not only the reporting of sectoral policy output during the legislative process can cause a higher prevalence in public discourse, but—once implemented—policies can also lead to feedback effects and politicization. Policies targeted to replace, for example, fossil fuel-based energy with renewable, low-carbon energy generate private distributional effects for firms and individuals. They create winners and losers and these distributional *consequences may lead to an increased politicization of media discourse.* Accordingly, we would assume that such policy feedback and politicization effects emerge after sectoral policy output (*assumption 2b*).

[28] Herbst (1998).

[29] Howlett et al. (2009).

As a Swiss singularity, we introduce the role of direct democracy separately. While governmental policy-making clearly is a factor determining discourse on specific energy policy issues, the role of direct democratic decision-making on the energy policy discourse is less clear. In general, to what extent direct democracy helps or hinders a successful energy transition is still an understudied phenomenon.[30] Singular events such as referendums on energy policy issues require media space to trace arguments and the general debate.[31] Therefore, a mediated public debate around popular initiatives or referendums is supposed to heighten issue-specific salience (*assumption 3*).

In addition to these policy-specific factors, we refer to the independent role of news media (2) as a second explanatory factor that may explain variation within and between (sectoral) public discourse on energy issues. One of the basic functions of news media as an agenda setter is to communicate to people what issues to think about[32] and to provide a marketplace of ideas.[33] Moreover, news media can serve as an important actor especially in the early stages of energy transition that we focus on. In their agenda-setting and gate-keeping role,[34] media outlets can first bring ideas into the discourse; and they can, second, transport important alternatives and thus nuance ongoing debates on energy policy. Referring to the work of Eilders et al. (2004), Tresch[35] speaks of a dual role that newspapers take in referendum campaigns: "Through news coverage, newspapers inform the public about the issue positions and frames of the competing camps and convey information between political actors and citizens. In editorials and commentaries, in contrast, newspapers become political advocates in their own right that raise their voice, set an agenda, pursue policy options and try to shape public opinion". In sum, newspapers as agenda setters could seek to stress issues differently to encourage the wider public to focus on certain sectors more heavily (*assumption 4*). Thus, differences in salience between sectors may emanate from the newspapers' agenda-setting role in emphasizing certain issues.

4 Data and Methods

4.1 Data

The newspapers that form the basis of our analysis are the two newspapers of record with broad coverage in the German-speaking part of Switzerland: the Neue Zürcher

[30] Biber et al. (2016); see especially Rinscheid and Udris (2021).

[31] Marcinkowski and Donk (2012).

[32] McCombs and Shaw (1972).

[33] Entman and Wildman (1992); Van Cuilenburg (1999).

[34] Bernauer et al. (2015).

[35] Tresch (2012), p. 288.

Table 1 Newspaper data used

Newspaper	(A) Data basis: Total Articles (Scraping)	(B) Total MaxQDA (human-coding, climate change relevant[a])[b]	(C) Data universe for Structural Topic Model
Tages-Anzeiger	674,098	1615	1594
Neue Zürcher Zeitung	895,486	1886	1836

[a]Oehl (2015); Oehl et al. (2017)

[b]English translation of search string used: (climat! OR greenhouse! OR global warming) AND (renewable energ! OR energy polic! OR refining OR feed-in! OR emissio! OR emissions trading OR certificate trading OR (green OR white) AND certificate) OR combined heat OR cogeneration OR power solutio! OR energy solutio! OR CO2 OR carbon OR energy efficiency OR energy saving OR extraction OR exploitation OR geotherm! OR (solar w/5 (power OR energy) OR (wind w/5 (energy OR power)) OR hydro! OR agricultu! OR waste management OR forest OR wood!). For more information on the procedure, see Oehl et al. (2017); Oehl (2015) or Schaffer et al. (2021).

Zeitung (*NZZ*) and the *Tages-Anzeiger (TA)*. All published articles by the *NZZ* and the *Tages-Anzeiger* between of January 1997 and 31st of December of 2010 were scraped from wiso.[36] This procedure yielded over a million articles (see Table 1 below). Then, a search string was used to select potentially relevant articles. Afterwards, the articles were manually coded determining whether the articles were relevant, i.e. whether they covered climate change or energy policy issues. This substantially decreased the sample and led to the text corpus in column B of Table 1.

For our structural topic models, all the articles were then assembled into a common text corpus and preprocessed (column C in Table 1). This included the removal of stop words, punctuation and numbers. In addition, words with an extremely low or extremely high occurrence were removed by using a specific percentage as a threshold. While nearly every automated content analysis removes certain words, the exact definition of the limits, in this case the specific percentage, can vary.[37] In our case, words with less than 1% or more than 99% appearance were removed. The same applies to extremely short or extremely long articles. The last step of the preprocessing includes the removal of capitalization and the removal of word endings of conjugated verbs or plural nouns. This then leaves just the "word stem", which is especially useful for languages that change the word ending according to the sentence the word is placed in.[38]

---

[36]See Oehl (2015) and Oehl et al. (2017).

[37]Lucas et al. (2015), pp. 256–258.

[38]Lucas et al. (2015), p. 258.

Table 2 Example: two topics pertaining to renewable energy

energi, energien, erneuerbar, energieeffizient, energiepolitik, erneuerbaren, programm, massnahmen, …	**Renewable**
strom, energi, solarstrom, kraftwerk, wassserkraft, produzieren, solarzellen, pro, produziert, netz, kwh, …	**Renewable**

4.2 Structural Topic Model

Previous applications of automated text analysis have shown that the method offers a great advantage especially for large amounts of text dealing with the same general topic.[39] For the specific academic research area of climate change and climate policy, the method was successfully applied to analyze the public's perception of air pollution and climate change from open-ended surveys.[40] Further, topic modeling was used to identify the most central topics in a collection of more than 800 academic articles in the area of environmental sociology.[41] STM is also perfectly suited for this study, as we have already categorized the collected articles as relevant to the topic of "climate change".

In order to determine the most important factor in any topic modeling (the k number of topics), different models were calculated with k = 20/40/...80/100. Subsequently, these models were validated by analyzing the semantic coherence as well as the exclusivity of topics. The semantic coherence is maximized when the words that are most probable in a single topic frequently co-occur, while the exclusivity analyzes to what extent words which often occur in one topic tend to occur in another topic. Both validation steps were done by using a data-driven approach as well as human coding. In the end, the model with a k number of 100 was chosen as the best fitted model for our purpose. But a high number of topics also means that some topics of the same general subject overlap. As can be seen in Table 2, these two different topics of the same model both describe the supply of "renewable energy".

Since we are interested in the prevalence of general subjects such as, for example, "renewable energy sources" or "buildings", the prevalence of all topics that had the same overall theme was added up. It is therefore possible that the sectors in the following analysis can consist of one or multiple topics.

From the 100 topics assembled within the topic models, we identified 36 energy policy relevant topics; thus, the majority of topics were not relevant for our interest. For example, Table 3 shows that topics that were not relevant for our specific interest concerned the implications of global warming as well as international

[39] STM itself is the result of a multi-stage development of the Latent Dirichlet Allocation (LDA); see Blei and Lafferty (2009). While the LDA, as one application in the broader field of probabilistic topic modeling and mixed-membership models, does not allow the inclusion of covariates in its original form, STM does.

[40] Tvinnereim and Fløttum (2015); Tvinnereim et al. (2017).

[41] Bohr and Dunlap (2018).

Table 3 Example: two irrelevant topics from the STM

grad, erwaermung, celsius, global, globale, jahrhundert, meeressspiegel, anstieg, wuerd, wahrscheinlichkeit, temperatur, koennt, temperaturen, wert, etwa	**Implications of global warming**
klimakonferenz, uno, kyoto, bali, protokol, entwicklungslaend, konferenz, verhandlungen, industrielaend, usa, staaten, laender, industriestaaten, nairobi, montreal	**International negotiations**

negotiations. The data on energy policy output is from Schaffer and Bernauer (2014) and Schaffer et al. (2021).

5 Development of Energy Policy Discourse in Switzerland 1997–2011

The period of investigation for this chapter might be seen as the beginning of climate change related energy transition policy in Switzerland.[42] By the start of the period, a proposed CO_2 law had just been discarded after consultations had taken place. On the international level, the IPCC had released its 2nd assessment report; again confirming the workings of man-made climate change and the potentially disastrous consequences of an ongoing business as usual. Two years later, the international community agreed on the Kyoto Protocol, the first-ever binding international treaty to combat climate change. Having ratified an international agreement on climate change, states were supposed to comply by enacting policies to reach their prescribed goals.

Central to the national responses to climate change were policies that target energy production due to its large contribution to CO_2 emissions as well as *energy efficiency policies. Thus, energy policies helping to decarbonize the* economy by, e.g., switching from fossil fuels to renewable energy were a popular choice. This increased relevance of energy policy within governments' agendas led us to stipulate that the overall prevalence of energy policy topics within newspapers would increase over time (*assumption 1*). Figure 1 shows the prevalence of articles including energy policy topics with respect to all articles published in the respective Swiss newspapers of record, the *NZZ* and the *Tages-Anzeiger*.[43] Overall and counter to our assumption 1, there is no general upward trend throughout the time period. Instead, we can see that from 1997 up until 2002 there is a slight downward trend in the prevalence of energy policy topics within news media discourse. From 2002 onwards until around 2006, however, we observe a sharp increase in the prevalence of energy policy

[42] C.f. Rieder and Strotz (2018), p. 25.

[43] As our Fig. 1 reports the prevalence of energy policy topics in relation to all daily media content, reported % on the y-axis are very small.

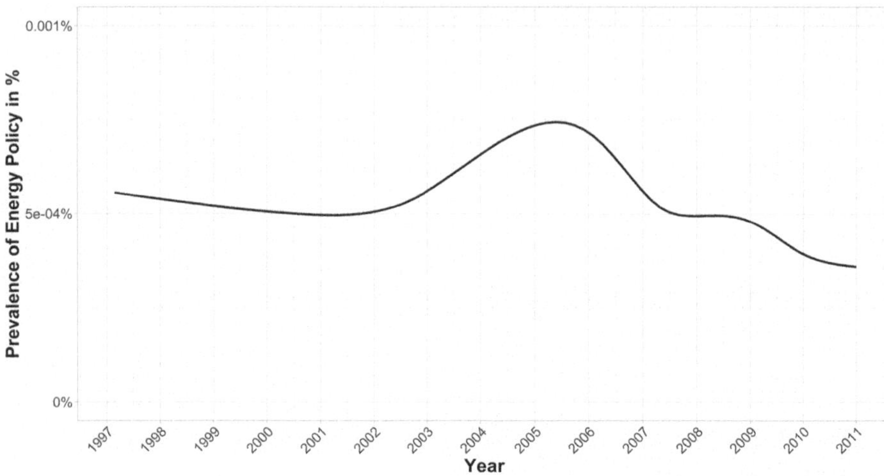

Fig. 1 Prevalence of energy policy topics with respect to total reporting by *NZZ* and *Tages-Anzeiger*

topics. From 2006 until 2011, again, the prevalence of energy policy topics in relation to total news reported decreases. If we recall our assumption, the main rationale for an increase was supposed to emanate from an increase in policy-making activity to target CO_2 emissions and, linked with this activity, public discourse on and politicization over energy policy.

Let us now take a look at the developments with respect to legislative activity on energy policy in Switzerland. We will concentrate on the largest and most relevant activities here.[44] Directly from 1997 onwards, the Swiss Parliament debated and drafted a revised version of the CO_2 Act to comply with the Kyoto goals of an 8% reduction of GHG emissions and passed the bill by 1999. This CO_2 Act is the main legal basis for regulating CO_2 emissions in Switzerland. Although it is an encompassing piece of legislation that generated a lot of debate about its design and about who would be responsible for its initiation, we can observe from Fig. 1 above, that there is comparatively little attention within the media discourse.[45] This is a notable finding suggesting a decoupling of the early policy process and news media discourse that has, for example, also been found by Tresch, Sciarini and Varone.[46] Nevertheless, the law contained a provision for a CO_2 levy[47] to be

[44]For more information on the history of Swiss energy policy, see Rieder and Strotz (2018).

[45]Also, the Energy Act (EnG) dates to this period (1998), which may also have contributed to an increase in public discourse with respect to energy.

[46]Tresch et al. (2013).

[47]The term "levy" is used "to distinguish the CO_2 levy from a conventional tax, since the revenue from the levy is not channeled into the national budget, but is returned in its entirety to the population (via reduction of health insurance premiums), to businesses that pay for it (in the form of a cut in old-age pension contribution), and the buildings program", IETA (2015), p. 3.

implemented if voluntary measures toward CO_2 reductions were not successful, which—literally—fueled the debate from 2002 to 2006, as we will show below.

So, what moves public discourse over energy policy topics? In our theoretical part, we have assumed that public discourse might be determined by news media reporting on (discussions of) upcoming legislative activity (*assumption 2a*). Contrarily, one might expect public discourse to be highest in the implementation and evaluation phase of a policy,[48] that is when the consequences from policies become apparent and a given issue is politicized (*assumption 2b*).

These differences in the timing of public discourse notwithstanding, actual policy-making in the area of energy policy is supposed to be linked to differences in news media attention. In Fig. 2, the bars represent energy policy output.[49] One may observe the peak of overall policy adoptions to occur somewhere around 2009, while the mode of the prevalence of energy policy in our news media data is clearly in the year 2006. Accordingly, one may speculate whether policy either follows public discourse with a 2–3-year lag or whether the cumulative change in policies from the years 2002–2004 triggered discussion in 2006. The former would rather support assumption 2a, while the latter would be in line with our politicization assumption 2b. In any case, there does not seem to be an apparent co-occurrence of governmental policy in the area of energy and the overall public discourse on energy. But before we turn to our more disaggregated descriptive analysis, we need to consider other important political events and their impact on the overall energy policy discourse, most importantly national referendums.

While the public does not have an active role in everyday energy policy-making, in a direct democratic setting as in Switzerland, referendums on specific issues will need to be voted on from time to time. Referendums are relevant for our analysis for two reasons: First, we might expect a lot of public discourse on the respective issue. Our assumption 3 accordingly stipulated that these popular referendums should go together with a high level of public discourse on energy issues, as media within direct democracies assume their role in informing the public.[50] Second, a "no" to a proposed law might imply that the respective policy has little chance of being implemented. Not considering referendums and the potential policies on energy that may *not* manifest (after a lost referendum) may bias our descriptive analysis. Within the time period in question for this chapter, there were seven referendums on issues of energy policy that are depicted and explained in Fig. 2. Notably, in 2000[51]

[48] Jann and Wegrich (2007).

[49] Various information sources were used to code policy output (Schaffer and Bernauer 2014; Schaffer et al. 2021) including IEA and EU databases, country reports to the UNFCCC, and information from national environmental and energy agencies to code the data for the dependent variable. Especially useful in this context were the IEA database on Climate Change Policies and Measures (IEA 2018) and the national communications (NCs), which Annex I countries to the Kyoto Protocol submit under the UNFCCC.

[50] Tresch (2012).

[51] In 2000, a referendum about energy taxes with the purpose to encourage renewable energies took place. The population had to express itself on three proposals: a popular initiative on solar energy (*Solar-Initiative*) and two governmental proposals, namely a measure for the promotion of renewable energies (*Förderabgabe*) and a constitutional article to introduce an eco-tax

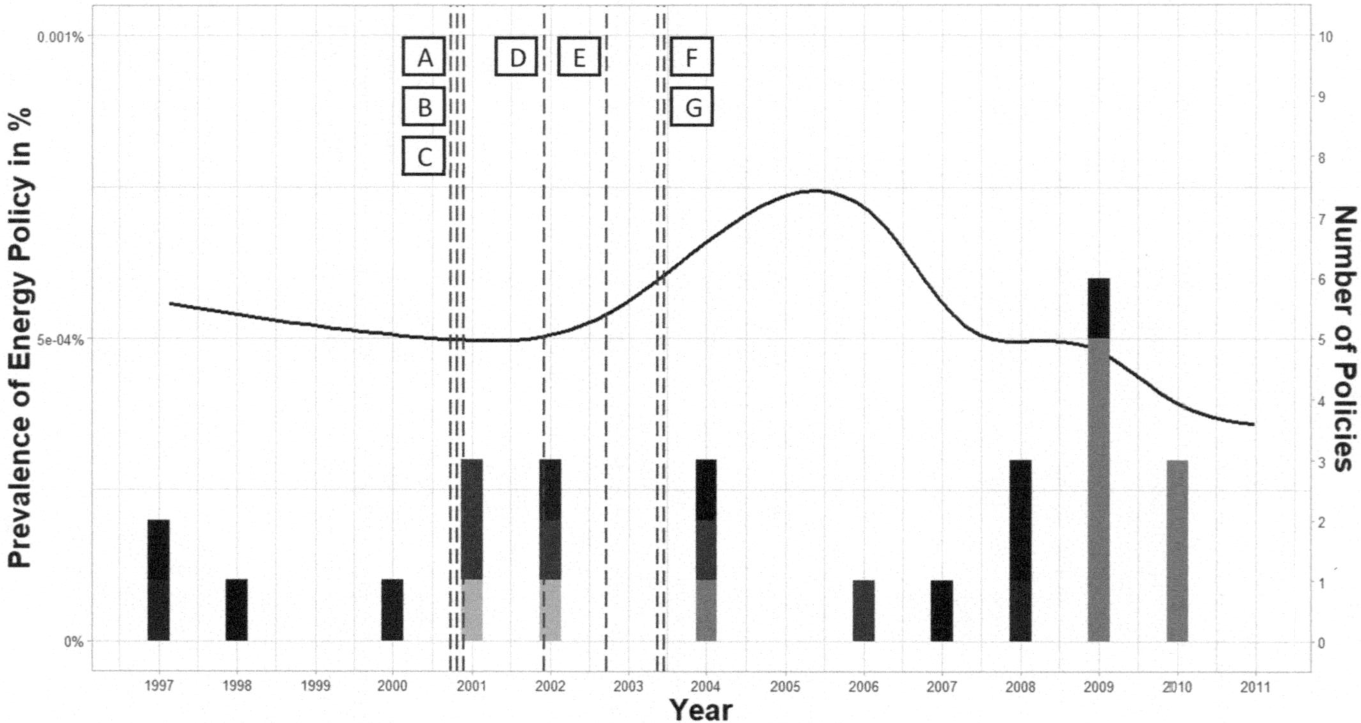

Fig. 2 Prevalence of topics over time. Bars indicate number of energy policy adoptions in a given year. Dashed lines mark times of popular referendums on energy policy topics during the period between 1997 and 2011. (**a**) 24.09.2000 Popular initiative on solar energy (*Volksinitiative 'für einen Solarrappen (Solar-Initiative)'*); (**b**) 24.09.2000 Government proposal for the promotion of renewable energies (*Verfassungsartikel über eine Förderabgabe für erneuerbare Energien (Gegenentwurf zur Volksinitiative 'für einen Solarrappen (Solar-Initiative)')*) (*Förderabgabe*); (**c**) 24.09.2000 Government proposal on a constitutional article to introduce an eco-tax (*Verfassungsartikel über eine Energielenkungsabgabe für die Umwelt (Gegenentwurf zur zurückgezogenen 'Energie-Umwelt-Initiative')*) (*Energielenkungsabgabe*); (**d**) 02.12.2001 Referendum on Energy tax not VAT (*Volksinitiative 'für eine gesicherte AHV - Energie statt Arbeit besteuern!'*); (**e**) 22.9.2002 Referendum Electricity Market Act (*Elektrizitätsmarktgesetz (EMG)*); (**f**) 18.05.2003 Popular initiative "*Strom ohne Atom*"

(nuclear phase-out) (*Volksinitiative 'Strom ohne Atom - Für eine Energiewende und schrittweise Stilllegung der Atomkraftwerke (Strom ohne Atom)'*); (**g**) 18.05.2003 Popular initiative "MoratoriumPlus" (*Volksinitiative 'Moratorium Plus - Für die Verlängerung des Atomkraftwerk-Baustopps und die Begrenzung des Atomrisikos (MoratoriumPlus)'*) (extension of nuclear construction stop)

the Swiss population rejected the introduction of incentive taxes to promote renewable energies, such as the "solar cent" or taxes on non-renewable energies to promote renewable energies.[52] Moreover, the draft of the Electricity Market Act (*Elektrizitätsmarktgesetz EMG*) was rejected in 2002. The initial purpose of this act was to liberalize the market for electricity, and it contained provisions on renewable energies. A proposition to phase out nuclear energy and to extend the moratorium on the construction of new nuclear power plants (*MoratoriumPlus*) was also rejected in 2003, showing little will from the Swiss population to go beyond the existing regulation in terms of energy supply or to promote renewable energies.[53] Comparing these referendum events that took place in a relatively short time period between 2001 and 2003 (see the dashed lines in Fig. 2) with the overall prevalence of energy policy in the news media discourse, again, there is no apparent co-occurrence. While this is not in line with our assumption 3, others have found that the level of media coverage and public discourse on referendum campaigns varies widely between issues. Marcinkowski and Donk,[54] for example, find in their study that the topic of international politics yielded a large number of articles, whereas immigration and traffic issues led to less coverage. Thus, we may conclude that either the topics relating to energy policy on the ballot did not spark an above-average discourse in the media, or we need to consider the specific sub-issue the referendum was about in order to account for the referendum's impact on media discourse.

In summary, the aggregated information from an overall consideration of public discourse on energy policy topics is not detailed enough to distinguish whether the observed peak around 2005 can be linked—for example—to an emergent discussion around the Electricity Supply Act from 2007 (*Stromversorgungsgesetz, StromVG*) or whether the final introduction of a CO_2 levy (as stipulated within the CO_2 Act) in 2007 was responsible for the heightened level of energy policy discourse. To this end, we have argued that one needs to account for different energy policy issues or sectors about which there was discussion and that structural topic models can assist researchers in these more fine-grained analyses.

Figure 3 depicts how the prevalence of topics related to different sectors[55] published in the respective Swiss newspapers developed over time. The y-axis

---

(*Energielenkungsabgabe*). The three proposals had in common that they would have raised a tax on non-renewable energies. Compared to other countries, the proposed levels of taxation were rather low, but there was substantial opposition from industrial associations, who campaigned against all three proposals. The coincidence with prices spikes in the oil market in the summer 2000 led to a rejection of all proposals in the popular vote.

[52] Wüstenhagen et al. (2003).

[53] After these 7 referendum decisions within only 3 years, the Swiss people were granted some 12 years until they were asked to vote on energy matters again in 2015, SFOE (2019), p. 29.

[54] Marcinkowski and Donk (2012).

[55] The following sectors are considered in our analysis: energy supply (power and heat generation), transport (public and private), buildings and appliances. The categorization used here is in accordance with Schaffer et al. (2021).

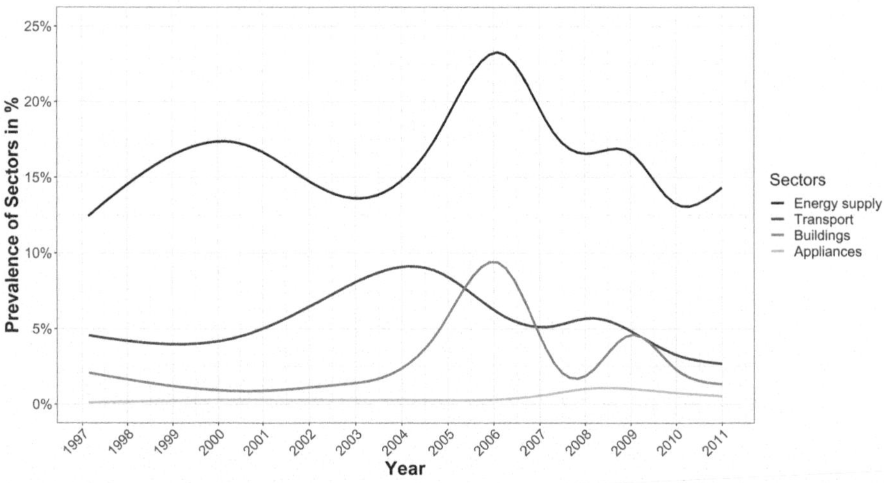

Fig. 3 Prevalence of topics regarding different sectors

shows the sector percentage in relation to all climate-change relevant articles (i.e. column C in Table 1) and not to the total of articles published in the newspaper.

So, do we see stark differences in how news media discourse evolved within those four sectors, and can we gain additional insight regarding the importance and timing of actual policy output? First, we see that there is variation in the prevalence of sectoral topics both over time and between sectors. Topics relating to energy sources in power and heat generation (energy supply) clearly enjoy the highest prevalence, while appliances apparently were not much of a discussion item within the public discourse. Second, similar to the overall picture, we also see the peak in media discourse concerning energy supply (and also regarding buildings) in the year 2006.

In Fig. 4, we further divide the topics within the energy supply category into topics pertaining to the different energy sources: nuclear, renewable or fossil. Here, we see a remarkable difference in the prominence of topics in the overall discussion. While most of the discourse in energy policy concentrated on how to deal with power and heat generated from *renewable sources* during the beginning of our period and peaking around the year 2000, topics pertaining to *fossil energy sources* were comparatively less prevalent in this first period. According to our disaggregated Fig. 4, the referendums on the solar initiative as well as the government proposal for the promotion of renewable energies *(Förderabgabe)* in 2001 seemingly did lead to comparatively high levels of public discourse on the topic of renewables within the two main newspapers of record. This observation supports our assumption 3 on the importance of media discourse in the event of a referendum and the value of a public debate over issues that interest the general public as a key element of democracy. After the lost referendums on solar energy and a promotion levy for renewable energy (*Förderabgabe*), however, topics pertaining to renewables dropped in prevalence and never reached the same amount of relative consideration within the media

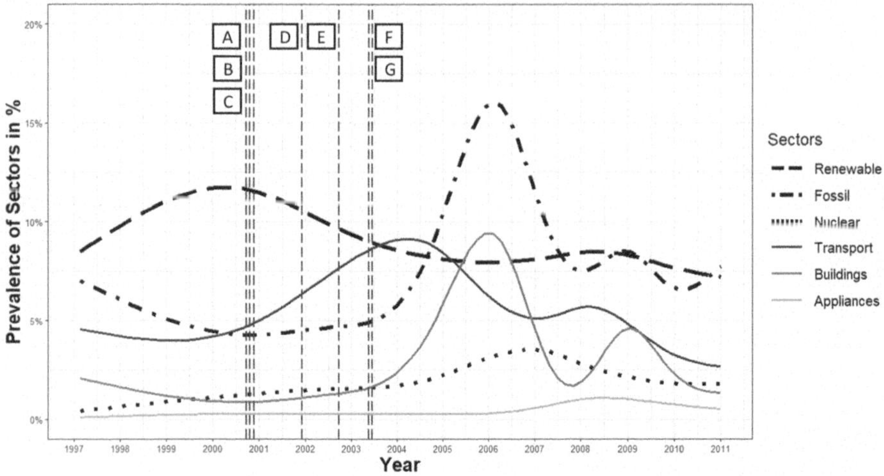

Fig. 4 Prevalence of topics regarding different sectors (accounting for different energy sources). Dashed lines mark times of popular referendums on energy policy topics during the period between 1997 and 2011. (**a**) 24.09.2000 Popular initiative on solar energy; (**b**) 24.09.2000 Government proposal for the promotion of renewable energies (*Förderabgabe*); (**c**) 24.09.2000 Government proposal on a constitutional article to introduce an eco-tax (*Energielenkungsabgabe*); (**d**) 02.12.2001 Referendum on Energy tax not VAT; (**e**) 22.9.2002 Referendum Electricity Market Act; (**f**) 18.05.2003 Popular initiative "*Strom ohne Atom*" (nuclear phase-out); (**g**) 18.02.2003 Popular initiative "MoratoriumPlus" (extension of nuclear construction stop)

discourse again. This is an unexpected finding as—following the rejection of the Electricity Market Act in the referendum in 2002 and facing the threat of the EU market liberalization—the question of renewables within the energy supply was a central one within elite discourse and it received increased parliamentary attention.[56] Moreover, the decision on the Swiss feed-in tariff (*kostendeckende Einspeisevergütung KEV*) as the prime mechanism to encourage renewable energy is associated with the adoption of the Energy Supply Act (*StromVG*) of the 23rd of March 2007 (in force from 1st of January 2008) and with the revision of the Energy Act of 1998 (*Energiegesetz EnG*) on the 1st of January 2009. These important decisions on the promotion of renewable energy seem not to be accompanied by an increased public discourse. From our visual inspection of relative topic prevalence, we may thus conclude that renewable energy was a comparatively uncontested issue during our period of analysis. From Fig. 4, we further observe that the prevalence of topics relating to power and heat generated from fossil energy sources moves somewhat counter to the renewables debate. Starting comparatively low, fossil energy topics received above-average attention between 2004 and 2007.

[56] For example, notable parliamentary initiatives regarding how to change the current approach with respect to renewable energy sources were proposed by Dupraz (2004), n. 03.462 and Speck (2003), n. 03.409.

Moreover, the prevalence of nuclear energy in the public discourse has also been comparatively low but steadily increasing to reach a peak around 2007, when nuclear energy also ranked prominently in discussions surrounding the Energy Supply Act and the preparation of energy perspectives up to 2035.

The above-mentioned accumulation of policies with respect to energy supply around the years 2007–2009 can be observed in Fig. 5 below. Here, the disaggregation of policies as well as the public discourse into different sectors can bring additional information to the overall picture. For example, we clearly see that policy output concerning sources of energy supply dominates the political agenda with respect to energy issues over the whole period, whereas there are only two policies associated with regulating appliances. Policy output thus generally corresponds to the levels of public discourse. What about the timing? For example, with respect to the building (residential) sector and regarding energy supply, the peak in public discourse is observed before the respective peaks in policy output. While this suggests that public discourse over different sectors happened before important and comprehensive policy-making within these sectors took place, our visual evidence is indicative at best. For the transport sector, the prevalence of transport topics within the news media in 2004 may be driven by discussions regarding the ordinance about an emission compensation obligation for importers of fossil motor fuels coming into effect in that year.

The question of how to deal with a potential tax on motor fuels as originally foreseen within the CO_2 Act marks the start of discussions surrounding the CO_2 tax from around 2004. As stipulated above, these discussions relating to the CO_2 levy (that was decided upon in 2005 and that came into effect by 2008)[57] can probably serve as a possible explanation for the bump in overall energy policy prevalence within the public discourse (as observed in Fig. 1). The CO_2 Act and especially the coalitional dynamics within the debates over the design of the CO_2 levy have already sparked a lot of academic interest.[58] To also look into this important debate in a bit more detail, we chose to pick topics (from our 100 topic STM) that included the word stem "*abgabe*" (levy). Accordingly, Fig. 6 provides a graphic representation of the discussion on the CO_2 levy.[59] "Abgabe" was listed as a representative word within four different topics (see Table 2). Moreover, given that a "climate penny" (*Klimarappen*) was presented as an alternative suggestion by the Swiss Petrol Union (*Erdöl-Vereinigung*[60]) to circumvent a levy on motor fuels,[61] we have also added the one topic representing the climate penny (*Klimarappen*). According to the 15 words

[57] IEA (2018).

[58] Ingold (2011); Ingold and Varone (2012); Ingold and Fischer (2014); Kriesi and Jegen (2001); Lehmann and Rieder (2002).

[59] For example, we did not use a topic that explicitly dealt with "foerderabgabe", as from the 15 words it became clear that this referred to an earlier debate around the referendums in 2001 (however, it obviously counted towards the (renewable) energy supply discourse).

[60] Avenergy Suisse (since 2019).

[61] Ingold (2011).

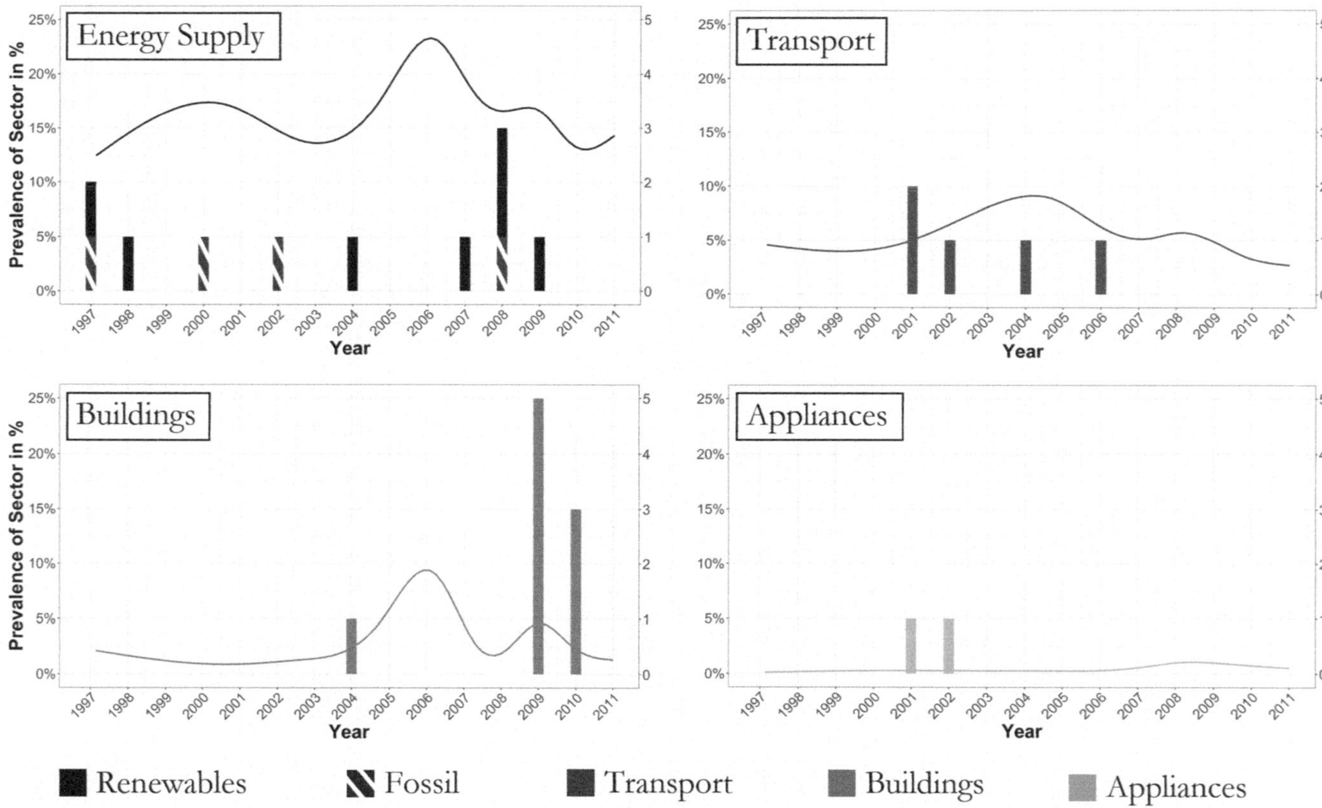

Fig. 5 Prevalence of topics regarding different sectors. Vertical bars indicate the number of energy policy adoptions in a given year per sector

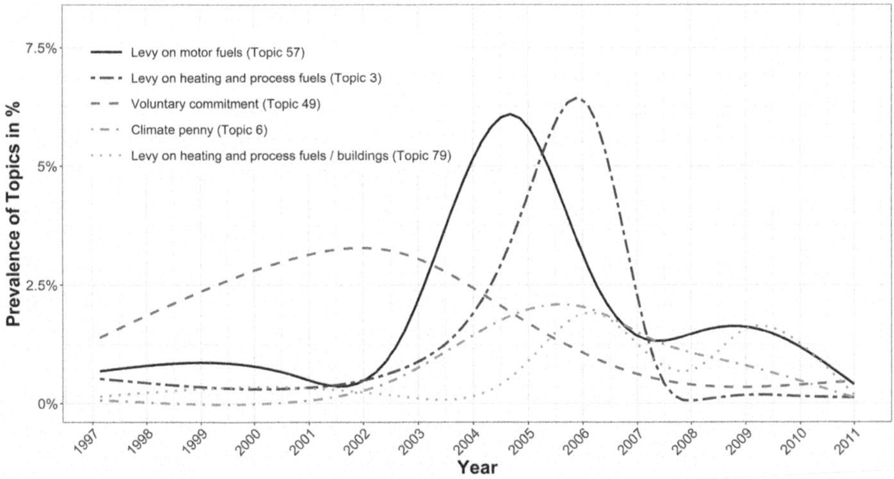

Fig. 6 Debate surrounding the introduction of a CO_2 levy

Table 4 Topics relating to the discussion surrounding the CO_2 levy

A: Topic (top 15 words ranked by prevalence)	B: Topic
abgab, *bundesrat, klimarappen, pro, lenkungsabgabe, treibstoffen, rappen, wuerd, liter, treibstoff, massnahmen, benzin, gesetz, inland, einfuehrung*	**CO_2 levy on motor fuels (Topic 57)**
abgab, *oi, klimarappen, klimaschutz, rappen, heizoel, nationalrat, liter, cvp, ausstoss, pro, bundesrat, vanoni, inland, lenkungsabgab*	**CO_2 levy on heating and process fuels (Topic 3)**
gesetz, wirtschaft, emissionen, ***abgab***, *redukt, massnahmen, ziel, freiwillig, unternehmen, reduktionsziel, erreicht freiwilligen, verpflichtungen, umsetzung, klimapolitik*	**Voluntary commitment (Topic 49)**
klimarappen, *stiftung, millionen, tonnen, inland, ausland, redukt, projekt, pro, bund, ziel, zertifik, rappen, franken, beitrag*	**Climate penny (Topic 6)**
abgab, *gebaeudesanierungen, bundesrat, nationalrat, franken, vorlag, wab, staenderat, parlament, heizoel, millionen, massnahmen, bevoelkerung, vorschlag, pro*	**CO_2 levy on heating and process fuels/buildings (Topic 79)**

most representative of these topics (column A in Table 4), we assigned headings for the reader to more easily relate to the (approximate) content of the topic (column B in Table 4). As the levy and the climate penny were mostly discussed together, we looked for the words that could best discriminate between the topics and assigned headings accordingly. To this end, the main difference between topic 57 and topic 3 is that 57 prominently deals with motor fuels (*treibstoffe*) whereas 3 concerns heating oil (*heizöl*). Topic 79 also includes heating oil as a top word but is referred to in the context of building renovations and can thus be discriminated from topic 57 (Table 4).

Figure 6 shows the prevalence of these singular topics on the CO_2 levy over time to zoom into the main discussion expected to have driven the observed overall peak around 2006 (c.f. Fig. 1). As mentioned above, the CO_2 levy was included in the 2000 CO_2 Act; however, it was not immediately effective. Voluntary agreements by industry to cut their CO_2 emissions were the initial measure to bring Switzerland in line with its 10% emission reduction goal defined in the Kyoto Protocol. Only if the voluntary agreements were not sufficient to reach this goal, in a second, subsidiary phase, a CO_2 levy (tax) would be introduced.[62] Accordingly, from Fig. 6 we can see that the first topic mentioning a levy and showing increases in prevalence within the public discourse is indeed the one associated with the voluntary agreements (topic 49). Prevalence of this topic increases steadily, representing the phase (2000–2002) in which the private sector could sign voluntary agreements to reduce CO_2 emissions. By 2002, however, it became obvious that the voluntary measures would not suffice to reach the 10% reduction goal compared to 1990 levels by 2010.[63] Thus, from 2003 onwards, debates over a potential CO_2 levy and whether it would be levied only on heating and process fuels (topics 3 and 79 in Fig. 6) or also on motor fuels (topic 57 in Fig. 6) began that ended with the formal introduction of the CO_2 levy on heating and process fuels in 2008. In the course of this debate, opponents of a levy on motor fuels mobilized, and the Swiss Petrol Union (*Erdöl-Vereinigung*) presented the climate penny (*Klimarappen*) as an alternative to the ongoing discourse (topic 6 in Fig. 6), which was later taken up by the government in public consultation and eventually led to the abandonment of a CO_2 levy on motor fuels.[64] These real-world developments are picked up quite well by our 5 topics; for example, the discussion around a levy on motor fuels (topic 57) and a levy on heating and process fuels (topic 3, topic 79) dominated the public discourse especially in the years between 2003 and 2008. Also, the topic "*Klimarappen*" gains in prevalence throughout this same period. After the Bundesrat had decided on a compromise solution, namely a levy on heating and process fuels in combination with the "*Klimarappen*", and parliament had voted upon it by 2005, questions on the concrete design dominated the discourse. In our Fig. 6, this is manifested by the increased importance of topic 79 that unites the levy on heating and process fuels and the building sector in the discussions from 2005 onwards. In this context, the set-up of how to recycle revenue from the levy back to the population and how to link revenue to further measures in the building sector through the Buildings Program (*Gebäudeprogramm*) was a topic of public discourse.

In making assumptions about the public discourse above, we mentioned potential differences between newspapers and their reporting on energy issues as one explanation. We assumed that newspapers might take different foci and stress different

---

[62] Lehmann and Rieder (2002).

[63] Ingold (2011); Prognos (2002).

[64] It is quite remarkable that a private actor and interest group proposed a policy alternative that later was adopted.

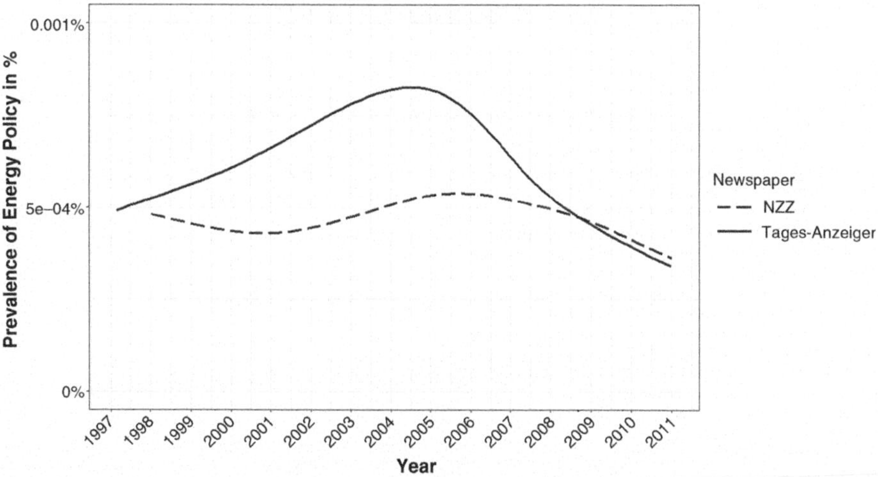

Fig. 7 Prevalence of energy policy topics with respect to total reporting by the NZZ (dashed line) and the Tages-Anzeiger, split by covariate "newspaper"

elements or sectors of a discourse. The newspapers used for our STM are two leading quality newspapers in Switzerland that are considered to have different ideological leanings. While the *NZZ* is considered to be more conservative, the TA is more center-left leaning.[65] In Fig. 7, we can see that for the overall prevalence of energy policy topics within the total articles featured in the newspaper, the only notable finding is that the TA seems to dedicate more relative space to topics of energy policy compared with the *NZZ*.

Again, using such an aggregated measure to compare the two newspapers may not show large differences between them. The devil might be in the details regarding which newspaper pushes a certain topic while potentially neglecting another. Taking the debate about the CO_2 levy presented above, we might take a look whether both newspapers reported on all topics or whether some topics (e.g. the climate penny) were discussed more often in one of the newspapers. The debate at the level of single topics is very well suited for such a detailed comparison. To this end, Fig. 8 shows the estimated mean difference in topic proportions for the two newspapers. Indeed, we can see some interesting variation. First, we cannot observe any difference between the two newspapers regarding the topic of voluntary commitment and the—arguably most controversial—discussion on a levy on motor fuels. Second, the reporting and discussion on the climate penny is comparatively based more within the *NZZ*. But the real difference lies in the coverage on the levy on heating and process fuels (combustibles). Here, topic 3 (***abgab***, *oi, klimarappen, klimaschutz, rappen, heizoel, nationalrat, liter, cvp, ausstoss, pro, bundesrat, vanoni, inland, lenkungsabgab*) mostly dominates the discussion within the *Tages-*

[65] C.f. Stauffacher et al. (2015).

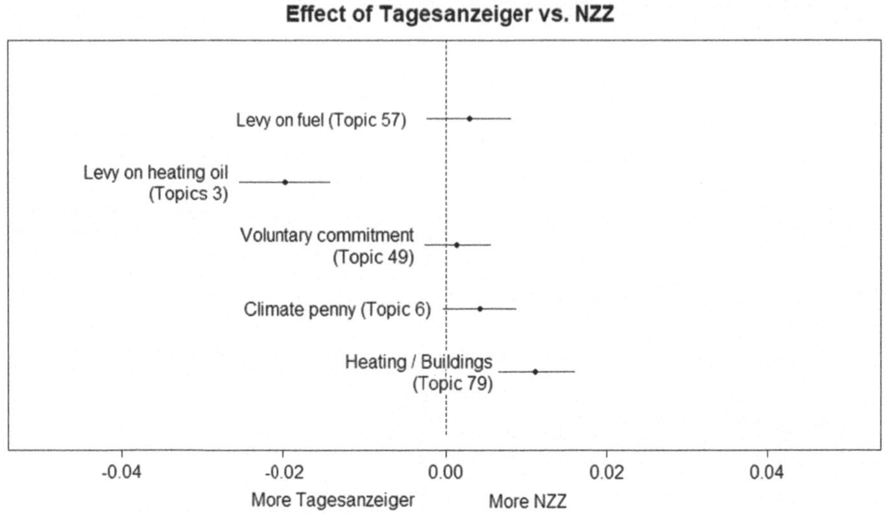

Fig. 8 Estimated mean difference in topic proportions based on covariate newspaper

Anzeiger, while topic 79 (***abgab**, gebaeudesanierungen, bundesrat, nationalrat, franken, vorlag, wab, staenderat, parlament, heizoel, millionen, massnahmen, bevoelkerung, vorschlag, pro*), which links the CO_2 levy to the building sector, is mostly covered by the *NZZ*. To what extent this relates to their more conservative platform remains open, but nevertheless very subtle differences in the coverage of certain topics can be observed. Overall, however, Swiss media rather stick to their non-interventionist style of reporting elite discourses.[66] Media and communication studies might find it interesting to explore these issues closer with respect to climate and energy policy.

In conclusion, we had expected a general increase in the importance of energy policy within the public and news media discourse during the early period of the Swiss energy transition. In our content analysis of all articles published by the two leading newspapers and consecutively using structural topic models, we found that the overall energy policy discourse was dominated by the discussions surrounding the CO_2 levy. While these discussions can explain most of the above-average increase in public discourse around the years 2004 and 2008, discussions on potential market mechanisms to promote renewable energy were also consistently led. While this is speculative given our exploratory analysis, one might argue that the heightened public discourse led to profound and stable compromises and served the idea that all parties were heard before passing legislation, which might, for example, have prevented a referendum on the Electricity Supply Act of 2008.

In any case, as energy policy-making does not necessarily progress in a uniform manner adding important legislation year-by-year, the discourse on energy policy

[66] Cammarano et al. (2010).

does not either. National and international circumstances, such as the financial crisis from 2008 onwards,[67] may possibly crowd-out discussions on energy or climate issues, while domestic debates on one energy policy issue (CO_2 levy) may sustain interest and potentially increase the prevalence of other energy policy issues (renewable energy remuneration) as well. Indeed, policy sequencing[68] may well describe the pathways observed in Swiss energy policy from 2008 onwards.

Looking at the developments presented here with hindsight in our explorative analysis of the public discourse, Switzerland did eventually meet its Kyoto Protocol targets, although some sectoral sub-targets were not met. Most notable for our descriptive analysis here is the transport vs. the building sectors trajectory. While the transport sector emissions were 10% above the 1990 level in 2012 (and should have been 10% below), the building sector's emission target was met and even undercut with a 16% reduction.[69] The proposed CO_2 tax on motor fuels, which represented a contested issue in terms of competitiveness but also inequality issues,[70] was replaced by the *Klimarappen* Initiative of the Swiss Petrol Union (*Erdöl-Vereinigung*). And although the emission gap that still exists in the transport sector has narrowed, a CO_2 tax on motor fuels has to this day not seriously re-entered the policy-making process—a case in point showing the political difficulty in seriously decarbonizing the transport sector.[71]

A central finding from our research is that it pays off to disaggregate reporting on the energy transition or equally climate change. Without a discussion on energy policy topics within the media, important topics such as the energy transition within the buildings and transport sector may not be discussed and thus are neither on the public nor on policy-makers' list of priorities.

6 Conclusion

Given the path-dependency of energy policy, it is of eminent importance to look at how topics evolve to account for today's realities. Our chapter aimed to contribute to and argue on three main points. First, in providing the whole picture, we suggested that energy policy and decarbonization pathways should not be addressed in an aggregated fashion, and we stressed the importance of disaggregating both the supply and demand of energy policies to more closely map the politics of energy. In this chapter, we chose to look into different energy-relevant sectors and visually traced the development of public discourse in each of these sectors. Our strategy seems warranted given the widely differing trajectories of topic prevalence

[67] Geels (2013); Scruggs and Benegal (2012).

[68] Pahle et al. (2018).

[69] IEA (2018).

[70] Thalmann and Vielle (2019).

[71] Thalmann and Vielle (2019).

concerning our four sectors. Whereas news media discourse regarding energy sources in power and heat generation (energy supply) as well as regarding buildings both peak at similar points in time, the prevalence of discussions surrounding transport issues peaks earlier, and appliances are barely featured within the public discourse. Our explorative analysis linking the sector-specific discourse to sector-specific policy output as well as political events (referendums) then showed that the news media discourse on energy policy was mostly driven by two major policy discussions: by the design of the CO_2 tax and the discussion around how to deal with renewable energy sources. In fact, the peak of the Swiss energy policy discourse—which happened between 2004 to 2008—occurs just before and during a peak in policy-making in the years 2007–2010. While our visual inspection cannot make a causal argument about discourse triggering policy-making, one may at least claim that the level of discourse in a sector is related to the level of policy-making (Schaffer et al. 2021). Vivid public discussions between 2004 and 2008 around those two topics might have helped reach a compromise and circumvent further referendums. Concerning the importance of media discourse around referendums on energy policy, we also found a meaningful connection especially with respect to referendums on renewable energy after disaggregating into different issues regarding energy supply. However, we do not see a connection regarding referendums on nuclear energy. One reason for this difference may be that public and news media discourse is higher with respect to comparatively "newer" topics (renewables) than on discussions surrounding nuclear energy where the public presumably already has formed an opinion and arguments are well known.

The second issue we wanted to highlight with our contribution pertains to the timely study of policy contestation and the politicization of energy policy. We argued to look beyond policy adoption and to systematically study how policies affect politics.[72] Energy transitions have non-neglectable distributional effects, which can be used to campaign against more stringent energy policy (as one could observe with the 2021 referendum on the revised CO_2 law).[73] While winning coalitions may help to break carbon lock-in,[74] increased politicization from losers of the process may have negative consequences on their continuation or change towards more ambition. In our explorative analysis we could observe only slight feedback effects due to the discussion on policy alternatives to the CO_2 levy on motor fuels. It remains to be seen whether politicization and an increase in contestation of energy policy happened within the decade from 2010 to 2020.[75] Given the only slight increase in energy prices (compared to other countries embarking on

[72] Béland (2010).

[73] Schaffer (2021); Schaffer and Magyar (2021).

[74] Meckling et al. (2015).

[75] Rinscheid and Udris (2021) give a first indication in their analysis of three energy-related referendums and find—for two of these—more media attention compared to a baseline of other referendums in the same period; see also Duygan et al. (2021), who find contestation of the Energy Strategy 2050 in their stakeholder survey.

energy transition and heavily subsidizing renewable energy such as Germany) and the overall satisfactory performance of Switzerland due to strong efficiency gains, we would expect only a moderate contestation. Nevertheless, the popular rejection of the complete revision of the CO_2 Act at the ballot in June 2021 may continue to lead to a higher level of contestation in the public debate as the climate crisis unfolds and action is needed.[76] Politicization of the public discourse is further assumed to go hand in hand with political parties distinctly positioning themselves and competing on energy policy issues.[77]

A third goal of our contribution was to explore how new unsupervised content analysis methods can inform policy analysis and studies on energy transition. Topic models can help identify certain topics and their prevalence over time, while structural topic models can add further relevant insights by using different document-level covariates. In our case, we differentiated between the coverage of the two main newspapers of record in Switzerland, the *NZZ* and the *Tages-Anzeiger*. We found that with respect to energy policy topics and their general salience within the discourse, there was little meaningful difference. As expected, the newspapers stressed different issues in their reporting. For example, the *NZZ* emphasized retrofitting buildings in connection with the discussion on the CO_2 levy, while the *Tages-Anzeiger* did not. As energy policy becomes an ever more contested issue, the agenda-setting of media outlets or their power to structure the discourse might as well increase in importance in the future. Communication scholars may be interested in further exploring these developments.

For future research, the obvious extension is to scrutinize how the public discourse evolved in the 2010s. The guiding question would be whether the level of discourse did actually again reach the heights experienced around the years 2004 to 2008. Can we still see that there are sectoral differences, or has energy politics become more encompassing to include all sectors, for example with the discussion of the Energy Strategy 2050? Our data and explorative analysis may serve as groundwork for such efforts.

References

Aklin M, Urpelainen J (2013) Political competition, path dependence, and the strategy of sustainable energy transitions. Am J Polit Sci 57(3):643–658

Bauer MW (2005) Public perceptions and mass media in the biotechnology controversy. Int J Public Opin Res 17(1):5–22

[76] https://www.nzz.ch/schweiz/gegner-des-co2-gesetzes-reichen-referendum-ein-ld.1596012.

[77] Schaffer and Lüth (2021).

Béland D (2010) Reconsidering policy feedback: how policies affect politics. Adm Soc 42 (5):568–590

Béland D, Howlett M, Rocco P, Waddan A (2020) Designing policy resilience: lessons from the affordable care act. Policy Sci 53:269–289

Bernauer T, Jahn D, Kuhn PM, Walter S (2015) Einführung in die Politikwissenschaft. Nomos, Baden-Baden

Biber E, Kelsey N, Meckling J (2016) The political economy of decarbonization: a research agenda. Brook Law Rev 82(2):605–643

Blei DM, Lafferty JD (2009) Topic models. In: Srivastava AN, Sahami M (eds) Text mining: classification, clustering, and applications. Chapman and Hall/CRC, pp 71–94

Bohr J, Dunlap RE (2018) Key topics in environmental sociology, 1990–2014: results from a computational text analysis. Environ Sociol 4(2):181–195

Broadbent J, Sonnett J, Botetzagias I et al (2016) Conflicting climate change frames in a global field of media discourse. Socius 2:1–17

Cammarano S, Jarren O, Donges PS (2010) Politische Kommunikationskultur im Wandel. Stud Commun Sci 10(1):29–43

Cao X (2012) An interest groups and partisan politics model for renewable energies. Working Paper Series Explaining Renewable Electricities. Penn State University

De Wilde P, Leupold A, Schmidtke H (2016) Introduction: the differentiated politicisation of European governance. West Eur Polit 39(1):3–22

Dupraz J (2004) Elektrizität aus erneuerbaren Energien. Bessere Rahmenbedingungen. Parliamentary Initiative 03.462

Duygan M, Kachi A, Oeri F, Oliveira TD, Rinscheid A (2021) Energy policymaking in Switzerland. In: Hettich P, Kachi A (eds) Swiss energy governance. Springer, New York

Eilders C, Neidhardt F, Pfetsch B (2004) Die Stimme der Medien. Pressekommentare und politische Öffentlichkeit in der Bundesrepublik. VS Verlag für Sozialwissenschaften, Wiesbaden

Entman RM, Wildman SS (1992) Reconciling economic and non-economic perspectives on media policy: transcending the "marketplace of ideas". J Commun 42(1):5–19

Geels FW (2013) The impact of the financial–economic crisis on sustainability transitions: financial investment, governance and public discourse. Environ Innov Soc Trans 6:67–95

Gilens M (2001) Political ignorance and collective policy preferences. Am Polit Sci Rev 95 (2):379–396

Golan G (2006) Inter-media agenda setting and global news coverage: assessing the influence of the New York Times on three network television evening news programs. J Stud 7(2):323–333

Herbst S (1998) Reading public opinion: how political actors view the democratic process. University of Chicago Press, Chicago, London

Hermwille L (2016) The role of narratives in socio-technical transitions—Fukushima and the energy regimes of Japan, Germany, and the United Kingdom. Energy Res Soc Sci 11:237–246

Howlett M, Ramesh M, Perl A (2009) Studying public policy: Policy cycles and policy subsystems, vol. 3. Oxford University Press, Oxford

Hughes L, Urpelainen J (2015) Interests, institutions, and climate policy: explaining the choice of policy instruments for the energy sector. Environ Sci Pol 54:52–63

IEA (2018) Energy Policies of IEA Countries: Switzerland 2018 Review. Available at https://webstore.iea.org/

IETA (2015) Switzerland: An emissions trading case study. Available at https://www.ieta.org

Ingold K (2011) Network structures within policy processes: coalitions, power, and brokerage in Swiss climate policy. Policy Stud J 39(3):435–459

Ingold K, Fischer M (2014) Drivers of collaboration to mitigate climate change: an illustration of Swiss climate policy over 15 years. Glob Environ Chang 24:88–98

Ingold K, Varone F (2012) Treating policy brokers seriously: evidence from the climate policy. J Public Adm Res Theory 22(2):319–346

Isoaho K, Markard J (2020) The politics of technology decline: discursive struggles over coal phase-out in the UK. Rev Policy Res. https://doi.org/10.1111/ropr.12370

Jahn D, Korolczuk S (2012) German exceptionalism: the end of nuclear energy in Germany! Environ Polit 21(1):159–164

Jann W, Wegrich K (2007) Theories of the policy cycle. In: Fischer F, Miller JG, Sidney MS (eds) Handbook of public policy analysis. Taylor and Francis, Boca Raton, pp 43–62

Jenner S, Chan G, Frankenberger R, Gabel M (2012) What drives states to support renewable energy? Energy J 33(2):1–12

Jenner S, Ovaere L, Schindele S (2013) The impact of private interest contributions on RPS adoption. Econ Polit 25(3):411–423

Kammerer M, Crameri F, Ingold K (2020) Das Klima und die EU: Eine Diskursperspektive auf die deutsche und schweizerische Klimapolitik. In: The European social model under pressure. Springer VS, Wiesbaden, pp 599–623

Kern F (2011) Ideas, institutions, and interests: explaining policy divergence in fostering 'system innovations' towards sustainability. Environ Plan C Gov Policy 29(6):1116–1134

King G, Schneer B, White A (2017) How the news media activate public expression and influence. Science 358:776–780

Kriesi H, Jegen M (2001) The Swiss energy policy elite: the actor constellation of a policy domain in transition. Eur J Polit Res 39(2):251–287

Lehmann L, Rieder S (2002) Wissenschaftliches Wissen in der politischen Auseinandersetzung. Fallstudie zur Genese des CO2-Gesetzes im Auftrag der Arbeitsgruppe Transdisziplinarität der Energiekommission der Schweizerischen Akademie der Technischen Wissenschaften (SATW), SATW-Bericht (24)

Lucas C, Nielsen RA, Roberts ME, Stewart BM, Storer A, Tingley D (2015) Computer-assisted text analysis for comparative politics. Polit Anal 23(2):254–277

Lüth M, Schaffer LM (2021) The electoral importance and evolution of climate-related energy policy: evidence from Switzerland. Working paper

Marcinkowski F, Donk A (2012) The deliberative quality of referendum coverage in direct democracy: findings from a longitudinal analysis of Swiss media. Javnost-The Public 19 (4):93–109

Markard J, Suter M, Ingold K (2016) Socio-technical transitions and policy change – advocacy coalitions in Swiss energy policy. Environ Innov Soc Trans 18:215–237

McCombs ME, Shaw DL (1972) The agenda-setting function of mass media. Public Opin Q 36 (2):176–187

Meckling J, Jenner S (2016) Varieties of market-based policy: instrument choice in climate policy. Environ Polit 25(5):853–874

Meckling J, Kelsey N, Biber E, Zysman J (2015) Winning coalitions for climate policy. Science 349 (6253):1170–1171

Meckling J, Sterner T, Wagner G (2017) Policy sequencing toward decarbonization. Nat Energy 2 (12):918–922

Oehl B (2015) Public Demand and Climate Change Policy Making in OECD Countries – From Dynamics of the Demand to Policy Responsiveness. PhD Thesis, ETH Zürich. https://doi.org/10.3929/ethz-a-010432416

Oehl B, Schaffer L, Bernauer T (2017) How to measure public demand for policies when there is no appropriate survey data? J Publ Policy 37(2):173–204

Pahle M, Burtraw D, Flachsland C et al (2018) Sequencing to ratchet up climate policy stringency. Nat Clim Chang 8(10):861–867

Prognos (2002) Standortbestimmung CO2-Gesetz. Prognos, Basel

Rieder S, Strotz C (2018) Die schweizerische Energiepolitik. In: Stadelmann-Steffen I, Ingold K, Rieder S, Dermont C, Kammermann L, Strotz C (eds) Akzeptanz erneuerbarer Energie.

Universität Bern/Interface Politikstudien Forschung Beratung/EAWAG, Bern, Luzern, Dübendorf, pp 22–44
Rinscheid A (2015) Crisis, policy discourse, and major policy change: exploring the role of subsystem polarization in nuclear energy policymaking. Eur Policy Anal 1(2):34–70
Rinscheid A, Udris L (2021) Referendum campaigns in Swiss energy policy. In: Hettich P, Kachi A (eds) Swiss energy governance. Springer, New York
Sampei Y, Aoyagi-Usui M (2009) Mass-media coverage, its influence on public awareness of climate-change issues, and implications for Japan's national campaign to reduce greenhouse gas emissions. Glob Environ Chang 19(2):203–212
Schaffer, LM (2021) Who's afraid of more ambitious climate policy? Distributional consequences and inequality perceptions in ratcheting up for the paris agreement. Working paper
Schaffer L, Bernauer T (2014) Explaining government choices for promoting renewable energy. Energy Policy 68:15–27
Schaffer LM, Lüth M (2021) Domestic political consequences of climate change: the evolving party competition over climate and energy policy. Working paper
Schaffer LM, Magyar Z (2021) Climate change policy: distributional implications and preferences on redistribution – evidence from Switzerland (Pre-Analysis Plan). Retrieved from https://osf.io/sn9tg
Schaffer L, Oehl B, Bernauer T (2021) Are policymakers responsive to public demand in climate politics? J Publ Policy
Scruggs L, Benegal S (2012) Declining public concern about climate change: can we blame the great recession? Glob Environ Chang 22(2):505–515
Sewerin S, Béland D, Cashore B (2020) Designing policy for the long term: agency, policy feedback and policy change. Policy Sci 53(2):243–252
Speck C (2003) Elektrizitätsmarkt. Sichere Versorgung. Parlamentarische Initiative 03.409
Stauffacher M, Muggli N, Scolobig A, Moser C (2015) Framing deep geothermal energy in mass media: the case of Switzerland. Technol Forecast Soc Chang 98:60–70
Stokes LC, Breetz HL (2018) Politics in the US energy transition: case studies of solar, wind, biofuels and electric vehicles policy. Energy Policy 113:76–86
Swiss Federal Office of Energy (SFOE) (2019) 20 Jahre schweizerisches Energiegesetz. Available at https://energeiaplus.com
Thalmann P, Vielle M (2019) Lowering CO_2 emissions in the Swiss transport sector. Swiss J Econ Statist 155(1):10
Tresch A (2012) The (partisan) role of the press in direct democratic campaigns: evidence from a Swiss vote on European integration. Swiss Polit Sci Rev 18(3):287–304
Tresch A, Sciarini P, Varone F (2013) The relationship between media and political agendas: variations across decision-making phases. West Eur Polit 36:897–918
Tvinnereim E, Fløttum K (2015) Explaining topic prevalence in answers to open-ended survey questions about climate change. Nat Clim Chang 5(8):744–747
Tvinnereim E, Liu X, Jamelske EM (2017) Public perceptions of air pollution and climate change: different manifestations, similar causes, and concerns. Clim Chang 140(3–4):399–412
Unruh GC (2002) Escaping carbon lock-in. Energy Policy 30(4):317–325
Van Cuilenburg J (1999) On competition, access and diversity in media, old and new: some remarks for communications policy in the information age. New Media Soc 1(2):183–207
Vliegenthart R, Walgrave S (2008) The contingency of intermedia agenda setting: a longitudinal study in Belgium. J Mass Commun Q 85(4):860–877
Ward H, Cao X (2012) Domestic and international influences on green taxation. Comp Pol Stud 45:1075–1103
Wittneben BB (2012) The impact of the Fukushima nuclear accident on European energy policy. Environ Sci Pol 15(1):1–3
Wüstenhagen R, Markard J, Truffer B (2003) Diffusion of green power products in Switzerland. Energy Policy 31(7):621–626

Lena Maria Schaffer is Assistant Professor for Political Science and International and Transnational Relations at the University of Lucerne, Lucerne, Switzerland.

Alessio Levis is student at ETH Zürich, Zürich, Switzerland

The Influence of Policy Risk on Swiss Wind Power Investment

Anna Broughel and Rolf Wüstenhagen

Contents

Abstract Wind energy is one of the most affordable and fastest-growing sources of electricity worldwide. As a large share of wind power generation occurs in the winter season, it could make an important contribution to seasonal diversification of domestic electricity supply. However, the development of wind energy projects in Switzerland has been characterized by long and complex administrative processes, with the planning phase taking up to a decade, more than twice as long as the European average. The objective of this chapter is to quantify the risk premium that lengthy permitting processes imply for wind energy investors in Switzerland and to suggest ways to reduce policy risk. The data have been gathered through 22 confidential interviews with project developers and several cantonal permitting agencies as well as a review of federal and cantonal regulatory documents. Furthermore, a discounted cash flow model was built to compare the profitability indicators (IRR, NPV) and the levelized cost of electricity (LCOE) of a reference case to scenarios with various risks—for example, delays in the permitting process, downsizing the

This chapter is a significantly revised and updated version of a manuscript that has previously been included in the final report of a project which has received funding from the Swiss Federal Office of Energy (see Wüstenhagen et al. 2017, pp. 10–35). The authors bear the entire responsibility for the content of this chapter and for the conclusions drawn therefrom.

A. Broughel · R. Wüstenhagen (✉)
University of St. Gallen, Chair for Management of Renewable Energies, St. Gallen, Switzerland
e-mail: anna.broughel@tetratech.com; rolf.wuestenhagen@unisg.ch

P. Hettich, A. Kachi (eds.), *Swiss Energy Governance*,
https://doi.org/10.1007/978-3-030-80787-0_14

project, or changes in the regulatory environment such as phasing out feed-in tariffs. The model shows that the highest profitability risks are related to the availability of a feed-in tariff, but other changes in the permitting process can also have a critical impact on the project's bottom line. The findings illustrate a significant policy risk premium in the pre-construction stage faced by wind energy project developers in Switzerland.

1 Introduction

The Swiss Energy Strategy 2050 (ES2050), which established ambitious energy efficiency and renewable electricity production targets and a ban for new nuclear power plants,[1] was accepted by 58.2% of the voters in a May 2017 referendum.[2] As a consequence, wind energy projects, together with other renewable energy sources, were granted the status of "national interest", thus leveling the importance of renewable power generation with other national interests, such as landscape protection.[3] Another important implication was that no *new* feed-in-tariff payments ("*kostendeckende Einspeisevergütung* KEV") would be earmarked for renewable energy after the end of 2022. Since January 2018, the previous KEV system has been changed towards a system of feed-in remuneration with direct marketing.[4]

ES2050 recommends a target of 11,400 GWh of new renewables (without hydropower) in 2035[5] and it is expected that wind energy will play an important part in fulfilling this goal. By the end of 2018, there were 75 MW of wind energy capacity installed in the country, producing roughly 122 GWh of electricity, which corresponds to the electricity consumption of 35,000 Swiss households.[6] These numbers suggest that in order to meet the federal production targets, wind power needs to see significant growth in the coming years. Administrative and regulatory issues[7] are among the major barriers to the development of renewable energy projects in Switzerland and internationally.[8] Leading Swiss governmental and industry stakeholders have identified the duration of administrative processes as an area of

[1]Swiss Federal Office of Energy (2016a).

[2]Federal Chancellery (2017).

[3]Energy Act (*Energiegesetz, SR 730.0*), Art. 12.

[4]For the sake of brevity, we use the term "KEV" in this chapter to refer to Swiss feed-in tariffs, including the system of feed-in remuneration with direct marketing introduced in 2018.

[5]Energy Act (*Energiegesetz*).

[6]Suisse Eole (2019).

[7]The words "administrative", "planning", "permitting", and "regulatory" costs are used interchangeably to refer to the costs borne by the project developer before the construction of wind turbines takes place.

[8]Battaglini et al. (2012); Burkhardt et al. (2015); Dong and Wiser (2013); Ceña et al. (2010).

concern: it can take more than 10 years to obtain all the necessary permits to construct a large wind energy project.[9] By comparison, the average pre-construction lead times are 4.5 years in Europe, with a considerable variation by country.[10] The long duration and complexity of the permitting process result in reduced attractiveness of the Swiss market for foreign and domestic investors, who prefer shorter administrative procedures.[11] This preference is financially sound: administrative costs are 'sunk' and increase the levelized cost of electricity (LCOE), thus directly impacting project profitability.

There are several types of costs that are connected to permitting procedures. The first type is easily quantifiable—these are *direct* monetary expenses, such as permitting fees or expenses on environmental impact assessment (EIA) and ecological compensation. We argue that administrative delays incur additional *indirect* costs, which have a detrimental and significant effect on the financial attractiveness of a wind project due to opportunity cost of capital and foregone profits. Moreover, delays give rise to regulatory and policy risk and uncertainty with respect to the federal support scheme and possible changes in environmental and spatial planning laws. Taken all together, we posit that direct and indirect costs of permitting and associated risks constitute a significant barrier for wind energy project development in Switzerland.

The aim of this chapter is to quantify the cost of regulatory and policy risks (the "risk premium") faced by investors in Swiss wind energy projects. The research focuses on the question: How can the policy risk premium for planning and permitting of wind energy projects be quantified and reduced? To answer this question, we describe wind energy project permitting procedures, summarize empirical data on their costs and duration, and analyze the impacts that regulatory risks have on LCOE under different scenarios.

Our analysis is informed by a review of publicly available documents and interviews with federal and cantonal authorities. The aim of the interviews was to cross-check information obtained from public documents and identify the most important bottlenecks. Industry-related data were gathered through 22 confidential interviews with wind energy project developers in German and French-speaking parts of Switzerland.

The results have significant policy relevance. To invest in renewable energy, project developers have to recover the cost of electricity production ("hard cost") as well as the associated risk premium ("soft cost"). While technological and market risks can be reduced through careful due diligence by the project developers, political and regulatory risks are harder to manage.[12] Quantifying the risk premium induced by the administrative process will allow a more precise calculation of adequate levels of public support, which will help policymakers balance the multiple

---

[9] Guy-Ecabert and Meyer (2016); Suisse Eole (2016).

[10] Ceña et al. (2010).

[11] De Jager and Rathmann (2008); Lüthi and Wüstenhagen (2012).

[12] Noothout et al. (2016); Bürer and Wüstenhagen (2008).

objectives of providing investor confidence, securing low-carbon electricity supply, protecting local landscapes and the environment, and maintaining affordable electricity prices.

The rest of this chapter has the following structure. First, we classify the risk categories faced by wind project developers and visualize the complexity of the administrative process for building large wind energy projects in Switzerland. Then, we quantify the policy risk premium based on the calculation of project profitability and LCOE under eight different scenarios. Finally, policy implications and recommendations for risk reduction are derived, informed by the model results and interview insights.

2 Risk Categories in Wind Energy Investment

This section investigates ten risks from the wind energy project developer's perspective, adapted from Noothout et al.[13] Careful consideration and weighting of wind energy project risks are paramount for successful project completion. While some risks are regulatory in nature and can be somewhat mitigated, a number of other factors need to be accepted "as is", exposing the project developer to cumulative project risk.

Policy design risk, policy change risk and administrative risk are the most relevant for our research, since they cannot be easily managed by the project developer. **Policy design risk** is connected to opportunities and threats arising from how the policy instrument is designed by the authorities, including duration and size of support and existence of a support cap. Since 2009, Swiss authorities have been offering feed-in-tariffs (KEV), a fixed remuneration paid for electricity produced from renewable sources for the duration of 20 years.[14] The KEV ensures that electricity generators receive compensation for the green power they produce and shields the project cash flows from the price volatility of the electric power markets. Moreover, wind projects that are ready to be built enjoy preferential treatment in the KEV system.[15]

Even though KEV offers an attractive and stable revenue stream, there are several challenges with the current implementation of this policy instrument in Switzerland, which translate into considerable risk for developers. The first challenge is the risk of not receiving KEV (considered by Scenarios VI–VIII in section 4.2). In fact, in the third quarter of 2019, only 40 wind turbines with an installed capacity of 62 MW benefited from KEV support.[16] Another 438 wind projects with a capacity of 1014 MW were approved for KEV support should they be built, and an additional

[13] Noothout et al. (2016).

[14] Swiss Federal Office of Energy (2016b).

[15] Swiss Federal Office of Energy (2016a).

[16] Pronovo (2019a).

356 planned wind energy projects with a nominal capacity of 843 MW were on the KEV waiting list, unlikely to get approval before the 2022 expiration of the feed-in tariff system.[17] Relieving this bottleneck could contribute significantly to achieving Switzerland's renewable energy goals. If half of the currently planned projects were implemented by 2035, this would lead to an expected annual power generation of 1637 GWh or 14% of the ES2050 target.[18]

Policy change risk: The second challenge is uncertainty about the subsequent support scheme after the KEV system is discontinued. Article 38 of the revised Energy Act specifies a sunset clause that phases out feed-in tariffs after 2022, suggesting that the majority of wind projects on the waiting list are unlikely to receive KEV support.[19] The design of a possible public support scheme after 2022 is currently unknown, which is a source of considerable uncertainty for project developers.

Administrative risks can be recognized as a significant hurdle to wind power development in Switzerland, as they have been internationally.[20] The risk stems from complex permitting procedures (described in detail in Sect. 3), variations of procedures by canton, changing requirements for environmental impact assessment (EIA), long administrative lead times, multiple opportunities for objections on the cantonal and municipal level, and the high number of authorities involved. The administrative risks bring about additional costs (e.g., new environmental impact studies), cause project delays (e.g., pending court cases), and introduce uncertainty (e.g., regarding a project's chances of receiving financing).

Social acceptance risk: Another important risk in the planning phase is connected to social acceptance, which includes acceptance by the markets, local communities, and society in general.[21] Note that social acceptance is closely intertwined with administrative risks, since projects with significant opposition from the local population or the NGOs are often delayed and are less likely to receive the necessary permits. Generally, Swiss public opinion polls show high approval ratings of wind energy: a favorable public opinion has been a defining trend in Switzerland for more than a decade.[22] Even though intense political campaigns ahead of voting can lead to opinion swings,[23] local voters accepted 19 out of 22 specific wind energy projects in the past 7 years.[24]

Public support for wind energy does not mean that all stakeholders are on board with wind energy development. Often, there is a highly organized and influential

[17] Pronovo (2019b).

[18] Own calculation based on data from Pronovo (2019a).

[19] Swiss Federal Office of Energy (2016a).

[20] Ceña et al. (2010); Lüthi and Prässler (2011).

[21] Wüstenhagen et al. (2007).

[22] Geissmann (2015); Ebers and Wüstenhagen (2016); Ebers Broughel and Hampl (2018); Tabi and Wüstenhagen (2015); Tamedia (2017).

[23] Rinscheid and Wüstenhagen (2018); see also Rinscheid and Udris (2021).

[24] Perret (2019).

opposition, which presents a variety of arguments against wind power development. These concerns are usually related to impacts of wind turbines on different aspects of local life: environmental (impacts on local flora and fauna, landscape change), emotional (place attachment), technological (contestation of wind technology), health-related (impact of noise, flicker), and economic (unfavorable perceived cost-benefit ratio of wind power development). In the academic literature, the issues of social acceptance are discussed in the context of environmental equity and fairness of renewable energy generation.[25] The project developers usually search collaboration and compromise with the opposition, which might involve commissioning of additional studies, introduction of ecological mitigation measures, changing the location of turbines, reducing the number of turbines, and switching off turbines when birds and bats are most likely to be impacted. Our estimations show that these factors may have significant financial consequences for the project developer. Social acceptance risks can be addressed through a careful stakeholder management strategy, but they cannot be fully avoided.

A wind project might receive dozens of objections, most of which are settled out of court. When a compromise cannot be found, the courts are likely to get involved. The task of the court is to weigh the conflicting interests: for example, environmental protection versus domestic energy supply.[26] Court cases have considerable impacts on the project's cash flow. Court deliberations lead to direct monetary expenses, such as remuneration for lawyers, expenses for commissioning new studies and project managers' work hours. The objections often lead to considerable delays, putting the project on hold for the duration of the court deliberations. Municipal courts are likely to hear a case in about 6 months, while the cantonal courts might require a year to reach a decision. A federal court is likely to need several years to announce their verdict. Multiple court cases might delay the project to the extent that it can no longer be realized.

Grid access risk: The project developer greatly depends on the availability of a grid connection; therefore, this is among the first points to be clarified in the initial project stages. If there are no suitable connection options available, the developer usually abandons the project idea because building new electric infrastructure can be prohibitively expensive. Generally, project developers tend to seek a close collaboration with the local grid operators.

Financing risk: Due to the stability of the Swiss financial system and currently very low interest rates, the developers are able to finance wind projects with relatively low cost of capital. Yet, financing of the existing wind projects in Switzerland was greatly facilitated by receiving a KEV, thus connecting the financing risk of project development with federal policy-making. The interviewees have reported that without the KEV, their projects are unlikely to obtain financing, as they would be exposed to volatile electricity prices, making it harder to present a clear

[25] E.g., see Wolsink (2007); Wüstenhagen et al. (2007).

[26] Plüss (2017).

investment case. In the absence of KEV, a long-term power purchasing agreement (PPA) might make the wind project financially attractive, if it covers LCOE.

Technology risk relates to the level of maturity of wind energy technology. Even though wind turbines are a novelty in many regions, wind power is a mature technology. The developer cannot influence the maturity of the best available technology, but a project can be designed to use the most appropriate technological solution, given local wind conditions, altitude, and environmental impacts. In recent years, technological progress has permitted the construction of increasingly larger turbines for increasingly lower cost, which tremendously improved the cost efficiency of wind energy per MW of installed capacity. One of the challenges of rapid technological development is that in the case of serious delays, by the time the project obtains all the necessary permits, the technology specified in the permitting documentation may be outdated or even no longer available. In this case, some permitting steps need to be repeated.[27] On the other hand, some project delays can also be an advantage, as they allow the developer to gather further information about the site and employ more efficient wind turbines as they become available on the market.

Management risk is related to the overall experience level of the project developer to successfully plan, commission, operate, and decommission or repower the wind project. Our interviews identified a significant learning-by-doing effect, as project developers learn about the complex permitting procedures. An experienced project team has the potential to reduce management risk.

To complete the picture, project developers are subject to **market design** and **country risks**, which equally apply to all electricity producers. These two risks pertain to such factors as: political stability, level of corruption, economic development, design and functioning of the electricity market, the legal system, and exchange rate fluctuations. The Swiss electricity market is partially liberalized, with the second stage of liberalization depending on an electricity trading agreement with the EU. The electricity market is dominated by public utilities, which makes the entrance of smaller players more challenging.[28] This stands in contrast with many private wind energy developers who are active in such countries as the US, Germany, the UK, or Sweden.[29] At the same time, Switzerland is a rather small market, which makes large-scale renewable energy developments challenging. As a result, many Swiss developers have built or acquired wind projects abroad.[30]

[27] One standard practice is to use approximate turbine characteristics in the beginning of the permitting process and avoid specifying the turbine model for as long as possible.

[28] Ebers Broughel et al. (2019).

[29] E.g., Bergek et al. (2013).

[30] Blondiau and Reuter (2019).

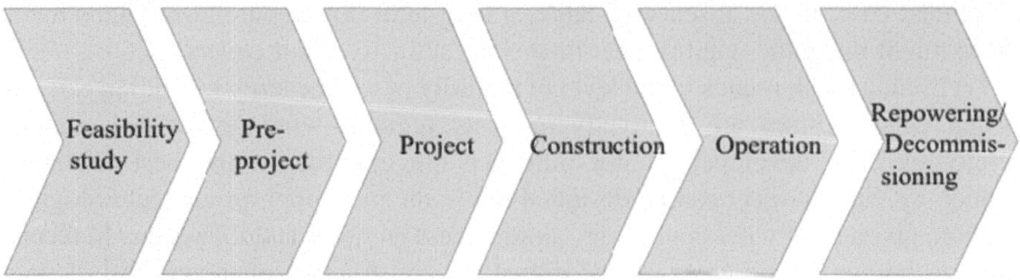

Fig. 1 Wind power project development process

3 Wind Energy Project Development Process

Wind energy projects are subject to a rigorous technical, financial, ecological, and geological evaluation, with the involvement of multiple stakeholders.[31] Fig. 1 shows the project development process of a wind park, consisting of six distinct steps: feasibility study, pre-project, main project, construction, operation, and repowering or decommissioning.

In Switzerland, the pre-construction stage (first 3 project steps) can last between 6 and 7 years without objections and stretch up to 15 or more years in case the project faces regulatory hurdles or opposition. In this stage, the project developer expects to spend 5–10% of the total budget on planning and permitting activities, which might range from several hundred thousand Swiss francs (in case no EIA is needed) to 3–6 million CHF. It must be noted that exact development costs are difficult to predict, since the requirements for implementing wind projects have increased tremendously, putting an upward pressure on pre-construction budgets. Moreover, pre-construction costs do not linearly increase with project size, as they are made up of fixed costs (independent of project size) and variable costs (dependent on project size, but also on location, the situation in the community, objections, cantonal planning decisions, etc.). Thus, larger projects tend to expose project developers to higher pre-construction risks (and expenses) because they require more extensive EIAs, more permits for wind measurement towers, complex technical planning, and coordination among multiple jurisdictions and landowners. On the other hand, in case of larger projects, the development costs are spread over a larger installed capacity, thus reducing cost per megawatt. To mitigate pre-construction risks, project developers were observed to form partnerships for the development of larger projects (cost sharing) or to develop a small lighthouse project first (cost-minimizing). In both cases, potential project failure would result in smaller monetary losses.

Exact pre-construction steps somewhat vary by developer, prior experience, and the jurisdiction. The initial "exploratory" stage of the project results in the feasibility study, which usually takes 1–2 years to complete. The study includes rough wind

[31] Twele and Liersch (2011).

potential evaluations, an initial consideration of environmental impacts and accessibility options, a preliminary geological assessment of the grounds, an evaluation of suitable wind turbines, and an initial financial appraisal. In this phase, the approximate project location and the number of turbines are proposed. This is also the time for the initial contact with local stakeholders. The authorities are contacted for information on permits and zoning requirements. Consent of the land owner(s) is of paramount importance, and it is usually secured through a contract. Interconnection options are discussed with the grid operator. Most project developers have applied for KEV by submitting a free-of-charge online application to the relevant agency, Pronovo (formerly Stiftung KEV). This is a rather fast and straightforward procedure. If the KEV approval is granted, the project developer has to notify the authorities of the project status every 2 years.

At the pre-project stage, all of the previously mentioned points get a deeper and more detailed assessment. The project developer obtains reliable wind speed data, by installing a wind measurement tower to monitor wind speeds, usually for 1 year. A more detailed pre-project file is submitted to the municipal and cantonal authorities for evaluation, so that the project can be integrated in the zoning plans.

The main project builds upon the outcome of the pre-project and includes a number of detailed studies, which are made to satisfy the building permit application and requirements of the Federal Inspectorate for Heavy Current Installations.[32] This stage can take several years and often stretches out longer due to delays. The main project file usually includes the following components: a detailed wind speed evaluation, a road access assessment, an interconnection study, contracts with the landowner, a technical plan, a business plan, and a full EIA with suggested measures of ecological compensation. The EIA, compulsory for projects over 5 MW, is an especially important part of the project plan, as it assesses the project's influence on flora, fauna, landscape, and noise exposure.[33] The EIA often represents a stumbling stone for project developers. Authorities, courts, and external stakeholders can require additional environmental studies, which range in cost between 30 and 300 kCHF each and take months (and sometimes several years) to complete. Generally, the authorities recommend clustering wind power developments, thus avoiding locations with high natural value.[34] Finally, the municipality decides whether to grant the project a construction permit, which takes several years with a possibility of a referendum. After the project receives all necessary permits, the construction phase begins. In order to install wind turbines, a number of infrastructural improvements (clearing forests, building roads) are often needed.

The next phase is the operational phase, which is the longest phase of the project cycle. It can last 20 years or more, and this is actually the first time when the project is generating revenues. During this time, the project developer might also implement ecological compensation measures to mitigate project impacts on flora, fauna and

[32] https://www.esti.admin.ch/en/esti-homepage

[33] Federal Council (2016).

[34] Federal Office for Spatial Development (2017).

local residents. After the end of the operational phase, the project can be either decommissioned or repowered with new turbines.[35]

While the six steps of the project development process seem straightforward, the picture becomes more complicated when the complexities of the administrative process are taken into account. In Fig. 2, we mapped out the permitting steps and the stakeholders involved, with arrows denoting the most significant interdependencies.

As evident from this visualization, the project developer has to obtain permits or decisions from a number of federal agencies, including aviation authorities, military authorities, the Federal Inspectorate for Heavy Current Installations, the Federal Office for the Environment, to name a few. To simplify this permitting process, the Federal Office of Energy has set up a one-stop-shop called "*guichet unique*"[36] to allow project developers to have a single point of contact with relevant federal authorities, instead of having to coordinate among multiple agencies. Even though federal authorities play an important role in the permitting process, the permitting authority lies with the cantonal and municipal agencies responsible for energy, zoning, the environment, and building.[37]

4 Quantification of the Policy Risk Premium

4.1 Methodological Approach

The following section focuses on the quantification of the risk premium, which was done by comparing the profitability and the LCOE of a reference project (risk-free scenario) with several risk-adjusted scenarios, when the project witnessed regulatory challenges. The calculations were based on the discounted cash flow model, expressing project profitability in terms of the Net Present Value (NPV) and Internal Rate of Return (IRR), which are standard project evaluation methods in finance.[38] For the calculation of project cash flows, the authors use annual Free Cash Flow to Firm (FCFF) values.

The LCOE calculations were based on an established method of accounting for project expenses and predicted electricity production at certain periods of time. LCOE was calculated with the following formula[39]:

[35] Deloitte (2015).

[36] Swiss Federal Office of Energy (2019).

[37] Federal Office for Spatial Development (2017).

[38] Brealey et al. (2012).

[39] Adapted from Kost et al. (2018).

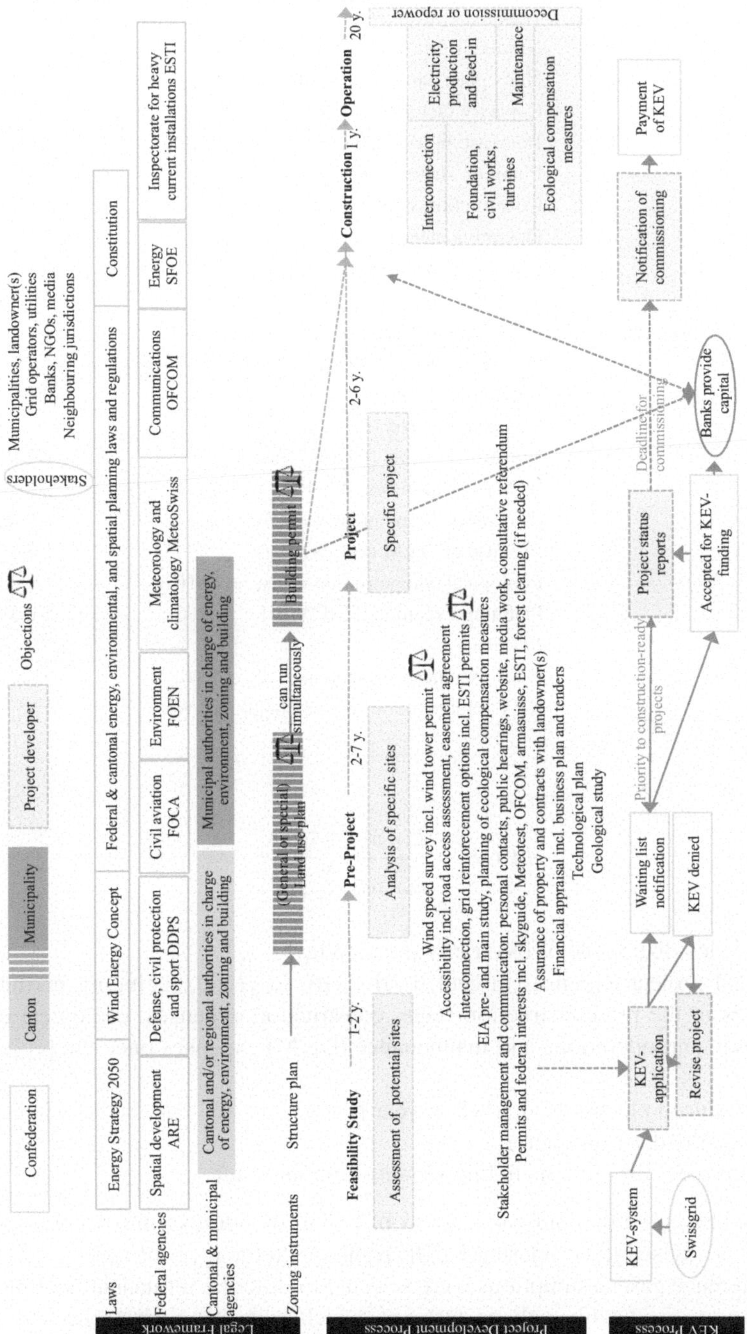

Fig. 2 Planning and permitting of wind energy projects in Switzerland

Table 1 Reference case assumptions

Input Parameters	Value
Technical parameters	
Number of turbines	9
Nameplate capacity per turbine (MW)	3
Capacity factor (%)	20.9%
Decrease in turbine power output (%/year)	1.6%
Planning stage (years)	7
Construction stage (years)	1
Operating stage (years)	20
Financial parameters	
WACC	3.97%
Depreciation, years	20
Corporate tax rate (%)	17.81%
Inflation rate (%)	0%
Building and O&M	
Construction cost (CHF/MW)	2,200,000
Interconnection cost (CHF)	660,000
Operations & maintenance (CHF/year)	594,000
Increase of O&M cost (%/year)	1%
Ecological compensation measures (CHF)	1500,000
Planning expenses (CHF/MW)	130,000
Revenues	
KEV remuneration in years 1–5, ct/kWh	21.5
KEV remuneration in years 6–20, ct/kWh	13.5

$$LCOE = \frac{\sum_{t=0}^{n} \frac{A_t}{(1+WACC)^t}}{\sum_{t=0}^{n} \frac{M_{t,el}}{(1+WACC)^t}} \tag{1}$$

- LCOE is levelized cost of electricity in ct/kWh;
- A_t are all project expenses in cent (0.01 CHF) in year *t*, including permitting expenses in the pre-construction stage, construction expenses, ecological compensation, and operations and maintenance (O&M) expenses once the project is built;
- M_t is produced electricity in kWh in year *t*;
- WACC is the discount factor;
- n is the project lifetime, including pre-construction stage.

It should be noted that our calculations of LCOE do not take into account taxes, so caution is advised in comparing LCOE results with the level of feed-in tariffs.

The reference case assumptions were selected to describe a financially attractive wind energy project with realistic features, which have been cross-checked with project developers during the interviews (Table 1). The reference case presents a planned wind park consisting of 9 wind turbines, with a capacity of 3 MW each (27 MW in total). The capacity factor, which is a measure of annual electricity generation per MW installed, is 20.9%, based on the average production values of wind energy projects in Switzerland in 2015.[40] The turbines' efficiency decreases at a rate of 1.6% per year.[41] The project developer expects the planning to take 7 years, construction to be completed in 1 year, and the turbines to generate electricity for 20 years. The project developer discounts her annual cash flows at the weighted average cost of capital (WACC) of 3.97%.[42] The inflation rate is set at zero for simplicity. The capital expenditure is fully depreciated in 20 years. The corporate tax rate is 17.81%, which is an average corporate Swiss tax rate.[43] The model assumes 1-year intervals for cash flows, which occur at the end of each year.

The construction cost of the reference project is 59.4 million CHF (2.2 million CHF/MW) and it costs 660 kCHF to connect the project to the power grid. After the construction, there is an annual expense of 594 kCHF (1% of construction costs) for operations and maintenance (O&M), which increases at a rate of 1% per year. The project developer expects to receive a feed-in tariff of 21.5 ct/kWh for the first 5 years of operation, followed by a lower KEV rate of 13.5 ct/kWh for the remaining 15 years.[44] During the interviews, the project developers reported production costs ranging from 10 to 20.5 ct/kWh.

Ecological compensation measures are carried out in the year of construction only if the project is realized, and they represent the NPV of all expenses on ecological compensation over the project's lifetime. They are assumed to cost 1.5 million CHF, which is due to the high number of planned turbines and increasingly stringent ecological requirements. After 20 years of power production, the developer expects to sell the turbines in the second-hand market, which should cover decommissioning costs; so the decommissioning is assumed to be cost-neutral. Note that project expenses in the reference case are rather conservative, tending to underestimate the project's risks rather than overestimate them.

In the beginning of the project, the developer earmarks a planning budget of 130,000 CHF per MW of planned capacity (3.5 million CHF), corresponding to about 6% of construction cost. For the reference case, project planning and ecological compensation expenses were informed by the values summarized from the interviews (Table 2). This represents a rather conservative assumption, given that the international literature reports planning budgets reaching 10% of the construction cost.[45] The planning expenses include wind measurements, environmental studies

---

[40] Wind Data (2017).

[41] Staffell and Green (2014).

[42] Swiss Federal Office of Energy (2016c).

[43] KPMG (2016).

[44] For reasons of simplicity, we assumed the standard feed-in tariffs for wind energy in years 6 to 20 rather than taking into account the exceptions specified in Appendix 1.3, section 3.2, of the Energy Ordinance (*Energieverordnung*, SR 730.01); Swiss Federal Office of Energy (2016b).

[45] Krohn et al. (2009); Blanco (2009).

Table 2 Estimation of average expenses of wind project planning

Project planning expenses (kCHF)	Mean	Min	Max	SD
Ecological compensation measures	844	100	1700	536
EIA pre-study and main studies	417	100	700	164
Coordination with stakeholders and PR	550	200	1100	288
General technical planning	398	100	1500	480
Wind speed measurements	243	80	530	152
Planning of grid interconnection	109	50	200	58
Federal permits and interests	20.5	9	35	7.7
HR expenses, accounting, controlling, legal advice	500			
Municipal court cases (1/2 year delay)	30–50/case			
Cantonal court cases (1 year delay)	30–50/case			
Federal court case (2 years delay)	50–100/case			
Insurances, land rent, leases	50			

and mitigation measures, salaries for lawyers, engineers, financial managers, as well as PR and stakeholder management expenses. The minimum and maximum values vary considerably depending on the interviewee, which can be explained by differences in project accounting, varying project complexity, and project experiences. Still, Table 2 presents a useful illustration of project planning expenses.

One of the most significant cost categories is connected to EIA and ecological mitigation measures, often accounting for half of the planning budget. EIAs take 1.5 to 6 years to perform and range in total cost from 100 kCHF for simpler studies to 700 kCHF for longer and more complex estimations. Similarly, all except for one interviewee reported ecological compensation measures in excess of half a million Swiss francs. Coordination with stakeholders was a significant cost category for some project developers, leading to spending of up to 1.1 million CHF over the project lifetime. In contrast, other developers planned several hundred thousand Swiss francs on such activities per year during the planning stage, depending on the type of activities carried out (organization of site visits and informational meetings with or without catering; noise simulations; preparation of dossiers, website, posters, and flyers; communication campaigns; support of local community activities).

The technical dimension of the project requires planning by experienced engineers, which can be done in-house or outsourced to an engineering company, costing on average about 400 kCHF (might include geotechnical study, road access survey, etc.) and taking 4–5 months to complete. Similarly, wind measurements depend on project complexity and can be completed in several stages, costing from under 100 kCHF to more than half a million CHF. Obtaining the permit for wind measurements can take several months for approval and can be subject to objections. Planning for interconnection might cost about 100 kCHF.

One of the cost categories that are most difficult to predict is the HR expense for project management and expenses for legal advice, as these directly increase with project delays, the number of objections, the number of subsequent court cases, and

Table 3 Summary of scenarios

Scenario	Description	Details
I	Delays	3- or 10-year delay in permitting
II	Lower capacity factor	Reduction of capacity factor to 19.9% or 17.9% due to switching off of turbines
III	Lower installed capacity	7 or 5 turbines are permitted instead of 9
IV	Planning costs increase	Increase of planning costs to 200 kCHF/MW or 400 kCHF/MW
V	Combination scenario	Low risk: 3 years of delay, capacity factor is 19.9%, 7 turbines permitted, planning budget is 200 kCHF/MW High risk: 10 years of delay in permitting, capacity factor is 17.9%, 5 turbines permitted, planning budget is 400 kCHF/MW
VI	KEV phased out	Electricity sold at market price of 4 ct/kWh or 8 ct/kWh
VII	KEV payments delayed	Payments delayed by 1 or 2 years, electricity sold at market price of 4 ct/kWh
VIII	KEV payments reduced	KEV reduced by 10% or 20% in all years

court instances involved. We made a conservative estimation of 500 kCHF over the planning period but also provide mean values for legal expenses per court case, which would be added to the planning budget as they arise. Finally, we include the cost of insurances, land rent and leases, estimated at 50 kCHF.

In order to evaluate marginal impacts of different administrative hurdles, we compute the NPV, IRR, and LCOE in the reference case and different scenarios. Each scenario investigates two levels of risk: low risk and high risk. The overall aim of the scenarios is to determine which factors have the highest impact on project profitability and hence represent the most severe policy risk.

Scenario I investigates changes in profitability and LCOE as a result of a 3-year (low risk) and 10-year (high risk) delay in project development in the pre-construction stage. The planning budget increases by 100 k CHF for every year of delay, which accounts for additional project management hours, legal advice costs and coordination efforts.

Scenario II illustrates the detrimental effect of policy-induced reductions in the project's capacity factor. Full load hours are usually predicted based on wind measurements in the pre-construction stage. Yet, decreased hours of operation can be a measure of ecological compensation, as the turbines might have to be switched off to protect migratory birds or vulnerable bat species. The turbines in the reference case operate with 1831 full load hours a year (20.9% capacity factor), while Scenario II evaluates the changes in LCOE if the turbines work with a capacity factor of 19.9% (low risk) and 17.9% (high risk). A similar negative effect is expected in **Scenario III**, where there are fewer turbines (5 in the low-risk case or 7 in the high-risk case) permitted than originally planned. In **Scenario IV**, we investigate cost overruns that increase the planning budgets to 200 kCHF (low risk) and 400 kCHF (high risk) per MW of installed capacity (Table 3).

Scenario V combines multiple administrative hurdles and is, in many ways, mirroring the reality of several Swiss wind projects. First, low project risks from Scenarios I–IV are combined: planning takes 10 years, the planning expenses increase to 200 kCHF/MW, only 7 out of 9 turbines are permitted, and the capacity factor is reduced to 19.9%. In the high-risk combination scenario, we investigate a 5-turbine project with a pre-construction stage of 17 years and a planning budget of 400 kCHF/MW, with a capacity factor of 17.9%.

Finally, we investigated the impacts of the level and duration of KEV payments on the project's profitability (represented by IRR and NPV). Since LCOE does not account for project revenues, it is not calculated here. We investigated whether wind energy projects will be developed in Switzerland without KEV (**Scenario VI**) and what levels of electricity market prices are necessary to make wind projects financially attractive. For modeling simplicity, we disregarded electricity price volatility and assumed a constant price of 4 ct/kWh, which was the average spot price for Swiss base load electricity in the day-ahead market between July 2015 and July 2016[46] and which is also within the range of the Swiss Federal Office of Energy's electricity price projections.[47] The low-risk Scenario VI assumes the market price to be 8 ct/kWh.[48] Additionally, we looked at project profitability if KEV payments are delayed by 1 or 2 years and the electricity is sold at the market price of 4 ct/kWh (**Scenario VII**). Finally, we calculated profitability changes due to an overall reduction in KEV support (by 10% or 20%) (**Scenario VIII**).

4.2 Results: The Price of Policy Risk

This section provides an indication of the magnitude of the policy risk premium faced by project developers due to challenges in the pre-construction stage. We compare LCOE in the risk-free scenario to the eight scenarios with policy risks introduced in the previous section. The LCOE of the reference case is 12.57 ct/kWh. Under the base case assumptions, the project is a reasonably attractive investment with an IRR of 6.68%, an NPV of 10.3 million CHF and a payback time of 10 years after construction. The following scenarios illustrate marginal impacts of policy risks on the reference case.

Scenario I A 3-year delay increases LCOE by 0.16 ct/kWh and results in 1.76 million in losses in NPV (Fig. 3). A 10-year delay in project development creates 4.42 million in losses in NPV for the investor, increasing LCOE by 0.37 ct/kWh.

---

[46] Bloomberg (2016).

[47] Swiss Federal Office of Energy (2016c).

[48] Because of price volatility in the electricity market, it is challenging to predict a wind project's revenues over its lifetime of at least two decades. This assumption is representative of the electricity price level when KEV was initially introduced. In late 2019, wholesale prices were 4 ct/kWh (www.epexspot.com), corresponding to the high-risk scenario.

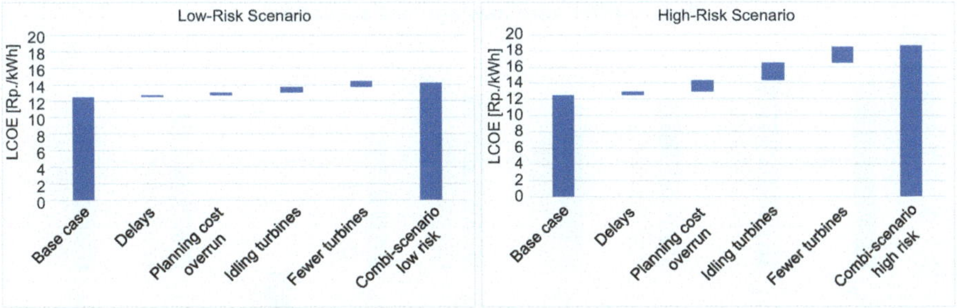

Fig. 3 Risk-adjusted LCOE in Scenarios I-V (high vs. low risk)

Note that these numbers account for only 100 kCHF in additional expenses per year of delay, thus increasing the planning budget by 300 kCHF and one million CHF altogether. Despite these rather small changes in the planning budget (0.5% and 1.7% of construction cost), the estimated profitability losses and LCOE increases are considerable. This observation illustrates an important lesson learned: project delays have a much larger impact on project profitability than is obvious from the direct additional expenses.

In addition to direct costs, delays in project development are connected to indirect costs, such as the opportunity cost of capital. During the years of permitting, the capital earmarked for the project is not productive; yet, it could have been invested at a profit elsewhere. A simple calculation of the opportunity cost shows that if the project developers in the reference case invested their planning budget of 3.5 million CHF into a financial vehicle with an annual yield of 3%, they would have obtained 105 kCHF in revenue per year. In 15 years, the project developers would have earned nearly two million CHF on their initial investment. In case of a wind project, the developers do not see any return on their investment for the duration of the permitting stage. Thus, the idling capital should be of the same level of concern as idling wind turbines.

Moreover, administrative delays make the project developer forego profits from electricity production, which also could have been reinvested. Depending on the assumptions, foregone profits from electricity generation also run into hundreds of thousands of francs, funds that cannot be reinvested if the project gets delayed. Even though opportunity costs of capital and foregone profits do not enter the financial accounting of the project developer, they should not be neglected, since they reduce the overall attractiveness of the project.

Scenario II Major profit-reducing events can occur if not all planned turbines are permitted or the turbines remain idle due to restrictions. Switching off wind turbines can be a measure of environmental conservation. The reduction in capacity factor by one percentage point to 19.9%, brings about an average loss in NPV of 2.8 million CHF and increases LCOE by 0.63 ct/kWh. If the capacity factor decreases to 17.9%, the NPV losses amount to 8.4 million CHF compared to the reference case. If this high risk is present, the LCOE increases by 2.11 ct/kWh.

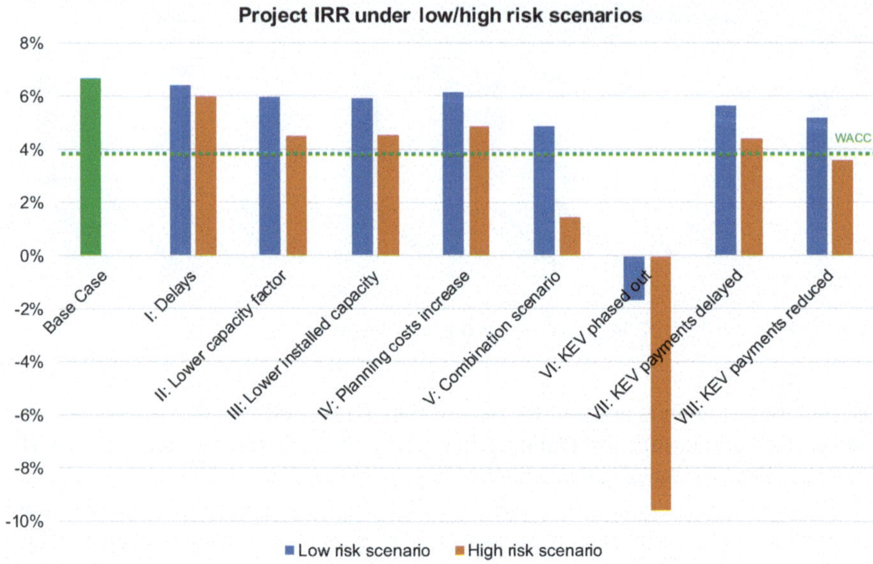

Fig. 4 Impact of policy risk on project's internal rate of return (IRR)

Scenario III A significant decrease in profitability is experienced if multiple turbines are not permitted. If only 7 of the 9 originally planned turbines can be built, LCOE increases by 0.73 ct/kWh. If only 5 turbines are permitted, LCOE climbs by 2.04 ct/kWh. Thus, reducing the capacity factor to 17.9% due to the switching off of turbines has roughly the same impact on LCOE as having 4 of the planned 9 turbines not permitted. The reference project needs at least 14 MW of production capacity to break even. If the project faces additional costs and delays, it requires larger capacities to counterbalance the permitting expenses. This illustrates the sensitivity of wind projects to the number of hours the rotor is allowed to turn and the number of turbines in the park.

Scenario IV The planning budget is likely to increase when the project is experiencing delays. If the planning costs increase to 200 k per MW of installed capacity, the project developer will not only have to invest 1.89 million CHF more into the project in the pre-construction stage, but the LCOE also increases by 0.38 ct/kWh. In a high-risk case, the planning costs would reach 400 kCHF/MW, which would increase LCOE by 1.44 ct/kWh, making the project only marginally attractive with an IRR of 4.88% (Fig. 4). From the interviews we have learned that some project developers would abandon a project if the planning cost reaches half a million CHF per MW. The planning costs for abandoned projects need to be implicitly won back by successful projects, putting an upward pressure on the required level of KEV payments.

Scenario V So far, the calculations estimated the marginal impacts of policy risks on project profitability and LCOE levels. The low-risk combination scenario illustrates a case that is fairly representative of many Swiss wind projects: 3 years of delays, a lower than planned capacity factor of 19.9%, 7 turbines permitted, the planning budget amounting to 200 kCHF/MW. The IRR of the combination scenario is 4.87%, which is still higher than WACC but does not represent a high-yield investment. At the same time, LCOE would rise to 14.22 ct/kWh, which is higher than the nominal KEV remuneration in years 6–20. This implies that the profitability of the project would be substantially lower than initially projected.

If we combine the high-risk scenarios (10 years delay, reduction in capacity factor to 17.9%, 5 turbines permitted, increase of planning costs to 400 kCHF/MW), LCOE rises to the unsustainable level of 18.67 ct/kWh. The cumulative policy risks would reduce the IRR below WACC, yielding a negative NPV, which suggests that an economically rational developer would abandon the project, as it will not be profitable. The combination scenario illustrates how multiple policy risks that are present in reality can have a significant negative impact on a project's financial performance. Unless minimized, these policy risks can hamper the prospects of development of wind energy projects.

Figure 3 presents the effects of the policy risks illustrated in Scenarios I–V on the risk-adjusted LCOE of wind energy in Switzerland. In order to make a positive investment decision, a project developer would compare LCOE with achievable revenues, i.e., remuneration from KEV or electricity sales.

Scenarios VI–VIII The highest risks to a project's financial viability are related to the unavailability, reduction, or delays of KEV payments. In line with the information received during the interviews, we find that no wind project can be developed without KEV in the current market conditions. If KEV payments are not available for 1 year and the electricity price is 40 CHF/MWh, the profitability of the whole project drops by 1.03 percentage points, which would cost the project developer 3.5 million CHF. Delaying KEV for 2 years in the initial years of operation is equivalent to not allowing 4 out of 9 wind turbines to be built in NPV terms. A relatively high market price for electricity is required for the project to be financially viable in the absence of a feed-in tariff: with the assumed WACC (3.97%), the wind project's NPV was positive when the average market price of electricity reached 13.5 ct/kWh for all years of operation. A minimum KEV support of 16.0 ct/kWh is required for all years of operation to maintain the profitability of 6%. If the level of KEV support is reduced by 10%, the project's NPV decreases by more than 5.84 million CHF (1.51 percentage point loss in terms of IRR). More significant reductions of KEV, say by 20%, are likely to deter investment, as the net present value of cash flows turns negative and IRR (3.08%) is below WACC. Note that the relationship between the reduction of KEV and losses in profitability is not one to one: if KEV is reduced by 10%, the profitability decreases by more than 22%.

Figure 4 summarizes the discussions in this section, illustrating how the initial project IRR of 6.68% would be affected by the policy risks discussed in Scenarios I to VIII. The dotted green line represents the assumed weighted average cost of capital of 3.97%. Policy risks can significantly reduce the expected rate of return, and let it fall below WACC and even to negative absolute values in some cases, suggesting that the project would turn unprofitable if the assumptions in some of the high-risk scenarios materialize.

5 Conclusion and Policy Implications

The profitability of a wind park is determined by an interplay of project risks and returns. Most risks in wind energy development occur in the permitting stage, while returns are only realized after the project is built (see Fig. 5). In order to incentivize investment in wind power, policymakers can (1) reduce the risks in the planning stage, (2) compensate investors for taking those risks through higher returns, or (3) shorten the planning stage to reduce uncertainty about both risks and returns. Many Swiss wind energy projects currently have a high-risk/high-return profile. Project developers are facing significant risk in the planning stage, and they receive attractive returns (in the form of the KEV) in those (few) cases where the project can actually be built. For projects not completed before the expiration of feed-in tariffs at the end of 2022, financing crucially depends on parliamentary decisions about any follow-up scheme or on their ability to secure a long-term power purchase agreement (PPA) at sufficiently favorable conditions. From a societal point of view, shifting

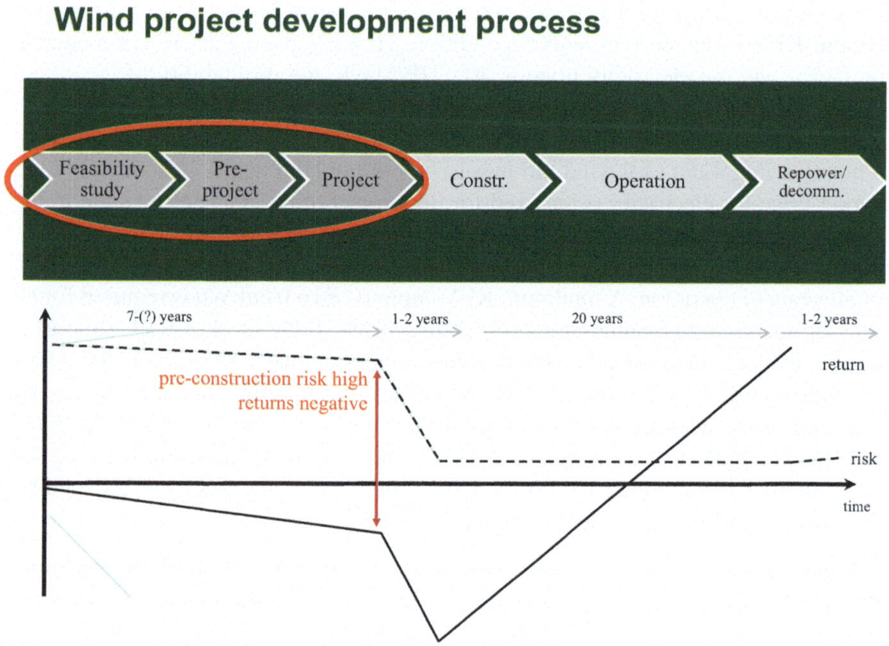

Fig. 5 Risk-return profile in wind energy project development

more projects towards the low-risk/low-return end of the spectrum would be preferable.

Above all, this implies decreasing project risks in the pre-construction stage. Possible measures include simplifying and streamlining permitting procedures, creating regulatory clarity, and expediting court cases. An important consideration is to implement such measures in a way that maintains social acceptance of wind energy by relevant stakeholders. Successful wind projects are characterized by an alignment of interests between investors and local communities, which can for example be facilitated by enabling financial participation of the local population in the project[49] or public support for the planning of community wind projects.[50] An approach that has had positive effects on social acceptance in some regions of Switzerland was to gain experience with one or a few turbines before planning an extended project. This allows concerns of the local population, e.g., about noise, to be contrasted with first-hand evidence and can, through word-of-mouth, facilitate further development of wind energy also in neighboring regions.

While a large number of measures is available to improve administrative procedures and reduce the policy risk premium, coordinating the variety of stakeholders in a federal democracy is not an easy task. The upside of successfully engaging in this task is to secure a clean, affordable domestic supply of electricity – which is ultimately what a majority of the population voted for in the 2017 referendum about the Energy Strategy 2050.

References

Battaglini A, Komendantova N, Brtnik P, Patt A (2012) Perception of barriers for expansion of electricity grids in the European Union. Energy Policy 47:254–259

Bergek A, Mignon I, Sundberg G (2013) Who invests in renewable electricity production? Empirical evidence and suggestions for further research. Energy Policy 56:568–581

Blanco M (2009) The economics of wind energy. Renew Sust Energ Rev 13(6–7):1372–1382

Blondiau Y, Reuter E (2019) Why is the grass greener on the other side? Decision modes and location choice by wind energy investors. J Bus Res 102:44–55

Bloomberg (2016) Bloomberg ticker for Swiss base load day-ahead power: LSWBHRBS Index

Brealey RA, Myers SC, Allen F, Mohanty P (2012) Principles of corporate finance. Tata McGraw-Hill Education

Bürer MJ, Wüstenhagen R (2008) Cleantech venture investors and energy policy risk: an exploratory analysis of regulatory risk management strategies. In: Wüstenhagen R, Hamschmidt J, Sharma S, Starik M (eds) Sustainable innovation and entrepreneurship. Edward Elgar Publishing, pp 290–309

Burkhardt J, Wiser R, Darghouth N, Dong CG, Huneycutt J (2015) Exploring the impact of permitting and local regulatory processes on residential solar prices in the United States. Energy Policy 78:102–112

[49] Tabi and Wüstenhagen (2015).

[50] Scottish Government (2013).

Ceña A, Iuga D, Simonot E, Fichaux N, Wokke S, Strom S (2010) Wind barriers: administrative and grid access barriers to wind power. European Wind Energy Association (EWEA), Brussels
De Jager D, Rathmann M (2008) Policy instrument design to reduce financing costs in renewable energy technology projects. Project report for the IEA Implementing Agreement on Renewable Energy Technology Deployment (RETD). Ecofys, Utrecht
Deloitte (2015) Establishing the investment case: Wind Power. August 2015. Available at https://www.scribd.com/document/294176431/Deloitte-Establishing-the-Investment-Case
Dong C, Wiser R (2013) The impact of city-level permitting processes on residential photovoltaic installation prices and development times: an empirical analysis of solar systems in California Cities. Energy Policy 63:531–542
Ebers A, Wüstenhagen R (2016) 6th consumer barometer renewable energy in collaboration with Raiffeisen. University of St. Gallen. Available at www.iwoe.unisg.ch/kundenbarometer
Ebers Broughel A, Stauch A, Schmid B, Vuichard P (2019) Consumer (co-)ownership in renewables in Switzerland. In: Lowitzsch J (ed) Energy transition: financing consumer coownership in renewables. Palgrave McMillan, pp 451–476
Ebers Broughel A, Hampl N (2018) Community financing of renewable energy projects in Austria and Switzerland: profiles of potential investors. Energy Policy 123:722–736
Federal Chancellery (2017) Vorlage Nr. 612, Vorläufige amtliche Endergebnisse, Energiegesetz (EnG) vom 30.09.2016. Available at https://www.admin.ch
Federal Council (2016) Zugvögel und Windenergie: Weltweit erste kombinierte Studie zu Schlagopfern und Vogelzugintensität. Press Release. Available at https://www.admin.ch
Geissmann M (ed) (2015) Social acceptance of wind energy projects: winning hearts and minds. State-of-the-art Report. Country Report for Switzerland. IEA Wind Task 28. Available at http://www.socialacceptance.ch
Guy-Ecabert C, Meyer F (2016) Leitfaden zur Optimierung der Praxis bei der Planung von Windparks. 31 March 2016. Swiss Federal Office of Energy, Bern
Kost C, Mayer J, Thomsen J, Hatmann N, Senkpiel C, Philipps S et al (2018) Levelized cost of electricity – renewable energy technologies. March 2018, Fraunhofer Institute for Solar Energy Systems ISE, Freiburg
KPMG (2016) Clarity on Swiss Taxes. Available at https://home.kpmg/ch/en/home.html
Krohn S, Morthorst P-E, Awerbuch S (eds) (2009) The economics of wind energy. Report of European Wind Energy Association. Brussels. Available at: http://www.ewea.org
Lüthi S, Prässler T (2011) Analyzing policy support instruments and regulatory risk factors for wind energy deployment—a developers' perspective. Energy Policy 39(9):4876–4892
Lüthi S, Wüstenhagen R (2012) The price of policy risk — empirical insights from choice experiments with European photovoltaic project developers. Energy Econ 34(4):1001–1011
Noothout P, De Jager D, Tesniere L, van Rooijen S, Karypidis N, Brückmann R et al (2016) The impact of risks in renewable energy investments and the role of smart policies. Diacore report. Fraunhofer ISE, Ecofys, eclareon, EPU-NTUA, LEI, TU Wien. February 2016. Available at http://publica.fraunhofer.de/starweb/pub09/index.htm
Perret L (2019) Recherche sur l'acceptation et énergie éolienne. Presentation at NRP70 Event on Social Acceptance. Bern, 26 June 2019. Available at https://api.nfp-energie.ch/api/de/content/file/35e733e7e019d194810f4c9221ec9727
Plüss K (2017) Interessensabwägung beim Bau von Wasser- und Windenergieanlagen. Schriften zum Energierecht, Band 4.Dike Verlag, Zurich/St. Gallen
Pronovo (2019a) Pronovo-Cockpit. 3rd quarter 2019. Status as of 1 October 2019. Available at https://pronovo.ch/de/services/berichte/
Pronovo (2019b) Facts EVS. Available at https://pronovo.ch
Rinscheid A, Udris L (2021) Referendum campaigns in Swiss energy policy. In: Hettich P, Kachi A (eds) Swiss energy governance. Springer, New York
Rinscheid A, Wüstenhagen R (2018) Divesting, fast and slow: affective and cognitive drivers of fading voter support for a nuclear phase-out. Ecol Econ 152:51–61

Scottish Government (2013) Community and Renewable Energy Scheme (CARES). Available at http://www.gov.scot

Staffell I, Green R (2014) How does wind farm performance decline with age? Renew Energy 66:775–786

Suisse Eole (2016) Windjahr 2015: Deutlich höhere Windstromproduktion, aber keine neuen Anlagen. Press release, 19 February 2016. Available at https://www.suisse-eole.ch

Suisse Eole (2019) Windenergie in der Schweiz in Zahlen. Fact Sheet, 22 February 2019. Available at https://www.suisse-eole.ch

Swiss Federal Office for Spatial Development (2017) Concept for wind energy for Switzerland. Available at https://www.are.admin.ch

Swiss Federal Office of Energy (2016a) Energy Strategy 2050. Available at http://www.bfe.admin.ch

Swiss Federal Office of Energy (2016b) Feed-in remuneration at cost. Available at http://www.bfe.admin.ch

Swiss Federal Office of Energy (2016c) Überprüfung der Gestehungskosten und der Vergütungssätze von KEV-Anlagen. May 2016. Available at https://www.admin.ch

Swiss Federal Office of Energy (2019) Guichet Unique Windenergie. Available at https://www.bfe.admin.ch

Tabi A, Wüstenhagen R (2015) Befragung der Anwohner von möglichen Windparks in der Ostschweiz. University of St. Gallen. November 2015

Tamedia (2017) Die meisten finden ein Windrad als Nachbar okay. Follow-up survey on the popular vote on the Energy Act, 20 May 2017. Available at http://www.20min.ch

Twele J, Liersch J (2011) Planning, operation and economics of wind farm projects. In: Gasch R, Twele J (eds) Wind power plants: fundamentals, design, construction and operation. Springer, Berlin, pp 480–519

Wind Data (2017) Standorte von Windkraftanlagen in Betrieb. Produktion 2015. Available at http://wind-data.ch

Wolsink M (2007) Wind power implementation: the nature of public attitudes: equity and fairness instead of 'backyard motives'. Renew Sust Energ Rev 11(6):1188–1207

Wüstenhagen R, Wolsink M, Bürer MJ (2007) Social acceptance of renewable energy innovation: an introduction to the concept. Energy Policy 35:2683–2691

Wüstenhagen R, Blondiau Y, Ebers A, Salm S (2017) Lowering the financing cost of Swiss renewable energy infrastructure: Reducing the policy risk premium and attracting new investor types. Report SI/501293-01. Swiss Federal Office of Energy. Available at https://www.aramis.admin.ch

Anna Broughel is a senior energy economist at Tetra Tech and an adjunct professor at Johns Hopkins University and at the University of Maryland College Park. Her most recent research reviewed over 120 international energy scenarios for 2040 and beyond, developing scenarios for post-COVID19 energy futures. Prior to joining Tetra Tech, she worked at the U.S. Department of Energy as a Science and Technology Fellow. During her post-doctoral training at the University of St. Gallen in Switzerland, she researched social acceptance of wind energy and other energy technologies. She holds a PhD in economics and policy from the State University of New York in association with Syracuse University, where she was a Fulbright scholar.

Rolf Wüstenhagen University of St. Gallen, Chair for Management of Renewable Energies, St. Gallen, Switzerland.

A Survey of Stakeholders' Views and Practices

Energy Policymaking in Switzerland

Mert Duygan, Aya Kachi, Fintan Oeri, Thiago D. Oliveira, and Adrian Rinscheid

Contents

Abstract Along with policy proposers and individual voters, key stakeholders play a crucial role in shaping the socio-political acceptance of energy policy. Understanding a broad landscape of energy stakeholders' views and practices thus should be a central theme in energy transition research. The Energy Strategy 2050 (ES2050), a sweeping energy transition policy package in Switzerland, was adopted in 2017. Concrete policy goals implied by ES2050 are yet to be implemented. Although there

---

Authors are listed alphabetically.

M. Duygan
University of Basel, Faculty of Business and Economics, Basel, Switzerland

Swiss Federal Institute of Aquatic Science and Technology (Eawag), Department of Environmental Social Sciences, Dübendorf, Switzerland

A. Kachi (✉) · F. Oeri · T. D. Oliveira
University of Basel, Faculty of Business and Economics, Basel, Switzerland
e-mail: aya.kachi@unibas.ch

A. Rinscheid
University of St. Gallen, Institute for Economy and the Environment, St. Gallen, Switzerland

P. Hettich, A. Kachi (eds.), *Swiss Energy Governance*,
https://doi.org/10.1007/978-3-030-80787-0_15

is a large body of social acceptance studies focusing on individual voters, we have a relatively scant empirical understanding of how stakeholders in this domain perceive the policy goals and how perceptions are linked to their organizational characteristics. To elucidate Swiss energy stakeholders' perceptions on key action targets implied by recent energy policies in Switzerland, we analyzed data from our original survey with 364 organizations. We examined their views on concrete policy goals related to electric mobility, deep geothermal energy, wind energy, hydropower, and planned phase-outs of renewable energy subsidies. When asked to rate how realistic these goals appear to them, the majority of the stakeholders responded negatively. Furthermore, our findings indicate that, despite the considerable diversity and the overall pessimism in their feasibility perceptions, those that consider goals to be realistic are more likely to be active in the media. This is a concerning finding as the public might receive a biased impression via the media about the level of consensus among the stakeholders, who could, at times, be seen by the public as experts on the topic.

1 Introduction

A lack of socio-political acceptance poses a hurdle to the pursuit of new energy policies and technologies. Apart from policymakers and individual voters, key stakeholders play a crucial role in shaping socio-political acceptance.[1] Thus, understanding a broad landscape of energy stakeholders' perceptions and practices should be at the core of energy transition research.

In the context of socio-political acceptance, a large body of research has focused on the role of citizens. So-called social acceptance studies investigate determinants of public support for energy technologies, infrastructures, or policy packages.[2] According to these studies, policy support does not only depend on citizens' perceptions and socio-economic statuses but also on characteristics associated with the decision-making process such as fairness and civil society participation.[3] The literature also stresses the role of policy communication, e.g., communication frames and sources of information, as a potential determinant of public support.[4] In this volume, too, there are several important contributions that touch upon the topic of citizens' attitude formation.[5] Understanding voters' preference formation is certainly important as it can directly influence policy outputs through referenda or indirectly

[1] Wüstenhagen et al. (2007).

[2] Gross (2007); Tabi and Wüstenhagen (2017); Blumer et al. (2018); Rinscheid and Wüstenhagen (2019).

[3] Bidwell (2016).

[4] Druckman (2013); Aklin and Urpelainen (2013); Hansla (2011).

[5] Rinscheid and Udris (2021); Schaffer and Levis (2021).

through the electoral pressure that voters exert on politicians' policy stances as the median voter theorem implies.[6]

However, we are all aware that it is not only individual voters' preferences that are reflected in political decisions; there are also other stakeholders. Here, we define energy stakeholders as all actors that have a stake in the public rule-making for the energy system,[7] and in this chapter we specifically focus on actors that represent collective interests. There are numerous examples in energy and climate policymaking in which international and domestic lobbying by industry actors and interest groups have won the policymakers over, when the collective policy preference held by the public seemed to be the opposite of what the powerful stakeholders preferred.

To mention a few examples, the European Union (EU)'s decision in 2011 to include the aviation sector in the EU ETS was foiled by multiple international lobbying efforts despite a relatively high level of public support for the measure.[8] Also in 2011, there was a contentious policy debate in Germany regarding the extension of stipulated lifespans for nuclear reactors. According to an opinion survey, voters were on average against the extension; and yet, the new policy was enacted by the governing coalition due to a small group of powerful stakeholders.[9]

Despite the significant influence of energy stakeholders on policymaking, surprisingly little is known about perceptions and activities of these actors. This is in part due to the inherent difficulty in collecting data on stakeholder characteristics and perceptions of policies held by the stakeholders. This challenge also applies to our understanding of energy policymaking in Switzerland, where the Energy Strategy 2050 (ES2050)—an energy policy directive that requires a fundamental realignment of energy systems—was adopted recently. From the energy governance point of view, this is clearly a deficit both for practitioners and energy researchers.

To elucidate Swiss energy stakeholders' perceptions on key policy targets implied by recent energy policies in Switzerland, we analyze data from our original survey with 364 organizations that have been involved in energy legislation during the past 3 years. We inspect their views on concrete policy goals related to electric mobility, deep geothermal energy, wind energy, hydropower, and planned phase-outs of renewable energy subsidies. We hope the chapter serves as a useful entry point towards future studies on energy stakeholders and their policy influence.

[6]Black (1948); Downs (1957).

[7]Breetz et al. (2018).

[8]Bernauer et al. (2014).

[9]Rinscheid (2015).

2 Energy Policymaking and Stakeholders in Switzerland

In Switzerland, the revised Federal Energy Act, commonly referred to as the Energy Strategy 2050 (ES2050), has been adopted in 2017. ES2050 is a broad energy policy directive aiming to achieve the goals of phasing out nuclear energy and increasing the share of renewable energy.[10] The final decision was made by public vote (referendum) on May 21, 2017. However, the implementation of each measure is expected to face a certain degree of acceptance and coordination challenges among various members of society.

This is why socio-political acceptance, in particular public acceptance, has been one of the key research topics in many branches of the SCCER (Swiss Competence Center for Energy Research) since its outset. SCCER Mobility and SCCER CREST have investigated ways to motivate the use of electric mobility by Swiss citizens. SCCER CREST also has a dedicated work package seeking paths toward effective curtailment of energy consumption based on public opinion panel surveys (Swiss Household Energy Demand Survey (SHEDS)). SCCER CREST and SCCER SoE (Supply of Electricity) have launched a new joint research program investigating public acceptance related to the expansion of hydropower (HP) and the introduction of deep geothermal energy (DGE) as ways to secure the baseload energy supply. All these efforts are meant to contribute to successful implementations of the ES2050, which aims at replacing all of Switzerland's nuclear generating capacity with renewable energy sources. Once again, many of these efforts focus on the determinants of public support for energy policy goals or technologies.

In contrast to the rich volume of studies focusing on citizens, we have a relatively thin understanding of how stakeholders in this domain perceive the various goals implied by the ES2050 scheme. This is what we will investigate in this chapter using our survey with more than 300 energy stakeholders. The adoption of new policies creates economic and ideological "winners" and "losers", which leads stakeholders to hold heterogeneous policy preferences. Wherever they can, these actors mobilize various financial and political resources to attain their policy goals. We must note, however, that their policy preferences do not automatically imply what policy goals they believe to be realistic based on their professional knowledge.

Especially in the case of ES2050 goals, there is a certain ambiguity on this. The policy process went through thorough administrative (consultation) and legislative steps between 2012 and 2017. From this dense process, one might expect that the level of consensus concerning the feasibility of the implied goals is high among the relevant energy stakeholders, who constantly engage with the topic. On the contrary, proponents and opponents of ES2050 used various narratives and evidence during the fierce political campaigns in the weeks leading to the referendum in 2017. There was ample contestation as to whether the policy package was financially too burdensome, whether the Swiss economy would benefit from it, and whether we could secure energy supply without nuclear energy.[11] One might interpret such a

---

[10] Swiss Federal Office of Energy (2018a).

[11] See Rinscheid and Udris (2021).

phenomenon as a consequence of sincerely divided perceptions by stakeholders (with a touch of exacerbation by political campaigners).

Thus, it is useful to inspect, first, whether and to what extent Swiss energy stakeholders' views vary. We answer this question by focusing on five common topics that are linked to Switzerland's energy policy: electric vehicles (EV), deep geothermal energy (DGE), wind energy, renewable energy (RE) subsidies including feed-in tariffs (FITs), and the expansion potential of hydropower (HP). In particular, we are interested in measuring the extent to which the stakeholders perceive the policy goals as realistic. Second, we examine the relationship between the actors' views and their "activeness" in politics and media. From these analyses, we will be able to identify sections of stakeholder topography that would benefit from further coordination efforts by the government in the implementation stage.

3 Empirical Studies on Stakeholder Involvement in Energy Policymaking

Before turning to the survey design, this section will outline how we identified key metrics that characterize energy stakeholders and their activities that are relevant in shaping policies. In doing so, we draw primarily on the political economy literature on lobbying; more concretely, the literature that addresses sources of stakeholders' success in their policy goal preference attainment.

As pointed out by prominent scholars in transitions studies, "consistently proving that special interests affect energy transition policies has turned out to be difficult".[12] For this reason, many existing studies on the politics of energy transitions neither succeed in properly conceptualizing what they aim to explain nor in systematically assessing the factors that make certain actors more politically influential than others. The political influence of stakeholders is often claimed to be captured by campaign spending data or anecdotal evidence. However, actual influence on policy is rarely ascertained and measured empirically in a convincing way.[13] Hence, most empirical studies that address stakeholder influence focus on other aspects, such as stakeholders' strategies (e.g., donations to politicians) and access (e.g., which politicians meet with lobbyists and how often). These might shed light on some of the ways through which actors exert political influence, but they are actually not the measures of influence.[14] One notable exception is a recent study that investigated what configurations of actor endowments (resources, networks, and discursive elements) are critical for their policy influence.[15]

[12] Cherp et al. (2018), p. 181.

[13] Bernhagen et al. (2014).

[14] Mahoney (2007).

[15] Duygan et al. (2021a).

In the remainder of the section, we will summarize how the literature has theorized various determinants of stakeholders' policy influence based on the five broad categories of actor resources that we identified. These are *financial resources*, *organizational capacity resources*, *informational resources*, *conflict capacity resources*, and *network resources*.

Studies using rational choice theory have demonstrated the importance of *financial resources* in conceptualizing lobbying as resource exchange.[16] To influence political outcomes, money can be either spent directly or converted to other forms of useful resources. The motivation of direct spending is to align policymakers' incentives with those of stakeholders through direct financial contributions.[17] Unlike popular views, however, empirical findings are mixed with regard to the link between actors' financial resources and their policy goal attainment.[18]

Stakeholders also differ in their ability to mobilize the motivational and material resources needed to establish effective instruments for the representation of their interests.[19] Intuitively, one might simply suppose that the size of organizations (e.g., the number of employees and branches) has an impact on their ability to organize political interests. However, the literature shows there are more nuanced organizational characteristics that are linked to the effectiveness of stakeholders' policy-related activities. For instance, the type of organizations' membership (individual versus collective) and organizational structure play a role.[20] We broadly categorize these organizational characteristics as *organizational capacity resources*.

Informational resources include both the level of technical knowledge and professionalization efforts. Since organizations can also convert financial resources to other essential resources such as human capital, these resources may be correlated with financial resource endowments (which should be an empirical question). However, the level of informational resources also depends on other factors—for instance, whether the organization actively invests in the professionalization of its staff and how much the organization's expertise is recognized by policymakers for other reasons than its financial resources.[21] This can be measured by the stakeholder's appearance in governmental documents and hearings. Moreover, political intelligence held by the organization can be exchanged for its access to direct interactions with policymakers (inside lobbying) such as in parliamentary committees or advisory boards of regulatory bodies.[22] In addition, organizations may also use informational resources to influence political outcomes through outside lobbying or constituency building, the form of lobbying that aims at the media and the public in the hope of generating support for one's own position.[23]

[16] Stigler (1971).

[17] Hillman and Hitt (1999).

[18] Walker and Rea (2014), p. 286.

[19] Offe and Wiesenthal (1980).

[20] Dür (2008).

[21] Hall and Deardorff (2006).

[22] Binderkrantz and Pedersen (2017).

[23] Kollman (1998); Weiler and Brändli (2015).

Vote-seeking politicians are generally concerned about their (re-)election probability, which depends on the employment rate, voters' personal income, and the government's ability to use tax revenues for the provision of public services. Therefore, some states are structurally dependent on private sector profitability and this leads certain industries and groups (e.g., the coal industry in Australia) to exercise influence on policymaking via their implicit *conflict capacity* against the state.[24]

Finally, the effectiveness of actor-specific resources in influencing policies can be amplified or suppressed by how the actors are embedded (e.g., the strategic or given position) in a network of multiple stakeholders.[25] Empirical studies confirm that well-connected stakeholders that collaborate with influential actors exercise disproportionate influence on political outcomes compared to less well-connected actors with a similar endowment.[26] Conceptually, we categorize various measures of actors' network embeddedness in *network resources*.

4 Methodology

To create measures for stakeholder resources that characterize their policy-related practices, we designed and implemented an original survey with organizations that are active in the energy policy domain in Switzerland. This section elaborates on the data collection methodology.

4.1 Who Are Swiss Energy Stakeholders?

The first question that arises upon designing such a study is the selection of relevant energy stakeholders in Switzerland. Hence, our empirical work starts with defining the targeted population in order to construct our sample for the analysis. Conceptually, stakeholders are all actors that have a stake in the public rule-making for the energy system.[27] To reiterate, our aim is to analyze perceptions, activities, and actors' resources that represent collective interest. Our target group therefore is not individual voters but organizational actors such as political parties, cantonal administrations, business associations, and other organizations.

The target population was determined using participation lists of federal consultation processes on Swiss energy legislation. In addition to the fundamental realignment of Swiss energy policy (ES2050) and its consultation process

[24] Levy and Egan (1998), p. 342; Stutzer et al. (2021).

[25] Hacker and Pierson (2014); Varone et al. (2016).

[26] Box-Steffensmeier et al. (2013); Baumgartner et al. (2011).

[27] Breetz et al. (2018).

from 2012 to 2013, we included the three arguably most relevant energy-related bills since 2016: *Klimapolitik*, *ES2050 Ordinance*, and *StromVG*.[28] After dropping individuals[29] and accounting for overlaps between consultations, the target group for our data collection comprised 740 organizations.

Although our aim was to approach all 740 organizations we defined as the population, identifying their contact information was anything but trivial. We were not able to contact 60 organizations from the initial sample, either because they no longer existed or because their contact details were unobtainable. This led us to invite 680 organizations to participate in our survey.

4.2 Survey Data Collection and Sample Characteristics

We designed and fielded an original survey in order to collect information on the characteristics, activities, and resources of stakeholders in Swiss energy policy. The pilot wave was launched in April 2019 and the main survey was fielded between May and September 2019. We communicated with the participants in German or French, depending on their contact information, and the participants were able to choose the survey language from German, French, and English.[30]

We conducted the pilot survey with 38 organizations, most of which were environmental NGOs and cantonal offices. After receiving their feedback, the set of included survey items remained unchanged for the main wave except for three items that were dropped after the pilot study.[31] This amounts to a total of 42 survey items. After minor adjustments in the wording and the order of several items, the main wave was launched with the remaining 642 organizations. Combining the pilot and main wave, we reached out to 680 organizations.

---

[28] *Klimapolitik*: A consultation on Switzerland's climate policy from 2016. This included the ratification of the Paris treaty as well as the revision of the CO_2 law.

ES2050 Ordinance: A consultation on the revision of 11 existing or newly introduced ordinances resulting from the first set of measures of ES2050 from 2017. The ordinance set detailed provisions in the context of the implementation of ES2050.

StromVG: A consultation on the revision of the Federal Electricity Supply Act from 2018. The revision aimed at completing the liberalization of the market by introducing the right to freely choose electricity suppliers also for small-scale consumers and households. Concurrently, it introduced measures that incentivize investments in domestic renewable energy in order to strengthen Switzerland's supply security.

[29] Note that individuals can also submit their opinions during consultation processes.

[30] Among the four official national languages of Switzerland, German and French are dominant in the political arena.

[31] The dropped items were on the number of business units occupied with political work, bill-specific lobbying behavior and resource allocation. They covered previously assessed concepts in a narrower context. After evaluating the survey length and the value-added of responses to these items, we decided to drop them.

Surveys with stakeholders are fundamentally different from surveys with individual citizens which are often used in public opinion studies in that responses require the organizations', not specific individuals', professional viewpoints. We made every effort to make the procedure transparent, and our survey was directed to people close to the competency of energy policy in order to avoid excessive communication within their organizations. To this end, we first sent personalized invitation letters with a fact sheet on the project and informed potential participants about the request to participate. Unless contact details were insufficient, no immediate action by the recipient was required. Ten days later, we emailed them personalized online survey links asking them to complete the survey within 16 days.[32]

After the online survey "deadline", all 463 organizations which had not explicitly indicated that they were not interested in participating and had not yet completed the survey were contacted again. This time we contacted them by mail with a printed survey along with a short reminder letter and a prepaid return envelope.[33] Respondents were able to choose between responding via the original online survey link or the hardcopy.

Among the 680 organizations that we contacted, we received 364 responses. This is a remarkably high response rate of 53.5% for a stakeholder survey. About 33% of the respondents completed the survey after our reminder by mail via the hardcopy survey. Our sample mirrors the population of energy stakeholders well with respect to their organization types (Fig. 1). Our sample consists of energy businesses (30%), business associations (23%), non-business associations (23%), cantonal administrations (6%), other businesses, municipalities, and communal/cantonal associations (4% each), and political parties and educational institutions (3% each).

4.3 Survey Flow

Figure 2 summarizes the survey flow. The heterogeneous sample required the use of two different versions of the survey. Given their unique organizational form and tasks, cantonal administrations completed a version in which two items had been adapted: (i) the term "your organization" was explicitly associated with the office the respondent was working for instead of the entire cantonal administration; (ii) the item asking about the number of employees following political events was adapted to cover energy policy events only. However, the survey *flow* remained the same for all types of participants.

Between *Welcome* and *Final Block* are seven substantive survey blocks. The welcome page clarifies that the data will be used only for research purposes and the

[32] The online survey was implemented with the survey software Qualtrics.

[33] It was typeset in LaTeX and compiled using SDAPS, an optical mark recognition program. While minor wording changes regarding survey instruction were necessary to account for the different format, no content-related changes were made. The document amounted to 14 pages.

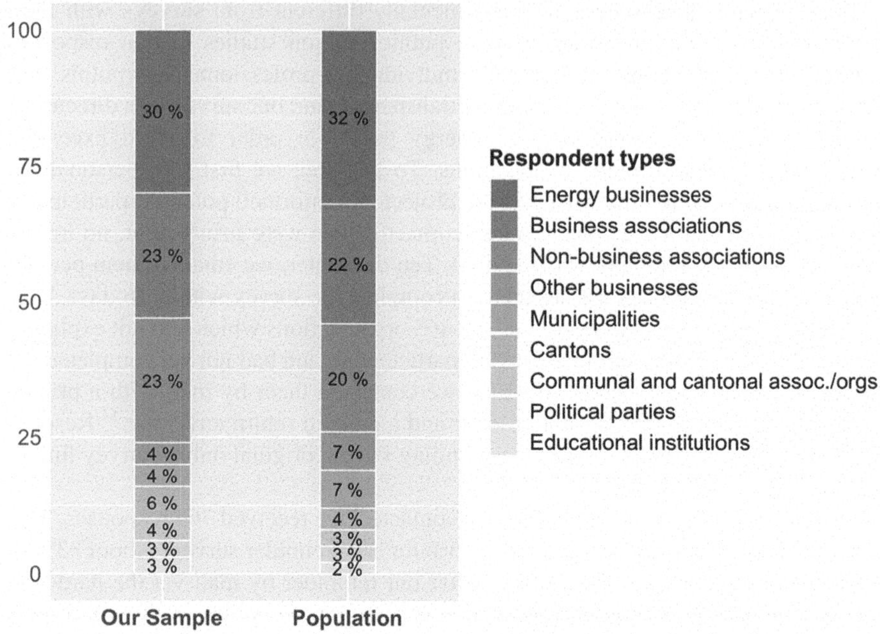

Fig. 1 Types of participating organizations ($N = 364$): Comparison with the population of Swiss energy stakeholders

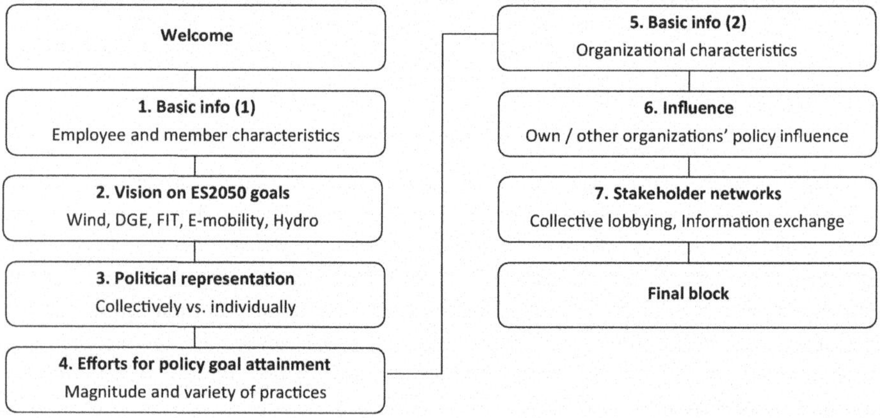

Fig. 2 Survey flow

results will be anonymized. Once respondents agree to participate, they answer questions on their organization's basic information. This block focuses on employee characteristics such as average age, education attainment, and opportunities for personnel development trainings. These questions are followed by a section that probes the organization's vision on various energy policy goals. Specifically, we ask whether the following goals associated with the recent energy policies look realistic from their professional point of view: new wind turbine installation, power generation capacity by deep geothermal energy, the role of feed-in tariffs, the share of electric mobility, and the expansion of hydropower generation capacity.

Next, we turn to practices employed by the organizations. In the fourth block on political representation of interests, we ask if the organization tends to take actions related to political representation alone or collectively (with other organizations) and if such collaborations come with a certain degree of adjustments ("costs") in their political goals. The fifth block, "4. *Efforts for policy goal attainment*", expands on related topics, focusing on the type and level of efforts exerted to follow political events or to attain policy goals. Key aspects covered in the subsequent block, "5. *Basic info (2)*," are the main fields of activities (e.g., sectors and types of energy production technologies), the organizational structure, and the budget.

The last two survey blocks ("6. *Influence*" and "7. *Stakeholder networks*") pose various questions about the positioning of the organization within the energy policy arena in Switzerland. First, we probe the participants' perceptions about other organizations' influence on policymaking in Switzerland as well as their assessment of their own influence on policy. Finally, we collect data on Swiss energy stakeholder networks—namely, with which other organizations the participant collaborates and/or exchanges information. The survey ends with an item asking whether the participating organization would like to receive a report based on the data. If so, then the participant should provide his or her email address. See Table 3 for the list of survey items.

5 Results

5.1 Diversity of Stakeholder Perceptions About the ES2050 Policy Targets

In this section, we inspect the Swiss energy stakeholders' views on five common topics that are linked to recent energy policies: electric vehicles (EV), deep geothermal energy (DGE), wind energy, renewable energy (RE) subsidies including feed-in tariffs (FITs), and the expansion potential of hydropower (HP). The following policy goals implied by ES2050 (Table 1) have been some of the focal points in the current policy debate.

5.1.1 Challenges Associated with the ES2050 Targets

We asked each participant to rate, all things considered, how realistic these targets are from the *organization's* point of view. Independently from their views on the feasibility, we also asked what the primary challenges associated with each goal are.

Table 1 Goals in five energy sub-domains of Swiss energy policy

EV	The share of electric vehicles of newly registered cars ought to reach 15% in 2022.[a]
DGE	Deep geothermal energy (DGE) is a viable option to produce baseload electricity. A substantial increase in electricity generation capacity by DGE should be considered.[b]
WIND	Around 800-900 wind turbines need to be constructed in Switzerland by 2050.[c]
RE	Feed-in tariffs for renewable energies will be phased out in 2022, and investment contributions and one-time payments will be phased out in 2030.[d]
HP—We asked about 4 detailed points. Hydropower is a viable option to produce baseload electricity. Potential measures to expand HP capacity in Switzerland are:	
...By new pumped storage.	
...By new small hydropower plants.	
...By expansion of existing plants.	
...By modernization of existing plants.	

[a]See Swiss Federal Office of Energy (2018b)
[b]Bauer et al. (2017)
[c]See also suisse éole (2017), p. 2; Stalder (2017); Morf (2020) for various estimates
[d]See Swiss Federal Office of Energy (2017), pp. 2–3; Swiss Federal Office of Energy (2018a), p. 12

They were able to choose as many types of challenges as they wanted from the provided list.

The question about the associated challenges mostly confirmed what we already knew from previous policy debates and research. As for EV, more than half of the respondents mentioned "weak infrastructure for electric vehicles" as a barrier and nearly a third mentioned "technological maturity", "high investment costs", "information deficits of consumers", and "low acceptance of EV by consumers". Power generation by DGE is currently only in a pilot and development phase (although heating by geothermal energy has been in use); however, two cities in Switzerland (Basel and St. Gallen) had their pilot projects halted due to seismic events caused by exploratory drilling.[34] The responses regarding DGE reflected these episodes—"seismic risks" (63%), "opposition by citizens" (54%), and "high investment costs" (49%) were mentioned by many respondents.

Hydropower (HP) is also considered to be a potential clean source of the baseload energy supply. HP has long been a major energy source in Switzerland and currently produces approximately 60% of all domestic energy. Here, the main debate is whether an expansion of current power generating capacity by any of the four methods mentioned in Table 1 is feasible. The result confirms previous research that the opposition by interest groups (mainly environmental NGOs) is the largest barrier (mentioned by 74% of the participants).

Turning to the goals related to the so-called new renewables, the biggest challenges associated with a major installation of wind turbines are the opposition by citizens and by interest groups; more than 80% of respondents mentioned these two.

[34]Ejderyan et al. (2019).

This mirrors Ebers Broughel and Wüstenhagen's contribution (in this volume) that emphasizes opposition by the local population or other stakeholders as an important factor that can lead to prohibitively high administrative risks in the implementation of wind power projects.[35] Finally, we asked what options should be considered to support the expansion of RE in Switzerland against the backdrop that phase-outs of some of the RE subsidies are planned by 2022 and some more by 2030. Half of the respondents are in favor of an extension of FITs after 2022 and nearly 40% of them are in favor of new market premium models after 2022.

5.1.2 Divergent Views on Feasibility

So far, on the aggregate level, our findings merely confirm mainstream views on the barriers linked to each subdomain. What is more intriguing is how divided the energy stakeholders' ratings are with regard to the feasibility of each goal. We asked whether each target summarized in Table 1 looked *realistic* from the organization's point of view. They could choose their responses from a Likert scale of *completely unrealistic*, *rather unrealistic*, *rather realistic*, *and completely realistic*. For the item on FITs and other subsidies, the question was phrased as "All things considered at this moment, from your organization's point of view, *do you think it is realistic that the targets of the Energy Strategy 2050 will be attained in this policy environment*?"

From Figs. 3 and 4, one can clearly see that the stakeholders' views are divided on many of the policy targets. When it comes to EV, the majority of them consider the target to be achievable; and yet, there are still 45% of them perceiving otherwise. There is a commonly held impression that DGE in Switzerland carries a negative legacy from the two cancelled pilot projects in Basel and St. Gallen due to seismic events. However, 38% of energy stakeholders consider this goal realistic, which is much higher than the proportion of respondents who think that wind turbine installations and the RE promotion under the planned phase-outs of RE subsidies are feasible. It is particularly noteworthy that those who hold negative perceptions about the feasibility of a large-scale wind energy installation have a strong view—more than 25% responded "*completely* unrealistic". Overall, a relatively pessimistic picture looms out of Fig. 3—the majority of Swiss energy stakeholders perceive the policy targets as unrealistic.

As for HP, we asked more nuanced questions based on on-going debates. Given the gradual phase-out plan of nuclear energy, HP is considered as one of the clean energy sources that could contribute to a stable baseload. In this context, an expansion of HP generation capacity is currently considered. At the same time, there is a wide-spread view that Switzerland has exhausted potential sites for HP facilities. Against this backdrop, it is rather surprising that around 50% of the participants consider the construction of new plants to be realistic. Capacity

[35] Ebers Broughel and Wüstenhagen (2021).

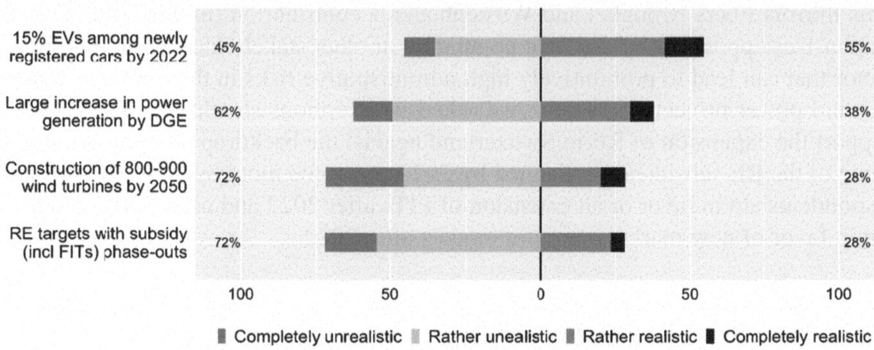

Fig. 3 "All things considered at this moment, from your organization's point of view, does this target look realistic or unrealistic?" (N = 303)

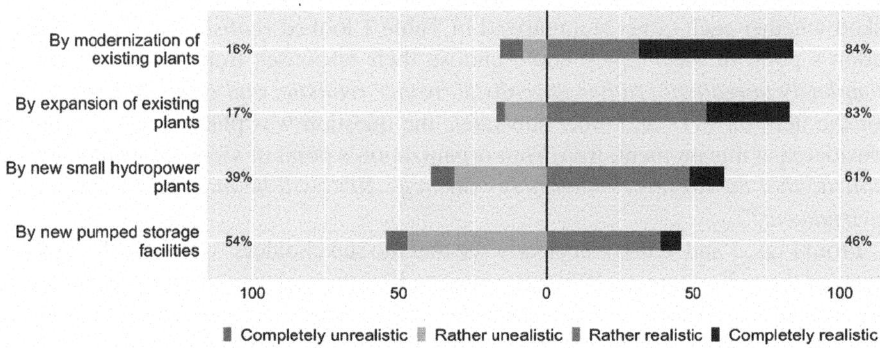

Fig. 4 "Hydropower represents an important part of the Swiss electricity generation mix. All things considered at this moment, does your organization consider the following measures to expand HP capacity in Switzerland to be realistic?" (N = 304)

expansion of existing facilities is considered to be realistic by more than 80% of the organizations.

5.2 *Diversity in Fields of Activity and Practices Related to Policy Goal Attainment*

Needless to say, these actors are diverse with respect to their fields of activity as well as their organizational characteristics. This section will give a glimpse on these aspects. According to our survey, at some point during the last 10 years 126 organizations have been active in the field related to HP, 119 in transport or mobility, 89 in wind, 54 in DGE, and 50 in nuclear. (The activity fields are not mutually exclusive.)

In the context of political influence, we should also pay attention to how active these organizations are in politics and the mediasphere. These two arenas of stakeholder activities relate to what political economists often label as inside and outside lobbying. The former refers to actors' efforts for policy goal attainment exerted directly on policymakers, and the latter includes various channels outside of the government (such as media) through which actors mobilize the public in a way that creates electoral pressure in favor of their own policy preferences.

We assess the level of political activeness by aggregating survey items that probe whether the organization has undertaken the following seven practices over the last 10 years: (i) definition of a political strategy regarding specific legislation, (ii) communication of information and political views to policymakers/administration, (iii) informal exchange with politicians, (iv) accessing non-public parts of the national parliament building ("*Wandelhalle*"), (v) participation in hearings of parliamentary commissions, (vi) participation in an official expert group to draft new legislation, and (vii) preparation and publication of political opinions and position papers. This composite index may not capture certain nuances. For instance, it measures neither the intensity nor the salience of *each* practice directly[36]. However, it certainly serves as a proxy for the organization's political engagement by the breadth of the activities. The distribution of the level of political engagement in our sample has a relatively clean bell-shaped curve with a slight skew to the left. On average, organizations have employed 4.22 practices out of the seven that were mentioned above with a standard deviation of 1.8. 42 organizations demonstrated a very high level of activity by engaging in all 7 activities. Interestingly, the mean level of political activeness remains nearly the same when stakeholders that are active in the mobility, DGE, wind, and HP domain are considered separately.

To measure the stakeholders' media-related activities, we used two items that ask if the organization has pursued (i) an active involvement in media debates, including opinion articles or interviews in print media, radio, television, and (ii) communication with the public via digital media such as Facebook, Instagram, Twitter, etc. Here, the responses were even more dispersed. 122 organizations engaged in none of the media-related activities, 94 in only one type of the activities, and 96 in both. Once again, there is no significant difference in this distribution when respondents that are active in the five subdomains are analyzed separately.

Finally, in the context of stakeholders' efforts for policy goal attainment, one might associate their policy influence with the level of financial resources held by the organizations. Such an inferential analysis is beyond the scope of the present chapter; however, it might be useful to note that here, too, variation is large. Figure 5 plots the distribution of the total annual budget of the organizations (top) and their budgets for political purposes (bottom). In political purposes we include political advocacy, information brokerage, and campaign financing.

---

[36]It might not capture the scope of competence in which actors engage in these practices either (Duygan et al. 2021b).

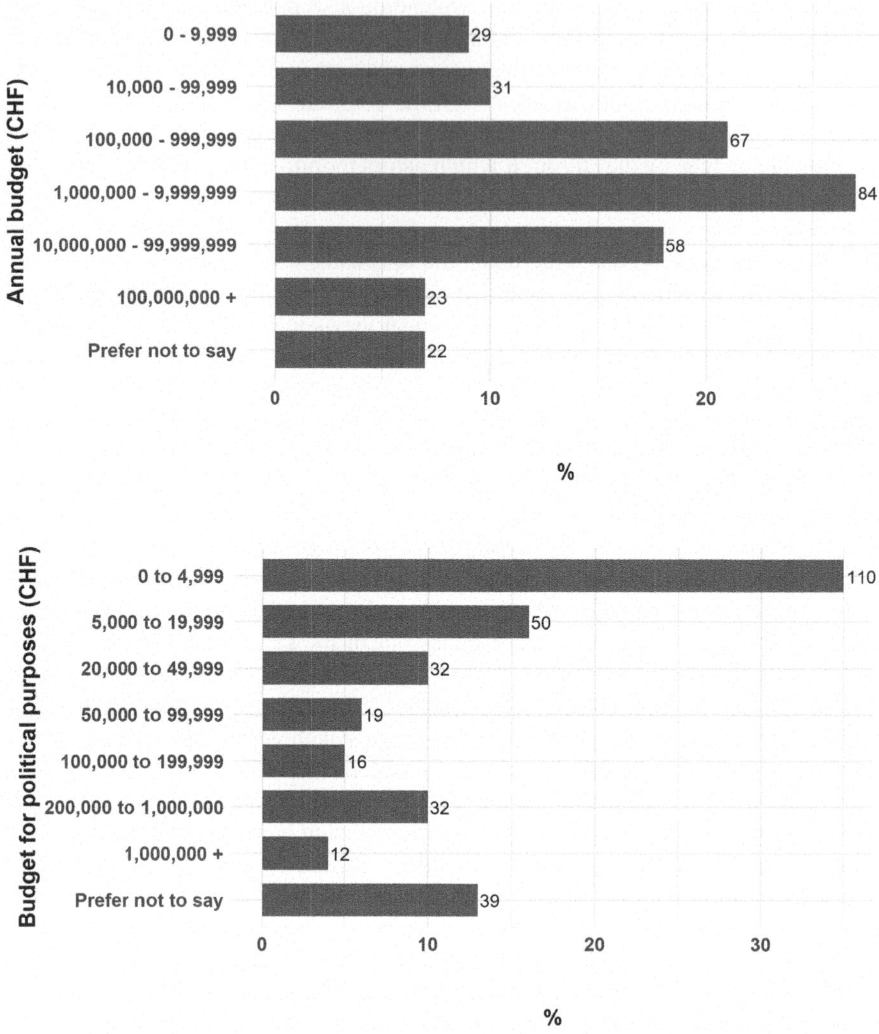

Fig. 5 Size of the budget of Swiss energy stakeholders: Total annual budget and budget for political purposes (N = 312)

5.3 *What Types of Stakeholders Perceive ES2050 Goals as More Realistic?*

Naturally, all these observations make us wonder what explains the dramatic diversity in the stakeholders' feasibility perceptions. Are there systematic patterns in the type of actors that view a certain policy target as more realistic than others? The question deserves more thorough investigations in the future; here we will highlight a

Table 2 Odds ratios from a logistic regression on each policy target

Dependent variable	EV	DGE	Wind
Active in the area of transport/mobility last 10 yrs	0.85		
Active in the area of DGE last 10 yrs		1.02	
Active in the area of wind energy last 10 yrs			0.59*
Active in the area of nuclear energy last 10 yrs	0.75	0.95	1.24
Activeness in politics	0.98	1.04	0.92
Activeness in media	1.46*	1.36*	1.50*
Technical aspects as challenges	0.42*	1.33*	0.42*
Voters, consumers, interest groups as challenges	0.82	1.05	1.14
Regulatory risks as challenges	0.86	1.27	0.87

Dependent variable (HP)	Modernization	Expansion	Small HP	Pump storage
Active in the area of HP energy last 10 yrs	0.92	0.89	0.64	0.97
Active in the area of nuclear energy last 10 yrs	1.21	2.33*	1.65	0.62
Activeness in politics	1.01	1.03	0.90	0.99
Activeness in media	0.93	0.68*	1.19	1.24
Technical aspects as challenges	2.04*	1.23	1.77*	0.83
Voters, interest groups as challenges	2.13*	1.72*	1.40	1.34
Regulatory risks as challenges	0.82	0.63	0.93	1.21

*Statistically significant estimates at the 95% confidence level

few interesting findings from our first-cut analyses. We devote this final section to reporting our first insights.

We answer these questions by studying the correlations between some of the stakeholders' characteristics and their feasibility views that are summarized in Figs. 3 and 4. More concretely, we focus on whether the organizations' feasibility assessment is linked to (1) their being active in the related energy subdomain (e.g., wind, HP, etc.), (2) how engaged they are in politics, (3) how active they are in media, and (4) what types of challenges they flagged for the policy goal in question. We categorized various challenges that the respondents marked into three groups: technological challenges (including construction and operational costs), risks associated with opposition (including voters and interest groups),[37] and regulatory risks. A measure for being active in the nuclear energy domain was also included as an additional control. The dependent variable, feasibility assessment, is a 4-point Likert scale from completely unrealistic (coded as 1) to completely realistic (coded as 4).

We estimated the correlations by running an ordered logistic regression for each of the ES2050 policy targets listed in Table 1, except for the RE subsidy goal. Table 2 summarizes the results as estimated odds ratios for each covariate. Each column represents regression results for a specific policy target.

[37] In the analysis for EV, we included information deficits by consumers in this category.

It turns out that being active in the sub-domain in question does not necessarily lead the actors to similar views on target feasibility. Only for the case of wind energy, being active in this domain systematically makes them think that the target is less realistic compared to those outside of the field.[38] The organization's perceptions on feasibility are not systematically linked to their level of political engagement. However, those that are more active in the mediasphere are 1.36–1.50 times more likely to respond that the EV, DGE, and wind energy target is realistic.

One might also ask whether the organization's attention to a certain type of challenge is more strongly linked to their feasibility assessment of the policy targets. Interestingly, our results suggest that stakeholders might acknowledge the possibility of facing opposition and regulatory risks, but these assessments do not systematically lead them to claim that the target is realistic or unrealistic. On the contrary, their assessment of technical challenges seems more directly linked to their feasibility assessment. However, as for DGE and HP, those that recognize greater technical challenges are the stakeholders that tend to claim that the policy target in question is *more* realistic.

One finding that stands out is the perception of an HP target. With regard to the question of whether HP generation capacity can be enhanced by expanding existing facilities, actors in the nuclear energy domain are 2.3 times more likely to claim that the goal is realistic. Similarly, those that recognize civil-society opposition groups as a challenge are more likely to consider the goal realistic.

6 Discussion

This chapter has illustrated some of the initial findings from a large-scale energy stakeholder survey in Switzerland ($N = 364$). Compared to public opinion surveys, recreuitment of participants into surveys with professional organizations is in general more challenging. In this sense, the survey data we presented here might serve as a reasonable entry point for practitioners and researchers who are interested in conducting systematic analyses on the complex links between energy policymaking and the influence of relevant stakeholders.

The discussion on the Energy Strategy 2050 began in 2011 and the policy was finally adopted after the referendum in 2017. As studies on social (voter) acceptance of energy policy goals flourish, we have seen an increasing number of insightful opinion surveys and survey experiments with population-representative samples that can identify sources of acceptance. However, we are yet to gain a *systematic* understanding about the landscape of energy stakeholders' views and activities around these goals. From the *energy governance* point of view, this is a clear deficit both for practitioners and energy researchers, as a more comprehensive understanding of the socio-political acceptance of the ES2050 and its various

[38] More specifically, for those active in the wind energy field, the odds of being more likely to say that the target is realistic are 40% lower.

implications may help address policy risks that could inhibit the realization of its goals proactively.[39]

In this chapter, we addressed this gap between different sides of socio-political acceptance by illustrating the diversity of energy stakeholders' perceptions. For multiple key policy goals associated with ES2050, we investigated how realistic the actors perceived them to be. It is quite astonishing that there was no consensus about the goal feasibility for any of the ES2050 policy goals. Moreover, on the aggregate level, the sentiment is pessimistic—there are more actors who perceive the goals to be unrealistic than those who perceive them as realistic. Given this sentiment, it also makes sense that the majority of stakeholders are in favor of extending renewable energy subsidies (or similar market incentives) after 2022 when the current incentives are planned to end.

However, it was challenging to pinpoint what types of actors (or what actor characteristics) are behind the polarizing views on target feasibility. Our survey data reveal that, for the most part, being active in the same energy subdomain does not always make the actors see the feasibility in a similar way, implying that divergent views do not only exist on the aggregate level but also within the sector. Most of the surveyed organizations actively engage in multiple practices to represent their political interests, too. Again, the degree of political activeness was not systematically linked to their feasibility perceptions either on the optimistic or the pessimistic side, implying that coordination efforts by policymakers are required at every end of the stakeholders' attitude spectrum.

One concerning element of our findings is that, despite the high level of diversity and the overall pessimistic views on policy goal feasibility, those that perceive the goals to be realistic are more likely to undertake media-related strategies at the same time. The public might receive a biased impression about the level of consensus among the stakeholders. A more detailed classification of the sources of divergent stakeholder views seems to be a fruitful avenue for future research. A systematic investigation of stakeholders' views and perceptions, as conducted in this study, may also allow us to strengthen integrative efforts further. A good example along this line might be the "Energy Transition Preparedness Index" proposed by Bürer et al.:[40] They highlight crucial elements of the energy-society system area that determines the pace of implementing energy system change.

Given that there is already a set of defined policy goals under the Energy Strategy 2050, perhaps one of the biggest challenges for politicians and the Federal Administration during the next years is to come up with effective modes of communication with their own citizens that help them make sense of the divergent feasibility perceptions that appear to exist "even" among the actors who are involved in energy topics on a daily-basis. This is indeed a hefty task for the government. Such communication by the government needs to be *transparent* to citizens, *fair* to diverse stakeholders, and *neutral* given its public function in order to make sure that the government is not mistaken as a user of manipulative narratives.

---

[39] Ebers Broughel and Wüstenhagen (2021).

[40] Bürer et al. (2021).

Table 3 List of items included in the Survey "*Diversity of Swiss Energy Stakeholders*" (June 2019)

Item	*Question*
Welcome	
	Welcome and thank you for your participation...
1. Basic information (1)	
	In the first part we would like to ask you some questions about the employees and, if applicable, about members of your organization. If you do not know the exact answers, we ask you to estimate as accurately as possible.
Q5	How many paid employees does your organization have? Please provide your details in full-time equivalents. If you do not know the exact number, please guess.
Q254	How many **unpaid** employees does your organization have? Please provide your details in full-time equivalents. If you do not know the exact number, please guess.
Q6	How old are the employees of your organization on average? If you do not know the answer, please guess.
Q7	What is the proportion of employees in your organization who have obtained a university degree? If you do not know the answer, please guess.
Q8	How often do employees of your organization participate in multi-day personnel development activities on average (e.g., internal training, professional development, executive education)? If you do not know the answer, please guess.
Q10	So-called "member organizations" can have both individuals (e.g., in the case of political parties) and/or other organizations (e.g., in the case of associations) as members. In non-member organizations (e.g., companies) there are no members, only employees or involved parties. How many members of each type does your organization have? Please choose one entry for **each** member type. In both drop down lists, there is also the option "None". If you do not know the exact numbers, please guess. (Matrix Question)
2. Vision on ES2050 goals	
Q19	According to the Energy Strategy 2050, around 800–900 **wind turbines** need to be constructed in Switzerland by 2050. All things considered at this moment, from your organization's point of view, does this target look realistic or unrealistic?
Q20	Regardless of your answer above, which of the following do you see as the biggest challenges to achieve this goal? (multiple answers possible)
Q22	According to the Energy Strategy 2050, deep geothermal energy (DGE) is a viable option to produce baseload electricity. All things considered at this moment, from your organization's point of view, does a substantial increase in **electricity generation capacity by DGE** look realistic or more unrealistic?
Q23	Regardless of your answer above, which of the following do you see as the biggest challenges for an increase of deep geothermal energy? (multiple answers possible)
Q25	According to the Energy Strategy 2050, feed-in tariffs for renewable energies will be phased out in 2022, and investment contributions and one-time payments will be phased out in 2030. All things considered at this moment, from your organization's point of view, do you think it is realistic that **the targets of the Energy Strategy 2050 will be attained in this policy environment**?
Q26	Regardless of your answer above, which of the following options should be considered to support the expansion of renewable energies in Switzerland? (multiple answers possible)
Q28	According to the recently published roadmap for the promotion of **electric mobility**, the share of electric vehicles of newly registered cars ought to reach 15 percent in 2022. All things considered at this moment, from your organization's point of view, does this target look realistic or unrealistic?

(continued)

Table 3 (continued)

Item	*Question*
Q29	Regardless of your answer above, which of the following do you see as the biggest challenges to reach this goal? (multiple answers possible)
Q31	Hydropower represents an important part of the Swiss electricity generation mix. All things considered at this moment, does your organization consider the following measures to expand **HP capacity in Switzerland** to be realistic? (please answer for each measure: By new pumped storage, by new small hydropower plants, by expansion of existing plants, by modernization of existing plants.) (Matrix Question)
Q32	Regardless of your answer above, which of the following do you see as the biggest challenges for the expansion of hydropower generation capacity? (multiple answers possible)
3. Political representation of interests—Collectively or individually	
	This block addresses the topic of political representation of interests. It can occur in different forms. We speak of interest representation as a collective when two or more actors agree on political positions and represent them together. This **does not** preclude a **simultaneous** representation of interests **as an individual organization**, without collusion with others. (by definition, membership organizations always act collectively. So here, interest representation as a collective is defined as activities conducted with other organizations that are **not members of your organization**. On the other hand, representing interests as a single organization means that there is no consultation with organizations that are not members of your organization.)
Q35	When you think about **Swiss energy policy in general**: has your organization undertaken the following activities as a collective **and/or** as an individual organization over the last 10 years? *(1) Definition of a political strategy regarding specific legislation. (2) Communication of information and political views to policy makers and/or administration. (3) Financial support of politicians. (4) Funding of institutions (e.g., political committees, parties) and/or activities (e.g., research). (5) Thematization in the public sphere (e.g., media contributions, signatures collection)* (Matrix Question)
Q36	To what extent do you agree or disagree with the following statement? *In Swiss energy policy, our organization is, in principle, willing to adjust its political demands, if this is necessary to enable collaboration with other organizations.*
Q38	To what extent do you agree or disagree with the following statement with regard to the **policy process of the ES2050**? *My organization would have had to adapt its political demands to be able to cooperate (more closely) with other organizations.*
4. Efforts for policy goal attainment	
	The following part of the questionnaire deals with the question of how your organization perceives its opportunities to represent its interests.
Q48	How important is political interest representation for your organization?
Q50	Please think about a typical legislative process of national energy policy, which **concludes in a referendum**. What proportion of time and financial resources does your organization devote to different phases within such a legislative process? Please select the shares so they add up to a total of 100%.
Q51	Is your organization competing with other organizations to recruit new members, raise income through donations, or secure funding?
Q52	Has your organization pursued the following activities during the last 10 years? (Multiple answers possible) *(1) Informal exchange with politicians. (2) Mandating other organizations or experts to follow the political events or actively represent interests of the organization. (3) Accessing non-public parts of the national parliament building*

(continued)

Table 3 (continued)

Item	*Question*
	(Wandelhalle). (4) Participation in hearings of parliamentary commissions. (5) Participation in an official working/expert group to draft new legislation. (6) Preparation and publication of political opinions and position papers. (7) Financing or conducting research. (8) Active involvement in media debates (e.g., opinion articles or interviews in print media, radio, television, etc.). (9) Communication with the public via digital media (e.g., Facebook, Instagram, Twitter, etc.). (10) Organization of expert conferences and/or public debates. (11) Funding of political advertising. (12) Funding and/or collection of signatures. (13) Demonstration call. (14) Other
Q53	Please indicate how many employees in your organization are commissioned to follow political events in general (not only energy specific) or actively represent interests of the organization (in full-time equivalents). If you do not know the exact answer, we ask you to estimate as accurately as possible.
5. Basic information (2)	
	In the following penultimate part we ask you to answer a few questions about your organization in general.
Q56	During the last 10 years, in which areas was your organization at least at some point active? *(1) Hydropower. (2) Nuclear energy. (3) Solar energy. (4) Wind energy. (5) Deep geothermal energy. (6) Other energy production. (7) Energy efficiency. (8) Trade of electricity. (9) Natural science research on energy. (10) Economic modeling research on Energy. (11) Social science research on energy. (12) Consumer information. (13) Transport/mobility. (14) International economic cooperation and development. (15) Other* (Multiple answers possible.)
Q57	In which year was your organization founded?
Q58	How many regional/local branches does your organization have?
Q60	Do representatives of these local branches have a say in your organization's policy stance on issues of national interest, such as the ES2050?* (*This question is shown if the response category (1) of Q58 was **not** selected.)
Q61	Organizations can make decisions in different ways, such as unanimity among members or board members, or other voting procedures. Please indicate what kind of decision-making is **mainly** used for important decisions in your organization.
Q62	What sources of funding are relevant to your organization? (Multiple answers possible)
Q63	What is the annual budget of your organization? If you do not know the answer, please guess.
Q65	You have clicked that you do not want to provide any details about the annual budget of your organization. We would like to point out once again that your information is treated absolutely confidentially and in publications conclusions with regard to your organization are in no way possible.By clicking on your budget category, you would provide information that is central to our research results. Of course, if you do not want to provide any information, we respect this.* (*This question is shown if the response category of Q63 = (9999))
Q66	What is the annual budget of your organization for political purposes (e.g., for political advocacy, information brokerage, campaign financing, etc.)? If you do not know the answer, please guess.
Q68	You have clicked that you do not want to provide any information about your organization's annual political budget. We would like to point out once again that your information is treated absolutely confidentially and in publications conclusions with regard to your organization are in no way possible.

(continued)

Table 3 (continued)

Item	*Question*
	By clicking on your budget category, you would provide information that is central to our research results. Of course, if you do not want to provide any information, we respect this. * (*This question is shown if the response category of Q66 = (9999))
Q69	What position do you hold in your organization?
Q70	How many years have you been working for your organization?
6. Influence	
Q12	The final questions relate to your organization in the context of Swiss energy policy. In the following, reference will always be made to other organizations. The term "organization" refers to all types of stakeholders in energy policy, such as energy companies, NGOs, political parties, umbrella organizations or even cantons and municipalities.
Q13	Please list those organizations that you consider to be **influential** in **Swiss energy policy** of the last 10 years. Please also list your own organization or individual members, if you count them among the influential organizations. (You can list as many organizations as you want. Additional text entry boxes will automatically appear. The order does not matter.)
Q14	Listed are the organizations you mentioned that have influence on Swiss energy policy. Please choose the **most influential** organizations; on the one hand, with respect to **Swiss energy policy in general** and on the other hand, with respect to the **Energy Strategy 2050 (ES2050) specifically**. In both cases you can choose **up to five** organizations; however, it is also possible to choose fewer.Energy strategy 2050 refers to new Energy Act, which was drafted by the Federal Council in 2011/2012 and submitted to consultation at the end of 2012. Between 2013 and 2016, the parliament discussed the law and the Swiss electorate approved it in 2017. *(Carry Forward Entered Choices—Entered text from "Q13")* (Matrix Question)
Q16	Please assess the influence of your organization on Swiss energy policy.
7. Stakeholder networks	
Q42	As a reminder, collective representation of interests is defined as activities in which two or more actors agree on political positions, which are represented in consultation with each other. Please list those organizations with which your organization has represented its interests collectively in **legislative processes of Swiss energy policy** over the last 10 years. (You can list as many organizations as you want. Additional text entry boxes will automatically appear. Please list only those partners who are not members of your organization. The order does not matter.)
Q44	Scientific, technical and political information plays an important role in energy policy. With which organization do you **exchange such information** with respect to the Swiss energy policy of the last 10 years? Below you can find those organizations with which your organization has represented interests in the collective in the past. Please **indicate** those organizations in the list with which you not only represented interests collectively but **also exchanged information.** *(Carry Forward Entered Choices—Entered text from "Q42")*
Q45	However, information can also be exchanged with organizations without representing interests together. Such information may be exchanged between **like-minded organizations** as well **as with representatives of the counterparty**. Please list **additional** organizations with which your organization exchanged information in the context of Swiss energy policy of the last 10 years. (You can list as many actors as you want. Additional text entry boxes will automatically appear. Please list only those partners who are not members of your organization. The order does not matter.)

(continued)

Table 3 (continued)

Item	*Question*
Final block	
Q72	You have the opportunity to be informed about the results of our analysis. If you would like to receive such a scientific report, please enter your email address here.
Q73	Do you have any further comments?
	You have reached the end of the survey. Please click on "Submit" to complete the survey. Thank you very much for your participation!

References

Aklin M, Urpelainen J (2013) Debating clean energy: frames, counter frames, and audiences. Glob Environ Change 23(5):1225–1232

Bauer C, Hirschberg S, Bauerle Y, Biollaz S, Calbry-Muzyka A, Cox B, Heck T, Lehnert M, Meier A, Prasser H-M, Schenler W, Treyer K, Vogel F, Wieckert H, Zhang X, Zimmerman M, Burg V, Bowman G, Erni M, Saar M, Tran M (2017) Potentials, costs and environmental assessment of electricity generation technologies. Technical report for the Swiss Federal Office of Energy. Paul Scherrer Institute, Bern

Baumgartner FR, Larsen-Price HA, Leech BL, Rutledge P (2011) Congressional and presidential effects on the demand for lobbying. Polit Res Q 64(1):3–16. https://doi.org/10.1177/1065912909343578

Bernauer T, Gampfer R, Kachi A (2014) European unilateralism and involuntary burden-sharing in global climate politics: a public opinion perspective from the other side. Eur Union Polit 15 (1):132–151. https://doi.org/10.1177/1465116513496878

Bernhagen P, Dür A, Marshall D (2014) Measuring lobbying success spatially. Interest Groups Adv 3(2):202–218. https://doi.org/10.1057/iga.2014.13

Bidwell D (2016) Thinking through participation in renewable energy decisions. Nat Energy 1 (5):1–4. https://doi.org/10.1038/NENERGY.2016.51

Binderkrantz AS, Pedersen HH (2017) What is access? A discussion of the definition and measurement of interest group access. Eur Polit Sci 16:306–321

Black D (1948) On the rationale of group decision-making. J Polit Econ 56:23–34. Available at https://www.journals.uchicago.edu

Blumer YB, Braunreiter L, Kachi A, Lordan-Perret R, Oeri F (2018) A two-level analysis of public support: exploring the role of beliefs in opinions about the Swiss energy strategy. Energy Res Soc Sci 43:109–118

Box-Steffensmeier JM, Christenson DP, Hitt MP (2013) Quality over quantity: amici influence and judicial decision making. Am Polit Sci Rev 107(3):446–460. https://doi.org/10.1017/S000305541300021X

Breetz H, Mildenberger M, Stokes L (2018) The political logics of clean energy transitions. Bus Polit 20(4):492–522

Bürer M, de Lapparent M, Capezzali M, Carpita M (2021) Governance drivers and barriers for business model transformation. In: Hettich P, Kachi A (eds) Swiss energy governance. Springer, New York

Cherp A, Vinichenko V, Jewell J, Brutschin E, Sovacool B (2018) Integrating techno-economic, socio-technical and political perspectives on national energy transitions: a meta-theoretical framework. Energy Res Soc Sci 37:175–190

Downs A (1957) An economic theory of political action in a democracy. J Polit Econ 65 (2):135–150. Available at https://www.journals.uchicago.edu

Druckman JN (2013) Public opinion: stunted policy support. Nat Clim Chang 3(7):617–617. https://doi.org/10.1038/nclimate1939

Dür A (2008) Interest groups in the European Union: how powerful are they? West Eur Polit 31 (6):1212–1230. https://doi.org/10.1080/01402380802372662

Duygan M, Stauffacher M, Meylan G (2021a) What constitutes agency? Determinants of actors' influence on formal institutions in Swiss waste management. Technol Forecast Soc Chang 162. https://doi.org/10.1016/j.techfore.2020.120413

Duygan M, Kachi A, Oliveira TD, Rinscheid A (2021b) Introducing the endowment-practice-institutions (EPI) framework for studying agency in the institutional contestation of socio-technical regimes. J Clean Pro 296:126396

Ebers Broughel A, Wüstenhagen R (2021) The influence of policy risk on Swiss wind power investment. In: Hettich P, Kachi A (eds) Swiss energy governance. Springer, New York

Ejderyan O, Ruef F, Stauffacher M (2019) Geothermal energy in Switzerland: highlighting the role of context. In: Manzella A, Allansdottir A, Pellizzone A (eds) Geothermal energy and society, lecture notes in energy, vol 67. Springer, Cham, pp 239–257

Gross C (2007) Community perspectives of wind energy in Australia: the application of a justice and community fairness framework to increase social acceptance. Energy Policy 35 (5):2727–2736. https://doi.org/10.1016/j.enpol.2006.12.013

Hacker JS, Pierson P (2014) After the "master theory": downs, Schattschneider, and the rebirth of policy-focused analysis. Perspect Polit 12(3):643–662. https://doi.org/10.1017/S1537592714001637

Hall RL, Deardorff AV (2006) Lobbying as legislative subsidy. Am Polit Sci Rev 100(1):69–84. https://doi.org/10.1017/S0003055406062010

Hansla A (2011) Value orientation and framing as determinants of stated willingness to pay for eco-labeled electricity. Energ Effic 4(2):185–192. https://doi.org/10.1007/s12053-010-9096-0

Hillman AJ, Hitt MA (1999) Corporate political strategy formulation: a model of approach, participation, and strategy decisions. Acad Manag Rev 24(4):825–842

Kollman K (1998) Outside lobbying: public opinion and interest group strategies. Princeton University Press, Princeton, NJ

Levy DL, Egan D (1998) Capital contests: national and transnational channels of corporate influence on the climate change negotiations. Polit Soc 26(3):337–361. https://doi.org/10.1177/0032329298026003003

Mahoney C (2007) Lobbying success in the United States and the European Union. J Publ Policy 27 (1):35–56. https://doi.org/10.1017/S0143814X07000608

Morf P (2020) Die Stromversorgung ist gefährdet. Finanz und Wirtschaft, 27 May 2020. Available at https://www.fuw.ch

Offe C, Wiesenthal H (1980) Two logics of collective action: theoretical notes on social class and organizational form. Polit Power Soc Theory 1(1):67–115

Rinscheid A (2015) Crisis, policy discourse, and major policy change: exploring the role of subsystem polarization in nuclear energy policymaking. Eur Policy Anal 1(2):34–70

Rinscheid A, Udris L (2021) Referendum campaigns in Swiss energy policy. In: Hettich P, Kachi A (eds) Swiss energy governance. Springer, New York

Rinscheid A, Wüstenhagen R (2019) German voters would prefer a more ambitious timeline to phase out coal. Nat Energy 4(12):1016–1017

Schaffer L, Levis A (2021) Public discourses on (sectoral) energy policy in Switzerland. In: Hettich P, Kachi A (eds) Swiss energy governance. Springer, New York

Stalder H (2017) Wo Windräder wachsen werden. NZZ, 28 June 2017. Available at https://www.nzz.ch

Stigler GJ (1971) The theory of economic regulation. Bell J Econ Manage Sci 2(1):3–21

Stutzer R, Rinscheid A, Oliveira TD, Loureiro PM, Kachi A, Duygan M (2021) Black coal, thin ice: the discursive legitimisation of Australian coal in the age of climate change. Humanit Soc Sci Commun 8:178

Suisse éole (2017) Gute Gründe für Schweizer Windenergie. Liestal, 28 March 2017. Available at https://www.suisse-eole.ch

Swiss Federal Office of Energy (2017) Wichtigste Neuerungen im Energierecht ab 2018, 2 November 2017. Available at https://www.bfe.admin.ch

Swiss Federal Office of Energy (2018a) Energiestrategie 2050 nach dem Inkrafttreten des neuen Energiegesetzes. Presentation, available at https://www.bfe.admin.ch

Swiss Federal Office of Energy (2018b) Roadmap Elektromobilität. Available at http://www.admin.ch

Tabi A, Wüstenhagen R (2017) Keep it local and fish-friendly: social acceptance of hydropower projects in Switzerland. Renew Sust Energ Rev 68(1):763–773

Varone F, Ingold KM, Jourdain C (2016) Studying policy advocacy through social network analysis. Eur Polit Sci Prev:1–15. https://doi.org/10.1057/eps.2016.16

Walker ET, Rea CM (2014) The political mobilization of firms and industries. Annu Rev Sociol 40:281–304. https://doi.org/10.1146/annurev-soc-071913-043215

Weiler F, Brändli M (2015) Inside versus outside lobbying: how the institutional framework shapes the lobbying behaviour of interest groups. Eur J Polit Res 54(4):745–766. https://doi.org/10.1111/1475-6765.12106

Wüstenhagen R, Wolsink M, Bürer MJ (2007) Social acceptance of renewable energy innovation: an introduction to the concept. Energy Policy 35(5):2683–2691. https://doi.org/10.1016/j.enpol.2006.12.001

Mert Duygan is Research Associate at the Faculty of Business and Economics, University of Basel, Basel, Switzerland and PostDoc at the Swiss Federal Institute of Aquatic Science and Technology (Eawag), Department of Environmental Social Sciences, Dübendorf, Switzerland.

Aya Kachi is Associate Professor for International Political Economy and Energy Policy at the Faculty of Business and Economics, University of Basel, Basel, Switzerland.

Fintan Oeri is a Ph.D. candidate at the Faculty of Business and Economics, University of Basel, Basel, Switzerland.

Thiago D. Oliveira is a former member of the Faculty of Business and Economics, University of Basel, Basel, Switzerland.

Adrian Rinscheid is International Postdoctoral Fellow and Lecturer at the Institute for Economy and the Environment, University of St. Gallen, St. Gallen, Switzerland.

Part IV
Concluding Remarks

Conclusions and Policy Implications

Aya Kachi and Peter Hettich

Contents

The term energy transition at times gives the impression that it is a process that starts with *the* incumbent regime and ends with *the* new regime at some point in time. This simplistic notion could lead to clumsy debates about what ought to be the new perfect regime, whether a newly-emerged system is indeed the one to which the society aspired, and why so (or why not). In the context of research on political regime transition—transitions between authoritarian and democratic regimes within a state, which has resemblance to the current studies on energy transition—these questions have fascinated political scientists for more than half a century. There is an important lesson learned by researchers in this field; that is, studying such a phenomenon by the normative or positive characterization of two end points would lead to a fairly dysfunctional proliferation of regime sublabels. In their seminal work "Democracy with Adjectives," Collier and Levitsky counted more than five hundred subtypes of democracy "precised" by adjectives that had eventually flooded the research field with little positive use.[1]

The work presented in this volume is a compilation of research highlights that represent numerous studies carried out by researchers within the Energy Governance Work Package (WP4) of the Swiss Competence Center for Energy Research, Society and Transition (SCCER CREST). As our Introduction has illustrated in detail, these

[1] Collier and Levitsky (1997), pp. 430–431.

A. Kachi (✉)
Faculty of Business and Economics, International Political Economy and Energy Policy, University of Basel, Basel, Switzerland
e-mail: aya.kachi@unibas.ch

P. Hettich
Institute of Public Finance, Fiscal Law and Law and Economics, University of St. Gallen, St. Gallen, Switzerland
e-mail: peter.hettich@unisg.ch

P. Hettich, A. Kachi (eds.), *Swiss Energy Governance*,
https://doi.org/10.1007/978-3-030-80787-0_16

researchers worked together under common scientific interests in providing recommendations to overcome governance challenges in the course of the energy transition in Switzerland. Despite the variety of disciplines involved in this group, the conscious decision not to "over-precise" the shared notion of governance has successfully guided the 4-year collaboration. We did not only circumvent the type of research inertia that the scholars of regime transition experienced previously, but also enabled the analysis of good governance by applying various theoretical frameworks and methods.

Researchers in the work package focused on identifying concrete challenges associated with the governance of energy transitions. More precisely, we investigated, given newly-available technologies and specific policy goals implied by the Energy Strategy 2050, what specific legal, political, investor-related, and voter-related challenges we need to overcome. One can view the findings of each contribution in this volume as concrete steps that are incremental yet collectively critical to the breakthrough of such a large-scale transition of energy systems—Charles Lindblom's distinction between comprehensive ("root analysis") versus successive limited comparisons ("branch analysis") comes to mind.[2] Naturally, when the Work Package was launched in 2017, our initial task was to break down the overwhelming objective into numerous but concrete issues to be tackled. As such, the findings presented in this volume should help identify basic designs and structural principles of good energy governance—i.e., governance that is more effective, efficient, and transparent.

As we outlined in the introduction chapter, this book first focused on macro perspectives in Part I, dealing with the interactions between the Swiss and European energy systems and policies. Part II then shifted the focus to domestic institutions through which interactions between state and non-state actors occur in ways that could drive (or hinder) the energy transition. Here we employed a broader definition of the relevant institutions and analyzed the implications of legal, political, and economic institutions (if markets can be characterized as economic institutions). Readers must have noticed that one of the most prominent focal points appearing in many chapters of Part II was that Switzerland's federal system requires us to consider the consequence of explicit multilevel governance. Finally, Part III put micro-level analyses into the focus. The contributions in Part III shed light on some of the emerging and more detailed issues to be considered concerning two types of key actors: voters and other stakeholders, e.g., industry players and interest groups. This section treated the institutional considerations mostly as a black box; instead, the chapters focused on actors' perceptions about policies and regulations, identifying ways to mitigate policy acceptance risks that might arise in the course of an energy transition in Switzerland.

Although this classification of the chapters by three relevant layers (macro, meso, and micro) and by the institution-actor distinction is convenient (and necessary) in laying out the contributions of the book, it is not necessarily helpful in providing

[2] Lindblom (1959), p. 79 et seq., 81.

recommendations for future policy implementation. Therefore, in the remainder of this conclusion section, we will summarize potential guiding principles that arise from our research in ways that synthesize multiple contributions in this volume.

Many of the recommendations relate to political, legal, and economic institutional structures and point to general considerations of good governance in network industries. Network industries tend to create vertically-integrated monopolies, which pose specific challenges when designing governance structures. More than in markets where competition may be effective without government intervention, competitive energy and electricity markets do not emerge without a design by the government. When designing the governance structures of energy markets, it is important to considert which level of government is best suited to effectively and efficiently overcome challenges. Effective multilevel governance may make it easier to strike a balance between concerns for the functioning of the system and the interoperability of the different actors. This is true in particular for the provision of fair and equitable access to the network for all users, as well as for concerns regarding locally optimized regimes and innovative modes of local governance. With the empowerment of local actors in ways that hold them accountable for potential failures, we might slowly overcome outdated modes of governance that are the result of entrenched interests of particular actors or that reflect axiomatic views of particular scientific disciplines, such as the current approaches to unbundling or to grid charges. By having the functioning of the system take centerstage, we may also deal with the fact that different administrative offices (independently based on each office's own motives) set diverse policy goals, which may result in inconsistent signals to private actors, giving rise to policy risks that deter potential investors.

Changes of governance can induce substantial shifts in private actors' behavior as well. Generally, changes in governance should preserve a level playing field among different types of actors in terms of market access and possibilities to innovate; in other words, we recommend that any deviations from this general principle should be accompanied by sufficient justification. For instance, this can mean that changes in governance should foster investments by private actors with financial rewards that are appropriate to the risks involved. Finally, our findings also implied that changes in governance would generate redistributive effects that need to be taken into account in the political process. Eventually, these first-order effects can also be transmitted back to the governmental actors. The altered investment landscape leads to heterogeneous and changing policy (outcome) assessments by the private actors. Therefore, governmental actors must consider whether their efforts for policy-industry coordination will be (re)allocated according to the changing level and location of contestation by key private actors.

The new set of collective knowledge we gained through the work represented in this volume also hints at the areas of energy governance that can benefit from further elaboration. One such aspect might be communication. Most of the aforementioned principles relate to economic and technical aspects of governance (including the legal and institutional technicality). This primarily involves business, industry, and governmental actors. However, some of the contributions in this volume vividly illustrate the importance of voters and policy discourses as factors that shape energy governance. Here, the media plays a significant role in connecting energy professionals and voters. Without going into normative or paternalistic discussions as to whether and to what extent voters need to be informed about the course of our energy systems, the research findings involving citizens—together with our own experience from the political debates that preceded the referendum voting for the Energy Strategy 2050—imply that policymakers ought to be conscious about their proactive communication design. One should note that such communication design benefits from longer-term planning in order not to fall in the vicious pattern of constantly reacting to inconsistent political narratives that are shot from left and right.

References

Collier D, Levitsky S (1997) Democracy with adjectives: conceptual innovation in comparative research. World Polit 49:430–451

Lindblom CE (1959) The science of "Muddling Through". Public Adm Rev 19(2):79–88

Aya Kachi is Associate Professor for International Political Economy and Energy Policy, University of Basel, Faculty of Business and Economics, Basel, Switzerland.

Peter Hettich is Director with the IFF-HSG and Professor for public law at the University of St. Gallen (St. Gallen, Switzerland).

The manufacturer's authorised representative in the EU is Springer
Nature Customer Service Centre GmbH, Europaplatz 3, 69115 Heidelberg,
Germany. If you have any concerns regarding our products, please
contact ProductSafety@springernature.com

Printed and bound by CPI Group (UK) Ltd, Croydon, CR0 4YY
30/09/2026
02225689-0016